Make Your Own PARTY

TWENTY BLUEPRINTS TO MYO PARTY!

Dedication

To my staff throughout the years:
you made my experience and evolution richer.

Scribe Publishing Company
91 N. Saginaw
Pontiac, MI 48342
www.scribe-publishing.com
All rights reserved.

Make Your Own Party
Copyright © 2022 Kelli Lewton

Photography: Emily Berger, eebergerphoto.com, and Alan Davidson
Design contributor: Kevin Miller
Editors: Allison Janicki and Jennifer Baum
Copy editing: Mel Corrigan, Ellie White, Jacob Whiten
Cover and interior design: John Wincek, aerocraftart.com

PRINTED IN THE UNITED STATES OF AMERICA

ISBN: 978-1-940368-08-5
Library of Congress Control Number: 2021951934

Publisher's Cataloging-in-Publication data:

Names: Lewton, Kelli, author.
Title: Make your own party / Kelli Lewton, C.E.C.
Description: Pontiac, MI: Scribe Publishing Company, 2022.
Identifiers: LCCN: 2021951934 | ISBN: 978-1-940368-08-5
Subjects: LCSH Parties. | Entertaining. | Cooking. | BISAC
COOKING/ Entertaining | COOKING/ Methods/Garnishing
& Food Presentation
Classification: LCC TX731 .L49 2022 | DDC 642/.4—dc23

Detroit Food & Entrepreneurship Academy is a 501(c)(3) non-profit that works
to inspire young Detroiters (ages 10-24) through culinary arts and food entrepreneurship. From cooking delicious healthy meals for friends and family, to
facilitating complex conversations with community, to developing artisan
food projects from scratch to market; students learn by transforming their
ideas into reality. Through this process, they grow as holistic leaders who are
healthy, connected, and powerful to affect change in our communities and
beyond. Learn more at www.detroitfoodacademy.org. #detroitfoodacademy

...ee Your Own
PARTY

TWENTY BLUEPRINTS TO MYO PARTY!

Kelli Lewton, C.E.C.

Scribe Publishing Company

Pontiac, Michigan

CONTENTS

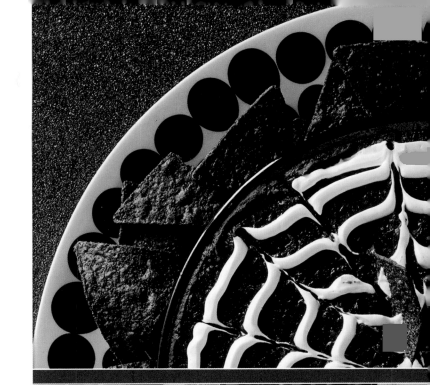

MISSION

If you're interested in branching out from your mother or grandmother's style of entertaining, then read on! My entire inspiration in writing this book is to give you permission to Make Your Own Party! People often say to me, "Hosting a party is so easy for you, but not for me." But here is the thing: they can (even if they don't know it yet), and you can, too. I'm here to provide the tools and insight to give you the confidence to do so!

Some of my most memorable personal events featured menu items as simple as a trio of salsa and tacos. Sure, I am a professional chef and have spent the better part of my life cooking and bringing events big and small to life, but in the end, it all comes down to having the heart, plan and desire to gather with others and enjoy food and community together. Ditch your mom's style if it does not serve you and pursue your inner event self! It may look a little boho with mismatched dishes, clean and modern or thrift-store chic. Perhaps you're inclined to blend many styles, and that is wonderful too.

Part I covers the anatomy of an event and my best tips for stocking your kitchen and pantry. Then in Part II, we'll put all these ideas to work with twenty blueprints for awesome parties that anyone can host with a little preparation.

Each chapter in Part II includes a theme, décor suggestions, recipes, tips and more. Use the plan in its entirety or take what inspires you and leave the rest. The endgame is to give yourself permission to *do you* and enjoy the journey along the way. Some cooking and organization might be needed to host guests, but if you throw out perceived "rules"—often unconsciously gathered from memories of fancy parties, weddings or professionally executed events—you will find your own road map to success. A dozen friends in your apartment courtyard? YES! Holidays with everyday dinnerware? Sign me up! Do not let the absence of expensive kitchen gadgets and fancy serving ware keep you on the sidelines of the event game!

Use this book and its guides and concepts to find the right fit for you, and remember that everything is just a guideline to build from. Do not let other people's rules or styles be a barrier. Listen to *your* intuition of what sounds good and is manageable for you.

My full heart's hope is that the *MYO Party* plans I share in this book will inspire you to enjoy life, food and communal experiences with your family and friends, creating beautiful memories along the way.

#PermissionToParty!

I am beyond grateful that you are sharing this journey with me!

Peace, health and happiness,

Chef Kelli

Who is Chef Kelli?

My twin sister tells the story that I started cooking before age ten and would pull up a chair to the stove to reach it. Maybe it runs in the family: my wonderful maternal grandmother frequently cooked delicious comfort food. I can still remember the smell and taste of her pot roast and mashed potatoes.

For me, growing up in a single-parent home meant constant financial uncertainty and a litany of other family issues that taught me many important life lessons. By age thirteen, out of necessity, I was already working at a local bakery, while my twin sister Karen worked at a Coney Island—a casual diner-type restaurant known for chili dogs that is ubiquitous in Detroit. Soon I moved from the bakery to join my sister in a work world with tips!

The Village Coney Restaurant was the start of my love affair with food. The cozy restaurant had only six booths and a counter, and by eleven a.m. on a Saturday, the smell of chili and coneys would permeate the restaurant, but my coveted Saturday morning shifts began at six a.m., flipping eggs in between waiting on customers. I began to recognize my true passion: cooking for others. That turned into a life-long career in hospitality.

From there I went on to work at several other restaurants, some high-end and others casual. As I moved up this food chain, it became more apparent that although being a server was quite lucrative, my heart was set on food preparation and the science behind it. I loved witnessing how food made people feel; I loved creating dishes that made people happy.

Like everything else in my young life, I jumped in full force with my high school sweetheart and was married at nineteen. Shortly after we were blessed with my daughter, Lauyren (who, by the way, is also an awesome cook!). I traveled some winding paths, all of which ended with learning cooking techniques and the creation of more food. After a short time off, I went back into the restaurant business. Hungry to expand my knowledge,

I enrolled in a culinary arts program at Schoolcraft College in Michigan—the same school that many years later allowed me to give back as a part-time culinary professor, which became a personal passion and a ministry of heart.

My college experience provided the real foundation for my art; everything came into focus as I found my true purpose. I studied French terms, classical cooking processes, American regional cuisine and so much more. It was a magical time and I advanced quickly, often being invited to regional and international culinary competitions. I was awarded six gold medals and even an international silver medal from Singapore! But most importantly: I learned a wealth of information about food composition and balance.

After graduating, I held numerous challenging positions in top restaurants. I opened an urban eclectic food and micro grocery store, Aunt Olive's, which became Michigan's first organic smoothie, juice and wheatgrass bar. Later, I started a home delivery business called Pure Food 2U, again a first in the community, with prepared organic meals delivered to homes and businesses.

But it was my company, Two Unique Caterers and Event Planners (2U), which I founded almost thirty years ago, that really set me free. Two Unique is an off-premise catering company, or as I call us, the Navy SEALs of the event world. No two events are ever the same—the location, people and details are always different. Two Unique is where it all came together for me, where my technical cooking skills met my love for art and expression.

Initially we operated out of a private school kitchen I leased. I remember many sleepless nights wondering if I had gotten in too deep or whether I could pull it off. With hard work and dedication, my worries evaporated, and the business grew from parties of twenty to parties of hundreds and then thousands.

From the beginning, I felt deeply connected to special events; they seemed magical. Leading up to an event, every idea felt possible. The food had to be special—from

scratch with no shortcuts—and then, like actors in a play, the prepared dishes needed to be set on a stage where they would come alive. I was obsessed with Martha Stewart and other hospitality figures and stylists as a young adult, and like them, I wanted every single detail to be picture perfect. When I started my company, dramatic décor, stylish vessels and other visual elements were not common at events. We were bringing something truly unique to our clients and their guests.

We kept evolving, growing, learning and cooking, and wonderful, talented people trusted and joined me. Our small team grew from two to three and then to well over 150. At Two Unique, our professional kitchen was like the living room for the entire food family. Relationships and teamwork were inextricable from the art of cooking: we collaborated, worked and cared for each other and the guests the way families do for one another.

Eventually, we moved out of the rental kitchen and bought a building for Two Unique. Then we bought the building next door and connected the two. We now operate out of a ten-thousand square-foot space home to our pastry and main kitchens, office, warehouse and tasting room. We host inspired, foodie dinners with winemakers, small events and social tastings for present and future clients (and once again, we have our eye on the building next door!).

But COVID-19 upended my career overnight. The stress of the instantaneous cancellation of literally every party in the book was soul crushing. My superpower—bringing people together to feast and celebrate—was rendered useless.

Now I can reflect on the past successes of Two Unique, which enables me to look forward to a brighter future. I am mindful of and thankful for my blessings and the people I love, and I grieve for our society's collective hardship and losses. The fact that this book was written during a difficult time only increases my sense of purpose and hope. Life is about living and doing the things that make you happy.

Two Unique

Our thirty-year journey brought experiences I could never have dreamed of in my younger years: serving US presidents, rock stars and celebrities and celebrating our clients' most special moments with birthday parties, weddings, corporate soirees, showers and huge outdoor events.

Events come to fruition in so many spectacular ways: from the perfect little micro-plate appetizers to an interactive food station, artfully plated dinner and décor that brings our events to life. Our work is guided by the principle that all the food we prepare should be born as close to the vine as possible. We are passionate about our style of cooking, which comprises high-quality ingredients, real food, local sourcing and sustainable ingredients whenever possible. This brings life to amazing prepared meals and events. My mantras are: "It all starts and ends with the food; that is what they will remember years from now," and "Every event is our most important event!"

One woman I have admired throughout my life is Oprah Winfrey, who tells narratives of joy, sorrow and continuously moving forward to become your best self and live your best life. If you have a dream, hard work will keep you moving forward toward the person you want to become. I feel blessed to have a career I love, and I hope my story serves as evidence that with dedication, focus, positive relationships with others and a little luck, you can bring your dreams to life.

ANATOMY OF AN EVENT

This section includes easy-to-follow décor and design concepts to help make your parties pop. Start with where to host your event—indoors or outdoors—and then consider seating, table coverings and other decorative elements. You'll also find suggestions for furniture and display materials and tips for incorporating fresh seasonal concepts and textures into your next *MYO Party,* and a special floral section with some petals of design wisdom from my best bud Kevin Miller.

There are many options available for rent or purchase to set up your own *MYO Party*, but do not overlook what is right in front of you. Shop within your home. I am willing to bet you have a lot more than you realize, and adding a few odds and ends from your local craft or thrift store are great options for building your own *MYO Party* supply arsenal to use for many years to come. Of course, there may be circumstances where renting items is the right option, so we have outlined those below as well.

Tables & Chairs

If you are having an outdoor event and want to get away from the folding table with dings that has been in your garage for years, try taking an indoor table from the kitchen, a coffee table or even a dining room table outside. I keep extra rugs rolled up in my "everything closet" and whip one of those over the cement or grass under a table from the house.

We cater a large variety of events in countless venues, and many of our clients rent indoor furniture for their outdoor events. If you entertain often, consider taking a trip to your local secondhand store or flea market. You can find weathered furniture like an old dresser that can do double duty as a bar or serving table. Something like that has a super boho feel and works wonderfully for events. These are inexpensive options that can be used outside or as a cool extra table for overflow. It may even find a permanent place in your home.

Of course, if you need to get your hands on something that involves a little less shopping and footwork, or if you just prefer folding something up and putting it out of the way, four-, six- and eight-foot plastic tables can be purchased online or at most big box stores. These covered tables work great for seating or serving tables. I keep three 36-inch round tables in my garage, as they are small enough to pop up most anywhere and can seat four to six people. They are great for a quick seating fix in the back-yard, on the deck or scattered in the house, and require little to no movement of regular furniture.

As far as seating goes, utilize your patio furniture seating if you are heading outside, and again, don't be afraid to take something from the inside outdoors. Benches make for great casual seating. Look around your house for more seating options, but if you are still in need of more, you can find a large assortment of folding chairs at many common stores. I have lightweight resin folding chairs that look as if they are made of wood that I purchased at Ikea. They also have a hole on the back of the chair in case you want to hang them up for storage. If you are looking for a more casual setting, use blankets and oversized pillows to create seating areas. This can be used both indoors and outdoors.

Let's say your *MYO Party* is a little larger than what you can accommodate with what you have in your home, or you're not interested in purchasing and storing folding tables and chairs. There are still many options for rent, and you will have plenty of choices. Below is a guideline to help you in your planning.

STANDARD ISSUE SNAPSHOT FOR RENTAL TABLES

- 36-inch round, seats 4 to 6
- 48-inch round, seats 6 to 8
- 60-inch round, seats 8 to 10
- 72-inch round, seats 10 to 12
- 6-foot rectangle, seats 6
- 8-foot rectangle, seats 8
- Tall 24- to-36-inch bistro tables are great for overflow or cocktail parties, and if you want chairs, taller bar-stool seats work well.

Higher-end rental companies will have more offerings beyond what I have listed and will often have a gallery of pictures that will help you dial into finding your look. You can rent everything from grand farm tables to whisky barrels with a wooden top!

RENTAL CHAIRS

Folding vinyl: Most often the least expensive option. These chairs are lightweight with vinyl backs and seats and metal legs. They normally are available in white, brown, black and sometimes clear plastic, which would be more expensive.

Wood: Wood comes in many colors as well and is a nice option. White wood is common for outdoor weddings. These chairs usually run for $2.50 to $4.50 per chair.

Chiavari: These are lovely, heavy-duty chairs that do not fold, but most often stack. They are usually more ornate and come in many colors, including white, brown, gold and silver, and come with a matching padded seat cover. We see these often at weddings. They can range in price from $8 to $15 per chair.

Plastic stackable garden chairs: These are like what you might pick up at Target or Walmart, but you may prefer renting these for a day rather than purchasing, as they take up a lot of real estate when stored.

There are a few options, but there are countless opportunities depending on your budget.

TABLETOPS

Hard Tabletops. I have a dozen or more hard portable surfaces that I use in food station displays. They function like a finished countertop at a party. I purchase them primarily from Ikea in all sorts of finishes (stainless steel, white, wood tones) and colors (white, black, wood tone, silver, yellow). These are a little heavier, so I store them in the box I purchased them in so the ends do not get dinged up. They can be tucked away under a bed, in the back of a closet or in the garage. When I need them, I just pop them out of the box and plunk them down on my table. This creates a clean and interesting finish where you can swag in some accent pieces or runners and forgo linen.

Another option with these tabletops is to put down a base linen, create a four- to six-inch riser with wood, metal or plastic blocks/boxes or even thick books tucked on the base table, and then set the smaller tabletop on the risers to create a floating effect on the tablespace. I have many hard, clear boxes for shoe storage that work great for a sturdy elevation under hard tabletops. A three- or four-foot tabletop slab placed on an eight-foot table adds interesting flow, elevation and dimension. In lieu of larger tabletops, we often use bookcase-size shelves. I am fond of the stainless steel or white shelves as they blend well with many types of décor. These are great for a little lift to place items on and give some height to alleviate overcrowding. Small lifts here and there help add interesting architectural elements to your table-scape, and these all work well on rental or lightweight folding tables or on your existing home surfaces.

Softer Tabletops. These can take many different shapes and forms. I am a big fan of Menards home improvement store. They have so many unexpected items that can translate into party décor pieces and are very inexpensive. I like the two- by four-foot faux boards that come in all sorts of patterns: brick, white birch, cedar, tin and much more. They are smaller and lighter than a full-size countertop, which makes them easier to store and versatile for design. Menards also has heavy plastic sheets in many colors, prints and designs. They are sold as two- by two-foot lightweight plastic squares that resemble the old vintage tin ceilings you might see in a building from the 1920s. You can also purchase larger sheets or panels up to four or five feet. Most of the materials are under twenty or thirty dollars and are lightweight and easy to tuck away for your next *MYO Party*.

Wallpaper or mural sheets often come with peel-off backs, which are easy to work with. You can purchase mosaic stick-on tiles or even pattern something yourself. Contact paper comes in so many designs. Take a clean foam board and peel then evenly adhere the paper to create your own custom piece in whatever length works for your tablespace. Maybe it's floral design, clean architectural geometric shapes, modern art, gerbera daisies or cloud wallpaper—the sky is the limit! Mural sheets or backdrops are also available on Etsy, with designs from Winnie the Pooh to modern art in all different sizes. These can range from twenty dollars and up. Other backdrop materials like metallic fringe curtains or paper streamers in different colors can create a great vibe for your event.

Natural materials like green preserved moss can be laid out for color and texture on top of simple or exposed-wood tabletops. I have used real sod and small picks to create a floating elevation for what I place on top. You can buy a two- by five-foot piece of sod for five or six dollars, and it is a great conversation piece.

TABLE COVERINGS

Table coverings are one of my favorite areas; it makes me feel like an artist with a canvas!

Tablecloths. This is the first line of defense in the pursuit of covering most tables. Tablecloths come in oodles of colors and prints with options from simple solid colors to bizarre patterns and everything in between. Most often the best options are found at a linen rental company. Many rental companies are national. They will ship the product and provide you with return packaging, so you only need to drop it in the FedEx box after the event. There are likely wonderful local vendors in your area, and it is always an exciting experience to be able to go to the showroom and see the items for yourself while supporting local businesses.

You can also visit your local fabric store to purchase fabric in the amount needed to cover a table, lay as a runner or use as an accent on your tablescape. For my daughter's wedding I wanted a sage green runner, so I purchased two large bolts of fabric (which cost less than what I would have paid renting). I started with a long white base linen draped three-quarters of the way down the sides of the tables, and then rolled out the sage green fabric right over the white linen and cleanly cut it right on the tabletop at the appropriate length. No hemming or sewing required! It was an amazing late summer wedding. We had a communal outdoor event with huge, long tables and organic living centerpieces of piled greens, herbs, grapes and small clusters of flowers. It was so pretty!

When calculating your linen requirements, measure the size of your table and leave extra room for overhang. I've outlined some basic calculations to assist you. You may go one size bigger if you want the linen to drop all the way to the floor. Tablecloths are a vast arena, and most often you will be working with a linen rental company to aid you in this design pursuit.

- 8-foot rental tables: Most often you would want a 90- x 156-inch base linen and cover it with a topper.
- 36-inch round: 90-inch tablecloth.
- 48-inch table: 90-inch or 108-inch tablecloth.
- 60-inch round: 108-inch or 120-inch tablecloth.
- 72-inch round: 120-inch or 132-inch tablecloth.

Other Table Coverings & Unexpected Accents. There are so many ways to cover a tabletop:

- Use actual hard tabletops, perhaps with a fabric runner or even decorative or textured placemats, to create an interesting pattern and color scheme.
- Large scarfs can be used for table accents along with clean vinyl or plastic floor mats purchased for the purpose of using on a tabletop.
- Inexpensive white or colored sheets can work in lieu of formal tablecloths for serving tables (not for seating tables).
- Craft butcher paper in white or brown could be the perfect pairing for something Tex-Mex or southwestern, or for a children's party with crayons on the table.
- Rolls of shiplap paper can be used in creative ways to etch a design on your serving table.
- I am not usually a plastic table covering kind of gal, but you can find interesting heavy plastic table covers for long tables measuring 54 x 120 inches, which is the perfect size for a serving table. They come in faux wood, grass and waterscapes and might be interesting for the right event. Consider the faux wood for a southwestern theme or grass for a sports theme.
- Use newspaper or comics glued onto foam core boards and placed on a table with a clear plastic sheet over top to create a fun surface for a themed event.

Props

This area is truly limitless. Props are fun elements in tablescaping that can highlight your theme and bring animation to your table. Most anything can become a table prop for the right cause or reason, from a porcelain bunny to interesting statues, pieces of pottery, fun baskets or boxes. Perhaps if you are creating something with an Asian-fusion feel, you might be drawn to some brass objects. Maybe clean and modern is your mode with glass pieces and white pottery. A wooden rooster might be the barnyard all-star on your rustic table—I have a giant one in my kitchen that has been known to moonlight at other people's parties. I am a fan of The Home Store, as it is a supreme knickknack prop warehouse that has great rustic elements like baskets, statues, runners, mats, wood crates and serving pieces. Other good spots for props are Home Goods, TJ Maxx, Target, flea markets and several online options. I have listed more at the end of the chapter.

Props can also be purchased from Etsy, which is one of my favorite online shops full of small artisans with very reasonable price points. Of course, the first place to start is with common objects in your home. If you are the DIY type, Pinterest and Esty have countless ideas for themes, and your search will eventually take you to props and images that will inspire you to find your own unique path. Many ideas for props will unravel in the chapters to come, but my best advice is that you have more in plain sight than you think!

Keys to Functional and Dramatic Table Design

The display:

- Will it be one-sided or two-sided (will people also see the table from the other side)?
- Where will foot traffic flow from?
- What is the proximity of serving tables to seating tables?
- Will there be access from all points of the room?
- What are the potential bottlenecks? There is a lot to consider here, but general crowd flow, location restrictions or even where you place the serving ware are good starting points.

Things That Hold Other Things

Whether you are rolling silverware in linen napkins or placing your heavy plastic utensils out, often you will need a vessel to keep them from spilling and rolling over your service area. There are so many easy, cute options from baskets to serving trays in clear plastic or white wood. If I were going in a rustic direction, I might choose a heavy porcelain pot to tuck my rolled silverware in. Sometimes I use wide-mouth floral vases to separate utensils, but flat, rustic wood pieces or even the right bowl will do the trick. Many chapters in this book are written with plates and utensils present on actual food stations. Of course, if you are presetting the table with flatware, this is not necessary. I certainly love a nice, pre-set table, but I also know it adds another huge layer to a more casual party as well as an additional expense.

Serving Your Guests

As you will see throughout all the wonderful photography in this book, food can find a home in so many places. I often pick up inexpensive odds and ends at flea markets or Salvation Army stores and work them into many food plans. The nice thing about my boho flea market picks is that most of the time, these pieces cost no more than a few bucks. I normally will not spend more than ten dollars on my reclaimed serving ware. I have a huge collection of mismatched mid-century Pyrex that I love to use whenever possible. Wood serving platters lined with a linen napkin, pewter and super clean stainless bowls that look like orbs cut in half are also great options for display. I have used cast iron and pie tins for themed events and colored pottery for others, depending on the theme and vibe I am seeking. I repurpose tin cans by cleaning them and tying raffia on the outside, and then I fill them with salsa and guacamole. The rule is: there are no rules. Not everything has to cost money or be super fancy. It all boils down to what you have, what you need and what you can repurpose and drive from there.

Melamine is often a good choice for a base set of platters. It is a high-density resin that looks nice and does not break. It is a nicer choice than a common plastic serving piece and comes in a large variety of colors and shapes. It might be useful to purchase one base set of serving vessels and then use them no matter the theme.

BASE SERVING COLLECTION

Here is a basic list to start your serving ware collection. As far as materials go, you can find pieces in various finishes: pewter, wood, ceramic, melamine, baskets, metal and more.

- 4 to 6 platters of 10 to 16 inches, round or oblong.

- A set of 4 to 8 smaller bowls (5 to 12 ounces) to use for condiments, nuts and other dollops of food. Ramekins are also nice for this purpose.

- 3 to 4 larger serving bowls, 1.5 to 3 quarts in volume.

- A few wooden items such as oval serving vessels, bowls and fun platters.

- 2 to 3 baking dishes, 2 to 4 quarts each that can double as serving dishes. I like the brand Staub, but there are many to choose from.

- 4 to 6 quarter-size aluminum sheet trays. They are great for holding silverware wraps.

- 1 to 2 cutting boards, 12 to 18 inches, for cheese platters, sliced turkey and so on.

- 1 to 2 pedestal serving stands.

- 14 to 16 pairs of small serving tongs. Stainless modern tongs are easy to find and inexpensive, and it looks great when all the tongs are the same, so buy them all at once!

- 8 to 10 slightly larger scissor-style serving tongs for salad and many plattered menu items. Again, it is nice to have uniformity in serving utensils.

- Serving spoons: 6 to 10 smaller teaspoons, 6 to 8 medium-size tablespoons and 8 to 10 larger true-size serving spoons.

CHINA, GLASSWARE, SILVERWARE AND MORE

This is an important conversation to have, as even though this book focuses more on food styles, menu creation and serving design composition, serving ware contributes just as much toward making parties memorable.

Many clients nowadays prefer a mix of formal and rustic serving ware, and there seems to be an evolution toward more casual party-throwing. I do not want to

deter you from using china at your event if you'd like, but rather want to give you permission to create a day that is a little more carefree if you choose. It doesn't have to be one or the other: mix it up! Most people do not want to own the amount of inventory needed to host more than twelve people and will seek out a rental company. This is a great option, as they will deliver the plates in crates and pick them up again after use. Most rental companies offer a variety of glasses, plates, silverware and charger plates in many shapes, sizes, textures and colors.

You may find that you are a hybrid person such as myself. I own silverware for up to forty guests and easy-to-wash satin ivory napkins that I roll silverware in for gatherings. I am also a big advocate of owning wine glasses, and I keep four dozen glasses boxed in my basement. I now stock only stemless, as their life span is more promising. I do have china as well, but depending on the occasion and if the guest count rises above twenty, I will jump to either the hard upscale plastic or bamboo plates to manage the added layer of heavy work. If you are an avid party-thrower, here are some suggestions.

Plates. Pick up an inexpensive white plate with a big face and very little rim, if any, in two different sizes. All food looks great on white, and any that break will be easy to replace. A good rule of thumb for plate sizes is to use five- to seven-inch plates for appetizers and other small bites, and eight- to eleven-inch plates for entrées.

A clean, modern plate style will also often cost less and is easy to replace as well as versatile. Look for serving ware that will accommodate most any party theme you are hosting. Often nice disposable plates can range from twenty-five cents to a dollar—if you shop the sales, you'll be surprised at how inexpensively you can purchase nice plates. Ikea is often a good resource for plates, wine glasses and more.

Another route to take if you are a little more boho is to start collecting plates in many different patterns (but a similar size) from thrift stores. The last set I purchased at the Salvation Army store was six bucks! They are often in sets of six, ten or more and are usually inexpensive. I personally LOVE a good mismatched plate party. You do you and have fun with it!

Glasses. It is never a bad idea to have a good stash of boxed wine glasses. I am now a fan of stemless glasses after seeing more than my fair share of glasses broken by a wagging dog tail, a little person's reach or just by accident. Four dozen would be a fair supply. Again, if you have space to store them, simple high- or lowball glasses are also great to have in the house for parties.

If you are renting glasses for an event, most often your inventory list will include one water glass and three to five bar drink glasses per person if you are having a full bar. It is very dependent on what you are serving to determine the correct supply of glasses. Often we will use rental glasses for events and then go to plastic backups for when they run out.

As mentioned above with plates, if you have a ton of storage and like a little chaos, you can shop mismatched beverage glasses at flea markets and thrift stores.

Silverware & More. Silverware falls into the same thinking as china and glassware: own a reasonable stock that is easy to replace if you lose one or two, or rent it as needed.

We have talked about rentals in many categories. There are several items you may need for your event that you may find at a rental company, such as chaffers, extra serving platters or bowls, portable bars, farm tables, string lighting or chandeliers. It is best to look at online galleries of rental companies in your area.

Out-of-the-Box Rentals

These items will usually come from design or production-orientated companies.

- Faux boxwood hedges
- Wooden or brick wall sections
- Huppahs or trellises
- Large pots with greenery
- Theatrical backdrops
- Larger cutouts or props that you might associate with something on a movie set
- Entire theme kits like the Oscars, gambling or tropical
- Faux walls
- Custom hanging lighting

Miscellaneous Prop and Serving Purchases

I own many fun odds and ends that are easy to store and reusable.

- Rain curtains: these are like hanging bead panels or shredded metallic hanging panel pieces.
- I have many Detroit-inspired vinyl canvases stored in large tubes that we use as backdrops or soft tabletop accents.
- Large fabric panels that hang from tall metal stations, often called pipe and drape: I have panels like this in all sorts of materials from icy blue sparkles to floral prints. Efavor.com is a great resource for these kinds of materials, and you will be surprised at all the other knickknacks you can find online from similar vendors.
- Deli/craft paper on a roll.
- Mixed woven baskets, cutting boards and trays for serving or as a prop.
- Galvanized trays and buckets.
- Mason jars in various sizes.
- Ramekins: good for holding small items and do double-duty as risers.
- Clear glass cylinder or square vases in various sizes.
- Fairy lights and Christmas lights.

Floral

CONTAINERS

Containers for florals can be anything from take-out Chinese cartons, painted mason jars or bottles, bottles wrapped in twine or fabric, small-produce wooden baskets, stone pottery, clear or colored glass, modern plastic boxes or tin buckets. I have used more than my fair share of little tin cans with succulents and a piece of raffia tied on the outside, as well as baskets of every flavor, urns, vintage kitchen equipment and bowls. You can even turn produce like pumpkins and gourds into containers with florals.

PLANNING YOUR FLORAL ARRANGEMENTS

When working on events, it is best to always start with a color scheme. This is the easiest way to set the vibe of your next party. Think about when your party will be in terms of the season. This will play a big role in what is available and can determine cost. Also, think about if the event will be outside in warmer weather or indoors. These are all important factors to consider when working with different types of florals.

Once you have decided on a color scheme, start thinking of the season and what types of flowers are available. With the technology now and flowers growing in different areas around the world, there are several options at our finger-tips. There are still a few specific flowers that are not always available, like peonies, tulips and hyacinths. Check ahead to ensure that your chosen beauties are readily available. Peonies, for example, are one of the most popular flowers we work with, and they are usually only available from spring to early summer. If they are not available, we often substitute with large garden roses. We let the roses fully bloom open and sometimes bend the outside layers of the rose petals back to create a large puffy bloom to look like a peony.

After you figure out the season, move on to thinking about where this event will take place. If it is going to be outside during the summer, I would consider using flowers that will last longer and suggest designing them in vases or containers that can hold a good amount of water. This will help keep your blooms hydrated and look-ing fresh all day long. For example, if you really want to use hydrangeas, you will want them in water during the whole event if it is taking place outside. You can even mist the head of the hydrangea with a spray water bottle before placing them on the table to keep them fresh. If you have a hydrangea bloom looking a little wilted prior to the event, pull the stem out and dip the head of the hydran-gea in a bowl or bucket of water, shake it off a bit, do a fresh cut on the stem and place the stem back into water and keep out of the direct sun. The hydrangea should rehydrate and come back to full bloom. If you're inside, you can consider using floral foam and putting that in an opaque container to hide it. Make sure to freshly cut each stem of your flowers/greenery as you add them into your arrangement. If you do not have access to a cooler or refrigeration, I would suggest doing this the morning of

Event designer Kevin Miller from Twigs and Branches

your event; otherwise, the day before works as well if you have refrigeration available.

Now that we know our season, venue and overall theme, it's time to create! When pulling your color scheme together, think about the vibe you are going for. If it is going to be more modern, consider blooms like calla lilies, steel grass, gerbera daisies and green dianthus. These are all more modern blooms with clean lines and will help create that modern look. If you want a theme with more tex-ture, bring blooms like peonies, garden roses, ranunculus, scabiosa and spray roses. You can add some texture with greenery if it makes sense with your style. There are vari-eties of eucalyptus and different types of ruscus that will help pull your look together. If you do not have any specific theme, the best way to pull a color palette together is by using paint swatches. You may not get the exact shade from that paint swatch, but if you have a few colors chosen and the blooms pull that scheme together overall, you're all set! If you are looking for some nontraditional color palettes, think of soft creamy yellows, blush pinks and deep burgun-dy. Maybe you are feeling chocolate and light blue or even peach and fuchsia. Do not be afraid to play with color.

As you start to design your arrangements, water is always important. When you are using different blooms and greens, the longer you keep them hydrated, the longer they will last. If you want to tuck blooms into your tablescape and do not have a good water source, think about using water tubes to tuck into backdrops or on your display tables. Make sure your flowers and greenery are always sitting in water while you are designing, and cut the stem of your flower or greenery on an angle to get the best source of hydration. After cutting, put the stem right back into the water, floral foam or water source in your arrangement. You can also make garlands with mixed greenery and floral wire. You will want to cut small bundles of your choice of greens and wrap your floral wire around it a few times, adding the next bundle on top to create the garland. Do this over and over until you have the length you want. At the end, cut your wire with some wire cutters and wrap the extra wire around a few times to finish it off. You can take a few sprigs of the greenery and tuck them the opposite way from the wire to have a finished look to your garland. Once you are done, wrap your garland up like a wreath, put it in a trash bag, add a little bit of water and tie the bag closed. Shake the bag gently to coat the garland with the water inside. Store this in a refrigerator or a very cool area (thirty-five to forty-five degrees Fahrenheit) overnight and your garland will be fresh and ready the next day! Colder temperatures, such as in an attached, unheated garage, make a perfect staging area for florals.

QUICK FLORAL TIPS

1. Use florals that tie into your season and overall theme.

2. Make sure to remove any stems that may sit below the waterline and cut them before putting them in arrangement.

3. Use floral preservation packets or make your own by adding a teaspoon of chlorine bleach, a teaspoon of sugar and a tablespoon of lemon juice per quart of water.

4. Keep flowers in a cool place and refrigerate if you can. Keep them out of direct sunlight. This will make your flowers last much longer.

5. Purchase flowers that have not fully bloomed for a longer life to your arrangements.

6. Make sure your chosen vases or vessels are clean to help aid in the prevention of bacteria.

7. Add fresh water every day or two.

WHERE TO FIND FLORALS AND GREENS

You may live in a place that has a wholesale floral market—it's worth looking into. I LOVE local farmers markets and growers, but sometimes in off seasons, it can be a challenge to purchase your favorite blooms. It is always better to purchase whole bunches of one type of flower and mix bouquets yourself when purchasing from open markets. I do not want to deter you from shopping local, and most often that is where I start, but occasionally what I find at Costco and Trader Joe's is less expensive than my wholesaler!

NON-FLORAL CENTERPIECES

There are lots of simple ways to bring your table to life without a floral arrangement.

- Cylinder vases of citrus fruits.
- Bowls of fresh peaches or large strawberries or blackberries.
- A steel bucket or basket with apples.
- Decorative purple or green kale set on a table or leaves put in a clean vase.
- Small gourds or pumpkins piled about or resting in vessels.
- Objects from nature such as cut branches and interesting twigs. Foliage and greenery can look great tucked into jars or large vases. Eucalyptus is nice and greens are far less expensive than most florals.
- Fresh herbs replanted in a short cylinder vase, mason jar tin or pot.
- Whole pomegranates, clusters of grapes, mandarin oranges, bosc pears or dried citrus slices.
- Succulents are easy and amazing if you can work those in. They are so inexpensive, and you can pot or plant them in most anything. Any potted plant is a good plan as it lives far beyond your event, and you can give them away as a favor.

Remember to always prep beforehand. Make sure you have everything you need before you start. Think of the goods and flowers that are necessary and the tools you need and create a list. The more you have organized, the smoother your designing will be. Do not forget to have fun and be creative! You will surprise yourself with all the beauty you can create.

Your Menu

You will find some solid innovative and approachable menu creations and recipes in this book. When thinking about a menu for an event, there are elements to consider, a few of which I have called out below.

Good menu writing takes many things into consideration:

WHO'S COMING?

Who are your guests? It is vital to cook for your audience. I have had this conversation with clients who are vegan. It's GREAT to be vegan, but if you are inviting two hundred other people who may not be vegan, it might be worthwhile to include a little dairy or fish somewhere. Entertaining is really supposed to show your heart for others, as well as recognizing someone's most special day. Find a middle ground if you can. If it will ruin your day, stick to what feels right to you.

WHAT TIME OF DAY?

Is it prime dinner hour or snacks and games at 8:00 p.m.? Is it a 1:00 p.m. weekend brunch, lunch or a little of both? If you are having people over anytime between 5:00 and 8:00 p.m., it is a good rule of thumb to have something a little more substantial, especially if they will be drinking. It does not have to look like a three-course meal, but maybe extra dips with bread and crackers or some charcuterie and a nice couple of side salads with hot dips. A great pasta and salad is an easy, delicious and very inexpensive menu to prepare.

WHAT IS THE OCCASION?

Weddings. Sometimes a couple will want to invite a large guest list, but they don't have the budget to support that. Oftentimes they suggest putting "hors d'oeuvres reception" on the invitation, assuming their guests will know to eat something before they attend. Nope. They won't get it. Your guests were invited to a wedding, and they do not understand they will not be served enough food and that they may leave hungry.

My suggestion is usually to lower the guest count to accommodate the budget. It's important to entertain people who are bearing gifts! Another option for a wedding on a tight budget could be to turn it into a more casual event, such as a house party or BBQ. You can invite a large group, but still serve a full meal, save money and stay on budget.

Graduations. As most often parents are breaking the bank to send their kids off to college, we don't usually see people planning graduation parties with the type of budget a wedding might call for. In this arena, it might be as simple as an amazing burger bar, taco stand or Greek salad station with grilled chicken and disposable plates. One tip I often share with clients is to have two sets of invitations: one goes out to family and other adults that calls for an open house from 1:00 to 4:00 p.m. and has a larger menu. The second set of invitations may go out to all the young family and school friends where you may overlap some menu items from the first wave of the party, but add more food like pizza, subs and such to help keep costs in line and cater to a younger audience. This will also help with street parking, crowd control and other resources.

Brunch. Brunch can be a cost-effective or expensive way to celebrate many of life's special days, such as Mother's Day, Easter, bridal or baby showers and so much more. A nice brunch could be as simple as an amazing bagel bar with trimmings, baked goods, an easy egg casserole or frittata and a crisp clean salad with some grilled chicken on the side. It can also be over the top with salmon platters and roasted beef tenderloin. There are many options here.

Birthday Parties. This is a large category. We could be talking about kids, which can be as easy as pizza and salad, or someone's milestone birthday with all the bells and whistles. It could follow an Italian or Parisian theme, or cater to the friend who loves BBQ. People do not expect over-the-top at a house party, so do not worry about serving prime rib. Of course, you can always hire your local expert like me to manage everything and make your special day turnkey!

There are many more party categories that I have not listed. My advice is to consider who you are entertaining, never let people leave hungry and plan your menus to stay within your budget. I would rather have a delicious plate of simple pasta and a salad than only three or four pieces of fussy appetizers and leave hungry.

Things to Think About When Planning Your Menu

Color: It is always nice to have a few bright colors on the table.

Variety: Add a fair combination of meats, larger sides and small bites.

Seasonality: Pick items that make sense for the season you are in. If it's fall, maybe a big pot of turkey chili with all the trimmings.

Texture: Some menu items can be soft like potatoes, others could be seared meats, rustic bread and crisp greens. Mix up your textures so it's not all one or the other.

Cooking Methods: It's hard to pull off complicated timing when you are serving larger crowds, so select items that are forgiving. I love braised short ribs, as they are fail-safe!

Cohesive Menu: Decide what will make sense together on the plate and include the right mix of vegetables, carbs and proteins. You will need to see everything on the same plate together, and if it gives you pause, rethink it.

Harmony and Balance: Select foods, dishes and accoutrements that work well together. That might feel like heirloom tomatoes with balsamic syrup, basil and sea salt. Don't forget all the little finishes, like a squeeze of acid from a fresh lemon or lime or a sprinkle of sea salt and a grind of pepper.

Dietary Restrictions: Be mindful that many of your guests may have allergies or dietary restrictions. Can you put croutons on the side to keep a salad gluten free? Nuts on the side? When you are making a sauce, can you thicken it with arrowroot or cornstarch rather than a typical flour-based roux? Perhaps put out small place card signs with menu item names or label items with their ingredients to help people navigate better.

The degree of difficulty to prep ahead and execute could be a chapter of its own, but to summarize, it is important to pick foods that you can prep ahead so when you are putting out your party feast, you are not stuck in the kitchen for countless hours and then exhausted. What can

you prep ahead? Many dishes can be prepared ahead of time and reheated or served at room temperature. For *à la minute* dishes, have everything cut and cleaned so you have an easy lift off. Trust me, everything seems to take longer than you probably expect it will, so being organized and allowing for extra time will be very helpful in the long run.

General Guidelines for Food Quantities
(per person)

- Passed hors d'oeuvres only: 10 to 12 bite-size pieces
- Passed hors d'oeuvres with dinner or food stations: 4 to 6 pieces
- Protein: 4 to 5 ounces for lunch | 6 to 8 ounces for dinner
- Starch: 3 to 5 ounces, depending on food density
- Vegetables: 3 ounces
- Bread: 1.25 pieces
- Salad Entrée: 3 ounces or 3 cups of lettuce plus added protein and other garnishes
- Side Salad: 1.25 ounces or a cup and a half of lettuce
- Sides, Cold and Hot: 4 to 5 ounces if only serving one side, 3 ounces each if serving two sides and 2 ounces each if serving three or more sides
- Assorted Tortes, Cakes and Pies: 1.75 pieces per person
- Tortes and Miniature Dessert Combination: .75 piece of torte and 2.5 pieces of miniatures
- Mini/Petite Desserts: 3.5 to 4.5 pieces per person

Drinks & Beverages

Depending on who you speak with, this category is either the first or second most important part of many events. There are so many options!

Every chapter in *MYO Party* has a suggested beverage or cocktail pairing. This is not to discourage you from serving other beverages that make sense for you, your family and friends, but rather to give you options you might not otherwise have thought of. If your entire family is over the moon about single malt scotch, then of course have some of that! My family loves wine, so this past Thanksgiving I made my own Turkey Day wine tour, starting from white and working onto reds. It was fun and everyone really enjoyed it. I had other beverages available, but wine was my focus and what most people drank. In the summer or maybe for a birthday bash, I would pick tequila-inspired drinks like a clean, skinny margarita or fruity watermelon and golden tequila drink. I suggest focusing on the theme and working the drinks from there. A full bar is certainly great, but what I have discovered over the years is that people tend to lean towards the "theme" drink, and stocking a full bar takes time and comes with a significant cost, and there are usually a lot of leftovers.

BEVERAGE CONCEPTS

Limited Bar with Specialty Cocktails. I often suggest to wedding couples that they each pick their own special namesake cocktail. Then we add beer, wine, sparkling liquor seltzers and maybe some bubbles to create a limited but interesting selection. At a wedding I booked recently, the bride's drink was a craft vodka cocktail and the groom's was a bourbon old fashioned. We added a couple kinds of vodka and served them touted as vodka sparklers with a variety of fruits, citrus, lemonade and sparkling water to be paired with. Kind of fun, right? Throw some hard seltzers and beer on ice, add a mocktail, self-serve hydration station with infused citrus fruit (served in decanters) and finally, for a few more non-alcoholic options, lemonade and iced tea would be a wonderful addition as well. Now it's time to party!

It is also fun to play off what is trending when planning your drink selection. If we were talking brunch, a Bloody Mary bar could double as a salad bar with celery, salami skewers, hot sauce, olives, pickles, peppers and more. Include sparkling waters and juices to drink with your vodka. What else might you need here? Champagne and maybe some Baileys for coffee would do it for me.

Beer & Wine. Nothing wrong with the beer and wine approach. If you are traveling this route, I would take the time to make some interesting selections instead of box wine (although I am told there are some excellent box wines in the world now). I am a bottle wine girl

and have a little cellar I work on constantly. Maybe you have wine flights that match your menu or small cards that describe the notes in the selection of wine. Good wine does not have to be pretentious or expensive, so do your homework or talk to your local wine merchant. Same thing with beer: it is not your dad or grandpa's beer world anymore. It's common to see notes of vanilla in porters, raspberry undertones in ale and oodles of other botanical creations. I am sure there are many local microbreweries in your hometown. Craft beer is alive and well; check it out! With a nice beer and wine reception, I would also include nonalcoholic options like sparkling waters or maybe cider in the fall.

Craft Cocktails. I have many hipster clients who are much more interested in craft cocktails than their food menu. Social drinking has become a full-circle botanical experience for so many. My favorite local place for a good craft cocktail is at the Detroit City Distillery. It boggles my mind to see the amazing botanicals, bitters and infusions that these amazing craft cocktail scientists brew up.

Presentation is key, and craft mixology puts an emphasis not only on how the drink tastes, but also presentation. It is most often poured into a fancy glass and garnished with herbs, exotic fruits and other fun bells and whistles. If you have good bartender support, supplies and time to make some craft cocktails, it will be very memorable for your guests.

Soft Drinks or Soda Pop? That is a question on the minds of many. If I were hosting an event with younger guests, I might have iced buckets of vitamin waters and the smaller eight-ounce cans of pop (yes, we call it "pop" in Michigan!). At a bigger event with an open bar where 7&7 or rum and Coke is an option, then yes, soda pop is a go. At a more elegant event that may serve a few signature cocktails that don't call for any soda pop, you could nix it altogether and serve sparkling water instead.

Keys to Overall Event Success

Shopping. There are many places to shop for materials to build your *MYO Party* arsenal, and we've already mentioned quite a few. A good idea for holiday-themed items is to shop after the holiday, when many items are highly discounted, and stash them for next year. Craft, hobby, big box, home improvement and supply stores are filled with possibilities to help you pull off your next *MYO Party*. Thrift stores, flea markets, Etsy and even social networking marketplaces are also good options. Find a mom-swap or wedding re-swap group and keep your eyes open for what might be a good find to add to your collection. Shopping sales and close-outs and using coupons are all great ways to stock your *MYO Party* supply closet.

Plan Ahead. When it comes to entertaining, not having a plan is in fact a plan to fail! What can you do ahead?

- Pull out your serving platters and vessels. Organize and label them with what will go in each one.

- Purchase nonperishables (beverages, spices, paper goods, etc.) far in advance so you are not scrambling at the last minute.

- Prep, prep and prep! Chop those vegetables and make baked goods the day before if you can. Are there some foods you can make and reheat? Anything you can do beforehand, so you don't have so much going on in the kitchen the day of? Many recipes in this book give you prep-ahead tips. Use them.

- Send out invites and always ask for an RSVP.

Less Can Often Be More. Do not overwhelm yourself and remember that you do not have to have everything and the kitchen sink. Use the tips you find in these chapters; streamline drinks and prepare clean menus that are easy to execute and get you out of the kitchen so you can enjoy the party.

Work in Realms That Make You Comfortable. Choose a menu and set up a style that is your comfort level. Your party may not be the right time to try the soufflé you have never made before.

If You're Inviting Smaller Children, Make Accommodations for Them. Children with no purpose can often become a problem at holiday or social events. Head out to the dollar store and pick up some coloring books, have a bag of construction blocks they can build with or put some bubbles outside. It's never a bad idea to have a box of things for the littles to play with.

Arrange Your Space. It's good to take a step back and see your space filled with people. Often even just moving a chair can make all the difference for a good traffic flow. Scan your space for breakables that may be better tucked away and look for potential space to pop up an extra table for seating or a food station if need be.

Playlist. Music matters, so don't forget the jams! Plan, think about who is coming and have a good playlist queued up for the party. DON'T let someone turn on the TV. It is a party distraction for sure!

Most Importantly, Be Present at Your Party! You want to be present and enjoy your party, so use the prep tips provided, plan ahead, engage your family to help and put someone else in charge of stocking drinks while you are in the kitchen. Purchase some high-quality premade items to offset your menu so there is less work for you, and my most favorite tip: hire someone to help you. When someone is getting paid for a service and is not related to your event in any way other than to work, your results will be better than a friend who says they will help . . . but then spends two hours talking to Aunt Mary.

A special thanks to Luxe Linen for the fabulous linen they provided for many of our chapters. Visit them at luxeeventlinen.com.

KITCHEN BASICS

Walk into any kitchen store and you are bound to be overwhelmed by the floor-to-ceiling kitchen gadgets. Here I hope to break it down for you and give a little direction on what you need in your kitchen.

Knives

Knives are the most important tool in your kitchen, but I would advise against going out and buying a big, fancy block of knives. They are not necessarily the best quality, and they will probably contain knives you don't need. Instead, start out with the few that are necessary and build from there. Spend what you can afford while also buying the best you can afford. This is an investment. If treated properly, your knives will last a lifetime. Let's start with some standards.

Chef's Knife. Your chef's knife is the workhorse in your kitchen. It should feel like an extension of your arm. Most upscale kitchen stores have areas where you can test out the knife. Take advantage of this. Try several different knives and see how they feel in your hand. Get comfortable with the weight and length. Chop a few vegetables and choose the one that suits you. My go-to is a German knife, but my Japanese chef's knife can't be beat for precision and paper-thin slicing. The most important thing about a knife is that it is sharp. A dull knife is far more dangerous in a kitchen than a sharp one.

Paring Knife. A paring knife is another well-used knife in your kitchen. It is a small, short-bladed knife used for peeling, small cuts and intricate precision work, so again, it should feel very comfortable in your hand. Here, I stray a little from the "buy the best you can afford" philosophy. I have a few in my cutlery drawer and I tend to grab my less expensive paring knife. It's lighter and has a bit of flexibility in the blade which I find helpful for small, hand-held tasks.

Serrated Knife. A serrated knife, or a bread knife, is another mainstay in your kitchen cutlery drawer. The serrated blade is useful in slicing not only those crusty artisan breads we all love, but those delicate summer tomatoes we wait all year for. Again, this is another "try before you buy" situation. Buy what feels comfortable in your hand.

Boning Knife. A thin-tipped boning knife with a flexible blade is great for cutting around bone with precision.

Slicer Knife. A slicer is a long, thin blade used to thinly slice cooked roasts or charcuterie items, or to prep anything needing very thin cuts.

Honing Steel. A honing steel (sometimes referred to as a sharpening steel, which is misleading, because it does not actually sharpen the knife) is used to put the edges of the blade back into alignment. You carefully drag the blade of your knife along the steel several times to realign the cutting edges or hone back the burr.

Knife Sharpening Stone. While not a necessity in your kitchen, it's not a bad idea to have a sharpening stone. They are relatively inexpensive and easy to learn to use. Watch a YouTube video or two, and you'll be sharpening your own knives in no time. I'm not a fan of the electric sharpener. I've personally "chewed" up a knife or two of my own. If you're not comfortable sharpening your own knives, there are plenty of available local knife sharpeners just an internet search away. Check your farmers market. You may find a local sharpener there on the weekends.

While there are many other knives out there, what I've listed above covers the basic knives that every cook needs in their arsenal. As you grow as a cook and spend more time in the kitchen, you will no doubt want to add to your knife collection. New knives are always a good suggestion when asked what you want for an upcoming holiday or gift and you don't have room for another candle in your closet.

Pots and Pans

Pots and pans are another big investment in your kitchen arsenal. Again, I would advise buying the best you can afford. If you take care of your pots and pans, they will become lifelong fixtures in your kitchen. All-Clad is a good choice, but there are other good brands out there. You are looking for solid heavy-bottom pans that will hold and distribute heat evenly. This is another purchase where I would take a trip to a higher-end cooking store and talk to a knowledgeable professional who can give you a good in-person tutorial. Again, avoid the prepackaged sets and buy what you need. Here are a few must haves.

Stock Pot. Great for making stocks and sauces. A twelve-quart stock pot is a good size for most home kitchens.

Dutch Oven. A large, enameled Dutch oven that goes from stove top to oven. It is great for soups, stews, braising or anything that requires the initial high heat then slow cooking. I use mine daily. It lives on my stove top.

Saucepans. Here you may want to invest in a couple sizes, perhaps a two- and three-quart saucepan.

Skillets/Frying Pans. Both regular and nonstick skillets are a must in your kitchen. A couple different sizes are helpful.

Sauté Pan. A sauté pan has taller sides than a skillet and the sides sit at a right angle to the base. This allows for more surface area for searing and also offers protection against splattering.

Cast-Iron Skillet. A cast-iron skillet holds heat like no other. Once heated, this is a great pan for anything from searing to shallow frying and from making cornbread and pizzas to your family's favorite weekend pancakes.

Other Essentials

Sheet pans	9 x 13-inch casserole pans
Loaf pan	Roasting pan
Muffin tin	Round and rectangular cake pans

Kitchen Tools

Cutting boards	Metal spoons
Wooden spoons	Spatulas/turners

Vegetable peeler

Metal tongs

Whisks (balloon, French and flat whisks in a few sizes)

Ladle

Spider strainer

Heat-resistant silicone spatulas

Handheld citrus juicer

Stainless steel mixing bowls in various sizes

Box grater

Microplane grater

Mandoline slicer

Measuring cups

Measuring spoons

Offset spatula

Kitchen scale

Colander

Fine-mesh sieve

Piping tips (round and star)

Piping bags (disposable)

Round and square cutters of varying sizes

Meat thermometer

Candy/deep-fry thermometer

High-speed blender

Food processor

Immersion blender

Spice grinder

Salad spinner

Mortar and pestle

Mason jars

Butchers twine

Latex gloves

Knife Cuts

Below is a list of the basic knife cuts. For most cuts, it's helpful to start with a square or rectangular product, so start with whatever it is you are using and trim the edges to form a square or rectangle, trying to avoid as much waste as possible.

We'll use a potato as an example. Trim the sides of the potato so that you have a rectangular shape. Not only does this make it easier to get even and consistent cuts, but it allows for safety and stability when cutting. Start by slicing the potato into planks. Stack the planks and slice them into sticks, and then slice the sticks into dices. The size of the plank and dice depends on the cut you are going for.

Batonnet. This is a rectangular cut measuring ½ inch x ½ inch x 2½ to 3 inches. It is the "stick" before it becomes a medium dice.

Allumette (or Matchstick). This is a rectangular cut that measures ½ inch x ¼ inch x 2½ to 3 inches. It is the "stick" before it becomes a small dice.

Large Dice. Consists of a ¾-inch cube.

Medium Dice. Consists of a ½-inch cube.

Small Dice. Consists of a ¼-inch cube.

Mince. Something that is minced will basically melt into whatever dish it is added to. To mince garlic or onions, bring it to the small dice stage and then run your knife through it a couple of times until it is minced.

Brunoise. This is a ⅛-inch cube, the smallest of the dice cuts and is usually used for garnishes.

Julienne. This is a rectangular strip cut that measures ⅛ inch x ⅛ inch x 2½ inches.

Fine Julienne. These strips measure 1/16 x 1/16 x 2 inches.

Chiffonade. This means finely cutting herbs or leafy vegetables into thin strips. To chiffonade, neatly stack your herbs or greens flat, roll the leaves tightly together and run your knife through them, creating ribbons.

Seasoning

I'm a believer that you should season as you go. You are building layers of flavors. You need to season and taste your food as you are cooking. "Season to taste" usually refers to salt and pepper and it is exactly what it sounds like: taste, season a little, taste again and repeat until you are satisfied with the outcome. Resist the urge to dump a bunch of salt and pepper in at once. It's easy to build up flavors, but hard to walk them back.

Cooking Methods

Roasting and baking are the same thing. It's a dry cooking method where the heated air in the oven remains constant and cooks your food at an even rate. Roasting typically refers to meats and vegetables, while baking refers to desserts, breads, pastries, etc. Chef's tip: when roasting vegetables, preheat your sheet pan in the oven before adding your vegetables. You should hear a nice sizzle when your veggies hit the pan.

Broiling is similar to roasting, except the food is directly exposed to very high heat from the top. Broiling can be used to melt cheese onto a casserole or soup (think French onion), but you can also cook a steak or other whole cut of meat or fish. But be careful, as things can burn quickly.

Sautéing literally means "to jump" in French. The food is cooked with a little fat and is in constant motion either by stirring or shaking the pan. One reason consistency in knife cuts is important is because you want your food to cook at the same rate.

Searing or browning cooks an ingredient over very high heat for a short period of time. Unlike sautéing, you do not move the food until it has become fully browned. The purpose of searing is to give a flavorful exterior crust with a moist interior. Do not overcrowd the pan or you will end up with steamed and rather grey-looking food.

Grilling is a cooking method where dry heat is applied to the surface of food. Food is usually grilled on a rack over a heat source such as wood, charcoal or ceramic briquettes heated by a gas flame. Grilling can also be done indoors on a grill pan. It involves a significant amount of direct heat and quickly sears the outside of the food, producing a distinct slightly charred flavor as well as a nice crust. If food is grilled over a more moderate heat, it will produce a nice crust along with a smokier taste.

Frying can be done using two techniques: deep and shallow panfry. To deep fry, food is fully submerged in hot oil. Since it is completely submerged, the food gets a crunchy, crisp exterior that is hard to duplicate. Panfrying uses much less oil than deep frying and is a better method for more delicate foods that would otherwise fall apart in the deep fryer, like crab cakes or fritters.

Braising or stewing is a combination cooking method. Braising refers to large cuts of meat, whereas stewing refers to larger cuts of meat cut into smaller pieces. Both start out as a dry cooking technique (browning the meat in fat), and then pivot to a moist cooking method to finish cooking in liquid. Both typically use tougher cuts of meat that are cooked low and slow. Although braising/stewing requires a little effort in the beginning, after that it is a "set it and forget it" dish that transforms a tough cut of meat into something that will literally melt in your mouth.

Boiling brings water to a temperature of 212°F. The liquid rises rapidly to the surface. Boiling is a common cooking technique for pasta. Many recipes have instructions to bring to a boil and reduce it to simmer.

Simmering refers to cooking in a liquid that is just below the boiling point, between 180° and 205°F. You will see bubbles forming, but they should be gentle and not at a full rolling boil.

Poaching falls in the temperature range between 140° and 180°F. There may be tiny bubbles on the perimeter of the pan, but few to no bubbles in the water. Poaching is ideal for cooking delicate foods like fish or eggs that would otherwise be compromised by aggressive boiling.

Steaming uses boiling water without the ingredients touching the water itself. By placing a steamer basket above the boiling water, the ingredient cooks without losing any of its flavor.

Blanching also involves boiling water and is well known for setting the color of a vegetable. By placing a vegetable—green beans, for example—into boiling water for a brief time and plunging them into an ice bath, you end up with a bean that maintains its vibrant green color and still has a tender, crisp bite. When you are blanching vegetables, always have an ice bath ready and waiting. An ice bath is a bowl filled with ice and water and is used to stop the cooking process. You may have heard the phrase "blanch and shock" your vegetables. This is how you do it.

Shopping

With the internet today, there is virtually nothing you can't get your hands on, but I suggest shopping local first. Most cities have wonderful farmers markets that are open on the weekends, or check out specialty stores that cater to different ethnicities and small local butcher and seafood stores. By utilizing these stores and vendors, you are not only supporting your local community, but you are also dealing directly with the person who can offer you guidance and information. If you are looking for a particular cut of meat and it's unavailable, your local butcher can guide you to a great substitution. Also remember that butchers are some of the best chefs you will find—don't be afraid to ask your butcher for some cooking tips. Your local fishmonger can steer you towards what is fresh that day, and the farmers at your neighborhood weekend farmers market will be more than happy to not only provide you with the freshest in season produce but offer tips on

what to do with a food you may not have used before or give you a new twist on an old favorite.

STOCK YOUR PANTRY

Having a well-stocked pantry can be the difference between throwing together a quick meal with what you have on hand and eating last night's leftover takeout cold from the carton. If you have a few basic staples in your pantry, you can throw together a quick and healthy meal in no time at all. We've put together a list of staples, but of course, add your personal staples to the list based on what you need to throw together your quick and easy weeknight meals along with your party-planning menus and dishes.

CONDIMENTS & SEASONINGS

Good quality seasonings and condiments bring your dishes to their full potential, and acidic ingredients such as lemon or vinegar are also important factors in the quality of a dish. It is a true tenet of cooking to layer your food with seasoning as you go. You should always season raw meat. Often people will say they prefer to have guests add salt for themselves, but most often your dishes will not shine without seasoning. Seasoning post-cooking is nice for a finish, but it cannot do the whole job. Make sure to purchase good quality, fresh spices. Frontier is a good brand, as well as Spiceology, Smith & Truslow and the Spice House. My absolute favorite spice company is a local Michigan blender called High 5 Salts (find at foodgeekfoods.com). I am obsessed with the Fixer Upper Salt-Free Blend and use it in many dishes!

If you still have the spices from a ten-year-old wedding gift set, toss them! Spices do not actually spoil, but they do lose flavor and potency over time. Old spices will not serve your dishes well. If you are not sure of the age of a spice, sprinkle some in your hand and check for its aroma and color. If both are weak, it's time to toss! A good rule of thumb is that ground spices have a five- to nine-month shelf life, dried herbs about a year and whole species or seeds about two years or a little more. Purchase smaller quantities so they run out, and then purchase again. To keep your spices fresh for as long as possible, store them in tightly sealed containers and keep away from heat, direct sunlight and moisture.

BASIC DRY SPICE & HERB ARTISANAL

Sea Salt. Salt is probably the most important seasoning you will have in your spice rack. I am a big fan of Celtic Sea Salt (find at celticseasalt.com). It comes in super fine, regular fine and coarse varieties. The salt is baked in the sun as opposed to being fired in a kiln oven at high heats. This natural sea salt has a bit of a grey appearance since it contains minerals. Sea salt also comes in many designer varieties, from pink and black to smoked and mixed with other spices. I also recommend kosher salt for seasoning of all raw meat.

Black Pepper. For best flavor, do NOT purchase it ground. Have a committed small spice grinder, but there is also a wide variety of whole peppercorns that are sold in most stores in a disposable grinder.

Za'atar. I love this Middle Eastern spice blend that is light green with whole sesame seeds and a little sea salt and sumac. Za'atar is wonderful grilled on bread or sprinkled on meat and yogurt dips and cheeses.

Herbs de Provence. You've probably heard of this spice but may not know what it is exactly. *Herbs de Provence* is a French-inspired dry herb blend containing marjoram, rosemary, thyme, oregano and lavender. It is lovely sprinkled on grilled meats, in salads and more.

Sumac. Here is another Middle Eastern delight you may not be familiar with but will grow to love. We love including freshly ground organic sumac in zingy lemon dressing, hummus, Fattoush or on chicken and fish.

Star Anise. Often found in holiday baked goods, this will also add a zip when ground in soups and stews.

Smoked Paprika. If you imagine a classic deviled egg dusted with red powder, smoked paprika is what you're thinking of. It's also often used in potato salad or in meat braises. When using paprika, give it a toast in a nonstick pan with a little olive oil, then rub it on meat to bring up the flavor.

Turmeric Powder. As with many herbs and spices, turmeric shares a history in medicine and is said to reduce inflammation in the body. It's quite the superfood as of late. You will find it in the supplement aisle for your health and in the spice rack section for your cooking. It imparts a rich, woody flavor to Indian curries, lentil stews, rice and vegetables.

Allspice. This blended compound spice favors its name of "all," with cinnamon, cloves, nutmeg and black peppercorns. It is versatile in both sweet and savory cooking applications.

Nutmeg. This is a classic baking spice that has also crossed over to savory cooking applications. It is often added to cream sauces such as Béchamel. Nutmeg is also popular in many beverages, such as eggnog and assorted teas.

Ginger. Has a warm, bright note with a side order of sweet and is often found in Thai/Asian dishes as well as Middle Eastern-inspired and Indian cuisine.

Cumin. An essential spice to many Indian and Mexican or Southwest-inspired dishes, cumin is subtle with a warm undertone.

Cinnamon. Kind of like chilis, cinnamon has many categories and flavor profiles. The Vietnamese cinnamon is world-renowned for its high oil content and strong flavor. Cinnamon predominantly lives in the baking and pastry world but is also used in many savory cooking applications.

Cloves. Typically used in baking but also very popular in North African traditional cuisine and can often be found in notes of classic BBQ sauces.

Chipotle Chili Powder. Chipotle chiles are made from dried, smoked jalapeños and are great for adding just a hint of smoke to a dish such as BBQ recipes, dry rubs, sauces, queso dips and starchy bean or potato salads.

Red Pepper Flakes. I love a shake of these on so many foods, obviously pizza and Italian sauces, but they also add a little bright note to marinades and are also used in sausage making.

Ancho Chile Powder. Very popular in Mexican cuisine with its dark ruby color, mild heat profile and a little side of sweet.

Cayenne Pepper. It's straight up hot and many people don't use it as a common spice, but it is one of the spices I use the most. In lieu of black or white pepper I often just reach for a small sprinkle of cayenne.

Onion Powder. Always a good stand-by spice to add a little more depth to sauces and salad dressings.

Dried Basil. I will most always reach for fresh basil, but dry has its place too in soups and Italian sauces.

Italian Seasoning. This classic dried Italian herb blend, which was born from the comingling of oregano, fennel, marjoram. rosemary, thyme, basil and sage, is popular on the world stage, flavoring everything from spaghetti to Italian sauces to vinaigrettes.

Dried Bay Leaves. This aromatic herb with a woody undertone is most often used in long cooking projects such as soups and stews. Usually one or two will do the trick. Too many will cause bitterness in your dishes.

Dried Oregano. Like basil, my go-to is fresh oregano, but dried is super popular in Mediterranean and Italian vinaigrettes and other dishes.

Sage. Sage has a very distinct flavor and is easy to pick out of a crowd. It is a no-brainer with poultry and turkey and pairs well with pork or when making sausage and some dishes with cheese.

Marjoram. Most often better to add toward the end of cooking your dishes, marjoram carries light floral notes with a little woody undertone and pairs well with salad dressings, stews, marinades and meat dishes that cook for a long time.

Ground Cardamom. If cardamom is not on your spice rack, it should be! There are two varieties of cardamom: black and green, and yellow and white. Of course, it is the foundation spice of Chai Tea with its complex aroma of pine, fruit and a touch of menthol-like flavor. It will jazz up your rice dishes, curries, pastries and has now made it on to the craft cocktail scene. Go, cardamon!

Dill Weed. Where would ranch salad dressing and dip be without this? Use wisely in dressings, yogurt dips and vinaigrettes.

Rosemary. Wonderful in soups, stews and braised meat dishes. Flip to page 141 to see how it works in cookies, too!

Curry Powder. Curry powder is a mix of more than twenty herbs, spices and seeds. It is of course used in curries, but also finds its way into other sweet and savory dishes.

Ground Coriander. These ground seeds, which come from the cilantro plant, are used in many ways but often found in Mexican dishes such as tacos and guacamole.

Chili Powder. Chili powder is a great way to season in one swoop. It is a compound spice blend of chiles, garlic, cumin, coriander, oregano and cloves primarily used in Mexican and southwestern cuisine.

Taco Seasoning. I only suggest this if you purchase from a fresh spice house, as the big jars from the grocery store are often lackluster. This is a compound spice which can replace the need for multiple spices. Look for a blend that might have some of these players: toasted ancho, guajillo, New Mexico and arbol chiles, cumin, coriander and paprika. Taco seasoning is great in tacos, but works well in soups, beans and many other Mexican or southwestern-inspired dishes.

CONDIMENTS

This list could easily be over one hundred items long. I am listing some basic staples to keep on hand, but your lifestyle and tastes will drive your condiment collection.

Ketchup & Mustard. These all-American condiments can be used in so many applications besides burgers and fries. Purchase good quality ketchup and without added corn syrup. Mustard comes in a lot of varieties, but yellow, stone-ground and Dijon are a great start.

Honey & Jam. A must for adding that little pinch of sweet to most foods. Often, I eliminate sugar in a recipe in favor of the nectar of honey. I always purchase local, and in Michigan we have some serious local bees doing their thing! Jam should be your jam and besides the usual suspects like PB&J and morning toast, remember it in a quick vinaigrette in place of whole fruit. Jam layers well on assorted cheese or whipped brie and certainly many savory dishes.

Maple Syrup. One hundred percent real maple syrup is what I'm talking about. All the others are just a bunch of disguised high-fructose corn syrups. Yes, it does cost more, but you and your family are worth it. Like its friend honey, it can be used as a sweetener in place of sugar and drizzled into pastry dishes and savory dishes. My famous autumn turkey stew would not be the same without a little Michigan maple!

Mayonnaise. Mayonnaise can act as the base for so many different sauces! Flavored aiolis or tartar sauce are a few examples, and where would tuna or egg salad be without it? Find a good quality store-bought brand or try your hand at making it. It's much easier than you probably think.

Tahini. We would not have our celebrated hummus without it. This sesame paste is a great condiment for many other dishes, vinaigrettes and salads.

Soy Sauce or Tamari. Soy sauce and tamari are very similar and used in many Asian-inspired dishes. They are both derived from fermented soybeans, but tamari is processed without wheat, so it is the gluten-free option. If soy is not for you, try coconut aminos, which is a great substitute for soy.

Ponzu. This citrus soy sauce adds a bright, fresh note to Asian dishes.

Worcestershire. Your grandma probably had this in her pantry, too, and it's often used in meat preparations and sauces. Worcestershire is a concoction of vinegar, water, soy, garlic, sugar, molasses, tamarind extract and chili peppers.

Harissa. The North African pepper paste is traditionally made from bell peppers, chile peppers and garlic, and has assorted heat levels. I smear this on meat or salmon. Use it as a rub for vegetables before roasting. Harissa is an easy but not commonly used condiment that will make you look like a rock star.

Sriracha & Sambal Oelek. Sriracha is the go-to condiment in our street food aspirations of late, from burgers to bahn mi or maybe a spicy slaw for a fusion taco or topping. I put it on simple stir frys and cold noodle dishes at my house. Sambal oelek is also spicy, and with its birthplace in southeast Asia, it is a more simplistic chili sauce and is made with just chilis and vinegar.

Vinegars. Raspberry, balsamic, rice, champagne, white and cider are the core staples. Their obvious use is in vinaigrettes, but often vinegars are great for that splash of acid you need in sauce or soup making and marinades. The two I cannot live without are coconut vinegar and Bragg apple cider vinegar. Bragg has a cult following, as it is touted to heal most ailments and help you lose weight to boot.

Oils. Olive, walnut, sunflower and sesame are good ones to have on hand. Purchase good quality oil as it is important for flavor as well as good health. I would opt out of highly refined vegetable oils for hot cooking and sautéing, as they are not stable under high heat, so choose more traditional fats for that application, such as clarified butter or ghee.

Panko Breadcrumbs. This is the only grain on this list, because everyone needs a little panko in their cooking world. Panko is a quick fix for a crunchy top on fish or chicken and provides stability for meatloaves and meatballs. It's a more interesting choice than fine breadcrumbs.

Final Notes

Mise en place, what does that mean? It's French for "everything in its place," and it's the key to success in the kitchen. The most important thing you can do in preparing for your event (or cooking in general) is to be organized and have a plan. Read over all the recipes so there are no surprises. Set up a workstation for yourself. Start with a large cutting board, have your knives, a bin with your tools and a garbage bowl all within reach. Make recipes and prep lists easily visible and use small bowls or deli containers to store your prep work. When I'm preparing for any large gathering, be it entertaining a large group of friends or just having my family over for Sunday brunch, I rely on lists for everything. I start with a timeline for the week (i.e., when to shop, what I can make ahead, etc.), and then I make a list with what I need to gather for staging and serving and pull out any special props or plates and gather them all in one place. For the day of the event, I prepare a schedule and tape it on the cupboard in front of me. It tells me what needs to be done, and if I get a little sidetracked or distracted, it recenters me.

1

Contemporary Oktoberfest

GF/Gluten Free, DF/Dairy Free, V/Vegetarian, V+/Vegan

Autumn is my favorite season in the mitten state. It is perfect in most every way, with apple picking, pumpkins, celebrated seasonal gourds and root vegetables. The air turns a little crisp and the landscape colors change to fall's golds and reds. Step up a traditional Oktoberfest event with a sausage and pretzel bar that will be a remembered crowd favorite.

Throw in a cup of chili and an apple-inspired dessert for good measure! The changing season provides a lot to celebrate. Go for rustic with an overtone of shabby-chic. Kraft paper can be a fun and economical table covering that you can also write on to label the dishes and condiments. Use wood crates as risers to create levels in the center of your table and wood boards and galvanized metal trays as serving pieces. You can find wood planks or circles at most any craft/home store. Add rustic metal elements using iron candle holders, pewter, pounded metal vessels or distressed wood pieces.

Add a breath of floral with amber-colored bud vases, old beer bottles and jugs with a tight cluster of dried wheat for easy and chic centerpieces. Painted mason jars look great filled with golden, brown or rust-colored flowers, rustic bundled greens and autumn berry branches and leaves. Fill jars with acorns or add small bales of decorative hay. Mid-century Pyrex vessels, twig orbs and small cone-shaped trees will add a natural luster. Small galvanized buckets with pinecones and gourds, tin buckets lined with parchment paper or bushel baskets would be great filled with pretzels and peanuts, popcorn, or other snacks. Disposable bamboo plates or simple kraft boats would be my go-to for guest plates, along with silverware wrapped with twine or raffia.

myo AUTUMN PRETZEL & SAUSAGE BAR

YIELD 8 SERVINGS

Soft and hard pretzels paired with a ton of fun sauces, smears and condiments can make any fall gathering a huge success! Kids, teens and adults alike can find something in this MYO mix.

You can find good quality frozen jumbo pretzels in most of your better grocery stores or food service outlets, but of course homemade is always tasty too! Pretzel balls (or knots as they are sometimes called) are also a fun mouth-pop with assorted smears and sauces.

JUMBO SOFT pretzels

YIELD 8 LARGE PRETZELS

1½ cups warm WATER *(110°F to 115°F)*

1 tablespoon SUGAR

2 teaspoons KOSHER SALT

1 envelope active dry YEAST

20 ounces all-purpose FLOUR

2 ounces unsalted BUTTER, melted

VEGETABLE OIL, for the bowl and pan

10 cups WATER

⅔ cup BAKING SODA

1 large EGG YOLK, beaten with 1 tablespoon water *(egg wash)*

¼ cup PRETZEL SALT

1 In the bowl of a stand mixer, combine warm water, sugar and salt. Sprinkle yeast on top. Set aside for 5 minutes or until the mixture foams.

2 Add flour and butter. Using the dough hook attachment, mix on low speed until well-combined. Change to medium speed and knead until the dough is smooth and pulls away from the side of the bowl, about 4 to 5 minutes.

3 Remove dough from the bowl. Clean the bowl and oil it well. Return dough to the bowl, cover with plastic wrap and set aside in a warm place for an hour or until the dough has doubled in size.

4 Heat the oven to 450°F. Line 2 half-sheet pans with parchment paper and lightly brush with oil. Set aside.

5 In a large stock pot, bring 10 cups of water and baking soda to a rolling boil.

6 Turn the dough out onto a lightly oiled work surface and divide into 8 equal pieces. Roll each piece of dough into a 24-inch rope. Make a U-shape with the rope and, holding the ends of the rope, cross them over each other and press onto the bottom of the U to form the shape of a pretzel. Place on the prepared sheet pans. Repeat with the remaining pieces of dough.

7 One at a time, place the pretzels in the boiling water for 30 seconds. Using a large slotted spatula, remove pretzels from the water and return to the sheet pans. Brush the tops with the egg wash and sprinkle with pretzel salt.

8 Bake for 12 to 14 minutes or until dark golden brown in color. Transfer to a cooling rack for at least 5 minutes before serving.

PRETZEL smears

Of course, mustard is the expected and perfect pairing for pretzels. Use a few tablespoons of "this and that" to pep up your MYO mustard madness.

Base Mustard

GF | DF | V   YIELD 2 CUPS

1 cup plus 2 tablespoons YELLOW MUSTARD

½ cup DIJON MUSTARD

¼ cup STONE-GROUND MUSTARD

2 tablespoons HONEY

Compound Mustard Flavors

GF | V

To ½ cup of BASE MUSTARD, add:

CHERRY: 3 tablespoons chopped reconstituted dried cherries and a pinch of black pepper. (To reconstitute dried cherries, soak in a tablespoon of water or orange juice for 10 minutes, drain and chop.)

STOUT: reduce ¾ cup stout beer by ¾ (making a syrup so to speak).

COWBOY: 2 teaspoons chopped roasted pepper, 2 teaspoons chopped grilled onions, ½ teaspoon cumin and a pinch of black pepper.

SWEET & SOUR: 2 tablespoons pickled red onions.

DILL: 1 teaspoon chopped fresh dill and 1 teaspoon onion powder.

DIABLO: ½ teaspoon sriracha.

THE MITTEN: 1 tablespoon Michigan maple syrup and 1 tablespoon chopped reconstituted dried cherries.

MOROCCAN: ½ teaspoon paprika, ½ teaspoon turmeric and ⅛ teaspoon coriander.

APPLE PECAN: 1 tablespoon chopped pecans, 3 tablespoons finely chopped roasted apples and 2 teaspoons Michigan maple syrup.

BLUE CHEESE: 3 tablespoons of finely crumbled blue cheese.

SOUTH CAROLINA: ¼ cup of your favorite barbeque sauce.

Base Mustard 2

To ½ cup YELLOW MUSTARD, add:

MELLOW YELLOW: 3 tablespoons chopped banana peppers.

MEXICAN VILLAGE: 2 teaspoons chopped pickled jalapeños and ⅛ teaspoon chipotle puree.

NON-MUSTARD SMEARS

You can find these and plenty of others at your favorite market:

- Nacho cheese sauce
- Bar cheese spread *(refrigerated counter)*

What would a pretzel be without a little sausage pairing? There are so many amazing sausages out in the world now. Even at the big box stores you will find fun flavors like Thai apple, apple chicken, brats, cheese this or that, kielbasa with extra smoke and so on and so forth. Grill sausages outside on the barbeque, roast them in the oven on a sheet pan or cook them on the stove top in a heavy-bottomed skillet. Serve sausages whole or slice on an angle about an inch thick for one-bite options. Your mustard smear creations will also work tastefully with your sausage selections. Consider some pickled items and raw veggies to round out your pretzel and sausage bar.

Suggested Sausages to Pair with Pretzel Bar

DF

1 pound ITALIAN SAUSAGE, cooked and sliced on an angle

1 pound KIELBASA, cooked and sliced on an angle

1 pound SPECIALTY SAUSAGE such as turkey apple cooked and sliced on an angle

harvest BABY KALE SALAD

GF | V

YIELD 8 SERVINGS

This kale and apple salad with blue cheese, maple glazed walnuts and balsamic dressing would be the great green food you could pair with pretzels, chili and sausage.

2 honey crisp **APPLES**, diced

1 **LEMON**, juiced

8 ounces **BABY KALE**

½ **RED ONION**, julienned

BALSAMIC MUSTARD VINAIGRETTE *(recipe follows)*

CANDIED WALNUTS *(recipe follows)*

4 ounces semi-firm **BLUE CHEESE**

½ cup chopped cooked **BACON** *(optional)*

1. In a medium bowl toss diced apples with the juice from the lemon.
2. In a large bowl toss apples, baby kale and onions. Lightly drizzle with vinaigrette and toss to coat. Arrange salad on a platter, top with candied walnuts, crumbled blue cheese and chopped bacon (if using).

Balsamic Mustard Vinaigrette

GF | DF | V

YIELD ½+ CUP

¼ cup plus 2 tablespoons **OLIVE OIL**

3 tablespoons **BALSAMIC VINEGAR**

2 teaspoons **DIJON MUSTARD**

Juice from half of **LEMON**

1 teaspoon **MAPLE SYRUP**

¼ teaspoon **SEA SALT**

⅛ teaspoon **BLACK PEPPER**

Pinch **CAYENNE PEPPER**

1. With a blender or an immersion stick, mix all ingredients for about a minute until vinaigrette comes together. You can also whisk together in a bowl or place in a large mason jar with a lid and shake until blended.

Candied Walnuts

GF | V

YIELD ½ CUP

1 teaspoon unsalted **BUTTER**

½ cup **WALNUT** halves

¼ teaspoon **SALT**

2 tablespoons **PURE MAPLE SYRUP**

1. Preheat the oven to 325°F. Line a small sheet pan with parchment paper and set aside.
2. In a small nonstick pan over medium heat, melt butter. Add walnuts, season with salt and toss to coat.
3. Add maple syrup, stir to coat and bring to a simmer. Do not stir after syrup starts simmering as this could cause the sugar to crystalize. Cook for 3 minutes or until most of the excess liquid has evaporated, being careful not to burn the sugar.
4. Transfer walnuts to the prepared sheet pan. Bake on the center rack for 6 to 8 minutes or until remaining liquid has evaporated. Set aside to cool.

Chef's Notes

Nuts are great for everything, including just snacking. Make a double or triple batch and store in an airtight jar at room temperature.

chipotle TURKEY CHILI

GF | DF   YIELD 8 TO 10 SERVINGS

2 tablespoons BUTTER or OLIVE OIL

3 pounds GROUND TURKEY MEAT *(dark or white, whatever you prefer)*

1 ONION, finely chopped

1 GREEN BELL PEPPER, medium dice

1 RED BELL PEPPER, medium dice

1 tablespoon chopped GARLIC

1 *(28-ounce)* can TOMATO PUREE

1 *(15-ounce)* can fire-roasted DICED TOMATOES

1 *(15-ounce)* can PUMPKIN PUREE

3 cups CHICKEN STOCK

2 cups medium diced SWEET POTATO

1 cup medium diced PARSNIPS

3 tablespoons dark CHILI POWDER

2 tablespoons CUMIN

2 CHIPOTLE CHILI PEPPERS *(in adobo sauce)*, minced

1 tablespoon SALT

2 teaspoons fresh-cracked BLACK PEPPER

1 *(15-ounce)* can CANNELLINI or NAVY BEANS

1. Heat oil or butter in a large, heavy-bottom stock pot over medium heat. Add ground turkey in small clumps and cook over medium heat, breaking up meat with a wooden spoon until browned.

2. Add onions and peppers and sauté for 3 to 4 minutes. Add garlic and sauté for another minute.

3. Add tomato puree, fire-roasted tomatoes, pumpkin puree, chicken stock, sweet potatoes, parsnips and seasonings. Bring to a boil, reduce heat and simmer, uncovered, 20 to 25 minutes until sweet potatoes and parsnips are tender.

4. Add beans and continue to simmer for 8 to 10 minutes.

5. Adjust seasonings as needed and serve or cool for service later.

Chef's Notes

If chili is too thick, add more stock to thin it out. This recipe is easily made vegan. Replace ground turkey with vegan meat alternative or lentils, and substitute vegetarian stock for chicken broth.

michigan BROWN BETTY

V

¾ cup plus 2 tablespoons all-purpose FLOUR

⅓ cup packed BROWN SUGAR

2 tablespoons plus ½ cup granulated SUGAR *(divided)*

1 teaspoon SALT *(divided)*

8 tablespoons unsalted BUTTER, cold, cut into small cubes

1 cup old-fashioned ROLLED OATS *(not quick cooking)*

3 pounds local MICHIGAN APPLES, peeled and cut into ½-inch chunks

2 tablespoons freshly squeezed LEMON JUICE

½ teaspoon ground CINNAMON

1 Preheat the oven to 350°F. Spray 2-quart baking dish with nonstick spray. Line a sheet pan with parchment paper.

2 For the topping, in a large bowl mix flour, brown sugar, 2 tablespoons granulated sugar and ½ teaspoon of salt. Gently cut butter into flour/sugar mixture using a pastry blender or by tossing with a large fork or two knives until mixture is the texture of coarse meal.

3 Add oats and use your hands to combine by squeezing the mixture together until large, moist clumps form. Wrap and place in the freezer for 15 to 20 minutes.

4 In a large bowl toss apples with lemon juice, cinnamon and remaining ½ cup granulated sugar and ½ teaspoon salt. Transfer to a shallow prepared baking dish and sprinkle with topping mixture.

5 Place the baking dish on the prepared sheet pan and bake 55 to 65 minutes until golden and bubbling. Let cool for 10 minutes before serving.

Chef's Notes

This is delicious on its own or served with vanilla bean whipped cream or ice cream.

PUMPKIN SPICED APPLE **cider**

GF | V+   YIELD 16 SERVINGS

½ gallon local APPLE CIDER

⅓ cup spiced PUMPKIN PIE PUREE

1 tablespoon WHOLE CLOVES

1 teaspoon ground ALLSPICE

1 teaspoon ground NUTMEG

2 CINNAMON STICKS, more for garnish

1. In a heavy-bottomed stock pot combine all ingredients and simmer over low heat for 15 to 20 minutes.

2. Remove cinnamon sticks and cloves. Ladle into mugs and garnish with fresh cinnamon sticks.

Chef's Notes

This is great for any fall gathering. Feel free to add dark rum for the adult version.

pretzel rack RECIPE

Just for fun, please enjoy this "recipe" from my husband Rich, who made the pretzel rack for our shoot. The ones I use at work are huge, and this is a nice tabletop size. The entire project took him about an hour and a half. The ingredients are available from a hardware or home improvement store.

TOOLS AND SUPPLIES:

Flat worktable *(with protection in case glue gets on it!)*

One 8-foot piece of ¾-inch COPPER PIPE

Small pipe cutter

One piece of SANDPAPER *(320 grit)*

Window cleaner

Paper towel

One package EPOXY GLUE *(5 minute to 1 hour set time)*

Disposable small paper plates to mix epoxy

Popsicle sticks to spread epoxy

Two ¾-inch COPPER ELBOWS *(90 degree)*

Four ¾-inch COPPER END CAPS

Two ¾-inch COPPER TEES

1. Cut the copper pipe into pieces of the following length using the pipe cutter:

    1 piece at 30 inches long, 2 pieces at 17 inches long, and 4 pieces at 6½ inches long

2. Lightly sand each piece and each fitting to bring out the bright copper color.

3. Lightly sand the inside of each fitting to assure good adhesion.

4. Clean each pipe and fitting with window cleaner and wipe with paper towel.

5. Build the upright:

    A Dispense about a teaspoon of epoxy glue and mix well.

    B Apply a light coat of epoxy glue to the inside of each opening in each of the two elbows.

    C Place an elbow on each end of the 30-inch piece of pipe.

    D Place one of 17-inch pieces of pipe into the other opening of the elbow.

    E Wipe off any of the excess epoxy.

    F Lay the assembly flat and do not move until the glue has hardened.

6. Install end caps:

    A Dispense about a teaspoon of epoxy glue and mix well.

    B Apply a light coat of epoxy glue to the inside of each of the 4 end caps.

    C Place one end cap on one end of each of the 6½-inch pieces of pipe.

    D Wipe off any excess epoxy.

7. Assemble the feet:

    A Dispense about a teaspoon of epoxy glue and mix well.

    B Apply a light coat of epoxy glue to the inside of each of the 2 opposing ends of each Tee. Do not apply epoxy to the "stem" of the Tee.

    C Insert one of the 6½-inch pieces into each of the 2 opposing ends of the Tee.

    D Wipe off any excess epoxy.

    E Lay each foot assembly flat and allow the glue to harden.

8. To use, simply insert the upright into the stem of the feet Tees. When done, disassemble the feet for easy storage!

Builder's Notes

The copper will develop a natural patina over time. If you prefer the bright copper finish, the pretzel rack can be sprayed with a clear acrylic paint or polished with paste wax to help retard oxidation.

2

Tailgate Tricks

GF/Gluten Free, DF/Dairy Free, V/Vegetarian, V+/Vegan

35

Tailgating is always a fun way to start the game, so why not make it look good, too? It does not have to be complicated to create a great look for your next tailgate. I like to start with my color scheme, or you can think of the teams playing and pick your favorite. My colors are maize and blue, so I have the quintessential flags, cups and table coverings that speak to that.

I picked up a large vinyl mat a few years back that I use to cover my table surface. When the day is done, I wash it off with a little soap and water at home and throw it in my tailgate prop box. I normally try to freshen my décor box each season.

Speaking of the prop boxes, this is a great way to store all your décor and is easy for traveling and storage. Think of lightweight items like branded pendants you can hang from your open trunk door. A few themed throw blankets that act as décor are also good for those chilly mornings. Use large tin buckets or containers in your color scheme for transportation and to hold beverages over ice or pack with snacks like chips or homemade Chex Mix. If you have extra room in your vehicle, don't be afraid to bring some easily movable furniture like a small bookcase or petit table to display cups and plates. Multi-tier trays are helpful for display. I have always been a fan of the artificial Astroturf and have made amazing table coverings with that. Sometimes I stray from my normal swag and celebrate the season, rather than opting for the standard football fare décor. Think plaid blankets and rustic crates or buckets. Pick up a few mums from the farmers market and wrap the pots in burlap for a nice rustic feel. It never hurts to look on Pinterest to get inspired. Happy tailgating! GO, TEAM!

As for plates, serving vessels and such, the easier the better. Disposable kraft boats, plastic or melamine serving platters and recycled tins that you might paint like a football to hold utensils and napkins are all great options.

Touchdown Menu

Tailgates are fun and communal social gatherings to let your team spirit shine! For many of us it is a celebrated ritual. I am a University of Michigan band mom and come sunshine, rain or even snow, I am in the "Go Blue Zone" with food treats for my tailgate group. For us tried-and-true tailgaters, we are always trying to think outside of the box. Sure, the quintessential chili with toppings is great. Fun sandwiches out of the cooler with a menagerie of snacks, dips, cold salads and chips are an option. A breakfast casserole toted in your hot bag with bagels and cream cheese would be fun, but most everyone already has those menus, so I thought I would take you on a journey of my new obsession: food combinations grilled in foil packets! It is a fun, interactive grill concept where you mix-n-match thinly sliced veggies and meat with herbs and spices, fold tightly in foil and toss on the grill. This allows each guest to have their own designer-grilled tailgate food experience!

Your packets can range from steak sandwich options to fancy gourmet concoctions to impress even the snobbiest of professional tailgaters. The food will be hot and fresh. Fire up a packet when you are ready, and it takes about five to fifteen minutes to warm or cook your packet. Eat right out the foil packet, slide it on a bun or put it on a plate. Of course, this concept would also be amazing for outdoor cookouts, camping trips and long holiday weekends with family at the cottage. I love the unique presentation and the fresh, tasty outcome of this cooking technique.

When thinking about foil packet tailgate meals, there are different ways to approach your menu planning. I will show two example stations below to get your ideas churning, along with a few of my tried-and-true recipes.

CONCEPT ONE:
Build an MYO Bar; They Will Come and Create!

This approach lets your family and friends' inner cook get a touchdown. You'll need to plan your theme: it could be deconstructed kebabs with all sorts of veggie options, oils, seasonings or pestos, or maybe a hearty BBQ using sliced cooked sausages mixed with peppers, onions and potatoes. A southwestern dish can be achieved using chicken, seasonings, tomatoes, cheese, corn, BBQ sauce, herbs and spiced oils. Maybe you prefer Greek street food and your MYO platter has gyro meat, chicken, olives, vegetables, pickled or sliced onions, peppers, garlic sauce, feta, pita and hummus on the side. There are countless options available, from Asian to Jamaican and everywhere in between. The nice thing here is everyone gets to choose what and how much they want.

CONCEPT TWO:
You Build It and They Will Still Come with a Cheer!

Here you will preplan the foil packet menu with some good food combos in mind to please a diverse group of people, from young people that may like more kid-friendly food, to guests looking for a light square or something hearty for your hungry sports enthusiast.

The nice thing about either road you travel is that both prep and cleanup are a breeze!

MYO Basic Blueprint Foil Packets

FOIL: Tear your heavy-duty foil into 12 x 14-inch long sheets, including a few extra pieces.

FAT: Fat is important as it helps raw, or in some cases partially-cooked or cooked ingredients, from sticking to foil. About a tablespoon per packet will usually do the trick. Butter or a butter alternative, olive oil, coconut oil, avocado oil and flavor-infused oils all work well. Pesto is great as it includes oil, herbs and garlic which adds a nice flavor punch. A chef trick for MYO packets is to put your fats in squeeze bottles. This makes them easy to transport and use. Make sure they are individually wrapped tightly.

PROTEIN: Ground meats like chicken, turkey, beef and lamb work well as they cook quickly when crumbled and they most often contain some percent of fat. Thinly sliced chicken and steak or beef work well. Stay away from big pieces or whole breasts. Sliced cooked sausages are great, and you do not have to worry about slicing them

thin since they are already cooked. Do not overlook shrimp or slices of a more hearty fish like salmon. There are lots of plant-based meats and tofu options for our veggie or vegan sports fans.

VEGGIE PARTY: The sky's the limit here. Try mushrooms, onions, sliced squash or zucchini, asparagus, bell pepper chunks or strips, green beans, little sweet peppers or even frozen vegetables. The important thing to remember about veggies is to manage their cooking time. For example, you would want to slice your potatoes or carrots thinner so they cook at the same rate as your mushrooms and onions.

CONDIMENTS & SPICES: As with any type of cooking, you cannot forget about a dash and a sprinkle of seasoning in your packets. Sea salt and pepper are a must, and you can keep layering from there. Try fresh or dry herbs or other special seasonings that match your flavor profile. Maybe add BBQ spices, onion or garlic powder, paprika, cumin, Italian seasoning, Za'atar and chopped garlic. Sauces such as BBQ, Worcestershire, soy and hot sauces will all work, depending on your taste. Pesto, ketchup, a splash of citrus juice, wine or stock will all give your packets extra flavor and provide some liquid to aid in the steaming process. I would also include cheese in this category. Add a sprinkle of feta or Parmesan and, if you are starting with base ingredients that are more cooked than raw, you could lay a slice of cheese on top before sealing the packet. The Philly steak recipe is a good example of cheese going on top of a cooked item which will be reheated later on the grill.

FILL & FOLD: Tear heavy-duty aluminum foil into 12 x 14-inch long sheets. Lay your piece of foil out and start to build, starting with raw meat on the bottom, then veggies, fat, spices, flavoring agents and condiments. Do not overcrowd your packet, as you need to allow room for steam to build and help carry the even cooking process of ingredients. Fold the two long edges toward one another and fold over twice, then crimp tightly. Fold and crimp each short end of the foil toward the middle so that the edges are all tightly sealed and no juices leak out. Store the packets in the refrigerator if you have premade them.

GO TIME: Getting your grill set up should be the first order of business when you reach your tailgate site. Heat the grill to medium-high before you start grilling. The general rule is about 9 to 15 minutes cook time, depending on what is inside. For example, shrimp and thin veggies may cook in a little under 8 minutes, but pieces of chicken with larger cut veggies will take longer. Of course, do not cook the heck out of them, but as you are steam cooking, it is hard to overcook to the point of being dry. If you are using the oven, bake on a sheet pan in a preheated 350°F for 25 to 30 minutes.

CHILI CHEESE "fries"

GF   YIELD 8 TO 10 PACKETS

8 to 10 pieces of heavy-duty ALUMINUM FOIL torn into
     12 x 14-inch sheets

NONSTICK SPRAY

4 to 5 large IDAHO POTATOES, rinsed and scrubbed, and cut into
     steak fries-size wedges *(about 4 per half)*

3 tablespoons OLIVE OIL

1 teaspoon SEA SALT

½ teaspoon PEPPER

8 to 10 slices of CHEDDAR CHEESE

1 cup of your favorite CHILI

½ cup shredded CHEDDAR CHEESE

¼ cup SCALLIONS or diced ONIONS

1. Preheat the oven to 375°F. Prepare foil sheets by giving them a coating of nonstick spray.

2. Take prepared raw potato wedges and cut in half to make 16 shorter pieces.

3. In a large bowl add potatoes and toss with olive oil, sea salt and pepper. Place on a sheet pan and roast for about 12 minutes until partially cooked but not soft.

4. Divide potatoes evenly among prepared foil sheets. Place a slice of cheddar cheese over potatoes and top with a couple ounces of chili, a sprinkle of shredded cheddar and scallions or onions. Crimp edges tightly and fold over to make a secure packet. Refrigerate or stash in a cooler to transport.

5. Place packets folded side up on BBQ and grill for 5 to 7 minutes.

STADIUM TEXAS BBQ beefsteak

GF | DF   Yield 8 to 10 packets

8 to 10 pieces of heavy-duty ALUMINUM FOIL, torn into
     12 x 14-inch sheets

1 pound raw ground CHORIZO

2 pounds or 4 heaping cups medium-diced cooked STEAK,
     STEAK TIPS or TOP-ROUND BEEF of your choice

4 tablespoons OLIVE OIL or fat of your choice

2 tablespoons finely chopped GARLIC

2 teaspoons CUMIN

¾ cup diced GREEN PEPPER

½ cup diced ONION

⅓ cup pickled JALAPEÑO PEPPERS

¾ cup of your favorite BBQ SAUCE

SEA SALT and BLACK PEPPER to taste

BUNS *(optional)*

1. Line up your foil sheets and crumble a few tablespoons of chorizo in the middle of each. Divide chopped steak evenly over chorizo.

2. In a small bowl whisk together olive oil, chopped garlic and cumin. Add diced peppers and onions and toss to coat. Divide evenly over meat. Top with pickled jalapeños, a couple tablespoons of BBQ sauce and a sprinkle of salt and pepper. Crimp edges super tight and fold over to make a secure packet. Refrigerate or stash in a cooler to transport.

3. Place packets folded side up on the prepared BBQ and grill for 8 to 12 minutes. You are basically just making sure the chorizo is cooked through.

4. Serve on a bun if desired, a plate or eat right out of the foil packet.

deconstructed
GREEKTOWN CHICKEN KABOBS

GF | DF   YIELD 8 TO 10 PACKETS

2 pounds medium-diced raw **CHICKEN BREAST**

8 to 10 pieces of heavy-duty **ALUMINUM FOIL**, torn into 12 x 14-inch sheets

2 tablespoons **OLIVE OIL**

1 teaspoon **SEA SALT**

½ teaspoon freshly ground **PEPPER**

2 cups chunky diced **GREEN** or **RED PEPPERS**

1 **RED ONION**, halved and cut in medium-thin strips

1 medium **ZUCCHINI**, cut into ½-inch circles

½ cup diced **TOMATOES**

½ cup **KALAMATA OLIVES** *(optional)*

¾ cup **GREEK SALAD DRESSING** or **VINAIGRETTE**, your favorite store-bought brand

½ cup of crumbled **FETA** *(optional)*

PITA BREAD *(optional)*

1. Place raw chicken in the center of each foil sheet.

2. In a small bowl whisk olive with sea salt and pepper. Drizzle over chicken.

3. Layer packets with peppers, onions, zucchini circles, diced tomatoes and olives if using. Top with a couple tablespoons of

Greek dressing. Fold packet and crimp sides tightly. Place in the refrigerator or cooler to transport.

4. Place packets folded side up on BBQ and grill for 12 to 15 minutes.

5. Top with crumbled feta and serve with pita bread if desired.

spicy SHRIMP FOIL PACKETS

GF | DF

2 pounds raw, 16/20 medium-size **SHRIMP**, peeled and deveined

3 tablespoons **OLIVE OIL**

1 teaspoon **CHILI POWDER**

1 teaspoon **CUMIN**, divided

½ teaspoon **SEA SALT**

¼ teaspoon **CHILI FLAKES**

1 *(15-ounce)* can **BLACK BEANS**, drained and rinsed

1 cup diced fresh or canned **PINEAPPLE**

½ cup small diced **RED ONION**

1 **RED PEPPER**, diced

1 medium **TOMATO**, diced

2 tablespoons minced **PICKLED JALAPEÑO**

1 tablespoon grated fresh **GINGER**

3 tablespoons fresh **LIME JUICE**

½ teaspoon ground **CORIANDER**

8 to 10 pieces of heavy-duty **ALUMINUM FOIL**, torn into 12 x 14-inch sheets

1 to 2 **AVOCADOS**, diced, or ½ cup **GUACAMOLE**

4 tablespoons chopped **CILANTRO**

1 Rinse the shrimp and pat dry.

2 In a large bowl mix olive oil, chili powder, ½ teaspoon cumin, salt and chili flakes. Add shrimp and toss to coat.

3 To make the salsa, in a medium bowl combine the black beans, pineapple, red onion, red peppers, tomato, jalapeño and ginger. Add lime juice, coriander and remaining ½ teaspoon of cumin. Gently stir everything together to combine.

4 Arrange foil sheets and divide black bean salsa mixture evenly, top with 4 shrimp (if you have extra, divide evenly among each packet). Fold packet and crimp sides tightly. Place in the refrigerator or cooler to transport.

5 Place the foil packets on the grill, cover and cook for 10 to 12 minutes until shrimp are opaque.

6 Peel open the foil packet, top with the diced avocado and cilantro if desired.

FOIL BBQ BANANA **split**

YIELD 1 PACKET

1 piece of heavy-duty **ALUMINUM FOIL** *(10 x 10-inch sheet)*

1 ripe peeled **BANANA**, split in half lengthwise

2 ounces **DARK CHOCOLATE BAR**

2 large **MARSHMALLOWS**, cut into quarters *(easier if you use scissors)*

4 **CARAMEL CANDIES**, cut in half

1 tablespoon *(or more)* toasted **SLIVERED ALMONDS** *(you can also use chopped walnuts or pecans)*

2 to 3 **GINGERSNAP COOKIES** or **GRAHAM CRACKERS**, broken up into pieces

VANILLA ICE CREAM *(optional)*

1   Tear heavy-duty foil into a 10 x 10-inch sheet. Crunch foil into a packet shaped like a banana split dish.

2   Place banana in the center and scatter remaining garnishes over the top. Crimp the foil together, leaving a 2-inch gap over the filling.

3   Place on a low grill for 5 to 8 minutes until gooey and melted. Serve over vanilla ice cream or eat right out of a foil banana boat.

blueprint MYO COMBINATIONS

As I shared in the above recipes, you can pre-make your packets and have them ready to grill when you get to your tailgate location. The following two recipes, or blueprints, allow you to just put out the goods and let people drive their own food game. The ingredients should be sliced, diced or prepared ahead of time, stored in containers and lined up buffet-style in a vessel that will allow them to sit on ice. Disposable aluminum pans will work well here. Have heavy-duty aluminum foil sheets torn and ready for your guests. A little "how to" instruction sign might be helpful for your guests as well. Whether you choose prepared packets, MYO packets or both, you're sure to have touchdown results!

MYO SIMPLE tailgate

YIELD 8 TO 10 PACKETS

2 pounds GROUND BEEF or TURKEY

1 pound cooked SAUSAGE, sliced

12 baby RED POTATOES, partially cooked and sliced into wedges or
1-inch circles

1 pound MUSHROOMS, cleaned and cut in half

2 RED or GREEN BELL PEPPERS, sliced into strips

1 ONION, halved and sliced into medium strips

1 cup GREEN PEAS

1 cup chopped fresh GREEN BEANS

1 cup CORN (fresh or frozen)

6 tablespoons BUTTER or OLIVE OIL

4 tablespoons fresh chopped GARLIC

½ cup PESTO

½ cup SALSA

½ cup BARBEQUE SAUCE

1 bottle WORCESTERSHIRE SAUCE

A couple small bottles of HOT SAUCES

SEA SALT and PEPPER

SOUTHWEST SEASONING BLEND

Any other seasonings or condiments you may like such as cheese or avocado and maybe a nice bakery bun to eat it with

Follow the cadence of the premade foil packets. Each packet should have protein, most often on the bottom.

1 Layer the vegetables.

2 Add fat to every packet.

3 Seasoning and a splash of sauce is a good idea.

4 Don't forget about extra add-on condiments for after-cooking, such as a sprinkle of cheese, a bun, a pita, a dollop of guacamole or avocado, extra pesto and so on.

myo GET YOUR BIG GAME ON!

YIELD 8 TO 10 PACKETS

1 pound raw STEAK, cut into medium cubes

1 pound raw CHICKEN, cut into small cubes

1 pound 16/20 SHRIMP, peeled and cleaned

4 cooked large SAUSAGE LINKS, cut on a bias

½ pound IMPOSSIBLE BURGER MEAT, crumbled

2 RED PEPPERS, cut into strips

1 ZUCCHINI, sliced into medium circles

1 YELLOW SQUASH, sliced into medium circles

1 ONION, halved then cut in thin strips

1 (10-ounce) package of BABY BELLAS, halved

2 cups partially cooked POTATO slices

1 cup CABBAGE, medium sliced

½ cup CARROTS, thin angle slice

½ cup GREEN ONIONS, thinly sliced on a bias

½ cup pickled JALAPEÑOS

½ cup OLIVE OIL in squirt bottle

SAUCES and CONDIMENTS (½ to ¾ cup of each or a few of your choice): Salsa, Asian or soy sauce, pesto, barbeque sauce, Italian or Greek dressing, spicy flavored oil

SEASONING BLENDS: Asian, Mediterranean, BBQ, Southwest, fancy flavored salts, ground pepper

FRILLS: Breads, rolls, cheeses, fresh herbs

1 Layer the vegetables.

2 Add fat to every packet.

3 Seasoning and a splash of sauce is a good idea.

4 Don't forget about extra add-on condiments for after-cooking, such as a sprinkle of cheese, a bun, a pita, a dollop of guacamole or avocado, extra pesto and so on.

GAME beverages

It seems that the majority of people have solid drink patterns like an iced bucket of beer or sparkling seltzer with alcohol. I would encourage you to have a nice selection of non-alcoholic beverages and provide lots of water. Make a fun iced tea or virgin fruity drink. Sometimes less is more, especially when most will be driving.

3

Eat, Drink, Be Scary & Merry!

Menu

GF/Gluten Free, DF/Dairy Free, V/Vegetarian, V+/Vegan

A Halloween party is fun for everyone from youngsters to adults. There are certainly countless concepts for your décor and menu. Your concept should match your audience and support your menu.

BRIGHT COLORS: Do not be afraid to stray from spiders, witches and scary masks in favor of pops of vibrant color such as hot pink, lime green, orange and purple. These bright colors can bring a unique and playful look to your gathering. Painting real or faux pumpkins in vibrant colors or even covering them in fabric will add interest to your tablescape. Add some bling with a few stick-on clear crystal gems in fun patterns to make your pumpkins stand out. Layer your table with colorful, shiny fabrics and add black accents like candle holders with bright taper candles for a spooky but fun tablescape. Need more color? Adding some colored drinking glasses in turquoise or blue is a great way to pull together this playful twist to Halloween.

PUMPKIN PATCH: There are so many fun ways to bring your pumpkin to the next level. Pick a theme and run with it! Use matte or metallic paints and materials to create swirls, textures and patterns either freehand or with stencils. Paint your pumpkin a solid color like black and use glow-in-the-dark paint to create ornate patterns and add different-size googly eyes to make a fun glow-in-the dark pumpkin! Use Mod Podge and attach spooky decorative paper to add a playful spooky element or tulle fabric to wrap around your pumpkin and tie it off on the stem to add some texture to your tabletop flair. One year I did a '70s theme with peace signs and swirls of color to create a tie-dye feel and set the tone for the whole party. Search painted pumpkins on Pinterest to give you some visual ideas.

FAMILIAR HALLOWEEN: Start with a neutral linen or a natural wood table as your base. Roll out black construction paper to create a runner down the table. Use white paint to add simple outlined bats or ghosts. Gather rusted wood bowls or cutting boards to elevate mini orange pumpkins clustered with some trailing down the table. Take tall mason jars and add simple raffia bows around them with a tea light inside. Take that same leftover raffia and create cute napkin ties for each place setting. Mix in a few terracotta pots painted black with a plastic liner inside to hold dips, veggie coins and crunchy snacks. Round out this look by tucking in a few dried leaves in yellows and oranges to add a pop of color and texture.

SERVING PLATTERS: You could go in many directions depending on your theme. Add colorful ceramic plates and dishes for your spooky party, or you can DIY your own platters. Take some old picture frames, paint them in fun colors and insert decorative paper or a spooky photo and attach a couple of brass handles. These could be clustered in different sizes and colors or just a few large ones. If you want your tablescape to be the star, opt for a neutral style using white plates and bowls and mixed wood cutting boards and platters.

fresh FLESH
(SMOKED SALMON & CREAM CHEESE CROSTINI)

YIELD 14 PIECES

14 pieces **SOURDOUGH BAGUETTE**, sliced about ¼-inch thick

2 tablespoons **OLIVE OIL**

5 ounces **CREAM CHEESE**

2 teaspoons of finely minced **RED ONION**

1 teaspoon **LEMON JUICE**

1 teaspoon finely chopped **CAPERS**

½ teaspoon freshly chopped **DILL** *(optional)*

1 *(6-ounce)* package of sliced, **SMOKED SALMON**

1 Preheat the oven to 325°F.

2 In a large bowl, toss sliced baguettes with olive oil. Transfer to sheet pan and bake for 5 to 7 minutes until lightly toasted. Remove crostini from the sheet pan and let cool for 10 minutes.

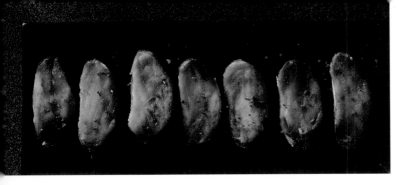

3. Place cream cheese, red onion, lemon juice, capers and dill in the small bowl of a food processor. Pulse 4 to 5 times until all ingredients are combined.

4. Spread whipped cream cheese mixture evenly on each crostini. Stretch a piece of sliced smoked salmon over the top of prepared crostini, trimming edges where needed.

5. Place assembled crostini on a serving platter.

Chef's Notes

Make the cream cheese mixture up to three days ahead of time and keep in an airtight bag for fast execution an hour or two before your guests arrive. This is a great small-bite recipe for any occasion. Consider arranging the salmon to be folded on top instead of stretched if using it outside of the Halloween zone.

GRAVEYARD **bones**

GF | DF   YIELD 10 SERVINGS (ABOUT 30 BONES)

Heavy-duty **FOIL**

3 slabs **PORK SPARERIBS**

⅓ cup **YELLOW MUSTARD**

FOR THE DRY RUB

¼ cup smoked **PAPRIKA**

2 tablespoons **GARLIC POWDER**

2 tablespoons ground **CORIANDER**

2 tablespoons **CUMIN**

2 tablespoons **CHILI POWDER**

1 tablespoon granulated **GARLIC**

1 teaspoon smoked **SEA SALT**

1 teaspoon **RED PEPPER FLAKES**

2 teaspoons **KOSHER** or **SEA SALT**

¼ cup **BROWN SUGAR**

Favorite **BBQ SAUCE**

1. Preheat the oven to 275°F. Tear 6 long heavy-duty foil sheets 3 to 4 inches longer than your spareribs in length.

2. Make sure the membrane is removed from the back of the ribs. Most often the butcher will do this if you purchase your ribs at the meat counter. If the whitish membrane is on the backside of ribs, using a boning knife, carefully cut under the membrane enough to grab a good hold of a corner, set one hand on the backside of the rib and with the other hand, pull off the membrane.

3. Lay out ribs on a work surface or cutting board and lightly brush both sides with a very light coating of yellow mustard.

4. In a medium bowl or in a food processor combine all the dry rub ingredients until well blended with no clumps. Coat each mustard-rubbed side of the ribs with dry rub and place in center of heavy-duty foil sheet. Fold over sheet of foil, crimping edges, then turn crimped packet, crimp side down, on to another sheet of foil and repeat. Place racks on a large sheet tray.

5. Bake low and slow for 2 ½ to 3 hours until temperature reaches 190°F and meat looks like it will fall off the bone. Unwrap ribs on tray and let rest 15 minutes before service.

6. Arrange on oblong serving platters to resemble skeleton bones and serve with your favorite BBQ sauce for dipping.

Chef's Notes

You can put the rub on the ribs the night before, roasting them the day of your gathering, or you can also prepare the ribs up to three days in advance and reheat them in foil to keep moist.

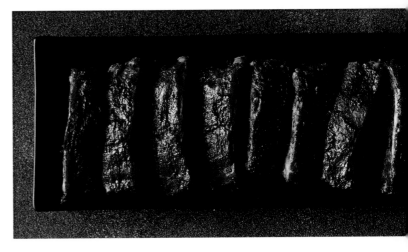

black widow DIP WITH BAT WINGS

GF | V   YIELD 8 TO 10 SERVINGS

2 tablespoon of OLIVE OIL

¼ cup minced WHITE ONIONS

2 teaspoon ONION POWDER

2 teaspoon CUMIN POWDER

1 teaspoon SEA SALT

¼ teaspoon CAYENNE

2 (15-ounce) cans refried BLACK BEANS

⅔ cup of prepared SALSA *(your favorite brand)*

1 cup SOUR CREAM

2 tablespoon LIME JUICE

1 (12-ounce) bag black corn TORTILLA CHIPS

1   Heat olive oil in a sauté pan over medium heat. Add onions and sauté for a minute or two. Add spices and continue to cook for another minute over medium-low heat.

2   Add refried black beans and salsa to pan and meld by stirring with a wooden spoon. Continue stirring ingredients over low heat for another couple of minutes. Remove from heat and cool for 20 minutes before transferring to the refrigerator for 30 or more minutes.

3   Mix sour cream and lime juice and place in a piping bag. Or you can snip one of the bottom corners of a ziplock bag to create a makeshift piping bag.

4   Spread black bean dip on a flat 10-inch serving platter or plate and pipe sour cream in a circle/spiral from center of plate to the edges (like a bullseye target). From the center, drag a toothpick through the dip to the outside of the plate to create a cobweb effect. Serve with black corn tortilla chips.

Chef's Notes

Make black bean spread up to 3 days before.

STUFFED PEPPER mummies

1 tablespoon OLIVE or BLENDED OIL

6 ounces bulk MEXICAN CHORIZO SAUSAGE

½ small ONION, finely chopped

¼ teaspoon RED CHILI FLAKES

½ teaspoon ONION POWDER

½ teaspoon CUMIN

2 tablespoons finely chopped CILANTRO

4 ounces CREAM CHEESE, at room temperature

4 ounces shredded SHARP CHEDDAR CHEESE

2 ounces QUESO FRESCO

1 teaspoon WATER

1 EGG, lightly beaten

FLOUR, for dusting

2 sheets PUFF PASTRY or DANISH DOUGH, thawed

18 large GYPSY PEPPERS *(about 4 inches long, also called sweet mini peppers)* cut in half lengthwise, seeds removed and stems intact

OPTIONAL FOR MUMMY "EYES"

¼ cup SOUR CREAM

1 tablespoon canned sliced BLACK OLIVES, roughly chopped

1 Preheat the oven to 350°F. Line sheet pan with parchment paper.

2 Heat oil in a medium skillet. Add chorizo in crumbles, stirring occasionally. Once meat is browned, add onions and spices. Continue to cook over medium-low heat for another 3 to 4 minutes until cooked through.

3 Drain extra fat from the chorizo mixture and transfer to a medium mixing bowl to cool. Once cooled, add cream cheese, cheddar cheese and queso fresco and mix thoroughly with a spoon or place in the small bowl of a food processor and pulse for a quick minute until just mixed through.

4 Prepare egg wash by mixing water and egg together. Set aside.

5 Lightly sprinkle a work surface with flour. Lay out pastry dough and lightly roll to remove creases and flatten a little. Using a sharp knife, cut dough into thin strips lengthwise.

6 Fill each pepper half with cream cheese mixture, mounding it slightly. Wrap each pepper half all the way around with a strip of dough, leaving space between successive wraps and pinching ends and tucking them around the backside. Place peppers on the prepared sheet tray and brush tops of peppers with egg wash.

7 Bake until pastry is golden brown, 10 to 12 minutes. Transfer to a serving platter and let cool for 5 to 8 minutes.

8 For mummy eyes, place sour cream in a pastry bag or a resealable plastic bag with the corner cut off and pipe 2 dots of sour cream onto each pepper for eyes. Place an olive piece on each sour cream dot and serve.

PUMPKIN PATCH **cheeseball**

V   YIELD 8 TO 10 SERVINGS

8 ounces CREAM CHEESE, at room temperature

8 ounces PUB CHEESE

8 ounces shredded CHEDDAR CHEESE

3 tablespoons minced GREEN ONION

2 tablespoons prepared HORSERADISH

½ teaspoon GARLIC POWDER

½ teaspoon ONION POWDER

1 teaspoon HOT SAUCE

Pinch of CAYENNE

1 BELL PEPPER STEM for garnish

Crackers, pretzels, chips and crudités

1 Using a hand mixer or a stand mixer fitted with the paddle attachment combine cream cheese and pub cheese and mix until smooth. Add cheddar cheese, green onion, horseradish and spices and continue to mix until combined.

2 Scoop mixture onto plastic wrap and use wrap to form a ball (the creases in the plastic wrap will give the cheese ball indentations that will mimic a pumpkin). Chill for a few hours or overnight.

3 Remove from refrigerator about 20 minutes before serving. Add pepper stem to the top and serve with crackers, pretzels, chips and crudités.

Chef's Notes

If you are looking for a little extra crunch, roll your orange cheese ball into 1½ cups of crushed Cheez-It crackers.

DEVIL'S **eyes**

DF | V   YIELD 16 PIECES

8 EGGS

⅓ cup MAYONNAISE

1 tablespoon DIJON MUSTARD

1 teaspoon WHITE VINEGAR

½ teaspoon SEA SALT

¼ teaspoon coarsely ground BLACK PEPPER

4 GREEN OLIVES *(with pimento centers)*

1 Place eggs in a stock pot and cover with water. Bring to a boil, reduce heat to medium and cook eggs for 10 minutes.

2 Remove from heat and tilt the pot over the sink to drain water, place in the sink and run cool tap water over eggs until eggs are cool enough to handle before peeling.

3 Cut a small slice from the top and bottom of each egg to create a stable bottom for the egg. Cut the egg in half vertically.

4 Scoop out yolks and place in a small mixing bowl. Take egg whites and gently rinse them in a bowl of water to wash away any specks left from the yolk. Turn whites upside down on a work surface lined with paper towels and let dry.

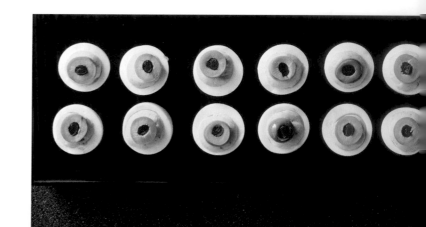

5 Mash yolks with a fork to break the yolk down in small pieces. Add mayonnaise, Dijon mustard, vinegar, salt and pepper and mix well.

6 Spoon or pipe yolk mixture into clean white bases and smooth the top of yolk to be more rounded than flat.

7 Slice olives in thin circles and then place the bullseye center on egg to resemble an eyeball.

two unique STUFFED POTATO GHOSTS

GF | V YIELD 36 PIECES

18 **FINGERLING POTATOES** (be careful to select uniform potatoes that are not too small)

1 large **BAKING POTATO**

⅓ cup **SOUR CREAM**

¼ cup crumbled **GOAT CHEESE**

1 tablespoon whole unsalted **BUTTER**

1 teaspoon **SEA SALT**

¼ teaspoon **WHITE PEPPER**

½ teaspoon **ONION POWDER**

5 slices thinly sliced **MONTEREY JACK CHEESE** (cut into thin rectangular strips the size of the fingerling potato halves)

6 **BLACK OLIVES**, cut into small pieces to place as eyes on potato ghosts

36 paper-thin slices of **GREEN ONION** (just one thin ring) to place as mouth

1 Preheat the oven to 350°F.

2 Place fingerlings and large potato on a sheet tray and bake until cooked through, about 20 minutes for the fingerlings and 35 to 40 for the large potato. Cool, cut in half lengthwise and scoop potato flesh into a large bowl.

3 Add sour cream, goat cheese, butter, salt, white pepper, onion powder and mash together.

4 Place about 1 tablespoon of potato mixture into each fingerling half and smooth.

5 Top with a strip of Monterey Jack cheese. Melt cheese over potato for just a minute or two in the oven. Remove and decorate eyes with olive slice pieces and green onion "ring" mouth.

Chef's Notes

You can prep potatoes the day before. Place cheese strips on top, cover and hold in the fridge until the next day. Pull ghost potatoes an hour or so before service to bring them down in temperature. Pop them in the oven just before service to melt the cheese and decorate as instructed.

boo BARK

v

4 cups **MILK** or dark melting **CHOCOLATE**

12 to 14 **ORANGE-AND-BLACK SANDWICH COOKIES**, broken up into large chunks

¾ cup **CANDY CORN** *(¼ reserved)*

½ cup **PRETZEL THINS**, broken a little

⅓ cup **M&M'S** *(divided in two)*

⅓ cup **HEATH CANDY**, chopped coarsely *(divided in two)*

A variety of Halloween food **SPRINKLES**

Spooky **CANDY EYEBALLS** *(small jar or about ¼ cup)*

1 Prepare sheet tray with parchment paper.

2 Melt chopped chocolate or use chocolate discs over a double boiler on medium heat. Once melted, remove 20% of the chocolate and place in a separate bowl.

3 Mix broken cookies, ½ cup candy corn, pretzel thins, half of the M&M's and half of the chopped Heath candy into a larger bowl with melted chocolate. Once incorporated, spread evenly onto the prepared sheet pan and sprinkle remaining candy randomly on top. Place in the fridge for 5 or so minutes until chocolate is close to set. Remove tray, drizzle remaining chocolate and adorn with Halloween sprinkles and spooky candy eyeballs.

4 Return to the fridge to set chocolate for 10 minutes or set the tray in a cool place for 30 minutes. Once set, cut into desired size pieces. Wear kitchen prep gloves during this process so you don't leave fingerprints.

5 Store bark in an airtight container for up to two weeks.

WITCHING HOUR MEETS happy hour

There are so many interesting ways to serve beverages for Halloween: mason jars, science beakers, test tubs, long skinny tumblers or martini glasses.

swamp water (NONALCOHOLIC)

GF | DF YIELD 8 TO 10 SERVINGS

16 ounces of PINEAPPLE JUICE

32 ounces of LIME or GREEN APPLE SODA

16 fun-colored GUMMY WORMS

1 Mix juice and soda together. Pour into fun glasses, such as beakers or mason jars with ice.

2 Decorate rim of glass with a gummy worm hanging halfway into glass or skewer on cocktail stick and place on top.

spooky-tini WITH BLOODSHOT EYEBALLS

GF | DF | V YIELD 8 TO 10 SERVINGS

Tangy fresh lemonade with frozen grapes as eyeballs is such a fun and festive Halloween drink. A mild honey such as orange blossom, would be a good choice to complement the lemon juice.

1 can natural LIMEADE

4 cups cold WATER

2 cups of your favorite VODKA

32 ounces LIME or APPLE SODA

16 frozen RED or BLACK GRAPES for eyeballs

1 Mix ingredients together and pour into fun glasses.

2 Add ice and garnish with a frozen "eyeball." Serve immediately.

4

Modern Pumpkin Party

Menu

GF/Gluten Free, DF/Dairy Free, V/Vegetarian, V+/Vegan

55

Fall is in the air, so consider celebrating pumpkin at your autumn cocktail party with interesting fun-filled pumpkin and squash flavors paired with craft beer and cocktails with a shimmer of caramel and pumpkin.

My idea here is something that strays from the familiar bales of hay and the super rustic trimmings you will often find with many things fall. This concept feels very grown up, with architectural, clean surfaces and muted earth-toned accents in the way of linens or a crisp, modern table runner that feels more industrial. Chilewich.com is one of my favorite resources for table runners. Your runner can also be more intricate with a woven sisal material and simple elements added on top. Bring your modern design home with white pumpkins. These are often referred to as ghost pumpkins in the gourd family. You can also find light sage green Cinderella pumpkins for a larger tablescape. Your favorite local farmers market is a good resource for finding these. Accent your table using fresh herbs, eucalyptus or other clean monolithic greens in thin cylinder vases. Nestle a collection of small green apples into a white bowl or clear vase and add some large white gerbera daisies. Finish this look with white ceramic or wood spheres and light wood candle holders with thick white pillar candles on top. For serving, enrich your modern design by using clean wood boards and white platters accented with a little autumn greenery.

pumpkin MAPLE BRIE

v

YIELD 10 SERVINGS

1 *(13-ounce)* wheel of BRIE

½ tablespoon BUTTER

1 tablespoon APPLE CIDER or WATER

2 tablespoons dried CHERRIES or CRANBERRIES

¼ cup canned PUMPKIN

1 tablespoon MAPLE SYRUP

½ teaspoon PUMPKIN PIE SPICE

¼ teaspoon SEA SALT

1 sheet PUFF PASTRY, thawed

1 EGG, beaten with a tablespoon of water *(egg wash)*

¼ cup SUGARED WALNUTS *(recipe follows)*

Crackers, crostini or baguette slices for serving

1   Preheat the oven to 350°F. Place brie in the freezer for 10 minutes to make it easier to cut.

2   In a medium skillet over medium-low heat melt butter. Add cider or water and cherries or cranberries. Simmer, stirring often for 2 to 3 minutes. Add pumpkin, syrup, pumpkin pie spice and salt. Continue simmering for an additional 3 to 4 minutes until most of the liquid evaporates. Set aside to cool.

3   Spray 9-inch stoneware or glass round baking dish with nonstick spray. Unfold the puff pastry sheet and give it a little roll. It should be large enough to wrap around the wheel of brie. Place pastry in the prepared pan.

4   Remove brie from the freezer and butterfly by slicing horizontally into 2 equal pieces.

5   Place the bottom half of brie onto the pastry. Spread ¾ of the pumpkin mixture on it, then top with remaining half of brie. Spoon remaining pumpkin filling onto the center on top of brie (like a big belly button) in about a 2-inch circle. Fold dough over top of brie, making a neat little brie package.

6 Brush exposed pastry with egg wash and bake for 20 minutes until bubbly and golden.

7 Remove from the oven and top with sugared walnuts. Serve with crackers, crostini or baguette slices.

Sugared Walnuts

GF | V+   YIELD 2 CUPS

⅓ cup granulated SUGAR

1½ teaspoons ground CINNAMON

Pinch CAYENNE PEPPER

Pinch ground NUTMEG

½ teaspoon SALT

2 cups RAW WALNUTS

2 tablespoons COCONUT or OLIVE OIL

3 tablespoons MAPLE SYRUP *(divided)*

1 Preheat the oven to 300°F. Line a sheet pan with parchment paper.

2 In a small bowl combine sugar, cinnamon, cayenne, nutmeg and salt. Set aside.

3 In a medium bowl add walnuts, oil and half of the maple syrup. Toss to combine. Sprinkle with sugar mixture and stir until walnuts are evenly coated. Pour onto the prepared sheet pan, spreading out to an even layer.

4 Bake for a total of 12 to 15 minutes until golden brown and fragrant, tossing/stirring once at the halfway point to ensure even cooking.

5 Remove from the oven and immediately drizzle with remaining maple syrup.

6 Enjoy warm or let cool completely on the pan. They will crisp up as they cool.

7 Store in an airtight container at room temperature for 2 to 3 weeks (or in the freezer for up to 1 month).

Chef's Notes

Prepare the filling up to a week before using. It would also be great as a smear on bread or crackers by itself.

SQUASH & PUMPKIN flatbread WITH KALE & PROSCIUTTO

YIELD 4 WHOLE FLATBREADS OR 32 SQUARES

6 tablespoons OLIVE OIL *(divided)*

12 to 15 fresh SAGE LEAVES

KOSHER SALT, to taste

1 cup GREEN KALE, cut into thin strips

2 cups medium-diced HARD SQUASH *(butternut is good, or your favorite)*

¼ teaspoon each, SEA SALT and PEPPER

1 *(15-ounce)* can PUMPKIN PUREE

¾ cup *(or 6 ounces)* GOAT CHEESE

⅓ cup HONEY

2 teaspoons chopped CHIPOTLE PEPPER

Couple pinches of CAYENNE PEPPER

4 large naan or pizza FLATBREADS

8 slices of PROSCIUTTO

1 cup shaved PARMESAN

1 Preheat the oven to 375°F. Place a sheet pan in the oven.

2 In a small sauté pan over medium-high heat add 3 tablespoons olive oil. Add sage leaves and fry for 30 seconds or until lightly crisped. Remove from oil, place on a paper towel and season with kosher salt. Reserve oil.

3 In the same pan heat the remaining 3 tablespoons olive oil over medium heat. Add kale and give a quick one-minute sauté just to melt the greens. Remove kale and drain on a paper towel.

4 In a large bowl add diced squash and some of the reserved sage oil and toss to coat. Season with salt and pepper. Carefully remove sheet pan from the oven, spread diced squash out evenly on pan and roast 15 to 18 minutes, moving around occasionally with spatula, until golden and cooked through. Remove from the oven and set aside to cool.

5 Increase oven temperature to 400°F. Line a sheet pan with parchment paper.

6 In a small food processor blend pumpkin puree, goat cheese, 1 tablespoon reserved sage oil, honey, chipotle, salt and cayenne until smooth. Season with salt and pepper to taste.

7 Place naan or flatbreads on the prepared sheet pan. Smear with pumpkin/goat cheese spread, lay 2 pieces of prosciutto on each flat and sprinkle sautéed kale and roasted squash. Top with a drizzle of remaining reserved sage oil and shaved Parmesan. Bake 5 to 7 minutes until golden.

8 Remove from the oven and sprinkle with crumbled fried sage leaves.

9 Cut each naan into 8 pieces (could be bigger or smaller depending on the bread flat you choose, but 2 x 2 is a good size).

Chef's Notes

These will hold well frozen. Make pizzas and just melt cheese to glue everything down. Cool, wrap individually in plastic wrap and freeze. Remove from the freezer an hour before you want to serve them. Place on a sheet pan and bake 400°F for 5 to 7 minutes until bubbly and crisp. If you have a rack to sit on the sheet tray, this is even better so air circulates for improved crispness.

squash BRUSCHETTA
v   YIELD 24 PIECES

3 cups peeled and diced **BUTTERNUT SQUASH**

3 cups peeled and diced **ACORN SQUASH**

¼ cup **OLIVE OIL**

1½ teaspoons **SEA SALT**

½ teaspoon **BLACK PEPPER**

¼ cup **APPLE CIDER** or **JUICE**

¼ cup dried **CRANBERRIES**

1 cup **KALE**, coarsely chopped

½ cup **RED ONION**, finely diced

3 tablespoons pure **MICHIGAN MAPLE SYRUP**

2 tablespoons **APPLE CIDER VINEGAR**

1 tablespoon fresh **SAGE**, chopped

24 pieces **CROSTINI** *(sliced baguette, toasted)*

1 cup whole milk **RICOTTA CHEESE**

1 Preheat the oven to 425°F. Place sheet pan in the oven.

2 In a large bowl add butternut and acorn squash and olive oil. Toss to coat. Season with salt and pepper.

3   Carefully remove the hot sheet pan from the oven. Pour squash onto the sheet pan and bake until golden brown, about 20 minutes, turning pan and tossing with a spatula halfway through cooking. Set aside to cool.

4   In a small saucepan add apple cider and dried cranberries. Simmer over low heat for 2 to 3 minutes until liquid reduces and cranberries plump. Set aside to cool.

5   In a large bowl combine the cooled squash, plumped cranberries, kale, red onion, maple syrup, apple cider vinegar, sage, sea salt and pepper. Toss to coat and adjust seasoning if needed.

6   Top crostini with a smear of ricotta and a heaping tablespoon of squash mixture.

turkey MEATBALLS WITH CRANBERRY GLAZE

DF   YIELD 18 TO 20 MEATBALLS

1 cup fresh **CRANBERRIES** *(or frozen, thawed and blotted dry)*

1 teaspoon **OLIVE OIL**

1½ pounds **GROUND TURKEY** *(I prefer to use 50% white and 50% dark meat)*

2 **EGGS**, whisked together

¾ cup shredded **APPLE** *(gently squeeze extra juice out)*

½ cup plus 2 tablespoons fine **BREADCRUMBS**

1½ teaspoons dried **SAGE**

1 tablespoon fresh chopped **PARSLEY**

1 teaspoon **ORANGE ZEST**

1 teaspoon **SEA SALT**

½ teaspoon **BLACK PEPPER**

FOR THE CRANBERRY ORANGE GLAZE

1¼ cups fresh or frozen **CRANBERRIES**

1 cup **ORANGE JUICE**

1½ tablespoons **MAPLE SYRUP**

¼ teaspoon **GINGER**

GARNISH

1 tablespoon chopped **PARSLEY**

1   Preheat the oven to 350°F. Line a sheet pan with parchment paper.

2   Spread cranberries out evenly on the prepared sheet pan. Drizzle with olive oil and bake for 20 minutes until they become shriveled and slightly dried. Remove from the oven and set aside to cool.

3   In a large bowl, add turkey and remaining ingredients. Mix well until thoroughly combined. Gently fold in cooled oven-dried cranberries.

4   Roll the mixture into 18 to 20 medium meatballs and place on the prepared sheet pan. Bake 18 to 20 minutes until slightly golden on top and cooked through.

5   While the meatballs are baking, prepare the glaze by placing glaze ingredients in a blender or food processor. Pulse until smooth.

6   Before serving, gently toss or brush meatballs with the cranberry glaze and sprinkle with parsley. Serve cranberry sauce on the side for a quick dip.

Chef's Notes

Get a jump on your prep and make the meatballs ahead of time (up to three days to keep fresh). The day of, bake and glaze as outlined above. You can also make, shape and freeze the raw meatballs on a sheet pan. After frozen, transfer to a ziplock bag. They will be great for three months for a quick grab-and-go appetizer on the fly.

*For a gluten-free option, substitute breadcrumbs for gluten-free breadcrumbs.

AUTUMN DEMI salad

GF | V   YIELD 12 SERVINGS

2 cups chopped **BABY GREENS**

2 cups **BRUSSELS SPROUT SLAW** *(you will find this bagged in the lettuce aisle)*

½ cup dried **CHERRIES**

½ cup crumbled **GOAT CHEESE**

½ cup finely diced **RED PEPPER**

¼ cup toasted **PEPITAS** *(pumpkin seeds)*

¼ cup small diced roasted **SQUASH**

⅓ cup your favorite **BALSAMIC VINAIGRETTE**

FOR SERVING

1 dozen 6-ounce **PLASTIC CUPS** *(the wider mouth cups that you might serve wine in)*

1 In a large bowl, combine chopped baby greens and brussels slaw. Divide into cups.

2 Evenly sprinkle remaining ingredients over cups and drizzle with your favorite balsamic dressing.

PUMPKIN hummus

DF | V   YIELD 2 CUPS

1 pound prepared **HUMMUS**

¼ cup **PUMPKIN PUREE**

1 teaspoon chopped **CHIPOTLE PEPPER**

½ teaspoon **SEA SALT**

PITA CHIPS and **CUCUMBER** coins for serving

1 In a large bowl, mix hummus, pumpkin puree, chipotle and salt until smooth and combined.

2 Serve with pita chips and cucumber coins.

PUMPKIN PIE martini

YIELD 6 MARTINIS

FOR THE RIM

¼ cup MAPLE SYRUP

¼ cup ground GRAHAM CRACKER crumbs

MARTINI

5 ounces VODKA

3 ounces salted CARAMEL BOURBON

4 heaping tablespoons PUMPKIN PIE PUREE

½ cup CREAM *(or coconut milk for a non-dairy option)*

½ cup APPLE CIDER

1 tablespoon real MICHIGAN MAPLE SYRUP

CINNAMON STICKS for garnish *(optional)*

1 Lightly brush the rim of the martini glasses with maple syrup and dip in crushed graham cracker crumbs. Set aside.

2 Fill a cocktail shaker with ice. Add martini ingredients and shake to combine.

3 Pour in prepared glass and garnish with cinnamon sticks.

CARAMEL BOURBON BEER bomb

YIELD 1 COCKTAIL

1 *(12-ounce)* OKTOBERFEST PUMPKIN BEER

1 ounce SALTED CARAMEL BOURBON

FOR SERVING

Pint GLASS

1 Pour beer in glass and top with salted caramel bourbon.

5

Charcuterie Party

Menu

GF/Gluten Free, DF/Dairy Free, V/Vegetarian, V+/Vegan

Although now trendy, charcuterie is rooted in times long past. It was a popular use in European culture for the otherwise unusable meat trimmings. The word "charcuterie" hails from the French word for the person (*charcutier*) who fabricates and sells meats (also referred to as the "pork butcher").

Many of the curing and preservation techniques practiced today were used in the ancient Roman Empire to preserve meats. This craft has evolved in creative and delicious ways from small to enormous charcuterie feasts! Modern charcuterie has expanded in many dimensions. Although your mind goes to meat when you hear charcuterie, it is not unusual to find dips, spreads, jams, chocolate squares, dried fruits and more on a charcuterie board.

Charcuterie is the perfect fit for easy, prep-ahead entertainment. The gamut ranges from large, impressive boards or platters trimmed with an array of salamis, salumi, mousses and pâtés to pickled items such as olives, cornichons and onions. It is not uncommon to find fish pairings such as a trout pâté, whitefish salad and smoked fish. Nuts, mustards and jams are always a way to round out your board.

Your party plan can go so many ways in this arena, from elegant to rustic. I personally like the rustic feel here, as it is an invitation for less-formal eating. Remember that your spread is in fact your living centerpiece and perfect for spilling down a large island or table. Start with a base of a muted-colored linen or chalkboard paper where you can write pertinent info with a sharpie or chalk. Do not fret about wooden boards; you may have more in your cupboards than you realize. Everyday cutting boards, interesting trays you have around the house, regular or cute little aluminum sheet trays, ceramic platters and marble or slate slabs will all make a great visual impact. Stay in the rustic theme by using small mason jars to capture pickled items, jams or sauces.

Less is more here with décor, which is why edible botanicals feel like such a great fit when rounding out your table. Let all the bold rustic foods lead you. Tucking in bouquets of herbs like rosemary, thyme and mint, and greenery like eucalyptus, olive branches and kale add color, scent and texture. Clusters of berries, grapes and nuts will add a pop of color and feel old world while lending to the vibe of organic, functional décor. Wooden risers and metal buckets with orbs or produce will add a nice feel to your layout. School your guests by adding a fun printed map with a tour of your charcuterie spread. Add chalkboard signs listing ingredients with suggested wine or beverage pairings. Lately, I have seen "jarcuturie": individual short, largemouth jars nestled with an array of little mouth-pop treats. These would be fun as a ready-made option for your guests. For serving, salad plates or kraft boats with bamboo or polished heavy plastic utensils feel right at home here.

Base Camp Supplies
MEATS

This is a large conversation, since there is such a large array of meats, including cured/smoked salami and salumi. Salumi refers to larger whole muscle parts, where salamis are tumbled and extruded. Traditional types of dry cured salami are twenty to thirty percent fat and are seasoned in many diverse ways with spices and herbs. Classic types of salami include hunters, *tartuffi*, *felino*, *calabrese*, *soppressata*, *ungherese*, chorizo and *picante*. Varieties of salumi include prosciutto, pancetta, *coppa*, *guanciale*, *spalla*, *lardo* and *lonza*.

PÂTÉS & MOUSSES

Pâtés and mousses are growing in variety in most of your upscale grocery stores. Common varieties include country, liver, peppercorn, mushroom, herb and more. They usually come in small tubs ranging from four ounces to a pound. *Foie gras* (mousse made from fattened goose or duck liver) is quite expensive and often found on fancy boards and used in many culinary dishes. Although not a classical go-to, I always like to have a fish component on my boards; it adds a nice diversity for guests. Mousses, spreads, trout, salmon (fresh or cured) or white fish are all great options.

CHEESE

I am certain there are more flavors of cheese in the world than ice cream flavors! Harder, more traditional cheeses such as comté, gruyere, parmigiano-reggiano, *mimolette*, *manchego* and harder goat goudas are quite popular. Other common varieties include camembert, aged cheddar, white cheddar, fontina, jarlsberg, cotswold, French raclette, Cypress Grove humboldt fog and a wide variety of blue cheeses. Newer on the scene are cheeses that have been fabricated with fruit and spice: pumpkin, chia, dried cherry, stilton with apricot and the list goes on and on. I personally like jazzing up my trays with a fun seasonal cheese. Goat cheese or whipped brie bowls studded with dried fruits, fresh black berries and chopped nuts with a drizzle of honey are also a nice addition to a modern collection. Cheeses presented in wedges or slices and a selection of one or two softer smears makes for a nice balance.

PICKLES

Pickles are super important to trim out a legitimate charcuterie experience. Add small pickles like cornichons, teardrop peppers ("sweeties"), peppadews, assorted olives and zesty pickle chips from sweet to hot for your spread. Pickled vegetables such as mushrooms, roasted peppers, carrots, cauliflower, red onion, okra, asparagus, fennel, green beans, bell pepper strips and cucumbers add a nice variety. You will find a quick-pickle recipe later in this chapter.

BREADS AND COMPANY

This is an important area, as it is often the vehicle our meats and spreads travel on to be eaten. I like an array of breads in the shape of a *bâtard* or baguette such as sourdough, multigrain bread, raisin-walnut, and my newfound favorite, pretzel, which you can find in a short, stubby baguette-like form or purchase as rolls and slice them into crostini-size discs. Speaking of rolls, this can be a great way to add a diversity of flavors without buying more than you need. Pick up a couple varieties of rolls and slice them into discs. Some will be a little smaller depending on the shape of the roll, but that is fine. Turn your sliced

breads into crostini by tossing them with a little olive oil, a sprinkle of sea salt and pepper, placing on a sheet pan and baking in a preheated 350°F oven for around seven to ten minutes. When I choose pretzel bread or rolls, I like to toss them with a little melted butter and an extra sprinkle of sea salt before baking.

CRISP AND CRUNCH

Thick-cut sea salt potato chips are wonderful if you have any fish pâtés or tapenades/dips. Crackers come in so many varieties from seeded and fruited to wheat, rye, savory and a little sweet. Higher-end crackers normally live in the cheese or international section of the grocery store, which is my normal go-to, but there is nothing wrong with plain-Jane saltine crackers served with a little white fish or trout spread. Trader Joe's has a nice assortment of nuts, crackers, pretzel rolls and sourdough baguettes at reasonable prices.

FRILLS, FRUITS, SPREADS AND JAMS

A cluster of red, green or black grapes or a combination of colors are nice. Plump strawberries cut in half, whole blackberries and raspberries, slices of pear or apple snuggled next to blue cheese or camembert, dried orange slices, apricots, cherries or cranberries are delicious options. Roasted vegetables, cured tomatoes or small crudites are also a nice add-on. Place a nice variety of condiments such as chutney or interesting mustards like tarragon, cracked pepper or herb. You will find some quick and easy mustard preparations in the "Modern Oktoberfest" chapter. Savory jams and tapenades such as herb tomato, olive, bacon jam and sweet fig or a little square of honeycomb are popular. Finish your spread with squares of dark chocolate by the cheese or fruits. There are so many options to choose from, but stay in the dark, over-seventy-five-percent-cacao zone (I like the super dark ninety-percent cacao). Finally, add a sprinkle of Marcona almonds or your favorite nut.

charcuterie BLUEPRINT

YIELD 8 TO 10 SERVINGS

3 to 4 dry **CURED MEATS**, 8 to 10 ounces of each

3 **CHEESE SELECTIONS**, 5 to 6 ounces of each

2 to 3 **PICKLED ITEMS**, ½ cup or so of each

8 to 10 ounces **SMOKED FISH MOUSSE** *(optional)*

4 to 6 ounces **LIVER MOUSSE** or **COUNTRY PÂTÉ** *(optional)*

3 to 4 ounces **MUSTARD**

3 to 4 ounces **JAM**

8 to 10 or so **STRAWBERRIES**, some cut in half

8 to 10 **BLACKBERRIES** or **RASPBERRIES**

Medium bunch of **GRAPES**

¼ cup **MARCONA ALMONDS**

2 to 3 sleeves of **CRACKERS**

20 pieces toasted **CROSTINI**

¼ to ½ cup assorted **DRIED FRUITS**

Large platter or serving area *(19 x 12 inches)*

1 Lay out all your supplies. Organize your meats by rolling or folding some to create diversity. Crumble and slice the cheeses. Roast veggies and prepare your dips and tapenades in advance. Fill small bowls or jars with spreads, mustards and smaller pickled items.

2 For layout, think about placing cheese wedges and bowls in place first and use that as a focal point to work from. Proceed by arranging sliced meats and cheeses. I always like to describe placing meats and cheese like fanning out a deck of cards. Use strong lines to create curves and leave clean areas to place your other ingredients.

3 Fill in board with smaller items like dried fruits and nuts.

4 Use berries and grapes to add focal points of color.

5 Place alike foods together to keep the board easy on the eyes. It will aid in making it look clean and modern.

6 Add contrast to your board by mixing up the colors. Keep flavors that go nicely together near each other and away from clashing components with pickles, spreads and fruits.

7 Reserve smaller or more neutral items for last to fill in the empty space. Nuts and crackers work great for this. Once you have placed all your main components, sprinkle nuts or scoot in some crackers, crostini and herbs to fill in all the empty spaces on your board.

The sky's the limit. Just because it is not on the list above does not mean it cannot be part of your custom board.

Chef's Notes

This is an easy one to get a jump on preparation. Pickles, jams and tapenades can be made weeks in advance. A selection of dry goods can be tucked away in the pantry ready and waiting. You can certainly purchase cured meats weeks ahead, but if you are going to purchase them sliced, pay attention to use-by dates. If you purchase sliced from the deli, the average shelf life is about a week. The other nice thing about a charcuterie spread is that, in theory, you can buy everything you need already prepared from one of the nicer markets, but you'll still look like a superstar!

smoked TROUT PÂTÉ

GF   YIELD 10 SERVINGS

⅓ cup SOUR CREAM

¼ cup CREAM CHEESE

¼ cup MAYONNAISE

2 tablespoons prepared HORSERADISH

2 tablespoons finely chopped DILL

2 tablespoons fresh LEMON JUICE

1 tablespoon LEMON ZEST

1 tablespoon chopped CAPERS

1 tablespoon minced SHALLOT

2 teaspoons DRY MUSTARD

½ teaspoon SEA SALT

Pinch of CAYENNE

1 pound cleaned SMOKED TROUT, flaked into small pieces

1. In a large bowl add sour cream, cream cheese and mayonnaise. Stir to combine thoroughly.

2. Add remaining ingredients except trout, and incorporate into the cheese mixture.

3. Gently fold in flaked trout until just combined. Adjust seasoning as necessary.

4. Serve with crackers, thick-cut potato chips and crostini (my favorite is pretzel bread crostini).

2U SPICED nuts

GF | DF | V   YIELD 3 CUPS

1 large EGG WHITE

¼ cup BROWN SUGAR

1 teaspoon CAYENNE PEPPER

¾ teaspoon fine SEA SALT

½ teaspoon BLACK PEPPER

½ teaspoon CHILI POWDER

¼ teaspoon ground ALLSPICE

¼ teaspoon ground CUMIN

¼ teaspoon ground GINGER

3 cups assorted NUTS (walnuts, pecans, almonds or your favorite combination)

1. Preheat the oven to 300°F. Line a sheet pan with parchment paper.

2. In a large bowl beat egg white until soft and foamy.

3. In a separate bowl add the remaining dry ingredients and stir until combined.

4. Whisk the dry ingredients into the egg white.

5. Add nuts and stir until well coated.

6. Spread mixture in a single layer onto prepared sheet pan.

7. Bake nuts for 12 to 15 minutes, stirring with metal spatula every 5 minutes. Remove from the oven.

8. Reduce oven temperature to 250°F. Return nuts to the oven and continue to bake until medium brown, about 10 minutes.

9. Cool and break up any that stick together.

10. Store nuts in an airtight container in a cool, dry space for up to one month.

TOMATO jam

V+

YIELD 4 CUPS

4 cups diced fresh TOMATOES, or 4 cups canned

½ cup granulated SUGAR

½ cup BROWN SUGAR

3 tablespoons BRAGG APPLE CIDER VINEGAR

2 tablespoons LEMON JUICE

1 teaspoon grated fresh GINGER

½ teaspoon CHILI FLAKES

½ teaspoon SEA SALT

⅛ teaspoon CORIANDER

1. In a nonreactive saucepan add all ingredients. Bring mixture to boil and reduce to very low simmer. Continue to cook for 35 to 45 minutes, until thick and syrupy. Allow jam to cool.

2. Transfer jam to a ceramic container or glass jar and place in the refrigerator for at least 6 hours so the flavors come together. Jam can be kept in the refrigerator for up to 14 days.

spicy BEER MUSTARD SEEDS

V

YIELD 2 CUPS

½ cup YELLOW MUSTARD SEEDS

¼ cup BROWN MUSTARD SEEDS

½ cup BRAGG APPLE CIDER VINEGAR

½ cup of BELGIUM BEER

2 tablespoons WATER

2 tablespoons organic HONEY

1 tablespoon and 1 teaspoon BROWN SUGAR

1 tablespoon prepared HORSERADISH

½ teaspoon CHILI FLAKES

½ teaspoon SEA SALT

1. In a bowl or glass jar combine mustard seeds.

2. Add Bragg apple cider vinegar, beer and water and stir. Let sit covered at room temperature for 12 to 14 hours until liquid is absorbed.

3. In a small bowl combine remaining ingredients. Stir into plumped mustard seeds.

4. Place mixture in a food processor and give it 4 to 5 pulses until it reaches desired consistency.

5. Store in an airtight container or jar in the refrigerator for up to 8 months.

quick PICKLED RED ONIONS

GF | V+   YIELD 2 CUPS

2 RED ONIONS, cut in half and thinly sliced into strips

½ cup WATER

½ cup BRAGG APPLE CIDER VINEGAR

2 tablespoons RED WINE VINEGAR

1 tablespoon WHITE SUGAR

1 tablespoon BROWN SUGAR

⅛ teaspoon lightly crushed CORIANDER SEEDS

1 teaspoon SEA SALT

1. Place prepared onions in a glass jar or stainless-steel bowl.

2. In a small saucepan mix water, vinegar and sugar and heat until sugar is dissolved and mixture is almost to a boil.

3. Add crushed coriander seeds and sea salt.

4. Pour mixture over prepared onions and let cool.

5. Store onions in the refrigerator to pickle overnight. Best if used within two weeks.

OLIVE tapenade

V+   YIELD 2 CUPS

1 ½ cups pitted KALAMATA OLIVES

½ cup green pitted ITALIAN OLIVES

2 tablespoons CAPERS

3 cloves of GARLIC

3 tablespoons chopped PARSLEY

3 tablespoons LEMON JUICE

¼ teaspoon dried THYME

Couple pinches of CAYENNE PEPPER

4 tablespoons OLIVE OIL

1. In a food processor combine pitted olives, capers and garlic and pulse until chunky.

2. Add parsley, lemon juice, thyme and cayenne pepper. Blend while slowly drizzling in olive oil.

3. Transfer to serving bowl or store in an airtight container in the refrigerator.

euro CHOCOLATE "SALAMI"

YIELD 2 ROULADES

¾ cup **HEAVY WHIPPING CREAM**

1 pound **DARK CHOCOLATE**, chopped small *(about 2 ½ cups)*

¾ cup roughly chopped **PISTACHIOS**

¼ cup diced **FIGS**

¼ cup diced dried **APRICOTS**

¼ cup dried **CHERRIES** or **CRANBERRIES**

¼ cup diced dried **PEARS**

GARNISH

BERRIES, **WHOLE PISTACHIOS** and additional **DRIED FRUIT** (optional)

1   Heat cream in a small, heavy-bottom saucepan until just before it comes to a boil.

2   Place chocolate in a heat-proof mixing bowl. Add hot cream and stir until incorporated. Add pistachios, figs and dried fruit and stir until combined. Let cool for 10 to 15 minutes until set a little but still moldable.

3   Place 2 long sheets of plastic wrap (about 18 inches long) on a work surface. Spread chocolate mixture onto prepared sheets, keeping a couple inches at each end free. Roll and start to twist ends to make a sausage shape. Repeat with the second piece of plastic wrap. Roll ends very tight and secure with a piece of string. Place in the refrigerator for 20 minutes to set.

4   Slice chocolate "salami" into ¼- to ½-inch slices and place on a serving platter. Garnish with fresh berries or dried fruits with a sprinkle of whole pistachios and sea salt.

Chef's Notes

Chocolate "salami" can be made up to a week ahead of time. Store wrapped tightly in the refrigerator.

bourbon

Bourbon naturally complements smokey flavors, many of which will be prevalent at your charcuterie party. Bourbon also has a sweet undertone which aids in tempering heat from spice and can make for many craft cocktail pairing options.

whiskey factory
COCO COFFEE OLD FASHIONED

GF | V   YIELD 4 SERVINGS

6 ounces DETROIT DISTILLERY BOURBON

5 ounces WATER

4 ounces ESPRESSO

3 ounces *CRÈME DE COCO*

4 teaspoons local HONEY

4 dashes ORANGE BITTERS

8 COFFEE BEANS

1   Put all ingredients in a cocktail shaker. Add ice and shake thoroughly.

2   Divide into four rocks glasses filled with a couple of large ice cubes.

3   Garnish by adding 2 coffee beans into each glass.

CRAFT BEERS. Craft Beer is a great go-to for an MYO charcuterie bash! You could read an entire book on the matter and still not know all there is to know. I suggest going to your favorite neighborhood wine/beer shop and talking to someone who can guide you through what is hot and local. In Michigan we have some amazing breweries and I like to use local whenever possible. I have included an outline on a few basic principles.

AMERICAN IPA. India pale ale and American pale ale were first in line during the early days of American craft brewing. Where pale ales showcase American hop character in closer balance with malt, IPAs are all about letting those hop aromas and flavors take the spotlight. Big, bold American hops are front and center here, though the pale and caramel malt profile also has complementary sweetness.

AMBER OR RED ALE. Amber or red ale is another style that was present early in the American craft brewing movement. The name of the style is an indication of its malt profile, which is based on simple pale malt but features medium to dark crystal malts to provide color, caramel flavor and a moderate initial sweetness. The balance between hops and malt in this style varies.

STOUTS AND PORTERS. Today stouts enjoy a wider style diversity than porters, with examples ranging from the light and dry Irish stout to the big and heavy imperial stout. Porters still tend to be everyday straight-forward drinking beers that utilize a lower amount (if any) of roasted barley or black pate malt, allowing for a more mellow roast character.

AMERICAN WHEAT & HEFEWEIZEN. Both American wheat ale and German Hefeweizen share a similar wheat-focused grain as well as a lightly bready flavor profile and fluffy mouthfeel. The similarities mostly stop there. The big differences between these styles comes from the yeast and hops used in each.

BROWN ALE. Modern brown ales are a twentieth-century development. This style of English brown ale is a mild beer with caramel-focused malt flavor. It lacks the full roast flavor you would find in porters or stouts.

6

Give Thanks

GF/Gluten Free, DF/Dairy Free, V/Vegetarian, V+/Vegan

Thanksgiving is the gateway for the festive holiday season. Unless we are starting a new tradition of our own, the normal way to go for most is to keep the traditions that have been shared and handed down. I would suggest keeping a couple of treasured favorites and stepping up your turkey game to include some fresh and modern sides that could create some new traditions for years to come!

Thanksgiving can be transported into many directions, from fancy gold and silver tones to a simple autumn rustic feel with gourds, light burlap ribbons and wood tones. With your serving table, use interesting greens such as eucalyptus, Italian Ruscus and ornamental rosemary tucked and clustered to create a runner down the center of your table. Once your runner is created, add simple elements such as pomegranates, two-toned yellow and red apples, dried oranges and small Bosc pears. Put petit sunflowers clustered in small bud vases and sprinkle them down the table for impact. Keep the stems short so the heads of the flowers sit right on top of the bud vase opening and give the illusion of floating on the table. Light metal décor or candlesticks would be nice, too. Decorate your surroundings with some of your favorite seasonal gourds or pumpkins, then add accents like throw blankets, decorative pillows and table linens in warm hues of red, yellow and orange. Place accent bowls with tiny, variegated gourds to bring warmth to any room. There are plenty of opportunities for serving vessels here. Wood boards and metal or ceramic serving trays would fair nicely on the backdrop of your aromatic greenery. Maybe you have serving pieces in warm fall tones that can be brought in to add a funky mid-century modern vibe.

A TANGLE OF ROOT **vegetables**

GF | V+   YIELD 8 TO 10 SIDE SERVINGS

2 large SWEET POTATOES

3 large IDAHO POTATOES

3 large ORANGE CARROTS

3 PURPLE CARROTS

3 YELLOW CARROTS

3 large PARSNIPS

1 small ONION

5 tablespoons OLIVE OIL

2 tablespoons HARISSA PASTE

2 tablespoons MICHIGAN MAPLE SYRUP

2 teaspoons SEA SALT

4 tablespoons PUMPKIN SEEDS

2 teaspoons chopped ROSEMARY

1. Preheat the oven to 400°F. Once hot, heat 2 large sheet pans in the oven for 5 minutes prior to roasting vegetables.

2. Using a spiralizer (a little gadget that turns vegetables into little rings known as zoodles) or a peeler (slicing vegetables lengthwise to create small "sheets" of vegetables), cut all root vegetables into spirals or sheets. Slice onion into thin circles. Soak cut purple carrots in cool water for 10 minutes and drain.

3. In a large bowl add oil, harissa, maple syrup and salt. Stir until combined. Add vegetables, pumpkin seeds and rosemary. Toss until everything is evenly coated.

4. Carefully remove hot sheet pans from the oven and evenly spread vegetable mixture onto trays. Return to oven and roast for 10 to 15 minutes or until the edges of the vegetables start to singe a little, lightly giving the vegetables a toss with metal spatula every few minutes.

You can prep "zoodles" up to a day ahead if you hold them in water to keep from browning. When you remove from water, gently blot completely dry on paper towels or a clean kitchen towel. If you are unable to find purple and yellow carrots, substitute with orange. I called for pumpkin seeds in the recipe, but most any nut would be great for crunch, including walnuts or pistachios.

GREEN BEAN PORTOBELLO **bundles**

GF   YIELD 20 BUNDLES

3 *(8-ounce)* packages fresh *HARICOTS VERTS (French green beans)*

6 tablespoons extra-virgin OLIVE OIL, divided

1 tablespoon BALSAMIC SYRUP

¾ teaspoon SEA SALT, divided

½ teaspoon BLACK PEPPER, divided

4 portobello MUSHROOMS, wiped cleaned and cut into ¼-inch slices

4 teaspoons fresh LEMON JUICE

10 PROSCIUTTO slices, cut in half lengthwise

½ cup shaved PARMESAN cheese

1 Preheat the oven to 450°F. Lightly oil sheet pan with olive oil or nonstick spray and set aside.

2 Bring 4 quarts of water to a boil in a large stock pot. Season water with sea salt.

3 Add green beans and cook until crisp-tender, about 3 to 4 minutes. Be careful not to overcook; you want them to maintain their bright green color.

4 In a large bowl add ice and water to create an ice bath (this will stop the cooking of the green beans). Drain beans and plunge into the ice bath. Drain again and blot dry thoroughly with paper towels or a clean, lightweight kitchen towel.

5 In a small bowl whisk together 3 tablespoons oil, balsamic syrup, ⅛ teaspoon salt and ⅛ teaspoon pepper. Add mushrooms and toss to coat. Spread mixture evenly on the prepared sheet pan, being careful not to overlap. Roast for 5 minutes, move mushrooms around to ensure even roasting and continue to roast for another 7 to 8 minutes. Remove mushrooms from the sheet pan and set aside to cool.

6 In a large bowl whisk together remaining 3 tablespoons of olive oil, lemon juice, ⅛ teaspoon salt and ⅛ teaspoon pepper. Add beans and toss to coat.

7 Gather beans into 20 bundles of about 10 beans each. Intermittently line up portobello strips with bean bundles. Place 1 bundle at the end of 1 prosciutto piece and roll up lengthwise. Repeat to create 20 bundles.

8 Arrange assembled bundles, seam side down, on sheet pan. Bake for 4 to 5 minutes or until beans are warmed and prosciutto begins to brown. Remove from the oven and switch the oven to broil. Sprinkle each bundle with Parmesan and broil for a minute or until Parmesan is bubbly and golden.

You can most certainly make these in the morning, wrap them and bake just before serving.

A TRIO OF CRANBERRY chutney

Cranberry chutney/jelly can often be an overlooked dish, but if we reimagine the old-school cranberry situation and put some new swag in it and then serve it as a sexy trio, you are bound to get some new cranberry chutney fans! In addition to being a great meal accruement with dinner, chutney is just as yummy served with soft cheeses or as a topper for brie or goat cheese accompanied by crackers. It is great to incorporate with leftovers, as a spread on your next-day turkey sandwich, stirred into pancake batter, spread on French toast or eaten with bagels and cream cheese. There are so many places in the world for a good cranberry chutney.

Chunky Pecan Cranberry

GF | V+   YIELD 3 CUPS

1 cup **APPLE CIDER**

½ cup fresh **ORANGE JUICE**

¼ cup **SUGAR**

¼ cup pure **MICHIGAN MAPLE SYRUP**

1 small **CINNAMON STICK**

1 *(1-inch)* piece fresh **GINGER**

½ teaspoon **SEA SALT**

½ teaspoon whole **CLOVES**

⅛ teaspoon dried crushed **RED PEPPER**

1 *(12-ounce)* package fresh or frozen **CRANBERRIES**

½ cup dried **APRICOTS**, finely diced

2 teaspoon **ORANGE ZEST**

½ cup chopped toasted **PECANS**

1. In a large saucepan over medium-high heat add the first 9 ingredients (apple cider through crushed red pepper) and bring to a boil. Reduce heat to low and simmer, stirring occasionally, for 10 minutes. Remove cloves with a slotted spoon and discard.

2. Add cranberries, increase heat to medium and bring to a boil, stirring occasionally, 4 to 5 minutes or just until cranberries begin to pop. Discard cinnamon stick and ginger and stir in apricots and orange zest. Top with toasted pecans.

3. Cool completely. Serve immediately or chill and serve within 3 to 4 days.

Pickled Cranberry Relish

GF | V+   YIELD 3 CUPS

1 large navel **ORANGE**, zest and fruit

⅓ cup of **WATER**

½ cup **SUGAR**

¼ cup **APPLE CIDER VINEGAR**

2 cups fresh or frozen **CRANBERRIES**

¼ cup **GOLDEN RAISINS**

¼ cup dried **MICHIGAN CHERRIES**

2 tablespoons finely chopped **SHALLOTS**

½ cup chopped **WALNUTS**, toasted

2 tablespoons chopped **PARSLEY** *(optional)*

1. Zest the orange and then remove the peel. Chop the fruit and reserve.

2. In a medium saucepan, bring water to a boil. Add sugar and apple cider vinegar. Continue to boil until the sugar has dissolved. Add cranberries, raisins, cherries, shallots, orange zest and chopped orange. Reduce heat to medium-low and simmer for 2 minutes, cool and store in the refrigerator overnight.

3. Before serving, stir in toasted walnuts and spoon chutney from excess liquid into a serving vessel. Top with parsley if desired.

Spicy Cranberry Chutney

GF | V+ YIELD 2 CUPS

¾ cup SUGAR

2 large JALAPEÑOS, preferably red, seeds removed and finely chopped

1 tablespoon LEMON JUICE

1 teaspoon LEMON ZEST

½ teaspoon SEA SALT

¼ teaspoon CAYENNE PEPPER

½ cup WATER

1 (12-ounce) bag fresh or frozen CRANBERRIES

1 tablespoon grated GINGER

1. In a saucepan over medium-high heat add sugar, jalapeños, lemon juice and zest, salt and cayenne pepper. Add ½ cup water and stir with a wooden spoon to dissolve sugar. Bring mixture to simmer and cook for 2 minutes.

2. Add cranberries and ginger and bring to a boil. Reduce heat to medium-low and cook, stirring occasionally, until cranberries have softened and no liquid remains in the pan, about 12 to 15 minutes. Remove from heat and allow to cool.

3. Taste and adjust seasonings with a pinch more cayenne if you like it hotter. Store in the refrigerator for up to two weeks.

Chef's Notes

Chutney, like many cooked jams and pickled items, has a great shelf life, so go ahead and make it a week or two in advance.

market BRUSSELS SPROUTS & BUTTERNUT SQUASH

GF | V YIELD 8 TO 10 SERVINGS

2 tablespoons OLIVE OIL, divided

3 cups BUTTERNUT SQUASH, peeled and cut into ½-inch cubes

½ cup dried CHERRIES

¼ cup APPLE CIDER

6 cups BRUSSELS SPROUTS, washed, trimmed and halved

½ cup WATER

1 teaspoon SEA SALT

½ teaspoon BLACK PEPPER

½ cup small diced WHITE ONIONS

½ cup chopped PECANS

FOR THE GLAZE

½ cup APPLE CIDER

2 tablespoons BUTTER, melted

2 tablespoons MICHIGAN HONEY

1 ORANGE, zest and juice

2 teaspoons APPLE CIDER VINEGAR

½ teaspoon BLACK PEPPER

1. In a large sauté pan heat 1 tablespoon olive oil over medium heat until hot. Add diced squash and stir to coat. Stir occasionally, until squash starts to brown. Add cherries and apple cider. Cover pan and cook until squash is cooked through. Remove the lid and continue cooking to evaporate any leftover liquid. Remove squash from sauté pan and set aside.

2. In the same pan, add the remaining 1 tablespoon of oil and heat over medium-high heat. Place the brussels sprouts cut side down in the hot oil and season with sea salt and black pepper. Reduce heat to medium and cook until lightly browned. Add onions and continue cooking for about 5 minutes until tender.

3. Whisk the glaze ingredients together.

4. Add the squash and cherry mixture back into the pan. Stir in the glaze and simmer for a minute to coat. Adjust seasoning and top with chopped pecans before serving.

rustic BOURBON WHIPPED SWEET POTATOES

GF   YIELD 8 TO 10 SERVINGS

5 pounds SWEET POTATOES, peeled and cut into medium-large chunks

1½ tablespoons OLIVE OIL

8 slices thick-cut BACON, chopped

½ cup WHITE ONION, diced small

¼ cup BOURBON

½ cup APPLE CIDER, divided

¼ cup unsalted BUTTER

15 large SAGE leaves

½ cup whole MILK

½ cup DARK BROWN SUGAR

1 teaspoon CINNAMON

½ teaspoon SEA SALT

¼ teaspoon fresh CRACKED PEPPER

Pinch of CAYENNE PEPPER

1   In a large stock pot add sweet potato chunks, cover with cold water and season with sea salt. Bring the potatoes to a boil and cook until they are fork tender, about 20 to 25 minutes and drain and leave in the pot covered with a lid to keep warm.

2   In a sauté pan over medium heat add olive oil. Add the chopped bacon and cook until bacon begins to brown. Add diced onions and continue to cook until onions are close to caramel in color. Reduce heat to low. Add bourbon and cook until most of the bourbon has evaporated. Add ¼ cup apple cider and reduce liquid again for 3 to 4 minutes until sticky but not swimming in liquid. Use a slotted spoon to remove the bacon and onion mixture and set aside to garnish the top of sweet potatoes for serving.

3   In a small sauté pan melt butter until hot. Quickly fry sage leaves for about 30 seconds until crisp. Remove with a slotted spoon and place on a paper towel to dry.

4   In a small saucepan heat milk, brown sugar, the remaining ¼ cup apple cider, cinnamon, salt, pepper and cayenne until warm.

5   Using either a stand mixer with the whisk attachment or a hand mixer, whip warm liquid into drained sweet potatoes until smooth and creamy.

6   Serve topped with reserved bacon/onion mixture and fried sage as a garnish or mixed into whipped potatoes.

pieBOMB.COM

Upset the pie cart this Thanksgiving with a fun bite-size approach to dessert. Ditch those big slices of pie for little pie mouth bites!

base concept
Oven Baked EZ Pie Balls

YIELD 10 TO 12 SERVINGS

It is so simple to nest assorted prepared pie fillings (cherry, apple or blueberry) into pie or Danish pastry dough circles.

2 prepared roll PIE CRUSTS *(8 to 10 inches)* or Danish dough also works nicely

1 *(20-ounce)* can desired PIE FILLING

1 egg beaten with a tablespoon of WATER *(egg wash)*

3 tablespoons coarse SUGAR

1   Preheat the oven to 325°F. Line a sheet pan with a silicone mat or parchment paper.

2   Cut prepared pastry into 2 ½- to 3-inch circles using a round cutter or trace the same size lid of a jar over dough with a knife.

3 Place a heaping tablespoon of pie filling into the center of the dough ball, pinch top to seal and roll ball in the palm of your hands quickly if you need to shape it a bit due to pinching. Place on the prepared sheet pan, pinched side down.

4 Brush the pie balls with egg wash and sprinkle with coarse sugar.

5 Bake for 9 to 12 minutes until golden brown.

Pumpkin Pie Balls

1 cup PUMPKIN PUREE

3 ounces CREAM CHEESE, softened

1 large EGG

⅔ cup granulated SUGAR, divided

3 teaspoons PUMPKIN PIE SPICE, divided

1 teaspoon pure VANILLA EXTRACT

Pinch SEA SALT

1 package DANISH DOUGH or PUFF PASTRY sheets *(Danish preferred)*, thawed

2 tablespoons melted BUTTER

FOR THE GLAZE

½ cup POWDERED SUGAR

1 tablespoon MILK

Dash of VANILLA

1 Preheat the oven to 350°F. Line a large sheet pan with parchment paper.

2 In a large bowl add pumpkin, cream cheese, egg, ⅓ cup sugar, 2 teaspoons pumpkin pie spice and vanilla. Using a hand mixer, beat until smooth. Season with a pinch of salt.

3 Unfold Danish dough and cut into 18 2 x 2-inch squares.

4 Dollop a rounded tablespoon of pumpkin mixture onto each square. Pinch all corners together and seal to create a ball.

5 In a small bowl mix remaining ⅓ cup sugar with the remaining 1 teaspoon pumpkin pie spice. Brush balls with melted butter and roll in sugar mixture and place on the prepared sheet pan. Bake for 25 to 30 minutes or until balls are golden and puffy.

6 While pumpkin balls are baking, make the glaze. In a medium bowl add powdered sugar, milk and vanilla and mix until smooth, adding more powdered sugar or milk to reach desired consistency.

7 Serve slightly cooled with glaze for dipping.

Pecan Pie Balls

1 8-inch prepared PECAN PIE

½ cup ground CHOCOLATE WAFER COOKIES

1 cup melted DARK CHOCOLATE for dipping

1 Crumble pecan pie into the bowl of a stand mixer fitted with the paddle attachment. Add cookies and stir until mixture comes together. Place in the freezer for 10 to 15 minutes.

2 Using a 2-ounce scoop, scoop pie mixture and roll into balls. (Wear food-prep gloves. This is sticky business.)

3 Place chocolate in a microwave-safe bowl and heat for 20 seconds. Stir and repeat 2 to 3 times until melted or place chocolate in a small bowl over a pot with simmering water (double boiler) and stir until melted.

4 Line a sheet tray with plastic wrap or parchment paper and put on fresh prep gloves. Spoon a little melted chocolate in your hand and quickly roll a pecan ball into the chocolate. Place on the prepared sheet pan and repeat until all the balls are coated. Place in the fridge for 2 minutes to set chocolate and repeat with a second coat.

5 Place pecan balls in a cool place to set up and store in an airtight container in a cool place for up to two days. Refrigerate if storing for a longer period of time.

FRILLS

Consider inserting a short stick or cute pick into the base of your pie orbs and serve them on platters. Create a fun topping bar with whipped cream, an icing drizzle or dip, chocolate and caramel sauces and assorted sprinkles.

Chef's Notes

Use your imagination here! Purchasing small, prepared cans of pie filling or mini pies works without the expense or overload of trying to have so many varieties of large pies.

SALTED CARAMEL **chai**

GF   YIELD 8 TO 10 SERVINGS

Chai beverages with pie is a winning dessert combo!

1½ cups **HALF AND HALF, WHOLE MILK** or **MILK SUBSTITUTE**

2½ cups liquid **CHAI CONCENTRATE** *(Oregon or Tazo are good brands)*

6 ounces **SALTED CARAMEL WHISKEY, BOURBON** or **VODKA**

4 ounces **KAHLUA**

GARNISH

WHIPPED CREAM and **CINNAMON** for serving (optional)

1 In a saucepan over medium heat add half and half or milk and chia concentrate until hot, but not boiling. Remove from heat. Stir in liquors.

2 Serve in a short mug or glass that will manage a hot beverage. Top with a little whipped cream and a sprinkle of cinnamon if desired.

'Tis the Season

GF/Gluten Free, DF/Dairy Free, V/Vegetarian, V+/Vegan

This is maybe the holiday that calls for the most décor all year, as it typically encompasses your interior and exterior. Are we thinking of decking out the mantles and shelves? Do we need a place setting to match? Is there a serving buffet that we want to tie in with all the other components?

You can intermix these ideas in so many ways, from the garland down your tablescape. Splashes of elements in one area could easily be used in another. Does your décor want to feel a little more natural, with eucalyptus, dried fruits, small brown pears and oranges, frosted pinecones and cut wood chargers with sprigs of forest green and white? Or maybe your jam is shiny and bright, with silk floral elements, festive bulbs and garlands of beads with pops of fresh floral and ribbon. Whichever direction you choose, the main idea is to pick a feeling or theme and try to stick with it all the way through.

Putting together fresh garlands is a great way to add festive décor to your mantle, stair railing or even a bookcase. Grab inspiration from nature and use scented greenery like pine and cedar, and add contrasting colors using magnolia and silver dollar eucalyptus. It's best to add these greeneries closer to your event or the holiday because they will dry out over time. If you are looking to use faux, maybe mix a few faux garlands to create the look of a fresh greenery. Use a smaller, more streamlined style and a larger, fluffier style and intertwine them with each other. This will help create the fullness of a fresh garland for years to come. Once your garland is in place, start layering. Add in your large pieces first. Large ornaments come in different shapes and sizes and can fill in gaps. Take some of your smaller ornaments and cluster them together with floral wire and tuck them in to create multiple textures and interest. Add decorative branches, berries and even some glittery faux feathers to incorporate more focal points and elements of interest within the garland. Ribbon is another great addition to make your garland look robust and add color and texture! Complete project garland with your favorite colorful, glittery or patterned ribbon to help tie the entire look together.

Weave the ribbon in and out, going around the ornaments and covering any empty gaps that may be exposed and voilà! Your garland becomes a whimsical focal point for your home.

Now that your home is dressed, let's get to work on the tablescape. Tuck in fresh sprigs of green every so often down the center of your table, leaving space in between for other decorative items. Add an extra layer of dried fruits and pinecones. Consider using brightly colored fruits such as kiwis, oranges, pomegranates, grapefruit and strawberries. Nestle them organically into your communal food masterpiece to add a pop of color and a sweet, refreshing element.

Incorporating taper candles to your tablescape is a great way to add height without being in the way of your guest and is also a good opportunity to add a burst of color or to give a wow factor. Consider matching your candle's color to your napkin to tie everything together. Mix up your candle holders (metal, glass, wood, etc.), but keep them consistent with your theme. Candlelight also creates an ambiance within the room that will allow your centerpiece to have a focal point for your space. For a festive place setting, consider a wood charger or something with texture to pull color from the center of the table. Poke a hole in some dried fruit and loop velvet ribbon or twine through the fruit. Finish with a little place setting tag with your guest's name and wrap it around a simple folded napkin. Tuck in a sprig of evergreen for a little added texture and color. Adding little touches to the place setting will complete the table.

Today with our feast we chose a very simplistic Scandinavian style of set up with fresh cedar, soft yarn garland on the walls, warm wood and a few china serving pieces—simple but beautiful on our wood table with no linen.

BEEF TENDERLOIN **platter**

DF   YIELD 10 TO 12 SERVINGS

1 whole **BEEF TENDERLOIN** *(4 ½ to 5 pounds)*, cleaned

1½ teaspoons **SEA SALT**

1 teaspoon freshly ground **PEPPER**

⅓ cup **OLIVE OIL**

1 tablespoon **DIJON MUSTARD**

2 tablespoons **ROSEMARY**, chopped

1 tablespoon **PARSLEY**, chopped

1½ tablespoons chopped **GARLIC**

1 bundle/bouquet of **THYME** or **ROSEMARY** to garnish platter

ACCOUTREMENTS

1 cup prepared **HORSERADISH SAUCE**

¼ cup **DIJON MUSTARD**

½ cup **STONE GROUND MUSTARD**

18 to 20 petite **BRIOCHE ROLLS** or your favorite rolls, sliced ¾ way through

1. Preheat barbeque grill to medium and preheat the oven to 350°F.

2. Place whole tenderloin on work surface. Season with salt and pepper.

3. In a small bowl mix olive oil, mustard, herbs and chopped garlic. Using food service gloves massage the tenderloin all over with the oil mixture.

4. Place the whole tenderloin on the barbeque grill and cook for about 4 minutes. Turn the tenderloin 30 degrees to give the roast cross marks and cook for another 2 minutes. Flip the entire tenderloin and repeat. The goal here is to sear both large sides, giving it a nice crust and locking in juices.

5. Once both sides have a nice sear, remove the tenderloin from the grill and place seared tenderloin in a large roasting pan or on a sheet tray. Place in preheated oven and roast for 18 to 25 minutes until a meat thermometer reads about 128° to 132°F. This will land you at a nice medium finish, which will look pink but not bloody. Of course, cook the tenderloin to your desired doneness.

6. Let meat rest for 30 minutes and then slice into ½- to ¾-inch slices, keeping the slices together to place on platter.

7. On a large platter, working from the outside of your platter in, shingle tenderloin slices off, setting slices a little over the one before to create sweeping rows, saving a spot for mushrooms and other garnishes.

8. Serve with accoutrements.

Chef's Notes

- If you want to use the oven to sear the tenderloin, place the roast in a preheated 425°F oven for 8 minutes and reduce heat to 350°F and continue as outlined above.

- A tenderloin platter is often the "wow" dish on a holiday table. You may consider having some extra garnish to add to your platter, such as roasted peppers, sautéed onions or olives. Think about ½ to ¾ of a cup of extra garnishes if desired.

- A great time saver is to cook your tenderloin the day before, leave whole and refrigerate. A couple hours before serving, pull the tenderloin and slice as instructed above. It is easy to slice when it is cold. Arrange the platter, garnish, wrap with plastic film and let sit on the counter to bring up to room temperature before serving. A tenderloin platter does not have to be hot. Room temperature is great, but I do not suggest cold as it is less flavorful.

- If a whole tenderloin is too big for your crew, you can often purchase a half roast at a good butcher counter.

balsamic ROASTED MUSHROOMS

GF | V+

YIELD 8 TO 10 SERVINGS AS A GARNISH

1 pound baby bella MUSHROOMS

3 tablespoons OLIVE OIL

¾ teaspoon SEA SALT

¼ teaspoon freshly GROUND PEPPER

¼ teaspoon RED PEPPER FLAKES

2 tablespoons BALSAMIC SYRUP

1. Preheat the oven to 400°F. Once heated, place a sheet tray in the oven and heat for 5 to 8 minutes.

2. In a medium bowl add mushrooms. Drizzle with olive oil and sprinkle with salt, pepper and red pepper flakes, giving mushrooms a good mix or rub with your hands.

3. Carefully remove the hot sheet tray from the oven and spill mushrooms on to the tray, making sure you don't overcrowd it. Place in the oven and roast for 12 to 15 minutes, stirring with a spatula every 4 or so minutes.

4. Remove from the oven and let cool for 5 minutes. Drizzle with balsamic syrup and give them a stir to thoroughly coat.

5. Garnish tenderloin platter (see recipe , p. 87) with mushrooms or serve on the side in a bowl.

Chef's Notes

- Usually the baby bellas are very clean, but if they look a little gritty, take a clean, damp paper towel and give them a quick rub.

- Make your mushrooms up to three days in advance. Remove from the fridge and let them come to room temperature or give the mushrooms a quick pop in the oven to take the chill off.

jeweled STUFFED HOLIDAY TURKEY BREAST

YIELD 8 TO 10 SERVINGS

1 large 4- to 5-pound TURKEY BREAST, skin on *(or two smaller)*

CIDER GINGER MAPLE GLAZE

1 cup APPLE CIDER

1 small nub fresh GINGER, peeled and sliced *(about 1 heaping tablespoon)*

⅓ cup pure MAPLE SYRUP

5 tablespoons unsalted BUTTER

2 tablespoons ORANGE JUICE CONCENTRATE

1 tablespoon ORANGE ZEST

2 fresh SAGE leaves, chopped

½ teaspoon CINNAMON

JEWELED STUFFING

2 tablespoons unsalted BUTTER

½ cup diced ONION

1 bulb FENNEL, cleaned and cut in thin strips

16 dried APRICOTS, sliced in strips *(about 3 pieces per apricot half)*

8 dried black or golden FIGS, chopped medium

¼ cup dried CHERRIES or CRANBERRIES

1 PEAR, peeled and diced medium

¾ cup CHICKEN or VEGETABLE STOCK

2 tablespoons BROWN SUGAR

¾ teaspoon SEA SALT

½ teaspoon PEPPER

¼ teaspoon CINNAMON

⅛ teaspoon ALLSPICE

⅛ teaspoon ground GINGER

2½ cups cubed DAY-OLD BREAD

7   Stuff turkey breast with stuffing. Place the dressed breast on the prepared sheet tray. If you have extra stuffing, bake in a small, covered casserole dish for the last 20 minutes.

8   Carefully pull the skin of the turkey breast back and brush with some of the cider glaze.

9   Place the stuffed turkey into the oven and roast, basting every so often with cider glaze. Cover the turkey with foil if it starts getting too dark; this can happen around the 30-minute mark. Cook turkey 45 to 55 minutes or until meat thermometer inserted into the thickest part reads 160°F.

10   Transfer turkey to a cutting board and let rest for at least 10 minutes.

11   Meanwhile, put the drippings from the pan into a small sauce pot and reduce about 30%. Slice turkey. Place on a platter and brush with reduced pan drippings.

PECAN MUSTARD RUBBED SALMON **platter**

YIELD 10 SERVINGS

Nonstick spray

3 tablespoons **DIJON MUSTARD**

2 tablespoons **COARSE MUSTARD**

2 tablespoons unsalted **BUTTER**, melted

2 tablespoons **MAPLE SYRUP**

¾ cup **PANKO BREAD CRUMBS**

½ cup finely chopped **PECANS**

1 tablespoon **ORANGE ZEST**

1 tablespoon finely chopped **PARSLEY**

1 teaspoon **SEA SALT**, divided

½ teaspoon freshly ground **BLACK PEPPER**, divided

10 (4-ounce) **SALMON FILLETS**

1 **LEMON**, sliced into wedges for serving (optional)

GARNISH

1 **ORANGE**, sliced in circles

A bouquet of **HERBS** such as rosemary

1   Preheat the oven to 400°F. Line a large sheet pan with foil and spray with nonstick spray.

2   In a small bowl combine mustards, melted butter and syrup.

1   Preheat the oven to 350°F. Line a sheet pan with parchment paper and a roasting rack. Coat a 9 x 13-inch baking pan with non-stick spray.

2   Prepare a pocket in the turkey. Using a long slicer knife or a chef's knife, slowly work the blade to each side to create a space without piercing all the way through. Set aside.

3   To make the glaze, in a medium saucepan over medium-high heat add apple cider and fresh ginger and reduce by half. Remove from heat and whisk in maple syrup, butter, orange juice concentrate, orange zest, fresh sage and cinnamon. Set aside.

4   To make the stuffing, in a large sauté pan over medium heat melt butter. Add onion and fennel and sauté for 3 to 4 minutes.

5   Add dried fruits, pear, stock, brown sugar, salt, pepper and spices. Reduce heat to low and simmer for 2 to 4 minutes.

6   Add bread cubes with cooked fruit mixture and toss to mix everything together. Place in a baking pan and bake for 30 minutes. Allow to cool before stuffing turkey.

ROOT VEGETABLE hash

GF   YIELD 10 TO 12 SERVINGS

1 cup **PARSNIPS**, thinly sliced on a slight angle

1 cup medium diced **RUTABAGA**

1 cup medium diced **TURNIPS**

3 tablespoons **OLIVE OIL** *(divided)*

2 cups medium diced **SWEET POTATOES**

3 tablespoons unsalted **BUTTER**

8 slices wood-smoked **APPLE BACON**, diced *(optional; add another tablespoon of butter if omitting)*

2 cups variegated **CARROTS**, sliced medium-thin on a slight angle

½ cup julienned **ONION**

1 large bunch of **KALE**, chopped medium to large pieces

1½ teaspoons **SEA SALT**

1 teaspoon freshly ground **BLACK PEPPER**

1 tablespoon chopped **PARSLEY**

1 tablespoon chopped **ROSEMARY**

1 Preheat the oven to 375°F. Line 2 sheet pans with foil.

2 In a large bowl add parsnips, rutabaga and turnips. Toss with 1½ tablespoons of olive oil, season with salt and pepper and place in a single layer on the prepared sheet tray. Repeat the process with sweet potatoes. Roast for 15 to 20 minutes, occasionally tossing with metal spatula to ensure even cooking. Sweet pota-

3 In a second bowl combine panko, pecans, orange zest, parsley, ½ teaspoon salt and ¼ teaspoon of pepper.

4 Place salmon on a work surface and season fillets with remaining ½ teaspoon salt and ¼ teaspoon black pepper. Brush or spoon mustard mixture over salmon fillets, press salmon fillets into panko mixture and place an inch apart on the prepared sheet pan. Lightly spray salmon with nonstick spray.

5 Bake for 12 to 15 minutes until the salmon is firm to touch.

6 Let salmon rest for 5 minutes. Line up on a serving platter and garnish with sliced orange wheels in a row on the outer perimeter of the platter and nestle in the bouquet of herbs. Serve lemon wedges alongside if using.

Chef's Notes

You can also roast the salmon as a whole side versus individual fillets. Simply place roasted salmon on a large serving platter and serve with a small spatula, allowing guests to help themselves by cutting into the side. You can make the glaze 3 or more days in advance and store it in the fridge. Panko mix can also be made ahead of time and stored in the freezer and pulled out an hour before preparing the dish.

toes will take 4 to 5 minutes longer than other root vegetables. Let cool for 20 minutes.

3 In a large heavy-bottom sauté pan over medium heat melt butter. Add diced bacon and cook for 3 to 4 minutes until a little crispy. Use a slotted spoon to remove bacon and let drain on a piece of paper towel.

4 Add carrots and cook for a couple minutes. Add onions and continue to cook over medium heat for a minute or two then add roasted root vegetables and cook over medium-high heat for about 3 minutes until crispy, flip with metal spatula and cook for another 3 to 4 minutes until the second side is crispy. If the pan starts to stick, add a little more butter or olive oil.

5 Close to the end of cooking on the second side, add chopped kale and cover pan with a lid for a quick minute. Remove the lid and stir the kale into the hash.

6 Season with sea salt, pepper and herbs.

Chef's Notes

- Variegated carrots are the multi-color regular size carrots—yellow, orange and purple—most often in a bag next to the orange ones. If you cannot find them, no stress, just use all orange carrots.

- You can prep the veggies a day or two in advance so you are ready to sauté just before dinner without the extra mess or fuss of prep.

holiday HARICOT VERT

GF | V+   YIELD 8 TO 10 SERVINGS

2 pounds trimmed HARICOT VERT

½ cup SUN-DRIED TOMATOES, chopped and reconstituted or packed in oil sun-dried tomatoes

½ cup toasted PEANUTS, chopped

6 to 8 BASIL leaves, chiffonade

1 tablespoon extra-virgin OLIVE OIL

Juice of one LEMON

½ teaspoon SEA SALT

BLACK PEPPER to taste

1 Blanch or steam beans 2 to 3 minutes until cooked but still al dente.

2 Transfer beans to a large bowl, add remaining ingredients and toss together. Adjust seasonings to taste. Place beans on serving platter.

'TIS THE SEASON salad

GF | V   YIELD 10 SERVINGS

VINAIGRETTE

½ cup OLIVE OIL

6 SHALLOTS, sliced

¼ cup BRAGG APPLE CIDER VINEGAR

3 tablespoons ORANGE JUICE

2 tablespoons DIJON MUSTARD

1 tablespoon HONEY

1 teaspoon ORANGE ZEST

A pinch each of SEA SALT and PEPPER

SALAD

4 cups shaved BRUSSELS SPROUTS (or purchase bagged in produce aisle)

4 cups KALE, cleaned and chopped

½ cup toasted ALMONDS

2 GREEN APPLES with skin on, diced

½ cup julienned RED ONIONS

1 cup shaved PARMESAN

½ cup POMEGRANATE SEEDS

1 Heat olive oil in a small heavy-bottom saucepan. Add sliced shallots and fry until crispy (about a minute). Use a slotted spoon to remove shallots and drain on a paper towel. Set oil aside to let cool or pop in the fridge for 10 minutes.

2 To make the dressing, combine cooled oil, Bragg apple cider vinegar, orange juice, mustard and honey and whisk to combine. Stir in orange zest and season with a pinch of salt and pepper.

3 In a large bowl mix brussels sprouts and chopped kale. Dress with ¾ of the prepared dressing. Let salad rest with dressing for at least 15 minutes at room temperature or up to 2 hours in the fridge.

4 When ready to serve add fried shallots, almonds, diced green apple and red onion and gently toss. Place salad in a serving bowl and sprinkle shaved Parmesan, pomegranate seeds and drizzle a little extra reserved dressing if needed.

Chef's Notes

To keep apples from oxidizing, hold them in a little lemon water if you chop more than 30 minutes before service.

GINGERED PEAR CRANBERRY ALMOND **tart**

V   YIELD 8 TO 10 PIECES

4 medium PEARS, firm, sliced ¼-inch thick

1 tablespoon fresh LEMON JUICE

4 tablespoons melted BUTTER

2 tablespoons LIGHT BROWN SUGAR

1 teaspoon VANILLA

1 teaspoon CINNAMON

½ teaspoon ground GINGER

1 sheet PUFF PASTRY, thawed but kept cold

FLOUR, for dusting

¼ cup dried reconstituted CRANBERRIES *(cover with boiling water, let sit 10 to 15 minutes until soft)*

3 tablespoons sliced ALMONDS for garnish

WHIPPED CREAM *(optional)*

ICE CREAM *(optional)*

FRANGIPANE

¼ cup BUTTER

¼ cup SUGAR

1 EGG

½ cup ALMOND FLOUR

2 tablespoons ALL-PURPOSE FLOUR

1 teaspoon pure VANILLA

½ teaspoon LEMON ZEST

1 Preheat the oven to 375°F. Line a sheet pan with parchment paper.

2 In a large bowl add sliced pears and lemon juice and toss to coat.

3 Add butter, brown sugar, vanilla, cinnamon and ginger. Toss together until everything is evenly coated. Set aside.

4 To make the frangipane, combine butter and sugar and beat until creamy. Add egg and mix until incorporated. Add almond flour, all-purpose flour, vanilla and lemon zest. Continue mixing until everything is well incorporated.

5 Roll out puff pastry on a surface dusted with flour to measure 9 x 11 inches. Carefully place pastry on the prepared sheet pan. Use a small paring knife to score the long sides of the pastry, about 1 inch from the edge, being careful not to cut all the way through the dough. Dock the center of the pastry with a fork. Spread frangipane down the center of the pastry and top with pears, shingling and overlapping slightly. Top with reconstituted cranberries.

6 Bake until the edge is puffed and golden, about 15 to 20 minutes.

7 Let cool and cut into 8 to 10 square pieces. Garnish with sliced almonds. Serve warm or room temperature with ice cream or whipped cream, if desired.

OLD SCHOOL eggnog

GF | V   YIELD 10 TO 12 SERVINGS

12 large **EGG YOLKS**

1½ cups **SUGAR**

½ teaspoon **SEA SALT**

8 cups whole **MILK**

3 whole **CLOVES**

2 tablespoons **VANILLA EXTRACT**

2 cups **HEAVY CREAM** *(we love Calder Dairy)*

Pinch of **NUTMEG**

Bourbon or **DARK RUM** *(optional)*

1 In a large bowl, whisk egg yolks, sugar and sea salt until fluffy and light lemon colored. Set aside.

2 Place milk in a heavy-bottom pot with cloves and heat milk slowly over medium heat until it is hot but not boiling. Remove whole cloves with a spoon.

3 Place your whisked egg yolk bowl on a damp towel or in a mixing ring (to keep it stable without holding with your hand). Using a measuring cup or a ladle, slowly stream in 4 cups of the hot milk into the egg mixture, whisking continuously. This is called tempering.

4 Once half of the milk has been tempered into the egg mixture, stream the egg/milk mixture back into the pot with the remaining 4 cups of hot milk. Stir continually over low heat until your eggnog reaches 160°F.

5 Add vanilla and carefully strain hot mixture through a fine-mesh strainer into a large bowl.

6 Quickly cool down your eggnog by placing the bowl over another large bowl with ice and water, and using a heat-proof rubber spatula, stir eggnog over ice bath for 15 to 20 minutes (you can stir intermittently).

7 Add heavy cream to eggnog. Transfer to serving pitcher.

8 To serve, set up a beverage station with the eggnog, bourbon or rum and a little shaker of nutmeg for people to mix their own.

Chef's Notes

After step 6, you can go two ways: step 7 as I have detailed above or reserve heavy cream until time of service then whip it into soft peaks and stir into base eggnog. It makes it feel a little thicker and fluffier.

Menu

GF/Gluten Free, DF/Dairy Free, V/Vegetarian, V+/Vegan

When planning a holiday cocktail or New Year's party this season, think about adding a little bling. Borrow a little this and that from the holiday décor you already have in place and give it a sparkling twist!

For your holiday party bling table, start with a white or pale-colored bed sheet or inexpensive fabric adorned with brush strokes of metallic or shimmer paint for a tablecloth or as an accent piece. You can pick up interesting linen online for rental or purchase with sparkles and bling, too!

Trim pine branches and pinecones from the holiday tree and spray them with a little frosted shimmer paint. Add sparkly bulbs and ornaments layered with battery-operated lights in a large vase or clear bowl with a few strands of polished beads and glass stones. Weave in some interesting metallic sparkling garland for a little extra table shine! Take twisted tinsel garland in your color scheme and have it trailing down your table or hanging from your fireplace or bookshelf. Consider shimmery faux snow layered in vases with pieces of blue icy accent linen. Purchase small four- by four-inch mirror tiles and paint your guests' names in gold or silver for place settings and gifts they can take home!

What's a holiday party without photos? Create a photo booth for your guest. Start with some wall-size panels of fringe curtains available online or at most party supply stores, add multiple balloons in monochromatic colors in hues of gold, silver or black and don't forget a fun prop basket that guests can grab from to create silly photo ops. Keeping your colors in mixed metallics will help everything stay cohesive and come together! Spray, sparkle, bling and repeat!

blackberry BRIE BITES

V   YIELD 24 BITES

In planning your amounts, based on this menu I would suggest 2 small bites per person.

1 *(8-ounce)* wheel of **BRIE**

2 sheets packaged prepared **PUFF PASTRY DOUGH**, thawed

⅓ cup **BLACKBERRY JAM**

24 toasted **WALNUT** halves

1 **EGG** and 1 tablespoon milk or water *(mixed)* to make egg wash

SPECIAL EQUIPMENT

2½-inch round cutter

1. Preheat the oven to 350°F. Line a sheet pan with parchment paper.

2. Cut brie into 24 cubed pieces and roll each cube into a ball.

3. Using the round cutter, cut puff pastry into 24 rounds.

4. Place each brie ball on pastry round and top with about ½ teaspoon blackberry jam. Gently press 1 walnut on top.

5. Pull up edges of puff pastry and twist the top to seal (like a Hershey's Kiss) and transfer to the prepared sheet pan.

6. Brush each pastry with egg wash.

7. Bake for 8 to 10 minutes until golden brown.

8. Serve warm or at room temperature.

Chef's Notes

Prepare brie bites ahead of time (without egg wash) and freeze on a sheet tray. After frozen you can store them in a ziplock bag in the freezer. When you are ready for a quick appetizer on the fly, pull brie cheese bites from the freezer, place on parchment-lined sheet pan and egg wash. Let thaw about 15 minutes before baking at 350°F for 8 to 10 minutes until golden brown.

old bay CRAB "MEATBALLS"

YIELD 20 TO 24 MEATBALLS

Cooking spray

16 ounces fresh jumbo lump **CRAB MEAT** (*picked through to remove any shells*)

1 large **EGG**

½ cup **MAYONNAISE**

½ cup and 3 tablespoons **PANKO BREADCRUMBS**

2 teaspoons **OLD BAY SEASONING**

2 teaspoons **LEMON ZEST** (*fine*)

1 teaspoon finely chopped **PARSLEY**

1 teaspoon **WORCESTERSHIRE SAUCE**

½ teaspoon **DIJON MUSTARD**

⅛ teaspoon **GARLIC POWDER**

1 to 2 tablespoons unsalted **BUTTER**, melted

AIOLI DIP (*optional, recipe follows*)

1. Preheat the oven to a low broil. Lightly spray a sheet pan with cooking spray.

2. In a medium bowl add crab meat and gently pick through to remove any shells, being careful to not break up the lumps.

3. In a separate bowl beat the egg, add the mayonnaise and whisk until well combined.

4. Add breadcrumbs, Old Bay, lemon zest, parsley, Worcestershire sauce, Dijon mustard and garlic powder. Stir until well combined. A little at a time, gently fold the wet mixture into the crab meat, being careful to avoid breaking up the lumps.

5. Scoop 1-ounce bites and gently shape them into balls.

6. Place the crab bites on a prepared sheet pan and brush with melted butter.

7. Broil for 5 minutes, checking every few minutes to make sure they do not burn.

8. Turn the oven down to 350°F and bake for an additional 5 minutes.

9. Let cool just a smidge, transfer to a platter and serve on a small cocktail fork or pick.

10. Serve with aioli dip, if desired.

This crab meatball mix freezes great. If you are pushed for time, assemble the crab mixture and freeze. Thaw, scoop and bake when you are ready.

Aioli Dip

½ cup MAYONNAISE

2 tablespoons fresh LEMON JUICE

½ teaspoon LEMON ZEST

1 clove of GARLIC, minced

1 tablespoon finely chopped PARSLEY

1 teaspoon SRIRACHA (optional)

1 In a small bowl whisk all ingredients together.

2 Serve alongside Old Bay Crab "Meatballs."

warm CAPRESE BALLS

V

YIELD 20 PIECES

3 tablespoons finely chopped, oil-packed SUNDRIED TOMATOES

1½ teaspoons OLIVE OIL

6 medium-large BASIL leaves cut in half lengthwise, then cut into wispy thin strips

½ teaspoon SEA SALT

¼ teaspoon freshly ground BLACK PEPPER

20 pieces of cherry size "ciliegine" fresh MOZZARELLA BALLS

⅓ cup FLOUR

1 EGG mixed with 1 tablespoon water

½ cup seasoned ITALIAN-STYLE BREADCRUMBS

Olive oil COOKING SPRAY

½ cup MARINARA SAUCE (you can use your own or a high-quality premade sauce)

1 Preheat the oven to 350°F. Line a sheet pan with parchment paper.

2 In the bowl of a small food processor add sundried tomatoes, olive oil, basil, salt and pepper. Process until smooth. Pour over mozzarella balls, making sure they are evenly coated. Place in freezer for 10 to 15 minutes.

3 Set up a breading station with three small bowls. In one bowl add the flour, in the second bowl the egg and water mixture and in the third the breadcrumbs.

4 Roll each marinated mozzarella ball in flour, dip into the egg wash, firmly coat in breadcrumbs and place on the prepared sheet pan. Freeze for one hour.

5 Remove the tray from the freezer and spray the breadcrumbs liberally with olive oil spray. Bake for 6 to 10 minutes or until lightly golden.

6 Carefully place mozzarella balls on a serving platter. Serve warm marinara dip sauce and picks for stabbing.

You can make and freeze these weeks in advance and they turn out great! Place the sheet tray with the prepared caprese balls into the freezer until they are frozen, then place them in a freezer bag and store in the freezer until ready to bake.

SMOKED SALMON **marbles**

GF   YIELD 24 PIECES

6 ounces **CREAM CHEESE**

6 ounces **GOAT CHEESE**

8 ounces **SMOKED SALMON**, chopped

1 tablespoon **LEMON ZEST**

1 tablespoon **LEMON JUICE**

1 tablespoon finely diced **RED ONION**

2 teaspoons chopped **CAPERS**

Sprinkle of **SEA SALT**

Pinch of **CAYENNE**

½ cup finely ground **PISTACHIOS**

Whole **PISTACHIOS** for garnish *(optional)*

PRETZEL STICKS, for serving *(optional)*

1. In a small food processor mix the cream and goat cheeses together.

2. Add remaining ingredients (except nuts) and mix until everything is just combined.

3. Scoop 1-ounce portions of salmon mixture and form into a ball.

4. Roll in ground pistachios and skewer with a pick or a small pretzel stick.

Chef's Notes

Make your cheese mixture up to three days before and then the day of, continue from step 3 above.

CHORIZO-STUFFED **dates**

GF | DF   YIELD 20 PIECES

10 ounces fresh **CHORIZO SAUSAGE**

1 cup **TOMATO JUICE**

½ **CHIPOTLE PEPPER** *(you will find chipotle peppers in a small can in the ethnic department of most grocery stores)*

20 medium **MEDJOOL DATES**

10 strips of **BACON** cut in half

1. Preheat the oven to 350°F. Line a sheet pan with parchment paper.

2. In a medium skillet add chorizo sausage and cook, rendering out the fat until brown, breaking up sausage as you go. Drain fat and set aside to cool.

3. In a small, heavy-bottom pot, add tomato juice and chipotle pepper. Cook over medium-high heat until reduced approximately by half.

4. Cut ¾ into the top of each date lengthwise. Hinge open and remove pit.

5. Stuff dates with a heaping tablespoon of cooled cooked chorizo and close date.

6. Wrap bacon strip around chorizo-stuffed date, overlapping a bit, and trim. Place the seam side down on the prepared baking sheet.

7. Brush dates generously with spicy tomato glaze and bake for 12 to 15 minutes until bacon is crispy. Use extra glaze for quick refresh brush before serving.

Chef's Notes

Make these far in advance. After you wrap the date with the bacon, place the dates on a sheet tray and put in the freezer until frozen. Once frozen, place the dates in freezer bags and store in the freezer. The day of your event, remove from the freezer a couple hours before and let thaw. Brush with tomato glaze and follow baking instructions.

BLOODY MARY SHRIMP shooters

GF | DF YIELD 20 SHOOTERS

2 cups spicy **TOMATO JUICE**

½ cup **VODKA** *(optional)*

2 teaspoons **WORCESTERSHIRE**

1 teaspoon prepared **HORSERADISH**

½ teaspoon **TABASCO SAUCE**

½ teaspoon **CELERY SALT**

½ teaspoon **KOSHER SALT**

¼ teaspoon freshly ground **BLACK PEPPER**

1 **LEMON** *(use a vegetable peeler to cut 20 strips or curls from the peel for garnishing shooter, then slice lemon into 4 wedges)*

¼ cup **KOSHER SALT**

20 16/20 **SHRIMP**, cleaned and cooked

CELERY LEAVES for garnish

SPECIAL EQUIPMENT

20 *(2-ounce)* shot glasses

1. To make the Bloody Mary mix, whisk together the first eight ingredients (tomato juice through black pepper) in a pitcher.

2. Rub the rims of each shot glass with lemon wedges and dip rims into kosher salt.

3. Carefully pour the Bloody Mary mix into each shot glass until three-quarters full.

4. Place a shrimp halfway into each glass, leaving the tail hanging over the edge. Garnish each shooter with a lemon curl and a few small celery leaves.

HOLIDAY RED VELVET cake pops

YIELD 40 TO 46 PIECES

1 box RED VELVET CAKE MIX

1¼ cups VANILLA BUTTERCREAM or your favorite vanilla frosting
(whipped and at room temperature)

3 cups DARK CHOCOLATE MELTING DISCS

½ cup RED CHOCOLATE MELTING DISCS

SPECIAL EQUIPMENT

48 3- to 4-inch white sticks *(any craft store or Amazon will have these)*

Styrofoam planks to place sticks with cake pops into

1. Bake cake according to instructions on box or make your favorite cake from scratch.

2. Let cake cool completely and then crumble into a medium mixing bowl.

3. Mix frosting into crumbled cake and combine thoroughly (I like to wear food gloves and mix with my hands). Scoop cake mixture into ¾- to 1-ounce balls and place on sheet tray. Refrigerate for an hour.

4. Melt chocolate over a double boiler (steel bowl over pot with water), stirring often. Be careful to just melt chocolate and remove from stove verses overheating. You can leave it on top of double boiler to keep it warm. Although chocolate certainly must be melted to dip pops, you do not want it hot.

5. Remove chilled pops and pierce the cake balls with white sticks about ½ inch into the ball. One at a time, dip the cake ball into melted chocolate and let extra chocolate run off back into the bowl.

6 After cake ball is dipped, place the stick into Styrofoam plank. Repeat process until all pops are dipped. Place balls in cool place until set and the chocolate is matte. Drizzle pops with melted red chocolate and let the chocolate set. Serve that day or store in an airtight container. Wearing food gloves, carefully remove cake balls from foam and place in an airtight container, being careful not to let them touch. Best to serve within a day or two of dipping.

7 Serve on tray, or I like to fill a fun, open-glass serving vessel with granulated sugar and float cake pops sticks into sugar.

Chef's Notes

Make cake balls far ahead of time. Roll, freeze on a baking sheet and then when frozen, remove from tray and place in ziplock bags. When ready to serve, more than half the work is done—just melt chocolate, secure sticks, dip, let set and serve.

SPARKLE & SIP station

V

Bubbles make everything feel upscale and fancy, and this is the season for that! Cater to various tastes and palettes by serving a glam MYO sparkle-and-sip station. Use a few or more of these concepts with a little MYO table card sign encouraging people to mix and match toppings. If using sorbet, consider pre-scooping balls and keeping them frozen until just before service and placing a few out at a time.

BASE OPTIONS

Dry champagne

Frosecco

Vodka or gin

RIMMED GLASS OPTIONS

Various colored sugars

Finely chopped chocolate

Citrus-zested sugar

GLAM FLAVOR OPTIONS

Blood orange, lemon and raspberry sorbet

Muddled or pureed whole raspberries, blackberries and cranberries

Pomegranate seeds

Soda water for any of the vodka or gin takers

GARNISH OPTIONS

Mint and basil leaves

Rosemary and thyme sprigs

Spiralized lemon or orange rinds

Chocolate-covered strawberries

COMBINATION IDEAS

HOLIDAY ROSEMARY CHAMPAGNE FIZZ: Champagne | Cranberries | Rosemary for garnish

FRENCH KISS: Champagne | Lemon sorbet | Raspberries | Lemon and mint to garnish

SPARKLING POM POM: Prosecco | Lemon sorbet | Pomegranate seeds

9

Love Picnic/
Valentine's

GF/Gluten Free, DF/Dairy Free, V/Vegetarian, V+/Vegan

The concepts below are written to serve six to eight people to include the kids or close friends and family for Valentine-inspired adventures. If you want to make this a Love Picnic for two, the recipes can easily be cut in half.

What is better than sharing a romantic night with your loved one at home? With a smidge of planning, your night is sure to be extra special! Plan your romantic picnic space in advance. If you're staying inside, perhaps a space close to the television with a romantic movie on standby or a cozy spot by the fireplace would work, or gather around your coffee table for fondue fun. You can transform a kitchen nook by pinning long sheets and twinkle lights to the ceiling to create an evening-under-the-stars feeling in your indoor space. Those of you living in warmer climates can head outside for an outdoor adventure. Create a romantic campsite in your own backyard by putting up a tent. Instead of the traditional camping gear, hang twinkle lights and fill your tent with cushions from your couch, cozy blankets and throw pillows or forgo the tent altogether and create a romantic oasis using patio furniture, blankets, pillows, outdoor lights, candles or battery-powered fairy lights in mason jars. Whatever space you choose, adding fluffy throws, blankets and lots of cushions and pillows will create a relaxed, romantic mood.

Whether you are going with a specific theme or color scheme, adorn your space with flowers and hand-cut paper hearts from your local craft store. Hang them using clothespins and yarn. Use vases you have around the house and add a little romantic scent with floral arrangements. Grab a roll of white paper, lay it across your table, serving area or on the floor leading up to your space and paint or draw large black XOXO's every so often and add some of your favorite love quotes. Create a table-scape using mixed cutting boards and other decorative platters to create a base to host your noshes and nibbles. I love adding different fabrics and ribbons to create pops of color. Make sure to include some fun activities. A pop-up dance party, fun game or, as mentioned above, a romantic movie in the wings with dim lighting and soft music lin-

gering in the background will set the perfect tone for your Love Picnic.

Now that we've set the scene, let's move on to the food. Stir a little sizzle into your Love Picnic by whipping up sweet and savory fondues! I suggest at least two savory styles and one sweet. Serving finger foods that you can dip and nibble on throughout the evening allows you to skip the quintessential heavy dinner that often comes with a food coma. Keep it simple. Fondue picnics are so easy to prepare ahead and most of the ingredients I have included will certainly fare well at room temperature. Prepare your fondue dipper selections a day or two ahead of time. The day of your romantic picnic, pull cold foods from the refrigerator and be sure to allow time for a quick warm-up for the meats. When it comes to beverage selections, fondues are so easy to pair with a variety of wines, beers, sparkling wines, champagne or fun infused waters. Little bites and sips will equal a carefree food and beverage adventure. A romantic picnic dinner is not very exciting when one of the two is in the kitchen all night, so plan and prep beforehand and say "yes" to romantic fondue for two!

FONDUE EQUIPMENT

Fondue has always been a communal pot. Cheese and chocolate are the most popular, but there is also broth (hot pot), oil and wine preparations to cook raw meats or blanch vegetables. The pot that holds fondue is formally known as a *caquelon* or a fondue pot.

Fondue pots come in many different shapes and varieties including enamel, ceramic, electric and iron. No worries if you do not have a fancy fondue pot; you can make fondue in most any heavy-bottom stock pot, double boiler or crock pot. The trick is keeping it warm while you are eating it. You can make your own makeshift warming station by placing the variety of fondues in glass mason jars and holding them in a warm water bath. Ceramic pots hold heat well. Place the hot pot on a trivet or heat-proof surface. You can create your own DIY fondue set-up by using a simple tin can with the label removed, adding a few notches for venting at the top and placing a tea candle in the bottom and a small bowl placed on top of the can. Another option is to use an oblong 4-inch-deep cake pan, with tea lights on the bottom and a metal roasting rack over the top of the tea lights. Put a heat-tempered glass bowl on top of the roasting rack above where tea candles are placed.

Chef's Notes on Preparation

Work ahead with fondue prep. Prepare your veggies ahead of time and store in airtight containers or ziplock bags. To save time, your proteins can be seared the day before and then have a quick flash in the oven to reheat before serving. Fondues can be made ahead of time, but they are so fast and easy to make, I recommend making them just before service so you don't run the risk of a reheated fondue breaking in texture and quality. Organize dry goods, pick an appealing platter or two and do not forget wooden skewers or fondue forks for dipping.

DIP, DUNK & DRIZZLE **fondues**

It is always nice to have a couple of flavors if you are not serving other finger foods. Below you will find three of my favorites. The brie is a quick and easy on-the-fly solution.

gruyère FONDUE

GF | V   YIELD 6 TO 8 SERVINGS

12 ounces **GRUYÈRE**, shredded *(Jarlsberg is great)*

2 ½ teaspoons **CORNSTARCH**

¾ cup dry **WHITE WINE**

1 tablespoon **DIJON MUSTARD**

Pinch of **CAYENNE**

1   In a small bowl toss shredded gruyère and cornstarch together and set aside.

2   In a large saucepan over medium-high heat add wine and bring to a boil.

3   Stir in cheese/cornstarch mixture, Dijon and cayenne.

4   Lower heat to medium-low and cook, stirring constantly in a figure-8 or zigzag motion, for about 3 to 4 minutes until cheese is melted and the mixture thickens slightly.

5   Keep covered in a warm place until ready to serve or put directly into fondue pot.

1. In a large pot over medium heat melt butter. Add onions, garlic and red pepper flakes. Sauté 2 to 3 minutes until caramelized and translucent.

2. Add stock and white wine. Cook for a minute or two until the liquid is hot but not boiling. Reduce heat to low, add cream cheese and stir until melted. Add spinach and artichoke hearts and stir to combine.

3. In a small bowl combine shredded cheeses with the flour and toss to coat.

4. Add cheese mixture to pot a handful at a time, stirring continually for a minute or so until melted and smooth. Remove from heat.

5. Stir in lemon juice, salt, chives and dill.

6. If fondue is a little too thick, add a few tablespoons of stock or white wine.

7. Keep in a warm space until ready to serve or transfer into a fondue pot.

four cheese
ARTICHOKE AND SPINACH FONDUE

YIELD 6 TO 8 SERVINGS

2 tablespoons unsalted, high-quality **BUTTER** such as Kerrygold

½ cup white **ONION**, diced small

1 garlic **CLOVE**, smashed

Pinch of **RED PEPPER FLAKES**

¾ cup **CHICKEN** or **VEGETABLE STOCK**

⅓ cup **WHITE WINE**

¼ cup **CREAM CHEESE**

1 cup baby **SPINACH**

½ cup chopped **ARTICHOKE HEARTS**

4 ounces shredded **SWISS CHEESE**

4 ounces shredded **MOZZARELLA**

2 ounces shredded **PARMESAN**

1½ tablespoons **ALL-PURPOSE FLOUR**

1 tablespoon **LEMON JUICE**

1 teaspoon **SALT**

1 teaspoon minced **CHIVE**

1 teaspoon chopped **DILL**

craft BEER FONDUE

GF | V   YIELD 6 TO 8 SERVINGS

1 clove of **GARLIC**, sliced in half

1 cup pilsner craft **BEER**

8 ounces shredded **PEPPER JACK CHEESE**

8 ounces shredded **SHARP CHEDDAR**

1 tablespoon **CORNSTARCH**

2 teaspoons sweet **BAVARIAN MUSTARD**

1 teaspoon prepared **HORSERADISH**

Couple pinches of **CAYENNE PEPPER**

1. Rub heavy medium stock pot with garlic clove halves. Discard garlic. Add beer and heat to a light simmer. Beer may foam a little; just stir.

2. In a bowl combine shredded cheeses and cornstarch, tossing thoroughly to coat.

3. Add shredded cheeses, a handful at a time, to simmering beer and continue stirring. Once cheeses are melted and smooth remove from heat. Add mustard, horseradish and a pinch or two of cayenne pepper.

4. If fondue breaks, thoroughly mix a tablespoon of cornstarch with an ounce of beer. Incorporate into fondue over low heat. If fondue seems too thick add a little warm beer.

5. Keep in a warm space until ready to serve or transfer into a fondue pot.

MELTING HEARTS **brie**

V   YIELD 6 TO 8 SERVINGS

1 *(8-ounce)* wheel of **BRIE**

2 to 3 tablespoons Amarena Toschi Italian **BLACK CHERRIES**

Fried **ROSEMARY**, crushed *(optional)*

CROSTINI and **CRACKERS**

1. Preheat the oven to 325°F.

2. Remove plastic wrapping from brie and carefully slice off the top layer of the rind. This works best if the brie is placed in the freezer for a few minutes beforehand. Return the brie to the wood base it was packaged in and place on a sheet pan. Bake for 10 minutes until brie is gooey, melted and starts to brown a little.

3. Transfer to a platter, top with Amarena Toschi cherries and sprinkle with fried rosemary. Serve with crostini and crackers.

Savory Fondue Dipper Suggestions

PICK 5 TO 6 OR MORE, ALLOWING 10 TO 12 PIECES TOTAL PER PERSON

Slices of cooked mild sausage, cubed hard salamis, cooked shrimp, chicken or beef satays; petit vegan, chicken, turkey or beef meatballs; assorted blanched vegetables such as cauliflower, broccoli and asparagus; tiny cooked fingerlings or baby red or Yukon gold potatoes and a variety of interesting cubed breads such as sourdough, multigrain or pumpernickel or small pretzel balls are always fun.

Chef's Notes on Fondue

It is better to purchase your cheese for fondue in brick style vs. pre-shredded. Commercially sold shredded cheese has caking agents added, which can make your fondue thicker. If you use pre-shredded cheese, pull back around ten percent on flour or cornstarch called for in the recipe. If your fondue is a little too thick or you make ahead and reheat, always feel free to add a little warm liquid to thin it out.

SEXY SPICED CHOCOLATE fondue

YIELD 6 TO 8 SERVINGS

8 ounces Belgian DARK CHOCOLATE, chopped

1 cup plus 2 tablespoons HEAVY CREAM

1½ teaspoons INSTANT COFFEE GRANULES

½ teaspoon ground CINNAMON

⅛ teaspoon CAYENNE PEPPER

Assorted "dippers" *(see below)*

1 In a double boiler add the chopped chocolate, heavy cream and coffee granules. Cook over low heat, stirring constantly, until chocolate is melted and mixture is smooth.

2 Add cinnamon and cayenne pepper.

3 Place in a fondue pot for service.

Sweet Dippers Suggestions

PICK 5 TO 6 OR MORE, ALLOWING 10 TO 12 PIECES TOTAL PER PERSON

Strawberries, apples, pineapple and pear slices, dried apricots and cherries pretzel rods, marshmallows, cubes of pound cake or angel food cake, assorted cookies like red velvet crackle cookies, shortbreads, toasted waffle cubes and petit cream puffs (you can usually find mini cream puffs frozen at higher-end grocery stores; it is fine if they are filled with custard) all work well here.

RED VELVET CRACKLE cookies

V

YIELD 15 TO 20 COOKIES

This is a great dipper for chocolate fondue.

3 cups ALL-PURPOSE FLOUR

¼ cup unsweetened COCOA POWDER

2 teaspoons BAKING POWDER

¼ teaspoon BAKING SODA

¾ teaspoon SALT

¾ cup unsalted BUTTER, softened

1⅓ cups granulated SUGAR

3 large EGGS

1 tablespoon MILK

1½ teaspoons VANILLA EXTRACT

2 teaspoons LEMON JUICE

½ teaspoon ORANGE ZEST

5 teaspoons RED FOOD COLORING

1 cup POWDERED SUGAR

1 Preheat the oven to 350°F. Line 2 sheet trays with parchment paper.

2 In a bowl whisk together flour, cocoa powder, baking powder, baking soda and salt until combined. Set aside.

3 In the bowl of a stand mixer fitted with the paddle attachment cream together butter and sugar until pale and fluffy.

4 Add eggs, one at a time, mixing until combined after each addition.

5 Add milk, vanilla, lemon juice, orange zest and red food coloring. Beat until combined.

6 With the mixer on low speed, add in first five ingredients and mix until just combined.

7 Cover bowl with plastic wrap and chill until firm enough to shape into balls.

8 Pour powdered sugar into a bowl.

9 Remove dough from the refrigerator. Scoop into 1.5-ounce portions (3 tablespoons each or use a 1.5-ounce ice cream scoop). With buttered hands, roll each dough portion into a ball and roll each ball into the powdered sugar to evenly coat. Transfer to prepared sheet pans and flatten slightly.

THE TIPSY **cupid**

V-

Edible iridescent powders add a festive and colorful glimmer to your Valentine's Day drinks. They come in a rainbow of colors and flavored and flavorless options. They are easily found at higher-end craft stores or online. I have included one drink recipe, but the iridescent powder is a good concept to use with so many drinks. Your "Tipsy Cupid" Valentine's cocktail could be something as simple as vodka, soda, a splash of cranberry and a little iridescent powder.

golden HEART

GF | V   YIELD 2 COCKTAILS

10-ounce chilled **SPARKLING WINE** or **PROSECCO**

1½ ounces **GRAND MARNIER**

⅛ to ¼ teaspoon edible gold **IRIDESCENT POWDERS**

Chocolate covered **STRAWBERRIES** (optional)

1 Mix sparkling wine, Grand Marnier and iridescent powder.

2 Divide between 2 wine or champagne glasses.

3 Garnish with chocolate covered strawberry if desired.

10 Bake for 13 to 14 minutes. Rest on sheet pan before transferring to a wire rack to cool completely.

11 To make heart-shaped cookies, cut the cookies with a cutter while they are still soft from the oven, cool and enjoy!

LOVE PICNIC BEVERAGE **pairings**

As I mentioned above, fondue is great paired with many beverages. In its traditional roots you would often find Riesling or similar wines with mild tannins as it brings out the nuttiness of cheese flavors, but I often serve a medium-body red or a crisp chardonnay at my cheese party and it goes well. As I always say, drink what you like. If you are serving a fondue with beer as an ingredient, it would be fun to feature a small craft beer flight. If alcoholic beverages are not your thing, no problem. The fancy sparkling water aisle of your supermarket offers plenty of options. To serve, garnish with fruits and a little sprinkle of the glitter powder I mention below in The Tipsy Cupid cocktail selection.

Unicorns Trending

The magical, mystical unicorn has become somewhat of a phenomenon over the past couple of years in many party plans including children's parties, baby showers, pride events and teenage and adult birthday parties.

Just a couple seasons ago I planned and catered a high school graduation party for a lovely young lady who wanted a unicorn theme, which, by the way, included a six-foot plastic blow-up unicorn sprinkler as a backdrop in the backyard, which a herd of kids did in fact take a run through! This theme is certainly present in the top ten themes for children's parties, often leaning more towards girls as it has an undertone of "fairy princess with a side order of mermaid." Many décor ideas, food concepts and recipes in this chapter could be used for a children's party, but I will gear this chapter more towards adults. Children's parties with this concept tend to be a little too sweet, in more ways than one. There are so many go-to ideas easily found in the children's category, so I will drive this more to an adult-themed party with many savory food options.

The sky's the limit with this concept, as it feels like it is from the sky adorned with rainbows and puffy white clouds. You can go in a couple directions here, from a solid rainbow-colored concept to light pastels with a splash of shimmer. With the pastel direction, it is a good idea to either mix gold or silver in the color palette. By adding those colors, it keeps the décor from looking too much like a baby shower or an Easter party.

Let's talk table coverings. For a base linen, white or a light-colored pastel is a safe bet if you have a lot of color or accents planned. My preference is to steer away from fluffy pleated skirting for serving tables, as it seems heavy and dated. TableclothsFactory.com makes an interesting table skirting that looks like the flaps inside a carwash, and the skirt has a twirl and cascade effect. They are sold in all sorts of colors. If you pick a more neutral color such as silver or pearl you can use the skirt again for a future event. If you want to elevate your unicorn party table, look no further than tulle. I think most unicorns would tell you that tulle fabric is their official pick for fluffy, shimmery party swag! I LOVE tulle! It is a thin see-through netting

that comes in every color you can imagine. Some are matte, others have shimmer and some have stars, dots and lots and lots of sparkles. The nice thing about tulle is that it comes in bolts of fabric spools from three to twelve inches, it is inexpensive and you can do a million things with it. You can use it as an overlay on top of your base linen, swag it in and out of your food display like a garland, cut pieces for a bow or knot wrapped on chairs or use it to drape walls or ceilings. I personally even wrap presents in it as it looks cool and is less expensive than fancy wrapping paper. Definitely consider tulle in your unicorn bag of party tricks!

Now that we have the base of your table laid out, let's decorate it. Tabletop décor can be very diverse here. Try filling clear glass vases with assorted colored puffy paper flowers. They come in a rainbow of colors, but instead of mixing them in the glass vases, choose three to five colors and fill each vase with only one color to create an interesting line of color blocking and height on your serving or seating table. A similar idea would be to pick up three to five colors of plastic pom poms. They would be fun strung together like a garland swag backdrop or woven into the tablespace. Paper streamers are a fun and inexpensive option as well. Glass Mardi Gras beads that match your color palette can be pooled on the table or nestled into glass bowls with some pastel or clear round ornaments or orbs. Small metallic silver bud vases with bright pops of solid-colored smaller flowers such as poppies, mini ranunculus, peonies, roses, bungalow roses, mini hydrangeas, smaller dahlia or button flowers, baby breath or pink pampas grass will add a fun fluff to your tablescape.

Let's talk balloons. I normally am not a big balloon person and if balloons are not executed with some restraint, they can take over your entire party. Here with our mystical, magical unicorn theme, balloons are a perfect fit. A few bouquets of pastel-colored balloons dotted with a couple silver ones offer a nice pop of color either tied behind the serving table or wound around a pendant lighting in the house. Use a few as an "X marks the spot" in the front yard indicating that your guests have arrived at the unicorn party palace!

When it comes to serving platters and vessels, keep it simple to not distract from the décor. Clean white or clear glass would be your best bet. I like the smaller eight-inch hard white plastic plates for this concept and menu.

PRISM FRUIT **kabobs**

GF | V+ YIELD 12 KABOBS

12 1-inch cubes each of **CANTALOUPE, HONEYDEW, WATERMELON** and **PINEAPPLE**

12 larger **STRAWBERRIES**, hulled

12 *(6- to 8-inch)* bamboo **SKEWERS**

1 Thread one cube each of cantaloupe, honeydew, watermelon and pineapple onto each bamboo skewer. Top each skewer with one strawberry.

2 Place on a serving tray and serve with coconut whip if desired.

Coconut Whip

GF | V YIELD 1 1/2 TO 2 CUPS

2 cans **COCONUT CREAM** *(refrigerated overnight)*

3 tablespoons **HONEY**

¾ teaspoon **VANILLA EXTRACT**

¼ teaspoon **CINNAMON**

Pinch sea **SALT**

1 Open cans of coconut cream and separate solid white matter from liquid, being careful to wipe any of the extra coconut syrup from solid cream. Place coconut cream in a medium-size mixing bowl.

2 Using a hand mixer, whip coconut cream until medium peaks appear. Add honey, vanilla, cinnamon and pinch of sea salt. Whip again on low speed until blended.

3 Place in a serving bowl alongside the fruit kabobs.

BEET HUMMUS WITH **rainbow** VEGETABLES

GF | V+ YIELD 2 CUPS

1 large or 2 medium **BEETS**

1 *(15.5-ounce)* can **CHICKPEAS**, drained and rinsed

1 small **ORANGE**, juiced

1 **LEMON**, juiced

¼ cup **TAHINI**

1 teaspoon **SEA SALT**

Pinch **CAYENNE**

GARNISH

Variety of rainbow-colored **VEGETABLES**

1 Preheat the oven to 425°F. Wrap beets in heavy-duty foil and roast for about an hour until tender. Let cool and place in the fridge. Once cooled, peel skin back and chop into medium-size pieces.

1 Preheat the oven to 400°F.

2 Place pizza rounds on a sheet pan and spoon sauce onto crusts. Sprinkle ½ cup of mozzarella cheese evenly over crusts.

3 Working in a bullseye pattern, arrange the vegetables in solid color blocks.

4 Top with remaining ¼ cup mozzarella cheese and sprinkle with Parmesan. Drizzle with olive oil.

5 Bake for 9 to 12 minutes until the cheese starts to bubble.

6 Remove from the oven and sprinkle with basil, a pinch of sea salt, pepper and red pepper chili flakes if desired. Cut each pizza into six slices.

Chef's Note

Pizzas will be fine prepared a day ahead, wrapped tightly and refrigerated. The day of, allow pizzas to come to room temperature before baking as outlined above. You can easily make this recipe gluten free using cauliflower or gluten-free crust.

2 In the bowl of a food processor grind chickpeas with orange and lemon juices and tahini. Blend until smooth. Add cooled beets, salt and cayenne. Blend until fully incorporated.

3 Spoon into a serving bowl and garnish with an array of colored vegetables, crackers and crostini.

RAINBOW pizza

V

YIELD 10 TO 12 PIECES

2 (8-inch) premade PIZZA ROUNDS or FLATBREADS

¾ cup prepared PIZZA or MARINARA SAUCE *(homemade or store bought)*

¾ cup shredded MOZZARELLA CHEESE *(divided, reserving ¼ cup)*

½ cup chopped BROCCOLI FLORETS, blanched

½ cup diced ORANGE BELL PEPPERS

½ cup diced YELLOW BELL PEPPERS

½ cup diced RED ONIONS

½ cup halved GRAPE TOMATOES

¼ cup shredded PARMESAN

2 teaspoons extra-virgin OLIVE OIL

2 tablespoons chiffonade fresh BASIL

Pinch of SEA SALT

Freshly ground PEPPER to taste

RED PEPPER chili flake sprinkle, if desired

citrus SWORDFISH STICKS

GF | DF   YIELD 10 STICKS

FOR THE CITRUS SPLASH

2 tablespoons LIME JUICE

2 tablespoons ORANGE JUICE

1 tablespoon LEMON JUICE

1 tablespoon HONEY

⅓ cup OLIVE OIL

2 GARLIC cloves, minced

1 teaspoon ONION POWDER

½ teaspoon SEA SALT

2 pinches CAYENNE PEPPER

8 fresh BASIL leaves

½ small bunch PARSLEY leaves

FOR THE FISH

1½ pounds SWORDFISH STEAKS *(sometimes easier to purchase in fillets)*, cut into 1-inch cubes

1 each GREEN, YELLOW and ORANGE BELL PEPPER, cleaned and cut into 1-inch squares

1 small RED ONION, cut into 1-inch squares

10 *(4- to 6-inch)* bamboo or wooden SKEWERS soaked in water for at least 20 minutes

SEA SALT

Sliced CITRUS ROUNDS for garnish, if desired

1 Preheat the oven to 350°F. Line a sheet pan with parchment paper.

2 Prepare citrus splash by blending all ingredients using a blender or an immersion blender.

3 Place swordfish cubes in a bowl, add ¾ of the citrus splash and toss to coat. Let marinate for 20 to 30 minutes.

4 Set up an assembly line with the bamboo skewers, fish and vegetables. Thread 2 pieces of fish, one each green, orange and yellow bell pepper and top with a piece of red onion.

5 Place swordfish skewers on the prepared sheet pan and season with a pinch of sea salt. Bake for 10 to 12 minutes until the flesh is white.

6 Transfer skewers to platter and drizzle with a few tablespoons of reserved citrus splash. Transfer any remaining citrus splash to a bowl and place alongside the serving platter. Garnish with slices of citrus if desired.

Chef's Notes

Prepare the fish, vegetables and citrus splash a day ahead of time. Do not marinate the fish until close to time of service as the fish will not fare well sitting in acid overnight.

RAINBOW slaw

GF | V   YIELD 8 TO 10 SERVINGS

FOR THE DRESSING

¾ cup whole-milk **GREEK YOGURT**

3 tablespoons **BRAGG APPLE CIDER VINEGAR**

2 tablespoons fresh **LIME JUICE**

1½ tablespoons **HONEY**

1½ teaspoons **SRIRACHA**

½ teaspoon **SEA SALT**

FOR THE SALAD

2 *(12-ounce)* bags **RAINBOW SLAW** or **BROCCOLI SLAW** mix

2 large **WATERMELON RADISHES** (or 6 red radishes) cleaned, thinly sliced
   and julienned

¼ to ½ of a small **RED ONION**, sliced into paper-thin julienned strips

¾ cup **SUNFLOWER SEEDS**

½ cup **GOLDEN RAISINS**

1 In a small bowl whisk all dressing ingredients together. Set aside.

2 In a large bowl toss slaw mix, radishes, onions, sunflower seeds
   and golden raisins together.

3 Pour dressing over salad and toss to coat.

vivid FRESH SPRING ROLLS
WITH THAI DIPPING SAUCE

GF | V+   YIELD 8 TO 10 ROLLS AND 1 CUP OF SAUCE

THAI DIPPING SAUCE

¾ cup sweet Thai **CHILI SAUCE**

⅓ cup **PEANUT** or **ALMOND BUTTER**

1 tablespoon **LIME JUICE**

1 teaspoon **BRAGG LIQUID AMINOS**

SPRING ROLLS

10 rice **SPRING ROLL PAPERS**

2 medium canned **BEETS**, sliced into ¼-inch planks

½ **YELLOW** and **RED PEPPER**, cleaned and julienned in thin matchstick-
   size strips

2 to 3 large **CARROTS**, peeled and cut into thin ribbons with a peeler

1 smaller **ENGLISH CUCUMBER**, cut into thin ribbons with a peeler

1 *(8-ounce)* package **EXTRA FIRM TOFU**, sliced into ¼-inch planks

1 ripe **MANGO**, sliced into ¼-inch planks

1 large bunch **MINT LEAVES**

1 large bunch **CILANTRO** *(leaves removed from stems)*

1 cup of **PEA SHOOTS** *(optional)* *(reserve a small handful for garnish)*

1. To make the Thai dipping sauce whisk all ingredients in a small bowl or give a quick buzz in a small blender. Place in a serving bowl and set aside.

2. Add about 1 inch of water to a deep dish or pie plate. Place one rice wrapper into the water and let soak for 10 to 15 seconds (keep remaining rice wrappers covered until ready to use). It should still feel firm when you remove it. Do not oversoak or the wrapper will become fragile and tear while you are wrapping. Lay your wrapper on a clean, flat work surface.

3. Starting at the side of the wrapper closest to you, lay a small line of the beet planks about ⅓ down from the top of the wrapper. Layer 1 to 2 pieces of each vegetable, a tofu and mango plank, a few mint and cilantro leaves and top with a few pea shoots. Be mindful not to mix your veggies. You want to see the beautiful colors in layers.

4. Fold the top over the fillings and gently roll over once. Fold in both ends of the rice wrapper and roll until completely sealed. Repeat the process until all are rolled. Note, there are two extra papers called for in the recipe in case one tears or breaks, or you may end up with two extra rolls!

5. Place on a platter (don't allow the rolls to touch, or they will stick to each other). Garnish with pea shoots and serve with Thai dipping sauce.

unicorn DONUT HOLE DIPPING BAR
V YIELD 12 TO 15 SERVINGS

This is a fun and easy go-to party dessert option and is a magical crowd pleaser. Who doesn't like a little sweet frosting, icing, chocolate or caramel dip dusted with some sprinkles or fairy dust!

2 dozen glazed DONUT HOLES

1 dozen powdered sugar DONUT HOLES

1 dozen chocolate DONUT HOLES

⁻ cup CHOCOLATE SAUCE or GANACHE

¾ cup CARAMEL SAUCE

½ cup PINK ICING

½ cup PURPLE ICING

½ cup WHITE ICING

¼ cup fun colorful SPRINKLES *(you can find unicorn sprinkles online)*

¼ assorted-colored COURSE SUGARS *(2 varieties)*

¼ cup crushed PEANUT or TREE NUT BUTTER

¼ cup NUTELLA

¼ cup RASPBERRY JAM

¼ cup pastel CHOCOLATE CHIPS

1 small shaker EDIBLE GLITTER

ICING

3 tablespoons unsalted BUTTER

3 tablespoons HEAVY CREAM

2 tablespoons CORN SYRUP

½ teaspoon VANILLA EXTRACT

½ teaspoon SEA SALT

2 cups of POWDERED SUGAR

Pink and purple FOOD COLORING

1. To make the icing create a double boiler by placing a medium metal bowl over a pot of simmering water. You do not want the water to touch the bottom of the bowl. Add butter, heavy cream, corn syrup, vanilla and sea salt. Whisk until butter is melted and ingredients are well combined.

2. Remove from heat and stir in powdered sugar.

3. Divide frosting into 3 small bowls or ramekins. Leave one bowl of frosting white and add a drop or two of purple food coloring

to one bowl and a drop or two of pink food coloring to the other. Stir to combine, adding more food coloring if needed to get desired color. Place all small toppings and sprinkles into petit serving bowls.

4   Serve on a platter with sprinkles, toppings and donut holes.

UNICORN horns

YIELD 1 DOZEN

1 pound **CARAMEL** loaf/block *(Peter's is a good brand)*
1 dozen long **PRETZEL RODS**
1½ cups **WHITE CHOCOLATE CANDY MELTS**
¼ cup pastel-**PURPLE CANDY MELTS**
¼ cup pastel-**YELLOW CANDY MELTS**
¼ cup light-**GREEN CANDY MELTS**
¼ cup **PINK CANDY MELTS**
3 tablespoons **SILVER**, pastel or white coarse sugar

1   Line a sheet pan with parchment paper and set aside.

2   Place caramel in the microwave for 30 seconds to warm up just a smidge. (If the caramel were set in a warm place for an hour, that would do the trick as well. You do not want to melt the caramel. You are just looking to make it easier to pull pieces into tufts.)

3   Wrap each pretzel rod by winding tufts of caramel in a circular fashion down the length of the pretzel leaving 1½ inch of the pretzel uncovered at the end.

4   Melt the white chocolate candy melts per package instructions.

5   Take a caramel-wrapped rod and over the bowl, spoon melted white chocolate over pretzel rods, leaving the 1½ inch on the bottom free and allowing the extra chocolate to drip into the bowl. Place pretzel rod on prepared sheet pan and repeat until all rods are covered. Let the white chocolate set up for 10 to 15 minutes or place in the refrigerator until set.

6   Melt the colored candy melts following package instructions.

7   Alternating colored candy melts, drizzle pretzels in single color blocks down the pretzel rod to cover white chocolate base.

8   Sprinkle sparsely with colored or coarse white sugar.

fruited WHITE WINE SANGRIA

GF | V+   YIELD 8 SERVINGS

1 bottle crisp **WHITE WINE CHARDONNAY** or **PINOT GRIGIO**, chilled

½ cup **COINTREAU**

2 tablespoons fresh **LIME JUICE**

½ cup **BLUEBERRIES**

½ cup **STRAWBERRIES**, hulled and quartered

½ cup sliced and quartered **KIWI**

½ cup diced **PINEAPPLE**

½ cup **RED** or **GREEN GRAPES**

12 ounces **SODA WATER** *(optional)*

1   Mix chilled wine, Cointreau and lime juice together.

2   In either a pitcher or 8 highball glasses, layer fruit in color blocks. Add ice cubes and sangria. Top with a spritz of soda water if desired.

Game or Movie Night Nosh

Menu

GF/Gluten Free, DF/Dairy Free, V/Vegetarian, V+/Vegan

The pandemic has changed what most of us do for fun and entertainment. Many of us stayed nested in our safe family pods while waiting for brighter days filled with hope. At Two Unique, we launched a home meal delivery service and an extended line of family snacks to help our customers stay safe. There have always been movie and game nights, but during the pandemic we saw these activities rise ten fold.

My family, too, bought countless new games to play and trade with families and neighbors. Although most of us have always enjoyed games, now we cannot imagine our lives without these kindred afternoons or evenings that always include a fun nibble to go along with a game, puzzle or movie night. Whether it is your small family game night or a twenty-person rotating euchre bash, let's serve up an unforgettable nosh!

Movie or game night is a great way to gather family and friends together for a fun night at home! Pull out all your games and set aside the ones you intend to play, while using the rest as your décor. Take extra game pieces and pile them in short cylinder vases. Scrabble chips could be used to spell out the name of dishes. Use the full or empty game boxes as risers for food displays and drinks. If you are using linen, go for bright, simple colors as a base and let your game boards and pieces be the design. Take a deck of cards and hole punch the top two left and right corners, stringing red yarn or string to create a garland to hang on the wall or front of the table. If you are looking for a little more pizzazz, add brightly colored gerbera daisies in simple bud vases for a fun pop of color and texture.

We are fortunate enough to have access to a local ceramic artist, Iggy Sumnik, and have used many of his ceramic art pieces for creating this theme in the photo shoot you will see in this chapter. I encourage supporting local business whenever possible. Another interesting route could be mid-century Pyrex bowls, platters and plates. Wood trays or shiny sheet pans are also a great option for serving platters. Create a "Family Movie/ Game Night" sign by taking a poster board, poking holes around the edge and stringing Christmas or fairy lights

through to add a little extra pop to your display. Create a snack bar in your kitchen using tin buckets or acrylic boxes to display packaged candies and other snacks, or fill paper cones loaded with candies and snacks that your guests can nosh on while watching the movie, playing games or as a grab-and-go to take home. Include a sign to display your snack bar menu. Those small felt letter boards are an affordable, fun option. Last, but certainly not least, no movie or game night would be complete without popcorn. We've included some fun popcorn recipes in this chapter—prepare and serve them in those fun red-and-white striped containers you can easily find online to give you that movie-theater feel.

Movie Night Can Be Romantic or Fun!

Clear the living room and bring in an inflatable mattress or pull one from a bedroom. Gather blankets and pillows and create different areas on the mattress for people to lay and sit. Do not forget about your couches and chairs. Pull them up to the mattresses to create an intimate setting and add extra seating. Use lanterns or simple cylinders and add battery-operated fairy lights that you can buy almost anywhere.

If a fort is your jam, use simple white sheets to build a fort that kids and adults will like. Draw the curtains closed to dim the lighting and hang some leftover white Christmas lights around your windows. Take your old DVD cases or videotapes and lay them out as a runner on your counter or coffee table. You can use this as a base for displaying snacks and drinks and it will double purpose as a conversation piece of favorite movies.

THIS LITTLE PIGGY WENT TO THE **party**

DF   YIELD 20 PIECES

Take a fun spin on pigs in a blanket by serving an array of precooked artisan sausages you can find at stores like Whole Foods or Trader Joe's. They come in several varieties including chicken chipotle, kale garlic, sage and spicy Italian lamb. The list goes on and on.

2 sheets **DANISH DOUGH** *(or puff, my preference is Danish as it is denser)*

4 large links precooked **CHICKEN CHIPOTLE SAUSAGE** *(usually a 12-ounce package)*

½ cup **YELLOW MUSTARD** or your favorite mustard

1. Preheat the oven to 350°F. Line a sheet pan with parchment paper.

2. Place dough on your work surface. Lay one link of sausage on dough and roll dough around sausage until covered. Trim extra dough and pinch seam. Repeat 4 times.

3. Place pastry-rolled sausage on a cutting board and cut into 5 equal pieces about ½-inch wide.

4. Place sausage coins meat side up (like a bullseye) onto the prepared sheet pan, leaving space between sausage coins to prevent them from touching once dough puffs from baking. Bake 15 to 18 minutes until golden brown.

5. Serve with your favorite mustard or mustard dip. Swing over to the "Contemporary Oktoberfest" chapter for mustard dip recipes.

fusion TURKEY WONTON CUPS

DF   YIELD 24 CUPS

This is my take on a fun turkey Asian taco cup. A little international twist would be fun for any game or movie night!

24 **WONTON WRAPPERS**

2 tablespoons **LIME JUICE**

2 tablespoons **SOY SAUCE**

2 tablespoons **WATER**

1 tablespoon minced **GINGER**

1 tablespoon **RED PEPPER CHILI PASTE**

¼ cup **CASHEW** or **ALMOND BUTTER**

2 tablespoons chopped **CILANTRO** *(divided)*

1 tablespoon **COCONUT OIL**

1 teaspoon **SESAME OIL**

½ pound ground **TURKEY THIGH MEAT** *(or breast if you desire)*

½ teaspoon **SEA SALT**

1½ cups **ASIAN SLAW MIX**

¼ cup shredded **CARROT**

2 tablespoons minced **GREEN ONIONS**

3 tablespoons finely chopped **ALMONDS**

1. Preheat the oven to 325°F.

2. Coat a muffin pan lightly with nonstick spray then nest wonton cups inside. Bake for 5 to 7 minutes until crisp.

3. In a small blender mix lime juice, soy sauce, water, ginger paste, red pepper chili paste, cashew or almond butter and one tablespoon chopped cilantro. Set aside.

4 In a heavy-bottom sauté pan, heat coconut oil and sesame oil over medium heat. Add ground turkey, season with sea salt and cook, chopping up with a wooden spoon to break into smaller crumbles, for 2 to 3 minutes until the turkey is about 70% cooked.

5 Add slaw mix, carrot and green onion. Stir and cook over medium heat for a minute. Reduce heat to low, cover and cook for 1 to 2 minutes until vegetables have wilted.

6 Remove the cover. Add the blended Asian cashew butter mixture to the pan and simmer for 3 minutes until your mixture is well coated.

7 Use a small spoon to fill wonton cups. Sprinkle the tops of cups with finely chopped almonds and a sprinkle of cilantro.

Chef's Notes

Make wonton cups up to a week ahead of time and store in an airtight container. The filling can also be made a day or two in advance. Warm it before filling cups and garnish the top according to recipe. These are fine served warm or at room temperature.

italian PIZZA FLATS

YIELD 2 FLATBREADS OR 10 TO 12 MEDIUM SQUARES

2 tablespoons OLIVE OIL

1½ cups thinly sliced BRUSSELS SPROUTS

¼ cup thinly sliced RED ONIONS

½ cup whole milk RICOTTA CHEESE

½ cup shredded PARMESAN CHEESE *(divided)*

3 small cloves GARLIC, minced

2 teaspoons fresh LEMON JUICE

1 teaspoon ONION POWDER

½ teaspoon crushed RED PEPPER FLAKES

½ teaspoon SEA SALT

2 pinches CAYENNE

2 FLATBREADS *(Stonefire makes a good one, or use a thin flatbread of your making or choice)*

6 slices PROSCIUTTO

½ cup crumbled GOAT CHEESE

¼ cup shredded MOZZARELLA CHEESE

1 Preheat the oven to 375°F. Line a sheet pan with parchment paper.

2 In a small heavy-bottom sauté pan heat olive oil over medium-high heat. Add sliced brussels sprouts and red onion. Sauté for about 3 minutes until the mixture is tender. Remove from heat and set aside to cool.

3 In a small bowl stir together the ricotta cheese, ¼ cup of the Parmesan cheese, minced garlic, fresh lemon juice, onion powder, crushed red pepper, salt and cayenne. Set aside.

4 Place the flatbread on the prepared sheet pan. Spread the ricotta cheese mixture evenly over the flatbread with a spatula. Top with brussels sprout mixture and lay prosciutto slices over the top (it's ok if they overlap a little). Sprinkle evenly with goat cheese, mozzarella and reserved ¼ cup of Parmesan.

5 Bake for 12 to 15 minutes or until the cheese is melted and the flatbread is golden brown and crispy.

6 Remove from the oven, cut into squares and serve.

Chef's Notes

These pizza flats are a great make-ahead-and-freeze item. Prep all the way until baking step, cover with plastic wrap and freeze. Pull out an hour before service, let thaw for 30 to 40 minutes and bake as instructed. Otherwise, they are fine to assemble a day ahead. Stash covered in the fridge and pop in the oven per instructions.

smashed GREEK HAND "FRIES"

GF | V　　　　　　　　　　　　　　　YIELD 10 TO 12 SERVINGS

1 pound of smaller NEW POTATOES

2 tablespoons unsalted BUTTER

2 tablespoons OLIVE OIL

½ teaspoon dry OREGANO

1 tablespoon chopped PARSLEY

1½ teaspoons LEMON JUICE

½ teaspoon SEA SALT (or to taste)

½ cup FETA, finely crumbled

½ cup store bought GARLIC SAUCE DIP (optional)

1　Preheat the oven to broil. Line a sheet pan with parchment paper.

2　Place potatoes in a medium pot and cover with water a couple inches over the top of the potatoes. Bring potatoes to a boil. Reduce heat to medium and cook about 15 minutes until cooked but still a little firm. Drain potatoes and let cool for 5 to 10 minutes. Once cool to the touch, place potatoes on a work surface and with the heel of your hand, smash the potatoes one at a time.

3　Melt butter in a small sauce pot, remove from the stove and add olive oil and oregano.

4　Heat a large heavy-bottom sauté pan over medium heat and add 2 tablespoons of butter/oil mixture. Once the pan is hot, add smashed potatoes. Be careful to not overcrowd the pan, it may take two batches. Cook potatoes on each side for about two

minutes until crispy and golden. Place crispy potatoes on the prepared sheet tray.

5　Add chopped parsley and lemon juice to the remaining butter and olive oil mixture and drizzle a little on each potato. Season with sea salt and top each potato with a little crumbled feta. Pop under the broiler on low for 2 to 3 minutes until golden and crispy. Serve with garlic dip if desired.

FANCY PANTS POPCORN trio

GF

There are oodles of pre-popped plain and flavored popcorn, or you can flavor your house-popped popcorn with dry spice blends found at most stores. I am a fan of the Trader Joe's spice aisle, as they have a great spice collection sold in smaller bottles for around $1.99. Two of my favorites are Cuban citrus garlic and the chili lime. Both are amazing! You can also purchase popcorn seasoning spice blends, but they are packing similar ingredients for the most part. As for the popping of your corn, some people do the brown paper lunch sacks with a little oil in the microwave, others microwave popcorn bags. I have the West Bend Stir Crazy Popcorn Machine and it delivers amazing popcorn every time.

Rosemary Parmesan Popcorn

GF | V　　　　　　　　　　　　　　　　　YIELD 12 CUPS

¼ cup extra-virgin OLIVE OIL

2 sprigs fresh ROSEMARY (divided)

1 large GARLIC clove, peeled and smashed

¾ teaspoon GARLIC SALT, plus more to taste

½ teaspoon ONION POWDER

¼ teaspoon freshly ground BLACK PEPPER

12 cups of popped POPCORN or ½ cup kernels to pop using the microwave, Stir Crazy air popper or stove top

⅓ cup freshly grated PARMESAN CHEESE

1　In a small heavy-bottom saucepan add olive oil, 1 sprig rosemary and smashed garlic clove. Stir in garlic, salt, onion powder and black pepper. Cook over low heat for a couple of minutes until very warm but not simmering. Remove from heat and let sit for 5 minutes.

2　Pull leaves from the second sprig of rosemary and finely mince.

3   Remove rosemary sprig and garlic clove from the warmed olive oil. Drizzle olive oil over popped popcorn and toss to coat. Sprinkle popcorn with grated Parmesan and minced rosemary.

4   Adjust seasonings to taste.

Hungry Dude Maple Bacon Popcorn

GF   YIELD 12 CUPS

1 pound thick sliced **BACON**

3 to 4 tablespoons reserved **BACON DRIPPINGS**

12 cups popped **POPCORN**

¾ cup **MAPLE SYRUP**

1 teaspoon **SEA SALT**

¾ teaspoon fresh **BLACK PEPPER**

4 tablespoons **CHEDDAR CHEESE POWDER** *(optional)*

1   Preheat the oven to 375°F.

2   Place bacon slices on a sheet pan and bake for about 12 to 14 minutes until cooked and crispy. Remove bacon from the pan with tongs and rest on a few sheets of paper towel to drain excess grease. Take another piece of paper towel and blot dry. Chop bacon into small pieces. Reserve 3 to 4 tablespoons of bacon drippings from the sheet pan.

3   Reduce oven heat to 300°F. Line a sheet pan with parchment paper. Spread popcorn evenly over the prepared sheet pan.

4   In a small bowl mix maple syrup, reserved bacon drippings, sea salt and pepper. Drizzle over popcorn and toss to coat. Toast in the oven for 5 to 8 minutes.

5   Remove from the oven and sprinkle cheddar cheese powder over top and then mix up a little with a spoon or tongs. Sprinkle with chopped bacon.

Buffalo Popcorn

GF | V   YIELD 12 CUPS

5 tablespoons unsalted **BUTTER**

4 tablespoons **FRANK'S REDHOT SAUCE**

2 tablespoons **RANCH SEASONING**

½ teaspoon **CAJUN SEASONING**

Pinch **CAYENNE**

1 ½ teaspoons **SEA SALT**

1 teaspoon freshly ground **BLACK PEPPER**

12 cups popped **POPCORN**

¼ cup grated **PARMESAN CHEESE**

¼ cup dry crumbled **BLUE CHEESE** *(optional)*

1   In a small saucepan melt the butter over low heat. Add Frank's RedHot, ranch, Cajun seasoning, cayenne, salt and pepper. Stir to combine.

2   Place popcorn in a large bowl. Drizzle with butter mixture, alternating with sprinkles of Parmesan and blue cheese. This is best when served warm!

Chef's Notes

There are so many wonderful popcorn seasonings available in most of your better grocery stores. If you do not want to make three or four different batches, consider picking up an array of fun seasoning shakers, finely grated cheese, hot sauces, and a few bowls with small candies such as M&M's (peanut and plain), crumbled Heath bars and so on. If you are looking for a cheese flavor but have vegan or dairy-free party goers, try substituting nutritional yeast for cheese.

COSMO CORN

GF | V YIELD 10 TO 12 SERVINGS

We use a local chip company, Better Made, for our puffed corn. O-Ke-Doke is another popular brand often found at Target. Be mindful to NOT purchase a pre-seasoned flavored corn. If you cannot find one on the fly, select one that may have just a little butter flavoring.

1 *(8-ounce)* bag plain **PUFFED CORN** with hulls removed

20 tablespoons unsalted **BUTTER**

1 ¼ cups **BROWN SUGAR**

5 tablespoons **LIGHT CORN SYRUP**

1 ½ teaspoons **VANILLA EXTRACT**

½ teaspoon **BAKING SODA**

1 Preheat the oven to 275°F. Set aside two sheet pans: one lined with parchment paper and one without.

2 Place puffed corn in a large heat-safe bowl.

3 In a high-sided pan, melt butter over medium heat. Add brown sugar and corn syrup and heat to boiling, stirring constantly to prevent burning. Boil for 2 minutes.

4 Remove pan from heat. Slowly and very carefully add the vanilla and baking soda while carefully stirring. This will cause the sugar and butter mixture to bubble up and boil like a volcano.

5 Once incorporated, working in a few batches, slowly pour mixture over the puffed corn, stirring gently between to completely cover.

6 Pour onto the unlined sheet pan, leaving any extra liquid behind in the bowl.

7 Bake about 30 minutes, carefully flipping the corn puffs every 10 minutes until brown and caramelized.

8 Immediately flip the caramelized corn onto the parchment-lined sheet tray and carefully separate the kernels so you do not have huge chunks stuck together. Let cool completely.

everyone LOVES RICE KRISPY TREATS!

V   YIELD 24 (APPROXIMATELY 2-INCH) TREATS

12 tablespoons unsalted **BUTTER**

3 pounds **MARSHMALLOWS** *(large or small)*

1 teaspoon **SEA SALT**

1 pound crisped **RICE CEREAL**

1   Line a 9 x 13-inch pan with parchment paper and spray well with nonstick spray.

2   In a heavy-bottom pot melt butter over medium heat. Add marshmallows in batches while continually stirring to prevent sticking and burning. Turn off heat once completely melted. Add salt and stir to combine.

3   Pour cereal into a large heat-safe bowl. Pour melted butter and marshmallow mixture over cereal and mix quickly and carefully until combined.

4   Immediately pour into the prepared pan. Spray your clean hands with nonstick spray and gently press mixture into corners and press evenly into the pan.

5   Let sit for at least 3 hours to set completely before cutting into desired squares.

VARIATION 1: SALTED CARAMEL

1   After step 2, turn off heat and add ¼ cup natural caramel flavoring. We use the brand Prova. Mix well before pouring over cereal.

2   After step 5, sprinkle a generous amount of sea salt over still-warm treats and let cool.

VARIATION 2: MOVIE CANDY

1   Add 1 to 2 cups of your favorite movie candy chopped into small pieces.

2   After step 3, let your mixture cool for at least 10 minutes and stir periodically to release the heat. Sprinkle your candies over the mixture and quickly fold in as best as possible, trying to avoid too much melting. Save a portion of your candies to sprinkle on top of the finished pan after step 5. Let cool completely before cutting, especially if there is chocolate involved. A few that work well in the treats would be mini or regular chocolate chips, crushed Butterfinger, Heath, or mini M&M's.

3   I also like to swap out regular marshmallows for mini cereal marshmallows.

OTHER FLAVORS

Remove 1 ½ cups of marshmallows from the base recipe and add ½ to 1 cup of Nutella or almond, cashew or peanut butter after your marshmallows are melted. You can still throw some candies in this party, too!

ROOT BEER BOURBON float

GF | V   YIELD 6 SERVINGS

8 ounces **BOURBON**

3 *(12-ounce)* cans **ROOT BEER**

1 cup of vanilla bean **ICE CREAM**

ORANGE PEEL slices or curls, for garnish

1   Line up 6 highball glasses or 10-ounce mason jars.

2   Place 5 to 6 ice cubes in each glass and divide bourbon evenly among glasses. Fill with root beer until glass is ¾ full and plop a small round scoop of ice cream on the top.

3   Garnish with orange peel or curl on the side of ice cream.

Chef's Notes

Rum works great in this recipe as well. You can go with RumChata and ditch the ice cream, since the RumChata is creamy. I am also a big fan of salted caramel bourbon and have poured it with root beer with very tasty results. This is also easy to offer as a non-alcoholic option to your guests.

Oh Baby!

GF/Gluten Free, DF/Dairy Free, V/Vegetarian, V+/Vegan

We have all seen so many adorable and fancy Pinterest concepts for baby showers. Some are twists from classic children's stories like Dr. Suess, *Winnie the Pooh* or *Where the Wild Things Are,* while others have animal-centric themes like elephants, whales, tigers, bears or "What will it Bee?" This is such a large open-ended category for theme and décor that is reliant on personal taste.

If you are dreading matching everything from napkins to table décor, don't stress. Not every baby shower has to have a theme. Go easy breezy with pastels of baby pink or blue, or keep it simple and clean with a combination of a favorite color or two that works well in the space. Our menu feels spring-forward, and there are so many botanical-inspired options to choose from. Start with clean, crisp white or pastel base linens. For a classic garden party, add some large, brightly colored puffy flowers. If a modern garden party is what you are looking for, gerbera daisies paired with tall greens in separate cylinder vases are easy options to create your tablescape. White serving platters and trays would work great and won't overpower a heavy floral presence. If you pull back and are more minimal on colors in the table décor, you could lean toward brightly colored ceramic serving pieces.

If you're looking for something less garden party and more gender neutral, try an "in the clouds" theme. Start with white linens as a base, add baby's breath in vases and DIY clouds hanging over guest tables. Create a cloud-like backdrop by gluing batting to a large 4 x 8-foot piece of foam board. Moons and stars with white, gold and even touches of blue make for a serene, sophisticated, gender-neutral look. Finish the look with silver and clear glass flatware and china.

A jungle theme is another great gender-neutral option. Start with playful stuffed animals as part of your centerpieces. Use simple tropical palm leaves and florals like ginger, pincushions or even just brightly colored roses in bud vases. Create a jungle-themed bar with green tablecloths, wood crates and a few safari hats for décor. Put bamboo sticks in simple vases for height and display different snacks and beverages in natural containers like wood trays or tin buckets.

You can even take your theme to another level—think vintage *Winnie the Pooh.* Add a look-alike stuffed bear with balloons tied to his paw as if he is about to float away, along with low overflowing centerpieces of florals like light-blue hydrangeas, pastel yellow roses and silver dollar eucalyptus. Use whitewashed crates and old antique tables and trays for serving. Jars of honey as party favors will really round out this theme.

There is no place like home, especially when welcoming a new baby into the family, so why not do a *Wizard of Oz* theme? Start with blue-and-white checkered tablecloths and add a light wood picnic basket overflowing with red roses for your centerpieces. Print memorable quotes from the movie to add to your tablescape. If you can get red poppies, add those in simple glass bud vases and sprinkle them around the room. Paint a few bricks yellow and stack them on tables as risers.

With a modern salad menu, one 8- to 9-inch plate will work great. It could be white or clear glass, or a modern plastic square plate. We have an abundance of white melamine plates in our repertoire that look very modern, and the cost is as low as a few bucks each. Even if you are using an upscale disposable plate, it is always nice to have silverware wrapped with a linen napkin at your seating tables. The selection of napkin color will help make the seating tables pop and tie into your theme.

Whatever direction you decide to go, add fun activities for guests to participate in. Create an interactive mimosa bar with plenty of options and a guide on how to mix and match. Add a selfie backdrop and include a basket of props for guests to create fun, memorable photos. Leave notecards at the tables and encourage guests to write a message to the mama-to-be to read on the baby's first birthday, and don't forget to include a fun party favor for guests to take home. Adding a few small thoughtful touches will make your baby shower one to remember.

veggie SHOOTERS

GF | V   YIELD 12 SHOOTERS

Some people like to make shooters in 2-ounce plastic shot cups, but I find them to be a little unstable and space for the dip in the bottom is smaller. I prefer to use the small 4- to 5-ounce hard, clear plastic wine cups, which are easy to find at your local party supply store or online. These would also be gorgeous in a 4-ounce clear-cut mason jar.

24 slices of **CELERY**, cut on a thin bias, around 2 inches long

12 slices English or Persian **CUCUMBER**, cut on a medium-thin bias

12 **ASPARAGUS** spears, trimmed and blanched

12 **GREEN BEANS**, picked and blanched

12 medium strips **YELLOW PEPPER**

12 medium strips **RED PEPPER**

12 **CHERRY TOMATOES** on a 2- to 3-inch long pick

24 multicolored **BABY CARROTS** *(or orange is fine if you can't source colored variety)*, cut 12 of the 24 in half lengthwise

12 **WATERMELON RADISHES**, cut into paper-thin slices and soaked in ice bath for 10 minutes or more *(optional)*

PEA SHOOTS *(optional)*

Garden Goddess Dip

V   YIELD ABOUT 2 CUPS

1 cup cleaned **PARSLEY STEMS**

¾ cup loosely packed **HERBS**, such as dill, mint and cilantro

2 tablespoons minced **CHIVES**

¾ cup whole milk **GREEK YOGURT**

3 ounces **GOAT CHEESE**

3 tablespoons **LEMON JUICE**

1 teaspoon **LEMON ZEST**

1 clove **GARLIC**

½ teaspoon **SEA SALT**

A couple pinches of **CAYENNE PEPPER**

1. Place herbs in a food processor and give them a little pulse.
2. Add remaining ingredients and pulse until pale green and smooth. It's fine to have recognizable pieces of herbs.
3. Adjust seasoning if needed.

SHOOTER ASSEMBLY

1. Spoon a couple ounces of Garden Goddess Dip into the bottom of a 4- to 5-ounce cup, being careful to pour dressing into the center of the cup to not smudge the sides.
2. Arrange taller vegetables in the back, position carrots point side down and place cherry tomato baton stick point down with tomato floating on top. Garnish with pea shoots if desired.

Chef's Notes

Make dressing up to 3 days in advance, and of course you can use hummus or your favorite veggie dip if the goddess is not your happy place. Prep veggies up to a day in advance and soak carrots, watermelon radish and celery in cold water overnight to keep from drying out.

heirloom TOMATO AND STONE FRUIT TOSS

GF | V   YIELD 10 TO 12 SERVINGS

1 pint petit heirloom multicolored **TOMATOES**, sliced in half or 4 large heirloom tomatoes sliced into ¼-inch-thick wedges, or a mixture of both

1 *(8-ounce)* container of "ciliegine" cherry-size fresh **MOZZARELLA BALLS**

3 whole **STONE FRUITS** of your choice, sliced into ¼-inch-thick wedges

1 large bunch of **BASIL** *(about 15 leaves)*, chiffonade *(reserve a little for garnish)*

3 tablespoons extra-virgin **OLIVE OIL**

¾ teaspoon **SEA SALT**

½ teaspoon fresh **CRACKED PEPPER**

3 to 4 tablespoons **WHITE BALSAMIC BLACKBERRY SYRUP**

1. In a medium bowl add tomatoes, mozzarella, stone fruit, basil, olive oil, sea salt and pepper and toss together.

2. Place salad on a serving platter, drizzle with white balsamic blackberry syrup and sprinkle reserved basil on top.

RAINBOW CARROT tabbouleh

V+   YIELD 10 TO 12 SERVINGS

1 cup cooked **WHITE QUINOA** *(follow directions on package)*

6 to 8 large multicolored **CARROTS**, peeled and shredded into thin ribbon strips *(should equal about 2 cups)*

6 large **RED RADISHES**, sliced paper thin

4 white **ICICLE RADISHES**, sliced paper thin

¾ cup flat **PARSLEY**, cleaned and chopped

¼ cup fresh **MINT**, finely chopped

¼ cup **RED ONION**, finely diced

¼ cup fresh **LEMON JUICE**

¼ cup **OLIVE OIL**

1 tablespoon **LEMON ZEST**

1 teaspoon **SEA SALT**

Sprinkle of **CAYENNE PEPPER** to taste

⅓ cup roasted, salted **SUNFLOWER KERNELS** *(reserve a couple of tablespoons)*

1 large **AVOCADO**, diced

1. In a large bowl add cooked quinoa, carrots, radishes, parsley, mint and onion. Toss together.

2. In a small bowl whisk lemon juice, olive oil, lemon zest, salt and sprinkle of cayenne.

3. Pour lemon/olive oil mixture over the tossed salad. Top with sunflower kernels and diced avocado. Adjust seasonings to taste.

4. Place in serving dish and garnish with reserved sunflower kernels.

White Balsamic Blackberry Syrup

V YIELD 1 1/4 CUPS

1 cup BLACKBERRIES

1 cup WHITE BALSAMIC VINEGAR

¼ cup HONEY

1 In a heavy-bottom saucepan add blackberries and vinegar. Cook over medium heat until reduced by half.

2 Strain through a fine-mesh strainer into a small bowl and stir in honey. Chill or let come to room temperature before using. Keep in the fridge for up to 3 months.

Chef's Notes

I love this blackberry-scented syrup and use it in all sorts of dishes when I want a little sweet-and-savory splash. It's amazing as a drizzle on chicken or fish. No white balsamic vinegar on hand? No problem. Just swap out the white for regular balsamic vinegar.

BEET ORANGE salad

V YIELD 10 TO 12 SERVINGS

2 NAVEL ORANGES, zest and juice

2 pounds YELLOW and RED BEETS

⅓ cup extra-virgin OLIVE OIL *(divided into half)*

Few pinches of SEA SALT and BLACK PEPPER

7 large ORANGES, a mixed variety *(navel, cara cara navel and blood orange are always pretty)*

2 tablespoons WHITE BALSAMIC VINEGAR

2 tablespoons fresh ORANGE JUICE

2 tablespoons HONEY

2 cups of ARUGULA

⅓ cup chopped toasted WALNUTS

1 Preheat oven to 375°F. Line two sheet pans with foil and set aside.

2 Zest one of the navel oranges and set aside. Juice both.

3 Peel raw beets and slice into ¼-inch-thick slices. Place yellow and red beets into separate bowls. Drizzle with 2 tablespoons oil and a couple tablespoons of reserved orange juice. Season with a sprinkle of sea salt and pepper. Toss to coat.

4 Place yellow and red beets separately onto prepared sheet pans. Roast beets for 25 to 30 minutes or until tender when poked with a fork. Chill beets.

5 Using a sharp paring knife, remove the peel and pith from the remaining 7 oranges. Slice into ½-inch-thick slices. Set aside.

6 To make the vinaigrette, in a small bowl whisk together the remaining olive oil, white balsamic, 2 tablespoons fresh orange juice, honey and reserved zest.

7 Sprinkle arugula on a serving platter to make a bed for the beets and oranges. Arrange orange and beet slices, overlapping a little. Drizzle with orange honey vinaigrette. Top with a sprinkle of sea salt and chopped toasted walnuts.

citrus SHRIMP

GF | DF   YIELD 10 TO 12 SERVINGS

2 pounds peeled and deveined raw 16/20 **SHRIMP**

¾ cup **OLIVE OIL**

2 tablespoons **ORANGE ZEST**

1 tablespoon **LIME ZEST**

1 tablespoon **LEMON ZEST**

½ cup fresh **ORANGE JUICE**

⅓ cup fresh **LEMON JUICE**

⅓ cup fresh **LIME JUICE**

2 tablespoons **HONEY**

2 tablespoons finely chopped **GARLIC**

1 teaspoon **SEA SALT**

¼ to ½ teaspoon **RED PEPPER CHILI FLAKES**

3 tablespoons **CILANTRO** *(divided)*

3 tablespoons chopped **PARSLEY** *(divided)*

1 Preheat the oven to 400°F. Place a sheet pan in the oven for 5 to 10 minutes to get hot before roasting shrimp.

2 Drain any liquid from raw shrimp and pat dry. Place in a large, gallon-size ziplock bag.

3 In a medium bowl whisk olive oil, zest, juices, honey, garlic, salt and chili flakes together. Take ¾ cup of this mixture and add to the shrimp in the ziplock bag. Add half of the chopped cilantro and parsley. Seal and let marinate for 30 to 45 minutes.

4 Place remaining marinade in a small saucepan over medium heat and reduce by 25%. Remove from heat and stir in remaining herbs.

5 Drain marinade from shrimp and discard liquid.

6 Carefully remove the preheated sheet pan from the oven and arrange the shrimp sparsely over the entire tray. Return to the oven and roast shrimp for 8 to 12 minutes until cooked through.

7 Arrange hot or room-temperature shrimp in a serving bowl and drizzle with reduced marinade.

kale PESTO GRILLED CHICKEN

GF YIELD 12 SERVINGS

Kale Pesto

GF | V YIELD 1 CUP

2 cups curly **GREEN KALE**, cleaned, stemmed and chopped

2 cloves **GARLIC**

3 tablespoons fresh **LEMON JUICE**

½ cup shredded **PARMESAN CHEESE**

½ cup shelled **PISTACHIOS**

½ cup **OLIVE OIL**

¾ teaspoon **SEA SALT**

Couple pinches of **CAYENNE PEPPER**

1 Place kale in a food processor and give it a quick buzz to break it up. Add remaining ingredients and pulse until mixture comes together and is spreadable.

Chicken

6 large *(6 to 7 ounces each)* **CHICKEN BREASTS**, butterflied into 2 pieces

1 cup **KALE PESTO**, divided

Sprinkle of **SEA SALT** and **PEPPER**

2 tablespoons chopped **PISTACHIOS**

¼ cup chopped **SUNDRIED TOMATOES** *(optional)*

1 Preheat barbeque grill to medium.

2 Place butterflied chicken in a mixing bowl. Add ½ cup of kale pesto and season with a sprinkle of salt and pepper. Mix until chicken is evenly coated.

3 Spray or lightly oil the grill grates to help keep the chicken from sticking. Place chicken on the grill and cook for about 3 to 4 minutes. Flip and cook for another 3 to 4 minutes until the internal temperature reaches 165°F when tested with a meat thermometer.

4 Place chicken on a serving platter with a smear of pesto or serve with the extra pesto on the side. Serve warm or at room temperature with a sprinkle of pistachios and chopped sundried tomatoes, if using, for garnish.

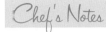

Chef's Notes

Make kale pesto up to a week in advance. It would be fine to prepare the chicken the day before and then do a quick reheat before service.

myo SALAD BAR

V

A salad bar checks all the boxes for hosting an afternoon event. With so many dietary concerns such as gluten and dairy free, vegan, vegetarian and raw, this is a thoughtful and tasty way to let your guest create their own special dish. I am not talking about some lettuce and vegetable toppings but rather an array of dishes and interesting salad sprinkles and toppings coupled with a side of this and that to make your early afternoon lunch soar in a contemporary and tasty way.

All of the dishes in recipes above *(or many of them)*

2 pounds of mixed baby **SALAD GREENS** *(they often are sold in the 1-pound plastic box containers)*

1 pound of **BROCCOLI SLAW MIX**

2 to 3 heads of chopped **ROMAINE**

1 cup **PEA SHOOTS** *(Whole Foods most always have them)*

1 cup **MICROGREENS** *(optional)*

2 cups sliced or diced **CUCUMBERS**

2 cups chopped **BROCCOLI FLORETS**

2 cups chopped **CAULIFLOWER**

1 cup diced **YELLOW PEPPERS** *(or color of your choice)*

1 **RED ONION**, sliced into thin strips

2 cups sliced **STRAWBERRIES**

1 cup **BLACKBERRIES**

2 cups cooked **MIXED QUINOA**

1½ cups crumbled **FETA**

1½ cups crumbled **GOAT CHEESE**

½ cup sliced toasted **ALMONDS**

1 cup **CHICKPEAS**

½ cup **OLIVES**

2 to 3 **VINAIGRETTES/DRESSINGS** *(the Green Goddess Dip would be great, or a fruited or poppy vinaigrette/dressing and an herbal vinaigrette such as Italian or Greek would work well. One quart total would be more than enough between the two or three varieties)*

A couple loaves of **BAKERY BREAD** or 15 or so rolls, sliced and toasted

Chef's Notes

You can get a big jump on all this a day or two in advance. This salad bar is a baseline. Feel free to add anything else that you like.

LEMON SHORTBREAD hearts

V

YIELD 12 COOKIES

½ cup European-style BUTTER, room temperature

⅓ cup CANE SUGAR

1 tablespoon LEMON ZEST

2 teaspoons fresh LEMON JUICE

2 teaspoons fresh chopped ROSEMARY

½ teaspoon VANILLA EXTRACT

1 cup ALL-PURPOSE FLOUR

¼ teaspoon SEA SALT

1. Preheat the oven to 350°F. Line sheet pan with parchment paper.

2. In a large bowl or the bowl of a stand mixer fitted with the paddle attachment, add butter and mix until pale. Add sugar and continue to mix, scraping the side of the bowl as needed. Add lemon zest, juice, rosemary and vanilla. Mix until completely incorporated.

3. Add in the flour and salt and mix on medium low until everything comes together and dough pulls away from the sides of the bowl, scraping down the sides and bottom as needed.

4. Remove dough from the mixer, form into a smooth ball and place on a lightly floured work surface. Pat the ball down into a round disc and using a rolling pin roll out dough to ¼-inch thickness.

5. Using a 2-inch heart (or round) cutter, cut cookies and place onto the prepared sheet pan. Put cookies in the refrigerator for 20 minutes or the freezer for 10 minutes.

6. Bake cookies for 13 to 15 minutes. They should be pale but lightly golden on the bottom and edges.

7. Transfer cookies onto a baking rack to cool. Store in an airtight container for up to 5 days.

Chef's Notes

Make dough in advance, roll, cut and freeze on a sheet pan, then transfer to a ziplock bag. Remove cookies from the freezer the day of or day before your event, place on a parchment-lined sheet pan and let sit for 10 minutes and follow baking instructions above.

LOVE BABY pie

V

These are super fun at a lady's event as a little sweet nibble rather than a piece of pie. You can be inspired by winter flavors or spring/summer fruited concepts.

Petit Pie Crust

3 cups FLOUR

¾ teaspoon SALT

1 cup cold unsalted BUTTER

3 tablespoons SHORTENING

1 teaspoon WHITE VINEGAR mixed into ¼ cup ice cold water

SPECIAL EQUIPMENT

Mason Jar Lids

Rolling Pin

1. Place flour, salt, butter and shortening into the bowl of a food processor. Pulse until it forms a crumbly mixture. Sprinkle in ¾ of the vinegar/ice-water mix and give it a few more pulses. Turn the dough out onto a lightly floured work surface and knead the dough just until it comes together (do not overwork the dough or you will end up with a tough crust), adding more ice water a few drops at a time if the dough appears dry. The dough should come together when you gather it into a ball without being sticky.

2. Divide dough into two balls. Flatten each ball into a disk, wrap and place dough in the refrigerator for an hour.

3 Place the lid insert into the ring upside down (using the rubber side on the bottom of the ring), place on a sheet pan covered with parchment paper and lightly spray lids with nonstick spray.

4 Working with one ball at a time, roll dough to ⅛-inch thickness on a lightly floured surface. For the bottom crust, using your mason jar lid as a guide, cut dough circles an inch bigger than your lid. Lightly press dough circles into prepared lids. For the top crust, cut the dough the same size as the lid you are using. Use a paring knife to score a vent in the center or use a small cutter and cut away a small hole in the center.

Chef's Notes

There are many ways you can top these little pie lids. With the traditional top (outlined above), you can bake them with no top and then add a meringue and crisp at the time of service, or serve with a dollop of vanilla bean whipped cream on top. Lattice-cut tops are also a nice finish. You can make these ahead of time, freeze and bake the morning of your event.

Pie Fillings

PEACH BLUEBERRY FILLING

3 tablespoons SUGAR

2 teaspoons CORNSTARCH

1 teaspoon LEMON ZEST

Pinch SEA SALT

1½ cups medium-small diced PEACHES

1 cup BLUEBERRIES

1 teaspoon LEMON JUICE

2 tablespoons unsalted BUTTER

EGG WASH *(1 egg mixed with 1 tablespoon of water or cream)*

Coarse SUGAR

1 In a medium bowl add sugar, cornstarch, lemon zest and pinch of sea salt. Stir to combine. Add peaches, blueberries and lemon juice. Toss well to coat. Let rest for 10 minutes. Drain off excess liquid.

2 To assemble your pies, add a couple tablespoons of filling to prepared pie crusts, top with a pinch of butter, place top crust over pie mixture and crimp edges of the two crusts together. Brush lightly with egg wash and sprinkle with coarse sugar.

3   Bake for 20 to 25 minutes until bubbly and golden.

VERY CHERRY PIE FILLING

2 cups frozen **SOUR CHERRIES**, thawed

1 cup **DARK CHERRIES**, thawed

1 cup **SUGAR**

1 tablespoon **LEMON JUICE**

3 tablespoons **CORNSTARCH**

½ teaspoon pure **ALMOND EXTRACT**

A couple pinches of **SEA SALT**

2 tablespoons unsalted **BUTTER**

EGG WASH *(1 egg mixed with 1 tablespoon of water or cream)*

Coarse **SUGAR**

1   Drain cherries in a mesh strainer over a bowl, giving them a light press to extract all the juices. You need ¾ cup of cherry juice. Add water if needed to reach this amount. Set cherries aside.

2   In a small saucepan add the cherry juice, sugar, lemon juice, cornstarch, almond extract and a pinch of sea salt. Heat over medium heat and whisk until liquid thickens and becomes clear. Let cool for 5 minutes. Stir in cherries. Let the mixture cool for 30 minutes.

3   To assemble pies, add a couple tablespoons of filling to prepared pie crusts, top with a pinch of butter, place top crust over pie mixture and crimp edges together. Brush lightly with egg wash and sprinkle with coarse sugar.

4   Bake for 20 to 25 minutes until bubbly and golden.

WATERMELON **sangria**

GF | V+   YIELD 10 TO 12 SERVINGS

Hands down this is one of my favorite light sips. It's one of those wine beverages that is delicious to sip on easily without the high alcohol content sneaking up on you.

8 cups chopped **WATERMELON**

¼ cup fresh **LIME JUICE**

1 bottle crisp **WHITE WINE**

1 liter **SPARKLING WATER** *(optional)*

12 **LIME WEDGES**

1   Place watermelon and lime juice in a blender and puree (most likely this will take 2 to 3 batches). You may need to crush watermelon with your hand to create more juice to aid in the blending process.

2   Strain pureed watermelon through a mesh strainer into a large vessel for mixing. Add white wine and mix thoroughly.

3   Fill wine glasses with 5 to 6 cubes of ice. Pour 5 to 6 ounces of watermelon mixture into each glass and top with a spritz of soda water if desired. Garnish rim with a wedge of lime.

13

South & West

Menu

GF/Gluten Free, DF/Dairy Free, V/Vegetarian, V+/Vegan

This event concept is a perfect event for a hot summer day! Of course, it could be inspired by a birthday, special occasion, wedding or summer family or friend reunion. It creates a taste for open-air BBQ, crisp salads, guacamole and salsa of many flavors served alongside ice cold beverages, margaritas and more!

I get a sense of warmth when I think of a southwestern theme. Think a little boho style with neutral tones with pops of color like turquoise, lemon yellow, fuchsia or even coral. Start your tablespace with a weathered wood table. If you don't have this, grab a neutral woven linen or burlap to act as a table cover. Build your tablescape with clay pots filled with cactuses and succulents or utilize other vessels like tin cans, mason jars, metal bowls or even colorful ceramic pots. Don't be afraid to add pops of color and texture with flowers like desert marigold, sage, golden cup, blue thistle or aloe plants. Add some stonewashed napkins and flatware tied together with simple leather string to complete your boho theme.

Yeehaw! Texas can be another great theme, with more of a cowboy feel. Use wood crates and trays for display and to act as risers. Add mason jars filled with wildflowers or loose white daisies along with a few prop pieces like a cowboy hat or some rustic horseshoes for added touches. Spill river rocks down the center of the table to create a runner effect and connect all your different elements. Use faux cowhide rugs as table linens or lay them on your wood benches or a few clustered under your dining room table. When thinking ranch vibes, you can use bandanas in multiple places. Roll them up, wrap them around mason jars and use them as cozies. Tie your flatware together with bandanas to use as napkins. They are even great as runners, too! Complete your Texas ranch-style table by repurposing tin cans and tapping holes in them to create candle holders. Add some galvanized buckets to hold utensils, napkins and other serving ware.

Whether you are heading to the lone star state of Texas in your own backyard, or looking to set a different desert vibe, both concepts will be great with wood crates for risers, cast-iron pans as serving dishes, mason jars or milk bottles for beverage glasses, pie tins for plates and wooden utensils for eating and serving.

base GUACAMOLE

V+ YIELD 2 CUPS

Make this wonderful base recipe and kick it up a notch with different accent flavors!

8 AVOCADOS, halved, seeded and peeled

3 LIMES, juiced

1 teaspoon SEA SALT

¾ teaspoon ground CUMIN

¼ teaspoon CAYENNE

½ medium ONION, diced

½ JALAPEÑO PEPPER, seeded and minced (optional)

2 ROMA TOMATOES, seeded and diced

2 tablespoons chopped CILANTRO

1 clove GARLIC, minced

1 Scoop out the avocado pulp and place in a large bowl with the lime juice. Toss to coat thoroughly. Drain and reserve the lime juice.

2 Add the salt, cumin and cayenne and mash together using a potato masher or fork.

3 Fold in onions, jalapeño, tomatoes, cilantro, garlic and 1 tablespoon of the reserved lime juice. Taste and adjust seasonings if necessary.

Chef's Notes

You can make your guacamole a day ahead. Top it with a thin layer of salsa to keep the guacamole from oxidizing and scrape off the salsa just before serving.

myo GUACAMOLE MIXER BAR

YIELD 10 TO 12 SERVINGS

MYO mix-in ingredients let guests swirl a little extra *pow* into their personalized portion. Surround your bowl of base guacamole with smaller ramekin serving vessels of "mixers" with tiny spoons.

1½ times recipe of **BASE GUACAMOLE** (above)

MYO MIXERS

¼ cup **CILANTRO**

4 tablespoons **GARLIC**

⅓ cup diced **TOMATOES**

¼ cup **SUN-DRIED TOMATOES**, chopped

10 to 12 **LIME WEDGES**

⅓ cup sliced pickled **JALAPEÑOS**, chopped

⅓ cup **BANANA PEPPERS**, chopped

⅓ cup roasted **CORN**

⅓ cup chopped **BACON BITS**

½ cup black or white **BEANS**

3 to 4 assorted small bottles of **HOT SAUCE**

SUMMER salsa

V+　　　　　　　　　　　　　　　　　　　YIELD 3 CUPS

4 large **TOMATOES**, diced *(about two cups)*

1 cup canned diced **MEXICAN TOMATOES** with green chilis

½ cup small diced **WHITE ONION**

1 whole seeded **JALAPEÑO**, minced *(optional)*

2 tablespoons *(about ½ bunch)* **CILANTRO**, chopped

2 to 3 tablespoons **LIME JUICE**

1 teaspoon **SEA SALT**

½ teaspoon **CUMIN**

Couple pinches of **CAYENNE PEPPER** *(optional)*

1　Place all ingredients in a mixing bowl and blend well.

2　Taste and adjust seasonings as necessary.

salsa verde WITH AVOCADO

GF | V+　　　　　　　　　　　　　　　　　YIELD 2 CUPS

1 *(14.5-ounce)* can **TOMATILLOS**

½ small **SPANISH ONION**, coarsely chopped

1 **AVOCADO**, peeled and seed removed, cut into chunks

1 **GARLIC CLOVE**, crushed

¼ cup pickled **JALAPEÑO**

¼ cup **LIME JUICE**

1½ teaspoons **SEA SALT**

Pinch **CAYENNE PEPPER**

¼ cup loosely packed fresh **CILANTRO LEAVES**, coarsely chopped

1　Preheat the oven to 400°F.

2　Once the oven comes to temperature, place a sheet pan in the oven for 5 minutes. Carefully remove and place canned tomatillos and onions on the hot pan and give them a little stir to spread out. Return to the oven for about 6 to 8 minutes to caramelize. Let cool for 10 minutes.

3　In a blender or food processor add cooled tomatillos, avocado, garlic, pickled jalapeño, lime juice, salt and cayenne pepper. Pulse until blended. Add cilantro and give it one last quick pulse or two. Adjust seasonings and chill.

SOUTH & WEST **street corn** BAR

Corn on the cob is a celebrated quintessential part of many south-western-inspired menus and cookouts. Let's take corn to the next level by allowing your guests to have an outdoor food experience they won't forget!

Grilled Corn on the Cob

16 ears of **CORN**

A couple large pots or bowls of cold **WATER**

Kitchen **TWINE**

1 Preheat an outdoor grill to medium.

2 Gently peel back corn husks without detaching and remove silk. Pull husks back and tie the end with kitchen twine. Soak corn in cold water for 10 minutes to prevent the husks from burning.

3 Place corn on the hot grill and cook 15 minutes or until tender, turning occasionally.

4 Remove corn from grill and carefully peel back husks.

5 Place corn in a warming dish so people can grab an ear and get to the smear and toppings!

myo SALSA MIXERS

Arrange your salsas with smaller ramekin serving vessels filled with "mixers" and tiny spoons. Although we have provided easy salsa recipes in this chapter, Trader Joe's has a large selection of quality salsas if you find yourself in a time crunch.

SUMMER SALSA

SALSA VERDE WITH AVOCADO

MYO MIXERS

ROASTED PINEAPPLE: ¾ cup diced grilled pineapple and 1 tablespoon of grated fresh ginger, mixed.

ROASTED VEGETABLE: 1 cup assorted chopped roasted vegetables.

GAZPACHO: ½ cup diced cucumber, ½ of a diced red pepper, ½ of a diced green pepper, mixed.

SOUTHWEST: ½ cup corn and ¼ cup cooked black beans, mixed.

Compound Butter

You'll find a few of my favorites below, but the sky's the limit when it comes to compound butters. Invent your own favorites if you like!

SRIRACHA GARLIC

6 tablespoons unsalted BUTTER, softened

1 heaping tablespoon SRIRACHA SAUCE

1 teaspoon chopped fresh GARLIC

RANCH

6 tablespoons unsalted BUTTER, softened

1 tablespoon and 1 teaspoon RANCH SEASONING MIX

TEX-MEX

6 tablespoons unsalted BUTTER, softened

2 tablespoons chopped CILANTRO

1 teaspoon chopped GARLIC

1 teaspoon ONION POWDER

1 teaspoon CUMIN

DIRECTIONS FOR ALL COMPOUND BUTTERS

1 Let the butter soften at room temperature. In a bowl, mix ingredients using a spoon or rubber spatula. If you make a large batch, consider using a stand mixer with the paddle attachment.

2 Place butter in a small serving dish or ramekin with butter spreader and leave at room temperature until ready to serve. If made ahead, be sure to pull from the fridge a few hours before serving.

TOPPINGS

CHEESES:

½ cup crumbled FETA

½ cup grated PARMESAN

¾ cup shredded SHARP CHEDDAR

¾ cup crumbled COTIJA CHEESE

FRILLS:

½ cup crumbled BACON

½ cup SOUR CREAM

¼ cup chopped CILANTRO

¼ cup chopped pickled JALAPEÑOS

20 wedges of LIME

3 to 4 tablespoons LIME ZEST

1 cup traditional STREET CORN SPREAD (recipe below)

Traditional Street Corn Spread

GF | V   YIELD 1 CUP

Although not a compound butter, it will be a star on your bar!

1 cup MAYONNAISE

2 tablespoons CHILI POWDER

1 tablespoon LIME JUICE

1 cup COTIJA or FETA CHEESE

1 Mix mayonnaise, chili powder and lime juice until well combined.

2 Gently fold in cotija or feta cheese or serve cheese on the side for guests to sprinkle on themselves.

Chef's Notes

The corn bar is a showstopper for sure! There are a few ways to approach Project Southwest Corn:

- Make 2 to 3 compound butters and display with add-on toppings.
- Serve only compound butter without toppings and frills.
- Use good quality butter (not compound, just plain) and serve with toppings and frills.

Compound butters and street corn spread can be prepared several days or even a week in advance. This is a very easy prep-ahead menu concept.

1. In a large bowl, add the salad ingredients and gently toss together.

2. For the vinaigrette, combine all ingredients using a blender or an immersion stick.

3. Drizzle the vinaigrette over the salad and toss to coat. Finish with fresh cracked pepper if desired.

citrus GUAJILLO CHICKEN

GF | DF YIELD 12 PIECES

FOR THE RUB

1 stick MEXICAN CINNAMON

1 tablespoon ANCHO CHILI POWDER

2 teaspoons MEXICAN OREGANO

1 teaspoon CUMIN SEEDS

1 teaspoon BLACK PEPPERCORNS

2 whole ALLSPICE BERRIES

1 BAY LEAF

2 tablespoons SEA SALT

2 tablespoons SUGAR

6 CHICKEN LEG QUARTERS cut into 6 thighs and 6 drumsticks

FOR THE SAUCE

2 whole dried GUAJILLO CHILIS

2 cloves GARLIC

1 LEMON, zest and juice

1 LIME, zest and juice

1 ORANGE, zest and juice

½ cup WHITE VINEGAR

¼ cup BROWN SUGAR

2 tablespoons HONEY

1. For the rub, in a small sauté or nonstick pan over medium heat add spices (everything except sea salt and sugar) and lightly toast. Remove from heat and let cool for a few minutes before grinding in a spice grinder. Place spices in a small mixing bowl or ramekin, add sea salt and sugar and blend with a fork. Rub chicken with prepared spice blend and rest in the fridge for 2 to 4 hours.

2. For the sauce, in a small dry pan over medium heat toast guajillo chilis and garlic cloves for about 1 minute until fragrant. Place

SEDONA SUMMER CHOPPED salad

GF | V YIELD 10 TO 12 SERVINGS

5 cups of CABBAGE SLAW MIX (or one 10- to 14-ounce bag)

2 cups chopped GREEN KALE

1 cup shaved BRUSSELS SPROUTS

1 cup COTIJA QUESO CHEESE, crumbled

1 pint GRAPE TOMATOES, cut in half

1 ENGLISH CUCUMBER, diced medium

½ to ¾ cup medium diced RED ONION

½ cup chopped BANANA PEPPERS

½ cup assorted BELL PEPPERS, diced small

⅛ cup fresh CILANTRO LEAVES, picked

2 AVOCADOS, cleaned and diced

Pepper grinder

FOR THE LIME VINAIGRETTE

1½ cups OLIVE OIL

½ cup fresh LIME JUICE

1 bunch fresh CILANTRO (leaves only)

¼ cup AGAVE SYRUP (or honey)

1 teaspoon fresh chopped GARLIC

Small handful (5 to 7) BANANA PEPPERS

1 teaspoon SEA SALT

Pinch of CAYENNE

toasted chili and garlic in a blender. Add remaining ingredients and puree. Pour puree into a medium saucepan over medium heat and reduce sauce, stirring occasionally, for about 10 minutes.

3　Preheat BBQ grill to 400°F. Turn the heat to low and add chicken. Grill chicken over low heat for about 6 to 8 minutes per side until an internal temperature reads 140° to 145°F.

4　Brush chicken with glaze every couple of minutes for another 4 minutes per side until the chicken reaches an internal temperature of 165°F.

Chef's Notes

The spice blend can be made weeks ahead and the sauce can be prepped up to 3 days ahead of time.

grilled SKIRT STEAK WITH CHIMICHURRI
GF | DF　　　　　　　　　　　　　　　YIELD 12 TO 15 SERVINGS

4 cloves **GARLIC**, minced

1 **FRESNO CHILI**, seeds removed, and minced

3 tablespoons minced **SHALLOTS**

3 tablespoons **RED WINE VINEGAR**

3 tablespoons fresh **LIME JUICE**

1 teaspoon **CUMIN**

1 teaspoon **SEA SALT**

½ teaspoon **RED PEPPER FLAKES**

¾ cup **OLIVE OIL**

½ cup chopped flat leaf **ITALIAN PARSLEY**

½ cup chopped fresh **CILANTRO**

3½-pound **SKIRT STEAK**

SEA SALT and **PEPPER**

12 to 15 sturdy bamboo or wooden **SKEWERS**, soaked in water for 10 to 15 minutes

1　Preheat the BBQ grill to medium high.

2　To make the chimichurri, in a medium bowl mix garlic, Fresno chili, shallots, vinegar, lime juice, cumin, sea salt and red pepper flakes. Whisk in olive oil. Using a fork, stir in chopped parsley and cilantro. Let sit for 10 minutes. Remove ¼ cup of the chimichurri and set aside. You will use this for basting while grilling. Save remaining chimichurri for plating and serving.

3   Lay skirt steak on your workspace and sprinkle with sea salt and pepper. Let meat sit for 10 minutes and then pat dry with a paper towel. Cut skirt steak in half vertically to give you a more manageable piece to work with and then cut 1-inch-wide strips that are 5 to 7 inches in length. You should end up with about 12 to 15 strips. Thread meat strips onto soaked skewers.

4   Once ready to grill, reduce heat on the BBQ to medium. Place skirt steak skewers on the grill and grill for 2 to 3 minutes. Flip and brush the grilled side of the steak with the chimichurri. Baste a couple times over the next few minutes while the underside is cooking. Discard any sauce that was used for basting.

5   Remove steak from the grill and place on a platter. Drizzle a few heaping spoonfuls of the reserved chimichurri and place the rest in a small bowl on the meat platter for guests to help themselves.

bourbon PEACH TACOS

V   YIELD 12 SERVINGS

12 (4-inch) FLOUR TORTILLAS

¼ cup granulated SUGAR

1 teaspoon ground CINNAMON

2 ½ tablespoons unsalted BUTTER, melted

SPECIAL EQUIPMENT

12 cup MUFFIN PAN

3-inch ROUND CUTTER

1   Preheat the oven to 400°F.

2   Using a 3-inch round cutter, cut a circle from each flour tortilla. You will end up with 12 3-inch round flour tortillas.

3   In a small bowl mix the sugar and cinnamon together.

4   Place tortillas into a large mixing bowl. Add melted butter, cinnamon/sugar mixture and toss until coated.

5   Flip the muffin pan upside down and place the tortilla rounds over muffin cups, gently pressing to form a cup. Bake for 5 to 6 minutes or until crisp. Remove shells and let cool.

6   Fill each taco with bourbon peach compote and a dollop of bourbon whipped cream (recipe below). Serve with "frills" if desired.

Bourbon Peach Compote

GF | V

¾ cup BROWN SUGAR

3 tablespoons unsalted BUTTER

3 tablespoons of BOURBON (optional)

3 tablespoons fresh ORANGE JUICE

1 teaspoon grated ORANGE RIND

1 teaspoon VANILLA EXTRACT

2 teaspoons ground CINNAMON

⅛ teaspoon ALLSPICE

⅛ teaspoon SEA SALT

6 ripe PEACHES, sliced

1   In a large heavy-bottom sauce pot skillet add the brown sugar and butter. Stir over medium heat until butter is melted and brown sugar is fully incorporated.

2   Stir in bourbon, orange juice, orange rind, vanilla, spices and salt. Add peaches and stir until peaches are well coated. Cook over medium-low heat until the peaches are soft, about 4 to 5 minutes.

Bourbon Whip

GF | V

1 ¼ cups HEAVY WHIPPING CREAM

3 tablespoons POWDERED SUGAR

1 tablespoon BOURBON

1 teaspoon VANILLA EXTRACT

½ teaspoon ground CINNAMON

1   Whip heavy cream and powdered sugar with an electric mixer on high until slightly stiff.

2   Reduce speed and add bourbon, vanilla and cinnamon. Mix until stiff peaks form.

FRILLS

½ cup CARAMEL SAUCE

1 quart vanilla bean ICE CREAM

WATERMELON **margaritas**

GF | DF| V+ YIELD ABOUT 12 DRINKS

A cool summer sip to pair with most any outdoor grilling party!

1 medium seedless **WATERMELON**, cubed *(about 9 to 10 cups)*

2 cups **WATER**

1 cup of fresh **LIME JUICE**

¾ cup **AGAVE SYRUP**

1½ cups **SILVER TEQUILA** *(I like the 1800 silver or coconut silver tequila)*

LIME WEDGES for serving

1 Place watermelon in a blender and puree. Add a little water from the 2-cup measure if it is not pureeing smoothly. Strain through a fine mesh sieve.

2 Mix watermelon juice with remaining water, lime juice, agave syrup and tequila.

3 Serve over ice and garnish with lime wedge.

Chef's Notes

Tequila can be omitted for a delicious mocktail.

Spring Things

Thoughts of replacing cold, grey skies with longer hours of sunshine and rising temperatures creates a path for entertaining, and our menu follows suit. Replace the heavy winter dishes and flavors for light, bright and easy dishes that will put a spring into your next gathering.

Whether it's Easter, Passover, a late morning bridal or baby shower or a "just because" family gathering, consider making some of these dishes your own.

When spring appears, I always think of color waking up in the world! Plants start to peak out of the ground and blooms abound. When thinking about a spring tablespace, I love a simple base, whether it is your natural wood table or a crisp white linen. Add layers with citrus- or pastel-colored accent linens or something with stripes or polka dots for a fresh and clean look. Simple bouquets of pastel tulips that will pop from your runner or table are a simple and readily available option, but there is so much to choose from in the floral season of spring. Colored gerberas, daisies, greens, hydrangeas, peonies and ivy are all great candidates.

Think in colors of yellows, pinks and even peach for taper candles to create height and ambiance. You can purchase a multitude of colored dripless candles online. If you desire to add more color, bring in a fun floral-patterned napkin and lay it on your plates in a trifold that hangs off the table or tie it in a simple knot that is placed off to the side of the plate. You can use colored glassware like green or blush to bring more fresh colors to your tablescape. Try other simple ideas like adding a woven basket for texture or tall cylinder vases filled with fresh carrots, radishes, asparagus and citrus fruits to weave in and out of your tablescape. If using vegetables, fill the vases with water for a great 3D look. This also helps to keep the vegetables from looking dry. Citrus fruits can be stacked in vases. Consider including a small pot of a low-growing herb like thyme to add color and fragrance to your table.

If you are going for an Easter theme, you can bring other elements such as light whitewashed wood pieces for risers or displays. Dig out those cute little porcelain décor bunnies that spend most of the year in the closet and add them to your tablescape. Use clean white and clear serving pieces to let your food pop. Mix up your place settings by using white dinner plates and adding a fun colorful or pattern salad plate or bowl. Wrap your flatware in a light-blush chiffon ribbon with a cute name tag.

BRUNCH-ISH

Although brunch has always been a mainstay in entertaining, it has taken on a new elevated status as of late. Food establishments are cashing in on the trend with hipster menus, Bloody Mary bars, craft cocktails, Bellini experiences and more, but it's a fun, often lighter and whimsical way to entertain at home as well! Room-temperature foods are great in the menu mix so you do not get stuck in the kitchen loading and unloading the oven. Think about a mix of larger-platter menu items and small bites for ease of presentation, table appeal and variety. This menu has a little bit of everything!

MYO SPRING smear

A fun version of power toast presented in little vignettes. The base could look like crostini of many flavors such as multigrain, sourdough, pumpernickel, bagel or pita chips and savory or sweet petit pancakes Note: all the smear recipes are gluten free unless eaten on crostini toast. You can always feature gluten-free toast on a separate platter.

SPRING GREEN PEA **hummus**

DF | V+ YIELD 10 TO 12 SERVINGS

2 *(15-ounce)* cans of **GARBANZO BEANS** *(drained but reserve about ¼ cup of liquid)*

2 cups of **GREEN PEAS** *(fresh and blanched or frozen)*

3 tablespoons **TAHINI**

¼ cup fresh **LEMON JUICE**

½ teaspoon **SEA SALT**, divided

2 tablespoons chopped **MINT**

1 tablespoon chopped **PARSLEY**

2 teaspoons **LEMON ZEST**

Couple pinches of **CAYENNE PEPPER**

18 to 22 pieces **CROSTINI** of many flavors, such as multigrain, sourdough, pumpernickel, bagel or pita chips or savory or sweet petit pancakes

1   In a food processor combine garbanzo beans, green peas, tahini, lemon juice and half the sea salt. Process until smooth (if mixture is a little too thick add reserved garbanzo bean liquid a little at a time until desired consistency).

2   Add chopped herbs, the remaining sea salt, lemon zest and cayenne, and pulse until just mixed. Adjust seasoning if needed.

3   Place in a serving bowl and place the bowl on a platter garnished with crostini.

FRILLS

- 8 to 10 red radishes sliced thin and soaked in cold water until time of service. Before service, drain, blot dry and arrange on a serving platter.

- 2 watermelon radishes sliced super thin and soaked in cold water until time of service. Before service, drain, blot dry and arrange on a platter. Watermelon radishes are sometimes hard to find, but they are worth the hunt as they are beautiful and tasty.

- Place a small bowl with pink sea salt on the platter with a demi spoon.

- Garnish with a neat pile of pea shoots (usually available at Whole Foods).

basil ricotta WITH HEIRLOOM TOMATOES

V YIELD 10 TO 12 SERVINGS

2 cups whole milk **RICOTTA**

2 tablespoons finely julienned fresh **BASIL**

2 tablespoons fresh **ORANGE JUICE**

2 teaspoons fresh zested **ORANGE**

¼ teaspoon **SEA SALT**

20 slices of assorted heirloom **TOMATOES**, cut into ⅛-inch slices or medium thin

18 to 22 pieces **CROSTINI** of many flavors, such as multigrain, sourdough, pumpernickel, bagel or pita chips or savory or sweet petit pancakes

Fresh **BASIL** for garnish

1   Place ricotta in a mixing bowl and add basil, orange juice, zest and sea salt. Mix thoroughly with a spoon.

2   Place ricotta mixture in a serving bowl on a platter. Arrange assorted heirloom tomatoes around the bowl and garnish with a bouquet of fresh basil.

Chef's Notes

All the spreads can be made a day or two in advance. Toast crostini just before service. Place breads on a separate platter or tucked vertically into an interesting bowl or serving piece.

GOLDEN eggs

GF | DF | V   YIELD 12 EGGS

4 ½ cups **WHITE VINEGAR**

1 ½ cups **WATER**

6 tablespoons **KOSHER SALT**

2 tablespoons **CORIANDER SEEDS**

2 tablespoons **YELLOW MUSTARD SEEDS**

2 tablespoons **SUGAR**

1 2-inch piece of fresh **TURMERIC**, thinly sliced, or 2 ½ teaspoons ground

1 teaspoon crushed **RED PEPPER FLAKES**

2 **BAY LEAVES**

1 small **WHITE ONION**, thinly sliced

12 hard-cooked **EGGS**, peeled

1 medium **CARROT**, peeled into thin ribbon strips with a vegetable peeler

1 To make the brine, in a medium saucepan add vinegar, water, salt, coriander seeds, mustard seeds, sugar, turmeric, red pepper flakes, bay leaves and onion. Bring to a boil over medium heat, stirring to dissolve the salt and sugar. Reduce heat, cover and simmer for 5 minutes.

2 Meanwhile, pierce each egg all the way through about 6 times with a toothpick or pin.

3 Put half of the carrots in the bottom of a decorative glass bowl or into individual 4-ounce mason jars.

4 Add eggs to the bowl or place one in each jar. Top with remaining carrots. Ladle in enough brine to completely cover the eggs. Allow to cool to room temperature, cover and refrigerate for at least 24 hours before serving.

5 The eggs will keep covered by liquid and refrigerated for up to 5 days.

mini FRITTATA TART

GF | V   YIELD 24 PIECES

1 tablespoon **OLIVE OIL**

½ cup **RED ONION**, diced small

½ cup **YELLOW PEPPER**, diced small

¼ cup **RED PEPPER**, diced small

½ cup shredded **MOZZARELLA**

2 tablespoons finely julienned **BASIL LEAVES**

12 large whole **EGGS**

1 teaspoon **SEA SALT**

½ teaspoon freshly ground **BLACK PEPPER**

½ cup crumbled **GOAT CHEESE**

¾ cup sliced **ASPARAGUS**, blanched

1 **ZUCCHINI**, sliced into ⅛-inch slices, lightly grilled or pan fried

SPECIAL EQUIPMENT

1 to 2 mini **MUFFIN PANS** (the flexible molds are great here)

1. Preheat the oven to 325°F. Prepare muffin tins with a heavy coating of nonstick spray.

2. Heat olive oil in a small sauté pan. Add red onion and cook over medium-low heat until onion is caramelized, about 2 minutes. Cool for 5 or so minutes.

3. In a bowl mix peppers, mozzarella cheese and basil. Divide evenly among the 24 muffin cups.

4. Beat eggs with salt and pepper until thoroughly combined. Divide equally between each prepared cup, being careful not to overfill (they will puff up as they bake). Bake for 15 to 20 minutes until cooked through.

5. Top each mini frittata with a sprinkle of goat cheese and a few slices of the blanched asparagus. Return to the oven until the goat cheese has melted and has a little color.

6. Let rest for a few minutes and gently side out with a small rubber spatula.

7. To serve, line a serving platter with grilled zucchini and top with mini frittatas.

Chef's Notes

These would be very nice plated on small grab-and-go plates with a little poof of salad or on a platter with crostini. You can make the frittatas a day ahead, being mindful to not overcook, and do a quick reheat before serving.

rainbow ROASTED CARROTS

GF | V   YIELD 10 TO 12 SERVINGS

2 pounds **BABY CARROTS** *(preferably rainbow)*, tops trimmed

3 tablespoons **COCONUT OIL**

⅓ cup **ORANGE MARMALADE**

Juice of two **ORANGES**

1 tablespoon **HONEY**

½ teaspoon **SALT**

¼ teaspoon freshly **GROUND PEPPER**

½ cup **GOAT CHEESE**

¼ cup chopped **PISTACHIOS**

1. Preheat the oven to 400°F. Place two sheet pans in the oven.

2. To blanch carrots, bring a pot of water to boil. Add carrots, reduce to a simmer and cook for about 3 minutes. While carrots are blanching, prepare an ice bath by filling a bowl with ice and water. After 3 minutes, drain the carrots and immediately place in the ice bath to cool. Remove, pat to dry and place in a large bowl.

3. In a heavy-bottom saucepan over low heat melt coconut oil. Add marmalade, fresh orange juice, honey, salt and pepper. Stir and cook for a quick minute. Add to the bowl with carrots and toss to coat.

4. Place carrots sparsely on a baking sheet and roast for 20 to 25 minutes, turning as needed. Carrots should look caramel in color.

5. Place carrots on a serving platter and sprinkle goat cheese and chopped pistachios.

SHAVED SPRING salad

GF | V+

4 cups ARUGULA

1 cup PEA SHOOTS

2 cups WATERCRESS

8 to 10 ASPARAGUS, shaved into thin slices *(with peeler or mandoline)*

4 stalks CELERY, shaved into ribbons and soaked in ice water for 10 minutes

6 to 8 large RED RADISHES, sliced paper thin and soaked in ice water for 10 minutes

¼ cup chopped MINT LEAVES

APRICOT VINAIGRETTE

¼ cup plus 2 tablespoons OLIVE OIL

¼ cup APRICOT PRESERVES

3 tablespoons CHAMPAGNE *(or white)* VINEGAR

2 tablespoons freshly squeezed LEMON JUICE

1 tablespoon LEMON ZEST

3 SHALLOTS, minced

4 tablespoons chopped TARRAGON LEAVES

Sprinkle of SEA SALT and fresh cracked PEPPER

GARNISH

2 tablespoons chopped CHIVES

1   In a large bowl toss all your greens, shaved vegetables, radishes and mint.

2   To make the apricot vinaigrette, in a small bowl whisk together olive oil, apricot preserves, vinegar, lemon juice, lemon zest and shallots together until combined. Stir in tarragon leaves and season with sea salt and fresh cracked pepper.

3   Lightly dress the salad with vinaigrette and toss to coat.

4   Place in a serving bowl and garnish with chives.

EVERYTHING salmon

GF | DF YIELD 10 TO 12 SERVINGS

1 whole fillet of **SALMON**

2 tablespoons **OLIVE OIL**, divided

Sprinkle of **SEA SALT** and **PEPPER**

¼ cup of **EVERYTHING SEASONING**

GARNISH

2 cups **ARUGULA**

½ cup thinly sliced **RED ONION**

1. Preheat the oven to 375°F. Line a large sheet tray with a Silpat mat or heavy-duty aluminum foil and a spray of nonstick spray.

2. Season fillet with 1 tablespoon of olive oil, sea salt and pepper. Sprinkle everything seasoning generously over the top of salmon and give a little pat down over flesh. Drizzle with the remaining tablespoon of olive oil.

3. Roast salmon for 15 to 18 minutes until the flesh is firm to touch.

4. Let salmon rest for 10 minutes. Using two spatulas, lift the salmon at each end and gently slide onto the serving platter. Garnish with a few handfuls of arugula and thinly sliced red onion.

citrus BLUEBERRY CAKE
WITH LEMON WHIPPED CREAM

V YIELD 9-INCH CAKE | 8 TO 10 SLICES

Citrus Blueberry Cake

2 **EGGS**

1 cup **SUGAR**

½ cup whole milk **YOGURT**

¼ cup **BUTTER**, melted and slightly cooled

1 teaspoon **VANILLA**

1 tablespoon **LEMON ZEST**

2 tablespoons **LEMON JUICE**

1½ cups **ALL-PURPOSE FLOUR**

1¾ teaspoons **BAKING POWDER**

¼ teaspoon **SEA SALT**

1¼ cups fresh **BLUEBERRIES**, divided

1½ teaspoons coarse **SUGAR**

1. Preheat the oven to 375°F. Spray a 9-inch springform pan with nonstick cooking spray and line the bottom with parchment paper.

2. In a medium mixing bowl combine the eggs and sugar. Beat on high speed until mixture is thick, pale and doubled in size, about 3 to 4 minutes.

3. Add the yogurt, melted butter and vanilla. Beat for another minute. Stir in lemon zest and juice.

4. In a separate small bowl add flour, baking powder and salt and mix with a fork until well combined. Add to your batter and mix until just combined.

5. Pour half of the batter into the prepared pan and spread evenly to the edges. Sprinkle ¾ cup of blueberries over the top. Add remaining batter and spread evenly. Top with remaining blueberries and sprinkle with coarse sugar.

6. Bake cake for 35 to 40 minutes until a toothpick inserted into the center comes out clean. Transfer to a wire rack and let cool for 20 minutes. Gently run a knife around the pan to loosen the cake, release the clasp and remove the outside ring of the springform pan to finish cooling.

7. Slice into 8 to 10 pieces and garnish with a dollop of lemon whipped cream (recipe below) on the side.

Lemon Whipped Cream

GF | V   YIELD 1 CUP

1 cup heavy **WHIPPED CREAM**

2 tablespoons **HONEY**

2 teaspoons **LEMON ZEST**

1. In a large bowl, combine heavy cream and honey. Mix until semi-firm peaks set (about double in volume). Stir in lemon zest.

NUTELLA, BANANA & CHIA sprinkle

GF | V+   YIELD 10 TO 12 SERVINGS

2 (7-ounce) jars of **NUTELLA**

½ cup shaved **DARK CHOCOLATE** or **MINI CHOCOLATE CHIPS**

¾ cup **CHIA SEEDS**

4 **BANANAS**, sliced into ¼-inch circles on a little bias

1. Place Nutella, shaved chocolate and chia seeds in individual small serving bowls. Place bowls on a platter.

2. Just before serving, slice bananas and arrange on the platter around bowls.

BEVERAGE

For a crisp, spring-centric cocktail, Limoncello will deliver a big citrus splash! Consider creating a couple of cocktails featuring Limoncello or create a mix-and-match bar. Include some prosecco and flavored sparkling waters (blood orange, lemon, lime, grapefruit), fill bowls with citrus wheels, berries and fresh herbs (mint, basil, thyme) and allow your guests to create their own cocktail.

limoncello

8 LEMONS to zest

1 750 mL bottle of VODKA *(25 ounces)*

1 ½ cups SUGAR

2 cups WATER

1 Zest lemons, being sure not to go too deep. You want only the zest, not the white portion of the peel.

2 In a large nonporous container such as a mason jar, combine the zest with the vodka. Cover and keep in a dark, cool place for 10 days.

3 Strain zest out with a cheesecloth and discard.

4 Add sugar and water to a saucepan and bring to a simmer. Cook, stirring until the sugar dissolves completely.

5 Allow sugar mixture to cool. Add to vodka and stir.

6 Store in the refrigerator for up to one month.

Backyard Street Food from Around the World

Menu

GF/Gluten Free, DF/Dairy Free, V/Vegetarian, V+/Vegan

Set the scene for a mid- to late-summer outdoor event with aromatic spices in the open air from a myriad of international street foods from the grill. Fresh marinated meats, all meant to be easy handheld backyard fare, paired with fresh corn tortillas, naan or pitas served with assorted vegetables, condiments, salads and fun accoutrements will make your outdoor event filled with bright, light and tasty food.

Using as much as you can around the house is always best. Grab your existing patio furniture or indoor furniture from the house and move it outside for your summer event. Add some throw pillows in bright colors. Even an indoor rug could be transported for a day to create a warmer outdoor space. Pull in any fun props, pottery or pieces that may help conjure the origin of dishes you are serving. Adding woven or jute rugs for pattern and texture coupled with soft lanterns or globes could bring up the mood after dusk.

To set the foundation for your table, you can go in many directions with linen from bright pops of color to soft muted whites or earth tones. Keep it simple by using already-potted plants. Succulents are low maintenance and when the party's over, you can place them around your home or give them as gifts. Natural materials like concrete and wood for plant containers always look good outdoors. We had some leftover wood from a project and cut some slices out of a four-by-four post to create risers for candles, clustered with concrete planters with succulents. For serving platters, think mismatched glass or ceramic plates, bold-colored platters or that funky serving piece you were never quite sure what to do with. Serving vessels as simple as a shiny stainless-steel sheet tray or a cast-iron pan will create the feeling of street food presentation.

KEEP THE BUGS **at bay**

Check out your local dollar store for inexpensive glass cylinders for our bug-repellent centerpiece.

MATERIALS

1 8-inch **GLASS CYLINDER**	**WATER**
1 **LEMON**, sliced	
1 **LIME**, sliced	Few drops of **ROSEMARY** essential oil
Few sprigs of **ROSEMARY**	1 floating **CANDLE**

1 Add sliced lemons and limes and rosemary to the glass cylinder then fill the vase three-quarters full with water. Add a few drops of the rosemary essential oil (5 to 7 drops per cylinder).

2 Add your floating candle and light it. This will look cute and help keep the bugs away!

KOREAN POW **shrimp**

GF | DF YIELD 12 SATAYS OR 32 PIECES

¼ cup **COCONUT AMINOS** or **BRAGG LIQUID AMINOS**

3 tablespoons **HONEY**

1 tablespoon **FISH SAUCE**

1½ tablespoons **GOCHUJANG** (Korean chili paste)

1½ tablespoons toasted **SESAME OIL**

3 to 4 cloves **GARLIC**, finely minced

Juice of ½ a **LEMON**

Pinch of **RED PEPPER FLAKES**

2 pounds raw tail-on **SHRIMP** (16/20 count)

2 teaspoons toasted **SESAME SEEDS** (garnish)

12 iceberg or bibb **LETTUCE LEAVES** (optional)

SPECIAL EQUIPMENT

12 8-inch bamboo **SKEWERS** (soaked in water for 20 minutes before preparation of satays)

GLAZE

1 tablespoon **COCONUT OIL** (liquid form or melted)

1½ teaspoons **AVOCADO** or **OLIVE OIL**

1½ teaspoons **SESAME OIL**

¼ cup freshly squeezed **LEMON JUICE**

¼ cup freshly squeezed **ORANGE JUICE**

1 small bunch cleaned chopped **CILANTRO**

1 small **FRESNO** or **JALAPEÑO PEPPER**, cleaned and sliced paper thin

1. In a medium bowl combine the aminos, honey, fish sauce, gochujang, sesame oil, garlic, lemon juice and pinch of red pepper flakes. Stir to combine. Add shrimp and toss to coat. Let shrimp marinate for 1 to 2 hours.

2. To make the glaze, in a small bowl whisk together oils, lemon and orange juice. Stir in cilantro and pepper slices.

3. Preheat your outdoor grill or cast-iron pan to medium high.

4. Drain and discard marinade from shrimp. Thread 2 shrimp on each bamboo skewer.

5. Cook shrimp for approximately 2 minutes on each side until cooked through.

6. Arrange on your serving platter. Brush with glaze and sprinkle toasted sesame seeds. Serve as is on the skewer or serve off the skewer with iceberg or bibb lettuce cups as a cool lettuce "taco."

crispy SEOUL SLAW

DF | V   YIELD 2½ CUPS OR 2 SIDES AS A CONDIMENT

3 cups ASIAN SLAW MIX

4 GREEN ONIONS, cleaned and sliced thin

¼ cup matchstick-cut RADISHES

½ cup MAYONNAISE

2 tablespoons LIME JUICE

1 tablespoon RICE WINE VINEGAR

1 tablespoon HONEY

1½ teaspoons GOCHUJANG

2 tablespoons chopped CILANTRO

SALT and PEPPER to taste

1. In a medium bowl combine Asian slaw, green onions and radishes.

2. In a small bowl whisk together mayonnaise, lime juice, vinegar, honey, gochujang and chopped cilantro. Taste and season with salt and pepper.

3. Add dressing to slaw salad and mix thoroughly.

4. Serve in a small bowl alongside Korean Pow Shrimp and lettuce cups.

MEXICO CITY carnitas

GF | DF   YIELD 2½ TO 3 POUNDS

1 3- to 4-pound **PORK SHOULDER** or **PORK BUTT**

1 tablespoon smoked **PAPRIKA**

2 teaspoons **CUMIN**

2 teaspoons **CHIPOTLE CHILI PEPPER**

2 teaspoons **CHILI POWDER**

2 teaspoon **ONION POWDER**

2 teaspoons **SEA SALT**

1 teaspoon **OREGANO**

½ teaspoon red pepper **CHILI FLAKES**

½ teaspoon **GARLIC POWDER**

¼ teaspoon **CINNAMON**

2 tablespoons **OIL**

Juice of 2 **ORANGES** *(reserve rinds)*

2 cups of **WATER**

2½ tablespoons **AGAVE SYRUP** or **HONEY**

½ **SPANISH ONION**, cut into 3 to 4 large chunks

2 **CHIPOTLE PEPPERS**, minced *(canned is fine)*

HOT SAUCE, to taste *(optional)*

1. Place pork on a cutting board fat side up. With a sharp boning knife, cut slits about ½-inch deep on a slight angle into your roast in rows about 1½ inches apart. You will end up with about 5 to 6 rows. Repeat the process in the opposite direction. Now the meat is scored.

2. To make the dry rub, combine all dry seasonings (paprika through cinnamon) together in a bowl. Mix until combined. Rub approximately 40% of the dry rub all over pork, getting into all the cut nooks and crannies.

3. Heat oil in a heavy-bottom Dutch oven or cast-iron pan. Once the pan is smoking hot, add pork and sear on all sides until golden brown (about 3 to 4 minutes per side).

4. Place seared pork into a heavy Dutch oven or deep square roasting pot.

5. Mix orange juice, water, agave and remaining seasonings. Add to pork along with onions and orange rinds. Cover and place on indirect heat on the barbeque grill for about 5 hours. Uncover every 30 minutes or so and baste the pork roast. In the final 30 minutes of cooking, remove the lid. If your pot or roasting pan seems a little dry, add more chicken stock or water. Roast pork until it reaches an internal temperature of 195° to 200°F. This is the temperature where the meat will tenderly flake with a fork.

6. Pour drippings and juice from pork into a saucepan and cook over medium-high heat until reduced by 35%. If you want your reduction a little spicier, add a few dashes of hot sauce to taste.

7. Once pork has rested for 15 to 20 minutes, use two forks to shred the meat. Place on a serving platter and drizzle with reduction. Serve with MYO Taco.

Chef's Notes

If you do not have a Dutch oven, use a heavy roasting pan with a rack in the bottom (like what you would roast a turkey in) and cover with heavy-duty foil. This can also be roasted in the oven at 350°F for 3 to 4 hours or until tender. You can make carnitas a day in advance and shred. Reheat with reserved juices. Many people like to render bacon fat or oil in a heavy sauté pan and sear shredded pork to make it crispy. This recipe will make a lot of tacos, but no worries, calculate about 3 ounces per person and freeze the remainder after your event for another taco, enchilada, nacho or pulled pork sandwich. Store the leftover dry rub in an airtight container. It can be used on any protein you want to spice up.

myo TACO BAR

GF YIELD 12 TO 14 TACOS

14 4- to 6-inch **CORN TORTILLAS**

1 cup **SALSA**, your favorite brand

¾ cup **SALSA VERDE**

2 to 3 **AVOCADOS**, sliced or mashed with a spritz of lime juice and sprinkle of sea salt

½ cup pickled **RED ONIONS** *(optional, find recipe in the "Charcuterie Party" chapter)*

½ cup pickled **JALAPEÑO** slices

1½ cups Mexican-style soft shredded **CHEESE**

summer GRILLING CHICKEN SHAWARMA

GF YIELD 8 TO 10 SERVINGS

3 pounds boneless, skinless **CHICKEN THIGHS**

MARINADE

¼ cup **OLIVE OIL**

3 tablespoons whole milk plain **YOGURT**

1 **LEMON**, juice and zest

4 small **GARLIC** cloves, crushed/chopped

2 teaspoons smoked sweet **PAPRIKA**

1½ teaspoons **SEA SALT**

1½ teaspoons **CUMIN**

1 teaspoon crushed **RED PEPPER FLAKES**

1 teaspoon freshly ground **BLACK PEPPER**

1 teaspoon **CARDAMOM**

½ teaspoon **CAYENNE PEPPER**

½ teaspoon ground **GINGER**

¼ teaspoon **TURMERIC**

GARNISH (OPTIONAL)

Pitas or naan **BREAD**, brushed with olive oil

Bibb **LETTUCE** cups

Sliced **TOMATOES** and **CUCUMBERS**

1 In a large bowl whisk the marinade ingredients together. Add chicken and toss to coat. Cover bowl and let the chicken thighs marinate in the fridge for 2 hours or overnight.

2 Heat your grill to medium-high. Spray grill with nonstick spray or coat a kitchen cloth with a little oil and brush on grill grates.

3 Grill chicken about 6 to 8 minutes on each side, turning a few times, until cooked through.

4 If using pitas or naan bread, brush with a little olive oil and warm on the grill for a quick minute while the chicken is resting. Wrap in foil to keep warm.

5 Remove from heat and let chicken rest for at least 5 minutes before slicing into strips. Serve with warm pitas or naan bread, lettuce cups and sliced cucumbers and tomatoes.

Tzatziki Sauce

GF | V YIELD 1½ CUPS

1 small **ENGLISH CUCUMBER**, grated

1 cup thick whole milk **YOGURT**

2 cloves of **GARLIC**, minced

1 tablespoon chopped **DILL**

2 teaspoons chopped **MINT** *(optional)*

2 teaspoons **OLIVE OIL**

1 teaspoon **LEMON ZEST**

1 teaspoon **SEA SALT**

Pinch **CAYENNE**

1. Drain grated cucumber in a basket colander over a mixing bowl for a couple hours. If you have time, cover it and let it drain overnight in the refrigerator. Transfer cucumber to a clean kitchen towel, and twist to ring out extra water.

2. In a large bowl, add cucumber with remaining ingredients and stir to combine. Cover and chill until time of service.

Chef's Notes

Feel free to make tzatziki sauce a day or two ahead of time. Just drain off any extra liquid that may develop on top. Chicken can marinate for more than a day if you want to get a head start.

shawarma MYO BAR

GF   YIELD 8 TO 10 SERVINGS

1 cup flavored or plain HUMMUS

1 cup TZATZIKI SAUCE

¾ cup FETA crumbles

1 large or two small TOMATOES, diced

1 small RED ONION, thinly sliced *(pickled would be even better)*

½ head ICEBERG LETTUCE, shaved

½ cup sliced PICKLES

10 6-inch PITAS or 5 larger pitas, cut in half

INDONESIAN BEEF satay

DF   YIELD 16 TO 18 PIECES

MARINADE

4 small SHALLOTS, chopped

3 GARLIC cloves, chopped

2 *(2-inch)* pieces of LEMON GRASS *(white part only)*, chopped

3 tablespoons LIME JUICE

3 tablespoons PEANUT OIL

1½ tablespoons FISH SAUCE

1½ tablespoons BROWN SUGAR

2 teaspoons CUMIN

1½ teaspoons SEA SALT

1 teaspoon FENNEL SEED

1 teaspoon TURMERIC

½ teaspoon ground CORIANDER

½ teaspoon BLACK PEPPER

SATAYS

1½ pounds SIRLOIN STEAK, cut into thin 1½- to 2-ounce strips

18 soaked bamboo SKEWERS

Grilled NAAN or LETTUCE cups *(or a combination)*

1. For the marinade, combine marinade ingredients in the food processor or blender.

2. Place sliced beef in a large ziplock bag and pour marinade over beef. Mix evenly and refrigerate overnight.

3. Heat grill to medium high. Spray grill with nonstick spray or brush grill with vegetable or olive oil.

4. Thread beef on soaked skewers.

5. Cook beef for about 1½ to 2 minutes on each side.

6. Serve with cucumber, peanut sauce, cucumber salad (recipes below) and naan bread or lettuce cups.

Peanut Sauce

GF | DF YIELD 1 1/4 CUP

½ cup PEANUT BUTTER

½ cup COCONUT MILK

1 (1-inch) piece fresh GINGER, roughly chopped

1 GARLIC clove

2 tablespoons LIME JUICE

1 tablespoon BROWN SUGAR

1 tablespoon FISH SAUCE

1 tablespoon KETCHUP

2 teaspoons SRIRACHA

1. Add all ingredients to the blender and blend on high until thoroughly combined.

2. Store in an airtight container. Pull from the fridge an hour before service.

cucumber SALAD

GF | DF | V+ YIELD 1 CUP

¼ cup RICE WINE VINEGAR

1 teaspoon SUGAR

¼ teaspoon SEA SALT

1 large ENGLISH CUCUMBER, sliced very thin on a mandoline

1 small RED ONION, sliced very thin on a mandoline

1. In a large bowl whisk together rice wine vinegar, sugar and salt until combined.

2. Add cucumber and red onion and toss to coat.

3. Place in a serving bowl or store in the refrigerator until ready to use.

churros WITH A TRIO OF SAUCES

DF | V YIELD 12 TO 14

2 cups WATER

1 cup VEGETABLE OIL

1 tablespoon SALT

10 ounces BREAD FLOUR

8 EGGS

OIL for frying

SUGGESTED TOPPINGS

Plain sugar

Cinnamon sugar

Powdered sugar

Cocoa powdered sugar

1. In a heavy saucepan heat water, oil and salt until boiling.

2. Add flour all at once and stir vigorously with a wooden spoon until the dough pulls away from the sides of the pan.

3. Transfer to the bowl of a stand mixer fitted with the paddle attachment and mix for 2 minutes to disperse the heat a little.

4. With the mixer running, add eggs 2 at a time, scraping down the bowl after each addition.

5. Mix batter until the dough is shiny and smooth and when you drag a spoon through, the track closes in about 2 seconds.

6. Transfer the batter to a piping bag fitted with either a straight or a star tip.

7. Heat frying oil to 350°F.

8. Pipe churros into dough to desired shape and length, being careful not to crowd the pan.

9. Fry churros for 4 to 5 minutes total, flipping and turning as needed.

10. Drain churros on paper towels and roll in desired topping.

Matcha Honey Dip

GF | DF | V   YIELD 2 CUPS

1 can full-fat COCONUT MILK

¼ cup Michigan HONEY

1 teaspoon VANILLA

1¼ teaspoons MATCHA POWDER

1 Pour off and discard ¼ cup of the liquid portion of the coconut milk at the bottom of the can. In the bowl of a stand mixer fitted with the whisk attachment, add the remaining coconut milk, honey, vanilla and matcha powder.

2 Whip all ingredients until slightly thickened and a little frothy, about 3 minutes.

3 Store chilled in an airtight container.

Chocolate Tahini Dip

GF | DF | V+   YIELD 2 CUPS

1 cup TAHINI

½ cup WATER (plus more as needed)

¼ cup MAPLE SYRUP

¼ cup COCOA POWDER, sifted

1 teaspoon VANILLA

1 teaspoon SALT

1 Add all ingredients to a bowl and whisk together thoroughly.

2 Add additional water, 1 tablespoon at a time, until desired consistency is reached.

3 Store in an airtight container at room temperature.

Mexican Caramel Dip

GF | V   YIELD 1 3/4 CUPS

1 cup packed BROWN SUGAR

½ cup plus 2 tablespoons HALF AND HALF

¼ cup BUTTER

Pinch of SALT

½ teaspoon CHILI POWDER

¼ teaspoon CINNAMON

1 tablespoon VANILLA

1. In a small saucepan over medium-high heat add brown sugar, ½ cup half and half, butter, salt, chili powder and cinnamon. Bring to a boil, whisking constantly. Boil gently for 4 minutes while continuing to whisk.

2. Remove from heat and stir in vanilla and remaining 2 tablespoons of half and half.

3. Cool completely and store in an airtight container at room temperature.

tamarindo GRILLED PINEAPPLE

GF | V+   YIELD 10 SERVINGS

There is so much going on with our menu creation in this chapter, so I wanted to keep dessert simple and easy. Grilled fruit will work so well here! I chose pineapple but you could do melon with a little honey or most anything you like.

1 PINEAPPLE, skinned and cleaned

16 *(6- to 8-inch)* bamboo SKEWERS, soaked in water

⅔ cup TAMARIND PASTE *(find at most grocery stores in the international section)*

3 tablespoons BROWN SUGAR

2 tablespoons COCONUT OIL

¼ cup shredded COCONUT

1. Cut pineapple in quarters and remove the core. Take the 4 planks and cut in half lengthwise and take those 8 pieces and cut in half crosswise. This will give you 16 long chunks. Put each chunk onto a bamboo skewer.

2. In a small saucepan, add tamarind paste, brown sugar and coconut oil. Heat over medium heat, stirring until mixture comes together.

3. Brush pineapple chunks with melted glaze and place on low grill for a few minutes on each side, giving them an extra brush of sauce during grilling.

4. Remove from grill, platter and sprinkle with shredded coconut.

beverages

When approaching a fun and flirty outdoor situation that brings a melting pot of food ethnicities together, consider serving easy, lightly fruited beverages like tall bottles of flavored sparkling water with whole lemons, limes and oranges resting in ice for a little pop of color. Lighter craft beer or spiked fruit coolers like White Claw or Truly would also work great. Include an iced tea bar, virgin or spiked!

blackberry HIBISCUS MARGARITAS

GF | V+   YIELD 6 TO 8 SERVINGS

HIBISCUS TEA CONCENTRATE

3 cups **WATER**

¾ cup dried **HIBISCUS FLOWERS** *(Rishi sel's great hibiscus tea and Tazo has a concentrate)*

½ cup **AGAVE SYRUP** or **HONEY** *(or substitute 2 to 4 packets stevia to taste)*

COCKTAIL

8 to 10 muddled **BLACKBERRIES**

3 cups **HIBISCUS TEA CONCENTRATE**

1 cup **SILVER TEQUILA** *(I like 1800 Coconut Tequila)*

3 large **LIMES**, juiced

8 ounces lime-flavored or neutral **SPARKLING SODA WATER**

GARNISH

6 to 8 **LIME SLICES**

1. To make the hibiscus tea concentrate, bring 3 cups of water to a boil, add hibiscus tea and stir. Remove from heat and let steep for 30 minutes. Strain into a jar or glass container through a fine-mesh strainer and add sweetener of choice.

2. To make the margarita, add blackberries to a serving pitcher and use a wooden spoon to muddle the berries. Add hibiscus tea concentrate, tequila and lime juice. Mix thoroughly.

3. At time of service add sparkling water and serve over ice. Garnish with lime slices.

GREEN TEA CUCUMBER cocktail

GF | V+   YIELD 8 TO 10 SERVINGS

CUCUMBER SIMPLE SYRUP

¾ cup granulated **SUGAR**

¾ cup **WATER**

1 **CUCUMBER**, sliced

COCKTAIL

25 to 30 fresh **MINT LEAVES**, muddled

3 cups **GREEN TEA**, brewed and chilled

1 cup **LIGHT RUM**

½ cup **LIME JUICE**

½ cup **SPARKLING WATER**

GARNISH

10 (¼-inch) **CUCUMBER** slices with one small notch cut for garnish

LIME WEDGES

1. To make the simple syrup, combine sugar, water and cucumber in a small saucepan over medium-high heat. Simmer until sugar is dissolved, then strain and discard cucumbers (makes about 1 cup simple syrup).

2. In a serving pitcher add mint leaves and use a wooden spoon to bruise the mint leaves. Add chilled tea, rum, lime juice and simple syrup. Mix thoroughly.

3. At time of service add sparkling water and serve over ice. Garnish with cucumber slices and lime wedges if desired.

Boho Beach Party

Menu

GF/Gluten Free, DF/Dairy Free, V/Vegetarian, V+/Vegan

Kick off your flip flops and sink those toes in the sand! The beach can be an amazing platform for a memorable casual summer gathering. It is important to pick foods that are easy to execute without a lot of fuss. Foods that work well over a beach campfire or outdoor grill and a variety of cold dishes are the way to go with picnic menu selections!

Create an eating or serving platform using wood pallets at your beach party. Wood pallets can serve as a casual serving center as well as a functional eating space and are often a byproduct from warehouses, grocery stores or rental companies, so keep your eyes open for them (they're even on the side of the road sometimes). You can raise your pallet table using a few cinder blocks if you would like a little more room for your tootsies. At Two Unique we use pallets as backdrops, vertical planters, tables, art walls and more (Pinterest is a great resource for ideas). Add easy outdoor or indoor pillows piled whimsically together to create cozy seating for your guests.

For your table coverings, old newspapers are an easy option. You can add a soft white- or earth-toned muslin for a relaxed accent piece. Add a splash of color with checked blue gingham or striped napkins, fresh lemons and wildflowers to decorate your tablescape. Galvanized metal serving dishes, light wood pieces or white melamine platters all feel at home here. Kraft or white paper boats would be a thoughtful plate option to serve your guests, but bamboo plates or bowls could be fun too. Fill small buckets with wooden cutlery tied together with twine or raffia for serving utensils. These materials are easily found at your local craft store, but dig around your house or garage. You may find you have old, galvanized buckets you can clean up and repurpose. Larger ones are great for housing and icing your beach beverages. Clean them up, add a plastic liner and you have an easy MYO beverage station. While this is a fun beach picnic idea, it is easy to conjure this same eating style on your backyard patio, deck or even while camping.

boho BEACH SHRIMP "BOIL"

GF

This is the same principle as a classic east coast shrimp boil. Arrange your ingredients in a foil packet to throw on the grill or beach fire!

SPECIAL EQUIPMENT

Heavy-duty **FOIL**

3 pounds large *(12/15 count)* **SHRIMP**, peeled and deveined *(leaving tail on is fine)*

2 pounds smoked, cooked **ANDOUILLE SAUSAGE**, thinly sliced

6 to 8 ears **CORN**, each ear cut crosswise into 4 to 5 pieces

2 pounds small baby **RED**, **YUKON** or **MARBLE POTATOES** *(cut in half if they are on the larger side)*

1 large **ONION**, cut into medium slices

10 teaspoons **BUTTER**

10 teaspoons **CAJUN SEASONING**

SEA SALT and freshly ground **BLACK PEPPER** to taste, sprinkled into each packet

¼ cup coarsely chopped fresh **PARSLEY LEAVES**

1. Place grate over beach fire leaving a 4-inch clearance between the grate and the fire. Cut 10 sheets of heavy-duty foil 12 inches long and line them up on your work service.

2. Divide shrimp (about 4 per package), sausage (about ⅓ cup), corn (3 pieces), potatoes (2 to 3) and onions evenly among heavy duty foil sheets. Top with a teaspoon of butter and teaspoon of Cajun seasoning, a sprinkle of salt and pepper and a sprinkle of parsley. Fold the sides of the foil packets together, enclosing the food completely and sealing the packets.

3. Place foil packets on the grate over prepared fire and grill until cooked through, about 10 to 12 minutes.

Chef's Notes

This method works great on a gas or charcoal barbeque as well as the little grills at state parks. You can also bake packets in the oven at 350°F for 10 minutes.

maine LOBSTER ROLLS

Nothing says east coast summer like a lobster roll! Pair this station with the foil packets or use it as a standalone for your beach party.

1¼-pound cooked **LOBSTER MEAT**, chopped into a medium dice *(keep claws in bigger clumps and use to garnish on top of rolls)*

⅓ cup finely diced **CELERY**

⅓ cup **MAYONNAISE**

2 teaspoons freshly squeezed **LEMON JUICE**

1 teaspoon **SEA SALT**

Pinch of **CAYENNE**

3 tablespoons melted **BUTTER**, divided

6 New England-style **HOT DOG BUNS** *(these are the buns that have the sides trimmed)*

1 teaspoon minced **CHIVES**

Dash of **PAPRIKA**

MYO LOBSTER TOPPINGS *(see below, optional)*

1. In a medium bowl add lobster meat and celery. Gently mix together.

2. In a small bowl add mayonnaise, lemon juice, sea salt and cayenne. Stir to combine. Gently fold mayo mixture into lobster meat. Chill until ready to assemble lobster rolls.

3. Brush melted butter onto outer naked sides of each bun.

4. In a nonstick pan over medium heat toast the buns on both sides until golden (about a minute per side).

5. Divide lobster salad evenly between the buns. Drizzle with remaining melted butter and top with chives and a sprinkle of paprika if desired.

MYO LOBSTER ROLL TOPPINGS

Consider creating a MYO lobster roll bar by serving them alongside a few toppings. Display toppings in small bowls presented on a platter with petit spoons for serving.

1 AVOCADO, cleaned and diced (squeeze a little lemon on top to keep avocado from browning)

12 slices BACON, cooked and chopped

1 (8-ounce) bag of seasoned SHOESTRING FRIES

1 cup of crushed POTATO CHIPS (dill-flavored chips are super tasty)

1 cup CORN SALSA

1 cup VINAIGRETTE COLESLAW

½ cup sliced BANANA PEPPERS

summer WATERMELON SALAD

GF | V   YIELD 10 TO 12 SERVINGS

Watermelon paired with a sprinkle of feta cheese, fresh mint, a splash of virgin olive oil and lime juice is the quintessential refreshing summer salad of sweet with a little salt!

8 cups medium-diced seedless WATERMELON

⅓ cup virgin OLIVE OIL

Juice of 3 fresh LIMES

1 teaspoon pink SEA SALT

¼ teaspoon freshly ground PEPPER

1 cup sheep's milk FETA, crumbled

2 ounces of AGAVE or HONEY

½ cup fresh MINT LEAVES, chopped

1. Add watermelon cubes to a large bowl.

2. Prepare the vinaigrette by whisking together (or place in a jar and give it a good shake) olive oil, lime juice, salt and pepper. Drizzle over watermelon and gently fold together to coat, being careful not to break up the chunks of watermelon.

3. Sprinkle with feta and fold together, again, being careful not to overmix.

4. Place in a serving dish and drizzle with agave or honey and top with fresh mint.

confetti CHOPPED SALAD JARS

GF | V YIELD 10 SALAD JARS

AVOCADO HERB DRESSING *(recipe follows)*

1½ heads iceberg **LETTUCE**, chopped

¾ cup shredded rainbow **CARROTS**

1 cup chopped **CELERY**

1 pint multi-colored heirloom **TOMATOES**, halved

1 cup blanched chopped **GREEN BEANS**

1 cup grated *(some call it riced)* **PURPLE CAULIFLOWER** *(white, green or yellow is fine too)*

½ cup medium diced **RED ONIONS**

1 cup medium diced **ENGLISH CUCUMBERS**

½ cup thinly sliced **RADISHES**, soaked in ice water

¾ cup **GREEN PEAS**

SPECIAL EQUIPMENT

10 wide-mouth pint **MASON JARS**

1. Place a few tablespoons of avocado herb dressing in the bottom of each mason jar. Add a big handful of chopped iceberg lettuce and add the remaining vegetables in layers (I listed ingredients in a colorful plan if you want to follow that), adding a couple more tablespoons of avocado ranch midway through.

2. Screw lid on and pack in the cooler for the beach.

Avocado Herb Dressing

GF | V YIELD 2 1/2 CUPS

1 cup whole milk **YOGURT** or **SOUR CREAM**

1 cup **BUTTERMILK**

2 ripe **AVOCADOS**

2 tablespoons **LEMON JUICE**

1 teaspoon **DIJON MUSTARD**

1 clove **GARLIC**

½ teaspoon **SEA SALT**

1 tablespoon chopped **DILL**

1 tablespoon chopped **CHIVES**

1 tablespoon chopped **PARSLEY**

Couple pinches **CAYENNE**

1. In the bowl of a food processor add yogurt, buttermilk, avocado, lemon juice, Dijon, garlic and salt and process until smooth.

2. Add herbs and cayenne and give it a quick pulse to combine. Chill until time of service.

cookout S'MORES

Mix-and-match s'mores would be all the rage for a beach party cookout, but would also be amazing for an outdoor party, graduation, wedding or birthday. Purchase assorted graham crackers or even use simple cookies as a base for your marshmallow sandwich. Feature your toasted marshmallow pillows with a variety of chocolate squares and sauces for serious s'more building—perhaps even add some ice cream (if your destination is suitable for keeping it frozen) for a designer s'more ice cream sandwich!

Large fluffy **MARSHMALLOWS** *(I like the square ones from Whole Foods)*

A variety of **GRAHAM CRACKERS**: chocolate, cinnamon and regular

Assorted **CHOCOLATE SQUARES** approximately 1 x 1 inch: white, mint, nut or fruited

CHOCOLATE ganache or sauce

BUTTERSCOTCH sauce

CARAMEL sauce

ALMOND, CASHEW or **PEANUT BUTTER**

Assorted **CANDY TOPPINGS**: peanut butter cups, Heath, Snickers, etc.

Sliced **STRAWBERRIES**, whole **RASPBERRIES** or **BLUEBERRIES**

Raspberry **JAM**

SPRINKLES

9 *(12-inch)* wooden **STICKS**

1 Place 2 marshmallows on a long marshmallow toasting steel skewer or fork. Toast over campfire until golden and gooey.

2 Place marshmallow between graham crackers and chocolate square of your choice.

3 Smear with extra sauces, nut butter or jams if desired.

key lime BEACH JARS

v   YIELD 8 JARS

CRUST

2 cups **GRAHAM CRACKER** crumbs

6 tablespoons unsalted **BUTTER**, melted

5 tablespoons **SUGAR**

A few pinches of **SEA SALT**

SPECIAL EQUIPMENT

8 mason **JARS**

LIME CUSTARD

2 *(14-ounce)* cans sweetened **CONDENSED MILK**

7 egg **YOLKS**

1 tablespoon plus 2 teaspoons **LIME ZEST** *(divided)*

1 cup fresh **KEY LIME JUICE** *(bottled is also fine)*

⅛ teaspoon **SEA SALT**

1 cup of **WHIPPED CREAM** for garnish

1. Preheat the oven to 350°F. Set jars onto a sheet pan.
2. Crush graham crackers in a ziplock bag with your hands or a rolling pin. Pour crumbs into a mixing bowl, add melted butter, sugar and a couple pinches of sea salt. Mix thoroughly with a fork.
3. Spoon graham cracker crumb mixture evenly into each of the eight jars.
4. Lightly give crumbs a pat once in jars.
5. In a medium bowl combine condensed milk, egg yolks, 1 tablespoon of lime zest and juice and sea salt. Whisk until blended well.
6. Divide lime custard evenly amongst the eight jars.
7. Bake for 15 to 18 minutes until custard is firm.
8. Let cool at room temperature for about 30 minutes. Sprinkle remaining lime zest on top of jars, cover with lids and bands and refrigerate for at least two hours until chilled.
9. When ready to serve, pop off the lid and add a dollop of whipped cream, if desired.

MERMAID **lemonade**

GF | V+   YIELD 8 SERVINGS

4 cups **LEMONADE**

1 cup **WHITE RUM**

¼ cup **BLUE CURACAO**

ICE

10 **LIME** wedges

10 **LEMON** slices

10 paper **UMBRELLAS** *(optional)*

1. In a large pitcher stir together lemonade, rum and Blue Curacao.
2. Fill 10 thin highball glasses with ice and fill with the lemonade mixture.
3. Squeeze lime wedge into each glass and garnish with lemon wheel and paper umbrella if desired.

Soft Beverage Beach Ideas

Flavored sparkling waters are an easy option and you will find that most stores carry 8-ounce versions of crowd pleasers such as berry combinations, lemon and lime.

Urban Picnic

I LOVE this chapter because it lends itself to so many different concepts, from lazy summer picnics to retro city living, all with the ease and relaxation of being in good company with your friends and family. This party could be happening in your backyard, at a park down the street, around your favorite picnic spot or up north while camping.

For this section, I am going all-in with my wish list of all things cool and urban!

Depending on your circumstances of travel and dedication to conjuring your setting, you can head in many directions, from simple pop-up chairs and a picnic table to creating an interesting urban vibe with lots of trimmings.

If you are in your backyard, patio furniture will create a lovely seating area. Bring out oversize blankets and pillows for you and your guests. Maybe add a fun loveseat that comes outside for the day. String low-hanging bistro lighting over your outdoor area so that the lights hang just above your heads to create a lovely intimate space.

If you're taking the picnic on the road, a roll-up carpet could be a great place to work from to give your picnic space a good base layer. Wood pallets are a fun, inexpensive table option that you can often find at surplus box stores. If you're handy, add 4 x 4-inch legs to your pallet to create your table, or make them collapsible for easy travel. Use oversize pillows or low lounge chairs for seating, and interesting benches transported from your home or yard will offer additional seating for guests. When packing up your picnic supplies, use wood crates or containers that can double purpose as storage and extra serving spaces. An old trunk, large wicker baskets, metal end tables or tiered nesting tables can all be repurposed and used in this space. Fun streamers or twinkle lights weaved into the trees above will create a lovely ambiance as you head into the evening.

For your tablescape, try a simple runner of mixed cloth napkins that you can layer for a fun and colorful table base. If your picnic is indoors, use colored glass vases with votives. Outside, add battery-operated string lights that you can hang or weave through your tablescape or above in the trees if you will be heading into dusk. Fresh flowers always brighten up your table. Use simple bud vases for easy-pack travel containers. Pick bright, colorful blooms like pink garden roses, fuchsia peonies or a few stems of snapdragons from your garden, or create easy bouquets of field flowers and herbs spattered about. For serving vessels, I love the idea of old vintage Pyrex dishes here. For serving guests, think paper boats or recyclable bamboo plates and cutlery. Mason jars make salads an easy grab-and-go play. You'll want some fun activities for your guests, so don't forget to include some games. Maybe Yardzee, life-size Jenga or just some playing cards for after-dinner enjoyment.

Whether you are picnicking at home or taking your urban adventure on the road, this concept can be eclectic and mismatched with a retro feel, so just have fun with it!

detroit city FRIED CHICKEN

YIELD 8 PIECES

CHICKEN

1 whole all-natural **CHICKEN**, back removed, cut into 8 pieces *(2 each of leg, thigh, breast and wing)*

BRINE *(recipe below)*

2 quarts **PEANUT OIL**

FLOUR BLEND *(recipe below)*

4 whole **EGGS**, beaten

BRINE

2 cups **BUTTERMILK**

2 tablespoons **DILL PICKLE BRINE**

6 dashes of crystal **HOT SAUCE**

FLOUR BLEND

1 cup **ALL-PURPOSE FLOUR**

1 cup **POTATO STARCH**

1 tablespoon **SEA** or **KOSHER SALT**

1 teaspoon **BLACK PEPPER**

2 teaspoons **GARLIC POWDER**

1. Place chicken pieces in a gallon-size ziplock bag on a sheet pan.

2. For the brine, combine the brine ingredients and pour over the chicken. Seal the bag, removing as much air as possible, and place the chicken on the sheet pan in the refrigerator overnight. When ready to cook, pull the chicken from the brine and pat dry with paper towels. Discard brine.

3. Heat peanut oil in a medium-large heavy-bottom pot until a deep-fry thermometer reaches 350°F.

4. Set up a line for breading the chicken. In one bowl add the flour mixture, in another the beaten eggs and at the end of the line have a cooling rack on a sheet pan as a place to rest your chicken. Working with one piece of chicken at a time, dredge chicken in the flour mixture, shake off excess flour, dip in the beaten eggs, roll/press again in the flour mixture and let rest on the rack. Repeat with remaining chicken pieces.

5. With long metal tongs, carefully submerge a few pieces of chicken at a time into peanut oil, being careful not to overcrowd, and fry the coated chicken until an internal temperature of 165°F is reached, turning chicken in oil if any part of a piece appears to be exposed. Add more peanut oil if needed, being careful to maintain the 350°F temperature of the oil. Once cooked, remove chicken and place on a sheet tray lined with paper towels to blot dry. Serve hot or at room temperature.

SAUCE trio

Detroit Hot Honey

GF | V

YIELD 1/2 CUP

½ cup local **HONEY**

1 teaspoon **RED PEPPER FLAKES**

5 to 6 dashes **TABASCO** hot sauce

2 cloves **GARLIC**, crushed

1. In a small bowl, stir all of the ingredients until well combined.

2. Store in an airtight container until ready to use.

Hamtramck "Ranch"

GF | V

YIELD 1 CUP

½ cup **BUTTERMILK**

½ cup **SOUR CREAM**

1 bunch fresh **DILL**, chopped

2 tablespoons chopped **PARSLEY**

1 clove **GARLIC**, minced

2 tablespoons **WHITE VINEGAR**

1 tablespoon **ONION POWDER**

2 teaspoons **SEA SALT**

1 teaspoon **BLACK PEPPER**

1 tablespoon minced **CHIVE** *(optional)*

1. Add ranch ingredients to a small mason jar and shake to combine.

2. Store in the refrigerator until ready to use.

Dearborn Butter Chicken Sauce

GF | V

YIELD 1 1/2 CUPS

1 cup **GREEK YOGURT**

½ cup **TOMATO PUREE**

2 **GARLIC** cloves, minced

1 teaspoon chopped or finely grated **GINGER**

1½ teaspoons **GARAM MASALA**

1 teaspoon **CUMIN**

½ teaspoon **CAYENNE**

1 bunch **CILANTRO**, chopped

1. Add sauce ingredients to a small mason jar and shake to combine.

2. Store in the refrigerator until ready to use.

summer CORN AND AVOCADO SLAW

GF | DF | V   YIELD 10 TO 12 SERVINGS

SLAW

3 cups cooked CORN, fresh or frozen

1 (8-ounce) bag tricolor COLESLAW or BROCCOLI SLAW mix

1 pint cherry or grape TOMATOES, halved

1 cup ENGLISH CUCUMBER, medium dice

½ cup finely diced RED ONION

3 AVOCADOS, medium dice

VINAIGRETTE

⅔ cup blended OLIVE OIL

¼ cup fresh LIME JUICE

1 teaspoon grated LIME ZEST

1 large bunch CILANTRO, chopped (heaping ¼ cup)

2 tablespoons HONEY or AGAVE SYRUP

¾ teaspoon SALT

½ teaspoon BLACK PEPPER

1. In a large bowl add all the prepared vegetables. Gently toss together to combine.

2. In a small blender or food processor combine the vinaigrette ingredients. Blend together until emulsified.

3. Pour ½ cup of vinaigrette over salad. Gently toss together and refrigerate for an hour or more. Remove slaw from the fridge and drain excess liquid that may have leached from vegetables. Taste slaw and adjust seasoning and give it another drizzle of vinaigrette if needed.

crunchy PICNIC PEA SALAD

GF   YIELD 10 TO 12 SERVINGS

4 cups frozen or fresh blanched GREEN PEAS

1¾ cups dry roasted salted PEANUTS

1¾ cup small diced CELERY

½ cup small diced RED ONION

1 small bunch PARSLEY, chopped

12 strips of BACON, cooked and chopped medium

8 hard-boiled EGGS, diced (optional)

DRESSING

¾ cup SOUR CREAM

½ cup MAYONNAISE

3 tablespoons BRAGG APPLE CIDER VINEGAR

2 tablespoons SUGAR

2 teaspoons ONION POWDER

1½ teaspoons SEA SALT

¾ teaspoon BLACK PEPPER

1. In a large bowl add all the salad ingredients and toss to combine.

2. In a small bowl add the dressing ingredients and whisk together to combine.

3. Fold dressing into the salad until evenly coated. Taste and adjust seasonings if necessary.

Chef's Notes

It is easy to prep this salad a day or more in advance, but do not dress until close to time of service so peanuts are not soggy from sitting for hours in dressing.

CITRUS POTATO **salad**

GF | DF | V   YIELD 10 TO 12 SERVINGS

2 pounds FINGERLING POTATOES

1 teaspoon SALT

3 large CARROTS, peeled

1 medium WATERMELON RADISH, sliced into thin slices *(or ⅓ cup sliced red radishes)*

½ small RED ONION, sliced into thin julienned strips

3 tablespoons chopped PARSLEY *(reserve 1 tablespoon for garnish)*

½ teaspoon PEPPER

½ cup CITRUS VINAIGRETTE *(recipe follows)*

1   Place fingerling potatoes in a large pot and cover with water by an inch. Add a generous pinch of salt. Bring to a boil and reduce heat to medium. Cook until potatoes are tender, about 15 to 18 minutes. Drain well and allow to cool.

2   With a peeler, shred whole carrot from top to bottom to create long carrot ribbons.

3   In a large bowl add remaining salad ingredients. Drizzle with ½ cup of the citrus vinaigrette and toss until evenly coated. Adjust seasonings. Spoon into serving bowl and sprinkle with remaining tablespoon of parsley.

Citrus Vinaigrette

YIELD 1 1/2 CUPS

2 LIMES, juice and zest

1 LEMON, juice and zest

1 ORANGE, juice and zest

⅓ cup WHITE VINEGAR

2 tablespoons HONEY MUSTARD

⅔ cup BLENDED OIL

⅓ cup OLIVE OIL

1 teaspoon finely chopped fresh DILL

½ teaspoon SEA SALT

Couple pinches CAYENNE PEPPER

1   In a small blender add citrus juice, vinegar and mustard. Blend until incorporated. With blender on low speed, drizzle oils in a steady stream for about 30 seconds until fully emulsified.

2   Stir in citrus zest, dill, salt and cayenne pepper. Store in refrigerator for up to one week.

focaccia PICNIC SANDWICHES

After making or purchasing the best focaccia bread you can, there are no rules here. This is where you get to create sandwich pairings that you and your guests will love. If you have a lot of vegetarians, perhaps you're serving roasted vegetable or tomato mozzarella sandwiches. If you love meat and spice, maybe you will be making a picnic focaccia with salami, ham and muffuletta toppings. If you're a cheese head, then a soft goat cheese, havarti or gouda with fresh tomatoes, a little coleslaw and tomato jam might be your jam. Below I have shared some sandwich concepts to help you along your way! Check out the Contemporary Oktoberfest chapter for some great mustard and smear recipes.

VIRGINIA HAM: Swiss cheese | grilled onions | sliced tomato | lettuce | honey mustard smear

THE ITALIAN: Salami | ham | Italian muffuletta salad | yellow mustard

CALI TURKEY: Roasted turkey | gouda | avocado | sliced tomato | cucumber | pesto aioli

TURKEY BLT: Roasted turkey | applewood bacon | iceberg lettuce | tomato | cheddar | ranch smear

BEEF: Tender roast beef | white Vermont cheddar | pickled red onion | crisp lettuce

GREEK STREET: Red pepper hummus | sliced cucumbers | tomatoes | grilled zucchini | roasted peppers

THE VEGAN: Grilled vegetables | crisp lettuce | white bean smear, tomato jam or both

CAPRESE: Mozzarella | sliced tomato | garden basil | balsamic syrup

CHEESE HEAD: Goat cheese smear | gouda | dill Havarti | sliced tomato | vinaigrette coleslaw

THE MAKING OF A FOCACCIA SANDWICH

1 Lay focaccia on your workspace. If you're going to make two varieties, cut your bread sheet into 2 pieces.

2 Place your hand on top of the focaccia sheet and carefully run a serrated knife through the center of the piece to butterfly it. Place the top off to the side.

3 Build your sandwich from the bottom up. A couple of good rules to follow for any sandwich making:

- Create a moisture barrier on the bottom of the sandwich to keep ingredients from traveling with gravity and sogging out your sandwich. A moisture barrier could be a leaf of lettuce, smear of butter or soft cheese base layer.

- Place your heaviest ingredients on top of the moisture barrier. This will most likely be your main ingredient such as the meat, fresh mozzarella, etc.

- Start layering your toppings—onions, salads, slaws, tomatoes—then add your chosen condiment—mayo, mustard, tomato jam, pesto—and top it off with a slice of cheese if that is part of the plan.

- By keeping the heavier ingredients on the bottom, you will deliver a well-crafted sandwich where you are not left with a soggy-bottomed bread.

- Once your focaccia sandwich is composed, replace the top and give it a firm pat. Using a serrated knife, cut the sandwich into strips 2 to 2 ½ inches wide and 3 inches long. This will allow for a few nice bites at a picnic where there are many other food options. Take the time to measure your bread and do a little math to figure out how to get the most cuts.

4 Take the sandwiches and cut parchment or deli paper to a size close to the length of the sandwich, leaving ends exposed; it

will be a band around the sandwich. Seal with a piece of tape on the bottom and tie a little knotted twine around the paper. You cannot tape parchment paper because it does not stick, so if using parchment, omit the tape and just use twine. Deli paper works well with the extra security of tape.

5 Pack your sandwiches neatly in a box and place in a cooler or transport on a serving platter if serving immediately.

Chef's Notes

Optional: If you would like your sandwiches to be a little more compressed, wrap the whole sandwich snuggly with a couple layers of plastic wrap, lay them flat in the refrigerator and weigh them down with a heavy skillet, a couple large books or any weighted item for an hour or two before slicing.

Rustic Focaccia

This is a most special recipe from Certified Master Chef Jeff Gabriel. Chef Jeff is a big deal for many reasons: he is one of the ninety or so certified master chefs in the USA, he was my first mentor in culinary school, he has been teaching for over thirty years at Schoolcraft college in Livonia, Michigan and he is an amazing cook and baker and I am beyond grateful to call him my friend. This recipe from Chef Jeff has a step the day before which is well worth the time investment. You can find other recipes that skip this step, but I promise the extra work will not disappoint when you taste this amazing focaccia! Measurements are given in both weight and volume, so for this recipe I would encourage you to dig out your kitchen scale and weigh your ingredients for best results.

POOLISH

Poolish is a highly fluid yeast-cultured dough. It is a type of pre-ferment traditionally used in the production of French bakery products. A Poolish resembles a sponge from the sponge-and-dough system. Bread made with a pre-ferment will not only taste more complex with more of a wheat aroma and a pleasant tang, but it will have an improved structure, a deeper-colored crust and an extended shelf life. All these advantages from one additional pre-step.

1¼ cups WATER, room temperature

⅛ teaspoon dry instant YEAST

2¼ cups BREAD FLOUR

1   In a large bowl disperse yeast in water to dissolve.

2   Mix in flour until smooth and cover with plastic wrap.

3   Let sit at room temperature for 12 to 16 hours.

FINAL DOUGH

1 pound 4.8 ounces BREAD FLOUR (4 ¾ cups)

1.6 ounces WHEAT GERM, toasted (⅜ cup)

13.4 ounces WATER, room temperature (1⅝ cups)

0.6 ounces SALT (1 tablespoon)

0.13 ounces dry instant YEAST (1¼ teaspoon)

POOLISH (recipe above)

2 ounces OLIVE OIL (¼ cup)

OPTIONAL

Fresh ROSEMARY, chopped

PARMESAN CHEESE, grated

1   In the bowl of a stand mixer fitted with the dough attachment add all ingredients except olive oil. Mix on lowest speed for 3 minutes.

2   Increase mixer to next speed and drizzle olive oil in a slow steady stream. Mix for 3½ to 4 minutes, until gluten is developed.

3   Place the dough in a lightly oiled large bowl and cover tightly.

4   Let rise for 3 hours, folding the dough after each hour.

5   Generously oil a 12 x 16-inch sheet pan.

6   Flatten the dough to fit the sheet pan. If the dough is fighting back, let it rest a little longer.

7   Cover and let the dough rise for 1½ hours at room temperature.

8   After rising, poke holes in the dough with your fingers and brush with more olive oil.

9   You may top with fresh chopped rosemary and grated Parmesan cheese.

10   Bake in a preheated 450°F oven for about 20 minutes.

Chef's Notes

You can make sheets of focaccia days or weeks ahead of time. Let cool and wrap tightly with a few layers of plastic wrap and freeze. Pop out of the freezer the morning of and place in a 325°F oven for 5 to 7 minutes to give it a toast. You can serve focaccia bread as its own food with no fillings by using tasty toppings such as cheeses, pesto, grilled zucchini and Parmesan.

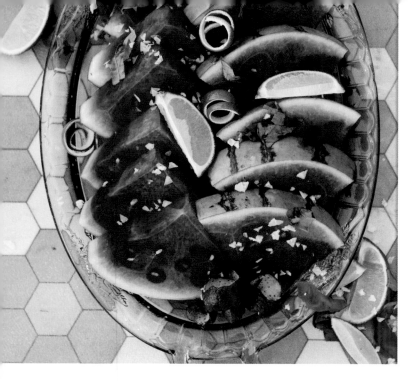

sliced WATERMELON WITH LIME WEDGES

GF | V+

Watermelon and lime are an easy and refreshing snack for your guests to enjoy, and who doesn't love fresh, cool watermelon on a hot summer day? No recipe here. Slice watermelon in half horizontally so you have a flat surface to work with. Cut watermelon into 1-inch-thick half-moons and slice each moon into 3 to 4 slices about 1½ inch thick. Serve with lime wedges and flaky sea salt for a little added flavor.

michigan CHERRY HAND PIES

V   YIELD 18 TO 20 PIES

Pie Crust

5½ cups ALL-PURPOSE FLOUR

4 tablespoons and 1 teaspoon granulated SUGAR

1½ teaspoons BAKING POWDER

1 teaspoon SALT

¼ teaspoon CINNAMON

6 tablespoons cold unsalted BUTTER

4 tablespoons cold VEGETABLE SHORTENING

10 to 12 tablespoons ICE WATER

1 In the bowl of a food processor fitted with the blade attachment add flour, sugar, baking powder, salt and cinnamon. Pulse to combine.

2 Cut butter and shortening into small cubes, add to bowl and pulse in short pulses until the mixture resembles small pea-size pieces.

3 Add ice water a couple tablespoons at a time and pulse carefully until your dough forms a ball.

4 Remove from the food processor and flatten into a disk. Wrap with plastic wrap and store in the refrigerator for an hour or more.

Pie Filling

2 cups pitted tart MICHIGAN CHERRIES

¼ cup dried MICHIGAN CHERRIES

¼ cup SUGAR

2 teaspoons fresh LEMON JUICE

¼ teaspoon CINNAMON

2 pinches of SEA SALT

1 tablespoon CORNSTARCH

3 cups VEGETABLE OIL or SHORTENING for frying

POWDERED SUGAR for dusting

SPECIAL EQUIPMENT

3½- to 4-inch round CUTTER

Deep fry THERMOMETER

1 Place pitted and dried cherries in a medium saucepan. Add sugar, lemon juice, cinnamon and salt. Cook over medium heat for 5 to 6 minutes until sugar dissolves and dried cherries have plumped a bit. Take a few large spoonfuls from the hot pot, place in a small bowl and stir in cornstarch.

2 Return the cherry mixture to low heat and simmer for 4 to 6 minutes until thickened. Cool and refrigerate for an hour or more.

HAND PIE ASSEMBLY

1 Remove pie dough from the fridge 10 to 15 minutes before rolling. Line a sheet pan with parchment paper.

2 Place pie dough on a very lightly floured work surface and roll dough to about ⅛-inch thickness. Using a 3½- to 4-inch round

- It is best not to fry hand pies before the day you plan to serve them, but if you want to get a jump, you can fry them earlier in the day and hold the pies at room temperature until service.

- If you want to skip a step, purchase already prepared pie dough from the market.

- If you are in a huge rush, pick up a can of pie filling and a box of premade crust, assemble the hand pies and bake them in the oven instead of frying.

- Of course, this concept would be great with most any fruit!

cutter, cut circles and place on the prepared sheet pan. Re-roll dough scraps and repeat. Place circles back in the fridge for 10 minutes.

3 Remove dough circles from the fridge and, one by one, fill with two tablespoons pie filling. Fold pie dough over to make a half-moon shape and use a fork to crimp the edges closed. Place on the same sheet pan and return to the freezer.

4 While the pies are in the freezer, in a medium heavy-bottom pot add about 3 cups vegetable oil or shortening and heat to 350°F. Line a sheet pan with paper towels.

5 Remove hand pies from the freezer and, using a small metal basket, slotted spoon or tongs, carefully (one at a time) place 5 to 6 pies into hot oil. Fry for 4 minutes or so, flip to the other side and repeat. Remove from hot oil and place on the prepared pan to drain excess oil. Repeat until all the hand pies are fried.

6 Place on a platter and sprinkle with powdered sugar.

Chef's Notes

- This is a great prep-ahead recipe. You could assemble the hand pies completely and freeze them on a sheet pan. After the pies are frozen, transfer them to a ziplock freezer bag and store in your freezer for frying or baking another day.

- If frying is not your thing, place pies on parchment-lined sheet pan, brush with egg wash and bake at 375°F for 10 to 12 minutes until golden brown. Dust with powdered sugar after baking or sprinkle coarse sugar on top before baking.

LEMON CURD yard jar

YIELD 12 4-OUNCE MASON JARS

Lemon Curd

GF | V YIELD 3 1/2 CUPS

12 large EGG YOLKS

1¾ cups granulated SUGAR

1 cup freshly squeezed LEMON JUICE

Zest of 3 large LEMONS

2 sticks of BUTTER, cut into 1-tablespoon slices

Couple pinches SEA SALT

GARNISH

1 pint BLACKBERRIES

1 To create a double boiler add 3 to 4 inches of water to a large pot and bring water to a simmer.

2 In a large metal bowl whisk egg yolks and sugar until combined. Add lemon juice and zest and place the bowl over the pot. Make sure the bottom of the bowl is not touching the water. Cook over medium-low heat, stirring occasionally for about 20 to 30 minutes until thickened and temperature reaches 175°F.

3 Remove from heat and strain lemon curd through a mesh sieve into another container or bowl. Add butter and salt and whisk. Strain a second time into another clean bowl or storage container. Place a piece of plastic wrap on top so it is touching the curd to prevent a skin from forming. Let cool for 30 minutes and then refrigerate.

Buttermilk Pound Cake

V

1⅓ cups **BUTTER**, softened *(high quality such as Plugra or Kerrygold)*

2½ cups **SUGAR**

6 large **EGGS**

1 tablespoon **LEMON ZEST**

1 teaspoon **VANILLA EXTRACT**

3 cups **ALL-PURPOSE FLOUR**

½ cup full-fat **BUTTERMILK**

1. Preheat the oven to 350°F. Generously grease and flour a 9 x 13-inch baking pan. Shake off excess flour and set aside.

2. Using either a stand mixer fitted with the paddle attachment or a hand mixer and a large bowl, beat butter until light and creamy, scraping down sides as needed.

3. Set the mixer to medium speed and add sugar ½ cup at a time. Continue to mix, scraping down the bowl as needed until sugar is combined and mixture is soft and pale in color.

4. Add eggs, one at a time, scraping down sides of bowl as needed.

5. Add lemon zest and vanilla extract.

6. Reduce the speed to low and gradually add ⅓ of the flour alternating with half of the buttermilk. Mix until ingredients are combined. Do not overmix.

7. Pour batter into the prepared pan and bake for 30 to 35 minutes until lightly golden and a wooden skewer inserted into the center comes out clean or with a few moist crumbs.

8. Allow the cake to cool for 20 minutes. Run a knife around the sides of the pan and carefully transfer the cake to a cooling rack.

LEMON CURD YARD JAR ASSEMBLY
SPECIAL EQUIPMENT

12 4-ounce mason **JARS**

1. Cut buttermilk pound cake into a little over 2-inch-wide strips (like long rails). You will end up with four "rails." Cut each rail into 1½-inch slices.

2. Place a slice of pound cake in the bottom of each jar, top with ¼ cup of lemon curd, another slice of pound cake and another ¼ cup lemon curd.

3. Garnish top with a blackberry or two.

Chef's Notes

You could certainly make these a day in advance, store in the refrigerator and top with the lid for transport.

RHUBARB STRAWBERRY lemonade

GF | V+   YIELD 1 GALLON OR 10 TO 12 SERVINGS

5 cups **WATER** *(divided)*

3 cups chopped **RHUBARB STALKS**

1½ cups **SUGAR**

Peel of 1 **LEMON**

¾ teaspoon **VANILLA EXTRACT**

2 pints **STRAWBERRIES**, sliced *(reserve ½ cup of slices)*

1½ cups freshly squeezed **LEMON JUICE**

GARNISH

LEMON SLICE

1. In a large, heavy-bottom pot bring 1 ½ cups of water, rhubarb, sugar, lemon peel and vanilla to a boil. Reduce heat to low and simmer for two minutes.

2. Remove from heat and stir in strawberries. Let steep and cool for 20 minutes.

3. Strain mixture through a fine sieve, pressing firmly with a wooden spoon. Discard solids. Place your rhubarb strawberry simple syrup in a large serving pitcher. Stir in remaining water and lemon juice. Refrigerate to chill. Before serving add sliced strawberries and serve over ice garnished with a lemon slice if desired.

Chef's Notes

The most time-consuming part of this recipe is the rhubarb sugar simple syrup. You can make the simple syrup days ahead and mix with lemon juice and water when you are ready to serve. The simple syrup would also be a great addition for a summer craft cocktail with vodka and a spritz of soda water. That would look like: 1 ½ ounces vodka, 2 ounces rhubarb syrup and 4 ounces sparkling water over ice. Rum would be a good option too!

Urban Picnic Behind the Scenes

I felt compelled to shout out some local brands rich in history that made the Urban Picnic chapter so special. You may also consider finding a special picnic site and celebrating your hometown's local brands!

LOCATION

Our urban picnic was in the city of Detroit at the Pierce House. This modern cinder block home was the brainchild of Cranbrook Architecture Master's students Matthew Miller and Thomas Gardner. Celebrated artist Beau Stanton created the vibrant murals. The house was later overhauled by Jason Lindy who currently operates it as a thriving boutique bed-and-breakfast. Many items in the home are made from local artisans and craftspeople, and the entire space is a constantly changing canvas of Detroit-themed artifacts.

Bea's Squeeze Lemonade

beassqueeze.com

Bea's Squeeze Lemonade is an amazing local company in the heart of Detroit with the best lemonade!

Better Made Potato Chips

bettermade.com

Cross and Peters Company was founded on August 1, 1930. The company was named after the founders' first names, Cross and Peter. Both set goals to make a better potato chip, hence the brand name BETTER MADE.

Display Group

displaygroup.com

Our benefactor for most of the outdoor furniture, Display Group is an amazing special event rental company in Detroit, Michigan and beyond! A big shout out to Cassie, who was our designer on the project and joined us at the picnic.

Star-Spangled Banner

Menu

GF/Gluten Free, DF/Dairy Free, V/Vegetarian, V+/Vegan

Take an MYO approach to your patriotic party by selecting three to four dogs from the menu below or get creative with pairings of your design. Place the toppings in small bowls, cute tins, mason jars or empty ten- to fifteen-ounce cans placed on separate themed trays with a menu card.

Purchase disposable white spoons that have a large enough handle to take a small-tip permanent marker and write the name of the condiment to help guests with their choices. Include a small food sign on each condiment tray to help guide your guests to make a successful hot dog creation. After your guests take the hot dog out of the heating tray and place it in a bun, they can move on to the different topping vignettes. It's no problem if you want to put hot dogs in buns ahead of time and place them out for your guests, but I would keep them separate if the guests are eating at sporadic times.

Summer is in full swing and this is such a fun holiday to decorate for. I think of family and friend gatherings in the backyard or maybe on the lake, enjoying some of the best backyard BBQ all year long and finishing with fireworks later in the evening. Often at Fourth of July parties you will find the quintessential Betsy Ross décor which is a great classic approach. American flags, banners, balloons, raffia and baby's breath leave you with a feel of patriotic times past. Another thought would be to approach the day with a modern look. I always like to stay with the classic colors of red, white and blue, but use them unexpectedly or in a more modern way.

For decorating your star-spangled party, think American flags, pennants, banners and balloons. Tie raffia on simple milk glasses to create vases and fill with florals like blue hydrangea, red roses, deep red poppies, red gerbera daisies or even eucalyptus. Maybe you have old watering cans hiding in the garage—fill them with full blue and white florals and place on your porch to welcome guests or use as a centerpiece on your picnic table. Keep things light and airy with simple blooms. I like to make the flowers look like they are popping out of the vase or containers like fireworks.

For your table, keep your linens crisp white to have all your colors pop. You can also bring in a blue buffalo check or gingham linen or napkin. As for serving pieces, think of crisp white trays, ceramic pieces and plates. You can lean a bit more rustic with galvanized pieces or maybe think out of the box with some vintage pieces from your favorite local resale store. Tin buckets, white milk glasses and mason jars all feel at home here and can be used for anything from utensils to serving snacks for guests. Easy disposable plates that match your party vibe or large paper boats would be fun with the hot dog party. Hard plastic plates in patriotic colors would work here. I often check the stores after a season has passed to see what I can grab at a discount and stash it for next year!

For icing beverages, shy away from the traditional old school coolers and opt instead for a big red wheelbarrow or galvanized tubs filled with ice. A red flyer wagon on the table with prepackaged snacks would make an easy display and an awesome conversation piece.

Since you will likely be outside, don't forget to decorate your yard. Create star templates and spray paint some red, white and blue stars on the lawn! You can turn them into a fun game for kids. Have outdoor games set up around the yard for your guests to enjoy. I love bistro lighting strung through trees or on your deck to create a more intimate area for your guests. You can usually find fun star-shaped lighting or even paper lanterns to dress it up as well. Set up little conversation areas around the yard with outdoor rugs, a few pillows and throw blankets and move your patio into the yard so your guests will have a comfortable place to hang out. Add a few citronella candles later in the evening if you plan to be outside after dark or are planning a fireworks display from your party spot later in the evening. All these thoughtful, fun touches will create an unforgettable star-spangled event that your guests are sure to remember for years to come!

HOT DOG **palooza**

The hot dog party is a great go-to menu for a patriotic party, but also works well for sports themes, graduations, birthdays, late-night wedding snacks or a just-because party. Fancy party dogs are also a very affordable food, and your guests will leave saying, "Wow, that was a fun idea!"

- Choose 3 or 4 pairings from the menu below.

- The general rule is 2 hot dogs per person. Use all-beef hot dogs, and you can mix it up with skin on dogs, kosher, vegan, etc.

- Provide 1½ to 2 cups of each condiment to match the themed dog. Look at each pairing as its own micro recipe. If two trays have coleslaw, you would need a cup and a half or more times two.

- For cheese, cut 4 to 5 slices of cheese into thin 1-inch rails so people can tuck them into their buns or use queso fundido.

- I like the ¼ sheet trays (9 x 13 inches) as a base to arrange condiments for each themed dog. These are easily available online or at your local restaurant supply store, but if you have large 10-inch dinner plates, that will work as well. Place your condiments in small ramekin bowls or short mason jars, place them up on the tray or plate and include a small menu card detailing each hot dog theme.

- Purchase white plastic or wooden spoons that have handles large enough to write on and print what each condiment is. This is optional as most things explain themselves, but it looks super cute and there are some condiments people might wonder about. For instance, could BBQ sauce be mistaken for ketchup?

- It's always a good idea to have yellow mustard and a ketchup bottle on the table for your guests who want a simple dog.

Hot Dog Blueprint Menu

Of course, design your own combos too!

CHICAGO STYLE: Tomatoes | onions | neon relish | pickles | yellow mustard

SOUTHERN BELLE: Chili | creamy slaw | corn

VEGAN PUP: Plant-based hot dog | vinaigrette coleslaw | chopped tomatoes | avocado

BACON SLAW DOG: Sweet and sour coleslaw | crisp bacon pieces

BIG APPLE DOG: Chili | diced onions

REUBEN DOG: Corned beef | Swiss cheese | sauerkraut | Russian dressing

LONE STAR STATE DOG: Queso fundido | grilled onions | pickled jalapeños

PIZZA PARLOR PUP: Marinara | mozzarella cheese | pepperoni

PIGGY BBQ: Grilled hot dogs basted with BBQ sauce | extra side of BBQ sauce | cheddar cheese | crispy onions

TURKEY DOG: Coleslaw | diced tomatoes | ketchup

2U TURKEY CLUB: Muenster cheese | coleslaw | chopped bacon | Russian dressing

PHILLY GRILL DOG: Provolone cheese | sautéed mushrooms | peppers | onions

BAHN MI: Mayo | thinly sliced English cucumber | thinly sliced jalapeño | diced red onion | fresh cilantro | peanuts | carrot slaw
(Carrot slaw is grated carrot with sugar and white or rice wine vinegar, soaked and drained before serving.)

Two Unique Golden Onion

GF | V   YIELD 8 TO 10 SERVINGS

1 tablespoon **OLIVE OIL**

2 large **SPANISH ONIONS**, diced

1 tablespoon **BROWN SUGAR**

2 tablespoons **WATER** *(or more as needed)*

¾ cup **MAYONNAISE**

¾ cup **CREAM CHEESE**, softened

2 teaspoons **BRAGG APPLE CIDER VINEGAR**

2 teaspoons **ONION POWDER**

¼ teaspoon **GARLIC POWDER**

Couple pinches **CAYENNE**

SEA SALT and **PEPPER** to taste

1 Heat olive oil in a large sauté pan over medium heat. Add onions and sprinkle with brown sugar. Sauté onion mixture, adding a tablespoon of water every few minutes to help the caramelization process along, stirring occasionally until onions are cooked through and golden. Remove from heat and let cool for 5 to 10 minutes.

2 In a food processor, add remaining ingredients and blend until mixture comes together. Add sautéed onions and pulse a few times until onions are incorporated, but you can still see flickers of onion pieces.

3 Place in a serving bowl and garnish with sea salt.

FREESTYLE: If preparing pre-arranged themed condiment trays is not your thing, you can take a freestyle condiment approach by labeling spoons to guide your guests instead of suggesting pairings in a menu. Again, the rule of thumb would be two hot dogs per person and 1½ to 2 cups of each condiment. Listed below are some condiment options.

Spicy Mayo	Cheese Sauce
Ketchup/Mustard	Chili
Relish	Jalapeños
Bacon	Pickled Onions
Barbecue Sauce	Crispy Onions
Salsa/Mango salsa	Chopped Onions
Sharp Cheddar Cheese	Chopped Tomatoes
Queso Fundido	

DIP duo

GF | V

Every summer party needs a delicious dip or two! Two of my favorites that we make at Two Unique are our Golden Onion and Spinach Artichoke dip. Put these out before the main attraction and pop back in the fridge for a later-day nibble. Serve dips with veggie coins of cucumbers and sliced carrots along with thick cut-potato chips, tortilla chips and crostini.

THE BEST EVER baked beans

GF | DF   YIELD 20 SERVINGS

10 pieces APPLEWOOD BACON, diced

⅓ cup chopped ONIONS

⅓ cup diced CELERY

⅓ cup diced GREEN PEPPERS

½ JALAPEÑO, seeds removed, and chopped

1 small BAY LEAF

1 teaspoon ground CORIANDER

½ teaspoon THYME

¼ teaspoon ground CINNAMON

3 (28-ounce) cans BUSH'S BAKED BEANS

⅓ cup BROWN SUGAR

⅓ cup YELLOW MUSTARD

⅓ cup BARBEQUE SAUCE

Spinach Artichoke

GF | V   YIELD 8 TO 10 SERVINGS

3 cups drained, coarsely chopped ARTICHOKE HEARTS

1 cup coarsely chopped BABY SPINACH

¼ cup small diced RED PEPPERS

⅔ cup MAYONNAISE

½ cup SOUR CREAM

1 teaspoon ONION POWDER

½ teaspoon GARLIC POWDER

2 teaspoons LEMON ZEST

2 tablespoons LEMON JUICE

¼ cup grated PARMESAN CHEESE

½ teaspoon SEA SALT

Pinch of CAYENNE

Fresh HERBS (garnish, optional)

1. In a large bowl add artichokes, spinach and peppers and toss to combine.

2. In a small bowl add remaining ingredients and whisk together.

3. Fold mayonnaise mixture into artichoke mixture. Adjust seasonings if necessary.

4. Place in a serving bowl and garnish with fresh herbs.

1. Preheat the oven to 300°F.

2. In a large sauté pan add bacon and cook over medium heat for 2 to 3 minutes until fat is rendered. Add onions, celery, green pepper, jalapeño pepper, bay leaf and spices. Reduce heat to medium-low and cook for 2 to 3 minutes until vegetables are soft. Remove from heat.

3. In a large baking dish add beans, brown sugar, mustard, BBQ sauce and bacon mixture. Stir to combine. Cover the pan with foil. Transfer to the oven and bake for 2 hours.

tangy SOUTHERN SLAW

GF | DF | V   YIELD 10 TO 12 SERVINGS

1 small *(or half of a large)* head of **CABBAGE**, thinly sliced or shredded

1 *(10-ounce)* bag of **BROCCOLI SLAW MIX** *(bagged in produce cooler section)*

1 medium **BELL PEPPER**, diced small

½ cup diced **RED ONION**

2 **CARROTS**, grated

1 cup **BRAGG APPLE CIDER VINEGAR**

⅓ cup **HONEY**

¼ cup granulated **SUGAR**

⅔ cup **SAFFLOWER OIL**

1 teaspoon **DRY MUSTARD**

1 teaspoon **CELERY SEEDS**

1 teaspoon **SEA SALT**

¼ teaspoon ground **BLACK PEPPER**

Pinch **CAYENNE PEPPER**

1. To process cabbage, cut into quarters and slice each quarter into thin shreds, leaving the core behind. Place in a large bowl with broccoli slaw, bell pepper, onions and carrots. Toss to combine.

2. To make the vinaigrette, in a blender add vinegar, honey and sugar. Blend on high until combined. Reduce speed to medium and slowly stream in safflower oil until emulsified. Add seasonings and pulse once or twice to bring everything together.

3. Add vinaigrette to the slaw mixture and stir until vegetables are evenly coated. Chill slaw in the refrigerator for a few hours or overnight.

4. Before serving, drain extra liquid and adjust seasonings if necessary.

SUMMER TOMATO LOVER'S **pasta salad**

V   YIELD 20 SERVINGS

VINAIGRETTE

¾ cup **OLIVE OIL**

¼ cup **TOMATO SAUCE** *(or ½ cup diced tomato, ground)*

¼ cup **RED WINE VINEGAR**

3 cloves **GARLIC**, minced

SALAD

¼ cup fresh chopped **PARSLEY**

20 **BASIL LEAVES**, chiffonade

1 pound of **ORECCHIETTE PASTA** or noodle of your choice, cooked

2 pints or 4 cups of multi-colored petit grape or heirloom **TOMATOES**

2 *(8-ounce)* containers of **BOCCONCINI**, sliced in half or 1 pound of fresh mozzarella, grated

1 teaspoon **SEA SALT**

¾ teaspoon freshly **GROUND PEPPER**

1. To make the vinaigrette, blend olive oil, tomato sauce, red wine vinegar and garlic and set aside.

2. In a large bowl mix salad ingredients.

3. Toss vinaigrette thoroughly with salad and adjust seasoning if needed.

4. Serve or store dressed until service.

myo SUMMER SHORTCAKE BAR

The sky's the limit with a fun MYO shortcake bar. Mix and match by adding sprinkles, fruit and even chocolate and caramel sauces for a festive sweet ending to a summer event. Below I share my Grandma Ruth's scone-style shortcake recipe, but if you are pressed for time, pick up some shortcakes or a classic pound cake at your favorite bakery or store.

Grandma Ruth's Scone-Style Shortcakes

V   YIELD 24 TO 26 PIECES

7 cups of **FLOUR**

¾ cup **SUGAR**

¼ cup **BAKING POWDER**

2 ½ teaspoons **SALT**

1 cup cold **BUTTER**, diced into small pieces

4 cups **HEAVY WHIPPING CREAM**

2 **EGGS**

3 tablespoons **MILK**

5 tablespoons course or raw **SUGAR**

1. Preheat the oven to 325°F. Line a sheet pan with parchment paper.

2. In the bowl of a stand mixer fitted with the paddle attachment add flour, sugar, baking powder and salt. Paddle until dry ingredients are mixed.

3. Add cold butter and mix on low for about a minute until butter is in small pea-size pieces and mixed with flour thoroughly.

4. With the mixer on low, stream heavy cream in quickly. Let paddle work in cream for five or six turns.

5. Turn dough onto lightly floured workspace and knead by hand to work out any dry pockets of flour. Form dough in a large square sheet about ½-inch thick.

6 Using a 3-inch ring cutter, cut circles and place on the prepared sheet pan. Lightly knead leftover ends into another ½-inch-thick sheet and repeat.

7 For the egg wash, in a small bowl whisk eggs and milk together.

8 Brush tops of shortcake scones with egg wash and sprinkle with a little coarse sugar.

9 Bake for 12 to 15 minutes until lightly golden and baked through.

10 Cool and platter for service or store in an airtight container.

Chef's Notes

- If your butter seems to warm a bit when cutting into small pieces, place it in the freezer for 10 minutes.

- A handy time saver is to make dough, roll, cut and freeze on a sheet pan with parchment in between layers. Pop out the freezer. Place on a parchment-lined sheet pan, thaw for 30 minutes, egg wash and bake.

- You can pre-bake scones. To store scones, lay parchment paper in between layers and freeze in an airtight container. Remove baked scones from the freezer. Place on a sheet pan, let thaw for an hour and then toast for 5 minutes in the oven at 325°F.

Toppings for Shortcake

YIELD 20 TO 25 SERVINGS

Of course, all of these are not essential—select 3 to 6 or all if you like!

ROASTED STONE FRUIT *(recipe at right)*

CHOCOLATE GANACHE *(recipe at right)*

MULTI BERRY MÉLANGE *(recipe at right)*

2 cups pitted, halved **CHERRIES** *(or cherry pie filling)*

3 cups **WHIPPED CREAM**

1 cup or 8-ounce jar **CARAMEL SAUCE** *(store bought is fine)*

1 cup or 8-ounce jar **LEMON** or **LIME CURD**

½ cup toasted sliced **ALMONDS**

½ cup chopped **CANDIED NUTS**

½ cup toasted **COCONUT**

¼ cup assorted **SPRINKLES**

½ cup **CRUSHED TOFFEE** or **HEATH**

½ cup **CHOCOLATE** shavings or curls

Roasted Stone Fruit

GF | V+ YIELD ABOUT 3 1/2 CUPS

¾ cup **SUGAR**

⅛ teaspoon **NUTMEG**

⅛ teaspoon **CARDAMOM**

½ teaspoon **CINNAMON**

Few pinches **SEA SALT**

Juice of two large **ORANGES**

1 teaspoon pure **VANILLA**

3 **PEACHES**, pitted and cut into eighths

3 **PLUMS** or Italian **PRUNE PLUMS**, pitted and quartered

3 **NECTARINES**

4 **APRICOTS**, pitted and quartered

Total fruit should equal about 4 heaping cups, feel free to alter to your liking or what is available

1 tablespoon of unsalted **BUTTER** or **COCONUT OIL**

1. Preheat the oven to 400°F.

2. In a small bowl add sugar and spices and mix.

3. In a medium bowl whisk together orange juice and vanilla. Add stone fruit and gently toss to coat.

4. Rub butter or coconut oil on bottom of a 9 x 13-inch oven-proof baking dish. Lay fruit, cut side up, in a single layer. Sprinkle with sugar and spice mixture.

5. Bake for 20 to 25 minutes. If fruit seems a little pale, but cooked through, place under the broiler for 2 to 3 minutes. Serve warm or room temperature.

Chocolate Ganache

GF | V   YIELD 12 OUNCES

8 ounces high quality DARK CHOCOLATE
½ cup HEAVY CREAM

1. Finely chop chocolate and place in a heat-proof glass or metal bowl.

2. In a heavy-bottom saucepan add cream and warm over medium heat until almost to a boil. You will see little bubbles begin to form around the edges.

3. Pour the hot cream over the chocolate and let sit for a minute. With a fork or small whisk, incorporate cream and chocolate until silky smooth.

Multi Berry Mélange

GF | V+   YIELD 2 1/2 CUPS

2 pints BLUEBERRIES
2 pints RASPBERRIES
1 quart STRAWBERRIES, quartered
½ cup SUGAR

1. Place berries in a shallow bowl and sprinkle with sugar.

2. With a tablespoon, stir berries just a little so as not to break them. Let sit for 30 minutes to an hour.

3. Drain excess liquid and place in a serving dish.

FATRIOTIC mocktail

GF | V+   YIELD 10 SERVINGS

Try this super easy, clean and crisp summer beverage. We have made it a mocktail, but you can always spike it with a little vodka if adults are looking for a cocktail.

3 cups WATERMELON cubes *(the size of regular ice cubes)*
2 pints BLUEBERRIES
1 *(2-liter)* bottle SPRITE
1 liter SODA WATER

1. Line two sheet pans with plastic wrap. On one tray, lay the cut watermelon in a single layer so they do not touch. On the other, lay blueberries in a single layer. Place both in the freezer for a few hours before serving until completely frozen.

2. In a large pitcher combine Sprite and soda water.

3. In tall clear glasses (or plasticware cups), add 6 to 7 cubes of frozen watermelon and a heavy sprinkle of frozen blueberries. Top with sprite and soda water mixture.

GF/Gluten Free, DF/Dairy Free, V/Vegetarian, V+/Vegan

Graduation parties come in all sorts of sizes, shapes and flavors. Often these parties entertain guest lists up to seventy-five or more. A vast majority of these landmark events end up happening in the family's house or backyard, which will come with uncharted territory for many, including questions like: Do I get a tent or no tent? How much seating do I need?

Should I make the food or hire a catering company and what food fare menu is best to host such a large, diverse group? Questions will arise in every area from décor to food and everything in between. So many big decisions, and we are here to help you with it all!

RENTALS

Let us start with talking about the real estate you will be working with. Is your house big enough to host everyone if the weather is questionable? If the answer is no, then consider a frame or canopy tent. Canopies are most often less expensive than a frame tent, so start there if it works with your landscape. The argument could also be made that the tent is not just for a rainy day but also to shield people from the bright sun and enclose a space to give you more of a special event feel. Usually the tent rental company will come out and do a quick measure and look for in-ground sprinkler lines and such. Try not to get caught up in shopping from various rental companies. You may save a dollar here and there, but my advice is to talk to a couple of reputable rental companies and go with the one that seems to offer the best overall. The touted "you get what you pay for" is often true in the rental arena. You do not want to end up with a budget tent that might fly away with a strong wind or be dirty.

When thinking of seating, there are a few factors to consider such as the timeline of your event and the number of guests attending. If your party is going to have a longer window of six hours or more, chances are that people will come and go. If your party has a narrow timeline of three to four hours, chances are at one point, usually around an hour and a half after start, it is possible that everyone will be there at the same time. A general rule of thumb is to allow seating for sixty percent of your guests. Consider adding a few stand-up cocktail tables for casual guest gathering and do not forget to include your own outdoor patio seating, tables or seating in the house for your calculations. Many styles of seating are possible; I like the long six- or eight-foot tables combined end-to-end to create long communal tables of twelve or more. Mix a few rounds to create more space for easy socialization. The rental company can review table and tent sizes to best suit your needs, and most can put your plan on their computer system to show you a visual of how the tables and chairs will lay out under the tent. Do not forget serving tables for drinks and food, and maybe a memorabilia table with pics of the graduate and take-away gifts for the guests.

LINEN

Often rental companies can accommodate linen. If that is not the case, there are plenty of specialty linen rental companies. Linen should be the base for your design format. Perhaps you want to go with the "tried and true" school colors, which is the most popular. You can go either high school colors or upcoming college colors. You can also opt for clean white base linen and pull in fun bright colors to reflect the season or even the graduate's favorite color. I had one client do shimmery blue as it was her daughter's favorite color and another who did a flower power vintage theme using assorted brightly colored linens. My sister snatched up an amazing deal on some interesting sheets with a cool design and placed them over round tables and knotted four sides of the overhang. It was super cute. If you're looking for something a little less expensive that also offers an easy cleanup, consider covering your long tables in white or kraft-colored deli/butcher paper and taping the ends down to keep the wind from blowing them out of place.

CENTERPIECES & DÉCOR

There are no hard rules here, but be intentional and keep in mind the entire scope of your vision and theme including tabletops, centerpieces and colors. Here are a few suggestions:

- Consider a picture of the graduate on each table in lieu of, or in addition to, a centerpiece. Keep an eye out for inexpensive frames that have some commonality in style or color (I often have luck at the At Home store; athome.com).

- If you are heading to the floral zone, think about the season and what is readily available. For my daughter's grad party, I placed three yellow gerberas in small separate four-inch cylinder vases and cut the daisy so its large head rested on the top of the small vase. I included a framed picture of her from a myriad of life stages nested in the middle of three vases on each table. It cost around ten dollars per table. Simple clay pots with geraniums are a great way to reuse plant décor in your landscape. Large mason jars with simple farmers market flowers make a great MYO centerpiece. I love mason jars as they are so versatile. Try painting them to add a pop of color, and they would look amazing with simple field flowers.

- Place writable chalkboard stickers on your vase or jar with a sentiment for the graduate.

- If your graduate is an athlete, use sports memorabilia. Fill mason jars with corn syrup and metallic confetti that people will be drawn to shake like a snow globe. Once I had a client place different superhero figurines into her centerpieces.

- Succulents are inexpensive and not too frilly. Plant them into small mason jars, wood bowls or tin vessels and then keep them or give them away to some of your special guests. Keep an eye out long before the party for a closeout on vases, jars and containers that would match your vision.

- Hang photos of the graduate from helium balloons to create a colorful cluster in the house. The floating photo memories are the perfect way to decorate your home for a graduation party or make a banner/garland capturing a timeline of photos that can be hung inside or out.

- Paper globes clustered on a piece of string, rope or ribbon as a garland against a wall or ceiling in a tent add an interesting pop of fun color.

- String twinkle lights in your tent, bushes or trees if your party is rolling into nighttime hours to add a special sparkle.

- Cluster balloons on tent poles or a bouquet on the front lawn so people do not have to look too hard for the address.

- Ribbon garland, linen panels draped behind a food station wall as a backdrop or sheer linen panels will bolster a mood setting. Check your local party supply store for festive banners.

- Tape white deli paper to the wall and have cups with colored pens or markers for guests to write a sentiment or future wish. You can also have a big jar with small note cards for people to write a wish and place it in the jar for reading later, or collect them at the end of the party and send a handful to your graduate every other week or so while they are up at school. It might ward off a smidge of homesickness or just make them smile.

- Make your own photo booth. Instant cameras have a vintage feel and create excitement and fun! Pick up a couple along with extra film and graduation props (hats, robes, funny large glasses, feather boas, oversize pencils, etc.). Suggest that your guests take two photos, one for your grad and one for the guest to take home.

- Create an Instagram hashtag for your grad's party so everyone can share their photos on the social platform.

- Do not forget music. Create a personal playlist and have extra speakers on hand if needed.

SERVING VESSELS AND PLATE WARE

The landscape is so vast in this arena, and you can go in so many directions with décor. White serving platters are most often a safe bet. You may be using chafing dishes for your hot items with a larger group. If your theme feels earthy, gravitate toward disposables such as bamboo and kraft boats. If you have a solid color theme, perhaps clear or white plates are the answer. Most often grad parties use disposable plates, and I would lean towards that for easier clean up at the end of the night.

Come Out and Play! DIY Yard Games

Graduation parties are often outdoors and can easily roll from day into evening, so why not provide the guests with some fun outdoor games to play? We have included a few simple DIY ideas below.

YARDZEE

Here's a super easy and fun DIY! Take a 4 x 4-inch wood post and cut out 6 perfectly square 4-inch cubes to make oversized dice. You can stain the wood and paint them with the dots to create your dice. We used an old tin bucket to shake them up and toss them on the ground. Keep score and see who wins!

GIANT JENGA

Another easy and simple DIY game you can make! Buy six 6-foot wood pieces measuring 2.5 inches wide by 1 by 1¼-inch thick. Cut these into perfect 7-inch-long pieces. These will create your timbers to stack. You can stain or paint these to customize them. Stack them 3 by 3 and create your Jenga—let's see who can keep it up the longest!

GIANT KERPLUNK

A childhood favorite supersized for your backyard! Take a large plastic planter, wrap it in chicken wire and use zip ties to adhere the chicken wire. Paint wooden dowels 4 different colors to slide through the gaps in the chicken wire and fill with some colorful plastic balls (the kind you would find in a child's ball pit) and you are all set!

TIC TAC TOE

Using a large slice of wood, paint the tic tac crosses. Once dry, use different colored rocks as your pieces.

snack CONES

Mix and match your favorite crunchy snacks, and then set them out and forget it. Choose vessels such as metal bowls or buckets with a liner, colored plastic bowls, tubs or large jars and fill with snacks and a small scoop. Let guests help themselves using paper cones and plastic or paper cups to carry away their own mix-and-match-made-personal snack.

Snack Supplies

There are countless healthy packaged snacks sold including veggie chips, petit rice cakes, pea straws, Hippeas and Skinny Pop. On the more traditional side, you will find a variety of flavored potato chips, popcorn, Frito chips, pretzels and nuts of many flavors. Depending on where you shop, packaged snacks can come in many different sizes, from 6-ounce bags all the way up to 40-ounce bags. Eight or more varieties will make a nice display, and depending on the size of your party, you may want to consider smaller bags to ensure you do not end up with a ton of leftovers. Go for the giant king-size bag if your guest list is larger. On average as a snack, 3 ounces would be a standard amount per person, so think about that when you are purchasing. Example: 75 people x 3 ounces per person = 225 ounces. Choose snacks, adding up ounces as you shop to meet your total amount.

GRADUATE MYO NACHO **blueprint**

This is a budget-friendly way to pump up your party offerings! Offer assorted-colored tortilla chips with oodles of toppings for ultimate nacho building that your guests can choose from. I like the medium-size brown kraft boats for these, as it keeps everything together for heaping ingredients onto chips.

MAIN FRAME

SOUTHWEST PULLED CHICKEN *(recipe below)*

TACO BEEF *(recipe below)*

3 to 4 large bags of **TORTILLA CHIPS** *(usually around 15 ounces per bag)*

COLD SAUCES

GUACAMOLE *(recipe below)*

BAJA SALSA *(recipe below)*

SOUR CREAM, 1½ cups

LIME CILANTRO SOUR CREAM, 2 cups *(juice of ½ lime and 2 tablespoons chopped cilantro mixed in with 2 cups sour cream)*

QUESO SAUCE, 4 cups, warm. You can make your favorite Queso Fundido or there are many good quality jarred varieties in the stores.

EXTRA SPRINKLES

3 cups shredded **CHEESES**	Grilled **ONIONS**, diced, ¾ cup
¾ cup pickled **JALAPEÑO**	Sliced **BLACK OLIVES**, ½ cup
¼ cup diced **RED ONIONS**	Shredded **LETTUCE**, 3 cups
¼ cup diced grilled **PEPPERS**	Diced **TOMATOES**, 2 cups

southwest PULLED CHICKEN

GF | DF   YIELD 3 TO 10 SERVINGS, ABOUT 2 POUNDS

½ cup of your favorite **SALSA**

2 tablespoons **OLIVE OIL**

1 tablespoon fresh chopped **GARLIC**

1 tablespoon ancho **CHILI POWDER**

1 tablespoon **CUMIN**

2 teaspoons **ONION POWDER**

½ teaspoon **SEA SALT**

Juice of two **LIMES**

1½ pounds boneless, skinless **CHICKEN THIGHS** *(or butterflied breasts or combination of both)*

2 tablespoons fresh **CILANTRO**, chopped

1. Preheat your outdoor grill to medium heat.

2. To make the marinade, in a large bowl add salsa, olive oil, garlic, all spices and lime juice. Stir until combined.

3. Add the chicken and mix until the chicken is evenly coated. Let the chicken marinate for an hour or feel free to prep the day before and marinate overnight in the refrigerator.

4. Grill the chicken for about 6 to 7 minutes on each side or until fully cooked. Remove from the heat and let cool for 5 minutes to allow juices to rest and settle.

5. Slice or dice chicken in thin strips and toss with cilantro.

TACO beef

GF | DF YIELD 8 TO 10 SERVINGS, ABOUT 2 POUNDS

Feel free to substitute ground turkey or plant-based meat in this recipe.

2 teaspoons **OLIVE OIL**

2 pounds 85 to 90% lean **GROUND BEEF**

½ diced **ONION**

1 tablespoon chopped **GARLIC**

2 tablespoons **CHILI POWDER**

2 teaspoons **CUMIN**

1 teaspoon **SEA SALT**

½ teaspoon **GARLIC POWDER**

¼ teaspoon **ONION POWDER**

1 cup mild **SALSA**

1. Heat a heavy-bottom skillet over medium heat. Add olive oil and add ground beef in crumbles, using a wooden spoon to break up beef. Cook for 3 minutes. Add diced onion, garlic and dried seasonings. Continue to cook over medium heat for 5 to 6 minutes.

2. Drain excess grease, add mild salsa, return to stove and simmer for 4 minutes over low heat.

3. Taste and adjust seasonings as needed.

guacamole

GF | V+   YIELD 2 CUPS

8 AVOCADOS, halved and seeds removed, and scooped out of peel

3 LIMES, juiced *(reserve 1 tablespoon)*

1 teaspoon SEA SALT

¾ teaspoon ground CUMIN

¼ teaspoon CAYENNE

½ medium ONION, diced

½ JALAPEÑO PEPPER, seeds removed, and minced *(optional)*

2 Roma TOMATOES, diced and seeds discarded

2 tablespoons chopped CILANTRO

1 clove GARLIC, minced

1. In a large bowl add the scooped avocado pulp and lime juice, toss to coat. Drain and reserve the lime juice.

2. Add the salt, cumin and cayenne and with a potato masher, mash the avocado mixture until smooth. Fold in the onions, jalapeño, tomatoes, cilantro and garlic until combined. Add 1 tablespoon of the reserved lime juice and adjust seasonings if necessary.

Chef's Notes

You can make your guacamole a day ahead if you top with a thin layer of salsa to keep the guacamole from oxidizing and then scrape off the thin layer of salsa just before serving.

BAJA salsa

GF | V   YIELD 2 1/2 CUPS

1 *(14.5-ounce)* can diced TOMATOES

1 *(10-ounce)* can diced TOMATOES WITH GREEN CHILIS

½ small diced WHITE ONION

3 CLOVES

½ JALAPEÑO, seeds removed, and chopped *(optional)*

2 tablespoons chopped CILANTRO *(about ½ bunch)*

Juice of 1 LIME

1 teaspoon HONEY

1 teaspoon RED WINE VINEGAR

1 teaspoon SEA SALT

1. Place all ingredients in the bowl of a food processor. Pulse on and off for 30 to 45 seconds until blended.

2. Taste salsa with a chip and adjust seasonings as needed.

slider MASTER PLAN

Graduation party hosts are always looking for a unique and fun food theme that is manageable, and sliders are a win as kids and adults love them! I recommend choosing three varieties of sliders, keeping in mind the age group's taste preferences. Perhaps more fancy and adventurous sliders for the adults and simpler ones for students and little people.

1. If you want to work ahead, no problem. Most slider varieties prep ahead great! Grill your patty, add toppings, place prepared burgers on a sheet pan and cover with foil. Heat the following day in a 350°F oven for about 8 minutes until heated through (or you can microwave in small batches). Some slider varieties may need to be finished the day of if they have cold or room temperature toppings such as slaw, lettuce or sprouts that should not be heated.

2. If you are not concerned about timing, preparing sliders the day of is great too.

3. Pick a fun vessel to hold your sliders. Paper boats, small sandwich paper wrappers or a plate that matches your theme of colors all work great.

4. Think about creating a brand for your graduate by making labels for the vessels that will hold menu items.

5. Do not be afraid to make your own burger blend; I like to take ground turkey and add chopped banana peppers, sautéed onions and peppers and a sprinkle of cracked pepper. This would be a great addition to the Middle Eastern burger profile.

6. When sizing your burgers or chicken, 2 to 2.5 ounces will give you the perfect size to fit in the slider size buns.

7. There are lots of choices in the slider buns world. Pretzel, wheat, white, sesame or Hawaiian rolls and biscuits are a few options. I have made suggestions below but feel free to mix your favorite buns with slider choices.

MYO OPTION

Pick 2 to 3 varieties of protein and serve them à la carte with chosen toppings on the side. Guests can grab a roll, choose their protein and fly how they want with their toppings.

Graduation Slider Collection

Choose two or three varieties and prep condiments accordingly. Two per person in total would be a good plan if you are serving other dishes.

ALL AMERICAN BEEF: Pickle pillows, ketchup, mustard, cheddar or American cheese, classic bun.

BACON & CHEDDAR BEEF: Chipotle mayo smears on pretzel roll.

CALIFORNIAN TURKEY: Whole grain roll, sprouts, goat or muenster cheese, fancy greens and avocado smear.

NASHVILLE CHICKEN HOT: Golden chicken, pimento cheese smear and pickle slices served on a biscuit or bun.

PULLED PORK: Crispy onions and cheddar, if desired, served on a pretzel roll.

CHICKEN, BACON & RANCH: Sliced cooked chicken breast, bacon, ranch, cheddar or Swiss if desired on a Hawaiian roll.

VEGAN BURGER: Multi-grain bun, salsa and guacamole (Impossible plant-based product or a lentil bean patty would be good here).

nashville CHICKEN HOTS

YIELD 12 SANDWICHES

2 EGGS

¾ cup BUTTERMILK

1½ tablespoons HOT SAUCE

1 cup ALL-PURPOSE FLOUR

1 tablespoon SEA SALT

2½ teaspoons freshly ground BLACK PEPPER

6 to 7 boneless skinless CHICKEN THIGHS

4 cups VEGETABLE OIL for frying

2 tablespoons CAYENNE PEPPER

1½ tablespoons HONEY

1½ teaspoons smoked PAPRIKA

1 teaspoon CHILI POWDER

¾ teaspoon GARLIC POWDER

12 SLIDER BUNS *(petit 2-ounce, brioche, biscuits or Hawaiian rolls)*

Thick-cut PICKLES *(optional)*

½ cup pimento-style prepared PUB CHEESE *(optional)*

1. In a medium bowl whisk together eggs, buttermilk and hot sauce.

2. In a second medium bowl combine flour, salt and black pepper.

3. Cut each chicken thigh in half and pat dry with a paper towel.

4. Take a piece of chicken and coat it in flour, then the egg mixture, then back into the flour. Repeat until all pieces are coated.

5. In a heavy cast-iron skillet heat oil until it reaches 325°F. When the oil is up to temperature, fry a few pieces at a time. Fry each piece until golden brown, with internal temperature measuring 165°F (about 5 to 7 minutes per side), allowing oil to return to temperature before adding the next batch of chicken. Place on cooling rack over sheet tray.

6. In a small bowl combine cayenne, honey, paprika, chili and garlic powder along with ½ cup of the frying oil. Stir well and brush on fried chicken pieces.

7. Serve on slider buns with thick-cut pickles and a smear of pimento pub-style cheese.

CHOPPED SUMMER greek salad

GF | V YIELD 10 TO 12 SERVINGS

Note: chop lettuce about half the size you would for a normal salad to make it more of a slaw.

1 head **ICEBERG LETTUCE**, chopped medium

1 head **ROMAINE LETTUCE**, chopped medium

2 cups **KALE SLAW MIX**

1 **ENGLISH CUCUMBER**, diced medium

1 package *(about 8 ounces)* grape or cherry **TOMATOES**

1 small **RED ONION** *(about ½ cup)*, diced small

1 cup **BANANA PEPPER RINGS**, chopped

1 cup **FETA CHEESE**, crumbled

1 cup **GARBANZO BEANS**

½ cup **BLACK KALAMATA OLIVES**, chopped a little bit

¼ cup chopped **PARSLEY**

1½ cups your favorite **GREEK DRESSING** or **VINAIGRETTE**

1 In a large bowl add prepared lettuce and slaw and toss together. Add remaining ingredients (except Greek dressing) and lightly toss.

2 Just before service, add a cup of Greek dressing, taste and add a little more if desired, and toss gently until everything is coated.

3 Place in a serving bowl or platter.

Chef's Notes

Split salad into 2 separate portions before mixing if your party will be longer so you can swap out a fresh batch a little later. You can also opt to serve the dressing on the side. If you do, you may need a little extra, so plan on an extra cup just in case people over dress, which they tend to do.

wicked cool ICE CREAM SANDWICH BAR

Premade or build-your-own ice cream sandwiches can be made with any type of cookie or ice cream. The possibilities are endless, and it might be fun to design a signature sandwich from your graduate's favorite flavors. When my twin nephews, Sam and Max, graduated, they each had their own signature sandwich. Sam's sandwich was a sugar cookie with Swedish fish ice cream and Max's was a chocolate-dipped cookie with Oreo cookie ice cream.

Store-bought or homemade cookies can be filled and frozen ahead of time, or the cookies can be presented on platters set with ice cream and your guests can decide what combinations they would like to create. It is perfectly fine to purchase premade cookies and give them a little pizazz by dipping a corner or the flat bottom in chocolate and then pressing them into sprinkles or crushed candy pieces. Think about using a local ice cream shop and you could be scooping flavors such as Mexican chocolate, Swedish fish, honey lavender, basil tangerine, bourbon pecan, mango and more!

Here are a couple of our favorite cookie recipes, but feel free to use your favorite.

COOKIE	ICE CREAM
Chocolate Chip	Vanilla
Peanut Butter	Chocolate
Oatmeal	Butter Pecan
Sugar	Any Fruit Sorbet
Chocolate Wafer	Mint Chip
Graham Cookies	Marshmallow

Banana Walnut Chocolate Chunk Cookies

YIELD ABOUT 10 COOKIES

2 cups ALL-PURPOSE FLOUR

1 cup WHOLE WHEAT FLOUR or ALL-PURPOSE FLOUR

2 teaspoons SALT

1 teaspoon BAKING SODA

3 sticks BUTTER *(room temperature)*

1 cup SUGAR

1 cup BROWN SUGAR

2 EGGS

1 tablespoon VANILLA

1 cup sliced BANANAS, mashed

2 cups ROLLED OATS

12 ounces CHOCOLATE CHIPS or chunks

1 cup WALNUTS, toasted and chopped

SPECIAL EQUIPMENT

2 ½-inch round cutter

1. Preheat the oven to 375°F. Line 2 sheet pans with parchment paper.

2. In a large bowl whisk together flours, salt and baking soda.

3. In the bowl of a stand mixer cream butter and sugars together until light and fluffy. Add egg, vanilla and banana and mix until smooth.

4. Scrape down the sides of the bowl, add oats and dry ingredients and mix. Add chocolate and nuts and mix until just combined.

5. Using a 2-ounce scoop, scoop dough into balls about 2 tablespoons each and place on prepared sheet pans about 2 inches apart.

6. Bake for about 12 to 15 minutes or until crisp around edges and set in the center. Cool on a wire rack.

Celebration Shortbread Cookies

YIELD 18 COOKIES

¾ pound unsalted BUTTER, room temperature

1 cup SUGAR

1 teaspoon VANILLA EXTRACT

1 teaspoon ALMOND EXTRACT

3 ½ cups ALL-PURPOSE FLOUR

¼ teaspoon SALT

½ cup multi color SPRINKLES

1. Preheat the oven to 350°F. Line 2 sheet pans with parchment paper.

2. In the bowl of a stand mixer fitted with the paddle attachment, add butter and sugar. Mix until well combined and pale in color.

3. Add vanilla and almond extracts and mix until combined.

4. In a medium bowl sift flour and salt. With the mixer on low speed, add flour mixture, one cup at a time, until just incorporated. Add sprinkles and mix until sprinkles are just combined. Do not overmix. You don't want to break up the sprinkles.

5. Dust surface with flour, remove dough and pat into a square, cover with plastic wrap and chill for an hour. (Make dough a day or two ahead if you like.)

6. Remove dough from fridge and roll out to ½-inch-thick sheet. Cut with 2 ½-inch round cutter. Place cookies an inch and a half apart on a prepared sheet pan.

7. Bake for 18 to 22 minutes until the edges begin to brown. Cool before serving.

8. If making ice cream sandwiches, pop cookies in the freezer an hour before assembling sandwiches. They will be easier to construct and you will avoid breaking them.

sparkling LEMONADE BAR

GF | V+

Lemonade is a crowd pleaser for all ages. Make a big batch of base lemonade and add other summer flavors listed below.

Simply Lemonade

YIELD 8 TO 10 SERVINGS

2 cups WARM WATER

1 cup SUGAR (can substitute ½ cup honey or agave syrup or 3 to 5 packets of unflavored Stevia)

2 cups fresh LEMON JUICE

6 cups COOL WATER

Couple pinches of SEA SALT

1 In a small, heavy-bottom saucepan add warm water and sugar and cook over low heat until sugar is dissolved. Remove from heat and cool, or place in an ice bath for a quick cool.

2 In a large pitcher, add sugar syrup, lemon juice, cool water and a couple pinches of sea salt. Stir to combine. If you prefer no sugar, omit the first step and replace the sugar syrup with 3 to 5 packets of unflavored stevia or swirl in honey or agave syrup to taste.

FLAVOR OPTIONS

BLACKBERRY BASIL: Add 2 pints of pureed blackberries with a table-spoon of basil to the base recipe.

STRAWBERRY LEMON: Add 1 quart of pureed strawberries to the base recipe.

SIMPLY LEMONADE: Float lemon slices in pitcher.

CITRUS PUNCH: Replace ½ cup lemon juice with ⅔ cup orange and ⅔ cup lime juice.

SPARKLERS: Offer an array of sparkling waters to mix with lemonade to make them sparklers.

ADULT COCKTAIL: This lemonade bar would also pair well with a vodka option for the adult faction at the party.

20

Easy Breezy Summer Shindig

Menu

GF/Gluten Free, DF/Dairy Free, V/Vegetarian, V+/Vegan

Create an easy, breezy summer party centered around MYO lettuce wraps, melon-inspired salads and sips of sweet summer tea (spiked if you like, too!). Set in your own backyard, work with existing outdoor furniture and add a little fluff with colorful pillows. Consider bringing indoor furniture out if you need more seating.

Use a crisp white sheet or tablecloth for your base linen with a pop of a bright accent runner or another layered linen. Keep in mind summer colors like violet, hot pink, yellow and even a fresh green. If you have trees or a pergola, hang some bistro lights. This will help designate your area and create an intimate space. Add a few brightly colored paper lanterns, usually found at home décor stores or online. Place your patio or indoor furniture right in the middle of your garden to get the fresh scents of your florals and herbs. Use your already-potted plants for centerpieces on the table and tuck large pots around your soft seating patio furniture to create a vignette. For your potted plants, think of geraniums,

zinnias, colorful petunias and trailing sweet potato vines for drama. Grab your old wheelbarrow, line it with some plastic and fill with ice for beverages or food that will need to be chilled. Use simple mason jars with fresh cuts from your garden to show off your beautiful blooms and fill the jars with tea lights for later in the evening. A few assorted-size bowls filled with fresh lemons and apples can be used during your event. Plates can be simple white ceramic to showcase all the beautiful pops of color in your dishes or colorful disposable plates with fun patterns for easy clean up. Don't forget that your food can double as a great centerpiece of color on simple white serving dishes.

SPICY THAI CHICKEN lettuce wraps

DF   YIELD 8 TO 10 SERVINGS

1 tablespoon OLIVE OIL

2 tablespoons SESAME SEED OIL

2 pounds ground CHICKEN THIGH

8 ounces WATER CHESTNUTS, chopped

½ cup small diced WHITE ONIONS

4 cloves GARLIC minced

1½ tablespoons grated fresh GINGER

⅓ cup HOISIN SAUCE

3 tablespoons SOY SAUCE

1 tablespoon LIME JUICE

2 teaspoons RICE WINE VINEGAR

1½ teaspoons SRIRACHA

1 teaspoon SEA SALT

½ teaspoon freshly ground BLACK PEPPER

1 tablespoon CORNSTARCH mixed with 2 tablespoons of COLD WATER
    (slurry)

GARNISH

3 GREEN ONIONS, sliced thin

½ cup shredded CARROTS

½ cup chopped PEANUTS

Small bunch of CILANTRO leaves

2 heads of BIBB LETTUCE

1 In a heavy-bottom skillet heat olive oil and sesame oil. Add ground chicken and cook, using a wooden spoon to break up bigger clumps. When chicken is about 70% cooked, add water chestnuts, onions, garlic and ginger. Continue to cook for another 2 to 3 minutes.

2 Add hoisin, soy, lime juice, vinegar, sriracha, salt and pepper. Simmer over low heat for 2 to 3 more minutes until all the flavors meld and chicken is fully cooked.

3 Add slurry and simmer until sauce thickens, about one minute.

4 Transfer to a platter or bowl and garnish with sliced green onions, shredded carrots, peanuts and cilantro. Serve with lettuce cups.

buffalo SHRIMP

GF   YIELD 8 TO 10 SERVINGS

BUFFALO SAUCE

2 tablespoons unsalted BUTTER

3 garlic CLOVES, minced

1 cup HOT SAUCE *(Frank's is a good brand)*

BUFFALO SHRIMP

1 tablespoon extra-virgin OLIVE OIL

2 pounds 16/20 SHRIMP, peeled, deveined, tails removed and butterflied

KOSHER SALT sprinkle

Freshly ground BLACK PEPPER sprinkle

GARNISH

10 to 12 BIBB LETTUCE leaves *(or romaine leaves)*

⅓ cup RED ONION, finely chopped or thinly sliced

3 CELERY ribs, sliced into thin ribbons with a peeler

½ cup BLUE CHEESE, crumbled

1 For the buffalo sauce, melt butter in a small saucepan over medium heat. Add garlic and cook for about 1 minute. Add hot sauce, stir to combine and set aside.

2 For the shrimp, heat oil in a large heavy-bottom skillet over medium-high heat. Add shrimp carefully to the hot pan and season with sea salt and pepper. Sauté until pink and opaque on both sides, turning with spoon or spatula to ensure even cooking, about 2 minutes per side. Turn off heat and add 80% of the buffalo sauce, tossing to coat (reserve the remaining sauce for an extra drizzle to serve with lettuce wrap).

3 Place shrimp in a serving bowl and garnishes in separate bowls so guests can make their own finished lettuce cup, or preassemble by adding a small scoop of shrimp to the center of each lettuce leaf and top with a sprinkle of red onion, celery and blue cheese.

VEGAN SUMMER **pea salad**

GF | V+   YIELD 8 TO 10 SERVINGS

6 cups fresh or frozen **GREEN PEAS**, blanched

½ cup small diced **RED ONION**

¼ cup chopped fresh **PARSLEY**

1¼ cups **VEGAN RANCH**, divided *(recipe follows)*

¼ cup **ALMONDS** *(optional)*

PORTO MUSHROOM BACON *(recipe follows)*

½ teaspoon **SEA SALT**

¼ teaspoon **BLACK PEPPER**

Pinch of **CAYENNE**

1   Combine the peas, onion, parsley and ¾ cup of the vegan ranch dressing. Stir to combine. Add almonds, portobello bacon and another ½ cup vegan ranch. Lightly mix and season with salt, pepper, and cayenne. Add more dressing if you like your salad creamier.

2   Taste and adjust seasoning if needed.

Chef's Notes

Sliced cucumbers and multigrain crackers would pair nicely with lettuce for a pea salad.

Vegan Ranch

GF | V+   YIELD 2 CUPS

1½ cups **VEGAN MAYONNAISE**

¼ cup **WATER**

2 tablespoons **LEMON JUICE**

1 tablespoon **WHITE WINE VINEGAR**

1 teaspoon **ONION POWDER**

½ teaspoon **GARLIC POWDER**

½ teaspoon **SEA SALT**

¼ teaspoon ground **BLACK PEPPER**

Pinch **CAYENNE**

4 tablespoons fresh **DILL**, **PARSLEY** or **CHIVES** *(mix and match to preference)*

1   In a large bowl add all ingredients (except herbs) and whisk to combine.

2   Stir in herbs.

Porto Mushroom Bacon

GF | V+   YIELD 1 CUP

2 tablespoons **OLIVE OIL**

2 tablespoons **MAPLE SYRUP** or **AGAVE**

1 tablespoon and 1 teaspoon **APPLE CIDER VINEGAR**

2 tablespoons **BRAGG LIQUID AMINOS** *(or tamari)*

1¼ teaspoons smoked **PAPRIKA**

1 teaspoon **SEA SALT**

½ teaspoon ground **BLACK PEPPER**

Pinch of **CAYENNE**

1 dash **LIQUID SMOKE** *(optional)*

4 **PORTOBELLO MUSHROOMS**, stems removed and gills scooped clean, sliced into ¼-inch-wide strips

1   Preheat the oven to 400°F. Line a sheet pan with parchment paper and set an oven-safe baking/cooling rack on top for crispiness. If you don't have a rack, just continue with parchment paper.

2   To make the marinade, in a medium bowl add olive oil, maple syrup, apple cider vinegar, liquid aminos, paprika, salt, black pepper, cayenne and liquid smoke (if using). Whisk to combine.

3 Add sliced mushrooms to the marinade. Gently toss to coat. Let marinate for an hour or longer.

4 Lay mushrooms on the rack or sheet pan, making sure to leave space between slices so as to not overcrowd.

5 Bake for 15 to 20 minutes until dark brown in color. Bake longer if you like yours crispier.

6 Remove from the oven, let cool for 5 minutes and gently peel off the rack or tray and dice.

asian NOODLE SALAD

GF | DF   YIELD 8 TO 10 SERVINGS

Eat with a fork or wrap in lettuce leaves.

FOR THE SALAD

1 (12-ounce) bag RICE NOODLES

1 (8-ounce) package tri-color COLESLAW MIX (green and purple cabbage with carrots)

½ head NAPA CABBAGE, cut in thin strips

2 cups finely shredded KALE

½ cup shredded CARROTS

4 SCALLIONS, sliced on a thin angle

1 RED PEPPER, cut into thin strips

1 bunch CILANTRO, chopped

FOR THE VINAIGRETTE

¼ cup OLIVE OIL

¼ cup FISH SAUCE

¼ cup fresh LIME JUICE

3 tablespoons SESAME OIL

3 tablespoons WHITE SUGAR

2 tablespoons minced fresh GINGER

1 tablespoon CASHEW BUTTER

2 cloves GARLIC, minced

½ JALAPEÑO, seeds removed, and minced

GARNISH

½ cup chopped CASHEWS, toasted (optional)

12 to 15 BIBB or ROMAINE LETTUCE leaves (optional)

1 Cook rice noodles according to package directions. Drain, rinse with cold water and set aside until ready to assemble salad.

2 To make the vinaigrette, mix ingredients together with an immersion blender until smooth.

3 In a large bowl add rice noodles and remaining salad ingredients. Toss to combine. Add vinaigrette and gently mix until the salad is evenly coated.

4 Place in a serving bowl or platter and garnish with toasted cashews.

5 Serve cold with lettuce leaves to make wraps if desired.

WATERMELON poke

V+   YIELD 8 TO 10 SERVINGS

2 tablespoons SOY SAUCE

2 tablespoons fresh LIME JUICE

1 tablespoon RICE or COCONUT VINEGAR

1 tablespoon toasted SESAME OIL

¼ teaspoon GARLIC POWDER

SALT and PEPPER to taste

3 cups cubed, seedless WATERMELON

3 small PERSIAN CUCUMBERS, diced medium

4 RED RADISHES, thinly sliced

1 WATERMELON RADISH, thinly sliced and then cut into strips

1 SCALLION, thinly sliced

1 AVOCADO, seed removed, and diced medium

SESAME SEEDS, for sprinkling

2 tablespoons pickled GINGER

3 LIMES, cut into 6 wedges

1 small bunch fresh CILANTRO leaves

1. To make the vinaigrette, in a small bowl whisk together soy sauce, lime juice, rice vinegar, sesame oil and garlic powder. Season with sea salt and pepper to taste.

2. In a large bowl combine fruits and vegetables with vinaigrette. Gently toss together to coat.

3. Place in a serving vessel, sprinkle with sesame seeds and garnish with pickled ginger, lime wedges and cilantro leaves.

MELON & **ricotta**

GF | V YIELD 8 TO 10 SERVINGS

1 CANTALOUPE, peeled and cleaned

½ HONEYDEW MELON, peeled and cleaned

1 cup of whole milk RICOTTA CHEESE

3 tablespoons MICHIGAN HONEY

¼ teaspoon SEA SALT

10 to 12 fresh BASIL leaves, julienned into thin strips

2 tablespoons WHITE BALSAMIC SYRUP *(recipe below)*

1. Place cleaned melons flat side down on a cutting board. Cut them into ⅛-inch slices on an angle.

2. In a small bowl mix ricotta and honey and season with sea salt.

3. Shingle melon on chosen platter and intermittently spoon a heaping tablespoon of ricotta on top of melon.

4. Sprinkle with prepared basil and drizzle white balsamic syrup.

White Balsamic Syrup

GF | DF | V YIELD 1/4 CUP

½ cup WHITE BALSAMIC VINEGAR

2 teaspoons MICHIGAN HONEY

1. Place vinegar and honey in a small saucepan. Bring to boil over medium heat, reduce to simmer, and cook until mixture is reduced by half, about 6 to 8 minutes.

tropical RICE PUDDING

GF | V+   YIELD 8 TO 10 SERVINGS

3 cups **COCONUT MILK**

1½ cups **COCONUT CREAM**

1 **VANILLA BEAN**, split into 2 pieces lengthwise *(or 1½ teaspoons vanilla extract)*

1 teaspoon **ALMOND EXTRACT**

2 cups cold **BROWN RICE**, cooked *(not overcooked)*

¼ cup **AGAVE SYRUP**

Couple pinches **SEA SALT**

GARNISH

2 **KIWIS**, slice and quartered   **SLICED ALMONDS**

2 **ORANGES**, supremed   ½ cup shredded **COCONUT**

¾ cup diced **PINEAPPLE**

1. Place coconut milk, cream, and vanilla bean in a heavy-bottom sauce pot. Bring liquid up to almost a boil and reduce heat to medium. Add almond extract, cold rice, agave syrup and salt. Simmer over medium-low heat for 10 minutes. Remove vanilla bean.

2. Reduce heat to low and continue cooking for another 10 to 15 minutes until liquid is absorbed and rice is fluffy. Remove from heat and cool.

3. Spoon rice pudding into a large serving vessel or individual serving bowls.

4. Garnish with fruit, sliced almonds and shredded coconut.

Chef's Notes

This is a great prep-ahead dessert. Make the rice pudding up to 3 days before, cut the fruit and garnish the morning of service. Feel free to switch up fruit—roasted pineapple or mango would be fun!

summer SWEET TEA SIPS

GF | V   SERVES 8 TO 10

Cool sips in the summer that let your guests choose different flavors to make their own icy drink work so well and do not require a recipe. Make 2 to 3 base teas, set up a tray with fruit purees and small berries and let your guests decide what fun swirl of puree would be their favorite.

BASE ICED TEA IDEAS

Choose 2 or all three

     2 quarts **BLACK** • 2 quarts **GREEN** • 2 quarts **HIBISCUS**

STIR-IN IDEAS

HONEY, small squeeze bottle 4 to 6 ounces

AGAVE, 4 ounces

PEACH, RASPBERRY, STRAWBERRY or **BLACK FRUIT PUREES**, ½ cup each

ASSORTED SELTZER SPARKLES are also fun to put a little fizz in a drink bar, 2 to 3 varieties, 1 liter each

Your favorite liquor: **VODKA, TEQUILA** or **RUM**, 1 ounce per drink

GARNISHES

HERBS: mint, thyme or basil, a micro bowl of each

FRUITS: peaches, lemons, limes, pomegranate, raspberries, blackberries, small bowl or 6-ounce mason jar of each

GRATITUDE

Many people in my life have come together in countless ways to support me in this quest to give all of you permission to party!

Jennifer, my publisher, and Mel, her first mate, thanks for believing in me and having patience. The COVID-19 pandemic really brought us to a halt in so many ways, but you held for me and the book.

My good friend and design contributor Kevin Miller, owner of Twigs and Branches. Kevin was a true partner with our centerfold photo shoots; he also contributed *MYO Party* content in this book.

Kevin, I am beyond grateful for your time and talent; you impress me every time we collaborate. From your stylistic eye with Fox 2 Detroit TV segments and shared events, to your time and talent that went into the amazing design elements and tips you've shared in this book, I thank you. I love how our styles meet and grow together in so many unexpected and beautiful ways! Your talent and passion are contagious, and I will look forward to a large DIY design book from you soon!

Carrie Sumnik, your efforts were monumental in the MYO book journey. You are one in a million and my chef gal pal. You started as my student and sous chef at Schoolcraft Culinary Arts College and blossomed into a wonderful cook, chef, educator and one of my superheroes on the MYO project! Thank you for taming my chaos, tasting countless recipes, proofreading and more.

A shout out to Deanna, my *everything* person on this project, from curator of interesting props to artist and office manager at Two Unique, you made long days of shooting manageable.

My gratitude is deep and wide for Schoolcraft College. Love to my tribe of brother and sister chefs, students and administrative staff. Thank you Schoolcraft for inspiring me to be better!

My first photographer, Alan Davidson, who got the ball rolling for *MYO Party* and then turned me over to the most talented Emily Berger. Emily, thank you for your amazing perspective, your over-the-top talent and your ability to capture my passion so that I have a vivid, visual story to share of the MYO journey.

Ida, my late mother-in-law, hosted magical holiday parties that were my first experiences being part of beautiful, large parties with over-the-top food, pretty bling, exquisite presentation and décor. I met her when I was only fourteen and I credit her for igniting the party spark within me.

My built-in best friend and twin sister, Karen, has been my true north star through all the beautiful and dark times of my life. Thank you, Karen, for always being full of encouragement. Thank you to my husband Rich, who is the most amazing "nerd" and who keeps all the stars hanging right in the sky even when I cannot see them. I am beyond grateful for my large, blended tribe of children: my daughter Lauyren, you are such a bright light in my life, and my bonus sons Anton and Aaron and their amazing wives Aubrey and Cindy, and to Rich's three sons, thank you for accepting me into your lives. To my entire family and beautiful littles (six grandchildren under six), thanks for always encouraging me even though my chosen profession kept me working long hours. When I missed out on happenings in your life, you always reciprocated with love and understanding, for which I'm eternally grateful.

Jim, my partner at Two Unique, thank you for all you do that has granted me the time to pursue this passion and goal, and for your encouragement. You mean more to me than words can express. To the entire tribe at 2U, I would be nothing without your time and talents. Every day when you all walk in the door, my heart says, "Thank you, God, they're here again today."

Kelli Lewton, C.E.C.

REAL FOOD ADVOCATE, CHEF AND
OWNER OF TWO UNIQUE CATERING

Chef Kelli Lewton lives and works by the tenet that food should be sourced as close to the vine as possible. Kelli's style of cooking combines high quality ingredients, dedication to local and sustainable farmers and an everlasting devotion to food.

Chef Kelli is a proud graduate of the prestigious Schoolcraft Culinary Arts College and has been teaching culinary arts as a chef instructor at Schoolcraft for over twenty years.

A leader in her industry, Chef Kelli is a regular guest host on Fox 2 News Cooking School and the recipient of several culinary awards. She is proud to have been of service to two US Presidents, numerous professional athletes, celebrities, CEOs and other wonderful customers all over southeast Michigan and beyond.

She likes to spend time with her friends and family and travel the world to experience all the new tastes that come with it.

Kevin Miller

EVENT DESIGNER

Since Kevin was very young, he had a true passion for gardening and grew up working in his parents' yard planting flowers, herbs and vegetables. He would leap out of bed every morning to water the flowers and explore the yard, looking for new sprouts and flowers born the previous day. Today Kevin has a deep love for travel, architecture and interior design, which inspires his design processes.

Kevin grew up in a large family and loved the constant family get-togethers, which has not changed over the years since his youth. These memories have encouraged him to start a family of his own with his partner, Brandon. Kevin and Brandon share a wonderful life together traveling and spending time cooking and entertaining their foodie family and friends. They love their fur babies: Great Dane Basil and Miss Sierra, a greyhound.

Kevin has been living his true passion of designing professionally since 2007, when at the young age of eighteen he launched his floral and design company, Twigs and Branches Floral (located now in Rochester Hills, Michigan). He finds beauty in everything, including nature, and has a passion for scouting venue sites and incorporating very natural unexpected elements whenever possible. Kevin is a regular contributor for design segments on Fox 2 Detroit and is passionate about bringing people's most special days to life with unique designs. With national and international events under his belt, Kevin is one of the most celebrated designers in Southeast Michigan and beyond.

INDEX

Skellefteå
in Heart and Soul

Text: Lars Westerlund
Principal photographers: Lasse Johansson and Torbjörn Lilja

INFORMATIONSFÖRLAGET

This book has also been published in Swedish under the title "Skellefteå i själ och hjärta"

© 1999 Informationsförlaget and the Author

Text: Lars Westerlund, Westerlunds Reportagebyrå, Skellefteå

Reference group: The presiding municipal council in Skellefteå and the Municipal Trade and Industry Office

Illustrations:
Lasse Johansson: 6, 7, 8, 9, 10, 11, 13, 14, 20, 21, 22, 24, 26, 27, 28, 29, 33, 34, 38, 39, 41, 42, 44, 45, 46, 47, 48, 49, 50, 51, 54, 55, 56, 57, 58, 59, 60, 61, 62, 63, 65, 66, 67, 68, 76, 77, 78, 79, 80, 82, 83, 84, 85, 86, 90, 91, 94, 96, 97
Torbjörn Lilja: Flyleaves, 12, 15, 23, 24, 30, 35, 36, 40, 41, 64, 66, 70, 71, 72, 74, 75, 81, 87, 88, 89, 90, 91, 92, 98, 100, 102, 103, 104, 106, 107, 108, 110, 111
Sofie Isaksson: 43, 52, 65, 77, 97, 101
Gösta Wendelius: 18, 19, 24, 25, 34, 41
Peter Jönsson: 32, 37, 83
Patrick Degerman: 18, 27
Erland Segerstedt: 48, 65, 100
Leif Andersson: 106
Michael Jacobsson: 17
Peter Lilja: Cover photo
Göran Sandgren: 51
FLT Pica: 95

Illustration editors: Nils Arvidsson, Arvidsson Design
and Catarina Sundberg, Westerlunds Reportagebyrå

Graphic design: Nils Arvidsson, Arvidsson Design, Skellefteå
Original: Avant Garde, Skellefteå

Publisher's project manager: Majbritt Hagdahl, Bokform, Stockholm

Repro: Repro 8, Stockholm

Printing: Grafedit Spa, Bergamo, Italien 1999

Translation into English by Jon Kimber

ISBN 91-7736-450-3

Informationsförlaget
Box 6884
S-113 86 Stockholm, Sweden
Tel: 08-34 09 15
e-mail: red@informationsforlaget.se
Home page: www.informationsforlaget.se

The cover portrays Skellefteå Landskyrka, the rural church in Skellefteå. The flyleaves show a view of Skellefteå and grazing young cattle at Drängsmark.

Contents

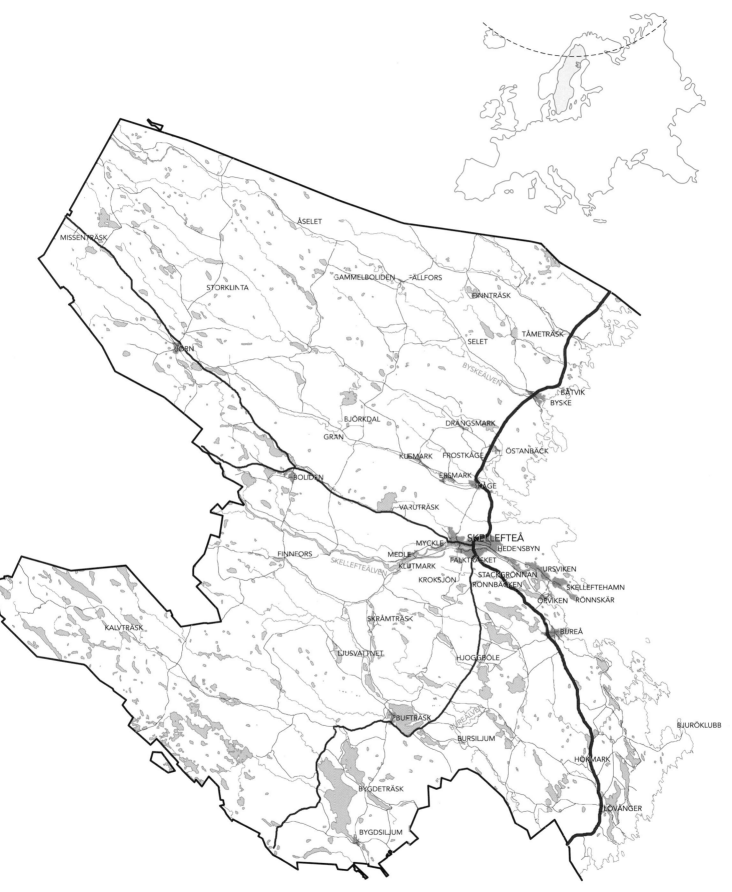

MISSENTRÄSK

ÅSELET

GAMMELBOLIDEN   FÄLLFORS

STORKLINTA   FINNTRÄSK

JÖRN   SELET   TÅMETRÄSK

BYSKEÄLVEN

BÅTVIK
BYSKE

BJÖRKDAL   DRÄNGSMARK

GRAN   ÖSTANBÄCK

KUSMARK   FROSTKÅGE

BOLIDEN   ERSMARK
KÅGE

VARUTRÄSK

MYCKLE   SKELLEFTEÅ

FINNFORS   MEDLE   HEDENSBYN
SKELLEFTEÄLVEN   KLUTMARK   FÄLKTRÄSKET
URSVIKEN
KROKSJÖN   STACKGRÖNNAN   SKELLEFTEHAMN
RÖNNBÄCKEN
ÖRVIKEN   RÖNNSKÄR

SKRÅMTRÄSK

KALVTRÄSK   BUREÅ

LJUSVATTNET

HJOGGBÖLE

BJURÖKLUBB

BUFTRÄSK

BURSILJUM

HÖKMARK

BYGDETRÄSK   BUREÄLVEN

LÖVÅNGER

BYGDSILJUM

Foreword

Throughout 'Skellefteå in Heart and Soul', you will experience what it's like to live in our community. Skellefteå has many different 'faces' – sparsely populated areas, farming districts, and built-up areas with prosperous trading, education and services.

People living here are offered a warm and creative environment where nothing is impossible. It's an enterprising environment that has produced everything from successful export companies to world-famous rock bands.

Those of us who have grown up in Skellefteå have come to appreciate its neighbourliness and its many activities. You can find societies catering for most interests, such as religion, sports, chess and drag racing. The locals of Skellefteå are always eager to give of themselves

and welcome newcomers into their circle of friends.

Picking berries and mushrooms is the best way for me to relax. Other examples of what people in Skellefteå like to do are fishing in the river Byskeälv or even in the middle of the city in the river Skellefteälv, skiing on the slopes of Storklinta and sailing from the harbours of Skelleftehamn or Kåge. We also have many opportunities to enjoy a high standard of theatre and music.

A community is never more than what its inhabitants make it. In my view, we have all managed to create a Skellefteå that offers its residents the very best conditions for living here.

Welcome to this encounter with Skellefteå and its people.

Lorentz Andersson
Lorentz Andersson
Chairman of the Municipal Board
of Skellefteå

Opposite: Skellefteå inhabitants meet on the broad pedestrian precinct in the centre of the town – window-shopping all year round thanks to heated pavements.

The gold caster in the Golden City

Sverker Lundgren has lived all his life in the village of Skelleftehamn. His workplace is the smelting works at Rönnskär. He has been the one to cast the gold bars since 1988.

"There aren't many gold casters in the world and I'm the only person in Sweden who does it for a living," says Sverker Lundgren.

A bar of gold weighs 12.5 kilos and is worth approximately one million Swedish Crowns. He produces between 500 and 600 bars each year.

A gold caster has to be conscientious and always keep his head.

"It wouldn't be particularly pleasant to have molten gold running on the floor. It has a temperature of 1,300 degrees Celsius."

Gold casting is the biggest attraction at the Rönnskär plant, and Sverker Lundgren has cast his bars in front of royals and government ministers. Security at the gold foundry is rigorous; both visitors and employees are searched before leaving the premises.

"Unfortunately it's necessary, because we handle such valuable products."

Through out time gold has exerted a magic power over human beings. All over the world people have died in

their hunt for the treasures of the mountain.

Gold is a symbol of power and wealth, and is used in jewellery, medals and coins. Gold bars are a common investment; it is also used by dentists and in the telecoms industry.

"I don't even wear a wedding ring myself," says Sverker Lundgren laughing. At the same time, he points out that, because gold does not deteriorate over time it is the most precious of all the metals. Almost all the gold that has ever been produced still exists in one way or other.

It was in 1924, when gold ore was discovered in Boliden, that the goldrush to Skellefteå began. The largest gold mine in the world was opened here. Washing and smelting plants were established. There are several mines within the municipality even today. Boliden runs mining operations in other parts of the county of Västerbotten, and also in Norrbotten and Dalarna. The company also mines in Spain and is co-owner of a very rich gold mine in Saudi Arabia.

"About six tons of mine gold is produced in Sweden every year," says Sverker. →

Above: Sverker Lundgren, gold caster at the Rönnskär plant.

Opposite: Gold casting at the Rönnskär plant. Most of the ore mined by Boliden in Sweden contains a certain amount of gold.

But all that glitters is not gold. On Skelleftefältet, the name of the ore-rich area in the northern part of Västerbotten, there is also silver, zinc and lead. And there is copper, Boliden's most important product. Following expansion of the Rönnskär plant, which will be finalized during the autumn of 2000 and will cost about two billion Swedish Crowns, copper production will amount to 230,000 tons per year.

"The construction is designed to allow the smelting works to be further extended in as smooth a manner as possible. The large investment in the Rönnskär plant gives those of us who work here with faith in the future."

However, Boliden is not the only player in the field. Terra Mining is the name of the local competitor. They run a rich gold mine in Björkdal.

"It seems that the ore will continue to bring prosperity to our area even in the 21st century," says Sverker Lundgren in conclusion.

Above left: Gold dust from Terra Mining's mine in Björkdal.

Above right: A serial number being stamped onto a bar of gold at the Rönnskär plant. The purity of the gold is a minimum of 99.99 %.

Opposite: Terra Mining obtains approximately 1.3 million tons of ore per year from open-cast mining at Björkdal. About 2.4 tons of gold is extracted from the ore.

Left: Rönnskär is the only smelting works n Sweden for copper, lead, gold, silver, and zinc clinker.

Top above: The Renström mine is one of the deepest in Europe. Mining takes place at depths of over 1,000 meters.

Top centre: One effect of the rationalizations at the Rönnskär plant is a huge improvement in productivity. In 1990, 50 tons of copper per man-year were produced. After the expansion of the smelting works at the beginning of the 21st century, a production rate of 350 tons per man-year is expected.

Top below: The Rönnskär plant is one of the 'cleanest' copper-smelting works in the world. There are several green areas within the plant site. Boliden's efforts have resulted in a number of environment-friendly processes, which are used not only in-house but are also sold all over the world by Boliden Contech.

13

In the head of an inventor

Kjell Lindskog now lives in the centre of Skellefteå but grew up on Mullberget nearby. He and school did not agree with each other, and Kjell left without any grades that might provide him with a career.

"I wanted to go to sea but my mother wouldn't let me. Instead, I started working in forestry," he says.

As a child he spent many hours in the basement of the house of the inventor Torsten Hellzén, and acquired an interest in product development. Scania in Södertälje discovered Kjell's talent in the field and gave him complex development tasks in their employ.

"But when I discovered that I could not get the same salary as the engineers, I quit and started my own company."

In Burträsk he started to manufacture racing cars for Formula V. His model was called the RPB. It formed the basis for a racing team that has twice won the Europa Cup.

However, it was difficult to keep afloat financially. In 1974, and 400 manufactured cars later, the company closed down. But Kjell has maintained his interest in racing and lives it out through his role as Chairman of SMS – the motor racing association in Skellefteå.

Instead of building cars, Kjell started to develop a new technique for manufacturing composite products. In 1996 the big break-through came. By then he had developed SQS, a unique security system for the transportation of valuable goods. Included in the system is a security bag with release codes that would take 60 billion years to break.

Kjell is an active member of the Skellefteå Idéforum – an association for local inventors.

"The association is a model for how inventors in Sweden can cooperate in order to develop their ideas."

Idéforum also works with the Skellefteå Nyföretagarcentrum, the main task of which is to promote business development. During the 90s the Nyföretagarcentrum has contributed to the establishment of several new enterprises within the municipality.

Skellefteå has a tradition of manufacturing stretching right back to 1885, when Ursvikens Mekaniska Verkstad was established.

Because it chose largely to utilize external suppliers for goods and services, the Boliden company played a major role in business development in Skellefteå at an early stage. One example is Skega in Ersmark, which developed in symbiosis with Boliden. It started by manufacturing rubber gloves for workers at the Rönnskär plant before moving into rubber lining for mining mills and 'O' rings.

Alvar Lindmark, who developed the rack-and-pinion construction hoist, is the most well known innovator from Skellefteå. Since the late 60s Alimak has been a world leader in this specialized field. And there are many more inventors who have left their mark on the international scene.

→

Above: Kjell Lindskog, innovator.

Opposite: Futurum is one of Sweden's best-known brand names. Since 1963 all development and manufacture of Futurum's kitchen fans has taken place in Byske.

Opposite: Alimak is world leader in rack-and-pinion elevators. The company's construction hoists have been seen at renovations of most of the major buildings in the world. Here, they are being used on the Statue of Liberty in New York.

Top left: Ericsson Erisoft is a company within the Ericsson Group. It works with the design, development and maintenance of software products and systems. The company has one of its units in Ursviken.

Top right: Skega was the first in the world to introduce rubber mill-linings in the mining industry. This took place in 1959, and meant a minor revolution in terms of function and operating costs. Svedala Skega's global product-and-development centre for mill linings is located in Ersmark.

Nils Bergmark, who produced the Futurum fan, is one of them. Göran and Birger Lundberg, who developed the back loader, and the Forslund brothers, who turned Skellefteå into a centre for hydraulics, are other important figures.

During the 90s some niche companies, with products for the future, chose to establish their operations here. Dentronic, a supplier of automated tooth-repair technology, is one example. A number of companies involved with optronics and electronics are also located in Skellefteå.

The IT industry is well developed, with companies such as Ericsson Erisoft, Enator and Consultec in the lead. There is also Paregos Mediadesign, which received the prestigious 'Multi Media Product of the Year' award in 1996. Another company in the same industry, is fast-growing Cidema, which is concerned with product development in a virtual-reality environment.

Kjell Lindskog points out that one of the main reasons why the industry of Skellefteå is so competitive and export-orientated is that it has people capable of doing business internationally.

"Whenever I go abroad I always meet someone from Skellefteå on his or her way somewhere or another. The key to success lies in their know-how. After all, an invention is worthless until there is a market for it," he says.

17

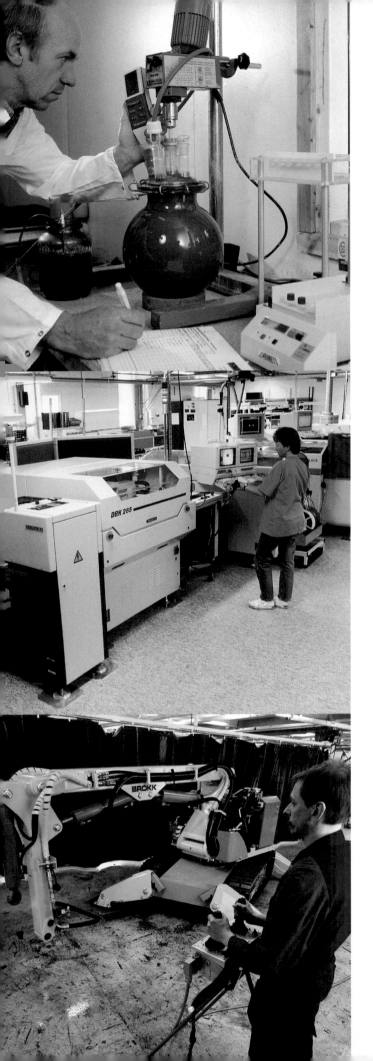

Top left: Miljöcentrum, the environment centre in Skelleftehamn, which was set up in 1995, is a gathering place for companies and individuals working with environmental care and environment issues. One of these companies is EkoTec, which specializes in the decontamination of polluted land. In the picture technician Peter Norlinder is performing a laboratory test.

Centre: Lövånger Elektronik manufactures circuit boards and electronic products.

Bottom left: Remote controlled demolition robots have carried the Skellefteå company Brokk out into the international market.

Opposite: The Ursviken division of Pullmax Ursviken, with its roots in the 19th Century, develops CNC controlled press brakes and guillotine shears.

Top left: Cidema is concerned with innovative product development in a virtual-reality environment. In the picture: Anders Backman, designer and Peter Johansson, site manager.

Bottom left: Paregos Mediadesign's operations are based on the power of curiosity. It develops games, multimedia presentations and educational material. Here it is a matter of interactive teaching – 'edutainment' at the sharp end of IT development. In the picture, from left: Kristina Elsisdotter, Daniel Wallström and Sofia Lindblom.

Opposite: Dentronic has developed care with a new automated technique of dental care as an alternative to manual treatment. It is a turnkey solution based on modern CAD/CAM technology.

Reaching the top
of the tree

Ingalill Tengman grew up in Åsele. After school she worked as a machinist in the wood industry. Unemployment eventually forced her to move to Skellefteå to study at the Medlefors Folk High School. She then continued on post-secondary vocational training (YTH).

"If it wasn't for the existence of YTH Wood in Skellefteå, I probably would have changed direction and done something completely different. But at YTH I made many important discoveries about the importance of combining theory and practice," she says.

Ingalill Tengman was recruited to the Trätek wood industry-research institute, which has a branch in Skellefteå. She first joined it as a project coordinator but took on full responsibility as site manager in 1992.

"We work with applied science and I benefit a lot from having worked 'on the floor' myself," says Ingalill. She thinks that one of Trätek's most important tasks lies in the de-dramatization of research.

Trätek in Skellefteå is well known both in Sweden and abroad for its skills in developing advanced wood-based constructions, such as wooden bridges. Scanning technology is another area of success, which has been developed in close cooperation with the Luleå University of Technology. Its Department of Wood Technology is located in Skellefteå. Three out of a total of four Swedish professors in the field work here. The Department educates engineers, and wood research is also being performed.

"Skellefteå offers the most comprehensive education in wood techniques in Sweden. The Master of Engineering course has a good reputation, and graduates generally find employment as soon as they finish," says Ingalill Tengman.

There are several companies in Skellefteå at the forefront of the wood industry. For example, Svenska Träbroar in Kroksjön is a leader in wooden bridges, and Martinsons Trä in Bygdsiljum is a major player in the glulam market. A number of fairly large saw mills are active within the municipality.

In her view, it is collaboration between companies that characterizes the wood industry in Skellefteå. Skellefteå Snickericentral (SSC), which was formed way back in 1958, offers a good example of this. Many companies achieved consensus within the framework of the collaboration, for example on marketing activities.

Stiftelsen Träenigheten, a foundation for unifying the wood industry, which is run by a number of players within the wood sector in conjunction with Skellefteå Municipality, is another forum that testifies to co-operation. Its cause is to promote research, education, development and regeneration in the wood industry. The Foundation regularly organizes a wood festival, and donates a prestigious prize to Swedish individuals who have made valuable contributions in the sector.

"There is no doubt that Skellefteå is well on its way to becoming the centre for wood-technology research and development in northern Europe," says Ingalill Tengman in conclusion.

Above: Ingalill Tengman, Site manager at Trätek in Skellefteå.

Opposite: The superb pine growing inland in the region constitutes the finest raw material found in any forest in the world.

Top left: Martinsons Trä in Bygdsiljum is one of northern Sweden's most modern privately owned sawmills.

Centre: Luleå University of Technology's Department of Wood Technology in Skellefteå has access to its own CT scanner, which is used by the department and Trätek researchers to study, amongst other things, the inner quality of timber.

Bottom left: Thinning with a harvester in a forest at Selet, Byske.

Opposite: In 1994, the local authorities built two wooden road bridges along Klockarbergsleden. The bridges were constructed by Martinsons Trä and one of them is supported on glulam wood beams.

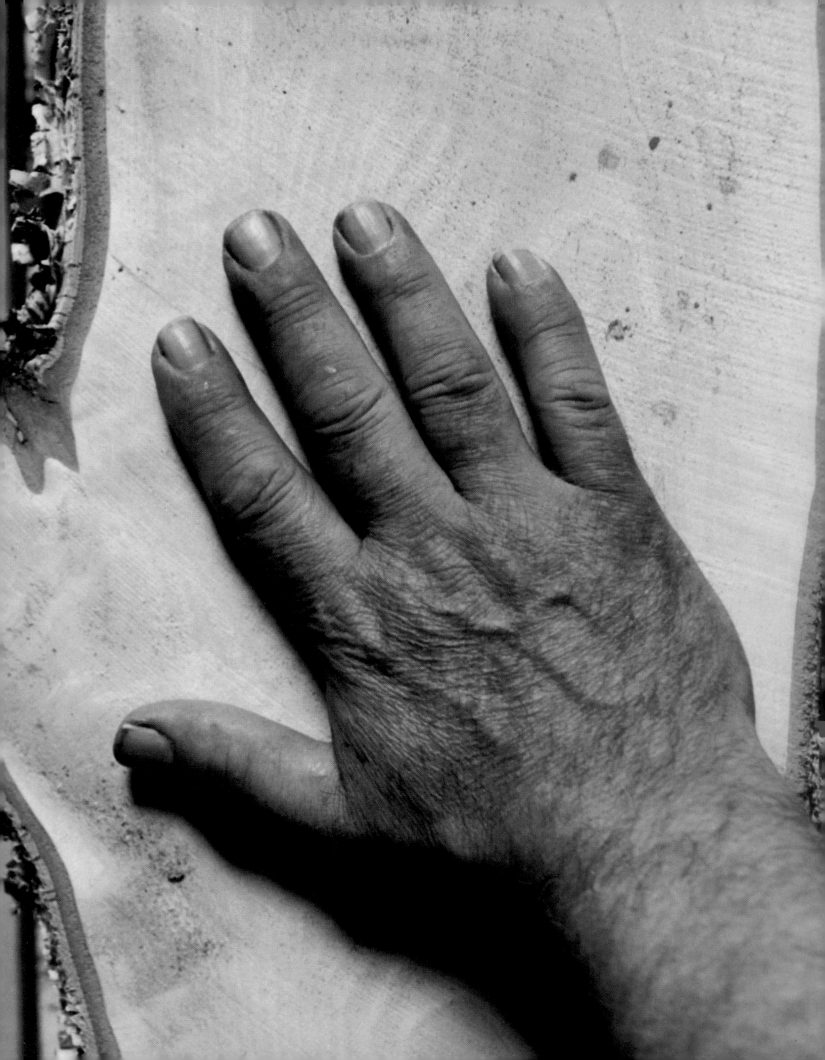

Left: There is a sound knowledge of wood in Skellefteå. Depicted here is the hand of an experienced woodworker at the Berglund joinery in Burträsk stroking a birch plank.

Top right: In 1998, the council-owned real estate company Polaris built the Ursviken TeknikCenter. It is the first modern timber building in Sweden with more than two storeys. The project was carried out in close cooperation with Trätek.

Centre right: The main building at the Varuträsk Mineral Park is built with a wood profile. Even the floor joists are made of solid wood.

Bottom right: Annika Marklund from Tuvan develops and designs her own furniture. The series named after her home village of Tuvan combines the styles of Gustavian, Rustic and Shaker.

Mobilizing energy for the future

Lars Atterhem grew up in Morön residential area. He obtained a Master of Engineering from the Royal Institute of Technology in Stockholm and majored in thermal energy technology. Following his years at university he joined Ericsson Radio to work on the development of air-traffic control systems. In 1986 Lars relocated to Skellefteå and was appointed by the Skellefteå Kraft power company to develop district heating. Today, he is head of the Heating business area.

Lars Atterhem lives at Långnäset in Burträsk and has, of course, a bioenergy pellet heater in his home.

"It is good for Skellefteå Kraft that we have divisions involved in both bio-energy and electric power. In-house competition benefits our customers in the end," says Lars.

Skellefteå Kraft, which is owned by the municipality, inaugurated its first hydro-power plant in 1908, on Finnforsfallet in the river Skellefteälv. It provided both local industry with power and the city with lighting. Skellefteå Kraft has steadily extended its network of power stations and increased its distribution area.

"We are the second largest municipal power producer in the country, with a turnover in excess of 1,000 million Crowns per year," notes Lars Atterhem.

The reason for this positive development lies in Skellefteå Kraft's innovative culture.

In recent years, Skellefteå Kraft has made major investments in bioenergy. From 1994 to 1997, under the management of Lars Atterhem, a 'combi-energy' plant was set up in the Hedensbyn industrial estate. It consists of a heating station and an integrated factory that produces biopellets. The production volume is approximately 100 million kWh power, 230 million kWh of heat and 130,000 tons of pellets per year. Given that electricity is produced through recycling energy from the factory's drying process, the plant is unique in the energy industry.

"On top of that, it's the largest pellet factory in the world," says Lars Atterhem.

When electricity, heating and pellet demands are high in Skellefteå – in general, for three months a year – the heating station and other production plants are run as usual. Production of pellets is determined by plans for deliveries to external customers.

Other European energy companies are standing in line to study the combi-energy plant in Hedensbyn.

"The plant is a model, with regard to both technical solutions and the efficient way in which it was built," states the British energy expert, D. C. Pike. Mr. Pike is an adviser to the EU Commission.

Before going ahead with building the pellet factory, Skellefteå Kraft negotiated a long-term agreement with the Stockholm Energi power company for a supply of 60,000 tons of pellets per year. As well as similar long-term deliveries to large consumers, Skellefteå Kraft also makes an effort to sell pellets on the local market in Västerbotten.

"There are many other innovators in Skellefteå working with the development of new types of pellet burners," says Lars Atterhem in conclusion. These days, he is frequently engaged as a lecturer on the European energy scene.

Above: Lars Atterhem, head of the Heating business area, Skellefteå Kraft.

Opposite: Skellefteå Kraft's combi-energy plant was put into operation in 1997. It consists of a heating plant and an integrated pellet factory. The pellet factory is the largest in the world.

Opposite: Skellefteå Kraft has around 58,000 customers in nine Swedish municipalities. Its distribution area covers 12,300 square kilometeres, an area as large as the Swedish province of Skåne. View of the town from the Vitberget mountain.

Top: 1908 saw the inauguration of the power station at Finnforsfallet on the river Skellefteälv. It was declared a heritage building in 1983 and now houses a museum – one of Sweden's most interesting monuments to power technology.

Bottom: Skellefteå Kraft produces around 2,700 GWh electricity a year. The largest proportion comes from its own hydraulic power plant. Here, the water is surging through the new power station at Finnforsfallet.

A multitude of encounters

Hans-Jörgen Ramstedt grew up in the Sjungande Dalen residential area. At the end of the 80s he went to Bolivia as an aid worker, where he also worked as a photographer and ran a chicken farm.

"I even got in touch with the cowboys and was put through a real baptism of fire. It was a childhood dream come true," he says.

When Hans-Jörgen returned to Skellefteå he supported himself as a freelance photographer, while at the same time setting up the Go West adventure company in Fällfors. His business concept was to offer visitors an opportunity to try tough, wild-west riding in the beautiful surroundings along the river Byskeälv. Activities include day trips and sleeping under the stars. In Fällfors he has built a saloon, where the riders can rest after their adventure on horseback.

"What I offer is a very strong sense of freedom."

In the city there is no shortage of activities for visitors, and the wildlife of the north is just around the corner. As well as wild-west riding you might take a wood-heated sauna in the middle of the river Skellefteälv, go underground in Varuträsk, or ride snowboard in Storklinta.

Hans-Jörgen notes that Skellefteå's power of attraction has risen dramatically during the 90s. A prerequisite is that restaurants, hotels and camping sites maintain a high standard and level of service.

"We have access to more than 1,000 beds in central Skellefteå," he says.

Hans-Jörgen Ramstedt thinks that Skellefteå is a cosy town. When he has visitors of his own, he usually takes them to Bonnstan and Nordanå.

"Many people are surprised that we have access to such fantastic oases right in the centre of the town."

The fact that he lives in the country, in Drängsmark to be precise, is no coincidence.

"The villages of Skellefteå are real treasures."

In 1998, twelve companies in the tourism industry in Skellefteå embarked upon the creation of a common quality standard. The aim is that every visitor should always be well taken care of. A quality standard reduces the risk of a guest ending up with a really poor deal or a recreational site 'missing the target'. The striving for quality also encompasses constant attentiveness on the part of all staff to anything that could convey a bad message to their guests.

The Government Conference on 'The Significance of Basic Industry to Employment', held in Skellefteå in 1997, put the entire visitor industry to a difficult test. The Expolaris Kongresscenter, which is run by the municipality in conjunction with its local collaborators, was made responsible for everything from flights to safety controls. After the conference, praise was received from the Swedish prime minister Göran Persson and his staff. One of the main speakers, Paul Weissenberg, chief secretary to one of the EU commissioners, was very much impressed by the Swedish government's choice of locating such a big conference in such a small town.

"It is not common in the other EU countries. Now I can see with my own eyes how you practise regional policy in Sweden," he declared at the conference.

Above: Hans-Jörgen Ramstedt, who runs Go West in Fällfors.

Opposite: The Winter Garden at the Expolaris Center. Here there are conference halls, hotels, public libraries and offices supplying 50 or so of Skellefteå's service companies.

Top left: The crafts fair at Folkparken in Skellefteå.

Bottom left: Stiftsgården, erected in 1802, was the residence of the vicar of Skellefteå until1963. Since then the building has been used as a training centre under the auspices of the Luleå diocese. It still has a consistently rustic style.

Opposite: Byske Camping is one of few five-star camping sites in Sweden. Tourism has a strong tradition in Byske. The first spa hotel was opened here as early as in 1932.

Lorentz Brännström, Medle, and his seven Siberian huskies, welcome many ride-hungry visitors each winter.

Hans-Jörgen Ramstedt of Go West offers tough riding
trips in the beautiful surroundings of Byske river.

Mother's cooking with Christmas-tree seasoning

Soolgerd Stenberg originally came from Burträsk but now lives in Myckle. She has worked with food and drink her whole working life. Over the year Soolgerd's cooking skills have brought gourmet standards to many of Skellefteå's restaurants.

"In the international arena Burträsk is now more famous than Skellefteå. That is presumably because of the tasty Västerbotten cheese that bears its name," Soolgerd tells us.

In 1980 Soolgerd left her job as restaurant manager at the Hotel Malmia and started two restaurants of her own – a small vegetarian restaurant in the town centre and Nordanågårdens Inn. Three years later she bought the famous director's villa in Ursviken and concentrated on the Disponenten Inn. "I rely primarily on a Norrlandic smörgåsbord, with herbs from my own garden," she says.

She collects many of the herbs straight from the forest. Among other items, Soolgerd uses dried berries as well as pine and spruce needles. "Instead of throwing away your Christmas tree you can actually eat it," she says laughing.

Mushrooms are another of her passions. "I have always picked mushrooms. In northern Sweden you weren't always particularly interested in using mushrooms in cooking, but the trend has changed."

In the forests around Skellefteå there are many different kinds of edible mushrooms, such as chanterelles, yellow chanterelles and Carl-Johans. There are also others that fungi experts pay dearly for.

"Luxury restaurants in Japan pay about 10,000 Crowns

per kilo for Goliath mushrooms. I have a pantry full of them," she tells us.

In order to encourage interest in local herbs and mushrooms Soolgerd arranges courses.

"There is a great potential for the production of Norrlandic herbs on a larger scale."

She is definite on the point that Västerbotten is Sweden's food county and has access to the finest ingredients. "As well as the fresh air, the light summers contribute to the vegetables being better than those in southern Sweden. And the clean environment gives farmers the opportunity to produce high-quality milk and meat products." When it comes to fish, salmon is the most popular. Trout and char are also regarded as delicacies.

"I would also like to strike a blow for whitebait. It's an under-rated delicacy," she says.

Deer and moose meat are often to be found on Skellefteå's tables.

"It isn't possible to serve moose steak in restaurants here. It is everyday food," says Soolgerd. She also has a high regard for hare, at which many will turn up their noses.

Fermented herring with thin bread is of course a 'must' in Skellefteå. Anyone who moves here has to enjoy – or at least put up with – the smell of fermented herring all over the place in high-season week during the autumn. Nearly every self-respecting village has a bakery that produces thin flat bread. And there are also companies that make unleavened bread on a large scale.

Above: Soolgerd Stenberg, who runs the Disponenten Inn in Ursviken.

Opposite: 'The Dish of Skellefteå' à la Soolgerd.

Opposite Skellefteå municipality has one third of the farming land of Västerbotten County. Here, cows grazing in a meadow at Frostkåge.

Top: 'Västerbottensosten' is the largest and heaviest of all the cheeses produced in Sweden – both literally and figuratively. It is the best known Swedish cheese abroad, and the special favourite of top Swedish chefs. Cheesemakers from Norrmejerier in Burträsk, the dairies that make the cheese.

Centre: Cloudberries are known here as 'Forest Gold'.

Bottom: Flat, thin, unleavened bread is produced in long strips here in Hökmark at the Lövångerbröd bakery.

41

A family with the riches of childhood

Robert and Helené Nyström got to know each other during their final years at school. Helené then moved with her family from Skellefteå to Slyberget, a village close to Gran, where Robert lived. He played drums in the pop group Paradox.

"The first time we met, the band were rehearsing in his room. The whole house was vibrating and Robert's dad sat in front of the TV with earphones plugged in," Helené tells us.

She soon joined Paradox as a singer, and love blossomed. The couple got engaged when they were 20 years old and moved into a cottage in her parent's grounds. Then they lived for a period in Ersmark before moving to the Anderstorp residential estate in Skellefteå.

Their first daughter – Maria – was born in 1983, and subsequent visits to the maternity ward came at two-year intervals. The results were Kristoffer, Markus, Andreas and Sara.

The four-room apartment in Anderstorp felt too crowded, so the family went out searching for a larger dwelling. In 1992 they found their dream home in a village called Klutmarks Station. In the 170-square-meter house, built in1912, there was room for child number six and Emilie came into the world. In 1998 daughter Emma was also born.

"We both wanted a large family. Financially it is no advantage to have many children, but we have our riches in the children instead. Contact with them means that you maintain your own childishness," says Helené beaming. "Mummy wants to have lots of children to help out in the garden," adds daughter Sara in a confident voice. She also tells us that the family have eight chickens

and a rabbit called Oscar.

Because of the closeness of the births, Helené has stayed at home with the children for most of the time, while Robert has brought in the money preparing rubber mixes at Svedala Skega in Ersmark.

All family members agree that life in the country is better than in town. "There is less pollution here," Sara explains.

The children like being out in the countryside. In the summer they are constantly building new huts and collecting insects. The villagers have jointly contributed to the construction of a communal swimming pool where a great deal of the summer is spent. And the family often travel to the child-friendly bathing site at Falkträsket nearby.

"As you might expect, in the winter a great deal of time is spent in front of the TV and playing computer games," says Robert.

The family have only good things to say about the midwives and maternity ward, and they have positive experiences of communal childcare.

Today, some of the children of the family go to primary school in Klutmark while the others attend secondary school in Sörböle. "They are happy at school and there doesn't appear to be any bullying," says Robert.

The Nyström family maintain that Skellefteå is a peaceful and safe place to grow up in. "It's much easier to keep an eye on the children here than in a large city. Even if something were to go wrong with one of the children I think it's possible to solve the problem early, because everyone knows everyone else in Skellefteå," Helené Nyström says in conclusion.

Above: The Nyström family at Klutmarks Station.

Opposite: Evelina and Paul Hedlund, Ljusvattnet, Burträsk, were the first to be born in Skellefteå in 1999.

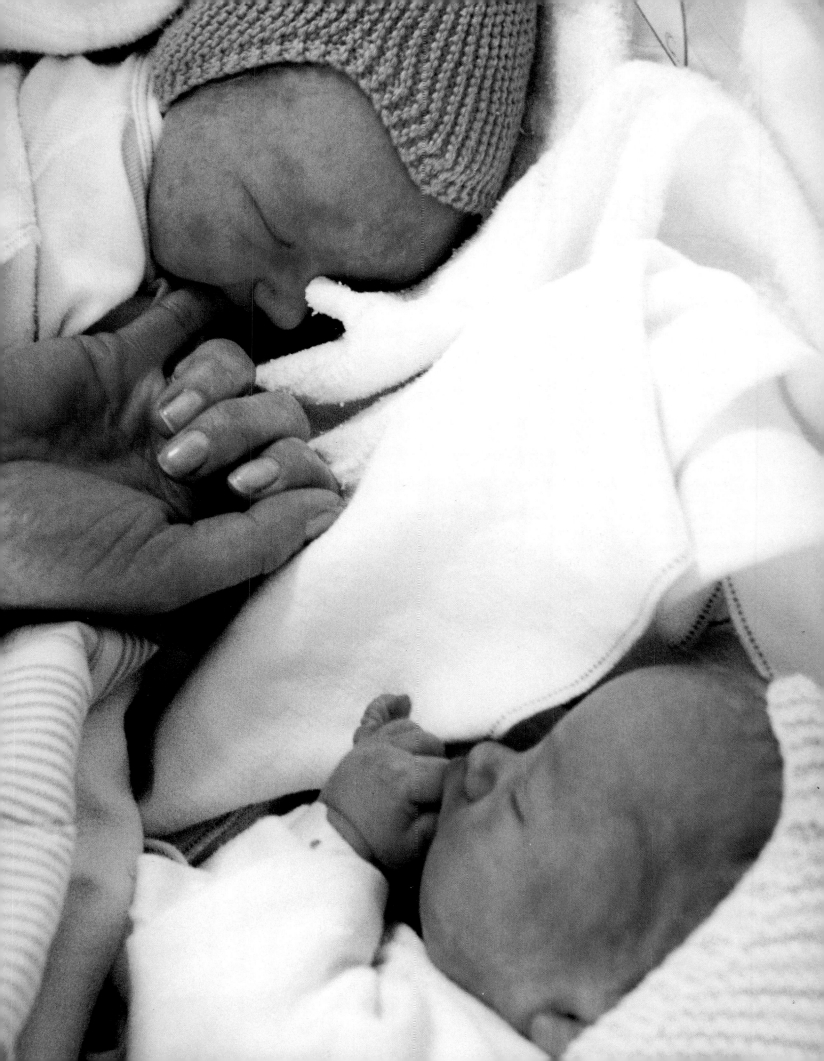

Opposite: A child in 'The Ship' at Nordanå play park in the Nordanå area.

Top: The village school in Skråmträsk.

Bottom: Elin Olsson and Maria Sundberg at school in Kåge – a school on the front lines of IT access.

Competence for all

Barbro Lundqvist grew up in the village of Aspliden in the municpality of Malå. Nowadays she lives in Sjungande Dalen residential area of Skellefteå. Barbro was always very interested in life's big questions and made up her mind early on to study theology. After studying at Uppsala she became a teacher in Skellefteå. She got her first job at Skellefteå Grammar School in 1967 and then moved on to the Balder upper secondary school, where she eventually became director of studies.

"I discovered that I liked being a leader," she tells us.

The next stage in her career was to become principal of the Skellefteå School of Nursing; and then she took up the post of director of upper secondary education. Today Barbro combines this position with that of chief executive of Skeria Utveckling, which is the municipality's education development company.

Barbro Lundqvist feels that compulsory education in Skellefteå and the town's upper secondary schools are of high standard. "We offer a broad program of upper secondary education, and the schools often participate in various trials to keep up with recent trends," she tells us.

Barbro also feels that local authority administered adult education and the folk high schools, Solvik, Edelvik and Medlefors, offer education of a high quality. "There aren't many Swedish municipalities of Skellefteå's size that have three such strong adult-education schools," she says.

Development of the Skeria area began at the beginning of the 70s. Wood technology and post-secondary

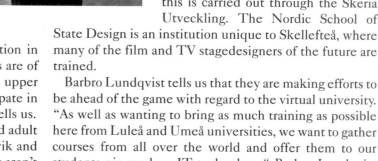

vocational education were the first to arrive. The big lift came when the Luleå University of Technology transferred its institute for wood technology to Skellefteå and masters degrees started to be awarded. Umeå University has also transferred a number of educational programs to Skeria, such as those for systems operators, sociologists, nurses and entrepreneurs. Skellefteå is well positioned between the two universities.

Barbro Lundqvist explains that one of the things that students coming from outside appreciate most is the location of the university. "It takes only three minutes to cycle from Skeria to the town square," she tells us.

In the field of qualified vocational training, Skeria Utveckling has been involved right from the start. Much of this is carried out through the Skeria Utveckling. The Nordic School of State Design is an institution unique to Skellefteå, where many of the film and TV stagedesigners of the future are trained.

Barbro Lundqvist tells us that they are making efforts to be ahead of the game with regard to the virtual university. "As well as wanting to bring as much training as possible here from Luleå and Umeå universities, we want to gather courses from all over the world and offer them to our students via modern IT technology," Barbro Lundqvist says.

Local politicians in Skellefteå are aiming to increase the student population at the Skeria area to 5.000 by the year 2005.

Above: Barbro Lundqvist, chief executive of Skeria Utveckling and director of upper secondary education.

Opposite: Skellefteå is a town with two universities. Both the Luleå University of Technology and Umeå University run courses in Skeria.

Opposite top: The Nordic School of Stage Design trains the scenographers, stage technicians and computer-graphics designers of the future. The very latest technology is available but creativity and artistry are still the most important attributes.

Opposite left: Pupils in the Arts and Crafts Department at Edelvik Folk High School working on a textile sculpture of a goat. From the left: Monika Stighäll, Malin Pettersson and Anna Morén.

Above: The cafeteria and library in Skeria are natural gathering places for students.

Young people with power

Stig-Arne Bäckman, who now lives at Anderstorp in Skellefteå, grew up in the Brännan area. He had great difficulties reading and writing, which caused problems at school. "I played truant for 115 hours to avoid giving a five-minute presentation on America," he remembers.

In protest against a system that did not want to know about dyslexia, he decided to be a defiant 'mod'. "I sat furthest back in class, chewed gum and argued with the teachers. That's how I learned how to use the language," Stig-Arne tells us.

Together with a few friends he started Club Palladium in 1966 and held rock concerts with local bands – such as the Turtles and the Human Beings. About the same time, the municipality opened its first youth recreation centre – called CeGe – and 16-year-old Stig-Arne was recruited as leader. Five years later he became manager of the Skrubben youth club in Sjungande Dalen. Stig-Arne became very much involved in drug issues and toured as an anti-drugs campaigner.

He gained a position as a social worker and in 1986 hatched the idea of Urkraft (primal power). Urkraft's mission is to offer nine-month-long courses of training to unemployed youths. "The starting point is that everyone has a primal power that can be brought to life".

The headquarters of the organization is in a large property on Tjärhovsgatan in Skellefteå. The house has been built with ecologically mindful hands. On the roof there is a large greenhouse where vegetables and herbs for the kitchen are grown, and flowers for the various departments. At Urkraft every day opens with a gathering at which everyone eats and shares relevant information. Then they get going with what has to be done that particular day – in the restaurant, cafeteria, gymnasium, bakery, TV station, conference centre, design school, and so on.

Most of what the participants learn in their training is connected with the practical production process. "What counts is 'learning by doing'. Variety in the training gives the opportunity for everyone to find a particular branch on the career tree," Stig-Arne Bäckman tells us.

Urkraft is an organization talked about with reverence throughout Sweden. The government, for example, have designated it as a national development centre, and requested Sweden's municipalities to send representatives to Skellefteå to see and learn how to tackle youth issues.

→

Above: Stig-Arne Bäckman, the man who inspired Urkraft.

Opposite top: Recycling rules on the premises of Urkraft. Even urine from the separate-compartment toilets is utilized as fertilizer in the greenhouse.

Opposite bottom: Urkraft arranges the annual Skellefteå Festival. It is unique in that young people themselves are the organizers.

Next spread: Around 20,000 people visit the Skellefteå Festival, which is held right in the centre of the town.

"Every year we have thousands of visitors. So we have developed the concept of a 'refresher course' for fatigued workers and politicians," says Stig-Arne. At various times he has functioned as expert and adviser to Sweden's Minister of Employment and to the Minister of Culture.

Stig-Arne Bäckman feels that a good environment in which youngsters can develop is being shaped in Skellefteå. And it is not only Urkraft that is paving the way.

"There are lots of fantastic youth leaders in Skellefteå doing a lot of work on the quiet. Among others, the Sweden Evangelical Mission (EFS), church organizations and various sports clubs are making great progress on that front," he says.

Left: Solkraft is an organization aimed at people currently excluded from the labour market. It has an overall perspective on the individual, and always looks towards what is healthy in each individual. Henry Karlsson is one of the workers at the Trivsel Bakery, run by Solkraft.

Opposite: The E4, is a down-town youth centre for the young people of Skellefteå. There are activities of all kinds, and around 15 different associations are represented. Mikael Andersson on his skateboard.

Pensioners shape an innovative future

The Mentor Group in Skellefteå comprises 20 or so pensioners with a full working life behind them. Its work is non-profit-making and consists of shaping exciting combinations of knowledge and entrepreneurship.

"It's one of the jigsaw pieces needed to make Skellefteå's future more innovative and enterprising," says the Mentor Group's chairman, Mats Bergqvist, who lives in Skelleftehamn.

He comes originally from Glommersträsk in Arvidsjaur Municipality. After studying at the Royal Institute of Technology in Stockholm, Mats worked as a metal forger at Sandvik's ironworks, as production director and chief executive in companies in the Höganäs Group, and as chief executive of Boliden Metall, Sorbinvest and Utvecklingsfonden.

"And in the last years before retiring I was chief executive of the risk-capital company KapN," he tells us.

The mentors all have different backgrounds and they work in a team supporting new businesses.

"It's great fun to follow the projects and see how the workers and companies mature."

What all the mentors have in common is that they believe they have something to contribute to the economy of tomorrow. The Mentor Group's end goal is to act as a resource pool. With their collective experience, the group's members can help to assess the business ideas of the future and facilitate the development of a network of new enterprises.

Lennart Nilsson is also a member of the Mentor Group.

He was part of the core team that built the association in 1997.

"The initiative came from Skellefteå Nyföretagarcentrum, the centre for new enterprises" says Lennart – who originally comes from Umeå and now lives in the Norrböle area in Skellefteå.

He has spent all of his working life in the Post Office. "My family and I came to Skellefteå in 1961 just for a short break in our careers. However, we appreciated the openness and pleasantness of the people so much that we stayed on," he tells us.

From 1980 until when he retired,1991, Lennart Nilsson was postmaster in Skellefteå. He has also been involved in bicycle sports for 55 years. As vice-chairman of the Swedish Cycle Federation and responsible for the international cycle contest, Postgirot, Lennart has made many useful contacts – which he can now pass on to young entrepreneurs.

"Our concept is that young people should contact us if they need help or support. In this way we can learn if our services are sought after or not".

He feels that brakes are often imposed on the community by middle-aged people who have climbed a fair bit up the career ladder and invested in a secure life.

"People of this kind seldom want to break new ground."

For himself Lennart Nilsson intends to go on mentoring for as long as the demand is there.

"It is important to keep old contacts warm. Lounging around on the sofa is not for me, that would make me restless and unbearable," he says.

Above: The Mentor Group in Skellefteå, with Mats Bergqvist and Lennart Nilsson in the foreground.

Opposite: The Free Church congregations run a home for the elderly through the Tryggheten Foundation.

Below: Sverre Lagerqvist, district medical officer at the Heimdall Care Centre on a home visit to Alida Eriksson.

Opposite: Bursiljum's senior dancers have a scheduled meeting once a week. Here are Yngve Andersson and Eva Hällgren on the dance floor.

A doctor with his heart in the right place

Kurt Boman grew up in a family of foresters in Kalvträsk, and both his parents were deaf and dumb. Such a close association with personal disability was a compelling factor behind his choice of career.

"I became interested in finding out how the human body actually works," he tells us.

Kurt also says that the need to use sign-and-body language in order to communicate with his parents has helped him in his role as a doctor. "It's not always the case that patients tell you how they really feel, but it's much harder to lie with body language."

Following his education Kurt worked as district medical officer in Boliden, and then ended up at the medical clinic in Skellefteå Hospital. There he has specialized in heart and cardiovascular diseases. He completed his doctoral dissertation on heart medications in 1983.

"It was very unusual in Sweden then for a doctor's public defence of a dissertation to take place outside a university hospital," explains Kurt, who has since become an associate professor.

In 1995 Umeå University Hospital placed a lecturer in Skellefteå Hospital, which now has several doctoral students.

At Skellefteå Hospital there is a very active research committee with representatives from most groups within health care. Their most sucessful research has been in the field of heart and cardiovascular disease. "Our studies into blood-clot formation and dissolution have earned great international interest."

Kurt Boman and his colleagues at the medical clinic have been deeply involved in the WHO-sponsored Monika project, which is aimed at developing new ways of preventing heart and cardiovascular diseases worldwide.

"Västerbotten is the region of the world where death from heart and blood disease is decreasing fastest. We're talking about half as many deaths over a period of ten years," Kurt Boman says.

He feels that within health care one should act more as an entrepreneur, when it comes to both internal developments and links with the business world. In partnership with businesses the health service in Skellefteå is working on the Medicin 2000 project, which will promote collaboration in medical developments.

"Among other things we have been involved in the development of the new catheters that are produced and marketed by Plastex in Skellefteå," Kurt tells us.

His own entrepreneurial spirit roams freely in the private sector. In 1976 Kurt opened a local department within Friluftsfrämjandet, the national organization for the promotion of open-air activities in his current home in Varuträsk. This association has carried out a number of projects to create a vigorous village community. The latest was the establishment of Varuträsk Mineral Park, where unique minerals from the closed Varuträsk mine are exhibited in different ways.

Above: Kurt Boman, head of research at the medical clinic in Skellefteå General Hospital.

Opposite: Serious work on quality development is in progress at Anderstorp Care Centre. In 1997 it obtained the 'Kvalitet i Norr' award – a prize given to the 'best' organization in the counties of Norrbotten and Västerbotten. Here, district nurse Pia Wernersson is performing an eye examination.

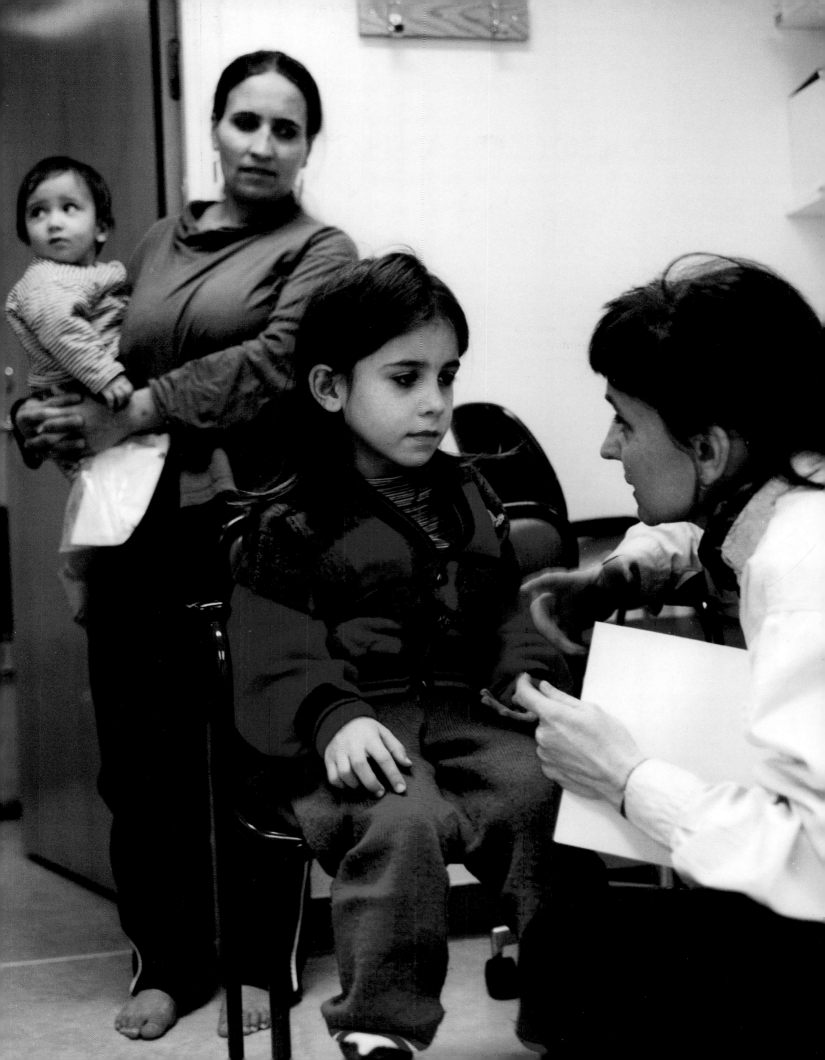

Wandering through the 50s town and in the countryside

Annika Sander grew up in Umeå. Her great dream was to be an archaeologist, and she realized that dream by studying cultural geography and archaeology at Stockholm University. After her studies she wanted to return north to search for archaeological remains in her home territory. Before the removal van left she participated in several excavations in southern Sweden. In the mid-70s Annika came to Skellefteå Museum and she immediately liked the atmosphere in the town. "It's a very pleasant place where people take their time to stop for a chat," says Annika.

As a cultural-environment archivist she worked right from the start with building inventories – in both town and country. "Skellefteå is probably the best preserved 50s town in Sweden," she says – adding that there are also clear traces of building from earlier periods.

The western part of Storgatan in the centre of Skellefteå is Annika's favourite area. "There are already four buildings with preservation orders and several more that could achieve the same status." Annika also has a favourite newly built area, namely Erikslid. "I feel happy just seeing the colossal houses there, which are not at all typical of Skellefteå. In some ways you are reminded of limestone cliffs and birds' nesting sites," she says.

She also puts in a word for the area around Bonnstan, with Lejonström Bridge, Stiftsgården, Landskyrkan and the Nordanå area. "There is no equivalent to this green oasis in any town in Sweden. It's quite simply unbelievably beautiful," she says as she looks out over the river Skellefteälv from her workplace window in

Nordanå. "There's a rich bird life on the river and sometimes I hear the curlew," Annika continues.

She also thinks that the larger villages in the municipality have gems of their own. In Lövånger Annika points to the church dwellings. In Byske you should direct your gaze at the church and the church cottages by the river. In Jörn the railway station and the old station hotel are worth a look. Boliden is a classical well-planned industrial community, which she feels is of national interest, and Skelleftehamn strongly bears the imprint of the Boliden company's building culture. In Kåge there are several fine buildings along Storgatan; and in Bureå it is most beautiful in the vicinity of the church close to the river Bureälv.

Annika Sander feels that the countryside is very close to the centre of Skellefteå. "To travel by car slowly through Klutmark is an uplifting experience. The same can be said of a trip on the southern side of the river from town and out towards Örviken." She also likes the area around Bygdeträsk and Bjuröklubb, which has a maritime cultural environment.

Annika, who herself lives in Östanbäck, states that approximately one third of Västerbotten's agricultural land is to be found in Skellefteå, as is demonstrated by the lively villages in open countryside. In the country there are lots of red-painted farms, and on these farms there are often several buildings with different functions, for example summer cottages, barns, and bakeries. "And there are the rounded-log huts, a distinctive feature of the countryside around Skellefteå," she says in conclusion.

Above: Annika Sander, cultural-environment archivist at Skellefteå Museum.

Opposite: In Burträsk there are many well-preserved wooden buildings. Here, craftsmen are fitting grooved metal sheeting to a quality-labelled apartment house in the village.

Left: The pedestrian precinct in Skellefteå.

Top left: Volleyball players on Möj igheternas torg
(Possibility Square) in Skellefteå.

Bottom left: Elephants walking along Nygatan in Skellefteå.

Top right: Trädgårdsgatan in Skellefteå with the Town Hall
in the background.

Bottom right: Outdoor restaurant on Möjligheternas torg.

Top left: The Erikslid residential area in Skellefteå.

Bottom left: Odenplatsen by Nygatan in Skellefteå.

Top right: The Expolaris Center in Skellefteå.

Bottom right: Skellefteå's central park with the cast-iron fountain 'Johanna in the Park'.

Opposite: The modernistic Kanalskolan in Skellefteå.

Next spread: The oldest wooden roadbridge is to be found in Sweden. It is a strut-frame bridge reinforced by trusses on some of its spans. Ever since 1737 the Lejonström Bridge, now 207 meters long, has been a key connecting link across the river Skellefteälv.

Top left: Church cottages in Bonnstan, the old town in Skellefteå. They were used for accommodation during the time of obligatory church attendance.

Bottom left: Time has stood still in the Nordanå area. Amidst the greenery there is a rich culture centre with Skellefteå Museum as its hub. In the picture, quilted statues that formed part of an exhibition held in the area in 1998.

Top right: A suspension bridge in Skellefteå, leading out to Kyrkholmen.

Bottom right: Warming up for a running competition in the Nordanå area.

Opposite: Burning of tar pile is a tradition over the holy weekend held in Skellefteå in June.

Next spread: Old buildings in Klutmark, combined with modern summer houses.

Top left: Potato fields in Myckle, with a typical Västerbotten farmyard in the background.

Bottom left: The small village of Gammelboliden outside Fällfors has five households and is locally renowned for the amount of snow that falls in the winter.

Top right: The chapel of the Bjuröklubb on the outskirts of the archipelago. The assembled fishermen before going out to sea.

Bottom right: With its conglomeration of small buildings, Lövånger's church community resembles a town of the Middle Ages. The cottages are now used as a youth hostel.

Opposite: In Åselet at Byske river there is a nature reserve of national interest. There is also a beautiful settlement environment on this delta landscape.

The musician that always returns home

Fredrik 'Fritte' Enqvist grew up in Boliden. When he was 10 years old the local anti-drug project 'Rocksnoken' visited the community centre. Just before the concert, after the orchestra had placed their instruments on the stage, Fritte sneaked up and performed a drum solo. "They were obviously impressed and I was taken on as one of the project's drum players," he tells us.

He was hooked on music and practised every day at Duvan youth centre, which has a fully equipped music room. "Skellefteå has very good recreation facilities for young people who are interested in music," says Fritte.

Together with some friends he formed a group that played hard rock. The House of Music on Mullberget in Skellefteå became the group's home. Local bands can cheaply hire practice rooms from the local council here. "The House of Music enables groups from Skellefteå to practice their skills up to a professional level without going broke."

In 1992 Fritte and his group Wade got their first record contract. He admits that the telephone call from the record company is one of the best things to have happened in his life. The Skellefteå-based record company was called A Westside Fabrication, and is run by Joakim Wallström. Joakim has launched several local pop groups that have done well on the international music scene – among them, The Wannadies, This Perfect Day and The Drowners.

An important reason for there being so many good pop groups in Skellefteå is the presence of a record company around the corner. "All the musicians know Joakim and getting a record contract is a goal that seems obtainable," says Fritte. He tells us that Joakim Wallström has received a "Grammis" award for his contributions to the Swedish music scene.

Another contributing factor to this success is access to the Rumble Road studio, run by the sound technician, Kjell Nästén. In Fritte's opinion this studio is one of the best in Sweden.

In Skellefteå there are 50 active pop groups. Fredrik Enqvist feels that all the bands are of a very high standard. Many members of the groups play in several bands at the same time. They often play one instrument in one group and another in the next. "It's good practice to try out different types of compositions and musical styles."

In 1997 Wade took part in a EU project 'Young Companies in the Music Business', which offered the opportunity to work professionally as a musician for one year. →

Above: Fredrik "Fritte" Enqvist, prominent figure in the pop group Wade.

Opposite top: The Wannadies is one of the most well known pop groups from Skellefteå. In 1998, they released an album entitled Skellefteå. "My Hometown", one of their greatest hits, is a tribute to their childhood town.

Opposite bottom: The Trästock Festival in Skellefteå is a music festival held annually where new and interesting music and culture is introduced. The festival is free and the emphasis on the many performers is local. Wade is depicted here, playing at Trästock in 1998.

"We were able to create material for a new record, practice, tour and establish international contacts."

The project resulted in Wade, who now play a slightly harder guitar-based pop-rock, signing a contract with an American company. For part of the year the group's members live in Los Angeles, making it easier to tour North America. "But I will always have my home in Skellefteå. The town is too good for me to leave. Large cities are so impersonal. It is in Skellefteå that I can develop as a musician and a person. Here everyone is on the same level. Even someone who is successful is just a normal Skellefteå guy and it's no good trying to pretend you're better than anyone else."

In musical terms, Skellefteå is no longer just a pop town. There are also lots of musicians here who play jazz, classical music and folk music, and do choral singing. The municipal music school in Skellefteå has a good reputation in Sweden, as does the music program at Anderstorp upper secondary school. "I myself learnt the basics of drumming at the municipal music school," says Fredrik 'Fritte' Enqvist, who is now mainly a guitarist and vocalist.

Top left: 95 percent of local school pupils have studied at the Skellefteå Municipal School of Music. This is a very high number compared with other municipalities in the country. One reason for this popularity is that the lessons at the school of music are free of charge. The school of music in Skellefteå is renowned for its high class of music teachers.

Bottom left: Skellefteå is the town of choirs. Lead by conductor Leif Åkesson, the Skellefteå Chamber Choir has been very successful in national choir competitions.

Below: A brass band at full blast on the town square in Skellefteå.

Top: Barn dancing in Ljusvattnet, Burträsk

Centre: The Skellefteå Dance and Ballet Society run an extensive operation among the children of Skellefteå. Depicted here is a performance for the public at the Nordanå Theatre.

Bottom: "Burträsksvängen" is a must for all lovers of folk music. Depicted here are Daniel Pettersson, Boliden, Daniel Fredriksson, Umeå and Gösta Pettersson, Boliden.

Opposite: A tranquil concert in the open during the Tjärholmen Festival in Byske.

Wordsmith with his hands on the wheel

Göran Lundin was born in Skellefteå, and his early years were spent with his family in the Älvsbacka area. Then they moved to Umeå. His great dream was to become a journalist, and he fulfilled this by attending the Department of Journalism, Media and Communication at Stockholm University. Göran worked as freelance and specializing as a foreign correspondent. Among other assignments, he covered Iraq and Turkey. "But I tired of this type of reporting after a few years and wanted to write fiction," he says.

Göran realized, however that he could not immediately make a living from writing books, so he chose to get a 'normal' job from which he could take a sabbatical when the time came to sit down at the typewriter. "I wanted to get back to my roots in Skellefteå and started as a driver with the Skellefteå bus company," says Göran. Ever since his return home he has lived in the Anderstorp residential area.

In 1981 Göran Lundin made his debut with 'Den svarte generalen', a historical novel about Haiti. Since his debut he has written about ten books. In some of them the main theme has comes from his everyday work 'Busschaufförren som försvann' is one example. "As a bus driver you get to meet a lot of people, and wonder what fates are concealed behind their appearances. Driving a bus is also an ideal way of letting your thoughts flow freely.

In 1991 Göran and another writer started the company Ord & Visor, which not only publishes its own books but also promotes other writers. Göran was now in a position to realize his dream of publishing a new edition of Kurt Salomonson's first novel 'Hungerdansen'. "His authorship has meant a great deal for my development," Göran tells us. Hjoggböle is a kind of literary centre in the municipality. As well as Kurt Salomonson, P. O. Enqvist, Anita Salomonson and Hjalmar Westerlund also have their roots here. Other renowned local writers are Sara Lidman from Missenträsk and Åke Lundgren from Kusmark.

Göran Lundin is of the opinion that there is a kind of special interest in writing books in Skellefteå municipality. It can be seen not least in the village chronicles that have been produced over the years.

Even among the youth of Skellefteå there is an urge to write. For example, the pupils of Kaplan upper secondary school publish a collection of poems each year under the title 'Tankarnas trädgård'.

Göran Lundin feels that the literary strength to be found in Skellefteå has been born out of the encounter between the hard struggle for survival and openness to new solutions – the hallmarks of the community.

The Västerbotten Theatre, based in Skellefteå, is a regional theatre that often makes its voice heard through its exciting productions.

The biggest public successes of the Västerbotten Theatre have been dramatizations of Sara Lidman's and Torgny Lindgren's works," says Göran Lundin.

Above: Göran Lundin, bus driver and author.

Opposite top: Each summer the Västerbotten Theatre puts on special performances. Locations vary. In these performances the Västerbotten ensemble works together with amateurs. Here, Jevgenij Schwarz's play 'The Dragon' is being performed on Vitberget.

Opposite bottom left: Roland Hedlund and Kajsa Ernst in a powerful scene from the Västerbotten Theatre production of Torgny Lindgren's "Hummelhonung".

Opposite bottom right: Sara Lidman from Missenträsk is one of the best known authors from the municipality. Her books have been sold in large editions and translated into several languages.

Artistic chaos out of security

Margaretha Holmlund has lived in Hjoggböle for the greater part of her life. Attached to her house is the ceramics workshop that is the scene of her creations. "I had a child at 18 and have never wanted to move around. But I have travelled a lot and got impressions from other places. I like the contrast between the calmness of life in the country and the pulse of the big city," she says.

Margaretha has always had a burning interest in art. Her mother, who came to Hjoggböle from Finland after the Second World War, was an early source of inspiration. "She had an unusual playfulness that was very contagious," says Margaretha. She tells us that her daughter Karolina, who is studying at the Royal Academy of Fine Arts in Stockholm, is also following the same path.

After upper secondary school, Margaretha earned her living as an art teacher, and in the mid-70s attended the Arts and Crafts course at the Edelvik Folk High School in Burträsk. Ceramics became her niche and her pots sold well. But, by her own standards, her great artistic leap forward did not come until 1986.

"I was on a course and met a sculptor who helped me become bolder. Only then did I allow my own chaos to appear in my work," she tells us, pointing out that you

have to be a complete person in order to find a healthy relation between order and chaos.

Her ceramics and sculptures attract considerable attention and have been shown at exhibitions in Sweden, Finland, Germany and Poland. Today, Margaretha combines a teaching post at the Edelvik Folk High School with creating her works of art. "I have an understanding employer who allows me to be free from my teaching post when I want to go into a creative period."

Margaretha Holmlund feels that there is a rich cultural life in the community. Two of the artistic tone-setters are the sculptor Torfrid Olsson from Bygdeträsk, and the painter Sture Meijer from Kåge.

Anyone who visits Skellefteå can, as a rule, find an art exhibition in 'Synvinkeln' in the Nordanå area. Margaretha Holmlund also thinks that Burträskbygden's art society has exciting exhibitions, as does the Anna Nordlander Museum in Skellefteå, one of three women's art museums in Sweden.

Handens Hus, which is also in the Nordanå area, is the central meeting place for woodworkers, handicraft specialists and artisans in Skellefteå. There they have an exhibition area, skilled advisers and the opportunity to attend courses.

Above: The sculptress, Margaretha Holmlund from Hjoggböle.

Opposite top: Art exhibition at Museum Anna Nordlander. The museum works to develop various forms of art performed by women.

Opposite bottom: Sculpture of ice and snow on the Town Square in Skellefteå. Behind it were the Solvik folk high school, the municipal authorities and the Skellefteå photography club.

Priest with a touch of insolence and a poor voice

Hans Marklund grew up in the Brännan area of Skellefteå and today lives right in the centre. His parents were involved in the Swedish Church, and after confirmation he adopted his own stance and became an active Christian. During his upper secondary school days he went to the US as an exchange student. "It was there that I decided to become a priest. I saw the church as a good forum for brotherly commitment. Also I was better at speaking than singing," he says.

After entering the priesthood in 1976, Hans immediately became a missionary. In Tanzania he spent almost five years building a youth club in the church. "Duties ranged from preaching to training the football team."

Back in Sweden Hans served in Luleå and Robertsfors before moving back to Skellefteå in 1990 to work as a local priest in the Anderstorp residential area. He was also involved in the treatment of alcoholics, following the Minnesota method. And then he became head of information for the Church of Sweden Aid international aid organization. "That involved some interesting years with many trips around the world."

Despite the experiences that such work involved, Hans longed to return to ordinary work as a priest, which gives close contact with people in times of both joy and sorrow. "You feel needed," Hans Marklund explains. He is now a local priest again, this time in the Morö Backe area.

Skellefteå is a municipality in which religion is taken very seriously. If you examine the full list of Swedish priests, you will find an over-representation of people from Skellefteå. Over the last 20 years four Swedish bishops have had their roots here.

"And many Christians from Skellefteå are working as missionaries." Hans believes that missionary commitment and strong entrepreneurship go hand-in-hand. "People from Skellefteå want to take part in developing organizations, and through the church community there are natural meeting places for networks to grow," he tells us.

Sweden's Evangelical Mission (EFS) has one of its strongholds in Skellefteå. It is a lay movement that grew up alongside the Swedish Church. In the town as well as the villages around the municipality there are prayer houses where EFS lay preachers take the services. "Today, the Swedish church and EFS work very well together," says Hans.

He believes that EFS plays an important role in forging the down-to-earth, character of Skellefteå's inhabitants. "The fact that people in Skellefteå are dismissive of hierarchies is probably a result of lay preachers' daring to stand up in the pulpit without any formal training for the priesthood," says Hans, who himself is known for straight talking and speaking out on sensitive issues.

In Skellefteå municipality there are many church buildings worth seeing. Hans Marklund thinks that the Skellefteå Landskyrka, the rural church, is one of the most beautiful. "It's shaped like a Greek temple. It gives a profound experience of God's greatness when full to capacity the first Sunday in Advent or at the Christmas and Midsummer services," he says.

Above: Hans Marklund, local priest in the Morö Backe area.

Opposite: Lucia procession at Byske Church.

Left: Finnträsk Church. In 1914, the village farmers decided to build a church based on drawings by the two villagers Robert and Gunnar Lundqvist.

Top: Celebrating the eve of May Day outside the church in Kåge. The arrival of Spring is celebrated outside churches in several places around Skellefteå. For Skellefteå's part, it takes place outside Landskyrkan.

Bottom: Christmas festivities at the chapel in Frostkåge. The chapel is a meeting-point for spiritualness and prayer of old. Today, the chapel occasionally has more wide-ranging uses.

Top: New Year prayers in Byske Church. Traditionally, churches have many visitors on New Year's Eve. It gives the opportunity to sum up the past year and allows an hour of peace and spiritualness.

Bottom: Boliden Church was designed by the architect, Peter Cellsing.

Opposite: Skellefteå Landskyrka, the largest rural church in Sweden, in winter garb.

Next spread: Church cottages in Bonnstan, the old town in Skellefteå. They were used for accommodation during the time of obligatory church attendance.

A stubborn swimmer who kept her buoyancy

Eila Nilsson grew up in Norsjö. She was trained as an assistant nurse and worked at the nursing home in her village. When Eila was 23 years old, her life changed drastically.

"I had diabetes and haemorrhages in my eyes. Nine months after the initial bleeding, I was totally blind," she says.

Eila put onto a rehabilitation program, and re-trained as a masseuse. She moved to Skellefteå and got a job at the rheumatology ward in the hospital. Because of the tremendous change in her life caused by the disease, Eila had become overweight and unfit. Now, it was a matter of finding a suitable form of exercise.

"I enjoyed swimming, because it was something I could do without an attendant," she says.

Eila Nilsson had taken part in some swimming competitions as a child. A trainer in the sports association for the disabled in Skellefteå discovered her talent as Eila covered lap after lap in the Eddahallen pool.

"After only 10 weeks of training I competed at the National Championships and got to the final of the 50-meters free-style," she says.

The achievement encouraged her and in 1992 she set a new world record for the 50-metres free-style. The year after that, she won gold in the European Championships. But she was now content with her accomplishments and fed up with success. When Eila got herself a guide dog she quit swimming completely so that she could put all her efforts into the training of the dog.

However, with the ParaOlympics of 1996 approaching, her competitive instinct re-emerged. She recharged her batteries and trained intensively in the outdoor pool in Kåge.

"Not many people believed in me then, and it felt great to prove them wrong. I won gold at both 50 and 100 meters free-style thanks to my technique and stubbornness," she says.

One of Eila's fondest memories in life was the home-coming, when masses of Norsjö and Skellefteå locals came to congratulate her as she got off the plane.

"It felt as if the whole of Skellefteå shared my delight with me. That is one of the advantages of living in a medium-sized town. Everything becomes very personal," she says.

Eila now lives in the residential area and works at Sinnenas Gym run by the Urkraft association. As well as giving massage, she lectures on personal development and crisis management.

"The best thing with sports in Skellefteå is its variety," maintains Eila.

"Almost everybody is involved and every weekend there is something exciting happening sports-wise. There are many clubs with excellent trainers, and we have great facilities within the municipality," she says.

It is not only Skellefteå's Eila Nilsson who has reached world class in sport. There is more than one European Champion, World Champion and Olympic Games medallist walking the streets of Skellefteå. They consist of ice-hockey players, free-style skiers, tennis players, cyclists, weightlifters, and so on. And if you go on to count National Championship winners, you will quickly run out of fingers.

"The most important thing is not to get a medal, but to achieve your own goals," says Eila Nilsson in conclusion.

Above: The swimmer, Eila Nilsson.

Opposite: Marie Lindgren from Burträsk won a silver medal in free-style at the Olympic Games in Lillehammer in 1994.

Top: Skellefteå KFUM Volleyball has a women's team in the élite series. Erika Lindström ensuring that the ball gets over the net.

Bottom: Skellefteå AIK is a club with a strong ice-hockey tradition that has brought up many international players. Johan Wikberg (in black) is playing for the junior team.

Top: Sunnanå Sports Club's women's team is in the top division. It has even won the National Championships. Malin Gustafsson (in blue) in a tussle with an opponent.

Bottom: Skellefteå Baseball Club has won the national league several times. Daniel Jonsson, Jonas Brännström and Erik Lundqvist celebrate a homerun.

Next spread: Skellefteå holds its Midnight Marathon each summer. The runners passing through Bonnstan.

Top: The children hold their own Midnight Marathon.

Bottom: Dragracing on Torsgatan in Skellefteå.

Opposite: Triathlon competition on the river Skellefteälv.

The search for a meaningful sparetime

Barbro Grebacken grew up in Jämtland in the village of Ås. After working for some time as a waitress in Stockholm she started studying geology at the Luleå University of Technology. She changed direction in the middle of her course and entered the world of wood technology. In 1986 she ended up as a student at the college of higher education in Skellefteå. "It was very easy to be accepted in town and I absolutely didn't feel like an outsider. I took Skellefteå to my heart," she tells us.

After school Barbro worked in quality control with Lovene Dörr, the door manufacturers, in Lidköping. She also ran her own company in the wood industry. The Grebacken family, however, longed to move back north. "I never liked the flat landscape and lack of winter snow in western Sweden."

Both she and her husband Pontus got jobs in Skellefteå in 1998 – he with Dentronic and she as a project leader with Trätek in Skellefteå. They found their house in Sunnanå on the Internet. "We live right on the edge of the forest, but still very near town," she says.

Everyone in the Grebacken family takes delight in the forest and the land. Each weekend they make an excursion together. In the summer it is often a cycling expedition, or else they go swimming. "The sea around Bureå is our favourite place for swimming. Grilling sausages at Rovön, which lies beside Lejonström Bridge, is also great, and so is taking a coffee break at Kyrkholmen."

Barbro tells us that the children became quite lyrical when they moved up to Skellefteå and the snow. In the winter the family goes both cross-country and downhill skiing. In the woods behind the house there is a 2.5-kilometer-long lit track where they train during winter evenings. Downhill skiing is mainly on the local sports association's ski slope in Bygdsiljum. "It's a very pleasant and wellcared for development with a main slope that is difficult enough for us grown-ups, and also nursery slopes where you dare to let the children loose. When the children get older we will probably start going to the Storklinta slopes, which are much tougher."

Barbro Grebacken's own favourite pastime is hunting. When she was 9 years old she accompanied her father moose-hunting and got the bug. Until 1990 she was there only to find the animals but then she got her hunting licence.

"To walk around in the forest listening for mooses is an indescribably exciting experience. For me it isn't necessary to shoot a moose, but I can't deny that it is a powerful feeling to bring down an animal. The adrenaline rush is very high," she tells us.

There are still not many women who hunt, so Barbro is sometimes met with amazed looks when she turns up with her gun. "But I'm used to it, because there aren't many girls in the wood industry either," she says.

Above: Barbro Grebacken.

Opposite: Fishing enthusiast Jan Marklund fly-fishing for salmon in the river Byskeälv considered by many to be the best for salmon in the whole of Sweden.

Top: Mushroom-picking in one of Skellefteå's forests.

Centre: Snowboarding on the Vitberget mountain near the town centre.

Bottom: Joggers on Rovön island in Skellefteå.

Opposite: Ronnbäcken's golf course lies in undulating forest and parkland. It has 27 holes.

Next spread: For Skellefteå dwellers a summer cottage is an important place to relax. This one is in Vättingen, Båtvik.

Left: Byske Camping is one of the largest camping sites in the country

Top right: The whole family out angling.

Bottom right: Children bathing in one of Skellefteå's many rivers.

Cincinnati
Majestic Vision

Cincinnati
Majestic Vision

Introduction
by Nick Clooney

Art Direction
by Bob Kimball

Sponsored by the
Greater Cincinnati
Chamber of Commerce

Cincinnati
Majestic Vision

Contents

URBAN
TAPESTRY
SERIES
TOWERY
PUBLISHING, INC.

By Nick Clooney

There are many ways to tell the story of Cincinnati, and over the years, I have tried most of them.

It is possible to trace the Queen City's history by focusing on the Ohio River, or on the hills that stand guard over its basin, or on the migrations that have changed its face, generation by generation. Cincinnati's commerce does have its story to tell, as do its educational institutions and the widely varied pursuits we crowd under the umbrella of "the arts."

The writer is tempted to scurry off, pencil in hand, to every neighborhood, giving the reader a smattering of that and a smidgen of this in the hope that the end result will convey some sense of the vibrant community Winston Churchill once called "the most beautiful inland city in America." This writer has succumbed to that temptation—and more than once. The results have been decidedly mixed.

So, let's you and I undertake an experiment. Instead of traveling at breakneck speed from Newtown in the east to Cheviot in the west and from Hebron in the south to Mason in the north, let's stay in one spot and see how much Cincinnati history might wash over us.

Picking the spot won't be easy. My guess is that we would learn more about the real Cincinnati if we were able to sit on the front stoop of one of the humble buildings that were homes to Cincinnatians who worked for a living, paid their rent, raised their families, found joy in homely things, and inched the city forward with their industry, honesty, and faith in the future. The problem with humble homes, however, is that they seldom survive a generation or two—victims of fire, flood, poverty, or the bulldozers of progress.

If we are to hear walls talk, they will have to belong to the home of someone prosperous, a substantial house that survived the depredations of time and whose residents could stay the wrecking ball with an imperious gesture. ▶

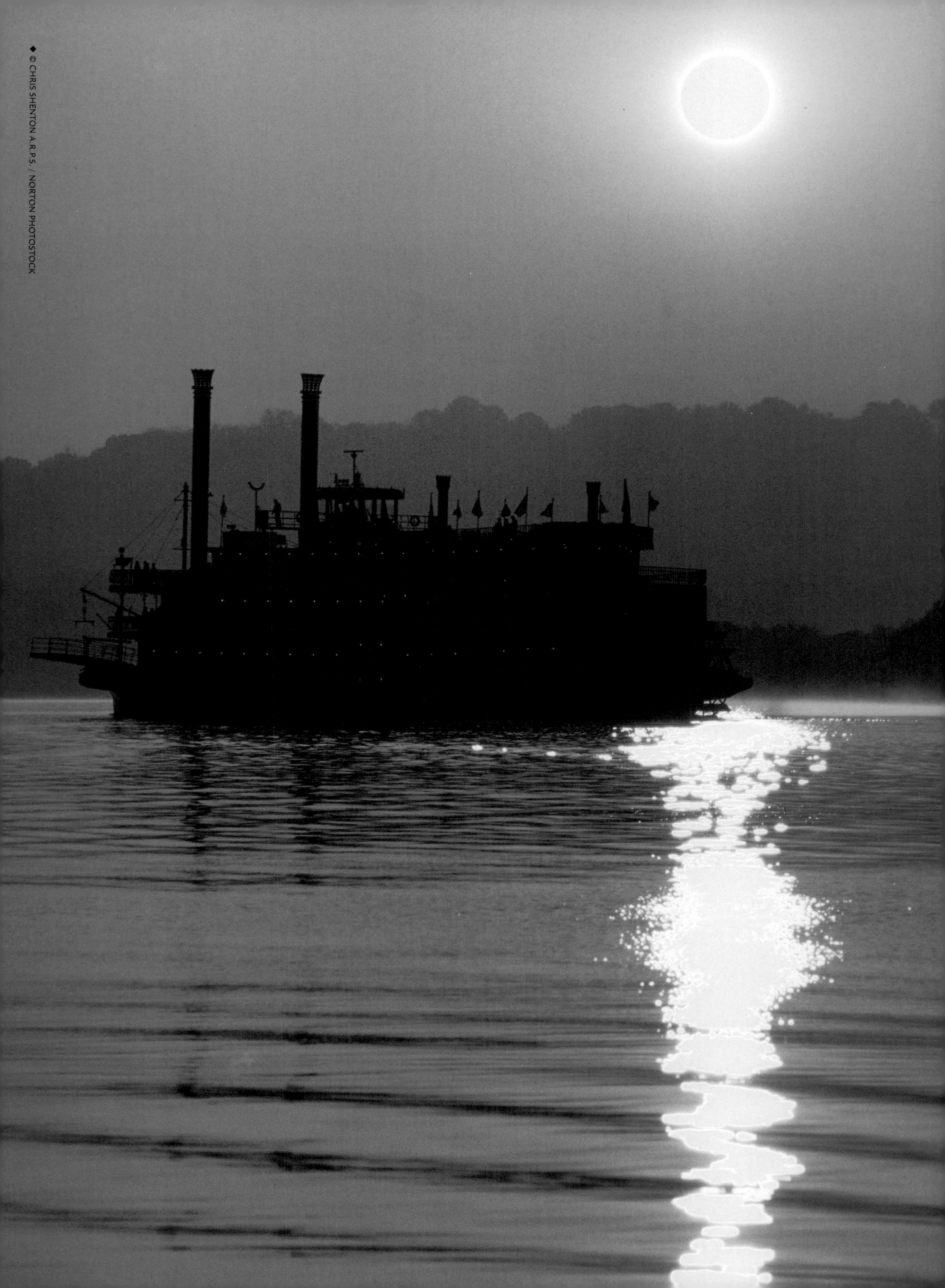

A home such as the one we now call the Taft Museum of Art at Fourth and Pike streets downtown, for instance. It didn't begin life as a museum, of course. It was a house—and what a house it was. Perhaps this is a place where we can pause and listen as the forces of change storm its formidable gates.

By the time the plans for the house that would become the Taft Museum were completed and its foundation begun in 1819, the city was already more than 30 years old and had been launched on a period of prodigious growth. The tiny huddling of cabins in 1788 named Losantiville; the fort called Washington; the fear of Indian raids; the name change to Cincinnati; the world-changing first sighting of the experimental steamboat *New Orleans* in 1811—all seemed distant memories, almost quaint. Cincinnati was a town "on the make," in no mood to dwell on yesterday. Toughs and teachers, saints and sinners crowded the waterfront.

For the next 30 years, Cincinnati would be the fastest-growing city in the fastest-growing nation in the Western world. In that period, it would be, by turns, America's leading meat packer, wine producer, and, finally, manufacturing center. Despite a few, brief setbacks, Cincinnati was America's boomtown, with all that implied.

Inevitably, those who were getting rich wanted to show off their wealth, and just as inevitably, the way they chose to do that was by building themselves spectacular homes.

And so it was with the house that is serving as our historical stoop: As 1820 dawned, Martin Baum began to frame up one of the most beautiful homes west of the eastern seaboard. The site was well out of the Ohio River's floodplain, far above the offensive odors and sounds of Rat Row and other riverfront hangouts for the rowdy elements of the burgeoning city. (There were enough rowdy elements to go around. The army garrison had years before been shifted from Cincinnati to Newport Barracks across the river, within sight of Baum's edifice, and already the pockets of prostitution, gambling, and saloons that often surround military bases were flourishing. The vice would outlast the barracks and cast a century-long shadow over Newport.) ▶

And up went the Baum house. By now, the area bounded by East Fourth and East Third, with Broadway to the west and Pike to the east, had become fashionable. There were still a number of small, middle-class homes and many shops, but the enclave was in the process of being dominated by large, single-family mansions with polished brass plates announcing some of the most famous names in Cincinnati.

Premium among them was Nicholas Longworth, who, a few years after the house was built, bought Baum's masterpiece and named it Belmont. Longworth had come to Cincinnati in 1808, and had soon begun buying and selling land. He was so successful that, by 1830, he was not only the richest man in Cincinnati, but, many whispered, maybe the richest man in the nation.

At the same time he was moving into Belmont, Longworth's vineyards on nearby Mount Ida were contributing to Cincinnati's successful wine industry. He called the collection of vine-growing fields on the side of the hill the Garden of Eden and, after a shattering blight killed their vines, the Longworth family presented the fields to Cincinnati. They became Eden Park. Earlier, Henry Wadsworth Longfellow, impressed by what he had seen on Mount Ida, wrote a poem to the Catawba grape in which he referred to Cincinnati as the Queen City of the West. And Queen City it has been ever since.

(A footnote regarding Longworth's Mount Ida: John Quincy Adams came to the city to dedicate an observatory at the top of the hill, after which Mount Ida was renamed Mount Adams in his honor.) ▶

Before we get too caught up in fashionable Fourth Street, it should be recalled that in 1835, Cincinnati was America's largest meat packer and, by 1845, was number one in the world. Most of that meat was pork, and the daily experience of those who would brave the streets of downtown Cincinnati back then is beyond the comprehension of today's Cincinnatian.

Imagine the sight of hundreds of pigs being driven through the streets of the city to any of a dozen slaughterhouses. Their droppings were everywhere. Strays wandered through residential streets and alleys, digging through garbage—their grunts and squeals a constant element of the city's sounds. When others called Cincinnati Porkopolis, it was not a compliment.

But the sounds were music to at least some ears. James Gamble, for instance, dealt with several meatpacking companies for their fat scraps to make soap and candles. When a man named William Procter came to town, he and Gamble were thrown together because they were married to two women who were sisters. Procter thought the business could be expanded with proper marketing, so, in 1837, they opened a shop at Sixth and Main streets, just three blocks from Longworth's Belmont. The site of their shop is currently the site for the international headquarters of the giant Procter & Gamble conglomerate, one of the biggest companies in the world.

What became of Porkopolis? Some 165 years later, it was metamorphosed into the Big Pig Gig, a five-month paean of praise to the pig, during which a grateful city honored its humble roots by calling on the arts community to salute the noble porker—its malodorous trips through the city long forgotten and forgiven.

Back in the 1830s, while teas and dances and dinners and conspicuous consumption of every description reigned on here at our mansion on East Fourth Street, darker forces were at work just a few blocks west. The great debate of the era concerned slavery, and Cincinnati could not escape its consequences. Ohio was a free state, but Cincinnati's merchants and manufacturers did a great deal of their business with the South. Kentucky, less than a mile away across the Ohio River, was a slave state. Cincinnati was deeply divided in its attitude toward the "Negro question."

There was one newspaper, the *Philanthropist*, that raised the banner of abolition in the 1830s. Even the mention of the word was incendiary in those days, and reaction to each proabolition editorial was an escalation in anger from forces of the status quo. In 1836, a mob of rowdies broke into the *Philanthropist*'s office, and took out its press, dragged it through downtown streets, and threw it into the river.

STAR

To emphasize the point, they then stormed the small African-American section of town, burning houses and sending residents fleeing. City officials and the business and religious communities, by and large, remained silent in the face of these outrages.

Not all onlookers were unmoved. Harriet Beecher Stowe, a temporary resident of Cincinnati, saw the conflict here at the North-South border in a way she never could have done in her native New England. She even attended slave auctions in Kentucky. The experience burned into her memory and seared across the pages of her *Uncle Tom's Cabin* in 1852.

What came to be known as the Underground Railroad was already active in Cincinnati. Most of those doing the dangerous work of getting escaped slaves out of the South were African-American, the majority of whose names were lost to history.

But this was not the case with their heroic work. Soon, on Cincinnati's rejuvenated riverfront, the Freedom Center will rise, a monument to the struggle for freedom and equality in our nation, using the courageous example of the Underground Railroad for inspiration.

Before we leave the critical period of 1820 through 1850, mention should be made of the Miami-Erie Canal, which played a major role in Cincinnati's prosperity, bringing produce and livestock to the city at a fraction of what it had cost the farmer earlier. As the canal wound through the city itself, it cut across downtown's North-South streets. The area north of the canal became an entryway for immigrant populations. At this time, many of those immigrants were German, so the canal came to be referred to, jokingly, as the Rhine, with the neighborhood north of the canal called Over-the-Rhine. Today's Central Parkway traces the route of the old canal, and the area north of the parkway is still referred to as Over-the-Rhine.

During the Civil War, Cincinnati was one of the nation's most important supply and transportation centers. The fighting never actually got to the city's door, although there were threats enough. A major battle was fought in 1862 in Perryville, Kentucky, just 150 miles south of Cincinnati, and bloody skirmishes struck much closer than that. Moreover, John Hunt Morgan led a Confederate cavalry detachment on a raid that was actually north of Cincinnati, so there was enough nearby combat to keep the city jittery for most of the war. ▶

After Appomattox, Cincinnati had to come to terms with a new reality. The great republic, with renewed energy after the cataclysm of war, was exploding westward. Cincinnati was no longer the nation's fastest-growing city, nor its leading manufacturer. While it was still an important center of commerce, many in Cincinnati thought it was time to focus more resources on the city's quality of life. The 20 years after the war saw an astonishing outburst of creativity, the result of which remains with us today: the completion of the Roebling Suspension Bridge through a coalition of private and public money; the formation of the nation's first all-professional baseball team; the erection of the Tyler Davidson Fountain, center-piece of Fountain Square; the magnificent Music Hall; the construction or expansion of public parks on prime real estate; a major enhancement to the University of Cincinnati (UC); the foundation of a world-class zoo; and the construction of the Cincinnati Art Museum and the Art Academy of Cincinnati. This is only a partial list, and it should be noted that every one of these assets remains a jewel in the Queen City's crown today.

And what had been going on all this time at Fourth and Pike streets, where the Longworths were living when last we checked in?

Longworth was a patron of the arts and wanted his beloved Belmont to have only the best. In a most unusual gesture for the time, he hired Robert Duncanson to paint extensive murals on the walls. Not only was Duncanson relatively unknown, he was also African-American. In 1841 America, that was virtually unheard of. Eventually, Duncanson became a leading American landscape artist, known and admired around the world.

After the Civil War, Belmont had a brief career as a girls' school, but in 1871, it was purchased by another wealthy Cincinnatian, David Sinton. Sinton had a 19-year-old daughter named Anna, and this was the home Anna loved beyond all others.

Fourth Street, still fashionable, had begun to change. Four blocks west was a tavern called the Mecca, which was headquarters for a man named George Cox. Though he never attained high elective office, Cox became the very definition of the big-city political boss. For 30 years, "Boss" Cox ran Cincinnati. While he initially brought a kind of order out of the social chaos of post-Civil War Cincinnati, the cost he exacted was exorbitant. Corruption, patronage, intimidation, vote buying: These were the coins of Boss Cox's realm. At the turn of the 20th century, Cincinnati was called "the worst-governed city in America."

In the meantime, Anna Sinton married Charles P. Taft and, after the death of her father, the couple moved into the beautiful home at Fourth and Pike. The Taft family seemed to excel wherever they hung their hats. It was on the porch

of what was now called the Taft Home that Cincinnati's William Howard Taft—Charles' half brother—accepted the nomination of the Republican Party for president of the United States in 1908.

It was at this time that Charles P. and Anna Taft embarked on an ambitious project to accumulate fine art. Interesting timing, because this was also the time the neighborhood was in flux. Factories were sprouting up all over the downtown area and thick, black smoke blanketed the city's basin. Former residents of the fashionable Fourth Street enclave fled. But not the Tafts. Not even when a factory moved in right next to them. Not even when the smoke began to damage the paintings.

Instead, the Tafts supported efforts to improve the neighborhood. They pushed for a green space that became Lytle Park. They encouraged the building of comfortable quarters for respectable working women. They sold a fine building to the Cincinnati Literary Club down the block. And they soon participated in building upscale apartments nearby to lure some upper-middle-class Cincinnatians back downtown, a venture that was only partially successful.

All of this was being done while winds of change were whirling around the core of Cincinnati. The great move to the suburbs had already begun. Public transportation allowed the growth of Walnut Hills, Westwood, even faraway Glendale.

Those winds of change, however, had even more profound implications. The nation was slowly tilting toward war, and it was war with the nation that a large proportion of Cincinnatians called their homeland—Germany. The First World War was a body blow to many Cincinnatians. Some few had divided loyalties, but most were perfectly clear about which side they were on. Recruiting was brisk. A number of German families changed their surnames, and shortly after the declaration of war against Germany in April 1917, the Cincinnati City Council changed the names of most streets that honored German places or historical figures. Gone were Bismarck, Bremen, German, and Berlin streets, for instance.

When the boys came marching home from over there, it was to an Ohio River frozen over and a rampant flu epidemic. But awaiting just beyond these immediate troubles was another period of boom times. The 1920s in Cincinnati featured

fun. Vaudeville was still around, but giving way to movie palaces. Dance bands were everywhere. There were amusement parks, roadhouses, bootleg liquor, bobbed hair, scandalously short skirts, and "sheiks." Ominously, Prohibition seemed to give rise to scofflaws and lent a certain legitimacy to underworld characters who gave the public what they wanted.

It was in the mid-1920s that Mary Emery a wealthy Cincinnati widow, dreamed the dream of a community based on the model of an English village, with rents targeted for people of all incomes. Unfortunately, cost overruns for Emery's beautiful Mariemont caused rents to be higher than she had hoped, closing out all but middle- to upper-middle-income families. Mariemont remains one of the city's most desirable neighborhoods, as it was when it opened in 1926.

All of this would become irrelevant in the triple whammy about to strike Cincinnati. The stock market crash, in 1929, led directly to the Great Depression. Stark numbers tell the story. In 1929, unemployment was 6 percent. By 1931, it was 19 percent. A year later, 28 percent. And in 1933, a heart-stopping 30 percent. Even those numbers don't tell the whole story. Many of those with jobs were underemployed. For instance, in the nadir year of 1933, one-half of Cincinnati's white workforce was employed full-time, but for Cincinnati's African-American workers, that percentage fell to one-third.

Yet, in these trying times, the city lifted two more of its landmarks to the sky: Carew Tower and Union Terminal. It was also at this time that the home in front of which we have figuratively been standing throughout this imaginary tour through the decades was codified as a landmark. Anna Taft had already decided that the house she loved would be a gift to the city she loved. When she died in 1931, the Cincinnati Institute of Fine Arts was ready to fulfill her wishes; Taft Museum opened in 1932.

By that time, only two of Cincinnati's five inclines remained open. They had been built in the 19th century to help horse-drawn wagons and buses get up the Queen City's famous hills. With the rise of electric trolleys and gas-powered autos, they were not as necessary to the city's transportation needs as before, and the Main Street-Mount Auburn, Bellevue-Clifton, and Fairview-Clifton Heights inclines were all closed. Still open were Price Hill and Mount Adams. Part of the charm of the inclines was the restaurants the rider could find at the summit. To

the west, it was Price Hill House, but because William Price, who operated the incline, disapproved of alcohol in any form, Price Hill House came to be known as Buttermilk House and the summit itself as Buttermilk Hill. There was no such compunction at the Mount Adams Highland House, where waiters were more than willing to slake Cincinnati's world-famous thirst just as soon as the government announced it was legal to do so again. Some said before. These last two bastions closed, respectively, in 1943 and 1948, and are still mourned by those of a certain age.

Just as Cincinnati was beginning to recover from the worst of the depression—unemployment had dropped to 20 percent—the Ohio River went on its most damaging rampage in recorded history. That is a considerable thing to say, because the river exceeded the flood stage of 52 feet with appalling regularity. A couple of times—1884 and 1913—the crest had even touched or passed the unimaginable 70-foot level.

Then came 1937. From January 18, when the Ohio first slipped out of its banks, to February 5, when it finally dropped back under flood level, Greater Cincinnati was pressed to its limits to deal with the raging torrent of muddy water. On January 26, the river actually reached 79.99 feet. One Cincinnatian had died and some 100,000 were out of their homes. Many communities never recovered. Flood wall construction was accelerated and, in a real sense, Cincinnati gave up and turned its back on the river.

By the mid-1930s, the federal government had created some 35,000 vital jobs for Cincinnati's breadwinners. These were not make-work projects. Under varying programs, government employees built Columbia Parkway, Laurel Homes in the West End, several major buildings at UC and the zoo, and the U.S. Post Office at Fifth and Walnut streets. Under President Franklin D. Roosevelt's U.S. Re-settlement Administration, some 1,200 people went to work on Greenhills, a sub-division for 1,000 families, including greenspace and a park. The applicants had strict income and personal guidelines. The homes were well built, and Greenhills, which had its first resident in 1938, remains an attractive part of Cincinnati today.

If the Great Depression and a 1,000-year flood were not quite enough, another world war was at hand and, on December 7, 1941, Cincinnati, like the rest of the country, jumped in with both feet. Before the struggle was over, some 92,000 Cincinnatians were in uniform. Of that number, some 2,300 never returned. ▶

About 2,500 years ago,
the Roman hero Lucius
Cincinnatus chose to be a farmer
instead of an emperor. In 1790,
Losantiville, settled two years
earlier, was renamed Cincinnati
by the Governor of the Northwest
Territory, Gen. Arthur St. Clair.
He thus paid homage to the
national honorary fraternal
organization of Revolutionary
War officers, the Society of
Cincinnati, of which
he was a member.

All those who did were profoundly changed. They would never look at themselves, their country, or their city in quite the same way again. They wanted a good life for themselves and their families, and they intended to get it.

No more crowded houses in congested cities with polluted air and uncomfortable public transportation. No more settling for a grade school or high school education. Men and women had sacrificed to have their chance at the American dream, and they were not going to settle for less than the best.

With sympathetic government programs, millions of Americans got their educations and became home owners. A backyard for the kids became the norm, not the exception, and so did a family car.

Cincinnati was turned upside down. Cornfields became communities overnight, it seemed. Roads had to be expanded, shopping malls invented, schools accommodated, hospitals erected. We began to hear about a "metropolitan area" and words such as "demographics." The term "baby boomer" entered the language.

Radio, where Cincinnati enjoyed a prominent position with the remarkable inventor Powel Crosley and his groundbreaking WLW setting the pace, was overwhelmed by television. Ruth Lyons, the master of both media with her various radio and TV programs, became an important opinion-maker in this new environment.

Amid the explosion of subdivisions at all points of the compass came an interesting reassessment of the inner city. Mount Adams became fashionable, and rehabbed homes there were suddenly among the most expensive in the city. There was a renaissance in the Mansion Hill area of Newport, downtown Covington, and sections of Over-the-Rhine.

More recently, the big expansion story in Greater Cincinnati has been Northern Kentucky. Long the poor relation of the metropolitan area, it was, in past times, known more for bickering and scandal than for growth and good government. Then, starting in the early 1980s, a number of things happened. The Cincinnati/ Northern Kentucky International Airport—located in Kentucky—began unprecedented expansion. I-275 was completed, uniting long-divergent communities, and

Northern Kentucky University was established and grew exponentially. The region, for the first time, had an identity, and businesses flocked to take advantage of the available workforce, convenient transportation, and relatively inexpensive land.

Cincinnati's riverfront has come alive, too. The Paul Brown Stadium for football and the up-and-coming Great American Ball Park for baseball keep the focus firmly on the Ohio River, as do floating restaurants and excursion boats. The annual Riverfest fireworks show over Labor Day and the occasional Tall Stacks events celebrate Cincinnati and its symbiosis with the 980-mile ribbon of water that brought those first settlers to this spot on the river bank back in 1788.

And how does that house up on Fourth Street, now called the Taft Museum, fit into the new Cincinnati? Not much of a stretch, really. As the millennium's odometer rolled over to read 2000, a Cincinnatian—Bob Taft—sat in the governor's mansion in Columbus.

Now it is time for a confession of sorts. This essay was commissioned by publishers who assumed that I "knew" Cincinnati. Though I did not disabuse them of the notion, the truth is that I don't know Cincinnati at all. Over six decades, I have collected thousands of mental snapshots of the city as I have beaten my narrow path through its history. That doesn't mean I "know" the city. What I believe it to be as I write these words will have little validity tomorrow, much less a year from now. For a city is a living thing, and its structures—on which I have spent so many words—are nothing but a framework for the quicksilver that makes a community thrive, grow, and change. Or not.

Buildings are symbols of how generations want to be remembered. Because, ultimately, a city is its people. Their generosity of spirit, vision, industry, and honesty will build on what went before—or their lack of those qualities will doom this great city to history's backwater.

For the record, if one Cincinnatian's observation is worth anything, the current crop of movers and shakers doesn't seem likely to be content with the backwater.

It could be an interesting century. ■

DELTA QUEEN

FIRST HELD IN 1988 AS PART of the city's bicentennial celebration, Tall Stacks combines two of Cincinnati's defining elements: its storied history and the rolling Ohio River. Nearly 20 historic steamboats from across the country dock at Public Landing (PAGES 30 AND 31) during the event, and attendees get into the spirit with costumes, music, tours, cruises, and races. Held every three or four years, the festival attracts hundreds of thousands of visitors annually, prompting the American Bus Association to name it the top tourism event of 1999.

UZZING WITH ACTIVITY, downtown Cincinnati rises high above the Ohio River, the tall skyskrapers reflecting its spirit of innovation and industry. In 2000, based on such criterea as housing, education, arts, development, and indentity, *Places Rated Almanac* ranked Cincinnati 11th on its list of the country's most livable cities.

Cincinnati

WITH A DIVERSE POPULATION and a scenic downtown, Cincinnati has a lot to love. Its cozy atmosphere makes the me-tropolis a perfect backdrop for many a happy occasion—whether a memorable wedding or a roman-tic New Year's.

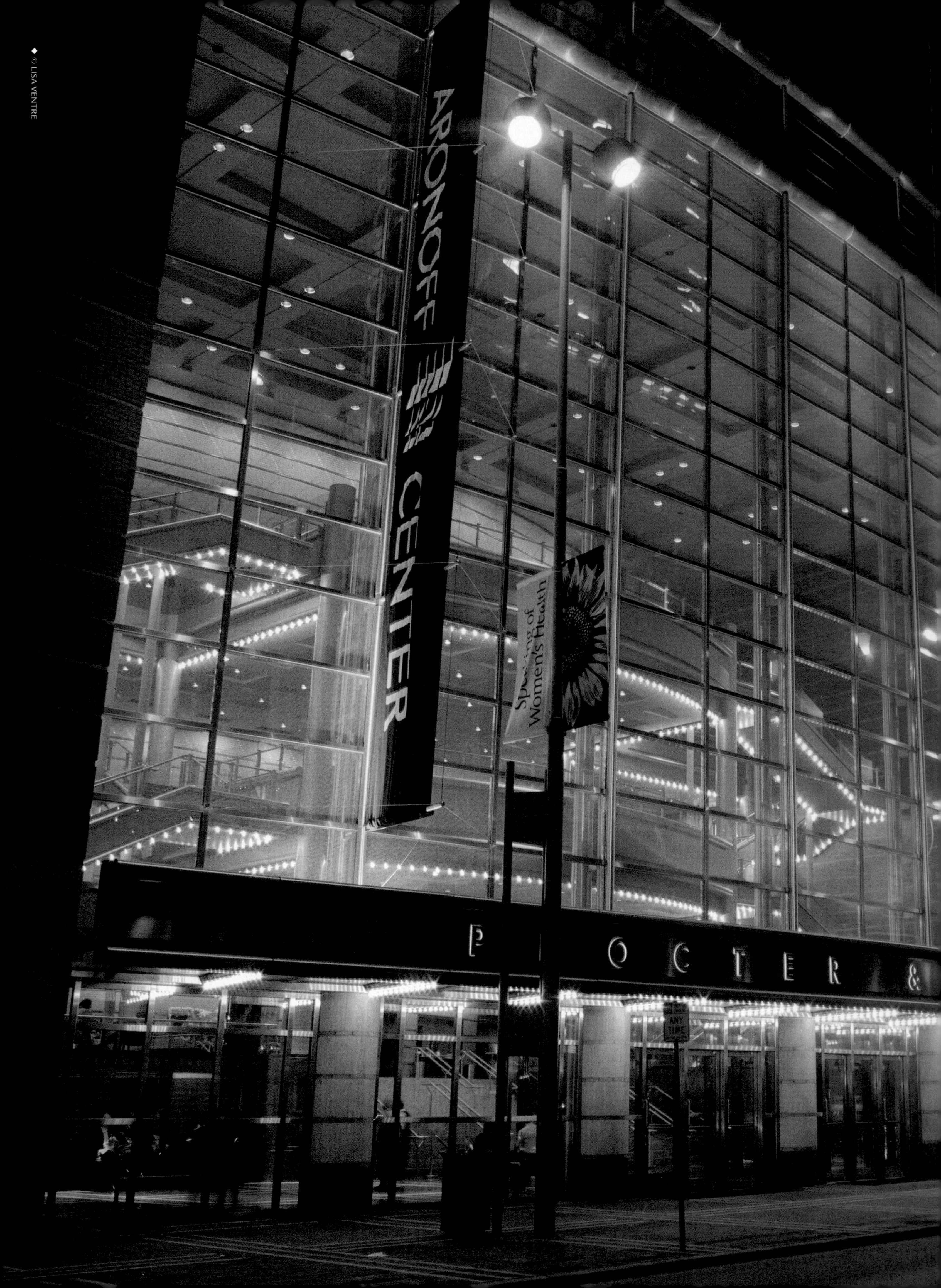

© LISA VENTRE

AT THE FOREFRONT OF DOWN-town Cincinnati's renaissance is the Aronoff Center for the Arts, which opened to great fanfare in 1995. Managed by the Cincinnati Arts Association, the center contains three stage areas, along with meeting space, offices, and an art gallery. Each year, more than 400,000 patrons visit the Aronoff to watch performances by the Cincinnati Ballet and the Cincinnati Opera, as well as visiting Broadway companies.

Ever get the feeling you're being watched? It might be one of Cincinnati's gargoyles, who perch upon building facades throughout downtown. Whether carved in stone or depicted in paint, the creatures have a bird's-eye view of the city's goings-on.

THE HISTORIC BUILDINGS around Plum Street frame a great deal of Cincinnati's civic and religious activity. Built in 1893, the red-granite City Hall (OPPOSITE) houses the area's governing offices, while nearby Plum Street Temple (LEFT) is home to the B'nai Yeshurun congregation. Both landmarks can be viewed from among the 12 immense Corinthian columns of St. Peter in Chains Cathedral (FOREGROUND LEFT AND OPPOSITE).

Cincinnati

Glass, lines, and curves define the structures at Cincinnati/Northern Kentucky International Airport, one of the fastest-growing airports in the world. Housing three Delta Air Lines terminals and Delta's locally based subsidiary, Comair, the airport services more than 500 flights a day to some 113 cities in the United States and abroad.

LOCAL ARCHITECTURE HOUSES both the everyday and the spectacular. Over low-lying buildings looms the immense Music Hall (OPPOSITE), constructed in 1878. One of the city's premier performance spaces—as well as one of its most impressive and imposing structures—the 3,397-seat hall is home to the Cincinnati Pops Orchestra and the Cincinnati Symphony Orchestra, and hosts the annual May Festival, the country's oldest orchestral and choral series.

WHETHER FOR WORSHIP OR recreation, Cincinnati has been showered with innumerable blessings. In addition to its many public parks, playgrounds, and swimming pools, the city counts more than 1,000 houses of worship throughout its neighborhoods.

Cincinnati

DURING SPRING AND SUMMER in Cincinnati, showers can appear suddenly and cease abruptly, sending umbrella-less locals running for cover. But younger Cincinnatians have a blast getting all wet (OPPOSITE).

HEART OF THE CITY: In 1871, local businessman Henry Probasco presented Cincinnati with what is now its most famous landmark—the Tyler Davidson Fountain (PAGES 52-54), named after Probasco's business partner and brother-in-law. Topping the fountain—which underwent extensive renovation in 2000—is the *Genius of Water*, whose inscription reads, "To the People of Cincinnati." Located in Fountain Square, the landmark isn't the only thing to light up the downtown area. Each Labor Day, the riverfront plays host to a spectacular fireworks celebration (PAGE 55).

DURING THE EARLY AND MID-1800s, Cincinnati's streets were filled with hogs being herded to market, and the ensuing stench and mess earned the city the dubious nickname Porkopolis. More than 150 years later, Cincinnati embraced that moniker as pigs once again filled the streets, this time as part of the Big Pig Gig. Between May and October 2000, 425 hand-painted fiberglass hogs hammed it up around town, striking comic poses and sporting outrageous pig-styles. Thanks to artist T.A. Boyle, hogs danced *Swine Lake* in front of the Aronoff Center (ABOVE), and Lynne, Scott, and Steve Hamons parodied Fountain Square with their *Styler-Davidson Sow-tain* (OPPOSITE).

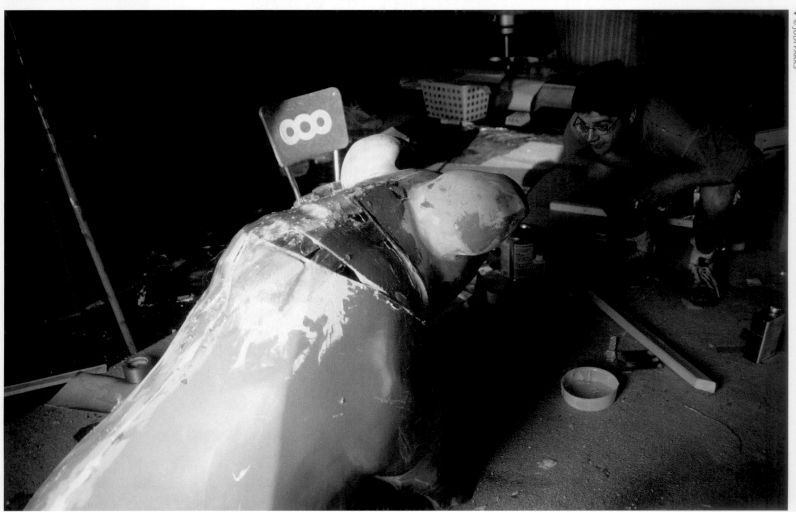

Cincinnati

HOG AGOG: HUNDREDS OF area artists, as well as several school groups, hit the pig time with their entries for the Big Pig Gig. Always colorful and creative— and never boaring—the herd was sponsored by local businesses and donors, then auctioned off for charity.

Cincinnati

C'EST UN PIG: LOCALS AND tourists alike went hog-wild for the Big Pig Gig's porks of art. Of the more than 900,000 people who toured the exhibit, some 462,000 were from out of town. An auction of many of the outdoor art pieces raised $839,000 for the local nonprofit organization ArtWorks and 240 other charities. According to a study conducted by the University of Cincinnati, the exhibit also pumped approximately $59.4 million into the local economy.

Cincinnati

I N Cincinnati, a study in astronomy quickly becomes a history lesson. In 1842, Ormby McKnight Mitchel, a professor at Cincinnati College, founded the Cincinnati Astronomical Society to raise money for a high-powered observatory on Mount Ida. In 1845, the first such facility in the nation was dedicated by former President John Quincy Adams, after whom the area was renamed Mount Adams. Today, the observatory (OPPOSITE TOP) still attracts star-struck citizens for educational and recreational programs.

For many Cincinnatians, a hot-air balloon is the perfect vehicle for touring the tristate countryside or just getting a new view on a sunset (PAGES 64-67). The area hosts a handful of hot-air-fueled events each year, including Balluminaria during the winter holidays and the annual Blue Ash Airport Days' balloon race.

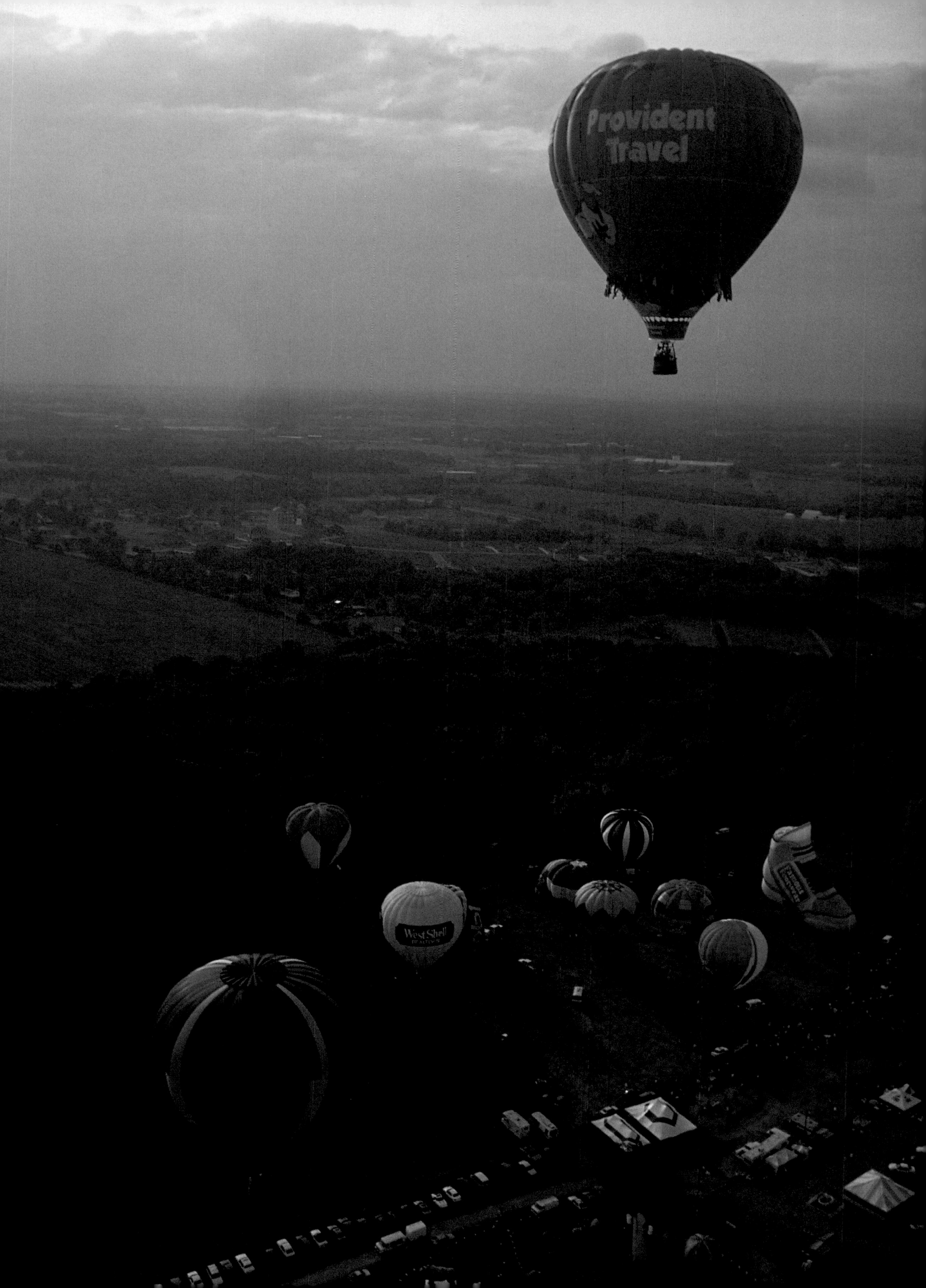

© TOM UHLMAN

Cincinnati

TRAIN OF THOUGHT: CINCIN-
nati's first railway station,
Union Terminal, is back on track
as the Cincinnati Museum Center.
Dedicated in 1933, the terminal
ceased railroad service in 1972, but
reopened as a knowledge station
in 1990. Today, it houses the Cincinnati History Museum, Cinergy
Children's Museum, Museum
of Natural History & Science,
Cincinnati Historical Society
Library, and Richard D. Lindner
Family OMNIMAX Theater, as
well as extensive murals painted by
German-born artist Winold Reiss
and colorful mosaics (PAGES 68-71).

CINCINNATI OFFERS ITS DIVERSE citizenry—whether canine, feline, or human—a unique window from which to view the world.

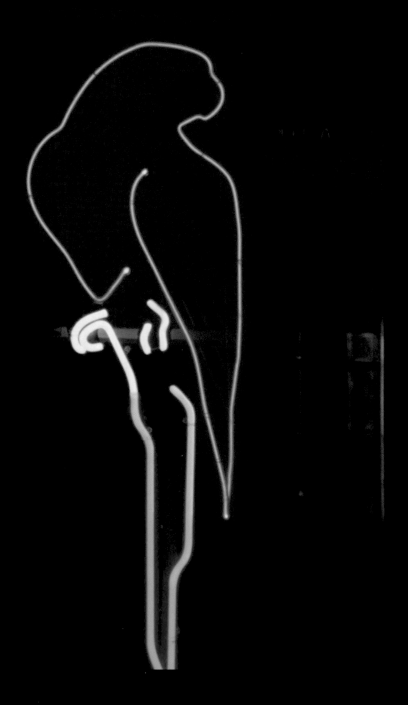

Cincinnati

ARCHITECTURAL FLOURISHES AND art deco details grace buildings around downtown, jazzing up Cincinnati's urban landscape and trumpeting the city's sense of style.

Majestic Vision

WILLIAM HENRY HARRISON

PRESIDENTS AND PRECEDENTS: Cincinnati has memorialized two of the country's chief executives in bronze. In Garfield Park stands the William Henry Harrison statue (LEFT), which commemorates the former North Bend resident and his monthlong presidential term in 1841. A statue of Abraham Lincoln (OPPOSITE), commissioned by the Charles P. Taft family and dedicated in 1917, keeps an honest watch over Lytle Park.

Majestic Vision

Cincinnati

INSIDE AND OUT, PLUM STREET Temple remains one of Cincinnati's most ornate architectural jewels. Designed by James Keyes Wilson in a combination of Byzantine, Gothic, and Islamic styles, the house of worship, constructed in 1866, was originally known as the Isaac M. Wise Temple in honor of its first rabbi, the founder of Reform Judaism.

Majestic Vision

God in the details: Religious images appear in multitude throughout the region, rendered in an array of media and placed in various settings (PAGES 82-85). The Cathedral Basilica of the Assumption (TOP AND BOTTOM) in Covington claims the largest stained-glass windows in the country, measuring 24 feet by 67 feet.

Cincinnati

WISE MEN CAME FROM THE EAST.

AN ANGEL OF THE LORD STOOD OVER THEM AND THE GLORY of

Cincinnati

BOTH LIFE AND DEATH PLAY important roles at the Spring Grove Cemetery and Arboretum, which, at 733 acres, is the second-largest nonprofit cemetery in the country. Since its dedication in 1845, more than 200,000 Cincinnatians have been laid to rest in its plots, including such prominent residents Charles P. Taft II and Nicholas Longworth II. Beautifully landscaped by German-born Adolph Strauch, the cemetery also contains some 300 varieties of trees, as well as numerous lakes and waterfalls.

FLOWING FROM THE CONFLU-
ence of the Allegheny and
Monogehela rivers in Pennsylvania,
the Ohio River has shaped and
defined Cincinnati's culture and
industry for decades.

DESPITE PERSECUTION DURING World War I, German culture has flourished in Cincinnati. The area hosts a number of German-themed celebrations, including the popular Oktoberfest-Zinzinnati. Each September, some 500,000 people attend the event, which takes up six downtown blocks and has grown into the second-largest gathering of its kind in the world.

ANTI-GERMAN HYSTERIA
(Continued from other side)

As a result of the anti-German hysteria during World War I, name changing became the rage. The Cincinnati City Council followed the trend by changing German street names on April 9, 1918. Among those changed were: German Street to English Street, Bismarck Street to Montreal Street, Berlin Street to Woodrow Street, Bremen Street to Republic Street, Brunswick Street to Edgecliff Point, Frankfort Street to Connecticut Avenue, Hamburg Street to Stonewall Street, Hanover Street to Yukon Street, Hapsburg Street to Merrimac Street, Schumann Street to Meredith Street, Vienna Street to Panama Street, and Humboldt Street to Taft Road.

Cincinnati

Catching some ZZZs isn't allowed when Cincinnati becomes Zinzinnati. In addition to supplying traditional German food, crafts, dance, and, of course, lots of beer, Oktoberfest also holds the world record for the largest chicken dance and kazoo march in 1999, featuring some 30,000 participants led by former Monkee Davy Jones.

Cincinnati

Lɪᴠɪɴɢ ɪɴ Cɪɴᴄɪɴɴᴀᴛɪ ɢɪᴠᴇs many people a reason to jump for joy. Whether taking the stage at the Aronoff Center (ʟᴇꜰᴛ) or pirouetting in the Opening Day parade for the Reds' first game of the season (ᴏᴘᴘᴏsɪᴛᴇ ʙᴏᴛᴛᴏᴍ), area residents dance to the beat of their own drummers.

Cincinnati

ELD ON THE GROUNDS OF Union Central Insurance in Forest Park, the Cincinnati Pops Orchestra's free Concert on the Green has been a local tradition since 1990. The performance draws thousands of families from around the area, who camp out on blankets and in lawn chairs to bask in the setting sun and enjoy the music.

SPICING UP LIFE IN CINCINNATI, the Gold Star ChiliFest, now held each July at Yeatman's Cove, celebrates the local delicacy and its many variations, and features live music, jalapeño-eating contests, and a Pepto-Bismol booth. Winning the cook-off means more than a hill of beans to its contestants, who travel to Cincinnati from around the region to cause a stir.

Northern Kentucky rang in the new millennium in grand style—and in G natural—with the Millennium Monument in Newport. Atop the world's largest carillon peals the world's largest swinging bell, the bronze World Peace Bell, which heralded the 25th anniversary of World Peace Day in October 1999 and tolled the closing of the 20th century some two months later.

Each year, hundreds of boys throughout the region earn merit badges and salute their country as members of the Boy Scouts of America. Cincinnati native Daniel Carter Beard helped form the organization in the early 1900s and served as a scoutmaster for more than 30 years.

N ESTING AMONG THE DETAILS and facades of buildings throughout Cincinnati, eagles eye the activity of the city's government and financial agencies.

VIETNAM

IN MEMORY OF THE
PEOPLE WHO SERVED.
1959 → 1975

ARMY
AIR FORCE
MARINES
NAVY

HANOI

NORTH
VIETNAM

DMZ (1954)

SOUTH

CINCINNATI SALUTES ITS FALLEN heroes with monuments and remembrances around the region. Each Memorial Day, Clermont County Vietnam veterans hold a vigil among the 500 crosses at Veterans Memorial Park in Union Township (ABOVE). Standing tall in Eden Park is the Vietnam Veterans Memorial (OPPOSITE), dedicated in 1984 to the memory of the more than 370 Greater Cincinnati residents killed or missing in action.

Cincinnati

WHETHER VISITING THE VET-erans Monument at Mount Healthy (ABOVE) or joining the ranks of men in uniform for the service at Fountain Square (OPPO-SITE), veterans and civilians alike—with heads bowed and hands over hearts—observe Memorial Day by honoring those who paid the ulti-mate price for freedom.

No emergency is too small or too dangerous for the area's fire departments and rescue teams. Established in 1853, the Cincinnati Fire Department (TOP)—the oldest full-time professional fire department in the country—answers some 6,000 calls each year. The Mason Fire Department promotes safety in the community by training lifeguards at Nixon Pool (BOTTOM) and demonstrating the jaws of life (OPPOSITE BOTTOM).

Cincinnati

RESIDENTS OF ALL AGES REVEL in the city's protective and provident environment. The Cincinnati Public Schools system oversees more than 60 elementary schools that instill life lessons in young students, and there are numerous senior citizen services that find housing and care for local elders.

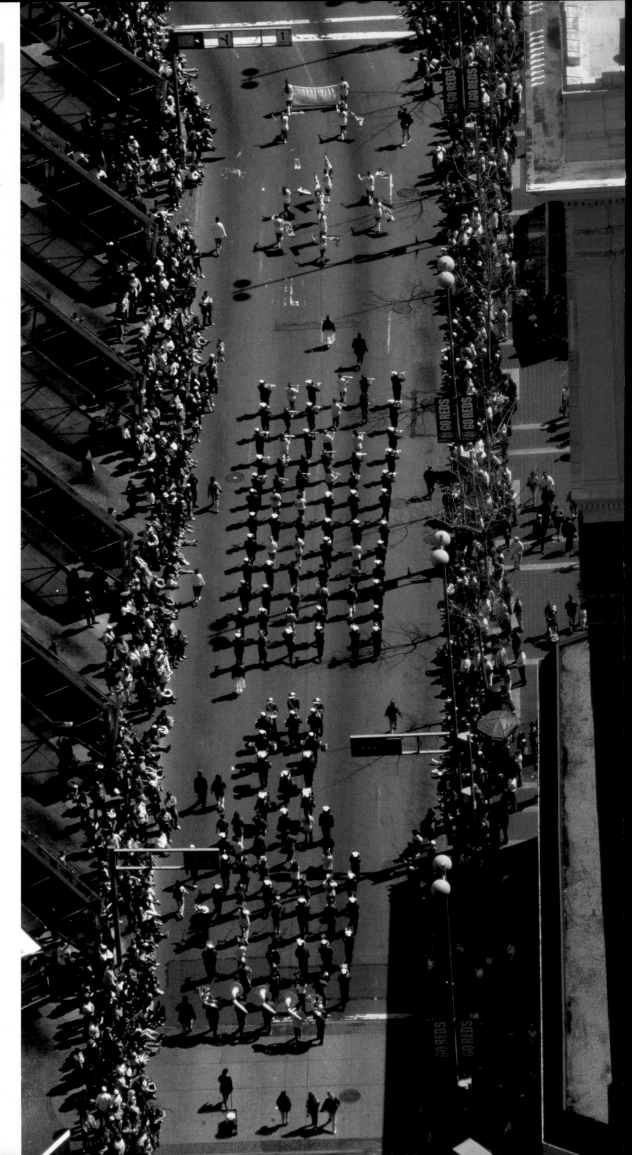

GIVING LOCALS AN OPPORTU-
nity to show their true colors,
the Reds' Opening Day parade—
a tradition since 1919—marches
for 18 blocks in celebration of a
new baseball season. In addition to
floats, balloons, and military and
high school bands, the parade also
features appearances by local celebrities, including former pitcher Joe
Nuxhall (OPPOSITE BOTTOM), who
acted as grand marshal in 1999.

Cincinnati

OPENED IN 1970 AS RIVER-front Stadium, Cinergy Field draws thousands of spectators to Reds' home games. In 2000, the park got a new playing field—Kentucky bluegrass replaced the Astroturf—but lost the center field section of seats, creating a view of the Ohio River. The modifications were part of the construction of the Great American Ball Park, which will replace Cinergy Field as the home of the Reds.

Cincinnati

AS NINE-TIME NATIONAL League pennant winners and five-time World Series champions, the Cincinnati Reds give their fans a lot to root for. Arriving in Cincinnati in late 1999, outfielder Dante Bichette (TOP) drew local cheers before being traded to the Boston Red Sox for two minor-league pitchers in August 2000. A true hometown hero, Cincinnati native Ken Griffey Jr. (OPPOSITE TOP)—acquired from the Seattle Mariners—managed to draw record crowds to home games—despite being out much of the 2000 season with injuries.

Cincinnati

TAKE ME OUT TO THE BALL game: If the Reds don't win, it's a shame, but the thousands of fans who attend have a ball just the same. A significant part of all the spectacle and excitement is Reds announcer Marty Brennaman (BOTTOM, ON RIGHT), who was inducted into the Baseball Hall of Fame in 2000.

Ohio's forested environs offer residents ample opportunity to escape the constant bustle of the metropolis (PAGES 122 AND 123). Encompassing 114 acres, the California Woods Nature Preserve (OPPOSITE) contains some 50 species of trees and more than 200 types of plants, as well as a network of winding trails.

Cincinnati

THAT NAME SURE RINGS A BELL: Although the city was named for a farmer—Lucius Quinctus Cincinnatus, who also ruled as dictator of Rome—Cincinnati has not been economically dependent on agriculture for more than a century. However, several small farms still remain, and reminders of the area's farming roots dot the countryside.

BUTTERFLIES AND BUTTERBALLS abound in Eden Park, where the Krohn Conservatory sponsors its Butterfly Garden show (RIGHT) each summer. With 1,000 butterflies representing more than 30 species, the event sets visitors' imaginations aflutter. While it didn't prove that pigs could fly, *Metamorphoswine* (OPPOSITE), created by local illustrator John Maggard, did delight passersby from its perch at the conservatory's entrance.

R UNNING MORE THAN 100 miles in length, the Little Miami River offers many big recreation options for Cincinnatians. Opened in 1991, the Little Miami Scenic Trail takes travelers—whether on foot, bike, or horse—from Milford to Springfield via several miles of lush forest (OPPOSITE).

WHETHER SPRINTING DOWN the field, skating on thin ice, or flying high above the half pipe, Cincinnatians get a real kick out of competitive sports.

Majestic Vision

Cincinnati

PEDAL POWER: AULT PARK is a haven for cyclists from around the region and across the country. Each summer, Cincinnati's fourth-largest public park is ablur with flocks of speed racers.

CINCINNATI PROVIDES ITS children with opportunities to participate in a variety of sports. An increasingly popular pastime, softball draws players of all ages—not to mention cheering crowds—to Rumpke Park in nearby Crosby Township.

THE NEW HOME OF THE BEN-
gals, Paul Brown Stadium
was named in honor of the team
founder, who brought the franchise
to Cincinnati in 1968. Dedicated
in August 2000, the 65,600-seat
stadium, which cost approximately
$460 million, hosted its inaugural
game on September 10, 2000,
drawing record crowds of avid fans
(PAGES 138-141).

Tickets Now On Sale!
(513) 621-TDTD
bengals.com

Provident Bank

Orange and black flood Paul Brown Stadium as the Bengals take the field for home games. During the 2000 season, thousands of fans—known for their fanatic devotion and outrageous fashion sense (pages 144 and 145)—turned out to cheer on players like wide receiver Peter Warrick (top), defensive end Glen Steele (bottom), and quarterback Akili Smith (opposite), the Bengals' first-round draft pick in 1999.

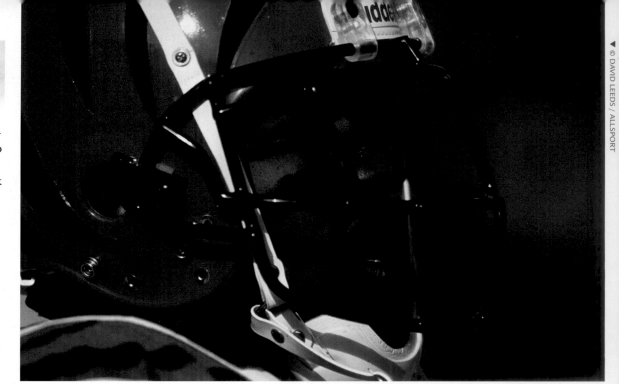

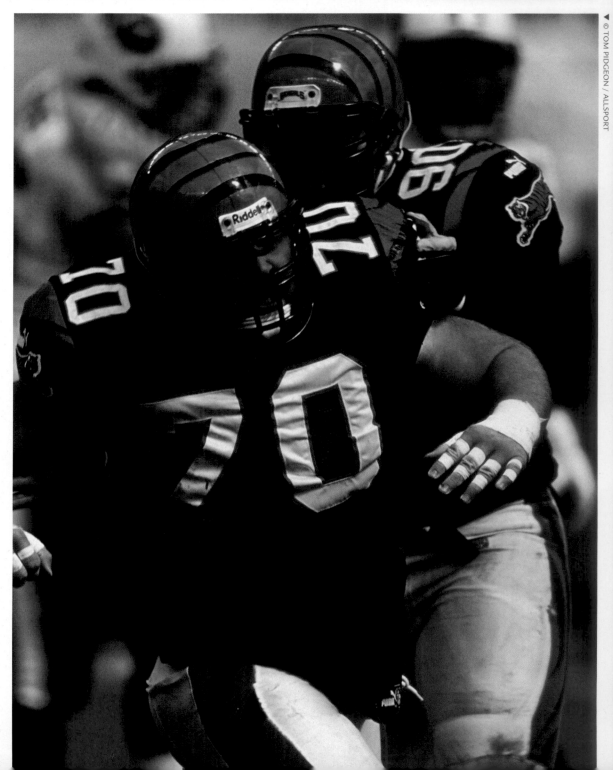

Cincinnati

LIONS AND TIGERS AND BEARS, oh my: Established in 1875 by German immigrant Andrew Erkenbrecher, the Cincinnati Zoo and Botanical Gardens is the second-oldest such facility in the country and certainly one of the finest. Unique, state-of-the-art habitats such as Big Cat Canyon and Jungle Trails are home to more than 700 species of animals—including some 100 endangered species—and more than 2,800 varieties of plants and flowers.

FOUNDED IN 1870, THE UNIversity of Cincinnati is one of the oldest and largest academic institutions in the state. Each year, some 34,000 students enroll in nearly 150 bachelor's and more than 120 graduate degree programs. Associate Professor of Biological Studies Bruce Jayne (OPPOSITE) has contributed a great deal to the understanding of reptile morphology by studying muscle function in lizards.

Cincinnati

Cincinnati

ONE OF THE CITY'S PREMIER performing arts centers, the University of Cincinnati-College Conservatory of Music plays a significant role in the area's cultural life. Ranked sixth in the nation by *U.S. News & World Report*, the conservatory stages more than 900 events every year, ranging from piano and voice recitals to dramatic productions to dance performances.

Majestic Vision

Cincinnati

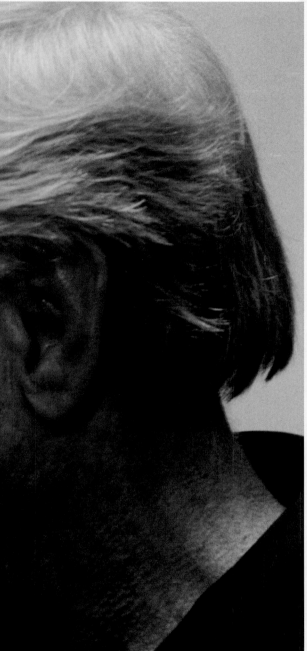

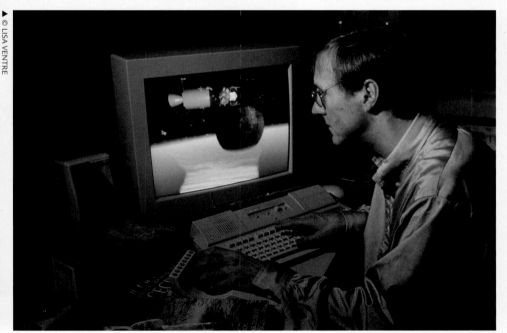

THERE ARE NO ACADEMIC dummies at the University of Cincinnati, which emphasizes a rigorous curriculum in all fields of study. Gary Lare (OPPOSITE, ON RIGHT), head of the Curriculum Resources Center and an accomplished ventriloquist, teaches students to think for themselves, but puts words in the mouth of his wooden partner.

WITH A DIVERSE STUDENT body and a highly skilled faculty, the University of Cincinnati has always worked to remain at the forefront of education—both in the laboratory and in the classroom. In 1906, it established the country's first cooperative education program, which today remains vital to both the school and its community.

Cincinnati

Two Taft homes have become museums commemorating one of Cincinnati's most prominent families. The Taft Museum of Art (ABOVE), former residence of Charles P. and Anna Taft, now serves as a showcase for the couple's extensive art collection. Charles' half-brother, William Howard Taft, is the only person to serve as both president of the United States and chief justice of the U.S. Supreme Court. His birthplace (OPPOSITE) today houses a historical museum and education center.

CINCINNATI'S STORIED HISTORY can be read in the architectural landmarks that comprise the downtown area. The Albert B. Sabin Cincinnati Convention Center (TOP) was named for the University of Cincinnati professor who discovered the polio vaccine, and the Procter & Gamble Towers (BOTTOM) serves as the headquarters for one of the city's largest companies, founded locally in 1837. At the time of its construction in 1845, St. Peter in Chains Cathedral (OPPOSITE, ON LEFT) was only the second cathedral in the country. City Hall (OPPOSITE, ON RIGHT), located across the street, was designed by local architect Samuel Hannaford, who was also responsible for Music Hall and the Mt. Lookout Observatory.

Cincinnati

WINTER SNOWS ONLY ENHANCE the elegance of Cincinnati's palatial homes, which reflect a variety of architectural styles— including Colonial and Tudor.

Cincinnati

LOCATED ATOP A HILL IN Mount Adams, Holy Cross-Immaculata Church (ABOVE)—constructed in 1859 and featuring murals painted by Johann Schmitt—continues to play a significant role in the area's Easter celebrations. On Good Friday, more than 10,000 Catholics from around the region ascend the 85 steps leading to the church (OPPOSITE), praying the rosary on each step.

Cincinnati

HOLY COMMUNION SERVICES at any of Cincinnati's churches offer participants an opportunity to reflect upon themselves and the world around them. The region supports some 230 Catholic parishes and more than 580 priests.

NATURAL LIGHT SUFFUSES Cincinnati's cemeteries and public spaces, creating a peaceful atmosphere amid the sheltering trees, stone markers, and religious architecture.

Cincinnati

WHATEVER THE SEASON, there's a lot in bloom at the Krohn Conservatory. Opened in 1933, the 36,000-square-foot greenhouse contains some 5,000 exotic plants in palm, desert, rain forest, and orchid exhibits. In addition, it hosts seasonal shows such as the popular Heirloom Garden and the Easter Lily Extravaganza Display.

CRYING FOWL: GREATER CINcinnati honors the many cultures that have contributed to its civic identity through statues around the area. In Eden Park stands the Cormorant Fisherman sculpture (RIGHT), donated by Cincinnati's sister city—Gifu, Japan—in 1992. Inspired by the Brothers Grimm's fairy tales, Eleftherios Karkadoulias designed the Goose Girl Fountain (OPPOSITE) in Covington's MainStrasse Village to commemorate the region's German heritage.

CINCINNATI HAS A FONDNESS for the vertical, as attested by the many sculptures and fountains—both for decorative and recreational purposes—that point skyward.

Majestic Vision

THE RUINS OF THE CINCINNATI Chamber of Commerce Building, which was built in 1888 and burned in 1911, comprise the H.H. Richardson Monument, named for the original structure's architect. Located in Burnet Woods, the monument contains 51 pink-granite slabs that form a 27-foot circle.

Cincinnati

OPENED IN 1886, THE CINcinnati Art Museum (ABOVE) maintains an impressive permanent collection composed of approximately 80,000 works of art representing 6,000 years. The Art Academy of Cincinnati (OPPOSITE), one of only a handful of museum schools in the country, enrolls some 200 students in four degree programs.

Cincinnati

A TROUBLED BRIDGE OVER water: Built in 1890, the two-lane Central Bridge was demolished over several weeks in 1992. In its place was constructed the state-of-the-art Taylor-Southgate Bridge, a four-lane crossway that was upgraded in 2000. Today, it is one of six bridges—including the Daniel Carter Beard Bridge (PAGES 178 AND 179)—that span the Ohio River connecting Cincinnati with Northern Kentucky.

SCAFFOLDING, CRANES, AND construction workers throughout Cincinnati serve as reminders of the city's near-constant expansion and progress, as well as its emphasis on preserving its past.

Cincinnati

RESTORING CINCINNATI'S historic structures puts many workers on top of the world. Along with private developers, the city continues to fund the restoration of its old buildings to meet increased market demand for retail and residential space—as well as to simply commemorate its rich heritage.

Cincinnati

FOR MORE THAN 50 YEARS, LEO Sunderman served blue plate specials of traditional sauerbraten, mock turtle soup, and pot roast from behind the counter at Stenger's Cafe, a mainstay in Over-the-Rhine. When Sunderman sold the restaurant to Doug Bootes in 1999, many loyal diners feared it was the end of an era. But while he did expand the menu and up-grade the kitchen equipment, Bootes has worked to maintain the cafe's cozy atmosphere and neighborhood status.

Cincinnati

Don't fret: Cincinnati resounds with music of all types played in an array of venues. The Blue Wisp (TOP) and Sonny's Café and Lounge (BOTTOM) offer some of the city's smoothest jazz in appropriately dark, smoky settings. For equally good music in a fresh-air environment, many of the city's streets serve as stages for its talented musicians.

Cincinnati

Named for former mayor and landowner General James Findlay, Findlay Market in Over-the-Rhine opened for business in 1855. The first cast-iron building in the country, the market has figured prominently in local history as the starting point for the Reds' Opening Day parade since 1919.

Cincinnati

F OR MANY LOCALS, A TRIP TO Findlay Market is a weekly event to be savored. The market hosts scores of area vendors selling a colorful cornucopia of fresh produce, meats, cheeses, candies, and homemade crafts.

Aone's sunset years, Cincinnati offers its senior citizens numerous living options, including several nursing homes and senior services centers. But whether shoveling or shopping, many older Cincinnatians still enjoy their independence and mobility.

SIGNS OF LIFE: AS SEEN IN FINER parking lots, brick walls, and driveways throughout Greater Cincinnati, ancient billboards serve as advertisements for still-profitable products, as well as reminders of brand names past, whose popularity has faded like the paint that once heralded their quality.

Cincinnati

MOVED TO MAKE A DIFFERENCE in their community, Dick and Anne Taylor (OPPOSITE) opened the Lord's Pantry and the Lord's Gym. Located at Liberty and Walnut streets, the Lord's Pantry provides food, shelter, and spiritual guidance to Cincinnati's homeless and underprivileged. At the Lord's Gym—housed in the Nicholas Hoyer Sports Club, which is named after the Taylors' grandson—Staff Minister Jerry Dubose and Trainer George Moore (ABOVE, FROM LEFT) help men in the neighborhood strengthen their bodies as well as their souls.

Cincinnati

DESCEND-CINNATI: WHEN winter hits the state, the landscape gets a soft blanket of snow and a rock-hard, icy shell. The surrounding countryside gives area climbers many opportunities to break the ice.

FOR SOME, SCALING SHEER walls is a job, but for others, it's a pastime. While window washers cling to the sides of downtown skyscrapers (OPPOSITE) in an effort to keep the city gleaming, climbers take advantage of the 90-degree inclines at Eden Park (ABOVE) to practice their techniques.

THE SKY'S THE LIMIT FOR CIN-
cinnati as it continues to grow
and prosper, giving many locals
a new angle on life in the city.

Cincinnati

A CLOSER INSPECTION OF Greater Cincinnati's many historic buildings reveals a world of miniature flourishes, as well as images of animals both mythical and real—and humans expressing a variety of emotions both protective and comical (PAGES 206-211).

Cincinnati

Cincinnati

Majestic Vision

Cincinnati

Mᴀɪɴ Sᴛʀᴇᴇᴛ ᴍᴀɪɴꜱᴛᴀʏꜱ: At Neon's Cigar Bar & Tavern, Terry Carter (ᴛᴏᴘ) stocks a large selection of more than 4,000 smokables, as well as a full bar of fine liquors. Just down the street, Greg's Antiques—run by Greg, Jeff, and Todd (ᴏᴘᴘᴏꜱɪᴛᴇ ᴛᴏᴘ) Starnes—has been a downtown fixture for years. Specializing in architectural items like mantels and windows, the store opened a second Main Street location in 1996.

PUTTING THE GREAT IN Greater Cincinnati, small communities like Reading, Blue Ash, and Deer Park surround the metropolis. In 2000, more than 850,000 people resided in Hamilton County, with less than half that number living within Cincinnati's city limits.

X MARKS THE SPOT: ESTABLISHED in 1831, Xavier University—an exclusive Jesuit institution with an expanding enrollment in excess of 6,000—offers an extensive curriculum and an experienced staff of experts to expand students' horizons. In addition, the school has defied expectations by becoming an exciting basketball powerhouse in the Atlantic 10 Conference; in 2000, the exceptional Musketeers, cheered on by exuberant fans, set an official school record by executing their fifth straight 20-win season.

Cincinnati

Cincinnati

THROUGHOUT CINCINNATI'S urban and suburban communities, family togetherness and friendly neighborliness create safe environments for children who are growing much faster than their rapidly expanding city.

Cincinnati

CINCINNATI GRINS LIKE A
Cheshire something-or-other
as feline fever strikes. Roaring
crowds root for local football
favorites the Bengals, named
after a species of tiger native
to Bangladesh.

Cincinnati

F ROM FISHNETS TO FACE PAINT, combat boots to logoed T-shirts, rebellion and individuality manifest themselves in the fashions worn by the young members of Cincinnati's burgeoning sub- and countercultures.

Cincinnati

Many Cincinnatians opt to use their bodies as canvases for art that is skin-deep. But while piercings often grow back, getting a tattoo removed will be a lost cauz for anyone unwilling to undergo surgery.

Majestic Vision

Cincinnati

Pyrotechnics and balancing acts turned the Cincinnati Museum Center into a three-ring Cirque du Bizarre for a fund-raiser in honor of AVOC—AIDS Volunteers of Cincinnati. The festivities drew more than 1,000 people and raised $170,000 for the organization.

Majestic Vision

RIDERS ON THE STORM OF competition—as well as those content to thunder around the neighborhood—see plenty of action in the Greater Cincinnati region.

For Cincinnati's athletically inclined youth, the city is a field of dreams. Lacrosse and soccer are just two of the sports that give local kids a leg up toward reaching their goals.

Majestic Vision

Cincinnati

THOROUGHBRED HORSE RACING makes tracks in venues all around Greater Cincinnati. Legendary Triple Crown jockey Steve Cauthen, a native of Northern Kentucky, launched his career on the one-mile track at River Downs (TOP). Across the Ohio River in Florence, Turfway Park (BOTTOM AND OPPOSITE) takes wagers year-round for either simulcast or live races.

Majestic Vision

Cincinnati

IT'S A TRUE LOVE AFFAIR EACH August when the top names in tennis converge on the courts of Mason's ATP Tennis Center for the Cincinnati round of the Tennis Masters Series. The event traces its history back to 1899, when Nat Emerson became the first winner of what was then called the Tri-State Tennis Tournament.

FANS OF THE UNIVERSITY OF Cincinnati men's basketball Bearcats rejoice practically every year as Coach Bob Huggins takes his team to the brink during the NCAA tournament. The team has contributed to March Madness each season since 1991.

G ETTING DUNKED MEANS ONE thing for a basketball and quite another for a kid about to make a splash in the waters of East Fork Lake. Throughout the Cincinnati region, parks and recreational sites provide fun aplenty for locals.

Cincinnati

SKATERS AWAY: EACH HOLIDAY season, Cincinnati's Fountain Square becomes an ice-skating rink for the young and the young at heart. But just when you think it is safe to get back in the water, the Newport Aquarium in Northern Kentucky tantalizes you with its *Surrounded by Sharks* and *Kingdom of Penguins* exhibits (BOTTOM AND OPPOSITE BOTTOM). And, although they might not have their own personal window washer like their cohorts across the river, the Cincinnati Zoo & Botanical Garden's tuxedo-feathered friends (OPPOSITE TOP) still have a great place to call home.

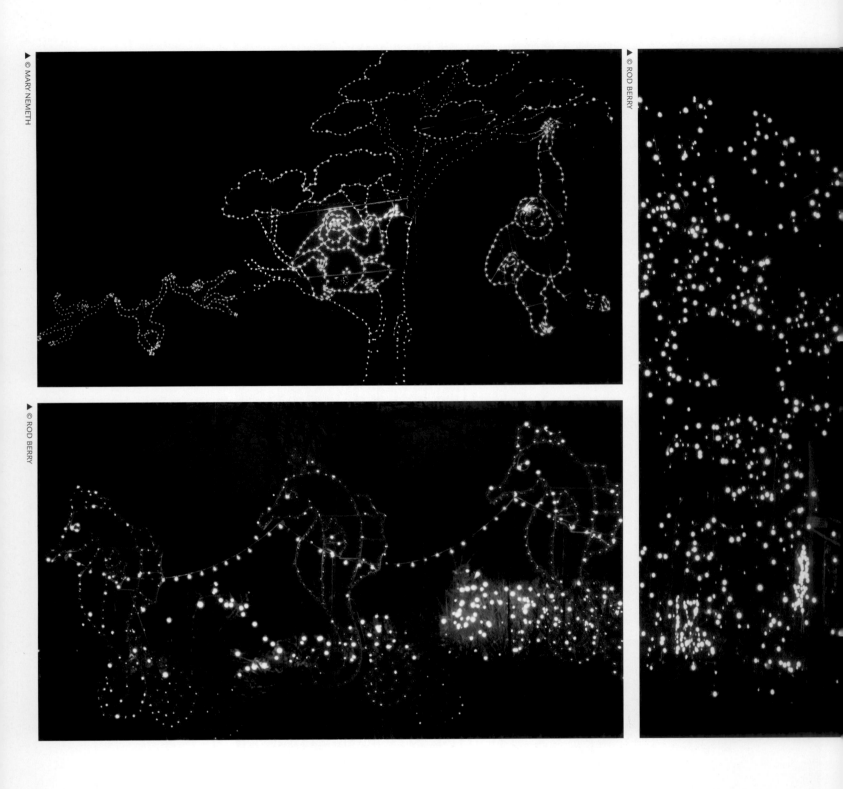

Cincinnati

THE STAFF AT THE CINCINNATI Zoo & Botanical Garden doesn't monkey around when it comes to holiday decorating. The PNC Festival of Lights and its 30-foot-tall nutcrackers help make the seasonal event a must-see.

Cincinnati

I T MIGHT BE TRUE THAT NONE of this trio will be pulling Santa's sleigh, but what holiday season would be complete without a reindeer or three to complete the bill?

IN THE TANGLE OF HOLIDAY shopping and travel, ornamental touches often mean the difference between tribulation and celebration. Cincinnatians keep the yuletide spirit alive with traditional poinsettias and other familiar decorations.

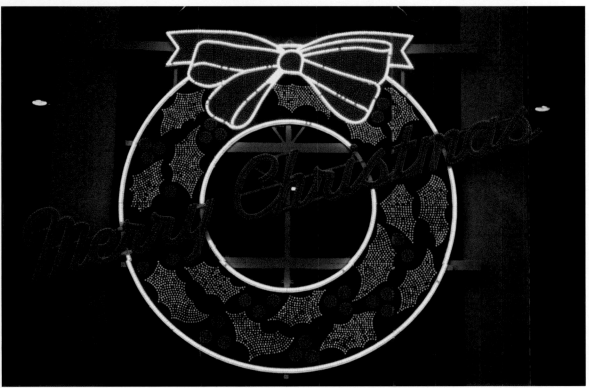

S CENIC DISPLAYS IN CINCINNATI give a whole new twist to the term *light rail.* Cast against a backdrop of the zoo's Festival of Lights, a train transporting visitors through the attraction threads its way among some of the 2 million lights that make up the dramatic show (ABOVE). Not to be outdone, historic Union Terminal toots its own horn in honor of the rails (OPPOSITE).

FADED GLORY: VINTAGE TRAINS at the Railway Exposition Company in nearby Covington confirm what lovers of the rails have always known—locomotives, cabooses, and historic Pullman dining cars are genuine works of art.

Cincinnati

FOLLOWING IN THE FOOTSTEPS of folks everywhere, Cincinnatians contribute to all walks of life, whether white- or blue-collar.

Opportunities abound in this region, composed of 13 counties in three states—and home to an estimated 2 million people.

Cincinnati

FROM SHINY AND SLEEK TO FAST
on the street, a man and his
auto are seldom parted. While
vintage vehicles might prosper best
in pristine surroundings, it requires
elbow grease—and a willingness to
get down and dirty—to keep the
drive alive.

MOTOR SPORTS FOUND A NEW home in 2000 when the Kentucky Speedway's 1.5-mile track heated up with racing events to thrill the more than 300,000 fans who filled the facility's seats during its inaugural season (PAGES 256-259).

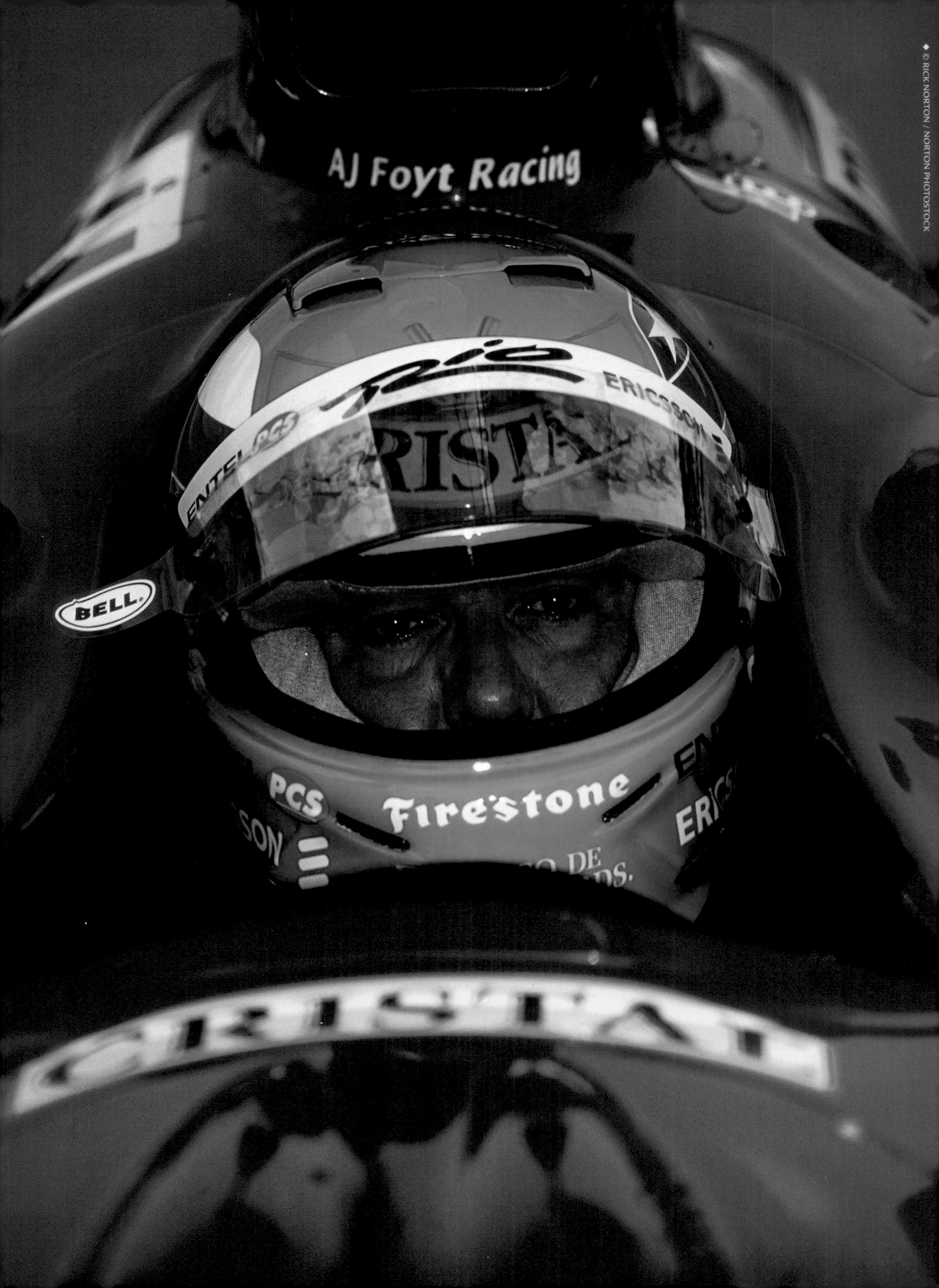

◆ © RICK NORTON / NORTON PHOTOSTOCK

Cincinnati

IT'S BUMPER-TO-BUMPER ON THE racetrack at Paramount's Kings Island (ABOVE), an amusement park north of Cincinnati where the cars are small, but the smiles are big.

Taking a break from watching the real thing, racing enthusiasts at Kentucky Speedway (OPPOSITE) rev their remote control engines around a miniature loop.

THRILL SEEKERS WON'T BE DIS-appointed at Paramount's Kings Island, where some 80 rides and attractions cover 364 acres (PAGES 262-265). Less-adventurous visitors can view the wonders of Ohio from the observation deck of the park's Eiffel Tower replica.

Cincinnati

Majestic Vision

Cincinnati

THE MODERNIZED VERSION of cheerleading incorporates dancing, increased athleticism, and big business. But for Cincinnatians with the right spirit, it's still a matter of root-root-rooting for the home team.

Cincinnati

BEHOLD THE JOYS OF SUMMER. Out of school and out-of-doors, local kids join their families for some good clean fun and a taste of that seasonal staple—the snow cone.

But beware the rains of spring (PAGES 270-275), which occasionally turn nearby attractions into casualties. Normally a site for a variety of recreational activities, Sawyer Point became a disaster area in 1997 when the Ohio River flooded the city before cresting at 64.7 feet.

Cincinnati

Cincinnati

Majestic Vision

Cincinnati

F OR EVERY ACTION, THERE IS an equal and opposite reaction. Kids of all ages turn playful in Cincinnati's many parks and play-grounds.

Cincinnati

It's a dog's life, but that's not really so bad for the pooches in Greater Cincinnati, where the daily routine is likely to involve a walk in the park with a rewarding drink to follow. Since 1931, Eden Park has been home to a kindred breed: a statue of the mythic wolf that suckled Romulus and Remus, the legendary founders of ancient Rome (OPPOSITE).

Cincinnati

Whether man-made or natural, flower power enlivens Cincinnati's vistas. The city offers 16,700 acres of parkland, including Hauck Botanic Garden and Krohn Conservatory.

Majestic Vision

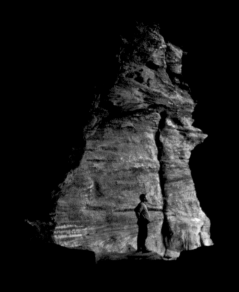

VISITORS TO CINCINNATI'S Ault Park cast a tall shadow against a deepening night sky (ABOVE). Cavers looking for a special treat can travel to Hocking Hills State Park in the southeastern part of the state to take in the wonders of sites such as Old Man's Cave, a hollowed-out section of the area's sandstone hills. But for true beauty, one need look no farther than the core of the city and Fountain Square's Tyler Davidson Fountain (PAGES 284 AND 285), a treasured fixture for more than a century.

Cincinnati

F ROM THE BANKS OF THE Ohio River, to the rolling hills of Northern Kentucky, to the suburban quiet of Southeastern Indiana, Greater Cincinnati has matured from its roots into a modern city with a majestic vision (PAGES 286-291).

Profiles in Excellence

A look at the corporations, businesses, professional groups, and community service organizations that have made this book possible. Their stories—offering an informal chronicle of the local business community— are arranged according to the date they were established in the Cincinnati area.

Adecco

American Financial Group

The Andrew Jergens Company

Aon Risk Services, Inc. of Ohio

Application Objects, Inc.

Ashland Inc.

Attachmate Corporation

Baldwin Piano & Organ Company

Balluff Inc.

Bayley Place

Belvedere Corporation

BF Goodrich Cincinnati

Burke, Incorporated

Chemed Corporation

Children's Hospital Medical Center

CIBER, Inc.

Cincilingua Inc.

Cincinnati Business Courier

Cincinnati Sub Zero Products

Cintas Corporation

City of Cincinnati

Clear Channel Broadcasting

Coca-Cola Enterprises

Cognis Corporation

College of Mount St. Joseph

Comair, the Delta Connection

Comfort Suites

Convergys Corporation

Custom Editorial Production, Inc.

Deloitte & Touche LLP

DigiTerra, Inc.

The E.W. Scripps Company

ENTEX IT Service, Inc.

Ethicon Endo-Surgery, Inc.

Fifth Third Bancorp

Ford Motor Co.-Sharonville

General Assembly, Inc.

Givaudan

Graydon Head & Ritchey LLP

Great Oaks Institute of Technology and Career Development

Greater Cincinnati Chamber of Commerce

Haberer Registered Investment Advisor, Inc.

The Health Alliance of Greater Cincinnati

Indiana Insurance

International Knife & Saw, Inc.

International Paper, Cincinnati Technology Center

Keane, Inc.

KeyBank and Gradison McDonald Investments, Inc.

kforce.com

Lockwood Greene

Loth Mbi, Inc.

LÛCRUM Inc.

Maple Knoll Village

Marriott Kingsgate Conference Center

Mazak Corporation

Metalex Manufacturing, Inc.

Metro and Transit Authority of Northern Kentucky (TANK)

Milacron, Inc.

ML Barnard

Northern Kentucky University

Norton Outdoor Advertising

Ohio National Life Insurance

Paramount's Kings Island™

The Payne Firm Inc.

PHC Group, Inc.

Portion Pac, Inc.

Premier Network Solutions, Inc.

Princeton City School District

Process Plus

Procter & Gamble Company

R.A. Jones & Co., Inc.

Radisson Hotel Cincinnati

The Regal Cincinnati Hotel

Reliance Medical Products

Rumpke Consolidated Companies, Inc.

SDRC

Sena Weller Rohs Williams, Inc.

Siemens Energy and Automation

Sisters of Charity of Cincinnati

St. Joseph Home

Steed Hammond Paul

Toyota Motor Manufacturing North America, Inc.

Twin Towers

The Union Central Life Insurance Co.

United Industrial Piping

The United States Playing Card Company

University of Cincinnati

Van Melle USA, Inc.

The Vernon Manor Hotel

The Western-Southern Enterprise

White Castle System, Inc.

Williamsburg Homes

xpedex

The YMCA of Greater Cincinnati

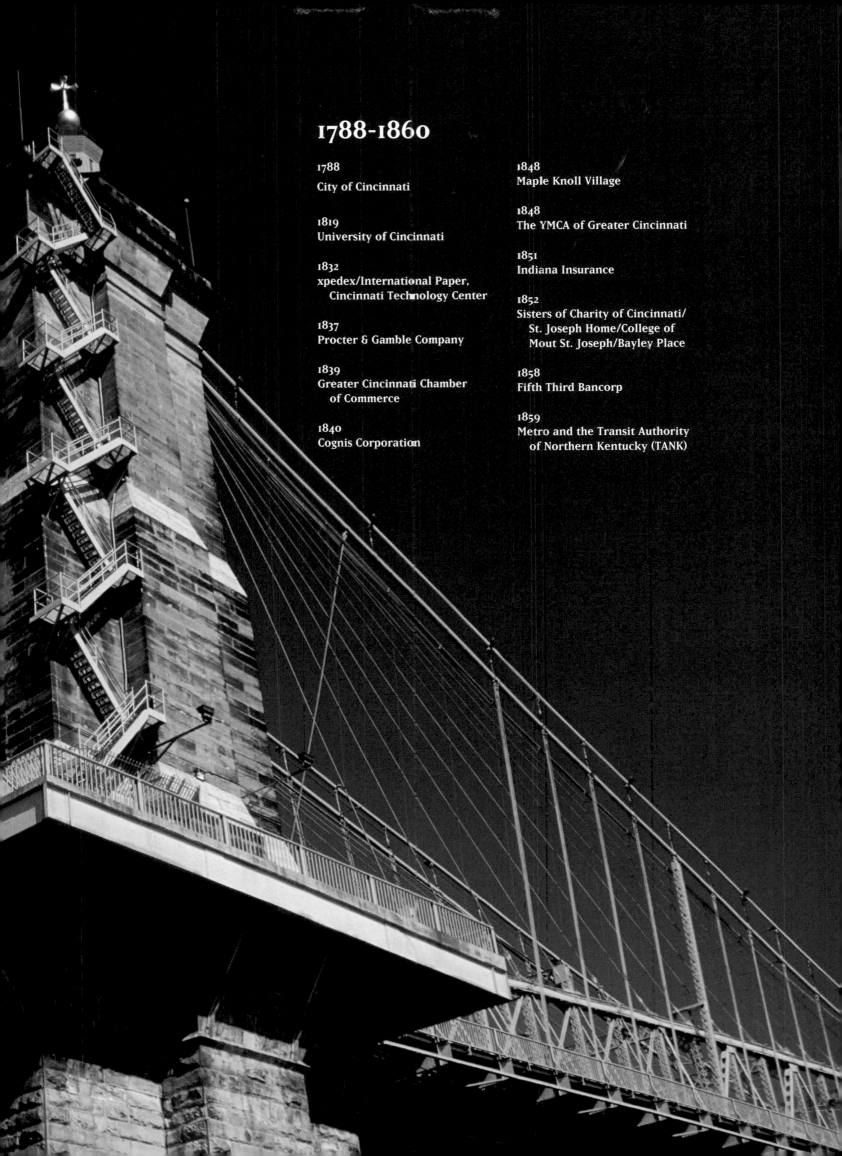

1788-1860

1788
City of Cincinnati

1819
University of Cincinnati

1832
xpedex/International Paper,
 Cincinnati Technology Center

1837
Procter & Gamble Company

1839
Greater Cincinnati Chamber
 of Commerce

1840
Cognis Corporation

1848
Maple Knoll Village

1848
The YMCA of Greater Cincinnati

1851
Indiana Insurance

1852
Sisters of Charity of Cincinnati/
 St. Joseph Home/College of
 Mout St. Joseph/Bayley Place

1858
Fifth Third Bancorp

1859
Metro and the Transit Authority
 of Northern Kentucky (TANK)

City of Cincinnati

THE CITY OF CINCINNATI—A CITY RICH IN HISTORY—IS WIRED FOR THE FUTURE. HOME TO A THRIVING BUSINESS COMMUNITY, CINCINNATI IS SURROUNDED BY ROLLING HILLS, WINDING RIVERS, AND VERDANT PARKS. IT IS, AS JOHN SHIREY, CITY MANAGER, POINTS OUT, "A CITY OF SURPRISES." ● WHILE MANY CITIES TOUT THEIR QUALITY OF LIFE, CINCINNATI HAS SOME IMPRESSIVE STATISTICS TO BACK ITS CLAIMS. RECOGNIZED IN RECENT YEARS BY *Places Rated Almanac,*

Employment Review, and *Entrepreneur* and *Fortune* magazines as one of the best places in America to live and work, Cincinnati provides residents with a safe, clean environment in which to raise their families.

A Great Place to Live

Understanding that housing and education are barometers of livability, Cincinnati has made substantial investments in both. The city recently contributed $100 million to Cincinnati Public Schools, an unprecedented step for a municipality. In addition, the city provides assistance annually to some 2,400 housing units. Cincinnati seeks to provide a wider array of housing alternatives for families, including single-family homes and modern loft apartments, and to encourage home ownership through an array of loan and grant programs.

Cincinnati is equally diligent in responding to residents' needs. Citizens with problems or questions can ask a customer service representative in City Hall for assistance or call a 24-hour hot line. The city does not wait to hear about citizen-reported problems; instead, it gets involved in prevention. Because Cincinnati is a city of neighborhoods, its City Neighborhood Action Strategy (CNAS) team works proactively by sending city employees into Cincinnati neighborhoods to address specific issues of concern.

While safety, sanitation, education, and housing may represent the meat and potatoes of livability, the amenities really make Cincinnati shine. Traditional favorites such as the world-famous Cincinnati Zoo, Museum Center, Cincinnati Art Museum, Music Hall, and Playhouse in the Park share the spotlight with new attractions like Paul Brown Stadium and the Aronoff Performing Arts Center. In the near

THE CITY OF CINCINNATI IS SURROUNDED BY ROLLING HILLS, WINDING RIVERS, AND VERDANT PARKS (TOP).

BUILT IN 1926 AND RESTORED IN 2000, THE TYLER DAVIDSON FOUNTAIN IS A SYMBOL THAT HIGHLIGHTS THE CITY'S COMMITMENT TO PRESERVE ITS HERITAGE (BOTTOM).

future, the National Underground Railroad Freedom Center, a new contemporary arts center, and a new Reds ballpark will grace downtown.

Cincinnati operates 45 community pools—four times as many as most cities its size—and is in the process of developing three new aquatic centers. The city also provides 29 community centers and is developing two new recreation centers. Cincinnati is home to some of the nation's most beautiful urban parks. "It's not often you find a city with as many amenities as Cincinnati has to offer in such a beautiful setting," Shirey says.

A Great Place to Work

Already home to numerous Fortune 500 corporate headquarters, the city is working hard to attract new employers as well. Cincinnati attracted and helped create more than 1,000 jobs within the city limits in 2000, and has aggressively pursued the development of enterprise zone projects. In 2000, the city created and approved 15 project agreements worth $63 million of new, private investment. Those projects will create or retain more than 2,400 jobs within the city by 2004.

To assist developers in the building process, Cincinnati created a development help center and appointed a development coordinator to serve as liaison for all development-oriented departments. To make plan submission simpler, faster, and less expensive, the city now allows developers to submit plans electronically.

The city's Department of Economic Development helps businesses find the assistance they need. Whether searching for financial or technical aid, businesses can count on this department for support. The department provides an array of federal, state, and local loan and financing programs, and can assist with employee-training programs. Because it works collaboratively with

organizations like the Cincinnati Business Incubator and the U.S. Small Business Administration, the city's Department of Economic Development can tap into the resources necessary to solve practically any problem.

To promote the city to businesses and organizations outside the area, the city owns and operates the Cincinnati Convention Center, a 300,000-square-foot facility that includes 162,000 square feet of exhibit space. The center, which can accommodate as many as seven different groups at any given time, has hosted such notable conferences as the African Methodist Episcopal and the International Fire Service Instructors conventions.

A Great Place to Grow

As one of the most wired cities in the country, Cincinnati provides access to high-speed, broadband telecommunications facilities, thanks to the aggressive expansions of Cincinnati Bell's ZoomTown and Time-Warner's Roadrunner. That technological investment has spurred so much Internet-related business in downtown that the Main Street area of Over the Rhine has been dubbed the Digital Rhine.

The City of Cincinnati is equally

resolved to preserve its heritage. Perhaps no symbol highlights that commitment better than the newly unveiled Tyler Davidson Fountain. Built in 1926 and beautifully restored

in 2000, the fountain stands as a bright reminder that Cincinnati celebrates a rich heritage. However, as Shirey notes, "Its best days are still ahead."

RECOGNIZED IN RECENT YEARS BY *PLACES RATED ALMANAC*, *EMPLOYMENT REVIEW*, AND *ENTREPRENEUR* AND *FORTUNE* MAGAZINES AS ONE OF THE BEST PLACES IN AMERICA TO LIVE AND WORK, CINCINNATI PROVIDES RESIDENTS WITH A SAFE, CLEAN ENVIRONMENT IN WHICH TO RAISE THEIR FAMILIES.

University of Cincinnati

WHEN W.B. YEATS WROTE THE WORDS "EDUCATION IS NOT THE FILLING OF A PAIL, BUT THE LIGHTING OF A FIRE," HE MAY NOT HAVE BEEN THINKING ABOUT THE UNIVERSITY OF CINCINNATI (UC), BUT HE CERTAINLY SHARED THE SCHOOL'S PHILOSOPHY. SO MUCH SO, IN FACT, THAT UC HAS MADE YEATS' AXIOM PART OF ITS ETHOS. ● AS JOSEPH STEGER, UC PRESIDENT, EXPLAINS, UNIVERSITIES THAT MERELY SEEK TO "FILL THE PAIL" WILL QUICKLY BE OUTMODED. UNDERSTANDING THAT CONCEPT, UC

has spent the past decade transforming itself from the old model to a new one that kindles aspirations, dreams, and lifelong learning. Toward that end, the university has focused on a handful of key themes—including pedagogy, globalization, interdisciplinary scholarship, and technological investment—that will help it light fires among its students for many years to come.

"Each of these initiatives is directed toward one goal: placing the University of Cincinnati among the best centers of learning and innovation in the next century," Steger says.

The Art of Learning

Tracing its roots back to 1819, UC has long been recognized as an innovator in education. The Reverend William Holmes McGuffey, who shaped the way Americans learn with his McGuffey readers, was an early president of the university. In 1906, the university went on to pioneer the concept of cooperative learning. Co-oping, a common feature in today's educational landscape, allows students to bridge the gap between academia and the workplace. By enabling students to apply what they learn in the classroom to real-world problems and bring the latest in workplace

innovation back to their university peers, the co-op experience changed 20th century learning.

Now, on the cusp of the 21st century, UC is again remaking education. Today, learning is not about a professor preaching to a group of passive students. It's about interaction—between professors and the 33,300-plus-member student body, as well as between fellow students—through interdisciplinary research and study, and electronically via the Web. It is about around-the-clock learning. UC understands that knowledge is not tucked away in journals and reference works or locked away in academics' heads. The era of "the sage on the stage" is over. Today, students and faculty, acting as members of a learning community, are exploring new ways to share information.

Faculty members have embraced this opportunity. They are working with peers in other departments to develop interdisciplinary programs that enable them to cooperatively explore areas that previously would have been outside the realm of traditional scholarship. That may mean leading a group of students on an excavation of a Trojan War battlefield or conducting a groundwater study that taps the expertise of academics from more than a half dozen disciplines, including engineering, geology, and medicine. It could also mean forging a new degree program, such as the legal nursing specialty developed to help nurses navigate the quagmire of managed care contracts.

Similarly, faculty and students are finding innovative ways to use technology to advance learning. Between 1995 and 2000, the university invested some $60 million in its electronic infrastructure. Thanks to that investment, professors can use technology not just as a research

DOTTIE STOVER

TRACING ITS ROOTS BACK TO 1819, THE UNIVERSITY OF CINCINNATI (UC) HAS LONG BEEN RECOGNIZED AS AN INNOVATOR IN EDUCATION.

tool or as a means of incorporating multimedia presentations into lectures, but also as a way to creatively realize their own particular teaching goals. It may mean performing a physics simulation on the Web that students can access 24 hours a day, using a CD-ROM to bring a Puritan-era text to life, or using a computer program to solve the algebraic elements of a problem enabling students to focus on the more challenging calculus.

Such practical applications are important to UC's mission. While other universities may embrace ivory-tower musing, UC is very much an application-oriented institution. Students are encouraged not merely to read about the global economy and international cultures, but to study abroad or co-op with a company in Japan or Germany. On campus, they are given an opportunity to form lifelong friendships, as well as to learn from classmates who represent 95 different countries and

faculty members whose research, roots, fellowships, and consulting engagements keep them active in more than 100 nations.

Architecture Reflects Mission

UC's approach to education is reflected in the very bricks and mortar that make up the university. Although described by the New York Times as "one of the most architecturally dynamic campuses in America today," UC's campus has not always been lauded for its aesthetic appeal. For years, the campus was a morass of tightly, illogically packed buildings. With land at a premium and a rapidly expanding student body, the university erected buildings where they would fit.

That began to change in 1989 when UC adopted a master plan to create "front doors" at various spots around the campus where visitors were likely to access the campus. Given UC's emphasis on practical-

ity, the massive building campaign, which has tapped the talents of such notable architects as Michael Graves, Frank Gehry, and Henry Cobb, is about more than creating an attractive campus, however. The master plan reiterates the university's underlying themes by connecting heretofore far-flung departments, thus facilitating interdisciplinary cooperation.

Most important, UC's campus makeover is a celebration of community that encourages interaction, collaboration, innovation, and informal communication. Those qualities foster the respect and community the University of Cincinnati is dedicated to forging.

"A university must be centered on learning," Steger says. "To place learning at the center requires respect for learners, an atmosphere that supports inquiry and discussion, as well as commitment to shared values."

CLOCKWISE FROM TOP LEFT: UC'S APPROACH TO EDUCATION IS REFLECTED IN THE VERY BRICKS AND MORTAR THAT MAKE UP THE UNIVERSITY.

UC STUDENTS SUCH AS ANCHANET PETERS (LEFT) AND ROBERT HATCHER TAKE ADVANTAGE OF AN OPPORTUNITY TO STUDY AT SIGMA SIGMA COMMONS.

LEV DAVYDOV, A UC GRADUATE STUDENT IN CHEMICAL ENGINEERING, RESEARCHES DIFFERENT SYSTEMS FOR BREAKING DOWN TOXIC ORGANIC COMPOUNDS INTO CARBON DIOXIDE AND WATER.

LIQUE COOLENL, A UC ADJUNCT ASSISTANT PROFESSOR IN CELL BIOLOGY, AND ONE OF HER STUDENTS EXAMINE BRAIN TISSUE AT THE UNIVERSITY'S VONTZ CENTER FOR MOLECULAR STUDIES.

A DISTRIBUTOR OF PAPER AND OTHER PRODUCTS IN THE TRI-STATE REGION, XPEDX IS ONE OF THE OLDEST COMPANIES IN CINCINNATI AND THE SECOND-OLDEST PAPER MERCHANT IN THE NATION. THE COMPANY, WHICH IS PART OF INTERNATIONAL PAPER, PROVIDES CUSTOMER SOLUTIONS THROUGH MORE THAN 120 DISTRIBUTION CENTERS AND 175 RETAIL STORES ACROSS THE COUNTRY. THE FIRM'S INTERNATIONAL HEADQUARTERS IS LOCATED IN COVINGTON. WITH

annual sales of $8 billion, xpedx has nearly 10,000 employees and 12 million square feet of warehouse space across the country.

xpedx succeeds because it is local to hundreds of customers in Greater Cincinnati and Northern Kentucky. With 24-hour-a-day operations, the company offers daily service to tri-state customers, providing printing papers, packaging supplies and equipment, facility supplies, and graphic imaging equipment and supplies.

xpedx has a significant presence in Southern Ohio and Northern Kentucky, with more than 700 employees in the area and an annual payroll of more than $30 million. International Paper has an additional 800 employees in the Greater Cincinnati area.

"WE WANT TO BE SEEN AS THE MOST CAPABLE, KNOWLEDGEABLE, AND DEPENDABLE SUPPLIER," SAYS TOM WEISENBACH, XPEDX GROUP VICE PRESIDENT FOR THE CINCINNATI/NORTHERN KENTUCKY REGION. "WE KNOW THAT IF OUR CUSTOMER SUCCEEDS, WE WILL SUCCEED."

A Rich History

The xpedx on Spring Grove Avenue can trace its history to 1832 when Goodman & Nixon opened in Cincinnati. The firm's name was changed to Chatfield Paper in 1865, and the company grew as it acquired other paper merchants. Changing its name to Zellerbach in

1988, the company became part of xpedx in 1998.

Another xpedx distribution center is located on Reading Road. Again, local heritage of that business speaks well of the company's long-standing history in the area. Saalfeld Paper began in 1919 in Covington on the site where the famous MainStrasse clock tower now stands. As the business grew, it moved to Cincinnati where it continues to operate now as part of xpedx.

Supplying Customer Solutions

The focus of xpedx is on three fundamentals: customer satisfaction, operational excellence, and people development. "Focusing on customers is most important," says Tom Weisenbach, xpedx group vice president for the region. "We need to keep our focus on our customers' needs and how their business requirements are changing. Operating excellence is how we run our business and respond to our customers. People development is critical as we better understand our customers and their needs."

Above all else, the company's success is driven by dedication to customer satisfaction. "We want to be known as our customers' most valued resource," Weisenbach says. "We want to be seen as the most capable, knowledgeable, and dependable supplier. We know that if our customer succeeds, we will succeed."

xpedx is totally focused on its target—providing customer solutions. In the 1800s, this meant providing paper to area businesses. Today, the company offers its customers an increasingly wide range of products, including paper, facility supplies, graphic arts, and packaging equipment and supplies.

But one thing has not changed: As Weisenbach says, "At xpedx, we deliver excellence."

WHETHER THEY'RE LEAFING THROUGH A MAGAZINE, MAKING A PHOTOCOPY, SELECTING A VIDEO, OR MUNCHING ON A SNACK, CHANCES ARE CONSUMERS HAVE AN INTERNATIONAL PAPER (IP) PRODUCT IN THEIR HANDS. THAT'S BECAUSE THIS DIVERSIFIED PAPER, PACKAGING, AND FOREST PRODUCTS COMPANY HAS MORE THAN 450 FACILITIES IN NEARLY 50 COUNTRIES AND OFFERS AN ARRAY OF PRODUCTS TO CUSTOMERS IN 130 NATIONS. ● THE CINCINNATI TECHNOLOGY

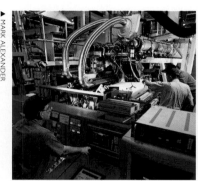

Center, home to IP's Packaging Development and Manufacturing Technology centers, conducts operations that are important to clients as well as to the company's global operations.

Given the Cincinnati Technology Center's central purpose, it's not surprising that Greater Cincinnati's location was a key factor in IP's decision to build here. Site Manager Robert Baillie says, "Cincinnati is convenient to our customers and to our mills. The Cincinnati/Northern Kentucky International Airport offers excellent domestic and international flight service that enhances our customers' ability to visit the facility and allows the staff access to our customers. In addition, Cincinnati offers a high quality of life for our employees and ready access to a large pool of highly trained people."

Packaging Innovations

The Packaging Development Center, which opened in 1996, demonstrates IP's commitment to technological innovation. Designed to meet customers' needs quickly and effectively, it includes a research library, 11 laboratories, and six pilot plants that bridge the gap between laboratory concept and full commercial production.

Efficient design and comprehensive approach enable the 200 IP staff members who are faced with a packaging challenge in the morning to present a prototype solution to a client by afternoon. That's a major benefit to customers, whether they are a quick-service restaurant chain or an international manufacturer of consumer goods. In addition to developing proprietary packaging and packaging products, the Packaging Development Center's professionals develop new applications for existing packaging and support customer use of current products.

Concern for Environment and Community

Working behind the scenes, the 300 engineering experts stationed at IP's Manufacturing Technology Center are engaged in a different kind of customer service. The group, which is responsible for making sure IP uses its resources in the most efficient, environmentally responsible method possible, serves the company's plants and facilities worldwide. Among the Manufacturing Technology Center's many functions are the management of IP's large capital projects and improvements, and technical troubleshooting support for the firm's mills and plants.

While IP's manufacturing and engineering experts spend much of their time in the field, when in Cincinnati, they are able to stay abreast of projects and developments around the world with the Manufacturing Technology Center's state-of-the-art videoconferencing facilities and computer links.

Though they may jet around the world to support IP and its customers, Cincinnati Technology Center employees have strong local ties and demonstrate their commitment to the area in a number of ways. For example, Cincinnati Technology Center is a partner in education with Milford and Loveland schools. Through these partnerships, IP employees act as mentors and tutors, while the company provides skill-enhancement opportunities for teachers and corporate educational grants.

Cincinnati Technology Center staff members likewise support the Clermont County United Way, Clermont County Chamber of Commerce, and Partnership for Greater Cincinnati, which promotes regional development. Far from a sideline, these civic activities are an important part of company operations, Baillie says. Responsible corporate citizenship "requires more than being accountable stewards of our resources and the environment," he says. "It means supporting the communities where we live and work."

CLOCKWISE FROM LEFT:
AT INTERNATIONAL PAPER'S (IP) PACKAGING DEVELOPMENT CENTER, LOCATED AT THE CINCINNATI TECHNOLOGY CENTER, A COEXTRUSION LAMINATING AND COATING LINE IS USED TO DEVELOP NEW PACKAGING FOR A VARIETY OF APPLICATIONS.

EMPLOYEES FROM THE CINCINNATI TECHNOLOGY CENTER SUPPORT CUSTOMERS WORLDWIDE.

IP OPENED ITS PACKAGING DEVELOPMENT CENTER IN CINCINNATI IN 1996.

Procter & Gamble Company

Founded in 1837 as a family-operated soap and candle business, the Procter & Gamble Company (P&G) has since blossomed into a $40 billion consumer products company that markets more than 300 brands to nearly 5 billion consumers in more than 140 countries. Based in Cincinnati, P&G is one of the largest employers in the tristate area with more than 13,700 employees at its numerous facilities, including its global headquarters, world-class research centers, and state-of-the-art manufacturing facilities.

Innovation and Technology

For more than 160 years, P&G has been dedicated to its purpose of providing products and services of superior quality and value that improve the lives of the world's consumers. With numerous category-leading brands, P&G is focused on continuing as a worldwide leader in consumer products in the 21st century. "Consumers place their trust in our brands to deliver value every time," says A.G. Lafley, president and chief executive. "From the first time a consumer uses one of our products all the way through each and every succeeding purchase, our goal is to delight the consumer. We accomplish this on the strength of our unique consumer understanding and product innovation capability."

P&G has been connecting knowledge and technologies to meet consumer needs throughout its history. This began in the company's earliest days with candles, which provided the technology base for making soap. That know-how enabled the company to learn about fats and oils, which in turn led to the creation of the vegetable-oil-based products Crisco and Crisco Oil. Crushing seeds to produce oil gave P&G expertise in plant fibers, which led to insights into making paper and absorbent products, such as diapers, feminine protection products, and paper towels. Because the science of fats and oils is also a fundamental base for surfactants, P&G became proficient in the manufacturing of detergents, which resulted in a greater understanding of hard water and calcium. P&G parlayed that knowledge into a greater understanding of teeth and bones. The result: toothpaste and, more recently, drugs to treat osteoporosis.

"This ability to transfer knowledge from one business to another has been an extraordinary factor in P&G's growth," Lafley says. "Historically, we have won biggest on the strength of superior product technology with products that set the performance standards in their categories and innovations that create entirely new categories."

P&G's innovative approach and ability to make insightful connections stretch across product categories—and retail store shelves—around the world, and has led to some of the world's most successful brands. The ever growing list includes such familiar names as Tide, Crest, Pantene Pro-V, Always, Bounty, Charmin, Pringles, Pampers, Olay, Vicks, and Dawn. Recent innovations have resulted in new-to-the-world products such as Febreze, Swiffer, and Dryel, and Internet ventures like Reflect.com, a customer-tailored cosmetics line sold via the Web.

The Greater Cincinnati area continues to play a leading role in P&G's innovative capability. P&G spends about $1.7 billion per year on research and development, and a large percentage of P&G jobs in the area are related to the R&D work being done at the company's growing list of technical centers. The newest examples include the

Based in Cincinnati, Procter & Gamble Company (P&G) is one of the largest employers in the tristate area with more than 13,700 employees at its numerous facilities, including its global headquarters, world-class research centers, and state-of-the-art manufacturing facilities.

quality of its products, packages, and processes. The company's focus on perfecting holistic, sustainable development strategies integrates its business goals with its commitment to the environment and corporate social responsibility.

P&G's focus on sustainability has already produced significant advances. Concern for the global water supply, for example, has led the Fabric & Home Care division to develop new cleaning methods that require less water or rely on cold water, nonpotable water, and even salt water. The need for better nutrition, particularly in developing countries, has led the firm's Food & Beverage division to develop a new nutrient drink to promote the growth and development of children.

"I view this as an opportunity and stimulus to innovate, to improve consumers' lives, while also making positive contributions to environmental quality and society, particularly in developing countries," Lafley says. "By providing products of superior quality and value to the world's consumers, we not only prosper as a company, but the communities in which we live and work prosper as well."

"CONSUMERS PLACE THEIR TRUST IN OUR BRANDS TO DELIVER VALUE EVERY TIME," SAYS A.G. LAFLEY, P&G PRESIDENT AND CHIEF EXECUTIVE.

Beckett Ridge Technical Center, a state-of-the-art global engineering and packaging prototyping lab located in West Chester Township, and the Fabric & Home Care Innovation Center, soon to be built at the site of P&G's first detergent manufacturing plant in St. Bernard.

Committed to the Environment and the Community

As a global corporation, P&G takes its civic responsibilities seriously. Along with its employees, it shares a sense of mission. "P&G is a company made up of extraordinarily dedicated men and women around the world who feel an enormous sense of ownership for the business and the communities in which they are located," Lafley says.

P&G is committed to using its resources—its money, people, and energies—wisely. As a result, the company provides financial support for a wide range of education, health, social service, cultural, civic, and environmental organizations. In the Cincinnati area, P&G is a major sponsor of the United Way campaign, the Fine Arts Fund, and numerous educational endeavors such as the Cincinnati Youth Collaborative. In addition, P&G's employees have a long tradition of

personal volunteer involvement, including partnering with schools on collaborative science projects and mentoring to encourage youths to remain in school.

P&G has espoused a similar commitment to the environment and to improving the environmental

P&G'S INNOVATIVE APPROACH AND ABILITY TO MAKE INSIGHTFUL CONNECTIONS STRETCH ACROSS PRODUCT CATEGORIES—AND RETAIL STORE SHELVES—AROUND THE WORLD, AND HAS LED TO SOME OF THE WORLD'S MOST SUCCESSFUL BRANDS.

Greater Cincinnati Chamber of Commerce

IN 1839, A GROUP OF 76 BUSINESS OWNERS CONVENED AT THE YOUNG MEN'S MERCANTILE LIBRARY IN DOWNTOWN CINCINNATI TO DISCUSS WAYS OF PROMOTING COMMERCE IN THE REGION—AT THE TIME THE LARGEST COMMUNITY WEST OF THE ALLEGHENY MOUNTAINS. OUT OF THOSE ENTHUSIASTIC DISCUSSIONS EMERGED THE GREATER CINCINNATI CHAMBER OF COMMERCE, WHICH MAINTAINS THE SAME SPIRIT VOICED AT THE GATHERINGS MORE THAN 150 YEARS AGO.

OHIO GOVERNOR BOB TAFT ADDRESSES THE TRANS-ATLANTIC BUSINESS DIALOGUE CONFERENCE, A PREMIER CONFERENCE ATTRACTED TO CINCINNATI IN 2000 WITH ENCOURAGEMENT FROM THE GREATER CINCINNATI CHAMBER OF COMMERCE AND THE PARTNERSHIP FOR GREATER CINCINNATI.

EACH YEAR, THE DOWNTOWN COUNCIL—NICKNAMED THE GREATER CINCINNATI CHAMBER OF COMMERCE'S ROCK AND ROLL DIVISION—PRODUCES OKTOBERFEST-ZINZINNATI, ONE OF SEVERAL MAJOR EVENTS THAT ADD TO THE CITY'S DOWNTOWN AND RIVERFRONT AREAS. ZINZINNATI'S OKTOBERFEST IS CONSIDERED THE LARGEST OUTSIDE OF MUNICH.

Today, as in 1839, the Chamber exists to serve its members and to strengthen the region's economic vitality and quality of life.

Twice named Chamber of the Year by the National Association of Membership Development, the Greater Cincinnati Chamber of Commerce has grown to become the fourth-largest chamber in the nation. Much of its growth can be attributed to a wide array of services: economic development, business retention, governmental advocacy, member benefit programs, business information, education and training, marketing, and volunteer opportunities. The Chamber's extensive palette of programs serves businesses, large and small, throughout the region.

A key theme for the Chamber at the turn of the new century has focused on regional cooperation, with the Chamber acting as a catalyst on many important fronts across 13 counties in Indiana, Kentucky, and Ohio. Nowhere is regional cooperation more evident than in the competitive arena of economic development. The Chamber spearheads the efforts of the Partnership for

Greater Cincinnati, a consortium of regional economic development partners, with a goal of promoting Greater Cincinnati nationally and internationally through a strong, unified message. The partnership's goal is job growth, especially in the high-tech and research and development industries.

Touting Cincinnati's Virtues

When it comes to promoting Greater Cincinnati as a region on the move, the Chamber and the partnership have plenty to talk about. The region's spirit is reflected in a new, $2 billion riverfront, with a futuristic stadium for the Cincinnati Bengals, an intimate ballpark for the Cincinnati Reds, a revamped Fort Washington Way, the National Underground Railroad Freedom Center, and an expansive park system.

National media have taken notice of Cincinnati's upswing. The *New York Times* reported that "Cincinnati exemplifies the cities driving the U.S. economy." *Fortune* added that the city is one of the top 10 in the nation to live and work, and Yahoo! rated Cincinnati in the top 25 "wired" U.S. cities.

Driving the economic growth for the region has been the Cincinnati/ Northern Kentucky International Airport, consistently named one of the top airports in the world for convenience, and home to Delta Air Lines' second-largest hub. The airport offers international, nonstop flights to London, Frankfurt, Paris, Zurich, Toronto, and Montreal, and direct service to Tokyo, Munich, and São Paulo. In all, the airport boasts more than 500 daily departures to more than 110 cities worldwide.

Greater Cincinnati is located within 600 miles of nearly three-fifths of the nation's population, and ease of transportation is one of the region's most important advantages.

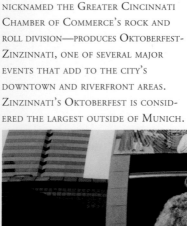

Three interstate highways pass through the city, and the Ohio River carries so much barge traffic that Cincinnati ranks as the fifth-largest inland port in America.

Another area of strength is the tristate's diverse economy, with no single company employing more than 2 percent of the workforce. That diversity, along with Greater Cincinnati's growing export business, has helped the city weather economic downturns better than most of its neighbors. Greater Cincinnati is home to seven Fortune 500 companies, as well as a growing list of international corporations and research and development centers.

Making Great Business Greater

In its leading role for small business, the Chamber has been an advocate for collaboration by regional chambers, bringing together resources for educational, networking, and legislative efforts. The alliance allows the chambers to serve members more effectively and to speak out to legislators on important governmental issues affecting business.

The Chamber's family of member benefit programs helps its member companies improve their bottom line. By leveraging the Chamber's strength in numbers, the programs deliver substantial group discounts on health insurance; workers' compensation group rating and claims administration; cellular telephone service; and discounts on business supplies. These member benefit programs have helped fuel a 50

percent increase in Chamber membership since 1990, with nearly two-thirds of the members participating in one or more programs.

Chamber educational programs cover a wide range of business topics, including a highly acclaimed strategic planning course, which enables growth-oriented companies to develop customized strategic plans. CEO roundtables offer executives the chance to discuss common concerns with an informal board of advisers, while the Chamber's Business Information Center provides important publications and data that businesses need to stay one step ahead. Networking opportunities allow businesspeople to meet potential customers in friendly, productive settings.

Perhaps the fastest-growing area of the Chamber's services is the Internet, with the Chamber maintaining high-traffic sites such as www.cincinnatichamber.com and its on-line information warehouse, www.trinet-online.com. Users can log on to cincinnatichamber.com to search a database of more than 10,000 businesses for key company information such as management personnel, number of company employees, and phone and fax numbers—putting valuable information at the click of a mouse.

As a new century dawns, the Greater Cincinnati Chamber of Commerce is more committed than ever to doing what its founders envisioned in 1839—making great businesses greater.

▶ PAULA NORTON / NORTON PHOTOGRAPHY 2

Cognis Corporation

C OGNIS CORPORATION IS ONE OF THE NEWEST ADDITIONS TO CINCINNATI'S BILLION-DOLLAR CORPORATE NAMES. BUT THIS RAPIDLY GROWING COMPANY IS FAR MORE THAN ANOTHER NEW FACE ON THE BLOCK. COGNIS, WITH ITS NORTH AMERICAN HEADQUARTERS IN CINCINNATI, IS A SOPHISTI-CATED, STRATEGIC BUSINESS DESIGNED TO FLOURISH IN THE COMPLEX AND COMPETITIVE GLOBAL CHEMICAL PRODUCT MARKETPLACE. FORMERLY A DIVISION OF THE GERMAN-

based Henkel Group, Cognis was established in 1999 as an independent entity, linking all of Henkel's worldwide specialty chemical businesses under a single, global corporate banner.

"The independent status of Cognis gives us a number of strategic advantages over our former position as a closely held Henkel operating division," says Robert T. Betz, president of Cognis North America. "As a separate business, it is easier for us to form close, protected technical partnerships with our customers. Our chemists and technicians often work with our customers in their laboratories, finalizing new technologies. Representing a separate business unit makes it easier for our people to build trusting relationships with our customers, especially when our customers may compete with Henkel in a consumer product or even an industrial market."

Betz sees increased financial flexibility as another distinct strategic benefit of the new Cognis organization. "With Cognis now operating as a separate subsidiary of Henkel Group, it allows us to compete for

financial resources anywhere in the global marketplace," Betz says.

From Cincinnati Roots to Global Branches

C ognis North America today serves a worldwide roster of diverse customers, yet the business started small. The company is a direct descendant of a tallow candle and lamp oil shop founded in 1840 in downtown Cincinnati by Thomas Emery Sr. Emery bequeathed the company to his sons, who in 1885

relocated the manufacturing facility from downtown to the present Cognis manufacturing site in Winton Place.

In the 1930s, Thomas Emery's grandson, John J. Emery Jr., began a long tenure as head of the firm. He directed a growing chemical product enterprise that built a national reputation for market and technical leadership in oleochemistry. In 1978, two years after John Emery's death, the original Emery family organization merged with National

WITH NORTH AMERICAN HEADQUARTERS IN CINCINNATI, COGNIS CORPORATION IS A SOPHISTICATED, STRATEGIC BUSINESS DESIGNED TO FLOURISH IN THE CHEMICAL PRODUCT MARKETPLACE.

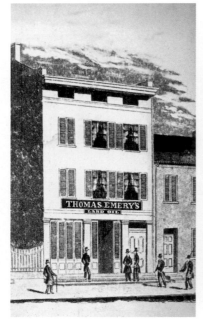

A DIRECT DESCENDANT OF A TALLOW CANDLE AND LAMP OIL SHOP FOUNDED IN 1840 IN DOWNTOWN CINCINNATI BY THOMAS EMERY SR., COGNIS SERVES A WORLDWIDE ROSTER OF DIVERSE CUSTOMERS.

Distillers and Chemical Corporation. The company later became part of the Quantum Chemical Corporation.

Henkel Corporation acquired Quantum's Emery Division in 1989, and it continued operation as the Henkel Chemicals Group. Henkel expanded the plant at the Winton Place site. The new investment broadened the base of the firm's chemical competencies, and expanded its research and production capabilities. In 1995, Henkel confirmed its commitment to the Emery oleochemistry legacy with the construction of the new Winton Place headquarters for Henkel Chemicals Group. The facility is now headquarters to Cognis North America.

"The formation of Cognis gave us a global vision and forced us to expand our understanding of what this company must be to succeed," Betz says. "Increased volume of business and enhanced profit and return on investment are responsibilities that our senior management team takes extremely seriously."

An Expanded Vision

Cognis is a chemical company with a decidedly global vision. With its world headquarters in Roermond, Netherlands, Cognis is a global leader in specialty chemicals. The company employs some 9,000 people worldwide and has service centers in some 50 countries on five continents. Cognis' world revenues in 1999 were $2.7 billion. North American operations accounted for approximately $1 billion of that

total. Cognis North America is headquartered in Cincinnati and uses the Queen City as its hub of operations for some 10 additional facilities in the United States and Canada.

Cognis is recognized as a world leader in chemical products made from renewable raw materials, such as oils extracted from corn, soybeans, coconuts, sunflowers, and rapeseed, as well as tallow from animal rendering. Cognis' technologies and innovative processes have made these renewable, environmentally

COGNIS' OPERATIONS ARE ALIGNED IN THREE BROAD GLOBAL BUSINESS SECTORS: OLEOCHEMICALS, ORGANIC SPECIALTIES, AND CARE CHEMICALS.

responsible chemicals ideal in a broad range of industrial manufacturing and consumer product applications, such as industrial and heavy truck lubricants, cosmetics, adhesives, detergents, food processing, paints, pharmaceuticals, plastics, and agricultural chemicals.

The Cognis product roster also includes organic intermediates and specialty chemical ingredients that improve end-product performance or enhance basic manufacturing processes. Industries served include

Technology Center, biotechnology studies are a fast-track project to engineer microorganisms genetically as biocatalysts to convert renewable agricultural feedstock into value-added chemical products. These chemical products would be too expensive or complex to create using traditional methods."

Focus on People

Products and technology only paint a portion of the Cognis corporate picture. It is people that complete the company portrait—Cognis employees and Cognis customers.

Cognis' new logo, the eye, symbolizes the critical role people play in the Cognis organization.

Company statements on the logo say "The eye is believed to be the window to the soul. We believe that in order to be a truly customer-focused company, we must have a depth of understanding of our customers' business. At the same time, the eye symbolizes Cognis' knowledge and expertise, and reflects our level of commitment, concern and dedication to our customers' success. The iris also represents the rainbow of expertise and diversity found in more than 9,000 Cognis employees worldwide."

Cognis uses a team-based structure at its Cincinnati headquarters and all of its locations throughout North America to empower employees to make decisions within their team that benefit the customer. The firm rewards success and encourages thoughtful risk-taking through its companywide innovation program.

Cognis is committed to providing its employees with ongoing education and training, as well as providing a safe, ethical, and environmentally responsible business culture for all of its employees. The company believes it is a combination of all of these factors that has allowed it to retain its most competent, talented, and motivated employees.

"Every year, we celebrate the 25-Year Club," says Betz. "These are current employees who have been with the company for more than 25 years. In 2000, we honored 230

adhesives, plastics, footwear, graphic arts, mining, paints, soaps and detergents, personal care, and nutrition and health.

Cognis' operations are aligned in three broad global business sectors: oleochemicals, organic specialties, and care chemicals.

Oleochemicals offer the largest and most complete spectrum of chemical products made from natural raw materials to customers worldwide. Cognis' Organic Specialties sector delivers chemical solutions that allow customers to optimize their processes and turn Cognis' technical innovations into practical product solutions. The organic specialties sector is Cognis' broadest product group and includes Synlube technology, textile technology, coatings and inks, plastics and polymer chemicals, performance monomer technology, the AgroSolutions division, and the Mineral Industry division and extraction technology. The Care Chemicals group focuses

on developments for detergents and household cleaners, cosmetics, and toiletries. Care Chemicals includes Cognis' nutrition and health segment, which is the world's leading supplier of antioxidants.

"We see our Care Chemicals business, spurred by an increased level of new customer alliances and product line acquisitions, emerging as our strongest near-future growth driver," Betz says. "With the growth we've experienced in graphic arts industry products, we are confident that our coatings and inks chemical segment also is capable of delivering solid annual growth rates."

Breakthrough Technology

Betz points to Cognis' long-term research and focus on biotechnology as one of the expected sources for company growth. "The potential for new technology in this area is extremely significant," notes Betz. "At our Cincinnati Research and

Cognis employees who have attained this remarkable level of tenure. I think this longevity and dedication says something about the strength of this organization and the level of commitment from our employees to serve our customers."

Thinking Globally, Remaining Community-Focused

Even as Cognis grows globally, its commitment to and investment in Cincinnati remains strong. In 1993, the Winton Place chemical plant became one of the first companies in the region to form a community advisory panel (CAP). The advisory panel is composed of 20 neighbors from the Winton Place and St. Bernard communities, including teachers, firefighters, police officers, health care workers, and homemakers. The panel brings employees and neighbors together to work on common issues such as community safety, health, and environmental practices; the panel also meets monthly with Cognis manufacturing and safety management. The CAP's guidance has been instrumental in cementing the company's bonds to its neighborhood and in anticipating community needs and concerns.

Working with local schools, Cognis employees have instituted

a grassroots Education Outreach program as well. Individuals from Cognis volunteer their time and talents to assist area schools in programs such as tutoring and mentoring. Cognis volunteers also act as resources for teachers and classes, and take part in instructional and career day presentations in their areas of expertise.

While the Cognis name is a new addition to Cincinnati's large roster of global corporate citizens, the company's dedication to innovation, customer satisfaction, and community involvement has already made it a leader in the region. Determined to continue its legacy, Cognis will set industry standards for decades to come.

INDUSTRIES SERVED BY COGNIS INCLUDE ADHESIVES, PLASTICS, FOOTWEAR, GRAPHIC ARTS, MINING, PAINTS, SOAPS AND DETERGENTS, PERSONAL CARE, AND NUTRITION AND HEALTH.

Maple Knoll Village

Located on 54 wooded acres in Cincinnati's Springdale area, Maple Knoll Village has been repeatedly recognized by *New Choices* magazine as one of the top 20 continuing care retirement communities in the United States. Offering a wide range of living options, including independent living, assisted living, and skilled nursing care facilities, Maple Knoll is designed to accommodate residents' changing needs. The organization is owned and operated by LifeSphere, formerly Southwestern Ohio Seniors' Services, Inc. (SOSSI), a not-for-profit corporation dedicated to serving older adults.

A Storied History in Cincinnati

Maple Knoll's facilities are state of the art, and its history is long and rich. Maple Knoll Village is the successor to three historic Cincinnati charities: the Widows' and Old Men's Home founded in 1848, the Maple Knoll Home founded in 1854, and the Bodmann Widows' Home founded in 1881.

Since its humble founding, the original, nine-room facility established by Lydia Beecher, stepmother of Harriet Beecher Stowe, has grown to hundreds of rooms located in a comfortable array of 157 cottages and 110 independent apartments that enable healthy individuals to remain self-reliant. Those needing assistance have access to Maple Knoll's 60 assisted-living apartments and 174 nursing care beds. A Geriatric Evaluation Center, in affiliation with University Hospital, operates at the village, and offers complete diagnostic evaluation for the older adult.

Maple Knoll caters to residents of varying financial means by offering financial assistance and providing a residential alternative for moderate to low-income individuals at The Meadows, a complex of 150 one-bedroom rental apartments operated under the auspices of the Department of Housing and Urban Development. Thanks to LifeSphere's 1997 merger with the Sycamore Senior Adult Multi-Service Center, Inc., Maple Knoll is aligned with two elderly housing projects—Corbly Trace in Mount Washington and Mount View Terrace in Reading—which, together, provide 94 apartments to area seniors. That merger likewise allied Maple Knoll with Anderson Senior Center and Sycamore Center. These services, combined with the existing Maple Knoll Center, expanded Maple Knoll's reach into the community. Today, the three centers assist 9,000 seniors living in their own homes.

"The merger has brought to the Greater Cincinnati area one of the most comprehensive systems designed to serve older adults in the nation," explains Ray Kingsbury, vice president of community services for LifeSphere. "Nowhere else can older adults and their families access such a wide range of programs and service options tailored to meet their specific needs. Our system offers unique opportunities for the vibrant, vital individual, as well as for those who may need some measure of assistance to maintain their independence."

With a zest for life, Maple Knoll Village resident and former trustee Martha L. Daniels personifies an energy and enthusiasm that belie her 90-plus years (top).

Maple Knoll Village residents love the Wellness Center's beautiful, heated swimming pool. Classes include arthritis aquatics, aqua aerobics, and water walking (bottom).

LifeSphere's mission expanded again in October 1999, when it welcomed its first residents at The Knolls of Oxford, an 85-acre continuing care retirement community in Oxford, Ohio. The Knolls provides 125 cottages, 50 apartments, 40 assisted-living apartments, and 30 nursing care beds.

Celebrating Life

But LifeSphere's mission is not merely to serve more people: It's to serve more people better. The organization accomplishes that mission by continually reviewing its services and amenities to ensure residents' physical, emotional, social, and spiritual needs are being met.

At Maple Knoll Village, amenities—such as a holistic wellness center, which includes an indoor, 25- by 60-foot, heated pool; state-of-the-art fitness equipment; whirlpool; fitness studio; lounge; and landscaped outdoor courtyard—are important components for achieving those goals. Equally important are the center's manicured grounds, which afford privacy as well as ample opportunities to socialize in communal features such as dining rooms, living rooms with entertainment centers and recreation tables, an arts-and-crafts studio, a full-service beauty shop, and a resource library.

No matter what their interests, residents can find a creative outlet at Maple Knoll. They can take a painting or crafts class, learn pho-

tography, attend a lecture or concert, or volunteer at the facility's popular radio station, WMKV (89.3 FM). The nation's only educational radio station designed for the listening pleasure of older adults, WMKV was recognized by the American Association of Homes and Services for the Aging as the Innovation of the Year following its 1995 inauguration.

One of Maple Knoll's most important features is that residents aren't cut off from the larger society simply because they live in a retirement community. Rather, they can interact with other members of the community while taking classes offered at Maple Knoll's campus through the University of Cincinnati's Learning in Retirement program, or by working with preschoolers attending the on-campus Montessori Child Center.

Other new and innovative programs are on the way. "We are work-

ing on exciting programs now that will greatly enhance the quality of life for our residents in the near future," says President and CEO Jerry D. Smart. Among those programs are the Eden Alternative and the Memory Garden.

The Eden Alternative addresses the three plagues that can overwhelm some nursing home residents: loneliness, helplessness, and boredom. The Eden Alternative brings the diversity and natural elements of the outside world to Maple Knoll. By encouraging interaction with children, animals, and plants, the program reminds residents and the broader community that seniors aren't frail and helpless, but an integral part of the community. That natural interaction alleviates boredom and lends purpose to seniors' daily lives, while enriching the lives of those around them.

The Memory Garden will be an enclosed garden filled with flowers, plants, statuary, and fountains. Because it will be accessible by a private elevator, nursing residents who might not otherwise be able to enjoy the outdoors unless accompanied by a friend or family member can have the freedom to enjoy a quiet oasis on their own.

By constantly striving to improve its facilities and nurture its residents, Maple Knoll Village promises to live up to its mission—to help older people live to their highest potential as individuals—for years to come.

CLOCKWISE FROM TOP: TAI CHI IS JUST ONE OF MANY HOLISTIC PROGRAMS OFFERED AT MAPLE KNOLL VILLAGE'S WELLNESS CENTER.

VOLUNTEERS CONTRIBUTE HUNDREDS OF LOVING HOURS AT MAPLE KNOLL VILLAGE, AND IT'S OFTEN DIFFICULT TO TELL WHO IS HAVING MORE FUN—THE VOLUNTEER OR THE CHILDREN BEING READ TO AT THE MAPLE KNOLL CHILD CENTER.

MAPLE KNOLL VILLAGE IS HOME TO WMKV 89.3 FM, THE NATION'S ONLY PUBLIC RADIO STATION DESIGNED EXPRESSLY FOR OLDER ADULTS. STAFFED LARGELY WITH VETERAN BROADCASTERS AND VOLUNTEERS, THE STATION HAS WON NUMEROUS NATIONAL AND INTERNATIONAL AWARDS.

The YMCA of Greater Cincinnati

As one of the oldest and largest not-for-profit community service organizations in Cincinnati, the YMCA of Greater Cincinnati has been working to meet the health and social service needs of children, teens, and families for more than 150 years. ● The roots of the YMCA of Greater Cincinnati go back to 1848 when seven men formed the Young Men's Association of Christian Inquiry. In 1853, the organization

became known as the Young Men's Christian Union and became affiliated with the national Young Men's Christian Association (YMCA) movement. By 1870, the association became incorporated, listing its objective as "the improvement of the spiritual, mental, moral, social and physical condition of young men."

Today, the mission of the YMCA is to put Christian principles into practice through programs that build healthy spirit, mind, and body for all, serving people of all faiths, races, abilities, ages, and incomes. The strength of the YMCA is in the people it brings together.

A constant source of community support, the YMCA of Greater Cincinnati is one of the oldest YMCAs in the nation, serving troops during the Civil War, World War I, and World War II. Two of the organization's oldest branches are still in operation. The University Branch, opened in 1915, serves the residents of the Clifton area, and members who live or work in the downtown Cincinnati area frequent the Central Parkway Branch, opened in 1917.

Eventually, the need for YMCA services grew beyond Hamilton County, incorporating communi-

ties throughout the tristate area. In 1987, the YMCA of Cincinnati and Hamilton County merged with the YMCA of Northern Kentucky to create the YMCA of Greater Cincinnati. Clermont County joined the association in April 1991. In 1995, the approval for a branch facility in Dearborn County, Indiana, made the YMCA of Greater Cincinnati one of the largest YMCAs in the United States, with a service area that spans three states, six counties, 20 branch facilities and 85 child care sites.

Tradition of Service

Setting the standards for community service organizations across the country, the YMCA has dedicated itself to finding innovative and meaningful ways to serve the community. In 1963, the Powel Crosley, Jr. YMCA was opened as the first suburban family branch, fulfilling the need to provide services for all ages. The year 1981 marked the opening of the first off-site child care center, which quickly became the largest fully licensed child care provider in the

Clockwise from top:
Jerry Haralson (left), YMCA of Greater Cincinnati president and CEO, with Henry Brown, chairman of the YMCA Metropolitan Board of Directors

The YMCA of Greater Cincinnati operates more than 85 child care sites throughout the tri-state area.

Serving more than 431,000 people a year, the YMCA offers a variety of programs designed for all ages in sports, health and fitness, character development, and other areas.

JOYCE PHOTOGRAPHY, TODD JOYCE

MARK BOWEN

MARK BOWEN

THE YMCA OF GREATER CINCINNATI IS THE LARGEST AREA PROVIDER OF PROGRAMS IN AQUATIC SAFETY, SWIM LESSONS, AND LIFEGUARD TRAINING (LEFT).

AREA YOUTH HAVE AN OPPORTUNITY TO SPEND A WEEK ENJOYING THE SUMMER AT YMCA RESIDENTIAL CAMPS. CAMP FELICITY IS LOCATED IN BETHEL, OHIO, AND CAMP ERNST IS LOCATED IN BURLINGTON, KENTUCKY (RIGHT).

city, serving some 4,500 children daily. In 1996, the YMCA of Greater Cincinnati became the first YMCA to implement a character development initiative, redefining the swim and gym image of the YMCA. With a full-time director of character development on staff, the YMCA has embraced the four core values of caring, honesty, respect, and responsibility. These values are integrated into every aspect of the organization, including the creation of a signature event to honor individuals of good character. Today, the YMCA is proud to hold the annual YMCA Character Awards, applauding 40 teens who demonstrate the traits of outstanding character values.

For many, the YMCA conjures images of physical fitness, but the organization is about a great deal more. "We are committed to serving the community through activities that will develop character in a child, provide positive role models for teens, and offer programs that an entire family can enjoy and participate in together," states Jerry Haralson, president and CEO. "By supporting youth and families today, we ensure our community will be in the hands of strong, responsible citizens tomorrow."

Building for the Future

Nowhere is the focus on the future more evident than in the recent, $32.6 million capital campaign that the YMCA has undertaken. In response to the development of a comprehensive strategic plan, the YMCA is answering the call of the community by focusing on four components: new facilities, teen programs, serving urban areas, and improving existing branches.

With many local communities experiencing rapid growth, the YMCA plans to build facilities in the Loveland area, Northern Kentucky, and Dearborn County. Fully equipped fitness centers, Family Aquatic Centers, Kids Clubs, and computer training centers are just a few of the amenities that will be housed in the new branches.

A new direction will be launched through the YTeens program, offering activities in the areas of fine arts, humanities, sports, business, leadership development, and social services. Part of the teen initiative includes the development of several teen centers, offering teens a place of their own with abundant social and educational opportunities. Teens will be able to choose from more than 20 venues, challenging them to develop positive character values in an exciting and educational atmosphere.

Reaching out to urban communities, the YMCA is creating new programs for its inner-city branches. Construction of the Carl and Edyth Lindner Family YMCA in the West End will make services even more accessible. In addition, the new branch will house the Bob Huggins Sports Pavilion, a super-size gymnasium that will offer both athletic and scholastic programs to Cincinnati residents.

Looking Ahead

Although the YMCA of Greater Cincinnati's founders might not recognize the organization that has grown to serve more than 431,000 residents each year, one thing hasn't changed and never will: the YMCA's commitment to developing a strong and healthy community.

"From generation to generation, the YMCA has offered individuals a place to grow and be productive to the best of their abilities," says Henry Brown, chairman of the YMCA Metropolitan Board of Directors. "I'm proud to be a volunteer for an organization that is making an investment in our future—our children."

TEENS ARE EDUCATED AND ENTERTAINED WITH YMCA ACTIVITIES FOCUSING ON LEADERSHIP, SOCIAL ISSUES, BUSINESS, TECHNOLOGY, SPORTS, AND ARTS AND HUMANITIES.

Indiana Insurance

RESPONSIVE, EXPERIENCED, PROFESSIONAL, COMPETITIVE. THOSE ARE THE QUALITIES CUSTOMERS OF INDIANA INSURANCE HAVE COME TO EXPECT, NO MATTER WHAT TIME OF DAY IT IS OR WHAT PROBLEM THEY MAY PRESENT. THIS ASSURANCE HAS BEEN PROVEN AFTER MORE THAN 150 YEARS IN THE INSURANCE BUSINESS: INDIANA INSURANCE KNOWS WHAT PEOPLE EXPECT, AND THE COMPANY KNOWS HOW TO EXCEED THOSE EXPECTATIONS. ● FOUNDED IN 1851 TO SERVE the needs of heartland residents, Indiana Insurance became a member of the Boston-based Liberty Mutual family of companies in 1999. As part of Regional Agency Markets, a division of Liberty Mutual Group, the Loveland, Ohio-based company is now part of one of the largest property and casualty multi-line insurers in the world. Indiana Insurance's reputable products, quality service, and commitment to independent agents have remained consistent throughout the company's history.

As part of a company that consistently ranks high on the Fortune 500 list, Indiana Insurance is widely recognized for its financial strength. The insurer holds an "A" (Excellent) rating from A.M. Best Company, the gold standard of financial strength. While other companies might wear such recognition as a badge of honor, this distinction simply marks Indiana Insurance's approach to business.

Independent Agents Make the Difference

The key to Indiana Insurance's success lies in its network of more than 1,000 independent agents. Because the company's insurance is sold only through those agents, consumers can be assured that they are receiving knowledgeable, objective advice from independent agents representing a variety of insurance companies. Because they are dealing with local agents, consumers know they are working with people who understand both their community and needs.

Trained to assess and understand each and every situation, independent agents and local underwriters know how to recognize and evaluate risk so they can protect client interests. In addition, agents receive valuable customer feedback so they can constantly improve their practices. The training and feedback, combined with years of experience serving regional clients with similar concerns, help Indiana Insurance representatives develop insights and solutions for local clients that representatives in some distant corporate office could never cultivate.

Serving Small and Midsize Businesses

Indiana Insurance writes property and casualty policies in Illinois, Indiana, Kentucky, Michigan, Minnesota, Ohio, Tennessee, and Wisconsin through five regional offices. In addition to the personal insurance lines the company offers, which include home owners, automobile, umbrella, inland marine, and watercraft coverage, Indiana Insurance offers a wide range of competitive commercial property and liability coverage to fit the

INDIANA INSURANCE IS LED BY PRESIDENT AND CEO RICHARD T. BELL (TOP).

INDIANA INSURANCE'S HEADQUARTERS IS LOCATED IN LOVELAND, OHIO (BOTTOM).

unique needs of the firm's business customers.

Because the operations of Indiana Insurance's customers vary widely—the company writes policies for retailers, light manufacturers, service firms, contractors, schools, churches, and other concerns—its products run the gamut. Through the firm's commercial coverages, clients can get a commercial business package, commercial auto, inland marine, umbrella, and property/crime policies, workers' compensation, employment-related practices liability, boiler/equipment breakdown coverage, comprehensive contractors policy, school program, and the Commercial Protector policy for business owners.

Business clients know they can depend on Indiana Insurance for exemplary service in the event of an accident. Indiana Insurance's loss-control consultants help small businesses diffuse that risk by offering on-site surveys to evaluate their current loss-prevention practices and accident-loss analysis. Larger businesses may take advantage of Indiana Insurance's five-step program that helps them identify real and potential loss sources and minimize their exposure. The company then takes its analysis one step further by helping clients develop an action plan—outlining their needs and expectations, and then recommending measures to strengthen existing programs.

Exemplary Customer Service

Indiana Insurance knows that the true test of an insurer's mettle is its responsiveness to loss, and the company has forged its reputation on its ability to respond quickly, fairly, and professionally. Recognized as one of the best regional companies in settling claims, the company understands that the events that result in the filing of a claim are often traumatic. Consequently, Indiana Insurance's employees do everything they can to assuage policyholders' concerns and promptly settle their claims. Policyholders can report a loss 24 hours a day and can count on speaking to an adjuster by the end of the next business day. In serious cases that involve hospitalization or damage that makes a policyholder's place of business uninhabitable, the company's on-call adjuster will respond within an hour of the reporting of the claim.

Indiana Insurance's reputation has been built by protecting families and businesses for more than a century. This has been accomplished by offering a variety of personal and commercial products and services designed to meet today's insurance needs. The company's tradition of

policyholder service has given generations of families and businesses the confidence to select Indiana Insurance as their carrier. Just as important, this quality of customer service will continue to make Indiana Insurance The Company of Choice for generations to come.

Sisters of Charity
of Cincinnati

Overlooking the Ohio River in western Cincinnati is the Sisters of Charity Motherhouse. This five-story, redbrick structure that dates back to the 1880s is the center for ministry, education, congregational leadership, and community life of the Sisters of Charity of Cincinnati. ● The Sisters of Charity of Cincinnati is an apostolic Catholic women's religious community that exists to carry out the gospel of Jesus Christ through service and prayer. Close to 600 sisters, using their professional talents in the fields of education, health care, and social services, live and minister in 25 U.S. states and four other countries.

Devoted Founders

The Sisters of Charity originated in Emmitsburg, Maryland, where Elizabeth Seton founded the first community of women native to the United States in July 1809. These women devoted themselves to the education of children and to the care of orphans, the poor, and the sick.

Shortly after its founding, the community began receiving requests from bishops around the country for sisters to serve in their dioceses. Such a request led to four Sisters of Charity arriving in Cincinnati in October 1829. This was the first permanent establishment of a women's community in the diocese of Cincinnati, which then encompassed the entire Northwest Territory. In 1852, the congregation separated from the Emmitsburg community to form the Sisters of Charity of Cincinnati.

In the late 1800s, the sisters established orphanages, parochial schools, and hospitals in the area.

The Sisters of Charity of Cincinnati Motherhouse, situated on a hill in Delhi Township overlooking the Ohio River, is the community's center for ministry, education, congregational government, retirement, and personal and community prayer (top).

From these beginnings grew such Cincinnati landmarks as the College of Mount St. Joseph in Delhi, Seton High School in Price Hill, Good Samaritan Hospital in Clifton, and St. Joseph Home in Sharonville.

Recognizing a need for its services beyond Cincinnati, the Sisters of Charity spread its ministries to other Ohio cities, then to other states, even responding to an appeal for missionaries in the New Mexico Territory in 1865.

Choosing Their Own Paths

Until the 1960s, young women choosing to answer the call to serve as Sisters of Charity of Cin-cinnati became primarily teachers or nurses. Like all of society, the Sisters of Charity witnessed significant changes during this turbulent decade. With the influence of the Second Vatican Council, the congregation began an assessment of ministry, lifestyle, governance, and sponsorship of institutions, and the sisters found new paths to explore for their ministries.

Today, Sisters of Charity members live out their mission in a variety of settings. Upon retirement, many return to the Motherhouse, volunteering their services wherever needed. All still carry on the work of Elizabeth Seton through service and prayer. They are joined in their mission by more than 100 associates, laywomen and -men who identify with the spirit of the congregation.

Over the years, some institutions founded or operated by the Sisters of Charity have closed, yet others continue. There are currently six nonprofit ministries in the Greater Cincinnati area sponsored by the Sisters of Charity of Cincinnati: Bayley Place Retirement Community, Delhi; the College of Mount St. Joseph, Delhi; arthConnection, Delhi; St. Joseph Home, Sharonville; Seton Family Center, Price Hill; and Seton High School, Price Hill.

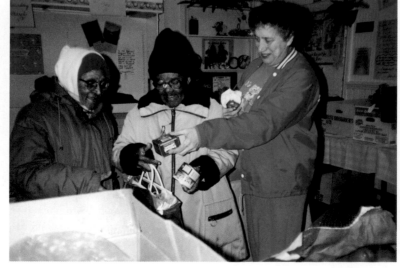

Since 1989, Sister of Charity Carol Ann Brockmeyer (right) has been improving the quality of life for Cincinnati's inner-city residents through the Vine Street Neighborhood Center. Volunteers from the area assist her in distributing food, paper goods, clothing, household items, and toys, all of which are donated and given freely.

ST. JOSEPH HOME, SPONSORED BY THE
SISTERS OF CHARITY, HAS BEEN DESCRIBED AS "A LITTLE BIT OF HEAVEN," "A VERY SPECIAL
PLACE," AND "A MIRACLE" BY STAFF MEMBERS, PARENTS, AND EVEN THAT TRADITIONALLY
CYNICAL LOT, REPORTERS. WHAT STRIKES A CHORD AMONG THESE OBSERVERS IS THE BOUND-
LESS AMOUNT OF LOVE THAT FILLS THE HOME, WHICH CARES FOR CHILDREN WITH SEVERE AND
PROFOUND MENTAL AND PHYSICAL DISABILITIES. ● FOUNDED IN 1873 BY SISTER

Anthony O'Connell as a home for unwed mothers and homeless children, the home's mission shifted to caring for children with special needs in 1976. Today, St. Joseph Home— also known as St. Joseph Infant and Maternity Home—is dedicated "to giving compassionate care, while at the same time challenging our residents to become the best individuals that they can," explains administrator Sister Marianne Van Vurst, a member of the Sisters of Charity.

While similar operations are frequently referred to as "facilities" or "institutions," St. Joseph Home is staunchly committed to being a home for its 47 residents, ranging from infants to young adults. A capable staff of men and women care for the nonambulatory and medically fragile residents.

The staff works closely with residents to develop strengths and improve weaknesses so they can feel more comfortable in their surroundings. For a resident to touch a special pad to operate a toy or listen to music, or to learn to drink from a cup on their own is a tremendous achievement. It takes a unique individual to fulfill the important role of caregiver.

The Hamilton County Board of Mental Retardation and Developmental Disabilities offers educational and vocational programs to St. Joseph Home residents. School-age children are able to continue their education at Hamilton County's Fairfax or Breyer schools. An additional classroom is available on the St. Joseph Home grounds for residents unable to attend off-site classes. Young adults attend General Assembly in Evendale, Ohio.

Residents at St. Joseph Home's Sharonville, Ohio, campus live in self-contained cottages nestled on 13 acres of rolling hills and wooded terrain. The cottages, which are connected by hallways, contain living

rooms, dining rooms, kitchens, bathing facilities, and four bedrooms that house two residents each. The St. Joseph Home's on-site staff of more than 140 professionals provide the children with around-the-clock care and act as an extended family. Two nurses' stations are easily accessible to the cottages, as are an indoor water-therapy pool, the Seton Educational Center, and the Home's chapel.

Because the number of children St. Joseph Home can accommodate is limited, the Home opened the Harold C. Schott Respite Center in spring 1998. Through respite care, the Home is able to extend its services to more members of the community.

Today, parents can bring their special-needs children to the Home for anywhere from a few hours to as long as two weeks. The break offers caregivers a respite so they can go about their own lives and attend to other responsibilities with peace of mind, knowing their children are being cared for by a capable, loving staff.

Volunteers Spread the Love

Dedicated as the St. Joseph Home staff is, they can only handle so many responsibilities at once. More than 125 tireless volunteers help spread St. Joseph Home's love. Whether they're reading to children, helping in the pool with water therapy, or simply being friends,

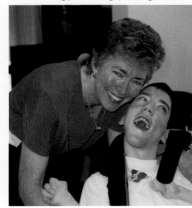

volunteers enrich residents' lives and help make St. Joseph Home the special place it is.

As a separate group within the volunteer community, more than 60 family members and friends share their time and talents as part of the St. Joseph Home Guild. Guild members sponsor fund-raisers, such as the annual St. Joseph Home Golf Classic; provide special assistance when needed; and operate the Top Bonanno Thrift Shop, located on the Home's grounds.

Staff and volunteers are quick to point out that, as much as they give, they take more from their experiences than they offer. While they add love to St. Joseph Home, the children multiply it.

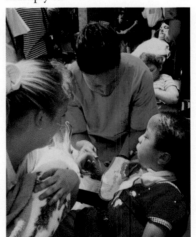

CLOCKWISE FROM TOP:
SOME SPECIAL FRIENDS HELP MIMI, A RESIDENT AT ST. JOSEPH HOME, FEEL THE SOFT FUR OF A RABBIT.

ONE OF THE FOCAL POINTS OF ST. JOSEPH HOME IS THE MEMORIAL GARDEN, WHICH STANDS AS A TRIBUTE TO RESIDENTS WHO HAVE DIED. THE NAMES INSCRIBED IN THE MEMORIAL GIVE THE GARDEN'S VISITORS AN OPPORTUNITY TO REFLECT ON THESE RESIDENTS' UNIQUE GIFTS.

ST. JOSEPH HOME VOLUNTEER MARILYN PARVIS SHARES A SMILE WITH RICK, A RESIDENT AT THE HOME.

College of Mount St. Joseph

Founded in 1920 and sponsored by the Sisters of Charity, the College of Mount St. Joseph is not just about developing great minds—it is also about molding great people. Located on 75 acres overlooking the Ohio River, the school takes a holistic approach to education, which means it encourages its some 2,300 students to develop not only their intellectual and academic abilities, but also their physical, spiritual, and emotional sides.

Academically, the College of Mount St. Joseph offers 45 degree programs, as well as graduate programs in education, religious studies, and physical therapy. Intimate class sizes encourage students to interact with faculty members and each other to promote a lively exchange of ideas. The college also offers an impressive NCAA Division III athletics program that enables students to choose from 11 different sports. In addition, the school encourages students to get involved in community service and focus on their career goals. Students have many opportunities to earn academic credit for community service and experiential learning.

The College of Mount St. Joseph's ambitious aim of helping students meet their full potential and its impressive track record for meeting that goal have earned the college national attention. Factors such as its retention and graduation rates and the academic profiles of its freshmen have kept the school on *U.S. News & World Report*'s list of the top 20 midwestern regional colleges for quality, value, and the best gradua-

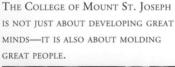

THE COLLEGE OF MOUNT ST. JOSEPH IS NOT JUST ABOUT DEVELOPING GREAT MINDS—IT IS ALSO ABOUT MOLDING GREAT PEOPLE.

tion rate. The *Templeton Guide* has also ranked the college as one of the top 100 nationwide in the area of character development.

Bringing Technology into the Classroom

A bastion of the liberal arts, the College of Mount St. Joseph is nonetheless at the forefront of technological innovation. In fall 2000, the college became the first in the area to adopt a universal computing requirement. Rather than technology for technology's sake, the school's Media-Rich Learning Infrastructure (MERLIN) program incorporates technology into the liberal arts curriculum by providing students with handheld computers and wireless technology. As a result, students have easy access to an array of multimedia resources in the classroom, around campus, at home, or wherever they might need them. What's more, MERLIN enables faculty members to incorporate a rich variety of resources into their instruction programs.

The College of Mount St. Joseph has incorporated technology into its liberal arts curriculum in a number of other important ways. It was the first local college to open a central-

ized student registration and financial aid service center, as well as the first to launch—in early 1999—on-line Web registration services. The campus is fully networked for technology, and the Center for Innovative Teaching helps faculty incorporate technology into their curricula. The college also offers a number of courses on-line, and provides American Bar Association-approved, on-line certification programs in paralegal studies and paralegal studies for nurses.

Embracing Diversity

Just as the College of Mount St. Joseph encourages developing the whole student, it also embraces the notion of a diverse student body. Students come from Ohio and some 20 other states, as well as from some 25 foreign countries. Adult students, many of whom take advantage of the school's accelerated programs and day care facilities, represent nearly 20 percent of the student body.

Many Mount St. Joseph students go on to establish their lives and careers in Cincinnati. More than 6,500 alumni live in the area, each one a testament to the college's academic prowess and an ambassador of its values.

DURING THE CENTURY AND A HALF THEY HAVE BEEN MINISTERING TO RESIDENTS OF THE CINCINNATI COMMUNITY, THE SISTERS OF CHARITY HAVE ANTICIPATED AND RESPONDED TO THE NEEDS OF A DIVERSE ARRAY OF CONSTITUENTS. SO IT WAS NO SURPRISE IN 1986 WHEN THEY BEGAN PLANNING BAYLEY PLACE, AN ASSISTED LIVING AND RETIREMENT COMMUNITY LOCATED ACROSS THE STREET FROM THE SISTERS' MOTHERHOUSE IN DELHI TOWNSHIP.

When Bayley Place opened in 1990, it became the first facility of its kind on Cincinnati's west side to offer care for the memory impaired. Today, Bayley Place provides 185 residents with dignified, compassionate care through its skilled nursing and assisted living facilities.

Meeting Emerging Needs

Because community needs are constantly shifting, the staff at Bayley Place has continued to update its services in response to demand. In 1993, Bayley Place pioneered the movement to provide assisted living facilities for residents suffering from Alzheimer's disease and dementia, becoming one of the first tristate facilities to provide assisted living apartments for memory-impaired residents. In 1995, Bayley Place expanded the program and added additional nursing facilities, seven additional assisted living apartments, and common space for residents and staff.

The Terrace, Meadows, and Woodlands units at Bayley Place all provide a homelike environment for residents who require supervision or assistance with personal care, but do not need skilled nursing care.

Staff members provide special programming to foster independence in a secure environment, while at the same time providing assistance with bathing, dressing, medications, and other activities of daily living as needed.

In 1999, Eldermount Adult Day program joined the Bayley Place retirement community to serve the needs of seniors living at home with their families. As part of that program, Eldermount provides transportation, supervision, and daytime care for about 30 seniors, allowing their caregivers a bit of respite time to themselves.

At the other end of the spectrum, Bayley Place's administrators understand that many modern seniors want a more independent living option. With that in mind, the facility broke ground on 78 independent living cottages in August 2000. When completed in 2003, the cottages will provide housing for seniors who are able to get around and care for themselves, but want the peace of mind that comes from knowing that Bayley Place stands ready to serve them should they one day need a little extra help.

Nurturing Mind, Body, & Spirit

Because residents' interests are as diverse as their needs, Bayley Place offers a diverse array of recreational and educational programs. Residents interested in taking computer classes, studying art history, or exploring other educational opportunities can take classes at the nearby College of Mount St. Joseph. Exercise classes are held on Bayley Place's scenic campus, and additional classes will be available when a new wellness center is completed in 2003. In addition, speech, physical, occupational, pet, art, and music therapies are all available to residents, depending on their needs and interests. Residents' spiritual needs are met through an active pastoral care program that includes daily religious services, Bible study classes, and prayer groups.

Through its holistic approach to care and its wide range of services, Bayley Place ensures that it will continue to serve its mission for many years to come: to provide a continuum of care for elders in a creative, homelike Christian community. In so doing, Bayley Place is well positioned to meet its ultimate goal of enabling older individuals to function and live at their maximum potential.

BAYLEY PLACE PROVIDES 185 RESIDENTS WITH DIGNIFIED, COMPASSIONATE CARE THROUGH ITS SKILLED NURSING AND ASSISTED LIVING FACILITIES.

Fifth Third Bancorp

CINCINNATI'S OLDEST AND LARGEST BANK, FIFTH THIRD BANCORP TRACES ITS ROOTS TO THE NATION'S WESTWARD EXPANSION, AND IN THAT SPIRIT, IT CONTINUES TO EXPAND TODAY. FOUNDED IN CINCINNATI AS THE BANK OF OHIO VALLEY IN 1858, THE BANK ACQUIRED ITS UNUSUAL NAME AS A RESULT OF ITS 1871 ACQUISITION BY THE THIRD NATIONAL BANK, WHICH COMBINED WITH THE FIFTH NATIONAL BANK IN 1908. TODAY, THE COMPANY IS COMPRISED OF 16 BANKING AFFILIATES

located in Ohio, Kentucky, Indiana, Michigan, Illinois, and Florida.

Fifth Third has enjoyed phenomenal success for the last quarter century. Despite the ups and downs of the economy and the banking industry, Fifth Third has reported record earnings and dividend growth every year since 1973. Today, the company has more than $70 billion in assets and more than 21,000 employees. Since 1980, the bank has increased earnings at an average rate of 16 percent, outperformed the Standard & Poor's 500 16-fold, and reported revenue growth that is twice the industry average. An investment of $1,000 in Fifth Third stock in 1980 would have grown to $203,025 by December 31, 2000.

That success, combined with the bank's high capital ratios and consistently strong credit quality, has led industry analysts to name it the number one bank in the coun-

CUSTOMERS CAN DO THEIR BANKING SEVEN-DAYS-A-WEEK AT FIFTH THIRD'S CONVENIENT BANK MART® LOCATIONS INSIDE KROGER GROCERY STORES.

try for nine consecutive years. A Fortune 500 company, Fifth Third was named the number one bank in the country in Forbes magazine's Platinum 400 list in January 2001. George A. Schaefer Jr., president and chief executive officer, attributes the bank's performance to hard work, sales effort, teamwork, cost control, and employees' willingness to give more than 100 percent to their jobs, a principle Schaefer refers to as "hustle".

Growth

Fifth Third Bancorp's growth is fueled by aggressive sales of its banking, investment, and e-commerce products. With attractive marketing campaigns, same-store sales of its loan and deposit products in its banking centers, strong sales incentives, and accountability for progress, Fifth Third is able to deliver top-notch products

PRESIDENT AND CHIEF EXECUTIVE OFFICER GEORGE A. SCHAEFER JR. ATTRIBUTES FIFTH THIRD BANCORP'S PERFORMANCE TO HARD WORK, SALES EFFORT, TEAMWORK, COST CONTROL, AND THE EMPLOYEES' WILLINGNESS TO GIVE MORE THAN 100 PERCENT TO THEIR JOBS, A PRINCIPLE HE REFERS TO AS "HUSTLE."

and services to its customers and solid returns to its shareholders.

In April 2001, Fifth Third partnered with Old Kent Financial Corporation, a $23.8 billion financial services company in Grand Rapids, Michigan, to become the premier banking operation in the Midwest. The merger between Fifth Third and Old Kent provided the most attractive, single opportunity in the bank's history to duplicate the local success that has fueled Fifth Third's impressive track record. Old Kent gave Fifth Third the opportunity to expand in the attractive markets of Chicago; Detroit, Traverse City, and Grand Rapids, Michigan.

Meeting Customers' Needs

A diversified financial services company, Fifth Third provides a broad array of products and services to every type of customer through four primary businesses: Commercial Banking, Retail Banking, Investment Advisory Services, and Midwest Payment Systems (MPS), the bank's data processing subsidiary.

Fifth Third works hard to deliver convenience. Customers can stop by the bank's nearly 1,000 banking centers or seven-day-a-week Bank Mart® locations and find a front-line sales force focused on delivering convenient, smart banking and investment products and services. Whether customers visit Fifth Third's banking center open 365 days a year at the Greater Cincinnati/ Northern Kentucky International Airport; access Fifth Third Online℠, the bank's Internet banking and investment service; dial up Jeanie® Telephone Banking; or stop by any of Fifth Third's more than 2,000 Jeanie® ATMs, they will find the same thing: great, quick service.

Fifth Third is Greater Cincinnati's number one home loan lender. The bank offers a complete line of home mortgage options to help customers acheive homeownership.

Fifth Third is a one-stop shop for the financial needs of businesses, too. The bank offers traditional funding for expansion, real estate, and venture capital opportunities, as well as financing for leasing, initial public offerings, and closely-held services. Additionally, Fifth Third has one of the largest foreign exchange trading desks in the United States, as well as international offices in Europe and Asia.

Fifth Third Bank Investment Advisors is one of the largest money managers in the Midwest with more than $173 billion in assets under care, of which it manages $33 billion for its individual, corporate, and not-for-profit clients. Fifth Third offers investment, trust, private banking, and brokerage services, including underwriting and public financing services.

Fifth Third's fourth primary business, Midwest Payment Systems (MPS), is one of the leading electronic funds transfer processors in the United States. MPS processes more than six billion e-commerce transactions for more than 85,000 financial institutions and merchants nationwide. Fifth Third is there when they use their credit or debit cards to purchase a suit at Saks Fifth Avenue or a book at Barnes & Noble.

More Than a Business

Fifth Third believes building a strong community builds a strong bank. In 1999, the company launched a $9 billion community investment called BLITZ: Building, Lending, Investments, and Technology Zones.

Through BLITZ, Fifth Third provides special financing for community development building projects, and promotes home ownership, small business growth, and credit availability through increased lending. The bank makes investments in low-income housing, tax credit, and venture capital projects. In addition, Fifth Third creates BLITZ technology zones by providing local community organizations with free personal computers to ensure

equitable Internet access for area residents. In the program's first year, Fifth Third made $3.2 billion available through BLITZ, surpassing its first-year goal by $700 million.

"BLITZ demonstrates Fifth Third's continuing commitment to the communities we serve," Schaefer says. "Even the name of our initiative mirrors the style and vigor with which we begin and build banking relationships in our communities."

In 1948, Fifth Third became one of the first financial institutions in the country to establish a permanently endowed foundation. Through the sound management of Fifth Third's investment professionals, the Fifth

Third Foundation has grown to $43 million in assets, and has provided more than $23 million to worthwhile projects since its inception.

Fifth Third spokesperson Johnny Bench, the former Reds catcher and All-Century Hall of Famer, came out from behind the plate in 1973 to pitch the area's first packaged checking service, the One Account. Bench's promotions have made the Fifth Third tag line, "Working hard to be the only bank you'll ever need®," recognizable throughout the community. Still, it is the determination and teamwork of the entire Fifth Third Bancorp team that continue to make those words ring true year after year.

Metro and the Transit Authority of Northern Kentucky (TANK)

WHEN OTHER ORGANIZATIONS SAY THEY ARE ON THE MOVE, THEY'RE SPEAKING RHETORICALLY. WHEN METRO AND THE TRANSIT AUTHORITY OF NORTHERN KENTUCKY (TANK) TALK ABOUT BEING ON THE MOVE, THEY MEAN IT LITERALLY. ● TOGETHER, THE TWO TRANSIT SYSTEMS OPERATE ABOUT 520 BUSES AND SUPPLY DAILY TRANSPORTATION TO ALMOST 83,000 RIDERS. IN FACT, ABOUT 35 PERCENT OF DOWNTOWN WORKERS DEPEND ON TANK AND METRO, OPERATED

by the Southwest Ohio Regional Transit Authority (SORTA), to get to their jobs.

City's Development Linked to Transit

Since its earliest days, Greater Cincinnati's development has both depended upon and paralleled the development of its transit system. Public transportation began propelling the community's growth in 1859 when the city introduced a system of horse-drawn railcars. Eventually, inclines were added, enabling urban dwellers to move up the city's historic hills and settle in neighborhoods such as Mount Adams, Mount Auburn, and Price Hill.

That tradition continues today on a greatly expanded scale. Each year, Metro and TANK buses cover more than 16 million miles and transport residents to the far corners of the tri state area. Whether they're headed to the Cincinnati/ Northern Kentucky International Airport, to their jobs downtown, or to such growing areas as Hebron, Kentucky, or Mason, Ohio, residents can count on Metro and TANK.

Both Metro and TANK do everything they can to make commuting easy and consistent. Through a program called the Guaranteed Ride Home, they offer reimbursement to preferred customers up to four times per year if they are forced to find alternative transportation because of unplanned overtime or a family emergency. Another program designed with convenience in mind is the DayTripper, which enables residents of Boone, Campbell, and Kenton counties who are not currently served by a fixed route bus service to call and arrange door-to-door transportation.

In an effort to meet local businesses' ever changing needs, Metro and TANK offer an array of programs and services. For example, transportation fairs held at local businesses allow employees interested in taking advantage of public transportation to consult a trip planner. JobBus helps connect both the job seekers and the employers in need of workers by providing transportation to

regional employment opportunities. An Employer Pass Program allows companies to purchase monthly bus passes and offer them as a valuable, tax-deductible benefit to workers.

"Metro and TANK work together to meet the needs of our business community," TANK General Manager Mark Donaghy explains. "We offer programs to make it easier for people to ride the bus, like the Guaranteed Ride Home program, and convenient routes geared toward commuters. We also work closely with employers to improve bus service for their employees and to educate them about the programs and services we offer."

More Than a Commuter Service

But Metro and TANK don't just serve commuters on their way to work. The two systems offer a vast array of services that cater to students, people with disabilities, and the elderly. Lift-equipped services, "kneeling buses" that lower the front step for easier boarding, and priority seating help make public transportation accessible to everyone.

The transit systems also facilitate fun. During the most recent Tall Stacks celebration, they accommodated more than 160,000 riders. That service alleviated congestion and enabled residents from throughout the area to enjoy the riverfront celebration without worrying about transportation and parking. Buses, which leave from strategic park-and-ride locations throughout the area, likewise alleviate the hassle of getting to and from the Cincinnati Bengals football games.

The Engine of the Future

Because Metro and TANK work in such close alliance, they are able to offer riders convenient transportation throughout the area. In 1997, the two systems opened a joint sales office in the heart of the downtown business district to make it easier for passengers to purchase passes and tickets and to gather information about both companies.

Metro and TANK will likewise serve the Riverfront Transit Center being constructed under the rebuilt Second Street. When completed, the facility will be capable of accommodating 20,000 passengers per hour, primarily visiting such signature riverfront events as Riverfest, Bengals football games, and Tall Stacks. It is slated to open in 2003.

While the transit systems' current services and planned improvements may be a boon to riders, they serve the larger population as well. With new highway construction costs running up to $70 million per mile per lane, road construction is an expensive way to alleviate traffic congestion. Public transit, conversely, is both affordable and effective: A full bus removes at least 45 cars from the road.

There's an environmental benefit as well. A full bus is six times more fuel efficient than a car, and each person who rides to work, rather than driving, removes more than 70 pounds of harmful pollutants from the air annually.

Collectively, those myriad benefits explain why public transportation will continue to be the engine propelling Greater Cincinnati's growth long into the future. "I'm excited about the future of Greater Cincinnati and the role public transit will play." Metro General Manager Paul Jablonski says. "Whether it's through additional park-and-ride lots, expanded services, light-rail, or a combination of those and more, Metro and TANK will continue to provide transportation that helps keep our region on the move."

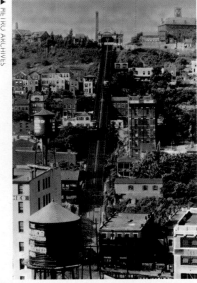

▲ METRO ARCHIVES

▲ METRO ARCHIVES

INCLINES OPENED UP ALONG THE HILLSIDES TO PROMOTE DEVELOPMENT AND GROWTH IN CINCINNATI. AT ONE TIME, THE CITY WAS HOME TO FIVE SUCH INCLINES, INCLUDING THE MT. ADAMS INCLINE, WHICH OPERATED UNTIL 1948 (TOP).

IN 1938, THE CINCINNATI NEWPORT & COVINGTON GREEN LINE—A TANK PREDECESSOR—OPERATED TROLLEY BUSES THROUGHOUT THE AREA. DOWNTOWN CINCINNATI HAS ALWAYS BEEN AN IMPORTANT DESTINATION FOR TANK PASSENGERS (BOTTOM).

1861-1899

1862
Baldwin Piano & Organ Company

1867
The Union Central Life Insurance Co.

1867
The United States Playing Card
Company

1871
Graydon Head & Ritchey LLP

1882
The Andrew Jergens Company

1883
Children's Hospital Medical Center

1883
The E.W. Scripps Co.

1884
Milacron Inc.

1888
The Western-Southern Enterprise

1891
Loth Mbi, Inc.

1898
Reliance Medical Products

1898
Siemens Energy & Automation, Inc.

Baldwin Piano & Organ Company

FEW COMPANIES CAN BOAST A HERITAGE AS RICH AS THAT OF BALDWIN PIANO & ORGAN COMPANY. FOUNDED IN CINCINNATI BY AN ITINERANT MUSIC TEACHER DURING THE EARLY DAYS OF THE CIVIL WAR, BALDWIN HAS GROWN FROM A STOREFRONT PIANO RETAILER TO THE NATION'S LARGEST PIANO BUILDER. ● ALONG THE WAY, THE COMPANY, NOW LOCATED IN MASON, OHIO, HAS SET MILESTONES IN MUSIC HISTORY BEGINNING AS EARLY AS 1900, WHEN ONE OF ITS

concert grand pianos became the first American-made piano to win the prestigious Grand Prix Award at the International Exhibition in Paris. Additional laurels followed during the next two decades at both the St. Louis and London expositions. Perhaps no praise was as resounding, however, as the 1965 declaration by a *Time* magazine music critic that the company's new SD10 Concert Grand was so remarkable that, "if Beethoven had had a piano like that, the course of music would have been radically altered."

A Marriage of Tradition and Progress

All of Baldwin's products continue to demonstrate the company's rich tradition and commitment to craftsmanship. Today, acoustic instruments are sold under three venerable names: Baldwin, Chickering, and Wurlitzer. The company also offers innovative Baldwin ConcertMaster computerized player piano systems and digital pianos bearing the name Baldwin Pianovelle.

Acoustic pianos range from upright models, such as the Hamilton and Acrosonic, to the company's prestigious concert grand. The company's uprights are a favorite of music teachers, schools, and churches because they offer superb tone, responsive touch, and exceptional durability. Families appreciate these heirlooms for the grace and elegance they bring to the home. At the top of the company's inventory is the nine-foot SD10 concert grand, which is preferred by many of today's finest pianists, composers, and conductors. In January 2000, the company's top-line Artist Series grands were reintroduced with a variety of enhancements to their tonal quality, touch response, aesthetic qualities, and structural attributes.

For those seeking a contemporary ensemble sound, Baldwin offers a full range of digital pianos. These instruments, with features that include a myriad of studio-quality sounds, effects, accompaniments, and multimedia capabilities, provide players with endless creative possibilities. Such features have made Pianovelle models a favorite of award-winning musicians.

The Baldwin ConcertMaster Complete Player System, a computerized version of the historic player piano, represents one of the newest innovations in the industry. A ConcertMaster-equipped piano enables listeners to enjoy "live," programmable, concert-quality music in their homes even if they don't play the piano. From solo music to piano with full orchestral accompaniment, and even vocals, ConcertMaster provides a complete spectrum of musical performances. Baldwin's new ConcertMaster CD system is offered to consumers who want an

easy-to-operate player piano system that can be attached to their upright or grand piano, whether new or old.

Artists Rave about Baldwin

Baldwin's commitment to building the highest-quality musical instruments has won it the endorsement of artists the world over. Whether their genre is jazz, pop, classical, or rock, musicians as varied as Dave Brubeck, Michael Feinstein, Ben Folds, Bruce Hornsby, Marian McPartland, Seiji Ozawa, and Earl Wild all sing the praises of Baldwin pianos. Legends like Aaron Copland and Liberace were likewise devoted to Baldwin pianos.

Through the years, the company's reputation for excellence has won it a spot on stages around the globe, including those of the Kennedy Center, Tanglewood, and Cincinnati's own Music Hall. Thanks to that type of dedication and talent, players and listeners alike are sure to enjoy Baldwin pianos for generations to come.

▲ GREG KUEHIK

BALDWIN PIANO & ORGAN COMPANY'S RENOWNED ARTIST GRAND PIANOS GRACE MANY OF TODAY'S MOST PRESTIGIOUS CONCERT HALLS.

THE AWARD-WINNING BALDWIN CONCERTMASTER SYSTEM LETS LISTENERS ENJOY "LIVE" MUSIC, EVEN IF THEY DON'T PLAY THE PIANO.

◄ GREG KUEHIK

WITH AN AMBITIOUS BUILDING CAMPAIGN, EXPANDING RESEARCH PROGRAMS, AND A VARIETY OF COMMUNITY OUTREACH PROGRAMS, CHILDREN'S HOSPITAL MEDICAL CENTER IS SEEKING TO BUILD ON ITS LONG TRADITION OF DELIVERING SKILLED, COMPASSIONATE PEDIATRIC CARE AND TO CEMENT ITS POSITION AS ONE OF THE WORLD'S PREMIER RESEARCH INSTITUTIONS. A PRIVATE, NOT-FOR-PROFIT ORGANIZATION THAT ALSO SERVES AS THE DEPARTMENT OF PEDIATRICS FOR THE

University of Cincinnati's College of Medicine, Cincinnati Children's has come a long way from its founding in 1883 in a three-bedroom, one-bathroom house. In fact, the 340-bed medical center resembles its earliest incarnation in just one respect: Its tradition of delivering compassionate care remains unchanged. Despite its growth, Cincinnati Children's still acts as an advocate for children by providing for their care throughout the Greater Cincinnati area, regardless of a family's ability to pay.

Building for the Future

Cincinnati Children's massive construction project bears testimony to its expanding mission. In an effort to bring care and lifesaving research to still more children, the center announced in 1998 a four-year construction plan that is adding an education center, garage, hospital, and research facility to its campus.

The Albert B. Sabin Education Center, named for the Cincinnati Children's researcher who developed the oral polio vaccine, advances the medical center's position as one of the nation's leading pediatric learning facilities. The six-story,

132,000-square-foot building, completed in November 2000, includes a 300-seat auditorium, a food court, offices, conference rooms, libraries, and a resource center.

A nine-story research tower also opened in fall 2000. Research has been a priority at the medical center since 1931, when the Children's Hospital Research Foundation was established. The 112,000-square-foot addition, the foundation's third expansion in only a decade, includes a brain tumor center, a gene therapy center, a clinical trials unit, and neuroscience programs.

A new hospital, adjacent to the existing Hospital Tower, is slated to open in 2002. The eight-story, 460,000-square-foot addition will consolidate clinical care—currently delivered in three separate buildings—into two adjacent, modern facilities. To meet the expanded center's parking needs, a three-story, underground parking garage was opened in March 2001.

Breaking New Ground

Significant as the brick-and-mortar expansion may be, it is only the physical manifestation of the dynamic growth occurring

within the hospital organization. For example, Children's Hospital Research Foundation, which brought the world such lifesaving technologies as the first functional heart-lung machine and the first artificial blood compounds to be used successfully as a substitute for whole blood, received research grants totaling $46 million in 1999. Cincinnati Children's ranks third nationally among pediatric research institutions in terms of funding from the National Institutes of Health.

In addition, Cincinnati Children's is exploring better ways to meet the needs of sick children and their families. The hospital is developing more interdisciplinary care programs for children with multiple illnesses, and is working on new and better pain management techniques for patients. The hospital is also expanding its network of suburban outpatient care facilities in an effort to bring convenient care to families living in Cincinnati's growing suburbs. Through these and a broad array of community outreach programs, Cincinnati Children's is working to ensure the health and safety of children from around the region and around the world.

CHILDREN'S HOSPITAL MEDICAL CENTER, WHICH SERVES AS THE DEPARTMENT OF PEDIATRICS FOR THE UNIVERSITY OF CINCINNATI'S COLLEGE OF MEDICINE, IS WORKING TO ENSURE THE HEALTH AND SAFETY OF CHILDREN FROM AROUND THE REGION AND AROUND THE WORLD.

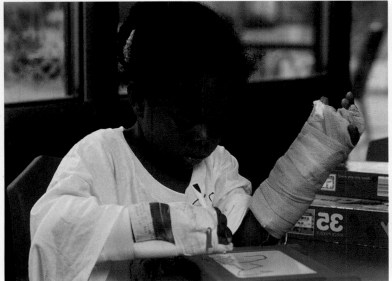
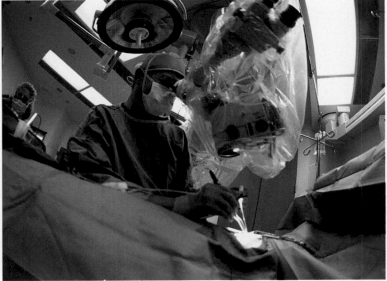

The Union Central
Life Insurance Co.

CINCINNATI IS RECOGNIZED AS A COMMUNITY WITH STRONG MIDWESTERN VALUES, FOUNDED ON THE IMPORTANCE OF INTEGRITY IN BUSINESS AND UNITY WITHIN FAMILIES. FOR FIVE GENERATIONS, THE UNION CENTRAL LIFE INSURANCE CO. HAS REFLECTED THOSE TRADITIONS IN THE FINANCIAL SOLUTIONS IT PROVIDES TO ITS BUSINESS AND FAMILY CLIENTS. ● LESS THAN TWO YEARS AFTER THE CIVIL WAR ENDED, UNION CENTRAL OPENED A STOREFRONT OFFICE IN DOWNTOWN

Cincinnati, then the third-largest city in the United States. John Peck, a young physician and businessman, viewed it as the ideal location for a life insurance concern. In 1867, Union Central became the first domestic life insurance company chartered in Ohio.

A History of Growth

William Procter and James Gamble were among the businessmen, clergymen, and physicians who provided the young company with financial backing. Together, they chose the company's name as a symbol of both the Union's survival and the city's central position in the nation's financial community.

Eventually, Union Central moved to a larger office and, in 1874, to a five-story building. In 1913, the company completed construction and moved into Cincinnati's first skyscraper—then the world's tallest building outside New York City.

The former headquarters tower remains a distinctive downtown landmark even today.

But once again, Union Central's growth called for a new home, and in 1964, the company moved its headquarters just north of Cincinnati to Forest Park. Today, its white-marble-and-glass structure houses more than 800 employees who support a nationwide network of field associates and representatives.

Union Central has been in operation for more than 135 years. With some $6 billion in admitted assets and $40 billion of life insurance in force, the firm ranks among the nation's 15 largest mutual life insurance companies. Union Central is licensed in all 50 states and the District of Columbia.

Union Central offers plans and options to meet a wide range of individual, family, and business needs: death and disability insurance, estate planning, tax-advantaged savings,

investing, business continuation and other business planning needs, and group benefits. The company's product portfolio includes individual life and disability insurance, annuities, group insurance, and group retirement plans such as 401(k)s.

Union Central prides itself on delivering customized, person-to-person financial solutions through professional field and home office associates. Among the company's subsidiaries are Carillon Investments, Inc., Summit Investment Partners, Inc., and Payday of America.

A Priority on Policy
Owners and Employees

We're committed to midwestern values: hard work, honest business practices, a belief in the value of relationships, and prudence in risk taking," says John H. Jacobs, president and CEO. "As a mutual company, our policyholders are our owners, and we have never forgotten

SINCE 1964, THE UNION CENTRAL LIFE INSURANCE CO.'S HEADQUARTERS HAS BEEN A STRIKING, WHITE-MARBLE-AND-GLASS BUILDING ON A CAMPUS-LIKE SETTING IN FOREST PARK, A NORTHWESTERN SUBURB OF CINCINNATI.

the promises we have made to them. Keeping those promises motivates everything we do."

With this philosophy, the company has grown and prospered, even through America's most turbulent years. Union Central's stability has been attributed to careful selection of policy owners, the level of service the company provides, and a conservative approach to investments. These practices are backed by the company's strong values.

"We believe that our daily lives at work can be guided and lived in accordance with values that allow each of us to find satisfaction from our work," Jacobs says. "Our employees have developed a unique company culture based on adhering to values, encouraging personal growth, and believing that each of us benefits when one person realizes his or her total potential."

Community Service in Action

Supporting people and organizations in need has always been important to Union Central and its employees. Most notable in its early activities was the relief the company provided during Cincinnati's 1937 flood. With thousands of homeless people along the Ohio River, Union Central opened its Third Street annex to serve as the Red Cross headquarters, while rescue and supply boats moored just outside.

Through the years, Union Central has maintained a time-honored tradition of practicing good corporate citizenship. At the local level,

the company is a committed supporter of United Way and the Fine Arts Fund. Support for other urban programs providing educational, cultural, and health services in the community continues to be a priority.

Union Central employees also touch the lives of people throughout Greater Cincinnati by volunteering. As part of the company's Community Involvement Council, employees raise money through a variety of activities and donate funds to various organizations. Union Central's volunteer efforts have provided pilot dogs for the visually impaired, built playgrounds and donated school supplies for kids, and brightened the holidays for nursing home residents.

Each summer since 1989, Union Central has welcomed thousands of guests to the spacious grounds of its headquarters for Concert on the Green. Area families are invited to enjoy the music of the Cincinnati Pops Orchestra. The combined efforts of the City of Forest Park and local businesses make this event possible.

Union Central has received the Good Scout Award from the Dan Beard Council of the Boy Scouts of America, an award given to corporations that provide outstanding leadership and support to the community. In addition, several times the American Heart Association has presented Union Central with the Heart at Work Company of the Year Award, in recognition of the

firm's leadership in promoting health awareness and education.

Union Central was also the recipient of the first Governor's Insurance Community Service Award, which was established to recognize insurance companies that support their communities through corporate contributions and volunteer efforts. Honoring the company for its community works, Ohio Governor George V. Voinovich stated, "Union Central and its employees are very deserving of this award for their tradition of outstanding philanthropic efforts, which have made many Ohio communities better places to live and work."

Creating financial solutions and better places to live and work are just a few of the ways Union Central contributes to keeping Cincinnati on the business fast track.

CLOCKWISE FROM TOP LEFT: THE HOLIDAY CHEERLINE FOR AREA NURSING HOME RESIDENTS IS ONE OF THE MANY WORTHWHILE PROGRAMS SUPPORTED BY UNION CENTRAL EMPLOYEES THROUGH THE FIRM'S COMMUNITY INVOLVEMENT COUNCIL.

EACH SUMMER, UNION CENTRAL WELCOMES THOUSANDS OF TRI-STATE NEIGHBORS TO ITS LUSH FRONT LAWN FOR CONCERT ON THE GREEN, FEATURING THE MUSIC OF THE CINCINNATI POPS ORCHESTRA.

WHEN IT WAS COMPLETED IN 1913, UNION CENTRAL'S FORMER HOME OFFICE—A 34-STORY SKYSCRAPER—WAS THE TALLEST BUILDING OUTSIDE OF NEW YORK CITY.

The United States
Playing Card Company

THE UNITED STATES PLAYING CARD COMPANY (USPC) IS THE WORLD'S LARGEST MANUFACTURER AND DISTRIBUTOR OF PLAYING CARDS. ITS LOCAL ANCESTRY DATES TO 1867 WHEN A.O. RUSSELL AND ROBERT J. MORGAN, WITH TWO OTHER PARTNERS, BOUGHT THE PRINTING ROOMS OF *The Cincinnati Enquirer*. THE NEW ENTERPRISE, RUSSELL, MORGAN AND COMPANY, BEGAN ITS BUSINESS PRINTING POSTERS FOR STAGE PRODUCTIONS, CIRCUSES, AND COUNTY FAIRS.

THE UNITED STATES PLAYING CARD COMPANY'S (USPC) HISTORIC CINCINNATI HEADQUARTERS FEATURES A FOUR-STORY TOWER OVER ITS MAIN ENTRANCE (LEFT).

INTRODUCED IN 1885, THE BICYCLE BRAND HAS NEVER GONE OUT OF PRODUCTION. TODAY, 9 OUT OF 10 AMERICANS RECOGNIZE THE BICYCLE BRAND NAME (MIDDLE).

USPC'S BEE BRAND APPEARS IN CASINOS WORLDWIDE (RIGHT).

The company then expanded into printed labels for goods in boxes, cans, and bottles. The firm outgrew its space on College Street, and a 53-by 90-foot lot was acquired on the east side of Race Street in downtown Cincinnati. A new, four-story building was completed and occupied by November 1873.

A Winning Hand

At that time, New York firms had long dominated American card making. Andrew Dougherty had begun his company in 1848, and The New York Consolidated Card Company, founded in 1871, had antecedents from 1832. Those two leaders colluded, fixing prices and dividing the market. On June 18, 1881, Russell, Morgan and Company ventured into the production of playing cards. These cards, as exemplified by the Congress brand, were of high quality and targeted to be competitive with the New Yorkers.

Early in 1883, the challengers renamed themselves The Russell and Morgan Printing Company, and moved to a six-story building newly built on Lock Street at the foot of Mount Adams. The company's Steamboat brand of cards, among others, was soon available. The Bicycle brand was introduced in 1885, named as such due to the great cycling craze at that time. The Bicycle rider back design that depicted a cupid astride a two-wheeler was introduced in 1887 and has never gone out of production.

In 1891, Russell and Morgan joined with Hinds and Ketcham, New York partners in label making, and with John H. Frey, a Cincinnati printer, to form The United States Printing Company. Two years later, the firm acquired The National Card Company of Indianapolis, whose factory continued to operate following the merger. Brands from this company included Rambler and Aladdin, which are still in production today.

Playing card manufacturing at United States Printing became profitable enough to operate as a separate entity and USPC emerged in 1894. That same year, the company bought The Standard Playing Card Company and thereby preserved its most popular deck, Gypsy Witch Fortune

Telling Cards. Even more dramatic that year was USPC securing its former competition, The New York Consolidated Card Company, as a subsidiary. Together, they cooperated with Dougherty in purchasing Perfection Playing Card Company, also located in New York.

Due to its growing operational needs, USPC relocated to Norwood in 1900. In 1907, A. Dougherty Inc. became part of USPC. Dougherty's Tally-Ho and other brands survived under the new arrangement. In 1914, USPC launched a Canadian subsidiary, International Playing Card Company, which began its own presswork in 1928. In 1929, USPC merged with a New Jersey-based card company named Russell (having no connection with A. O. Russell).

During the 1920s, the company greatly expanded its Norwood headquarters, which came to occupy more than 600,000 square feet. In keeping with the original Italianate architecture, a four-story tower, housing a clock and 12-bell carillon, was erected over the main entrance. The company then set up its own radio station, WSAI, with the primary purpose of teaching Bridge. Programming included music, news, stories, and public service announcements, as well as chime concerts from the company's bell tower; the broadcast

signal was strong enough to reach New Zealand. The station was sold to the Crosley Radio Corporation in the 1930s.

USPC has a collection of playing cards and books. It has become well-known in providing information for historians and collectors. The USPC collection was cataloged by Catherine Perry Hargrave. Her book, *A History of Playing Cards*, became a standard reference in its field.

In 1932, The New York Consolidated Card Co. and A. Dougherty, Inc. combined as Consolidated-Dougherty with offices in New York. Thirty years later, this business was brought to the Norwood headquarters and maintained as an autonomous division until it was dissolved in 1969. Nevertheless, Tally-Ho cards and the Bee brand, introduced by New York Consolidated in 1892, still endure as popular USPC products.

Beginning in 1969, USPC was distantly controlled by a series of corporations. During these transitions, USPC purchased Heraclio Fournier, S.A., the largest European card maker, in 1986. The following year, USPC acquired Arrco, the third-largest American card maker. USPC's Canadian factory closed in 1991,

although a sales and marketing organization continues in Toronto.

In 1994, USPC was restored to Cincinnati ownership through the resources of company management and other local investors. Recent changes in leadership have positioned the company for new growth in the new millennium.

Focus on the Future

USPC maintains a wide assortment of brands, including the old favorites. Experienced Bridge players choose Congress cards. The Bee brand appears in casinos worldwide. Nine out of 10 Americans recognize the Bicycle name. Decks

for Canasta, Pinochle, Euchre, Spades, Solitaire, Rummy, and Poker are packaged as Bicycle Games. Images from popular culture are featured in specially licensed decks for Disney, Warner Bros., Crayola, Coca-Cola, Harley-Davidson, and NASCAR, to name a few.

Card playing unites a great variety of people in a multitude of games, simple or sophisticated, old or new, serious or funny. Cards of distinctive craftsmanship and design also have educational, sentimental, and aesthetic value. In meeting all these conditions, The United States Playing Card Company preserves its founders' goals of diversity and quality.

CLOCKWISE FROM TOP: CARD PLAYING UNITES A GREAT VARIETY OF PEOPLE IN A MULTITUDE OF GAMES, SIMPLE OR SOPHISTICATED, OLD OR NEW, SERIOUS OR FUNNY.

FOUNDED IN 1867, RUSSELL, MORGAN AND COMPANY PRINTED POSTERS AND LABELS UNTIL TURNING TO PLAYING CARD PRODUCTION IN 1881.

USPC OFFERS DECKS FOR CANASTA, PINOCHLE, EUCHRE, SPADES, SOLITAIRE, RUMMY, AND POKER THROUGH ITS BICYCLE GAMES LINE.

Founded in 1871, the same year the Tyler Davidson Fountain was dedicated, Graydon Head & Ritchey LLP has a venerable reputation in Cincinnati. But the city's oldest general practice firm is anything but a relic. Indeed, Graydon Head & Ritchey owes its success and impressive tenure to its ability to evolve with the times and respond to the constantly changing needs of its clients.

In a world of start-ups that measure their track records in terms of days, Graydon Head & Ritchey recounts its history in decades. Founded as Matthews & Ramsey, the firm's distinguished alumni include a U.S. Supreme Court justice, a solicitor general, a U.S. senator, a U.S. congressman, and a governor, in addition to a number of highly regarded lawyers and judges.

Today, the firm's more than 60 attorneys, following in the footsteps of those distinguished alumni, adhere to the same tradition of serving the needs of their clients and the community. "Although there have been incredible changes in the practice of law since Graydon Head & Ritchey was founded some 130 years ago, some things remain constant: namely, our dedication to making our community a better place and our commitment to helping clients achieve success," says Michael A. Hirschfeld, chairman of the firm's executive committee.

A Tradition of Service

Hirschfeld attributes Graydon Head & Ritchey's longevity to its ability to deliver outstanding service. While other companies may pay lip service to the concept, at Graydon Head & Ritchey, customer orientation is at the center of every decision. That focus is so highly regarded that, in 1996, the company was named the first recipient of the Greater Cincinnati Chamber of Commerce's Customer Focus Award.

Graydon Head & Ritchey works hard to ensure client satisfaction. The firm continually asks clients for their feedback and, in response to their comments, has developed a variety of client service improvement initiatives, many of which are unique to the legal industry. What's more, the firm understands that, in today's business world, speed and accuracy are essential to success—and that a problem avoided is better than a problem solved. Bearing that in mind, the company works with clients to resolve their legal issues expeditiously, and to guide clients so that they can take proactive measures to minimize potential liability while maximizing opportunities for success. The firm's attorneys aren't just legal representatives to their clients—they are strategic partners.

The firm ensures satisfaction by making sure its expertise and practice accurately reflect the changing needs of the community. Technology and government regulations shape today's legal landscape in ways that would have been unimaginable 130 years ago. It is unlikely Graydon Head & Ritchey's founder, who had never seen a telephone, could have comprehended a global marketplace dominated by the Internet and electronic communication.

Those types of changes have kept Graydon Head & Ritchey's attorneys on their toes over the years; even today, the firm's attorneys are constantly focused on anticipating their clients' changing needs. The company's departments and service

While the world may be changing at an unprecedented pace, and new legal questions may be popping up faster than weeds in spring, one thing is certain: Graydon Head & Ritchey LLP is equipped to meet the challenge.

lines—bankruptcy and creditors rights; business and finance; commercial litigation and dispute resolution; commercial real estate; e-commerce; employee benefits; health care; human resources; international law; personal client services; and taxes—are a cross section of the legal challenges facing individuals and businesses today.

While Graydon Head & Ritchey's clients appreciate the firm's service, they aren't the only recipients. The firm has a long-standing history of service to the Greater Cincinnati com-

munity. In May 2000, the Cincinnati Bar Association recognized two Graydon Head & Ritchey attorneys, Bruce I. Petrie Sr. and Michael A. Roberts—as well as Peter J. Strauss, who retired from the firm in 1997—for their outstanding contributions to the community. Kent Willington was awarded the District One Award for Community Service by Lawyers 40 and Under by the Ohio State Bar Association.

Many other members of the firm work as part of Graydon Head &

Ritchey's Community Service Team to improve life in the community. Established in 1996 to promote hands-on community service opportunities for attorneys and staff members, the team has targeted a number of organizations through United Way. Whether painting the gym at St. Joseph's Orphanage, planting the garden at the Children's Home, or mentoring students at Washington Park Elementary School, staff members have risen to the challenge and walked the walk.

A Bright Future

While the world may be changing at an unprecedented pace, and new legal questions may be popping up faster than weeds in spring, one thing is certain: Graydon Head & Ritchey is equipped to meet the challenge. By relying on the highest-caliber professionals and delivering exceptional customer service, the firm will meet the challenges of tomorrow with the same aplomb that it has used to tackle those of the past 130 years.

"Through the years, the faces have changed at Graydon Head & Ritchey," Hirschfeld notes, "but the dedication of our attorneys and staff to clients, the community, and each other follows the tradition of our firm's founders and the many who came before us."

SEVERAL GRAYDON HEAD & RITCHEY ATTORNEYS HAVE BEEN RECOGNIZED BY THE CINCINNATI BAR ASSOCIATION FOR OUTSTANDING CONTRIBUTIONS TO THE COMMUNITY.

THE FIRM'S COMMUNITY SERVICE TEAM HELPS PROMOTE HANDS-ON COMMUNITY SERVICE BY MENTORING AT WASHINGTON PARK ELEMENTARY SCHOOL.

The Andrew Jergens Company

FOR NEARLY 120 YEARS, INNOVATION IN PERSONAL CARE HAS BEEN THE HALLMARK OF THE ANDREW JERGENS COMPANY. FROM ITS VERY START, JERGENS HAS INTRODUCED ONE NOTABLE INNOVATION AFTER ANOTHER, BEGINNING WITH ITS FIRST PRODUCT IN 1882, A HIGH-QUALITY, COCONUT OIL SOAP, MADE FROM THE PUREST SOAP-MAKING MATERIAL KNOWN AT THAT TIME. ANDREW JERGENS SR. AND CHARLES H. GEILFUS WERE THE FOUNDERS OF WHAT WAS THEN KNOWN AS THE

Andrews Soap Company. Today, under the ownership and innovative leadership of Kao Corporation, Jergens continues to break new ground by combining more than a century of skin care expertise with the latest global technologies.

Hard Work Leads to Soft Hands

With a $5,000 investment and some new ideas, Jergens and Geilfus started making products that were soon to be category leaders. Cincinnati proved to be an ideal location for the young business. As a meat-packing center, the area

provided the essentials for the company's growth and success: a steady supply of raw materials, a transportation network of rivers and canals, and a labor pool of hardworking immigrants.

In 1901, the company changed its name to The Andrew Jergens Company, and expanded into the lotion category when it purchased the formula for a benzoin and almond product that became Jergens Lotion. This lotion, with its famous cherry-almond fragrance, became synonymous with the name Jergens, and throughout the 1940s and 1950s,

Jergens commanded the hand lotion market. The characteristic fragrance continues to be fondly recognized by millions, and is still available in a variety of Jergens products.

In Partnership with Kao Corporation

A milestone in the company's history came in 1988, when it was purchased by Kao Corporation, a global manufacturer, marketer, and technology leader in the personal care, consumer products, and specialty chemical industries. Founded in Japan in 1887 as the Kao Soap Company, Kao has built its business on product innovation and technology. Today, Kao's product line includes more than 300 health and beauty, household, and food products that produce annual global sales of more than $8 billion in 27 countries.

The strength and synergy of this partnership has led to the world-wide distribution of Jergens products and the successful introduction of many Kao technologies tailored for the U.S. market. As Jergens President William Gentner notes, "Through our partnership, we can leverage Kao's vast resources in research, technology, and new product development to create exciting opportunities that have global reach."

An example of the collaboration between the two organizations is the recent implementation of an economic value added (EVA) measurement and management system. Originally developed by the U.S. consulting firm Stern Stewart & Company, EVA is a progressive management system designed to create shareholder value and profitable growth through precise measurement of true return on investment.

Jergens successfully implemented EVA in 1997 and, two years later, Kao followed, becoming the first Japanese company to utilize a true

THE ANDREW JERGENS COMPANY'S RESEARCH FACILITY WAS DEDICATED IN 1991 AND OCCUPIES THE FORMER SITE OF CINCINNATI UNION TERMINAL'S ROUNDHOUSE COMPLEX ON SPRING GROVE AVENUE.

THE BAN DEODORANT BRAND STRENGTHENS JERGENS' POSITION AS A MAJOR MARKETER OF PERSONAL CARE PRODUCTS.

EVA management system. According to Gentner, the use of EVA is fundamentally changing—and improving—business operations. "EVA is more than a measurement tool. It is about setting a world-class standard for performance, and then motivating and rewarding people for delivering against that standard. We are now more focused to direct resources toward our best opportunities for profitable growth. As a result, since introducing EVA, we have increased spending on new product innovation and improved information systems."

Jergens Today

Since becoming a part of Kao, Jergens has increased the pace of product innovation. The company's ultimate goal is to continually delight consumers with products that deliver unique and meaningful benefits and, as a result, generate profitable category growth for retail partners. Says Gentner, "The challenge to drive steady EVA growth has made Jergens more externally focused on retail customers and, ultimately, the consumer. Our mission is to develop innovative products based on original insights and technology."

With an exceptional team in Cincinnati and the resources of a technology leader like Kao, Jergens has been the source of some of the most inventive new products in the personal care category. With the launch of the Bioré facial care line in 1997, Jergens revolutionized the facial care category with the first pore strip in the United States. Bioré has won more than a dozen top industry awards for innovation, including the prestigious American Marketing Association Edison Gold Award for Best New Product Innovation.

In 1998, two new brands were added to the Andrew Jergens portfolio with the acquisition of the Curél and Soft Sense lotion brands from Bausch & Lomb. With the addition of these successful brands, Jergens has solidified its position in the lotion category with a strong competitor in each of the major segments: therapeutic, everyday, and specialty. In 2000, the acquisition of the Ban deodorant line from Chattem, Inc. further strengthened Jergens' position as a major marketer of personal care products.

Looking Forward

Given Jergens' successful record of innovation, strong brand equities, and extensive global resources, the company's future is promising. Founders Jergens and Geilfus probably would not recognize their former company today, but they would almost certainly be proud. After all, the Kao/Jergens philosophy to "contribute to the enhancement of people's lives by offering products which improve the quality of their everyday lives" is probably just what they had in mind.

THE COMPANY HAS BEEN THE SOURCE OF SOME OF THE MOST INVENTIVE NEW PRODUCTS IN THE PERSONAL CARE CATEGORY, AND BIORÉ HAS WON MORE THAN A DOZEN TOP INDUSTRY AWARDS FOR INNOVATION.

The E.W. Scripps Co.

In 1878, E.W. Scripps borrowed $10,000 from his brothers to start *The Penny Press* in Cleveland and a journalistic phenomenon was born. In the ensuing years, Scripps brought his recipe for affordable, clear, and politically independent newspapers into cities across the nation, including Cincinnati, where he acquired control of *The Penny Post* from his brother James, who had purchased it in 1881.

The E.W. Scripps Co.'s local newspapers, *The Kentucky Post* and *The Cincinnati Post*, began operating as *The Penny Post* in 1881, and took their current names in 1890.

Today, the 10,000 employees of the Cincinnati-based E.W. Scripps Co. perpetuate Scripps' entrepreneurial spirit and journalistic integrity by supplying the American public with information and entertainment through newspapers, television broadcasting, feature syndication, and cable television networks. Indeed, the Scripps motto—Give light and the people will find their own way—encapsulates the company's mission to uncover the news and educate the public.

Serving the Public Trust

At the core of Scripps' diverse enterprises is a unifying commitment to journalism and community service. While the newspapers E.W. Scripps originally launched to fight corruption and give voice to the powerless have grown into a media organization that includes 21 daily newspapers and 10 television stations, the company's emphasis on quality content, integrity, and serving the needs of local audiences remains unwavering.

Like the company's other news media, Scripps' local outlets—*The Cincinnati Post*, *The Kentucky Post*, and Peabody Award-winning WCPO-TV—strive to illuminate the topics that matter most to their hometown community. That goal is advanced through Scripps' local companion Web site at www.cincinow.com. The site, like Web sites offered in other Scripps markets, enables Scripps to transcend the time and space limitations of traditional media, and provide coverage as in-depth as it is broad.

The Leader in Category Media

Just as it shares news and laughter with its audiences, Scripps likewise shares their interests. In 1994, the company drew upon its tradition of informing the public when it launched Home & Garden Television (HGTV). Based on the groundbreaking idea of using television to provide viewers with the home- and garden-oriented news they had traditionally sought from shelter magazines, the Knoxville-based network has become one of the most trusted brands in cable television. Today, the 24-hour cable network brings the latest in home repair and remodeling, gardening and landscaping, and decorating and

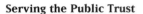

Scripps' hometown television station, WCPO-TV, won the George Foster Peabody Award in 2000 for its I-Team investigation into spending on the new Reds and Bengals sports stadiums.

design trends into more than 65 million homes in the United States. HGTV programming is also available in Canada, Australia, Japan, and the Philippines.

HGTV's success paved the way for additional cable networks. In 1997, Scripps acquired controlling interest in New York-based Food Network. By taking the programming out of the studio and into kitchens across the country, Scripps has kicked

the network up a few notches. Celebrity chefs and fun cooking and entertainment ideas have helped the 24-hour cable network attract more than 50 million subscribers in the United States. Meanwhile, the Do It Yourself (DIY) network, an offshoot of HGTV that launched in September 1999, provides practical how-to information in a slower, more deliberate and detailed format to those interested in tackling home

repair, remodeling, decorating, gardening, and craft projects.

Each network is interactive by design, with an accompanying Web site that provides additional information to viewers, as well as marketing opportunities for advertisers. Because category programming isn't limited by geography and can be extended through the Internet and other media platforms, category media represents a growing source of revenue for the company. With those opportunities in mind, Scripps announced plans to launch a fourth lifestyle-oriented network called Fine Living in 2001.

Carrying on the Tradition

While Scripps' journalistic mission is hard-hitting and informative, the company has a lighter side as well. In addition to its news and broadcast operations, Scripps operates United Media, a New York-based syndication and licensing business. The company licenses products and toys based on such timeless characters as Raggedy Ann and Andy, and syndicates a variety of widely loved cartoons, including PEANUTS and DILBERT.

Always mindful of its responsibility as a corporate citizen, Scripps recognizes the need to give back to the communities where it operates and to the journalistic community. The company's philanthropic arm, Scripps Howard Foundation, sponsors the prestigious National Journalism Awards, offers student scholarships, and provides financial support to high school and college journalism programs, as well as to community literacy programs. Such efforts recognize and help nurture the highest journalistic standards both now and in the future.

As the media industry changes, Scripps' innovative thinking and entrepreneurial spirit will be more important than ever, according to Scripps President and CEO Ken Lowe. "Scripps is a company that is constantly evolving," Lowe says. "New technologies in the 1930s and 1940s led us into radio and television. Going forward, advances in technology will continue to present us with opportunities. And we'll be there to program it."

CLOCKWISE FROM TOP LEFT: SCRIPPS CHAIRMAN WILLIAM R. BURLEIGH (LEFT) AND PRESIDENT AND CEO KENNETH W. LOWE.

SCRIPPS SUBSIDIARY UNITED MEDIA HAS BEEN HOME TO SNOOPY, CHARLIE BROWN, AND THE REST OF THE PEANUTS CHARACTERS SINCE 1950.

SCRIPPS CENTER, THE COMPANY'S HEADQUARTERS, IS LOCATED AT THIRD AND WALNUT STREETS IN DOWNTOWN CINCINNATI.

Milacron Inc.

IN THE MODERN BUSINESS WORLD, THE BEST COMPANIES THRIVE BY EVOLVING. UNDERSTANDING THAT, MILACRON INC., FORMERLY CINCINNATI MILACRON, SOLD ITS LEGACY MACHINE TOOL BUSINESS IN OCTOBER 1998 TO CONCENTRATE ON ITS GROWING PLASTICS AND METALWORKING TECHNOLOGIES SECTORS, FROM WHICH IT DERIVED THE BULK OF ITS PROFITS. THAT GROWTH, DRIVEN LARGELY BY NEW PRODUCT DEVELOPMENT AND MARKET EXPANSION,

CLOCKWISE FROM TOP: MILACRON INC. IS THE WORLD'S BROADEST-LINE SUPPLIER OF SYSTEMS TO PROCESS PLASTICS. ITS POWERLINE INJECTION MOLDING MACHINES ARE LEADING THE INDUSTRY-WIDE SHIFT TO ALL-ELECTRIC TECHNOLOGY.

MILACRON PRODUCES CARBIDE INSERTS AND STEEL TOOL HOLDERS IN NORTH AMERICA AND EUROPE FOR MACHINING A WIDE VARIETY OF METAL PARTS.

PACKAGING IS THE FASTEST GROWING MARKET IN PLASTICS PROCESSING. MILACRON'S BLOW MOLDING MACHINES PRODUCE A WIDE VARIETY OF BEVERAGE, COSMETIC, PHARMACEUTICAL, AND HOUSEHOLD CHEMICAL CONTAINERS.

as well as an aggressive acquisition campaign launched in 1993, convinced Milacron to chart a new course into the 21st century.

With its decision to spin off its machine tool business, Milacron returned to its roots. But the company is far from the small Cincinnati shop George Mueller, Fred Holz, and Fred A. Geier founded. Milacron has grown into a world leader in advanced technologies for the plastics processing and metalworking industries. The company maintains manufacturing operations in about a dozen countries and serves thousands of customers around the globe.

Traveling Full Circle

When Milacron, which employs about 2,000 people locally, was incorporated in 1884, its primary business was making screws and taps. Within just five years, the company had segued into making milling machines, and by the 1920s, it had become one of the largest makers of machine tools in the United States.

Although Milacron's metalworking technologies group, one of its two core business areas, still makes taps, that's only a small part of its business. The group, which maintains a facility in Oakley, Ohio, is the industry's broadest-line manufacturer of cutting tools, abrasives, and fluids for metal removal, as well as carbide die and wear parts.

Milacron has a long history of bringing new products to market in the metalworking technologies sector. One such product, developed shortly after World War II, was a water-based fluid to cool both the cutting tool and the workpiece during the metal-cutting process, and to wash away the chips created. Unlike commonly used oils, the new, synthetic fluids Milacron developed did not smoke or burn. The company went on to produce and sell grinding wheels that, along with the new fluids, became the mainstay of Milacron's consumable industrial products business through the 1980s.

Those early advancements have been accompanied in recent years by market-expanding acquisitions. Milacron acquired Valenite, the

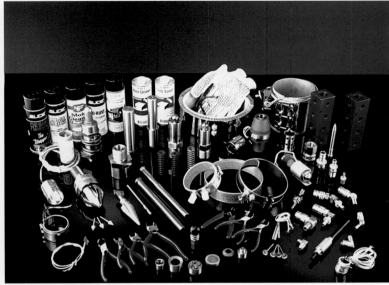

second-largest North American maker of carbide inserts and tool holders, in 1993. That purchase was followed in 1995 by the acquisitions of Widia, one of the largest European makers of carbide inserts and steel toolholders, and a series of companies that produce carbide and high-speed steel drills, end mills, and taps. These additions, plus continuous growth in the base business, catapulted Milacron to the number two position in North America and number three worldwide in metal-cutting tools and supplies.

A Future in Plastics

Today, Milacron's larger and faster-growing business is plastics technologies. Born when the company invented its first injection molding machine in 1968, this group has grown to be one of the world's broadest-line producers of machines, systems, tooling, and supplies for the plastics processing industry.

With operations locally in Batavia and Mount Orab, the group makes machines to process many types and sizes of plastic products—primarily through injection molding, blow molding, and extrusion technologies. These systems help customers produce products as varied as car parts, toys, pipes, electronic components, medical devices, utensils, and packaging.

The Milacron plastics group has expanded through a variety of acquisitions, including the 1993 purchase of Ferromatik, a leading

European manufacturer of injection molding machines, and the 1996 acquisition of D-M-E, a Detroit-based manufacturer of mold tooling technologies. Since then, Milacron has acquired a laundry list of top complementary firms in the industry, including Uniloy, Autojectors, Wear Technology, Master Unit Die, Northern Supply, and Nickerson.

Given its numerous holdings, Milacron relies on a worldwide distribution channel that includes direct sales, distributors, and catalogs. The company's products are also available through growing e-business channels, including Internet trade and supplier exchanges.

Finding a Better Way

A particular Milacron slogan dates back to a speech Geier, who served as Milacron's president from 1905 until 1934, made in the 1930s. In entreating Milacron employees to Find a Better Way, Geier coined a phrase that has become a corporate mantra. Today, the phrase is an integral part of Milacron's vision statement. It also serves as an appropriate counterpart to the company's core values, which emphasize customer satisfaction, employee opportunity, company growth and profitability, and integrity.

The company's emphasis on integrity shines through in Milacron's role as a responsible corporate citizen. The firm has a long history of community involvement. In 1906, Milacron, with the University of

Cincinnati, helped create the nation's first cooperative education program to provide on-the-job training for engineering students. Milacron continues to be an active participant in co-op programs today.

In 1915, the company was instrumental in establishing the Cincinnati Community Chest, the precursor to the modern-day United Way, which it actively supports. Milacron is also a major contributor to the arts, and maintains a foundation that supports educational causes.

Today, although few consumers realize it, Milacron's fingerprint is on such a broad array of products—including milk bottles, razors, airplanes, bicycles, faucets, and cell phones—that it would be hard to go through a day without handling a product the company helped to make. Milacron Inc.'s behind-the-scenes contributions are so widespread that they are the basis for another of the company's slogans, Helping the World's Leading Companies Make the World's Favorite Products.

CLOCKWISE FROM TOP LEFT: MILACRON SELLS MAINTENANCE, REPAIR, AND OPERATING SUPPLIES FOR PLASTICS PROCESSORS UNDER SEVERAL BRAND AND COMPANY NAMES.

MILACRON HAS A FULL LINE OF SOLID CARBIDE AND HIGH-SPEED STEEL ROUND TOOLS FOR BOTH NORTH AMERICAN AND EUROPEAN MARKETS.

MILACRON'S HOT RUNNER SYSTEMS SET NEW STANDARDS FOR LARGE-PART AND MULTI-CAVITY INJECTION MOLDING APPLICATIONS.

The Western-Southern Enterprise

NOW MORE THAN A CENTURY OLD, THE WESTERN AND SOUTHERN LIFE INSURANCE COMPANY IS EXPERIENCING ACCELERATED GROWTH DUE TO NEW PRODUCTS, NEW SERVICES, AND NEW WAYS OF REACHING THE CONSUMER. WHILE MANY LONGTIME CINCINNATIANS STILL THINK OF WESTERN AND SOUTHERN ONLY AS A LIFE INSURER, THE ORIGINAL PARENT COMPANY HAS BECOME THE FOUNDATION OF THE WESTERN-SOUTHERN ENTERPRISE, A

THE WESTERN-SOUTHERN ENTERPRISE CORPORATE CAMPUS INCLUDES THE COMPANY'S HEADQUARTERS ON BROADWAY BETWEEN FOURTH AND FIFTH STREETS IN CINCINNATI, AND A NUMBER OF NEARBY BUILDINGS (RIGHT).

THE GUILFORD BUILDING, A FORMER PUBLIC SCHOOL BUILT IN 1913, IS THE HOME OF WESTERN-SOUTHERN'S REAL ESTATE AFFILIATE, EAGLE REALTY GROUP; THE COMPANY'S CORPORATE UNIVERSITY, THE GUILFORD INSTITUTE; AND A FITNESS CENTER FOR ASSOCIATES. WESTERN-SOUTHERN'S RESTORATION OF THE GUILFORD BUILDING WON THE CINCINNATI PRESERVATION ASSOCIATION'S ANNUAL AWARD IN 1996 (LEFT).

diversified group of financial services companies whose subsidiaries offer financial services from life insurance to investment and real estate services, and employ more than 5,000 people nationwide. The company's growth in those many sectors—and its desire to perpetuate such growth—explains why Western-Southern has reorganized into a mutual insurance holding company.

Paving the Way for Growth

Maximizing opportunities and following through with consistently strong performance have been hallmarks of Western-Southern since its beginning. Founded in Cincinnati in 1888 with the goal of making insurance available to low- and middle-income consumers, Western-Southern has long adhered

to two guiding principles: place policyholders' interests first and provide financial safety through sound investment practices. This philosophy enabled Western-Southern to continue to grow during the Great Depression when other financial institutions failed; to accommodate policyholders' needs during the war years; and, throughout it all, to prosper. That ethos

continues today under the leadership of William J. Williams, chairman, and John F. Barrett, president and chief executive officer.

With its reorganization into the mutual insurance holding company structure, Western-Southern will maintain its ability to safeguard policyholders' assets while expanding opportunities for growth. Understanding that growth and economies

of scale are vital to future prosperity, the Enterprise plans to use internal growth and acquisition to increase the total assets it owns and manages to $50 billion by 2005. The new structure will help make this happen by giving the company the option of financing acquisitions with stock rather than with cash exclusively. This additional flexibility will enable Western-Southern to take advantage of growth opportunities as they arise.

"We believe that becoming a mutual insurance holding company translates to greater opportunities for our policyholders and our company," says Barrett. "It is a competitive measure that will allow us to offer more and better products and financial services, better meet our customers' needs, and enjoy even more success."

Diverse Services for Diverse Needs

During the past decade, Western-Southern has moved into several new markets by establishing or acquiring new companies. Currently, The Western-Southern Enterprise includes The Western and Southern Life Insurance Company, Western-Southern Life Assurance Company, Columbus Life Insurance Company, Capital Analysts, IFS Financial Services, Touchstone Advisors, Integrated Fund Services, The Integrity Companies, Fort Washington Investment Advisors, and Todd Investment Advisors. Eagle Realty Group, a full-service commercial real estate company, rounds out Western-Southern's diverse family of companies.

While making strategic acquisitions is necessary to expand and create economies of scale, Enterprise associates know that growth is also a matter of satisfying customers. At the most basic level, this means providing the high-quality products and services that have been promised, and Western-Southern associates are proud that Enterprise companies have an excellent reputation for doing this consistently.

The Western and Southern Life Insurance Company and Western-Southern Life Assurance Company have received outstanding ratings

from four of their industry's most respected independent rating services. The companies have received Standard & Poor's AAA (extremely strong) rating for financial strength; Fitch's AAA (exceptionally strong) for insurer financial strength; A.M. Best's A++ (superior) for financial strength, operating performance, and market profile; and Moody's Aa2 (excellent) for financial strength.

Convenience is another important aspect of the customer satisfaction equation. Western-Southern has made available an array of distribution choices enabling customers to communicate with the company anywhere, anyway, anyhow. A recently established client relationship center makes telephone and Web-based communication easily accessible. Customers preferring face-to-face communication can contact a Western-Southern sales representative in one of the company's 200-plus sales offices, located in more than 20 states. In all, more than 50,000 individuals—including career, independent, and general agents, as well as banks and financial planners—are licensed to distribute the products of Western-Southern Enterprise companies.

Investing Wisely

Western-Southern also understands that its customers expect the company to uphold the strong community values upon which it has staked its reputation. Western-Southern does this through a variety of community service initiatives that include, but also go beyond, funding.

Company philanthropic efforts are led by the Western-Southern Enterprise Fund, which provides support for health research, health care and higher education programs, and special initiatives. A few of the institutions that have benefited from Enterprise Fund contributions are the nursing school programs of Northern Kentucky and Xavier universities, Hoffman Elementary in the Walnut Hills neighborhood of Cincinnati, National Multiple Sclerosis Society's Greater Cincinnati MS Walk, United Way, Fine Arts Fund, Over-the-Rhine Coalition,

and National Underground Railroad Freedom Center.

While such philanthropic investments may sound unusual for an insurance company, they are just one more way Western-Southern demonstrates that wise investment and thoughtful allocation of resources pays off. "At Western-Southern, we've been making wise investments for more than 112 years," says Barrett, who became chairman of the Cincinnati United Way in 2001. "Investing in the community is about the wisest investment a company can make."

JOHN F. BARRETT, PRESIDENT AND CEO (LEFT), AND WILLIAM J. WILLIAMS, CHAIRMAN OF THE BOARD, HAVE HELPED TO BUILD THE WESTERN-SOUTHERN ENTERPRISE AND ITS SUBSIDIARIES INTO A FINANCIAL SERVICES GROUP THAT IS NATIONAL IN SCOPE.

Reliance Medical Products

An old adage claims that "the more things change, the more they stay the same," and Reliance Medical Products bears that out. Although the company sells its top-of-the-line medical equipment in some 80 countries and is an industry leader in technological advances, its commitment to craftsmanship is the same today as it was when the company was founded in 1898. ● Fred and Frank Koenigkramer, first-generation sons of German immigrants, formed their company after inventing a clog-free paint sprayer that farmers could use to paint their barns. Inspired by their success, the entrepreneurial brothers went on to obtain two patents for an improved barber's hydraulic chair, which they sold to their former employer, Cincinnati-based Eugene Berninghaus Company.

In 1920, the Koenigkramers introduced a complete line of barber's chairs under the brand name Reliance. Their product innovation was the hydraulic lift, which required only one lever for raising, lowering, revolving, or locking the chair. It was so popular that even the barber on *The Andy Griffith Show*, Floyd, had a Reliance chair.

The company entered the medical market in 1920, when a Missouri osteopath suggested that the broth-

ers build a treatment table. Product line extensions led Reliance into the podiatry and ophthalmology medical specialties, where the company developed an entire line of examination and procedures chairs, instru-

ment stands, and examination and surgical stools. Reliance still manufactures these products for ophthalmology, optometry, and several other medical specialties.

In 1988, Reliance Medical Products was purchased by Bern-based Haag-Streit AG. Shortly thereafter, Haag-Streit built a new, 100,000-square-foot facility in Mason, Ohio, to house the manufacturing operations, and a 25,000-square-foot office facility for the marketing departments of both Reliance and its sister companies.

A Leader in Medical Equipment

Chances are that anyone who has visited an ophthalmologist or an optometrist has had a close-up view of a Reliance product. The company draws on its vast experience in hydraulics to make an array

Reliance Medical Products founders Fred and Frank Koenigkramer formed their company after inventing a clog-free paint sprayer that farmers could use to paint their barns.

In 1988, Reliance Medical Products was purchased by Haag-Streit AG of Bern, Switzerland. Shortly thereafter Haag-Streit built a new 100,000-square-foot facility in Mason, Ohio, to house the manufacturing operations.

of ergonomically correct lift and examination chairs, mobile surgical stretchers and surgical tables, and the pendulum delivery systems and instrument stands found in many eye doctors' offices. In addition, Reliance, which introduces about three new products a year, makes an array of treatment cabinets, stools, instrument stands, and other office add-ons that enable doctors to furnish their examination rooms with state-of-the-art equipment.

Reliance products are popular with doctors; in fact, many report that when they retire, they are able to sell the Reliance chairs they purchased after graduation for more than they paid for them. The company recently conducted a search for the oldest Reliance chair still in use and the winner was a 1940 model.

A Marriage of Technology and Craftsmanship

A tour of Reliance's factory reveals the secret behind the company's success. The company's some 120 employees meld art and science to produce superior-quality medical equipment.

Reliance technicians ensure the equipment is calibrated not only to ISO 9001 certification, but also to the standards of EN 46001, the highest quality designation within the medical specialty field. The accuracy and precision of Reliance equipment is tracked by about 1,000 gauges. In fact, accuracy is not measured in inches or even fractions of inches, but is calibrated within millionths of an inch.

That kind of precision is artfully balanced against the comfort, appearance, and sturdiness of the product. Craftspeople wielding scissors and operating sewing machines to stitch fine upholstery onto solid Baltic birch frames are just as important in the creation of Reliance's showroom-quality furniture as are the firm's technicians.

Marrying the best of old-world craftsmanship and information-age technology is what Reliance is all about, according to Dennis Imwalle, president. "A lot of pride goes into making our products, and tradition is very important to what we do,"

Imwalle says. "Our motto is Precision through Tradition."

Union Based on Shared Values

Reliance shares its commitment to quality with its parent company, with which it works closely. Since Haag-Streit purchased Reliance, it has relocated the U.S. operations of several of its other companies to Mason. In addition to Reliance, Haag-Streit's holdings include Haag-Streit USA, Möller Microsurgery, Clement Clarke, and John Weiss.

Founded in 1858, Haag-Streit manufactures precision instruments for ophthalmology. The Haag-Streit slit lamp, its flagship product, is widely recognized as one of the finest slit lamps in the world. The company's other products include applanation tonometers, diagnostic contact lenses, ophthalmometers, corneal topographers, and the OCTOPUS projection perimeter, which is used to identify eye diseases such as glaucoma. Such technologically advanced products are only the beginning. Like the other Haag-Streit companies, Reliance, which maintains its own research

and development department, intends to continue to grow and prosper by developing and delivering high-quality products that meet customers' needs.

"It's so trite today to say you listen to your customers and provide what they want, but we really have a history of using that as our standard operating procedure," Imwalle says. "After all, that's how we got into this business back in 1920. We'll continue to invest in the latest manufacturing technology. In the future, we'll be more computerized and will make more sales on the Web, but our traditions aren't going to change. We'll still be listening to the customer."

DOCTORS OFTEN TELL RELIANCE THAT THEY PURCHASED A RELIANCE CHAIR WHEN THEY GRADUATED FROM COLLEGE, USED IT FOR THE LIFE OF THEIR PRACTICE, AND THEN SOLD IT FOR MORE THAN THEY PAID FOR IT WHEN THEY RETIRED. RELIANCE PROUDLY DISPLAYS A CHAIR FROM THE 1920S IN ITS LOBBY.

THE FX-920, RELIANCE'S NEWEST CHAIR, REVOLUTIONIZED THE MARKET WITH ITS STYLISH CURVES AND SLEEK DESIGN. LIKE ALL RELIANCE CHAIRS, THE FX-920 IS DESIGNED FOR DURABILITY AND MAXIMUM PATIENT AND DOCTOR COMFORT.

Siemens Energy & Automation, Inc.

WHAT A DIFFERENCE A CENTURY MAKES AT THE LARGE MOTORS AND PUMPS BUSINESS UNIT OF SIEMENS ENERGY & AUTOMATION, INC. FOUNDED AS THE BULLOCK ELECTRIC COMPANY IN 1898, SIEMENS STILL OCCUPIES THE SAME SITE IN THE CITY OF NORWOOD, OHIO, ON WHICH ITS PREDECESSOR BUILT THE COMMUNITY'S FIRST FACTORY IN 1904. BUT WHILE THE LOCATION'S THE SAME, IT IS DOUBTFUL THE BULLOCK BROTHERS WOULD RECOGNIZE THE WORLD-CLASS, TECHNOLOGICALLY

advanced industrial motors that Siemens produces today.

Siemens' Industrial Products Business Unit makes a wide selection of large electrical motors used by oil refineries, paper and pulp mills, mining operations, and petrochemical industries. Major customers include Dow Chemical, Cooper Industries, International Paper, and Shell Oil.

FOUNDED AS THE BULLOCK ELECTRIC CO. IN 1898, SIEMENS STILL OCCUPIES THE SAME SITE IN THE CITY OF NORWOOD WHERE ITS PREDECESSOR BUILD THAT COMMUNITY'S FIRST FACTORY IN 1904 (RIGHT).

A MEMBER OF THE SIEMENS NORWOOD TEAM SINCE 1987, MIKE KWIATKOWSKI IS TODAY GENERAL MANAGER OF THE FACILITY (BELOW).

▼ MAYHEW & PEPER

Global Power

Siemens Energy & Automation is part of New York-based Siemens Corp., a holding company for Siemens' U.S. operations, which in turn are part of the global Siemens AG organization headquartered in Munich. Siemens' annual U.S. sales are approximately $13 billion. Worldwide annual sales today exceed $60 billion.

◄ MAYHEW & PEPER

The company's Large Motors and Pumps Business Unit puts up equally impressive figures. Employing some 450 people, the Norwood plant generates about $100 million in sales annually, a figure that is continually growing.

"Every company must face the reality of competition and how it performs against customer expectations," says Mike Kwiatkowski, general manager of the Norwood facility. "In the large motor business, the market has become global. Therefore, we compete with manufacturers worldwide."

Siemens offers custom-engineered motors with ratings that range from 200 to 10,000 horsepower. The motors feature rugged, cast-iron enclosures that minimize vibrations and noise, which increases motor life and helps meet strict environmental standards.

Using standardized parts designed by Siemens' engineers for multiple uses, the Norwood operation can deliver built-to-order motors quickly at competitive prices. Siemens worldwide is supported in the United States by more than 200 authorized service centers and globally on every continent.

Siemens' motor division has developed a highly effective teamwork approach to its business. The plant's management and workers are dedicated to building and maintaining Siemens' reputation as a world-class supplier. Relations between Siemens' management and labor have become a model for U.S. industry.

World-Class Supplier

Kwiatkowski cites the following goals that Siemens shares with other world-class suppliers: to ship on time 95 percent of the time or better; to be easy to do business with; to relentlessly pursue the elimination of waste and the delivery of increased value to the customer; to develop products that are technologically superior to the competition; to foster employees who are involved and want to serve both their internal and their external customers; and to be the standard against which the competition measures itself.

By investing in new technologies and keeping a sharp focus on quality, Siemens strives to stay one step ahead of its global competition. The plant's business strategy has been to expand into the future by attaining higher standards, higher

voltages, lower noise levels, lower vibration levels, and reliability for longer product life, while holding down costs.

Siemens operates according to a certified quality performance system that has made it the industry benchmark for meeting and exceeding customer expectations. The company's closed-loop quality system has 10 distinct components: system management under a quality assurance manager who reports directly to the general manager of quality; product quality and reliability development; product and process quality planning; supplier quality assurance; continuous evaluation and control; special studies to investigate new or recurring problems; information feedback; ongoing calibration of measurement equipment; training and staff development; and careful monitoring of customer acceptance.

The underlying principle of this certified quality system is that, to maximize customer satisfaction, control has to start with order entry and end only when the product is in the hands of a happy customer who continues to remain satisfied and willing to give Siemens another order. The Norwood facility was the first Siemens Energy & Automation plant to achieve ISO 9001 registration.

Local Presence

The other side of Siemens' mission to be a world-class company in every respect is its dedication to the community. As a partner in education with Norwood Middle School, the company provides financial aid for science fairs and other special projects, and its employees serve as mentors to students, giving advice and feedback on school curricula. The partnership goes both ways: the students provide entertainment at Siemens' annual Christmas luncheon and volunteer once a month to clean up parking lots at the plant.

Siemens is also a longtime supporter of the annual Multiple Sclerosis Walk in Norwood, as well as of the Food Closet, which sup-

plies food and clothing for people in need.

An active member of the local business community, Siemens' Industrial Products Business Unit has two representatives on the Norwood Chamber of Commerce board, as well as one representative on the Greater Cincinnati Chamber of Commerce board. Finally, Siemens Norwood works with local colleges and high schools in co-op programs to help support and promote continual education.

With priorities in place and a solid corporate structure, Siemens Energy & Automation, Inc. is a boon to the Cincinnati community and a worldwide leader in the energy and automation industry.

EMPLOYING SOME 450 PEOPLE, THE NORWOOD PLANT GENERATES APPROXIMATELY $100 MILLION IN SALES ANNUALLY, A FIGURE THAT IS CONTINUALLY GROWING (TOP).

THE INDUSTRIAL PRODUCTS BUSINESS UNIT MAKES A WIDE SELECTION OF LARGE ELECTRICAL MOTORS USED BY OIL REFINERIES, PAPER AND PULP MILLS, MINING OPERATIONS, AND PETROCHEMICAL INDUSTRIES (BOTTOM).

Loth Mbi, Inc.

Loth Mbi, Inc. PROVIDES MORE THAN JUST NICE FURNITURE; IT PROVIDES OFFICE SOLUTIONS. THE FIRM UNDERSTANDS THAT COMPANIES MAKE HUGE INVESTMENTS IN THEIR OFFICES, FURNISHINGS, AND EMPLOYEES. THAT SAID, LOTH MBI WORKS HARD TO MAXIMIZE THOSE THREE ASSETS FOR EVERY CLIENT BY DESIGNING FLEXIBLE, ATTRACTIVE WORK SPACES THAT MAXIMIZE EMPLOYEE PRODUCTIVITY AND ARE ADAPTABLE ENOUGH TO GROW WITH COMPANIES' CHANGING NEEDS.

CLOCKWISE FROM TOP:
LOTH MBI, INC. MOVED TO A RENOVATED WAREHOUSE FACILITY IN 1998 THAT HOUSES THE COMPANY'S CORPORATE OFFICES, OFFICE RETAIL STORE, ASSET MANAGEMENT, AND PRE-OWNED FURNITURE DIVISION.

WERNDL EMERGE IS ONE OF THE MANY PRODUCT SOLUTIONS LOTH MBI OFFERS ITS CUSTOMERS.

LOTH MBI OFFERS FURNISHINGS FROM MORE THAN 100 SUPPLIERS AND IS THE AREA'S EXCLUSIVE AUTHORIZED DEALER OF STEELCASE, A LEADING GLOBAL OFFICE FURNITURE MANUFACTURER.

Loth Mbi's clients range from small to medium-sized businesses looking for office furniture, to value-oriented corporate customers looking for reasonable options, as well as major firms looking for full-service attention. The company brings more than 110 years of experience dating to 1891 and the expertise of some 130 staffers—including installers, designers, program managers, and account executives—to bear on every project.

"We bring a team to each project and try to make decisions that meet the unique interests of the client's entire operations," explains J.B. Buse Jr., president and CEO. "We supply our clients with more than just products. Thanks to the skill and expertise of our people, we add value by providing solutions."

While Loth Mbi's services are extensive, a great many people best know the company for its exemplary products. The firm offers furnishings from more than 100 suppliers, and is the area's exclusive authorized dealer of Steelcase, a leading global office furniture manufacturer. Consequently, Loth Mbi is able to meet every type of design and budget.

Explore, Plan, Provide, Maintain

To Loth Mbi, service is an ongoing proposition. Companies need products and services not only today, but also on a continuing basis as their work space needs change. Consequently, Loth Mbi helps clients study their spatial needs in light of long-term objectives. The company's consultants study clients' real estate usage, technological demands, and acquisitions and locations, as well as their organizational, cultural, and communications needs, to devise a plan uniquely suited to the clients' needs. Before designs are drawn or a stick of furniture is purchased, Loth Mbi team members discuss their findings and proposed solutions with clients to ensure their plan meets each client's objectives. Once clients have approved a plan, Loth Mbi provides top-quality furnishings and equipment from its vast selection.

Understanding that the need for furnishings can expand and contract with market fluctuations, Loth Mbi works with clients on an ongoing basis to supply additional furnishings, warehouse items that are not in use, and broker goods that are no longer needed. Recycling and repair services, so clients can keep their offices up to date at all times, are also provided. Indeed, clients can rely on Loth Mbi for everything from asset management and facility services to move management and work space design.

1900-1930

1901
Cincinnati Coca-Cola Bottling
   Company

1901
Sena Weller Rohs Williams Inc.

1901
Steed Hammond Paul

1903
Twin Towers

1905
R.A. Jones & Co. Inc.

1909
Ohio National Financial Services

1913
Givaudan

1920
Deloitte & Touche LLP

1922
Noveon Hilton Davis, Inc.

1924
The Vernon Manor Hotel

1925
KeyBank and Gradison McDonald
   Investments

1927
White Castle System, Inc.

1929
Cintas Corporation

Cincinnati Coca-Cola
Bottling Company

WHAT A DIFFERENCE A CENTURY MAKES," SAYS DOUG BECKER, SALES CENTER MANAGER OF THE CINCINNATI COCA-COLA BOTTLING COMPANY. WHEN THE CINCINNATI BOTTLING COMPANY OPENED ITS DOORS IN 1901, THE COMPANY PROCESSED SIX-OUNCE BOTTLES THAT WERE DELIVERED BY HORSE-DRAWN WAGONS. TODAY, THE MADISONVILLE SALES, PRODUCTION, AND DISTRIBUTION FACILITY SUPPLIES MORE THAN 150 BRANDS, INCLUDING COCA-COLA AND SCHWEPPES PRODUCTS,

Evian, Barq's Root Beer, Powerade, Dasani, and Minute Maid, and delivers them via $80,000 tractor-trailers.

A Long History of Success

The business of bottling Coca-Cola began in 1899 when two Chattanooga attorneys traveled to Atlanta, where the soft drink had been created 13 years prior to that date. They struck a deal with the Coca-Cola Company for the rights to bottle and distribute the soda throughout most of the United States. The company's owner, Asa Candler, although initially reluctant, finally agreed to the deal, and sold the rights for $1, a sum he never bothered to collect.

Just two years later, on December 4, 1901, Cincinnati became one of the first 10 areas in the world in which Coca-Cola would be bottled and distributed. The first Cincinnati bottling facility was located in downtown Cincinnati on Sycamore Street, and operated there without marked success. That changed in 1916, however, when William O. Mashburn Sr., a 36-year-old office manager at the company's national headquarters, purchased the Cincinnati operation. Mashburn promptly built a new, state-of-the-

art facility on Pioneer Street, and moved the company there. With conveyor systems and semiautomatic bottling equipment, the bottling plant was a wonder to visitors and a delight to employees.

During the ensuing decade, Mashburn extended his operations, opening warehouses in Aurora and Osgood, Indiana; Warsaw, Falmouth, and Maysville, Kentucky; and Hamilton, Georgetown, Lynchburg, and Clarksville, Ohio. He likewise purchased two additional franchises, the Cleveland Coca-Cola Bottling Company and the Springfield, Ohio Coca-Cola Bottling Company.

After his death in 1930, Mashburn's sons, William O. Mashburn Jr. and J. Cromer Mashburn, took over the company, which they moved to Dana Avenue. Since 1986, the Cincinnati operation has been a part of Coca-Cola Enterprises, a publicly traded corporation.

Employees Key to Success

Today, the some 800 employees of the Cincinnati Coca-Cola Bottling Company continue to operate in the tradition William O. Mashburn Sr. established years ago. Just as Mashburn, a Shriner

THE CINCINNATI COCA-COLA BOTTLING COMPANY HAS BEEN IN BUSINESS SINCE 1901.

WEBER & HARRISON INC.

and Rotarian, focused on giving back to the community, the local sales center remains an active member of the community. The company supports nonprofit organizations as varied as the Boy Scouts, Boys and Girls Hope, United Way, Habitat for Humanity, Ohio Reads, and countless others. In honor of its 100th anniversary, the Cincinnati company proudly announced the first annual Centennial Coca-Cola Cincinnati Public School Scholarship. "Coca-Cola has been a member of this community for 100 years," says Becker. "We are proud to establish this scholarship for Cincinnati Public Schools. We firmly believe that by supporting today's youth, we are investing in Cincinnati's future leaders."

In addition, Cincinnati Coca-Cola Bottling Company is quick to respond in the event of a disaster. In 1997, the company used its facility to bottle water for flood victims in Falmouth, Kentucky, and in 1999, the firm did the same for tornado victims in Blue Ash, Ohio.

The company has remained true to Mashburn's spirit of innovation as well. Its market service center was built on Duck Creek Road in 1983. The production and warehouse facility made history with the 1986 remodel that added a state-of-the-art operation and became one of the most advanced beverage plants in the world. In 2001, Cincinnati Coca-Cola Bottling Company produced an estimated 50 million cases and shipped them throughout Ohio, Kentucky, and Indiana.

Until recently, the highly automated plant was the only vertical production bottling facility in the nation. The Cincinnati branch office sells Coca-Cola products throughout a 50-mile radius, and is the fifth-largest sales center in Coca-Cola Enterprises' portfolio.

The Next 100 Years

Although the popularity of the Coca-Cola brand has fueled the company's growth over the years, Becker notes that it was the bottler's hardworking employees who guaranteed the products' unwavering quality and enabled the soft-drink company to meet consumer demand. Indeed, he attributes

the company's long-running success to its dedicated employees, loyal customers, faithful consumers, and helpful suppliers. "This is not just a birthday; it is a celebration of appreciation," says Becker.

As Cincinnati Coca-Cola Bottling Company moves into its second century, Becker says it will continue to bottle and to preserve the integrity of Coca-Cola products, and to serve all of the company's constituents. "For our customers, our aim is to provide superior service," says Becker. "As a corporate citizen, we will endeavor to enhance the quality of life in each and every local community. Finally, and most important, for our employees, we pledge to make Coca-Cola a great place to work and a source of pride, as we continue our rich heritage."

IN 2001, CINCINNATI COCA-COLA BOTTLING COMPANY PRODUCED AN ESTIMATED 50 MILLION CASES AND SHIPPED THEM THROUGHOUT OHIO, KENTUCKY, AND INDIANA.

Sena Weller Rohs Williams Inc.

SINCE 1901, SENA WELLER ROHS WILLIAMS INC. HAS BEEN HELPING CLIENTS INVEST THEIR CAPITAL WISELY. THE FIRM'S FORTE IS WORKING WITH CLIENTS TO UNDERSTAND THEIR NEEDS AND BUILDING SOLID, GROWTH-ORIENTED PORTFOLIOS THAT MEET THOSE NEEDS. ● SINCE ITS INCEPTION, THE COMPANY HAS FOCUSED ON DELIVERING EXCEPTIONAL SERVICE TO PRIVATE INVESTORS. "WE TOOK THE POSITION AT THE OUTSET THAT AN INVESTMENT COUNSELING FIRM

seeking an individual clientele should not be a merchandising enterprise, but, primarily, a well-informed source where the individual can get financial advice fitting to his or her own needs and interests," wrote W.H. Filmore, who founded the company more than a century ago.

While the company went through two name changes in the ensuing years, the principle of serving the needs of the individual investor remained constant. Today, the four partners for whom the firm is named are actively involved in the company and continue to offer fee-only investing services to clients who want to rely on a trusted adviser to increase their wealth.

"We understand the importance of communication and delivering the best possible service to those who invest with us," says William T. Sena, chairman. "Our focus today is the same one espoused by our founder, and it explains why several of our clients are the children and grandchildren of our earliest investors. Our clients know they can rely on us."

With 13 portfolio managers and 14 staff members, Sena Weller Rohs Williams is not interested in providing everything under one roof the way some larger firms do. "We focus on investing, and help coordinate financial planning or estate planning with other professionals," says Sena. "Our business focus ensures that we maintain our objectivity in selecting investments that are solely in the best interests of our clients."

Focus on Growth through Equities

But Sena Weller Rohs Williams has not developed such a loyal client base simply by offering personalized attention. The growth of clients' portfolios has demonstrated the validity of the company's equity orientation. "We consistently seek

to achieve above-average investment returns with limited risk," says Fred Weller, senior vice president. "We generally invest in companies that offer historically strong earnings growth and the promise of continuing this trend into the future."

While the company has adapted with the times and the changing nature of the investment business over the past century, Sena Weller Rohs Williams does not focus on trendy investments. The firm understands that no single investment method will consistently meet the needs of all investors, and that the need for conservation of principal,

income, and growth varies according to the client's circumstances. The company understands the importance of diversification, limiting capital risk, and asset balance. Sena Weller Rohs Williams takes a comprehensive approach to investing that considers market fundamentals and the relative valuation of investment alternatives to create the asset mix that will provide the highest potential return for growth, income, or conservation portfolios.

The firm has always been committed to the Greater Cincinnati community, as reflected by the involvement of the firm's employees in numerous civic, professional, and charitable organizations. David Osborn, senior vice president, is currently a trustee of the Cincinnati Society of Financial Analysts, and Weller and Peter Williams, senior vice president, are two of its past presidents.

As with its customer service, the key to the firm's investment success comes down to its consistency. Clients know what they can expect from Sena Weller Rohs Williams Inc. today, and a century's experience has taught them that they can count on the same unparalleled service and reliable results tomorrow.

THE DELOITTE & TOUCHE LLP MISSION INCLUDES "TO HELP OUR CLIENTS AND OUR PEOPLE EXCEL." LIVING UP TO THAT MISSION MEANS HIRING PEOPLE WITH BUSINESS KNOWLEDGE AND INDUSTRY EXPERTISE. EQUALLY IMPORTANT, IT MEANS HIRING PROFESSIONALS WITH A PASSION FOR PROBLEM SOLVING AND A COMMITMENT TO EXCELLENCE, AND HELPING THOSE PROFESSIONALS ACHIEVE THEIR ULTIMATE POTENTIAL BY PROVIDING GROWTH AND LEARNING OPPORTUNITIES.

"Our commitment to our employees strengthens the quality of service that we provide to our clients," says Gregory T. Bier, office managing partner. "We believe that outstanding people equal outstanding client service."

The professionals at Deloitte & Touche have helped the firm carve a niche for itself in the Cincinnati market. Operating from the Chiquita Center, the firm's more than 450 employees are dedicated to meeting clients' assurance, advisory, tax, and management consulting needs. A part of Deloitte Touche Tohmatsu, which employs more than 90,000 people in more than 130 countries, the firm has been active in Cincinnati since 1920. The office size in Cincinnati enables Deloitte & Touche to provide a wide array of value-added services locally in information technology, e-business, operations management, human resources, corporate tax, succession planning, employee benefits, mergers and acquisitions, and many other areas. In addition to those services, the firm has developed special expertise in many industry areas, including financial services, distribution, government, high technology, health care, insurance, manufacturing and consumer products, publishing and media, and real estate and construc-

tion. "Our size in this market allows us to support many specializations locally, which means many of our clients' specialized needs can be handled right here in Cincinnati," adds Bier. "This is a tremendous benefit to us and, more important, to our clients."

The coupling of its services and institutional understanding makes Deloitte & Touche a formidable force in the field of business services. This expertise has led such prominent local companies as Procter & Gamble, E.W. Scripps, Fifth Third Bancorp, Cincinnati Financial Corporation, and AK Steel to seek out the services of Deloitte & Touche.

The firm's professional advisers play an equally important role for emerging companies. In response to the ever changing needs of emerging companies, Deloitte & Touche created the Growth Company Services Group, which offers guidance on strategies for going public, writing effective business plans, managing mergers and acquisitions, e-business, and other areas of particular interest to growing firms. Bier adds, "Our Cincinnati Growth Company Services team does an outstanding job of adding value to our clients' operations. This group really focuses on doing whatever it takes to help our clients excel."

In addition to striving to exceed client expectations, the firm is dedicated to exceeding the expectations of its employees. Known as an employer of choice for its innovative human resources programs, Deloitte & Touche has been recognized as one of the 100 Best Companies to Work for in America by *Fortune* magazine for three consecutive years. "Again, the quality of professional services is directly linked with the quality of professionals delivering these services," Bier says. "Our innovative human resources programs, along with our outstanding clients in Cincinnati, allow us to provide tremendous opportunities for our professionals, helping us to recruit and retain the best and brightest, and ultimately provide exceptional service to our clients."

CLOCKWISE FROM TOP LEFT: DELOITTE & TOUCHE CINCINNATI'S LEADERSHIP INCLUDES (STANDING, FROM LEFT) JIM ELLERHORST, TAX MANAGING PARTNER; DENNIS FITZGERALD, AUDIT MANAGING PARTNER; (SEATED, FROM LEFT) TOM HABERMAN, ENTERPRISE RISK SERVICES MANAGING PARTNER; AND GREG BIER, OFFICE MANAGING PARTNER.

DELOITTE & TOUCHE AUDIT PARTNER NICK SOWAR AND TAX PROFESSIONALS MAGGIE DILLMAN (LEFT) AND NATALIE WEIS WORK TO PROVIDE QUALITY SERVICE BY MATCHING CLIENT NEEDS WITH A HIGHLY QUALIFIED, MULTIFUNCTIONAL TEAM OF DELOITTE & TOUCHE PROFESSIONALS.

GREG BIER IS OFFICE MANAGING PARTNER OF DELOITTE & TOUCHE CINCINNATI.

Steed Hammond Paul

FREDRICK MUELLER LAUNCHED HIS ARCHI-
TECTURAL FIRM MORE THAN A CENTURY AGO IN 1901, AND, WHILE STEED HAMMOND PAUL
MAY BE HOUSED IN A CINCINNATI SKYSCRAPER RATHER THAN A HAMILTON STOREFRONT,
THE FIRM'S BASIC VALUES AND COMMITMENT TO EXCELLENCE REMAIN UNCHANGED BY
TIME. ALTHOUGH THE FIRM HAS SWELLED TO SOME 110 EMPLOYEES AND MAINTAINS
OFFICES IN CINCINNATI, HAMILTON, AND COLUMBUS, IT IS STILL DEDICATED TO THE

notion that a building is not a monument to the architect, but an aesthetically pleasing response to the needs and values of a community.

Steed Hammond Paul's contributions to the Greater Cincinnati landscape are impressive. The firm, which specializes in public buildings and schools, designed the Hamilton branch campus of Miami University in the 1960s. As the firm grew in the Cincinnati area, it added its signature to a variety of buildings throughout southwestern Ohio, including the Fitton Center for Creative Arts, the Hospice of Cincinnati, and the new Fairfield Branch of the Lane Public Library.

In the past some 25 years, the firm's work designing schools defined the focus for Steed Hammond Paul. The firm's unique Schoolhouse

STEED HAMMOND PAUL'S CONTRIBUTIONS TO THE GREATER CINCINNATI LANDSCAPE INCLUDE THE LANE LIBRARY MAIN BRANCH (TOP) AND THE WALNUT HILLS HIGH SCHOOL ARTS AND SCIENCE CENTER LOBBY (BOTTOM).

of Quality process, which incorporates user feedback into the design while objectively considering the final product, reflects the needs of students, teachers, parents, taxpayers, and the community as a whole. This has made Steed Hammond Paul a trailblazer in the school construction arena. In 1997 alone, the firm helped open 10 new schools. The firm's consistent record of thoughtfully designed, user-friendly buildings has made Steed Hammond Paul the leader in the field and has translated into abundant projects.

Schoolhouse of Quality

The Schoolhouse of Quality process is an objective system for reflecting the collective voice of a school's users. Because the system is objective, it ensures that input from the most subdued participants receives the same consideration as that of the most vocal. Because the Schoolhouse of Quality process factors in the needs of the entire community—from the teachers, administrators, and students who use the schools every day to the parents who attend plays, games, and PTA meetings and the taxpayers who finance it—the process is comprehensive. The firm recognizes that

schools are not merely places of learning, but are community resource centers and, as such, must meet the needs of a broad variety of constituents. Even as the company takes on a wider range of projects including universities, early childhood learning centers, and private schools, it relies on its feedback process to ensure that each building is a bricks-and-mortar response to customer needs.

Steed Hammond Paul has an open approach to working with clients. The ability to consider the clients' needs and respond to them in every aspect of the design process has led many districts to commission repeat work. The Lakota Local School District contracted with Steed Hammond Paul to build nearly one new building a year during the 1990s. Numerous other projects—including Fairfield High School, Nagel Middle School in Forest Hills, and projects throughout Greater Cincinnati— likewise are testimonies to the success of Steed Hammond Paul's recipe for schools.

While Steed Hammond Paul owes its success to a century of sound projects, loyal clients, and talented architects, the firm's longevity can be attributed to its ability to flourish as

a community-based practice. Today, the community is larger and broader than in the past. Projects are subject to a myriad of global influences, thanks to technology and the diverse experience and exposure of the firm's staff, making Steed Hammond Paul's services ever more diverse and far reaching.

The Strength of a Team

The reason Steed Hammond Paul is so successful at listening to diverse points of view and uniting them into a cohesive product is because the company participates in that kind of interaction daily. The firm does more than don its team-building skills for clients; it uses them daily to help staff members realize their full potential.

"When I was playing basketball at UC [University of Cincinnati], I learned the importance of team building," explains Dale Heidotting, AIA, a senior vice president. "Everyone on the team had a specific skill and strength they brought to the team, and everyone had to work together in order to win games. It's the same here. Our team members support whoever has 'the ball' in order to meet not only team goals, but also the goals of the firm as a whole."

While many companies tout their teamwork, Steed Hammond Paul's low turnover and the easy camaraderie of its staff members provide solid backing to the claim. "What makes our firm truly different is an appreciation of the individual," says Gerald Hammond, company president and AIA Fellow. "By recognizing the special strengths of each person, we are able to provide oppor-

tunities for every member of this firm to shine in his or her own way."

Those changes are minor in light of what has not changed: the firm's consistent and unwavering focus on

the customer. Steed Hammond Paul's guiding principle of "architecture built around the customer" will continue to shape the firm's creations long into the new century.

THE FIRM'S UNIQUE SCHOOLHOUSE OF QUALITY PROCESS INCORPORATES USER FEEDBACK INTO THE DESIGN AND HAS BEEN USED IN THE FAIRFIELD HIGH SCHOOL AUDITORIUM (TOP LEFT), THE NAGEL MIDDLE SCHOOL LOBBY (TOP RIGHT), AND THE LAKOTA EAST HIGH SCHOOL (CENTER).

THE STEED HAMMOND PAUL SIGNATURE HAS BEEN ADDED TO THE HOSPICE OF CINCINNATI.

MANY ORGANIZATIONS PROFESS MISSION STATEMENTS, BUT TWIN TOWERS ACTUALLY LIVES ONE. WHEN DR. HENRY WEAKLEY, A METHODIST MINISTER, FOUNDED TWIN TOWERS IN 1899 AS A RETIREMENT COMMUNITY FOR AGING MINISTERS AND MEMBERS OF THE LAITY, HE PROFESSED, "THE MORAL WORTH OF A CIVILIZATION—A NATION, A CHURCH, OR A FAMILY—MAY BE EXPRESSED BY THE CARE IT GIVES ITS ELDERS." THERE IS NO HIGHER EXPRESSION OF SPIRIT AND HELPFULNESS TO

humanity, he wrote, "than in gracious ministry to the aged."

While a great deal has changed since that time, Twin Towers' commitment to serving the senior adult is as abiding as it was more than a century ago. The continuing care retirement community's mission remains the same: to provide life-enriching services and accommodations for senior adults through a caring, Christian community.

Meeting Changing Needs

As rich as its history may be, Twin Towers isn't stuck in the past. The company has broadened its mission to embrace new challenges and has expanded its services to meet the emerging needs of older Americans. Twin Towers' growth has meant extending its services to more residents: The community that cared for just 15 residents when it was founded is now home to about 600. Growth has also meant developing new living and care arrangements to ensure residents' needs are met.

"The continuum of care is the most important element of any retirement community," says Bill

Parker, Twin Towers' senior director of project management. "Our residents will tell us that they are looking to make the last move of their lives. When they come here, they know they will be able to age in a beautiful place and enjoy a high quality of life. That's very important."

Toward that end, Twin Towers has added independent living cottages and apartments, assisted living,

and skilled nursing facilities. That range of services ensures that active seniors can remain independent while enjoying the peace of mind that they will not have to leave behind friends and family members if they eventually require more care. In the same spirit, Twin Towers offers day care services for residents and senior adults of the community, so that their primary caregivers can work or attend to other obligations, knowing their loved ones are being cared for in a nurturing environment.

"We want to offer a full array of options to older adults," says Scott McQuinn, president and CEO. "We want to be flexible and versatile enough to meet their needs as they change and as new needs arise."

Twin Towers' emphasis on adaptability and responsiveness to its residents needs is seen in a number of ongoing improvements being made to the scenic, 120-acre facility. In 2001, the organization unveiled a massive, new wellness and community center. The new facilities include a lap pool, expanded exercise facilities, and enhanced multipurpose and common areas, promoting Twin Tower's focus on holistic health.

FINE AND CASUAL DINING IS AMONG THE AMENITIES FEATURED AT TWIN LAKES AND TWIN TOWERS (TOP).

WHEN RESIDENTS COME TO EITHER TWIN TOWERS OR TWIN LAKES, THEY KNOW THEY WILL BE ABLE TO AGE IN A BEAUTIFUL PLACE AND ENJOY A HIGH QUALITY OF LIFE (BOTTOM).

Offering New Options

At Twin Towers, health isn't simply a barometer of a person's physical well-being, McQuinn explains. Rather, the term encompasses an individual's physical, emotional, social, intellectual, spiritual, and vocational health. To balance all these measures of health, individuals must enjoy life-enriching experiences in a variety of areas. Understanding that, Twin Towers offers a beautiful chapel, an impressive art gallery, and a social dining area to help residents feel spiritually, emotionally, and socially connected. In addition, Twin Towers provides an array of creative and physical activities in which residents can take part. Shuttle service to shopping and community events is also available to broaden residents' entertainment options.

In focusing on holistic health, Twin Towers understands that individuals need to feel like important participants in a community. The implementation of an Eden Alternative program addresses this need at Twin Towers. Based on the principle that loneliness, helplessness, and boredom account for the bulk of suffering among older people, Eden communities emphasize companionship and interaction with children, plants, and animals to keep elderly residents engaged in the world around them.

Just as it is expanding the services and facilities available to its residents, Twin Towers is reaching out to older adults with a new facility in Montgomery, Ohio. Twin Lakes, a 56-acre, continuing care community, is located near the intersection of Montgomery and Perin roads. The red-brick complex, modeled in the Georgian style of architecture, offers the same types of amenities as Twin Towers, as well as similar housing options. The landscaped campus will include a scenic path for walking and bicycling; fine and casual dining; fitness and wellness programs; and a full calendar of events, lectures, and classes.

As with Twin Towers, however, the most important feature of Twin Lakes can't be drawn on a blueprint. This feature is the security residents enjoy by knowing that, whatever changes life brings, they are part of a nurturing, compassionate community that will embrace their needs.

CLOCKWISE FROM TOP LEFT: TWIN LAKES INCLUDES A LANDSCAPED CAMPUS WITH A SCENIC PATH FOR WALKING.

INTERACTION WITH PETS IS EMPHASIZED TO KEEP RESIDENTS ENGAGED IN THE WORLD AROUND THEM.

IN FOCUSING ON HOLISTIC HEALTH, TWIN TOWERS AND TWIN LAKES UNDERSTAND THAT INDIVIDUALS NEED TO FEEL LIKE IMPORTANT PARTICIPANTS IN A COMMUNITY.

AN ARRAY OF CREATIVE AND PHYSICAL ACTIVITIES ARE OFFERED AT BOTH TWIN LAKES AND TWIN TOWERS.

R.A. Jones & Co. Inc.

FOUNDED NEARLY 100 YEARS AGO, R.A. JONES & CO. INC. IS A LEADING DESIGNER AND SUPPLIER OF PACKAGING EQUIPMENT, SYSTEMS, AND ROBOTICS. THE COMPANY ALSO MANAGES ONE OF THE INDUSTRY'S LARGEST BASES OF PACKAGING EQUIPMENT, WITH MORE THAN 8,000 MACHINES AND 300 SYSTEMS INSTALLED WORLDWIDE. THE COVINGTON-BASED FIRM HAS CONTINUED TO THRIVE BY STAYING FOCUSED ON ITS CORE VALUES AND ITS COMMITMENT TO THE

Jones family of customers, suppliers, and employees.

R.A. Jones, which employs more than 500 people, traces its roots back to 1905 when Ruel Anderson Jones, a dentist by training, developed a soap press that embedded an advertising message into a cake of soap. Dr. Jones followed up on his invention a few years later when he launched a soap packaging machine, an invention that paved the way for the company's future.

R.A. JONES & CO. INC. IS HEADQUARTERED IN COVINGTON AND EMPLOYS MORE THAN 500 PEOPLE. THE FACILITY RESIDES ON A BEAUTIFUL, 33-ACRE TRACT WITH SOME 233,000 SQUARE FEET OF OFFICE AND MANUFACTURING SPACE.

ORGANIZED INTO CUSTOMER-DEFINED TEAMS, JONES' ACCOUNT MANAGERS AND TECHNICAL MANAGERS ARE INDUSTRY SPECIALISTS, WHICH ALLOWS THE TEAMS TO DEVELOP LONG-TERM RELATIONSHIPS WITH BUSINESS-PARTNER COMPANIES AND TO HAVE A VESTED INTEREST IN CUSTOMER SATISFACTION.

A Century of Innovation and Service

During the years since its founding, R.A. Jones has developed a variety of elegant solutions to tough packaging problems. Today, the firm manufactures a wide variety of packaging equipment that it markets to companies in the food, beverage, pharmaceutical, personal products, auto parts, and communications and electronics industries.

Whether trying to put facial tissues in a box or candy in a bag, Jones' clients know they can count on the venerable manufacturer to find a reliable solution. Jones, which manufactures the bulk of its products at its Covington facility, specializes in secondary packaging; the firm designs and manufactures machines that are used to put primary containers such as bags, bottles, tubes, and pouches into boxes.

Jones manufactures cartoners that can package products—as small as individual boxes of razor blades or as large as 32-can packages of soft drinks—into cartons for shipment. The company makes pouching machines that are used to create packages for such diverse items as single-serving sugar containers and dry soup mixes. Jones also makes multipacker machines that can pack layers of a product and divide items with cardboard separators.

Jones also makes tray-packing and pouching machines. Thanks to recent investments in servo-driven, wash-down cartoners and pouch machines, which meet high standards for food packaging, Jones is expanding into additional food markets.

Support after the Sale

Jones' clients know they can count on the company for service as well. Should a piece of equipment require maintenance, Jones'

highly skilled after-market services (AMS) team is on call 24 hours a day, seven days a week to correct the problem with minimal downtime. The company's reputation for reliability is so well entrenched, in fact, that Jones promises to stand by its equipment for 50 years as part of its 50-Year Promise.

Given the fact that many pieces of Jones equipment in the field today are more than 50 years old, that promise is more than idle chatter. It's an insurance policy safeguarding the equipment's productivity.

As important as longevity is, Jones understands that technology and business need change. That's why its industry-leading Conversions, Updates, and Rebuilds programs and the Jones Preventative Maintenance Group are available to help clients keep their packaging lines running at peak productivity. What's more, because members of Jones' staff collectively are fluent in 15 different languages, communication is never a problem, no matter where an international client is based.

Jones also understands that clients sometimes support multiple vendors,

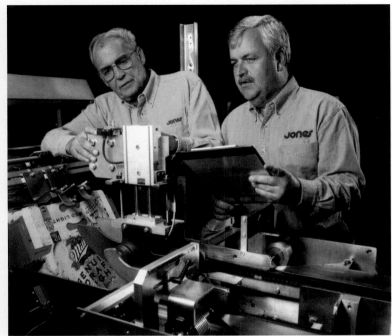

and that the success of a production line depends on the compatibility of many different pieces of equipment. The firm's integration services group helps clients overcome compatibility obstacles and the ensuing headaches by designing systems that link their various machines, even if they're not Jones products. The company's team of integration experts, which includes project managers, on-site coordinators, and systems and packaging-control engineers, helps clients achieve the operational line speed, up-time efficiency, and product-flow rates they need.

A Corporation with Family Values

Today, Jones is able to capitalize on the best aspects of both small and large firms. Although the Jones and Motch families, which owned and ran the firm for generations, sold it in 1998, R.A. Jones still operates according to the guiding principles set by its founder.

As part of IWKA, a $2 billion, German firm that operates several packaging machine companies as part of its PACUNION Group, Jones shares a long-term focus and a commitment to investing in cutting-edge technology with its parent. Jones benefits from IWKA's considerable resources, particularly in the area of research and development, while maintaining the entrepreneurial spirit for which it is so well known.

"When we stop and look back at our nearly 10 decades of successful operations and talk with our many longtime customers, we are reminded that Jones has established a proud

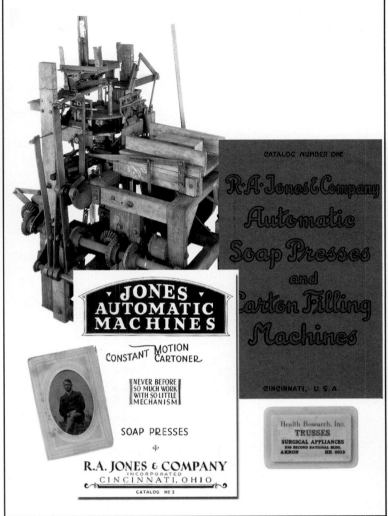

corporate heritage for excellence, reliability, and innovation," says Ralph J. Olson, president. "In 1905, Ruel Anderson Jones set a cornerstone of strong corporate and personal values. As we continue to build on his solid foundation, R.A. and his successors would be proud to see the manner in which we are guiding Jones into its second century."

CLOCKWISE FROM TOP LEFT: THE GOAL OF R.A. JONES IS TO SATISFY ITS CUSTOMERS' PACKAGING NEEDS BY PROVIDING TOP-QUALITY, HIGHLY RELIABLE MACHINERY WITH INNOVATIVE APPLICATION SOLUTIONS, WHICH ARE COUPLED WITH RESPONSIVE, COST-EFFECTIVE SERVICES.

IN 1905, RUEL ANDERSON JONES FOUNDED R.A. JONES & COMPANY AND BEGAN THE BUSINESS BY DEVELOPING AND MANUFACTURING A NOVELTY ITEM HE CALLED "ADVERTISING SOAP."

THE CRITERION 2000 IS THE BEGINNING OF THE NEXT GENERATION OF MODULAR-DESIGNED, SERVO-DRIVEN CARTONERS FROM JONES. IT CAN BE EASILY CONFIGURED AS A CONSTANT OR INTERMITTENT MOTION CARTONER, AND THE MULTI-AXIS DESIGN YIELDS SHORTER DELIVERY TIME, INCREASED RELIABILITY, GREATER EFFICIENCY AND FLEXIBILITY, REDUCED MAINTENANCE, AND STANDARDIZATION OF PARTS.

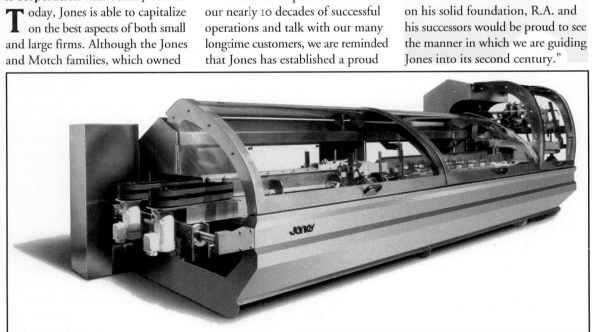

Ohio National Financial Services

I's not just Ohio National Financial Services' well-appointed new building, located north of Cincinnati just off Interstate 71, that is attracting attention. Ohio National has garnered national headlines in the past several years, thanks to dramatic growth and expansion into new markets, both in the United States and in Latin America. ● Tracing its origins to a one-room office in downtown Cincinnati, Ohio National was incorporated in 1909 and wrote its first policy the following year. By 1914, the company had $2 million of life insurance in force, and the numbers have only grown from there. Between 1979 and 2000, Ohio National increased its assets under management from $700 million to $9.3 billion, and total revenues were nearly $1.8 billion at year-end 2000.

Today, Ohio National's affiliates help meet the individual and financial needs of individuals and businesses in 47 states, the District of Columbia, Puerto Rico, and Chile, by offering a comprehensive array of products including life insurance, annuities, retirement planning products, mutual funds, and disability insurance. The keys to the company's success: building long-term relationships with customers and providing them with quality products and services.

"There's no question that building and protecting one's financial security in today's ever-changing environment presents opportunities and challenges for our customers," says David B. O'Maley, Ohio National's chairman, president, and chief executive officer. "We want to do all we can to examine ways to better serve our customers and, at the same time, further enhance the features of our core business products to meet their evolving needs."

Quality Products and Services

While focusing on growth, Ohio National has never sacrificed quality. During 2000, the major rating agencies reaffirmed the ratings of its life insurance affiliates: AA from Standard & Poor's for financial security characteristics, AA from Fitch for claims-paying ability, A1 from Moody's for financial strength, and A+ Superior from A.M. Best based on financial strength and operating performance to meet ongoing obligations to policyholders.

These ratings place The Ohio National Life Insurance Company and Ohio National Life Assurance Corporation among the top 7 percent of all life insurers. "Our outstanding ratings are not something we take for granted," O'Maley says.

Ohio National's team of dedicated professionals constantly work to ensure the products they market and the services they deliver to their clients are top of the line. New distribution channels, including a rapidly expanding network of banks and securities brokerage firms, complement Ohio National's long-standing agency network, and make the company's outstanding products accessible to more and more consumers.

At year-end 2000, more than 2,400 general agents and sales associates—and nearly 160 securities brokerage firms and banks with more than 15,000 representatives nationwide—offered Ohio National products. For clients who prefer to shop electronically, the company's term life insurance products also are available on several Internet sites, on which quotes and the initial application process are provided.

Expansion into New Markets

Today's marketplace is global in scope, and Ohio National recently entered the international marketplace. In April 2000, the company announced the acquisition of BHIFAmerica Seguros de Vida, one of the top 20 life and annuity companies in Chile. Now named Ohio National Seguros de Vida, the Santiago-based insurer recorded more than $25 million of written premiums in 2000, with nearly $225 million of consolidated assets. This acquisition, the first outside the United States, reflects the company's strategy to expand its core businesses into attractive, emerging markets.

"We believe the medium- to long-term prospects for the Latin American insurance industry are

David B. O'Maley serves as Ohio National Financial Services' chairman, president, and chief executive officer.

very attractive," O'Maley explains. "We further believe Chile is particularly strong due to a stable economy, its expanding private pension marketplace, and a growing acceptance of and desire for life insurance."

New growth initiatives announced in early 2000 also help Ohio National build its strategic growth areas of life insurance and asset accumulation products. In May 2001, the company announced plans to jointly own and operate a New York-based life insurance company to sell variable life insurance and annuity products. Plans call for the new company to be named National Security Life and Annuity Company (NSLA). The venture will allow the Ohio National enterprise to have access to the large New York market, and also capitalizes on the company's network of banks and brokerage affiliations. "We look forward to entering the New York market with a very competitive product portfolio offered by NSLA," O'Maley adds. "Variable products have been a competitive strength for Ohio National for more than 30 years."

Future growth of the company was further enhanced in 1998 when the company's policyholders voted overwhelmingly to approve a reorganization under a mutual holding company structure. Now, the policyholders of the former mutual life insurance company—The Ohio National Life Insurance Company—comprise the voting members of Ohio National Mutual Holdings, Inc., which in turn controls Ohio National Financial Services, Inc.

The new structure allows shares of stock of Ohio National Financial Services, Inc. to be sold to raise capital. Although the company has no immediate plans for a public offering, the potential availability of equity capital provides the company with a strong foundation for future growth.

A Place Where People Want to Work

Ohio National has made major commitments to create a healthy, vibrant workplace for its hardworking employees. The company moved into a state-of-the-art, 220,000-square-foot building in 1996. Equipped with ergonomic workstations, convenience store, walking trail, free garage parking, and fully equipped fitness center, the building helped Ohio National win a spot on *Fortune* magazine's list of 100 Best Companies to Work For in 1998 and 1999. Contributing to that recognition were the company's flexible hours, flexible benefit plans, comprehensive wellness program, and generous pension and profit-sharing plans, all of which highlight the company's commitment to its employees.

"We are proud to say that our business has continued to grow and prosper thanks to the support of our customers, and thanks to the significant efforts of thousands of dedicated and loyal associates in Cincinnati and across the country," O'Maley says. "Our business success and financial performance mark Ohio National as a financial services provider that has met the test of time and is eager to embrace the challenges of the future."

BETWEEN 1979 AND 2000, OHIO NATIONAL INCREASED ITS ASSETS UNDER MANAGEMENT FROM $700 MILLION TO $9.3 BILLION, AND TOTAL REVENUES WERE NEARLY $1.8 BILLION AT YEAR-END 2000.

Givaudan

ONE THING CAN CERTAINLY BE SAID OF GIVAUDAN: ITS WORK IS NEVER BLAND. THIS IS PARTLY BECAUSE THE COMPANY HAS ENJOYED TREMENDOUS GROWTH IN RECENT YEARS; PARTLY BECAUSE GIVAUDAN IS ONE OF THE LARGEST FLAVOR MAKERS IN THE WORLD, WITH OPERATIONS IN MORE THAN 40 COUNTRIES; AND MAINLY BECAUSE GIVAUDAN'S FOCUS IS ON MAKING WHAT WE ALL EAT AND DRINK TASTE BETTER. ● GIVAUDAN, BASED IN VERNIER, SWITZERLAND, OWES MUCH TO

brothers Leon and Xiavier Givaudan, who founded a flavor and fragrance company bearing their name in 1895, and to Claude Roure, who founded Roure in 1820. Roche, an international pharmaceutical, vitamins, and diagnostics company acquired both Givaudan and Roure, and later merged the two. Givaudan came to Cincinnati in 1997 when it purchased Tastemaker, a flavors company that was founded in the area in 1913. In June 2000, Roche spun off Givaudan Roure as a publicly held, independent firm known simply as Givaudan.

Although Givaudan manufactures both flavors and fragrances, its Cincinnati operation is dedicated to the flavor side of the business. Local operations include the company's global research and develop-

ment center, management, regional sales and marketing, and a manufacturing facility. The company also operates the only USDA-approved flavor manufacturing facility in the industry, located in nearby Devon, Kentucky.

Every Flavor Imaginable

Operationally, Givaudan is divided into business units: beverage, sweet goods, savory, and dairy. Collectively, the units develop flavors for everything from chicken to ice cream, a range that explains why Givaudan is a leader in the $4 billion flavors industry.

Givaudan strives to create sensory advantage for its clients by focusing on trends, and determining which aromas and tastes will most appeal to consumers and influence their eating and drinking habits.

Given the complexity of the task, Givaudan does not rely on a

ALTHOUGH GIVAUDAN MANUFACTURES BOTH FLAVORS AND FRAGRANCES, ITS CINCINNATI OPERATION IS DEDICATED TO THE FLAVOR SIDE OF THE BUSINESS.

standard calculus to create its flavor. As Bob Eilerman, senior vice president of research and development, explains, "Creating great flavors is an artful melding of science, creativity, and culinary art."

Although the company maintains a library of more than 1,000 flavors, the Givaudan flavor portfolio is actually far larger, given the number of customized flavors the company develops on a project-by-project basis. Still, there are certain ingredients Givaudan brings to every assignment through its core values: customer focus, a sense of urgency, and ambitious innovation. "The importance of those values cannot be understated, because they are the components necessary to fulfill Givaudan's mission—Creating Sensory Advantage—for its clients," says Bob Pellegrino, president of Flavors North America.

Research Is Key

In its never ending effort to create sensory advantage, Givaudan goes, quite literally, to the ends of the earth to stay that much further ahead in the field. One such effort, based in research and development, is Givaudan's TasteTrek™ program. As part of its TasteTrek's, Givaudan sends analytical scientists and flavorists around the globe in search of exotic and little-known fruits, spices, and other botanicals that serve as the inspiration for new flavors.

On one recent expedition, the Givaudan teams spent a total of two months exploring the rain forest canopy of Gabon in central Africa. Using an enormous blimp to explore the treetops, the researchers uncovered hundreds of previously unknown flavors and even cataloged a handful of new species. Sensitive to the delicate ecology of the regions the company explores, Givaudan

conducts its research according to the most assiduous environmental standards, and works with non-profit groups to help local people use natural resources in sustainable, environmentally responsible ways.

Givaudan does not always travel so far to develop its flavors, however. In fact, many are created in Cincinnati, using developments from the company's new, $20 million, global research center. Completed in February 2000, the 64,000-square-foot research facility features a state-of-the-art sensory and taste evaluation laboratory, a flavor-engineering laboratory, and biotechnology and analytical laboratories. Givaudan owes much of its success to the Cincinnati facility—part laboratory, part magician's workshop and artist's studio. Cincinnati is home to many of Givaudan's artists in lab coats, and is one of the reasons the company enjoys the sweet taste of success.

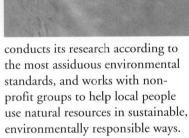

As part of the TasteTrek program, Givaudan sends analytical scientists and flavorists around the globe in search of exotic and little-known fruits, spices, and other botanicals that serve as the inspiration for new flavors.

Noveon Hilton Davis, Inc.

BORN AS A DOWNTOWN CONSULTING FIRM TO THE PRINTING INK INDUSTRY IN 1922, THE MANUFACTURING FACILITY THAT TODAY BEARS THE NAME NOVEON HILTON DAVIS, INC. HAS OCCUPIED TWO LOCATIONS AND BEEN THROUGH NUMEROUS METAMORPHOSES. STILL, THE PLANT—WHICH HAS MANUFACTURED EVERYTHING FROM PRINTING INKS TO PHARMACEUTICAL INTERMEDIATES DURING ITS LONG AND STORIED HISTORY—IS JUST BEGINNING TO HIT ITS STRIDE THANKS TO ITS

1998 acquisition by Noveon Hilton Davis.

The Langdon Farm Road facility currently operated by Noveon Hilton Davis opened in 1927. Even during its earliest days, the plant established itself as an important corporate citizen by signing a 99-year lease with the City of Norwood that enabled the municipality to establish part of the Fenwick Park from 10 of the plant's 85 acres.

A New Chapter in the Company's History

Sold by its founders in the mid-1940s, the facility traded hands a number of times prior to its 1998 acquisition by Noveon Hilton Davis, a $5.5 billion, multi-industry firm based in Charlotte. While many people still think of Noveon Hilton Davis as a tire manufacturer, the company no longer makes tires. Today, Noveon Hilton Davis' operations are concentrated in three areas: aerospace, performance materials, and engineered industrial products.

Noveon Hilton Davis purchased the Cincinnati facility as a strategic way to grow its performance materials business. This division supplies performance polymer systems and additives for a broad range of consumer and industrial applications in value-added growth markets such as personal care, pharmaceuticals, food, textiles, medical, electronics, transportation, and construction. The Cincinnati facility, which manufactures dyes, pigments, and color formers, is an important part of that sector.

"This is the largest plant in terms of employees in the entire performance materials group, and it's a vital part of Noveon Hilton Davis' overall operations," explains Mike Muirhead, plant manager. "Food ingredients are a growth area for the Performance Materials division, and this plant will play an important role in that because that's a key component of our operations here."

Although the plant's product lines fall into three general categories, the products into which they are ultimately incorporated are virtually limitless. For example, Noveon Hilton Davis, Inc. is the second-largest manufacturer of food colors in the United States. The company's water-soluble dyes are used to color a variety of food products, including soft drinks, candy, and dog food. The company also manufactures technical dyes used in products such as cleaning solutions, textiles, and paper, as well as cosmetic colors. Noveon Hilton Davis, Inc.'s pigments are used in the ink and paint industries, and its color formers are used to make carbonless-copy business forms and thermal fax paper.

Although the plant doesn't manufacture any consumer products, it would be difficult to go through the day without touching a product that owes its existence, at least in part, to Noveon Hilton Davis, Inc. Whether drinking a soft drink at a restaurant, painting the house, cleaning the kitchen, or changing the thermal fax paper in the office,

THE NOVEON HILTON DAVIS, INC. FACILITY MANUFACTURES DYES, PIGMENTS, AND COLOR FORMERS.

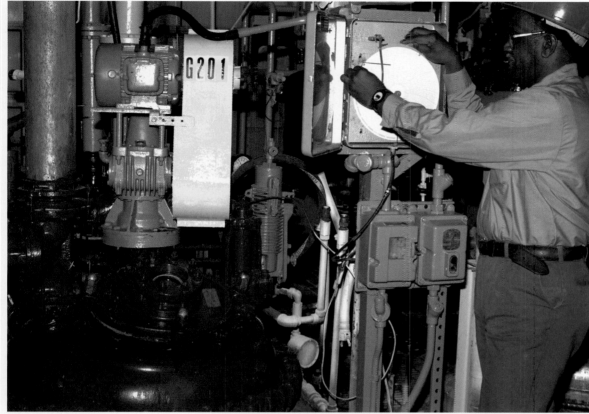

there's a good chance consumers are handling a product that contains ingredients born at Noveon Hilton Davis, Inc. "People may not think about us as they go through their days, but we think about them all the time," says Muirhead.

Caring about Its Employees

Noveon Hilton Davis' focus on people doesn't stop with its customers or the end users of its products. The manufacturer is equally concerned with the welfare of its some 250 employees, who work in three shifts each day to keep the facility humming 365 days a year. During its first full year of ownership, Noveon Hilton Davis reduced OSHA-recorded injuries at the plant—compared to the average annual injury rate over the previous 50 years—by 70 percent. As a result, workers are statistically safer on the job than they would be in their own homes.

Still, Muirhead insists that the strides Noveon Hilton Davis has made are only the beginning. "Our goal in the not-too-distant future is to make this an injury-free facility," he says. "We won't be satisfied with our safety record until we've achieved that."

Part of the Community

Noveon Hilton Davis, Inc. has demonstrated a similar concern for the community. The facility is investigating the formation of a Community Advisory Panel (CAP) in an effort to educate community representatives about the plant's operations and to share important updates about its plans.

"We want to get key community members involved," explains Muirhead. "We plan to meet once a month in an effort to take the mystery out of what we do here. We want to build a relationship with the community."

The site's community involvement, which began some 75 years ago when it leased parkland to the city, continues today. Noveon Hilton Davis, Inc. actively supports United Way, and its employees participate in mentoring and outreach programs in area schools. In addition, the company's on-site emergency medical technicians are available to the community, should a need ever arise.

"Everyone here understands the importance of being a good corporate citizen," Muirhead says. "After all, we don't just work in this community. We live here."

NOVEON HILTON DAVIS, INC. IS THE SECOND-LARGEST MANUFACTURER OF FOOD COLORS IN THE UNITED STATES.

The Vernon Manor Hotel

CROSS OLD-WORLD CHARM WITH HIGH-TECH AMENITIES, PLANT THE RESULTS IN THE HEART OF CINCINNATI'S HISTORIC UPTOWN DISTRICT, AND THE VERNON MANOR HOTEL IS THE RESULT. FROM THE MOMENT THEY TURN INTO THE HOTEL'S COBBLESTONED DRIVE, GUESTS KNOW THEY'VE ARRIVED AT A SPECIAL PLACE. ● MODELED AFTER THE STATELY ENGLISH MANOR THAT WAS ONCE HOME TO THE EARL OF PERCY IN HERTFORDSHIRE, ENGLAND, THE VERNON MANOR HOTEL

offers a boutique alternative to a downtown hotel. Built in 1924 as a retreat for wealthy Cincinnati residents from the busy downtown riverfront district, The Vernon Manor Hotel has since become the home away from home for hundreds of notables on their visits to the Queen City. Celebrities including former Presidents Lyndon Johnson, John Kennedy, and George Bush; the Beatles; and Tiger Woods have all been guests at The Vernon Manor Hotel.

Tradition Meets High-Tech

Despite its rich history, The Vernon Manor Hotel is anything but a stodgy relic. Thanks to a three-year renovation completed in 1999, the 177-room hotel is as fresh today as it was on the day it opened. The sumptuously paneled and chandelier-bedecked lobby, the rooftop garden, and other stately touches of a grande dame hotel coexist in exquisite harmony with electronic door locks, a 24-hour fitness room, and all the other amenities of a modern hotel. Located just minutes from downtown Cincinnati, The Vernon Manor Hotel has always

forged its identity on the marriage of charm and convenience.

The hotel's veteran staff understands that the life of a traveler can be exhausting even if the day has been filled with leisurely pursuits like squeezing in a Reds game or catching a Broadway show at the Aronoff Center for the Arts. That's why they are committed to making life more pleasant and convenient for road-weary guests. Rooms, which

range from one- and two-bedroom suites to individual rooms with king-sized or two queen-sized beds, have been renovated with all the extras, such as irons, ironing boards, and hair dryers, as well as luxurious, thoughtful touches like English-milled soaps. Other conveniences, such as on-site and valet parking, coffee and newspaper service, and area shuttle transportation, all of which are complimentary,

BUILT IN 1924, THE VERNON MANOR HOTEL WAS MODELED AFTER THE STATELY ENGLISH MANOR THAT WAS ONCE HOME TO THE EARL OF PERCY IN HERTFORDSHIRE, ENGLAND (TOP).

RANGING FROM ONE- AND TWO-BEDROOM SUITES TO INDIVIDUAL ROOMS WITH KING-SIZED OR TWO QUEEN-SIZED BEDS, THE GUEST ROOMS AT THE VERNON MANOR HOTEL HAVE BEEN RENOVATED WITH ALL THE EXTRAS, SUCH AS IRONS, IRONING BOARDS, AND HAIR DRYERS, AS WELL AS LUXURIOUS, THOUGHTFUL TOUCHES LIKE ENGLISH-MILLED SOAPS (BOTTOM LEFT AND RIGHT).

likewise make life on the road
a pleasure.

Business Travelers' Paradise

Business travelers in particular
will appreciate the hotel's two
24-hour business centers equipped
with workstations, halogen lamps,
telephones with dataports, fax machines, computers, and printers.
Those who prefer to work in the
privacy of their rooms will be grateful that guest rooms are equipped
with work areas and a telephone,
complete with voice mail and a
computer dataport.

The Vernon Manor Hotel likewise offers impeccable meeting facilities that include 13 private rooms
able to accommodate groups ranging
from five to 225. Although meeting
rooms are outfitted with state-of-
the-art audiovisual equipment and
satellite videoconferencing—making
them ideal for corporate functions—
the warmth of the intimate Oak Room
and the grandeur of the Regency
Ballroom make them equally fitting
for weddings and other celebrations.

Whether they've attended a
productive conference or caught
the bouquet at a friend's wedding,
guests seeking to unwind at the end
of a long day will enjoy The Vernon
Manor Hotel's award-winning Forum
Grill and English-style pub, Club
400. Named by the original owners
for the lively discussions and heated
debates that took place there, the
Forum specializes in steaks, chops,
and grilled seafood. Although its

breakfast, lunch, and dinner menus
are sure to delight guests, diners
won't want to miss the restaurant's
famous Sunday brunch that offers
a wide selection of entrées, a waffle
and omelet station, carved roasts,
poached salmon, and a sinful dessert station.

Club 400, which is open for
lunch and late-night snacks, offers
a fine selection of microbrews, cigars,
and single-malt scotches, and features live jazz on weekends. Room
service is likewise available for guests
who prefer to nestle in their rooms
and catch a movie on cable or
pay-per-view.

The hotel offers other on-site
services as well, including a florist,
barbershop, beauty salon, and auto-
detailing service, all of which make
it appealing to guests needing long-
term accommodations. The Vernon
Manor Hotel's 58 suites and apartments, all of which include newly
renovated kitchens featuring dish-
washers, microwaves, stove tops,
and refrigerators, are a charming
alternative to antiseptic extended-
stay hotels. Extended-stay guests
will appreciate the pampering the
hotel's staff lavishes. In addition to
having their beds made and receiving fresh towels daily, they'll enjoy
full daily housekeeping service and
have access to coin-operated laundry
facilities, daily coffee-to-go in the
lobby, free newspaper delivery to
their suites, free local calls, and
shuttle service to area shopping,
dining, and entertainment.

The Personal Touch

While The Vernon Manor
Hotel's charm and conve-
nient location just minutes away
from the downtown sports, entertainment, and business districts
may draw travelers the first time,
General Manager Michel Sheer
says it's the hotel's warm, attentive
staff that brings them back. One
of the prime advantages of a small
hotel, according to Sheer, is that
staff members can deliver the personalized service a larger hotel can't.
Guests shouldn't be surprised when
the desk clerk greets them by name
or the bartender learns their preferred brands of scotch.

More than fine dining and el-
egantly appointed rooms, Sheer
says, personalized service is what
makes The Vernon Manor Hotel
special. "Whether they stay with us
for a night or for several months,"
says Sheer, "our staff will make
guests feel right at home."

CLOCKWISE FROM TOP LEFT:
THE SUMPTUOUSLY PANELED AND
CHANDELIER-BEDECKED LOBBY WELCOMES
GUESTS TO THE VERNON MANOR HOTEL,
LETTING THEM KNOW THEY HAVE ARRIVED
AT A SPECIAL PLACE.

THE VERNON MANOR HOTEL LIKEWISE
OFFERS IMPECCABLE MEETING FACILITIES
THAT INCLUDE 13 PRIVATE ROOMS ABLE
TO ACCOMMODATE GROUPS RANGING
FROM FIVE TO 225.

NAMED BY THE ORIGINAL OWNERS FOR
THE LIVELY DISCUSSIONS AND HEATED
DEBATES THAT TOOK PLACE THERE, THE
FORUM SPECIALIZES IN STEAKS, CHOPS,
AND GRILLED SEAFOOD.

KeyBank and Gradison McDonald Investments, Inc.

FAMILIAR AS AREA RESIDENTS AND BUSINESS-
ES MAY BE WITH BOTH KEYBANK AND GRADISON MCDONALD INVESTMENTS, INC., MOST
OF THEM PROBABLY DON'T REALIZE THAT THE TWO ARE AKIN TO CORPORATE SPOUSES.
THAT'S SURE TO CHANGE, HOWEVER, AS PEOPLE LEARN MORE ABOUT THE EXPANDED
PRODUCTS AND SERVICES AVAILABLE, THANKS TO THEIR 1998 MERGER. ● WHEN
CLEVELAND-BASED KEYCORP ACQUIRED MCDONALD & COMPANY, OF WHICH GRADISON

FAMILIAR AS AREA RESIDENTS AND BUSI-
NESSES MAY BE WITH BOTH KEYBANK AND
GRADISON MCDONALD INVESTMENTS,
INC., MOST OF THEM PROBABLY DON'T
REALIZE THAT THE TWO ARE AKIN TO
CORPORATE SPOUSES.

McDonald Investments is a division, it forged a powerful partnership in the Cincinnati market. In bringing together KeyBank and Gradison McDonald as separate business units operating under a single corporate umbrella, KeyCorp assembled a team of highly skilled professionals dedicated to providing customers with world-class financial products and services designed to meet both their immediate and their long-term financial needs.

With the acquisition, KeyCorp, one of the nation's largest financial services companies with $83 billion in assets, greatly enhanced its presence in the Cincinnati market. Today, some 220 Gradison McDonald employees operating out of three convenient offices cater to consumers' investment needs, while 360 KeyBank professionals operating out of 25 KeyCenters meet their banking requirements. Combined, the two organizations offer customers a

full range of consumer banking products and services, as well as comprehensive investment banking services in areas such as brokerage services, capital markets, initial public offerings, and mergers and acquisitions. As a result, the two institutions are able to help clients find solutions to all their financial needs, no matter what they may be.

"The Key/McDonald Investments combination has been a natural fit from the moment the acquisition was

completed," explains Richard M. Curry, managing director of Gradison McDonald Investments and president of KeyBank's Cincinnati district. "The synergies between Key's balance sheet, capital base, and wide array of innovative products, along with McDonald's expertise in investments and depth of client relationships, benefit both Key and its clients. It's a win-win situation."

As Key's investment bank within a commercial bank, McDonald Investments includes high-powered groups specializing in private client services, taxable fixed income, fixed income capital markets, municipals, equity capital markets, investment banking, and public sectors. The company is part of Key Capital Partners, which also includes Key PrivateBank, a service focused on the financial and investment needs of high-net-worth individuals, and the Asset Management Group, which provides custom-made investment solutions to meet clients' financial goals.

Key Unlocks the Future

Recognizing that clients' needs are as diverse as the clients themselves, KeyBank offers a variety of services tailored to individuals and institutions to help them meet their financial goals. On the corporate side, the groups within Key Corporate Capital provide a myriad of services, including financing for commercial real estate, media and telecommunications, and health care organizations, as well as equipment financing and asset-specific financing solutions for global operations. Key Community Bank acts as a resource for small businesses by providing a full range of customized financial solutions and as a commercial banking resource for businesses of all sizes seeking credit-financing solutions.

Individuals can rely on Key Consumer Finance services to finance the purchase of their homes, cars, boats, and recreational vehicles, or for credit card services and educational loans. Key's Community Bank provides traditional banking services to individuals and businesses alike. Retail banking services are available in 27 geographic districts across the country to provide such services as checking, savings, money market accounts, certificates of deposit, and coin exchange.

Investing in the Community

KeyBank understands that the success of any community is based on the strength of its neighborhoods, and tries to reach beyond traditional lending practices to promote long-term economic stability in the communities where it operates.

Its HomeAssist program, a mortgage loan product for low- to moderate-income individuals and families, offers low down payment and down payment assistance, requires no private mortgage insurance, and has extended income-to-debt ratios, making it one of the most attractive mortgage programs in the city. The bank also offers a program to help individuals with no credit history or with past credit problems to establish or rebuild their credit records. Its LoanAssist product is designed to help individuals save money while establishing a credit record.

But lending programs aren't the only way in which the bank helps create a better community. KeyBank and Gradison McDonald contribute hundreds of thousands of dollars annually to area nonprofits and community agencies, including United Way, Fine Arts Fund, March of Dimes WalkAmerica, Junior Diabetes Foundation Walk, and Multiple Sclerosis Walk. KeyBank and Gradison McDonald also sponsor numerous fund-raising events that benefit a diverse array of organizations, including the Arthritis Foundation, FreeStore/FoodBank, and National Underground Railroad Freedom Center.

What's more, staffers contribute thousands of volunteer hours each year, most visibly on Neighbors Make the Difference Day, a single day during which KeyBank and Gradison McDonald employees provide more than 1,200 volunteer hours to 30 area agencies. Employees actively support area schools through Partners in Education, serve meals to the homeless through Tender Mercies, and find other venues to contribute to the community.

"Being part of the Cincinnati community means rolling up your sleeves and getting involved," Curry explains. "We're not just a company—we're part of the community, and we want to send a signal that we are committed to making this an even better place to live."

White Castle System, Inc.

WHITE CASTLE SYSTEM, INC. HAS THE RECIPE FOR SUCCESS. FOUNDED IN 1921 IN WICHITA, KANSAS, BY E.W. "BILLY" INGRAM AND WALT ANDERSON, WHITE CASTLE WAS AMERICA'S FIRST QUICK-SERVICE RESTAURANT CHAIN AND IS STILL GOING STRONG SOME EIGHT DECADES LATER. FAMOUS FOR ITS COFFEE AND ITS DIMINUTIVE EAT-'EM-BY-THE-SACK BURGERS, WHITE CASTLE, WHICH OPERATES MORE THAN 350 COMPANY-OWNED RESTAURANTS IN 12 STATES, HAS

become an American institution. Its secret is simple: good food, good prices, and loyal employees.

When White Castle opened its first Cincinnati-area restaurant in 1927, a local love affair with the company's unique steam-grilled burger was born. The family-owned chain operates 36 restaurants in the Cincinnati market, an area including Dayton, Southeastern Indiana, and Northern Kentucky. In addition, the chain operates a regional headquarters on Central Parkway and a bakery on Exon Avenue in Evendale. A manufacturing plant on Route 17 in Covington produces frozen ham-

burgers to be sold in grocery stores. Collectively, the area White Castle restaurants and affiliated operations employ some 1,200 people.

Opened years before McDonald's started flipping burgers, and at a time when hamburgers were still largely a novelty food served at ballparks and carnivals, White Castle restaurants broke down middle-class barriers for the hamburger. The company accomplished this with 100 percent, USDA-inspected beef patties, which are a precise two and one-half inches square and are steam grilled on a bed of onions. The burgers proved so popular that customers made a habit of purchasing them by the sackful and taking extras home to freeze, a practice that encouraged White Castle to begin selling frozen sandwiches through retail grocery outlets in 1986.

The restaurants themselves are equally distinctive. White Castle was among the first restaurants to feature stainless steel and porcelain enamel decor, building materials

that embodied the strength and purity befitting a "white castle." To satisfy the stringent standards for building materials, White Castle moved its headquarters from Wichita to Columbus, Ohio, in 1934, where it founded Porcelain Steel Buildings. The company still operates Porcelain Steel Buildings today under the name PSB Company, manufacturing steel fixtures and equipment.

Loyal, Hardworking Employees

One notable distinction between White Castle and its competitors stands behind the counter. White Castle employees are known for their tenure and their loyalty to the chain. Unlike many other chains that suffer high turnover, White Castle often employs the same people for decades. An estimated 15 percent of the company's employees have worked for White Castle for more than a decade, and more than 60 percent of the workers are full-time employees.

THE FIRST METAL BUILDING IN THE CINCINNATI AREA FOR WHITE CASTLE SYSTEM, INC. WAS PORCELAIN ENAMELED WITH EIGHT STOOLS; MOVED TO A NEW LOCATION IN 1945, IT BECAME KNOWN AS CASTLE NO. 15 (LEFT).

ONE OF THE FIRST WHITE CASTLE RESTAURANTS WAS LOCATED IN WICHITA IN THE 1920S (RIGHT).

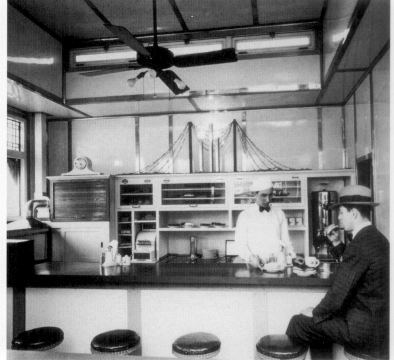

White Castle's generous benefits—which, for full-time employees, include health care coverage, life insurance, paid vacation, free food, a pension plan, and profit sharing—only partially explain employee longevity. Significant though the rewards may be, White Castle provides for its employees for reasons beyond just earning their loyalty. Founder Ingram's philosophy is frequently reiterated by his grandson Bill Ingram, who serves as the company's chairman of the board: "We have no right to expect loyalty except from those to whom we are loyal." In that spirit, White Castle celebrates its employees in a variety of ways, both large and small. For example, each fall, regional operations directors host a two-day celebration honoring employees who have worked for the chain for 25 years and rewarding them with a gold watch.

"We owe our success to the hard work of our employees and the loyalty of our customers over the past 80 years," says James Mundt, Cincin-nati director of regional operations, who joined the company in 1963 and, like all White Castle directors, put in his time behind the counter. "It's only right that we should recognize those long-term employees."

Devoted Customers

As any White Castle employee will point out, the restaurants have "regulars." While other quick-service restaurants tend to cluster near highway off-ramps and strip centers, White Castle moved toward such locations fairly late, and many of its restaurants are still located in urban areas near the main bus lines. While their clientele tends to skew a little older and a little more blue-collar than the traditional quick-service customer, the real mark of a White Castle customer is his or her fierce loyalty. "Our customers often visit our restaurants more frequently than other restaurants and tend to be more exclusive," explains Mundt.

Unlike other quick-service restaurants that have broadened their menus in recent years, White Castle remains faithful to its limited menu of hamburgers, cheeseburgers, fish, chicken, breakfast sandwiches, fries, onion chips and rings, mozzarella sticks, chicken rings, coffee, soft drinks, and shakes. Customers do not seem to mind.

"When you do something so well for so long, there's no point in tampering with success," Mundt says. "The restaurant industry is constantly changing. That's part of what makes it exciting. As we look to the future, it's hard to imagine the changes that will take place, but one thing is certain. We'll continue to focus on our hamburger sandwich—that's what's brought us this far—and we'll continue to rely on our excellent menu."

CLOCKWISE FROM TOP LEFT: WHITE CASTLE HAS ALWAYS FOLLOWED STRICT GOVERNMENT STANDARDS FOR THE BEEF THEY USE TO MAKE THEIR HAMBURGERS.

WHITE CASTLE NO. 44, LOCATED ON THIRD STREET IN COVINGTON, REPRESENTS THE MOST MODERN OF THE COMPANY'S BUILDING STYLES.

A SUBSIDIARY OF WHITE CASTLE, PORCELAIN STEEL BUILDINGS—TODAY OPERATING UNDER THE NAME PSB COMPANY—WAS ESTABLISHED IN 1934, ENABLING WHITE CASTLE TO MAKE ITS OWN STAINLESS RESTAURANT FIXTURES AND EXTERIOR PORCELAIN STEEL PANELS.

Cintas Corporation

THE POWER OF THE UNIFORM IS THE FOUNDATION UPON WHICH CINTAS CORPORATION IS BUILT. A LEADER IN THE UNIFORM RENTAL AND CORPORATE IDENTITY APPAREL INDUSTRY, CINTAS ALSO PROVIDES A WIDE RANGE OF ANCILLARY SERVICES, INCLUDING ENTRANCE MATS, SANITATION SUPPLIES, CLEAN ROOM SERVICES, AND FIRST-AID PRODUCTS AND SERVICES. CINTAS HAS MORE THAN 200 LOCAL OPERATIONS AND SOME 3,000 WEEKLY DELIVERY ROUTES IN THE UNITED

BASED IN CINCINNATI'S MASON AREA, CINTAS CORPORATION DESIGNS, MANUFACTURES, AND IMPLEMENTS CORPORATE IDENTITY UNIFORM PROGRAMS THAT IT RENTS OR SELLS TO CUSTOMERS THROUGHOUT THE UNITED STATES AND CANADA. THE COMPANY ALSO PROVIDES ANCILLARY SERVICES, INCLUDING ENTRANCE MATS, SANITATION SUPPLIES, FIRST-AID PRODUCTS AND SERVICES, AND CLEAN ROOM SUPPLIES.

States and Canada. Uniforms, which build teamwork, brands, and business, are popular work attire; more than 4 million people work every day in a Cintas uniform.

A Humble Start

Forced to find a way to support his family after the depression ended his circus career, "Doc" Farmer noticed that Cincinnati companies were using rags to clean machinery, then discarding them and buying replacements. Seeing an opportunity, he began collecting the discarded rags and laundering them in his wife's home washing machine. The rags were then resold to businesses; this work developed into an enterprise in 1929.

After Doc's son Hershell Farmer joined the business, the company was named Acme Wiper and Industrial Laundry. Eventually, the company outgrew the Farmer home, and the first plant was built along the Ohio River in Bellevue, Kentucky. The plant was washed away during the flood of 1937, and the family rebuilt in Cincinnati, serving America during World War II as an essential war facility by providing wiping

towels and workers' overalls to industrial giants.

A New Focus

Business flourished in the years following World War II. When Hershell's son Dick Farmer joined Acme in the 1950s, he saw uniforms as a natural extension of core competencies and championed the move into the uniform rental industry.

Acme began providing corporate identity apparel for every type of industry, and introduced many product innovations, including the use of polyester/cotton blends to make industrial clothing more durable. In the early 1970s, the company was renamed Cintas and the tag line The Uniform People was added to identify the company's focus.

Cintas in 2000

Cintas has grown steadily for more than 30 consecutive years. Its label is worn in the boardroom and the bakery, the garage and the grocery. Restaurants, hotels, hospitals, trucking lines, and service businesses all use Cintas products.

In addition to creating a professional image with the workforce, Cintas also works with its customers to create consistent brand images and professional appearances throughout the workplace. Cintas supplies its customers with entrance mats, sanita-

tion supplies, and first-aid services, small details that are very important to customers' ultimate success.

The company is recognized as a well-managed, innovative performer. Ranked as a *Fortune* 1000 company and listed as one of the 40 best-performing big companies in the United States in *Forbes'* Platinum List, Cintas also is a Moody's Dividend Achiever and one of America's finest companies, as determined by the Staton Institute.

The Spirit Is the Difference

The company attributes its success to its culture: everyone at Cintas is a partner in the business and its future—constantly striving to achieve and exceed expectations. "Cintas succeeds because we believe in working shoulder to shoulder with every employee—our partners," says Dick Farmer, now chairman of the board. "We stress integrity and honesty in everything we do."

The principles that guide Cintas today are the same principles that guided Doc Farmer in the 1920s: hard work, values, professionalism, and trust. "Together, we've built a company that provides great products and services for our customers, great returns for our investors, and great careers for our partners," Farmer says. "We're proud of our past and excited about our future."

CINTAS WORKS WITH A WIDE RANGE OF CUSTOMERS TO CREATE A CONSISTENT BRAND IMAGE AND A PROFESSIONAL APPEARANCE.

1931-1969

1931
Burke, Incorporated

1932
Rumpke Consolidated Companies

1940
Cincinnati Sub Zero

1949
Norton Outdoor Advertising

1949
Clear Channel Broadcasting

1955
Princeton City School District

1958
Ford Sharonville Transmission Plant

1959
American Financial Group

1962
International Knife & Saw, Inc.

1964
Chemed Corporation

1967
SDRC

1968
Northern Kentucky University

1968
Radisson Hotel Cincinnati

1968
The Regal Cincinnati Hotel

Burke, Incorporated

FOUNDED IN CINCINNATI IN 1931, BURKE, INCORPORATED HAS BECOME ONE OF THE MOST WELL-KNOWN NAMES IN THE FIELD OF MARKETING RESEARCH AND BUSINESS CONSULTING, AND IT NOW OPERATES IN MORE THAN 40 COUNTRIES WORLDWIDE. RECOGNIZED AS ONE OF THE TOP 20 RESEARCH FIRMS HEADQUARTERED IN THE UNITED STATES, THE $50 MILLION-PLUS COMPANY'S SUCCESS LIES IN ITS ABILITY TO GO BEYOND JUST COLLECTING AND ANALYZING DATA. BURKE'S

employee-owners work with their manufacturing and service clients to gain a competitive edge by helping them understand customers, accurately predict marketplace behavior, and implement solutions that improve business results. Since 1990, Burke has expanded its offerings to include services in stakeholder measurement and management, and strategic business consulting.

Comprehensive Services

Burke's services are concentrated in four critical areas: strategic marketing research, stakeholder value and loyalty management, strategic consulting, and training and development. By focusing on these areas, Burke enables its clients to enhance their organizational per-

formance by better understanding their customers' needs and preferences and by deepening their customers' loyalty.

"I think of our business as supplying management not just with data, or by stretching data further academically into information, but by stretching it into the right decisions," says Burke Chairman and CEO Ron Tatham. While marketing research may once have simply been a way to determine product preferences, according to Tatham, modern marketing research uncovers information that helps organizations become stronger—especially when the information is integrated with the analytical and consulting services offered by Burke. The company, which employs about 650

full- and part-time employees, accomplishes these goals through its four business groups.

Burke Marketing Research (BMR) provides full-service custom marketing research, analysis, and consulting for companies to help them understand marketplace dynamics. To do that, Burke offers an array of services, including product testing, brand equity research, pricing research, market segmentation, and strategic research.

Burke Customer Satisfaction Associates (BCSA) offers specialized services in customer value and loyalty measurement and management. The group's Secure Customer Index® provides industry best-of-class standards for assessing and improving customer-driven practices in order

BURKE, INCORPORATED'S COMMITMENT TO PROVIDING ITS CLIENTS WITH THE TOOLS NECESSARY TO SATISFY CUSTOMERS HAS MADE IT ONE OF THE TOP 25 RESEARCH COMPANIES IN THE UNITED STATES.

to improve customer retention and loyalty.

Burke Strategic Consulting Group (BSCG) offers in-depth experience in consulting and implementing strategic change through such means as employee assessment systems and value-based activity management. Working with BCSA, the group conducts extensive analyses to link employee and customer satisfaction to bottom-line business performance.

Burke's Training & Development Center offers both public and in-house educational seminars on marketing research, data analysis, customer satisfaction measurement, and qualitative research techniques. Through a curriculum of practical courses that runs the gamut from basic to advanced, Burke trains participants to uncover for themselves the information their organizations need to succeed.

In addition, Burke has developed a set of tools that measure the effectiveness of communications via the Internet. Burke Interactive gathers and disseminates research information through the Internet, enabling better understanding of marketplace dynamics, customers, employees, and other organizational stakeholders. Burke research about Internet research sets industry standards for collecting data through developing tech-

nologies and properly interpreting study findings.

No matter what their focus area, Burke professionals work with clients to establish trust, cultivate strong working relationships, and build long-term partnerships. That means tailoring their services to meet clients' individualized needs. Burke account teams often combine key competency areas to create multidisciplinary programs for clients that form the basis for Enterprise Value Management, a holistic approach to business operations.

Integrated Solutions, Global Perspective

Burke's global reach makes it a powerful partner to its clients. The firm opened its first European office in 1966 and has been an innovator in global business research for more than 35 years. Burke has had a long-standing partnership with Infratest Burke AG, headquartered in Munich. Together, Burke and Infratest Burke are able to provide business research and consulting services the world over.

According to Tatham, in today's competitive environment, managers are constantly bombarded with issues that will determine the future directions of their companies. By partnering with Burke, they are able to arm themselves with vital

information that is both comprehensive and in-depth. "Our job is to get accurate, timely, and actionable information to these people," Tatham says, "so they can make informed decisions that will create competitive advantage for their business."

Local Perspectives, Community Involvement

Burke employees also take an active role in local civic and charitable activities. In Cincinnati, Burke has participated in the Partners in Education Program for more than 10 years. The firm's work with Whittier Elementary School in Price Hill has included school cleanup projects, new clocks for all the classrooms, a pen-pal program, and various tutoring programs. Whittier student art is also on display in Burke's corporate offices. Since 1995, Burke volunteers have participated in the kindergarten-through-sixth-grade education program produced by Junior Achievement, which includes teaching a five-week course on business and economics in all grade levels.

Burke and its employees also participate in a number of other civic and charitable activities. According to Tatham, "While our business presence is worldwide, we believe we owe a personal presence to the community where we live, and our employees exemplify that belief in many ways. That type of involvement not only helps make our community stronger, but also makes us stronger as individuals and a company as a whole."

Rumpke Consolidated Companies

DRIVEN: THAT'S HOW RUMPKE CONSOLIDATED COMPANIES, ONE OF THE NATION'S LARGEST PRIVATELY HELD WASTE-HAULING COMPANIES, DESCRIBES ITSELF. DURING ITS NEARLY 70-YEAR HISTORY, RUMPKE HAS FORGED A REPUTATION FOR PROVIDING EFFICIENT WASTE REMOVAL BY GOING THE EXTRA MILE. ● RUMPKE, WHICH EMPLOYS NEARLY 3,200 WORKERS AND SERVICES CUSTOMERS IN 140 COUNTIES LOCATED IN FOUR STATES, TRACES ITS ROOTS TO A HUMBLE BEGINNING.

In 1932, William F. Rumpke was operating a coal and junkyard business in Carthage, Ohio, when he struck on the idea of purchasing pigs to eat the garbage, a common practice. Over the years the pigs—and the garbage business—grew.

A Family Business

Rumpke was joined by his brother Bernard in 1943, and together they expanded the business. In 1945, the Rumpkes purchased an 80-acre farm in Colerain Township. Two years later they purchased a farm adjacent to the property, increasing their holdings to 230 acres. Although government regulations

soon put an end to the brothers' pig farming, their garbage collection business had taken off.

In the 1970s, Bill Rumpke and Tom Rumpke—William's and Bernard's sons, who had started the company's commercial container operation—purchased the company from their fathers. The cousins, who continue to run the company today as copresidents, added more employees; new divisions, including Rumpke Recycling, Bear Necessity, Hydraulics, Power Components, and Iron Works; and acquired competitors to increase its size and competitive edge.

Those efforts have paid off in a

variety of ways and have won the company recognition on a number of fronts. In recent years, the company has been named to the *Cincinnati Enquirer*'s Top 100 list and Bill Rumpke and Tom Rumpke were named 1999 Entrepreneurs of the Year by the *Cincinnati Business Courier*. The company has won accolades within the waste removal industry as well. The Environmental Industry Association inducted founders William Rumpke and Bernard Rumpke into the waste industry hall of fame, and drivers Harold Caskey and Charles Elsaesser were named drivers of the year in 1999 and 2000, respectively.

Tom Rumpke credits the business' success and solid reputation to family involvement. Nearly 100 members of the Rumpke family, many of them members of the third generation, are involved in the waste business, and that makes a difference, according to Tom. "Our name is on the line," he says. "We have all come up through the ranks and know the business inside and out."

Finding Solutions to Tough Problems

Rumpke Consolidated Companies' employees and management team know that the environment is important to everybody, and that garbage is something most people would rather not think about. Therefore, the company has taken it upon itself to find solutions to tough disposal problems, to safeguard the environment, and to promote recycling.

Rumpke maintains its own environmental staff of engineers, geologists, and technicians to oversee its landfill operations, which have grown considerably to meet the needs of the various communities the company serves. Today, Rumpke operates 2,000 trucks; 10 transfer

COMPANY FOUNDERS WILLIAM F. RUMPKE AND BERNARD J. RUMPKE

stations, where waste is unloaded, compacted, and transferred to larger trucks; and 10 sanitary landfills in Ohio, Kentucky, and Indiana. All of Rumpke's landfills are classified Subtitle D, which means they meet or exceed all federal and state requirements for modern landfill design and construction.

The 444-acre Colerain Township pig farm is now home to the Rumpke Sanitary Landfill, one of the largest such facilities in terms of waste receipts in the state. Each day, the landfill receives an average of 6,500 tons of disposed waste, 90 percent of which is hauled by Rumpke. The site is outstanding not only for its size—the landfill occupies about 244 acres of the site—but also because it is home to the first methane gas recovery plant launched in Ohio. Rumpke works with Getty Synthetic Fuels (GSF), an operating division of Waste Energy Technology, to harvest the site's methane gas. The gas is purified, sold to the local gas and electric company, and used to heat more than 20,000 area homes each day.

"Rumpke is committed to finding solutions to important environmental issues," explains Bill Rumpke. "Finding a way to extract methane gas from garbage and put it to productive use for area residents is just one way we do that."

At the Forefront of Recycling

Rumpke Consolidated Companies' commitment to recycling goes back even further. As early as 1932, founder William Rumpke was pulling cardboard, metal, glass, and tin cans from the garbage. That effort, which continued for many years, accelerated in the 1980s when Ohio passed a law requiring solid waste districts to submit waste management plans detailing ways to reduce, reuse, and recycle waste materials. That law paved the way for the development of Rumpke Recycling, Inc., which opened in Circleville, Ohio, in 1989.

The company's launch of a recycling plant was followed in short order by the opening of Rumpke's St. Bernard material recovery facility in 1991. Capable of processing some 250 tons of recyclable material per day, the St. Bernard plant is Rumpke's largest material recycling facility. In all, the company operates nine recycling facilities.

To demonstrate Rumpke's commitment to recycling, one need only consider the numbers. When the St. Bernard facility opened, Rumpke was recycling between 2 million and 3 million pounds of material per month. Today, the company processes and markets materials for more than 400,000 commercial and residential customers, and recycles a total of 12 million pounds per month. That effort diverts several hundred garbage trucks from landfills each month.

Leader in Education and Community Involvement

Understanding that recycling and waste reduction are everybody's business, Rumpke's employees travel to schools and civic organizations to educate students and adults about the importance of these practices. In addition, Rumpke's employees participate in a number of organizations, including the Greater Cincinnati Earth Coalition, to promote environmental protection.

In addition to its environmental and educational efforts, Rumpke sponsors a number of civic events in Colerain Township, where nearly 1,000 of the company's employees work. The firm sponsors the township's annual Fourth of July and Taste of Colerain celebrations, assists in golf and bowling charity fund-raising events, and is active in the township's business association. Rumpke also supports Habitat for Humanity, the Cincinnati chapter of the Alzheimer's Association, the Cincinnati Museum Center, and the Christmas Caravan, which provide gifts to low-income families in Cranks, Kentucky.

Rumpke Consolidated Companies' outreach efforts, like its core business of waste hauling and disposal, are just another way that the company demonstrates its drive and underlying desire to serve the community in which it operates.

RUMPKE'S LARGEST LANDFILL SPANS 444 ACRES AND ACCEPTS NEARLY 8,500 TONS OF WASTE PER DAY.

TOM RUMPKE AND BILL RUMPKE GRACIOUSLY ACCEPT THE 1999 ENTREPRENEUR OF THE YEAR AWARD.

Cincinnati Sub-Zero

CINCINNATI SUB-ZERO (CSZ) HAS COME A LONG WAY SINCE OPENING ITS DOORS IN 1940 AS THE FIRST U.S. DISTRIBUTOR OF DEEPFREEZE BRAND FREEZERS. IN FACT, AS THE COMPANY CELEBRATED ITS 60TH ANNIVERSARY IN 2000, THE ONLY COMMONALITIES BETWEEN DEEPFREEZE DISTRIBUTING CORP., THE COMPANY OF THE 1940S, AND ITS MODERN SUCCESSOR ARE AN ABIDING COMMITMENT TO QUALITY AND A CONTINUED EMPHASIS ON TEMPERATURE CONTROL PRODUCTS. CSZ, WHICH

manufactures temperature-controlled equipment for medical and commercial use, began its transformation from distribution to manufacturing in 1949 when Robert Jacobson, the great uncle of Steven Berke, president and CEO, modified the DeepFreeze technology for use in other low-temperature-controlled applications. That shift spawned a company that today offers a full line of environmental-simulation and temperature-controlled equipment, as well as a line of patient temperature-controlled products used in hospitals throughout the world in the operating room, recovery room, and intensive care. Along with its lines of temperature-controlled products, Environmental Screening Services Corp. (ESSC), a wholly owned subsidiary of CSZ, provides testing and laboratory consulting services, with operations in Blue Ash, Ohio, and Detroit.

CSZ—a third-generation, family-owned business that moved to Sharonville, Ohio, in 1985—has four divisions geared toward the industrial, U.S. Postal System, and medical markets. In the industrial use area, CSZ makes heating and cooling systems that can be used to test products' reaction to rapidly changing temperatures. These systems include mechanically refrigerated production chilling chambers, calibration baths, environmental test equipment, stress screening equipment, and thermal shock temperature cycling units that are sold to the aerospace, defense, automotive, electronics, pharmaceutical, telecommunications, and metalworking industries.

Approximately 60 percent of CSZ's units are customized for particular applications and are used for diverse purposes—from designing a system used in the distillation process to trap enriched uranium, to the creation of a test chamber simulating the changing air temperature in a missile's environment. Closer to home, the units are used by pharmaceutical firms to design systems to control exothermic reactions, and by automobile manufacturers to test the effects of changing temperatures on air bag deployment and other automotive components.

All of CSZ's testing helps ensure reliability for the end user. "The

CINCINNATI SUB-ZERO (CSZ), WHICH OPENED ITS DOORS IN 1940, MANUFACTURES TEMPERATURE-CONTROLLED EQUIPMENT FOR MEDICAL AND COMMERCIAL USE.

THE QUALITY OF CSZ'S PRODUCTS IS AFFIRMED BY ITS ISO 9000 CERTIFICATIONS, WHICH HELPS TO ENSURE PRODUCT AND PROCESS CONSISTENCY (RIGHT).

CUSTOMIZED FOR PARTICULAR APPLICATIONS, APPROXIMATELY 60 PERCENT OF THE UNITS IN CSZ'S INDUSTRIAL MARKET ARE USED FOR DIVERSE PURPOSES (LEFT).

equipment can simulate a variety of hot and cold conditions, humidity, rain, snow, freezing rain, altitude, and sunlight to ensure product reliability under various operating conditions," explains Berke. "As a result, by the time the product reaches the end users, they know how temperature will affect their products."

In the health care arena, which CSZ entered in 1963, the company supplies a full line of localized heat and cold therapy products, including a wide variety of therapeutic pads designed for knees, elbows, and other specific applications; portable heating and cooling systems; and various heating and cooling blankets for use with water and air. CSZ also makes WarmAir Warming Tubes and FilterFlo Blankets so patients do not become hypothermic during and after surgery. CSZ is a leading manufacturer of hyper- and hypothermic units used to control patient body and blood temperature in surgery and in the intensive care and burn units.

The quality of CSZ's products is affirmed by its ISO 9000 certifications, which help ensure product and process consistency. In earning that quality designation for its medical products in 1996 and for its industrial products in 1998, CSZ took an important step toward expanding its operations in the European market. "You can't sell a medical product or most industrial products in Europe unless you have met ISO 9000 requirements," Berke explains. "By having that certification, we've really expanded our market."

Expansion Minded

But it's not just CSZ's markets that are expanding. The company itself is broadening its reach. In 1998, CSZ acquired from Indiana-based Zimmer, Inc. the inventory and manufacturing rights for Zimmer's line of thermal therapy products, a move that has increased sales and set a foundation for future growth.

Also in 1998, CSZ began bringing a number of formerly outsourced manufacturing activities in-house. Today, the company manufactures and powder-coats its own sheet metal in an effort to reduce inventory, lead time, and the cost of packing and shipping. CSZ also manufacturers its own disposable thermal air and water blankets, and operates a clean room, where sterile products to be used in surgery are packaged.

In 1999, CSZ added an additional ESSC testing facility in the Detroit area. The Detroit lab, like the Blue Ash facility, meets the American Association for Laboratory Accreditation's (A2LA) quality certification standards for contract test labs, and acts as an independent evaluator to verify clients' thermal testing. ESSC's in-house capabilities include environmental testing per military and commercial standards, environmental stress screening, root-cause failure analysis, process evaluation, training and education, soldering techniques, inspection training, and ISO 9000 quality system auditing and consulting.

The Raven Manufactured Products, Inc. division designs and manufactures a variety of products for various industries such as the postal and food industry. One of Raven's more popular products for the postal industry is the Integrated Parcel Sorter. The package sorting system saves the company's postal customers time and money by automatically sorting packages by zip code. All of Raven's products are designed to provide customers with solutions that will aid them in minimizing their costs.

Since its founding, CSZ's growth has been facilitated by a long serving and dedicated staff. The company employs about 220 employees, many of whom have worked for the firm for decades and have first-, second-, and third-generation family members who work there as well.

"Our employees are key to our success," Berke says. "They understand and are dedicated to CSZ's commitment to quality. We want to maintain our reputation as a quality provider of temperature-controlled products. By either developing, designing, distributing, or providing contract services, we aim to meet the customer's needs. Responding to customer needs is our primary goal."

Norton Outdoor Advertising

WHEN NORTON OUTDOOR ADVERTISING'S CLIENTS PURCHASE BILLBOARDS FROM THE KENNEDY HEIGHTS, OHIO-BASED FIRM, THEY GET A LOT MORE THAN PRIME ADVERTISING REAL ESTATE. THEY TAP INTO ALL OF THE INTANGIBLE, BUT IMMEASURABLY IMPORTANT, BENEFITS THAT COME FROM DOING BUSINESS WITH A FAMILY-OWNED AND -OPERATED FIRM WITH MORE THAN 50 YEARS OF EXPERIENCE. TRADITION, PRIDE IN CRAFTSMANSHIP, DEDICATION TO MEETING CUSTOMERS'

needs consistently, and a strong work ethic—at Norton, these are all part of the package.

A Long Tradition of Excellence

Some fifty years and two generations after Jerry Norton launched his firm from the backyard of his California, Ohio, home, Norton Outdoor Advertising has strengthened its base. Indeed, Norton, who used the earnings from his jobs as a peanut vendor and a set builder for the Albee Theatre to start the company in 1949, probably would not recognize the business he founded. Today, Norton Outdoor Advertising employs 25 people and maintains nearly 1,000 billboards throughout the Greater Cincinnati area.

Although he might not recognize the business, Norton would certainly be familiar with the faces. His sons Tom and Dan run the business as president and vice president of operations, respectively, and grandson Mike Norton is an integral part of the sales team for the company.

"It's not often that a family business continues into the third generation," says Tom Norton,

NORTON OUTDOOR ADVERTISING IS CONTRIBUTING TO THE DRIVE NICE CAMPAIGN, A NATIONAL EFFORT IN COOPERATION WITH THE FEDERAL HIGHWAY ADMINISTRATION TO COMBAT ROAD RAGE (TOP).

CINCINNATI BELL WIRELESS USED NORTON FOR THEIR SIMPLE RATE PLAN CAMPAIGN (BOTTOM).

who started riding along with his dad when he was just a toddler. "Lots of times, interest fades by then. But here there's a real pride in what we do, and that pride has actually grown with time."

A Set Goal of Consistency

When Jerry Norton launched the company, his primary business was in six- by 12-foot, eight-sheet posters that were mounted on the sides of downtown buildings. The posters represented an affordable advertising vehicle for local businesses like Frisch's and Coney Island and, unlike the expensive roadside billboards that were hard to come by in the wake of World War II, could be prepared quickly and economically.

Although Norton has expanded its offering since those days, the company's commitment to affordable advertising in high-traffic areas has not waned. The firm now markets 12- by 25- foot, 30-sheet posters and 14- by 48-foot bulletins in addition to the eight-sheet size it initially sold. While the signs of bygone days were traditionally located on corner buildings downtown, today's signs dot the city's highways and major thoroughfares.

The business has changed over the years. Tom Norton recalls calling on companies in decades past and having to convince them of the importance of advertising; signs were hand painted in the early days. Today, client firms often employ advertising agencies that come to Norton for help. While Norton

still maintains a talented creative department, most signs are designed on vinyl that is stretched across a signboard. Because the vinyl banners can be taken down and stored for future campaigns, they save advertisers money.

Still, Norton says, the fundamentals are the same now as they have always been. "We emphasize consistency," he says. "If you keep doing what you do year after year and doing it very well, you earn people's trust. That's exactly what we've done. The business has been our alter ego in a lot of ways. It's part of who we are, so we'll never compromise the work we do."

A National Reputation

While Norton's operations may be focused on Cincinnati, its reputation is national. Tom Norton has served as the chairman of the Outdoor Advertising Association of America (OAAA), and the company has been awarded OAAA's Five Star Award. That designation recognizes companies for the quality of their structures, sign maintenance practices, participation in the Traffic Audit Bureau's program to authenticate reach and traffic claims, and pro bono involvement in the community. In addition, Tom Norton has received the Miles Standish award, a special award given for excellence in the industry.

While Norton takes pride in its national recognition, serving local clients is its passion. Although the company represents both national and local advertisers, its roots and its future lie in serving local firms.

Serving the Local Community

Norton's abiding commitment to Cincinnati explains why the firm is so involved in supporting local nonprofits and community improvement initiatives. "When you have a public forum like we do, you get approached often for contributions," Norton says. "If we feel a cause is an important one and we can be of real help, we'll get involved."

Over the years, Norton has donated space and services to the Catholic Inner-City Schools, Children's Miracle Network, and Free Store. Currently, the company is contributing to the Drive Nice campaign, a national effort in cooperation with the Federal Highway Administration to combat road rage.

While these contributions tie up sign space and cost Norton Outdoor Advertising potential revenues, they are worth every penny. "It's an obligation that we have to the community," Norton says. "We serve the business interests of the community and benefit from that, and we have a tremendous public forum. It only makes sense that we use our displays as an opportunity to give back."

WHILE NORTON'S OPERATIONS MAY BE FOCUSED ON CINCINNATI, ITS REPUTATION IS NATIONAL.

Clear Channel Broadcasting

IF CINCINNATI HAS A VOICE, IT OWES THAT VOICE TO CLEAR CHANNEL BROADCASTING. A CONGLOMERATE OF SOME 1,200 RADIO AND 20 TELEVISION STATIONS IN THE UNITED STATES, CLEAR CHANNEL OPERATES WKRC-TV, THE LOCAL CBS AFFILIATE, AND EIGHT RADIO STATIONS IN THE GREATER CINCINNATI AREA. BROADCASTING FROM THE TWIN HILLTOPS OF MOUNT AUBURN AND MOUNT ADAMS, CLEAR CHANNEL STATIONS PROVIDE VIEWERS AND LISTENERS WITH

number-one-ranked, top-quality news coverage and a broad array of radio formats that appeal to every listener's taste.

Serving the Out-Of-Home Market

Whether commuting to work, traveling, or running errands around town, Americans spend a significant amount of time in their cars. Accordingly, Clear Channel's stations are extremely familiar to listeners. On the FM dial, they can choose from the album-oriented rock of WEBN, WOFX's classic rock, WKFS' (Kiss) contemporary hit rock, and WVMX's (Mix 94.1) adult contemporary format. Clear Channel's AM offerings include talk station WLW (the Big One), whose Clear Channel signal is so strong that it can reach as far as Canada on a clear night; talk sta-

tion 55-KRC; WCKY (Homer), the station for sports fanatics; and nostalgia radio WSAI.

For its part, WKRC-TV provides top-rated news, covering 75 half hours each week. Rob Braun, Kit Andrews, Tim Hedrick, and Brad Johansen, anchors of the station's 6 and 11 p.m. newscasts, are Cincinnati favorites. One-third of WKRC's 168-hour broadcast week consists of news and public affairs programming. The popular morning television anchor team includes Cammy Dierking, John Lomax, Steve Horstmeyer, and Chris Balish.

Collectively, the immense popularity of its stations in Cincinnati and 100 other U.S. markets has helped make Clear Channel a phenomenal success. During the 1990s, Clear Channel was a consistently top-performing media company on

the New York Stock Exchange. In addition to its U.S. properties, San Antonio-based Clear Channel has an equity interest in some 240 radio stations internationally. Additionally, the company maintains more than 750,000 outdoor advertising displays in some 40 countries throughout the world. SFX Entertainment is the newest Clear Channel acquisition, delivering top performing artists at locations around the world. All told, these global operations make Clear Channel the largest out-of-home media company in the world.

Better by the Bundle

Taken as individual properties, the Clear Channel stations are unique and powerful. Taken as a whole, they are an advertiser's dream.

CLEAR CHANNEL BROADCASTING'S TOP MAIN ANCHORS AT WKRC-TV ARE (FROM LEFT) TIM HEDRICK (WEATHER), ROB BRAUN (NEWS), BRAD JOHANSEN (SPORTS), AND KIT ANDREWS (NEWS).

By recognizing the common goals of radio, television, outdoor advertising, and entertainment, Clear Channel—because its divisions are the epitome of synergy—is able to deliver greater value than an individual medium could provide on its own. For advertisers, that means ample group buying opportunity and a chance to reach roughly 2 million tristate listeners via the combined forces of the various outlets. For radio listeners, Clear Channel provides easy access to WKRC-TV's around-the-clock weather forecasting services and frequent news updates.

The community as a whole benefits, as well, because the Clear Channel radio and television stations are able to band together to promote and sponsor events and fund-raisers that would be cost prohibitive for any one station to support. As a result, civic organizations are able to get the word out, guaranteeing a better draw for their events, and nonprofit organizations are better able to raise funds. Among the stations' many sponsorships is the annual Neediest Kids of All campaign, which provides essential items such as coats, shoes, and eyeglasses to area schoolchildren who would otherwise go without.

In addition, WKRC has produced television specials to promote local events. The station's 1999 production of "Burghley: The Life and Times of a Great English Country House" helped attract visitors to the Cincinnati Art Museum's special exhibit of treasures from the English manor. More recently, specials on dolphins and caves cultivated interest in Omnimax films that played at the Cincinnati Museum Center. WKRC has likewise teamed up with the *Cincinnati Enquirer* and used its high-profile status to salute outstanding youth through the annual Golden Galaxy Awards, in association with the Cincinnati Youth Collaborative.

In total, WKRC provides more than $3 million worth of free public service support to community groups in the tristate area. During

a typical year, the station airs some 10,000 public service announcements.

Whether promoting community events or helping to raise awareness of worthwhile causes, Cincinnati's Clear Channel Broadcasting stations are united in their support of the greater tristate communities. The stations are more than just the voice of the city: they are part of its heart, too. As a key senior Clear Channel executive once said, "We live here, too."

WKRC'S NEWS ANCHORS AT 6 AND 11 P.M. ARE ROB BRAUN AND KIT ANDREWS.

THE WKRC WEATHER TEAM CONSISTS OF (FROM LEFT) LAYNE MASON, MIKE BURESH, TIM HEDRICK, AND STEVE HORSTMEYER.

Princeton City School District

Although the current Princeton City School District was not formed until 1955, the overall community in which it sits demonstrated its commitment to education more than a century earlier. In 1852, the city of Glendale commissioned "a neat public school building" consisting of four rooms to educate the scions of some of Cincinnati's early entrepreneurs. ● Today, the district, its residents,

and its businesses remain no less committed to educating the area's youth. Drawn from six communities—Evendale, Glendale, Lincoln Heights, Sharonville, Springdale, and Woodlawn—the district's some 6,800 students represent a cross section of society.

A Community Dedicated to Education

The Princeton City School District is a nationally recognized, award-winning school district. Princeton is rich in diversity and is equally rich in the educational opportunities offered to each student. The district's 11 schools, including a high school, a junior high school, and nine elementary schools, provide educational opportunities that are extraordinary in their breadth and quality. Princeton offers a myriad of exemplary academics, extracurricular activities, and athletics, all of which encourage students to grow and explore the world around them.

"Princeton has an outstanding and comprehensive program that meets the diverse needs of our students, and we have an excellent

staff to work with every student," explains Dennis L. Peterson, Ph.D., district superintendent. "Performance by our students has been rising dramatically, and today's Princeton is a truly outstanding school district."

Despite their exemplary quality, the district's schools represent a tremendous bargain to residents. Thanks to the community's strong economic base and to district busi-

nesses such as Avon, Ford, GE Aircraft Engines, General Mills, and Procter & Gamble, Princeton has the fourth-largest commercial tax base of any district in Ohio—larger than those of Akron, Dayton, and Toledo. Thanks to that commercial support, real estate taxes are the second lowest in the region. For residents, that translates to a lot of education—$9,400 per pupil—for relatively low taxes.

Clockwise from top:
Princeton City School District boasts a student body eager to learn from both their teachers and each other as they explore all the district has to offer.

With 242 courses, including a variety of advanced placement courses, Princeton High School's curriculum is among the most comprehensive in the area.

Gifted fourth, fifth, and sixth graders have an opportunity to participate in an intensive magnet school program or in programs at each elementary school.

Preparation for College and Life

Located on a campus of more than 100 acres, Princeton High School is a model for public education. With 242 courses, including a variety of advanced placement courses, the school's curriculum is among the most comprehensive in the area. Princeton is one of only five school districts in Ohio to offer the International Baccalaureate program, designed to provide an integrated, two-year course of accelerated study to prepare academically talented students to attend colleges and universities throughout the world. In addition, Princeton High School students have access to nearby Scarlet Oaks, one of the career and technical schools operated by the Great Oaks Institute of Technology and Career Development.

The school's technological credentials are likewise enviable. Developing effective skills of technological fluency and collaboration is successful at Princeton because district teachers use technology in instruction at the earliest age. From the beginning use of computers in preschool, successive grades continue to build a foundation of computer skills that assure students develop technology fluency. Princeton High School boasts 10 fully equipped computer labs, and every classroom is Internet accessible.

Beyond that, Princeton's offerings are as varied as the students themselves. Young scientists can test their skills and broaden their minds in a high school physics lab lauded as one of the best in the nation. Because Princeton offers more than the traditional French, German, and Spanish courses, aspiring linguists have the opportunity to master Latin, Japanese, and Russian as well. Musicians of every type can find an outlet for their creativity, as Princeton High School is one of only 100 schools nationwide—and one of only three in Ohio—whose broad musical offering earned it a 2000 GRAMMY Signature School designation. Athletes can test their mettle on the fields and courts where several NFL and Division I NCAA players have honed their skills, or they can make use of the school's Olympic-sized swimming pool and foster other dreams.

Paving the Way in Younger Years

Students in Princeton City School District's lower grades have access to an equally wide range of opportunities. In addition to impressive early childhood development programs, the district offers educational alternatives including elementary schools with Montessori and traditional programs.

Elementary students, while mastering the three Rs, are also introduced to science, health, and social studies, and can explore the environment at the unique Princeton Nature Center. Technological literacy begins for students in the early grades, as computers are used extensively for word processing, as well as for retrieving and analyzing information. The visual and performing arts receive ample attention as well. Gifted fourth, fifth, and sixth graders have an opportunity to participate in an intensive magnet school program or in programs at each elementary school.

At the junior high school level, district students have the opportunity to identify and explore areas of interest. That might mean choosing a foreign language, taking an art course that provides exposure to a variety of media, or participating in music minicourses. In all, students can choose from 34 after-school activities and can tap into resources such as computerized reading and fiction libraries, as well as the Center for Applied Technology, one of the largest industrial technology and life management labs in the country.

Rich and diverse as the opportunities may be, in the end it is the Princeton community that represents the greatest educational resource. Princeton City School District proudly claims a staff of dedicated teachers, administrators, and support staff who tirelessly devote themselves to nurturing young minds and forging character. The district likewise salutes parents for their active support of the schools. Most important, Princeton lauds a body of students eager to learn from both their teachers and each other as they explore all that the district has to offer.

CLOCKWISE FROM TOP: MUSICIANS OF EVERY TYPE CAN FIND AN OUTLET FOR THEIR CREATIVITY, AS PRINCETON HIGH SCHOOL IS ONE OF ONLY 100 SCHOOLS NATIONWIDE—AND ONE OF ONLY THREE IN OHIO—WHOSE BROAD MUSICAL OFFERING EARNED IT A 2000 GRAMMY SIGNATURE SCHOOL DESIGNATION.

PRINCETON'S YOUNG SCIENTISTS CAN TEST THEIR SKILLS AND BROADEN THEIR MINDS IN A HIGH SCHOOL PHYSICS LAB LAUDED AS ONE OF THE BEST IN THE NATION.

TECHNOLOGICAL LITERACY BEGINS FOR STUDENTS IN THE EARLY GRADES, AS COMPUTERS ARE USED EXTENSIVELY FOR WORD PROCESSING, AS WELL AS FOR RETRIEVING AND ANALYZING INFORMATION.

Ford Sharonville Transmission Plant

In the modern business world, the concept of teamwork has become synonymous with productivity and profitability. Ford Motor Company's Sharonville Transmission Plant pioneered that concept nearly two decades ago. The plant—some 15 years after starting the revolution—is one of the most successful adopters of team-based production. ● In 1980, Sharonville was the worst Ford plant in

its class, complete with the highest production costs and the lowest-quality results. Employment had dipped, and there was talk of closing the plant. Then, two events took place that changed the course of the plant's history and set the stage for a new model of American business.

First, Ford and the United Auto Workers (UAW) union signed a letter of agreement on joint labor-management cooperation that emphasized the importance of employee involvement. Second, the company and UAW agreed to form a joint mutual growth committee at each plant location to initiate improvements that would bolster the manufacturer's competitive position. Those two movements, combined with the looming threat of closing the plant, set the stage for Sharonville's daring experiment.

In a move to forestall closing, the plant's mutual growth committee met and agreed to try out self-directed work teams at Sharonville. Depart-

ment 278 agreed to pilot the new method and, in November 1985, began training. The program's remarkable success induced Ford to award Sharonville the new electronic E4OD transmission, a move that stabilized the plant. This success convinced Sharonville that self-directed teams were the way to go.

Teamwork

Sharonville's teams consist of both hourly and salaried workers, and emphasize cross functionality.

Compensation is based on knowledge: the more operations in a department that a technician can run and set up, the higher his or her wage is. A salaried worker, who would formerly have been a supervisor, now acts as an adviser for each team, and team members are all trained in both technical and team skills. Team responsibilities include everything from meeting production schedule goals and assuring quality, to coordinating lunch and relief periods, to scheduling vacations.

THE FORD SHARONVILLE TRANSMISSION PLANT IS ONE OF THE MOST SUCCESSFUL ADOPTERS OF TEAM-BASED PRODUCTION.

At Sharonville, employee involvement and teamwork translate to a constant search for better ways to meet the plant's goals in areas of safety, quality, schedule, and cost. The premise upon which every decision is made is that it must foster continuous improvement and, as the plant's results demonstrate, this mark is rarely missed.

Thanks to the pride, cooperation, and foresight that Sharonville's employees demonstrated back in 1985, the plant is open and flourishing today. The sprawling facility covers more than 2.4 million square feet, and employs some 315 salaried workers and 2,400 hourly workers represented by UAW Local 863.

Since opening in 1958, the plant has expanded seven times and turned out some 35 million parts, including semiautomatic transmissions, converters, converter components, and gears for transmissions produced by Ford's Livonia, Batavia, and Van Dyke plants. Parts are used in Ford's light trucks and vans, as well as in its Expedition, Excursion, Navigator, Crown Victoria, Grand Marquis, Lincoln LS, Town Car, and Jaguar automobiles.

Much of the success of teams and of the Sharonville operation as a whole can be attributed to the strong partnership that labor and

management have developed. Management and UAW Local 863 have worked together in a continuous effort since 1979 to ensure that the plant's policies and procedures reflect both sides' joint interests. That pursuit has encouraged a relationship based on mutual respect and understanding. Union members understand that job security depends on productivity and profitability, and management knows that the quality of the product rests squarely on the shoulders of the employees.

Part of the Community

Ford Sharonville Transmission Plant's spirit of partnership and teamwork extends to the broader community as well. The plant has had a huge economic impact on the

region, thanks not only to the $200 million-plus in annual payroll and more than $4 million in property taxes it pays, but also to the charitable contributions the company and plant employees make. In 1999, Ford and plant employees contributed more than $428,000 to the United Way and other area charities.

"The Sharonville team is proud to be a member of the Greater Cincinnati community, and contributes in many ways to our community," says Vic Kane, plant manager. "Like Cincinnati, our future is bright with new products and upgrades of existing products on the way. Our strength is the employee teams that find innovative ways to contribute to our success."

MUCH OF THE SUCCESS OF TEAMS AND OF THE SHARONVILLE OPERATION AS A WHOLE CAN BE ATTRIBUTED TO THE STRONG PARTNERSHIP THAT LABOR AND MANAGEMENT HAVE DEVELOPED.

International Knife
& Saw, Inc.

Oₙₑ OF THE WORLD'S LEADING MANUFACTUR-
ERS OF INDUSTRIAL MACHINE KNIVES AND SAWS, INTERNATIONAL KNIFE & SAW, INC. SUPPLIES
MORE THAN 60,000 TYPES OF KNIVES AND SAWS TO A VARIETY OF INDUSTRIES, WITH
DIVERSIFIED PRODUCTS FOR EVERY APPLICATION. THE COMPANY, WHICH HAS OPERATIONS IN
NINE COUNTRIES ON FOUR CONTINENTS, MANUFACTURES CUTTING TOOLS THAT INCORPORATE
ADVANCED TECHNOLOGY AND ARE MANUFACTURED TO CLOSE TOLERANCE QUALITY CONTROL

WHATEVER THE APPLICATION,
INTERNATIONAL KNIFE & SAW, INC.
STANDS READY TO EXPAND IN ITS CORE
CUTTING BUSINESS, AND TO ENSURE
ITS LEADERSHIP POSITION NOW AND
IN THE FUTURE.

standards. Market specialists match each cutting tool to performance-specific applications and ship them from one of the world's largest inventories of standard sizes.

International Knife & Saw provides specialized technical assistance, resharpening services, and training seminars for a wide variety of cutting applications. Whether a customer needs to cut wood, pulp, paper, tissue, corrugated material, metal, diamond core, textiles, plastics, recycled materials, rubber, or even picture frames, International Knife & Saw stocks the blade to get the job done. As a result, the company's products are common fixtures in industries ranging from food processing to garment manufacturing, and the horizon is only broadening, thanks to the company's continued innovation.

A History of Expansion

International Knife & Saw traces its roots in the Cincinnati area back to 1962, when Jack Underhill launched American Custom Metals on Grand Avenue in Price Hill. That firm was purchased in 1977 by a private holding company that was later called TKC. The acquisition ultimately made the Ohio company part of International Knife & Saw, an international manufacturing subsidiary with operations in both Europe and North America.

Since then, International Knife & Saw has been on the expansion path. During the 1980s and early 1990s, the company made a number of strategic acquisitions in Germany and expanded in Canada with three major acquisitions. In 1991, the company expanded into South America, where the firm established a joint

venture in an industrial knife and saw distribution and service center in Concepción.

Also in 1991, International Knife & Saw expanded its operations into the Far East by entering into a sales and marketing joint venture in the Philippines, following that with a similar venture in Indonesia in 1992. During 1995, the company established its sales and distribution center location in Singapore as part of its plan to further penetrate developing markets.

In the mid-1990s, International Knife & Saw entered China through two manufacturing joint ventures. These ventures today provide the platform to expand the company's worldwide leading position in the industrial knife and saw market, as well as sell products domestically within China and export products to Europe and North America.

The Chinese joint ventures are set to provide a distribution network for International Knife & Saw to import its products from North America and Europe into China, supplying the 1.2 billion-person market as the economy expands and demands more cutting tool products.

Meeting Customers' Needs

Through its aggressive expansion efforts, International Knife & Saw has broadened its line of products and services through the years. Today, the company's nearly 1,500 workers, some 170 of whom are based in Erlanger, have developed cutting expertise in a variety of applications.

The firm operates the nation's largest computerized inventory of high-quality web-press, serrated-edge cutoff knives, and maintains a large inventory of circular slitters, collator slitters, standard or split perforators, and rotary cutoff blades. As a result, International Knife & Saw, one of

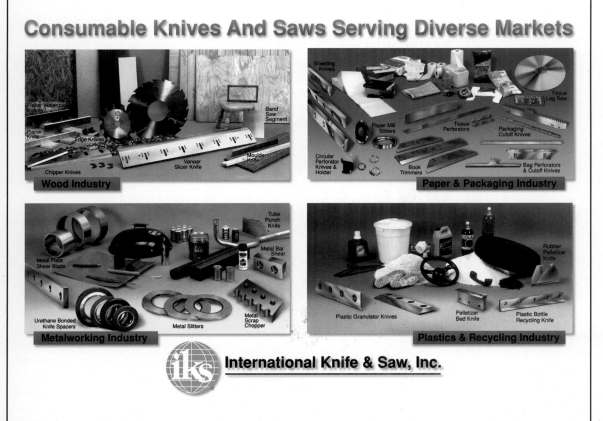

Consumable Knives And Saws Serving Diverse Markets

Wood Industry

Paper & Packaging Industry

Metalworking Industry

Plastics & Recycling Industry

International Knife & Saw, Inc.

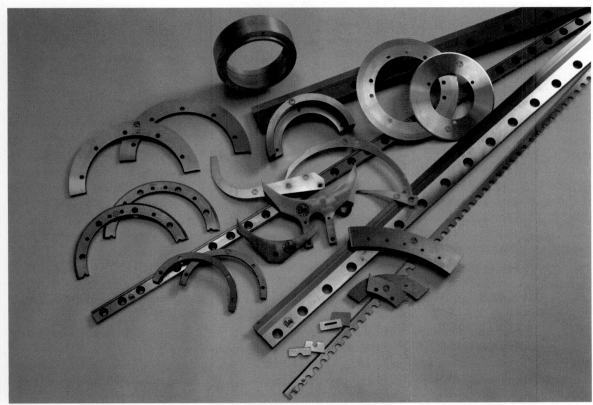

the nation's largest manufacturers of wood knives, wood saws, and industrial paper and packaging knives, has become the supplier of choice for a prestigious array of multinational firms. The company's customers include Weyerhauser Co., R.R. Donnelly, Georgia Pacific, Louisiana Pacific, International Paper, Kimberly-Clark, Fort James, and Procter & Gamble.

In addition, International Knife & Saw anticipates and responds to a number of medium-sized clients'

needs through an authorized dealer network. Working through hundreds of long-established distributors, International Knife & Saw helps smaller clients evaluate their cutting needs and find the solution that best fits their requirements.

Exploring New Applications

Even as it serves its traditional markets, however, International Knife & Saw continues to look for expansion opportunities. The company continues to evaluate strategic

acquisitions that will enhance its marketing position and strengthen its resharpening center operations.

What's more, International Knife & Saw is constantly evaluating new applications to grow the business. That might mean developing carbide slitters to cut computer boards, knives to cut roof shingles, or special blades to cut corn from the cob. Whatever the application, the company stands ready to expand in its core cutting business, and to ensure its leadership position now and in the future.

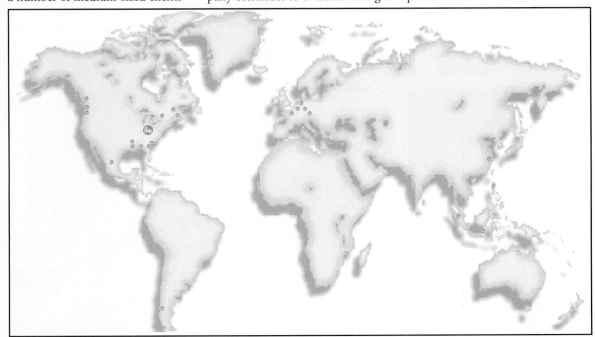

INTERNATIONAL KNIFE & SAW IS PART OF AN INTERNATIONAL MANUFACTURING SUBSIDIARY WITH OPERATIONS IN BOTH EUROPE AND NORTH AMERICA.

Chemed Corporation

Chemed Corporation, marking its 30th anniversary as a publicly traded company in 2001, has every reason to celebrate. The firm has spent the last three decades expanding both nationally and internationally, and with the growth of its three core businesses—Roto-Rooter Inc., Service America, and Patient Care Inc.—it is poised to continue in that vein. But no matter how far-reaching its enterprises, one point remains

clear: "Chemed's roots are in Cincinnati," says Chairman and CEO Edward L. Hutton.

Chemed traces its origins to the DuBois Soap Company (later DuBois Chemicals), which was founded in Cincinnati in 1920. The company was purchased by W.R. Grace & Co. in 1964 and was then merged into Grace's Specialty Products Group. Over the next decade, DuBois and the Specialty Products Group—under Hutton's leadership—metamorphosed into Chemed Corporation, a publicly traded company with Grace as its major shareholder.

Chemed became an independent company in 1982, when it traded a $250 million operating division and an additional $185 million in cash for Grace's holdings in the company. That same year, Chemed shares began trading on the New York Stock Exchange (NYSE).

During the next decades, Chemed's business changed dramatically, as the company added new businesses and discontinued less attractive ones. It sold DuBois and exited the specialty chemical business in 1991, the same year it moved its headquarters to the Chemed Center at Fifth and Sycamore streets. In

1997, it sold The Omnia Group— a distributor of disposable medical and dental supplies—to Banta Corporation for more than $50 million. That same year, Chemed sold its majority stake in National Sanitary Supply Co., a publicly traded Los Angeles-based sanitary maintenance distributor. Proceeds from the sale exceeded $100 million.

Those sales have enabled Chemed to focus its attention on its core businesses, Roto-Rooter in particular. Today Chemed, which employs more than 8,000 workers nationally

and more than 400 at its Cincinnati locations, is looking to build value through service-intensive companies on which consumers can rely.

Roto-Rooter Inc.

Roto-Rooter, the nation's largest provider of residential and commercial plumbing-repair and drain-cleaning services, is the crown jewel in Chemed's holdings. The Cincinnati-based company serves 90 percent of the U.S. population through company-owned branches, independent contractors, and franchisees. Chemed's largest subsidiary, Roto-Rooter also serves Canada and six overseas territories.

Chemed purchased Roto-Rooter, one of the most recognizable brand names in America, from its founding family in 1980 and took it public in 1985. For more than 10 years, Chemed maintained about a 60 percent ownership stake in the business. Recognizing Roto-Rooter's exceptional growth potential—it consistently reported double-digit annual growth during the 1990s— Chemed repurchased all outstanding shares in 1996.

Since then, Roto-Rooter has continued to grow, both internally and through acquisitions of franchises

and non-Roto-Rooter operations. Between 1998 and 2000, the company made 23 acquisitions and signed franchise agreements for China and Hong Kong and the republics of Indonesia and Singapore. Operating in highly fragmented industries, Roto-Rooter can continue to capitalize on its stellar reputation well into the future.

Service America and Patient Care

Service America markets major-appliance and heating, ventilating, and air-conditioning repair through service contracts and provides repair, replacement, and maintenance on a retail basis as well. After Chemed acquired Service America in 1991, this retail business surfaced as a diamond in the rough, with revenues growing at an average annual rate exceeding 40 percent. Like other Chemed companies, Service America is set apart from its competitors by delivering quality services through skilled service technicians.

Patient Care Inc. offers home health-care services—an often-preferred, quality, low-cost alternative to institutional care—in key markets in 10 states. More than 5,000 health-care workers, primarily home health aides, are on call to give 24-hour care to the ill, the disabled, and those who need assistance with daily living activities. Patient Care enjoys a reputation for rigorous quality-assurance programs and high-quality care.

Chemed as Incubator

Although three divisions represent Chemed's major operations today, over the years the company has helped a variety of businesses gain their footing. The company and W.R. Grace combined several of their health care operations and took Northern Kentucky-based Omnicare Inc. public in 1981. Today Omnicare is a leading geriatric pharmaceutical-care company, serving more than 600,000 residents of approximately 8,400 long-term-care facilities in 42 states. Publicly traded on the NYSE, Omnicare, for which Hutton serves as chairman, is also the nation's largest provider of professional

pharmacy, related consulting, and data management services for long-term-care, assisted-living, and other institutional health-care providers.

Currently, Chemed is focusing its entrepreneurial attentions on its Cadre Computer Resources Inc. subsidiary, an information technology consulting firm launched in 1992. Cadre's staff of consultants and programmers offers Internet development services, strategic e-commerce consulting, firewall security systems, and technological training.

There have been other success stories as well. Chemed was a founding shareholder of XL Capital Ltd. in 1986. The publicly traded insurance and financial products company, in which Chemed has only a small remaining interest, has since grown into a $10 billion financial services provider. Likewise, a separate investment in the preferred stock of Vitas Healthcare Corporation, the only national provider of hospice care, has produced substantial annual dividends.

A Common Business Philosophy

While diverse in products sold and markets served, Chemed's operating divisions and investments exhibit common business philosophies and similar characteristics.

"They are marketing- and service-oriented, rather than capital- or production-intensive. They are relatively recession-resistant and highly people-oriented businesses," Hutton says. "They are also industry leaders.

"In each of these companies, service is the key to success," Hutton continues. "Superior customer service adds value to every service offering and product line—value that customers recognize and appreciate; value that differentiates a Chemed company from its competitors."

THE CORPORATE MANAGEMENT TEAM, LED BY CHAIRMAN AND CEO EDWARD L. HUTTON (FRONT CENTER, RIGHT) AND PRESIDENT KEVIN J. MCNAMARA (FRONT CENTER, LEFT)

ROTO-ROOTER, THE LARGEST PROVIDER OF PLUMBING AND DRAIN-CLEANING SERVICES IN THE NATION, OFFERS SERVICES TO 90 PERCENT OF THE U.S. POPULATION THROUGH COMPANY OPERATIONS, INDEPENDENT CONTRACTORS, AND FRANCHISEES.

HIGH-TECH COMPANIES STAKE THEIR REPUTATIONS ON THEIR ABILITY TO INNOVATE AND INVENT, BUT FEW HAVE TAKEN THAT PRACTICE AS FAR AS SDRC, A MILFORD, OHIO-BASED FIRM THAT HAS CONTINUALLY REINVENTED ITSELF SINCE ITS INCEPTION. FOUNDED IN 1967 AS STRUCTURAL DYNAMICS RESEARCH CORP., SDRC TODAY EMPLOYS MORE THAN 2,500 PROFESSIONALS IN 77 OFFICES WORLDWIDE, AND HAS COME A LONG WAY FROM ITS DAYS AS A STRUCTURAL DYNAMICS FIRM.

No longer content to merely help customers design better products, SDRC has matured into a global provider of e-business collaboration solutions for the product life cycle. Coupled with process engineering and consulting services, the company's solutions facilitate innovation through collaboration, enabling industry leaders to optimize product development early in the design process, thus increasing productivity and significantly improving the time-to-market factor.

Collaboration toward Innovation

Although words like collaboration and innovation are part of the corporate lexicon these days, they aren't just words SDRC uses to describe itself. Rather, they are the ethos around which the company reinvented itself when it realigned its strategy for e-business collaboration and development.

"SDRC and our customers worldwide have been demonstrating the positive value that true collaboration and product knowledge management bring to product innovation and competitive excellence," says SDRC Chairman and CEO Bill Weyand. "We are evolving and realigning every facet of our company, from the boardroom to senior management to sales, in order to fully realize the significant growth opportunities created by the Internet."

At the heart of the company's strategy is the understanding that in today's competitive environment, companies must produce better, more innovative products and bring them to market faster if they are to remain viable. To do that, companies need tools that not only facilitate the design process, but also enable data sharing within the organization. That's where SDRC steps in.

As a global supplier of e-business collaboration solutions for the prod-

uct life cycle, SDRC's mission is to be the partner of choice for industry leaders. To address the emerging e-business and collaborative requirements of worldwide customers such as Ford Motor Company, Boeing, Nissan, Xerox, Lockheed Martin, ABB, Bosch, Siemens AG, Harley-Davidson, Mazda, and Bose, SDRC offers solutions for e-design automation, product knowledge management, and e-business integration.

If "innovate or die" is the objective, collaboration is the key to getting there, according to Weyand. The key to improving engineering productivity, reducing product development cycle time, and creating a category-killer product rests on an organization's ability to work together and share information, ideas, and knowledge. That holds true throughout a product's life cycle—from the definition of requirements through systems engineering, digital engineering, creation

SDRC'S WORLD HEADQUARTERS IS IN MILFORD, OHIO. FOUNDED IN 1967, THE COMPANY EMPLOYS MORE THAN 2,500 PROFESSIONALS THROUGHOUT NORTH AMERICA, EUROPE, AND THE ASIA-PACIFIC REGION.

in a digital factory, manufacturing, and maintenance.

SDRC's Approach

SDRC's e-business strategy emphasizes the need to maximize design information throughout the entire life of a product. Thus, each of SDRC's focus areas addresses the specific needs of a particular stage in the cycle.

Product knowledge management (PKM) is the portion of the collaborative product life cycle focused on creating and exploiting knowledge. Product data management (PDM) is the backbone of this stage and the engine for creating true innovation. By capturing customers' requirements very early in the process development life cycle and by understanding the impact of decisions on a product's ability to meet these requirements, SDRC's Metaphase and SLATE solutions enable clients to promote knowledge creation and foster subsequent innovation.

Through e-business integration, SDRC helps companies use Internet technologies to tie together product design, engineering, sourcing, sales, marketing field services, and customer service through shared information. By providing team members with the same data set, SDRC eliminates the chance for misinterpretation. Using SDRC's open, standards-based product, Accelis, companies introducing new products can integrate information from diverse databases,

as well as reduce time and the associated costs of delay and redesign work.

SDRC's e-design automation tools, which include I-DEAS, Imageware, and FEMAP, extend the benefits of Internet-based collaboration to product design. Customers may choose to implement an open, best-in-class application environment, or may build a fully integrated system that supports the digital design through a manufacturing environment in which all participants have access to design information via the Web.

SDRC in Action

Although the firm works behind the scenes, SDRC improves the processes used to design products consumers use every day. For example, the company helped Boeing reduce its internal costs by improving its business processes for airplane design and construction. Using its Metaphase technology, SDRC enabled the manufacturer to radically simplify its business processes and replace legacy systems and hundreds of separate computer applications with four integrated software systems. Those integrated systems serve as a single source of production data for 55,000 users, who are involved in every facet of product development.

SDRC partnered with Ford Motor Company to retool the automaker's design automation processes. Together, SDRC and Ford established

a technology center in Dearborn, where 200 SDRC employees support Ford with software training and implementation assistance. The program will allow Ford to increase its market leadership, reduce the time-to-market factor, cut vehicle development time, improve productivity, and share engineering information in a more timely and efficient manner.

Given the firm's ability to help companies implement such aggressive process improvements and realize valuable competitive advantages, it's no wonder SDRC's tag line is "getting there faster." Fulfilling that promise to current and future clients, SDRC will continue to be a leader in innovation.

Northern Kentucky University

A S ANY STUDENT KNOWS, A GREAT EDUCATION INCLUDES MUCH MORE THAN ACADEMICS. THE POSTSECONDARY EXPERIENCE OFFERS A CHANCE TO MAKE FRIENDS, LEARN NEW SKILLS AND TALENTS, DISCOVER POTENTIAL CAREER INTERESTS, AND—MOST IMPORTANT—DEVELOP CHARACTER. STUDENTS IN NORTHERN KENTUCKY AND THE GREATER CINCINNATI AREA ARE FORTUNATE THAT THEY NEED SEARCH NO FARTHER THAN NORTHERN KENTUCKY UNIVERSITY (NKU).

Academics and a Whole Lot More

The newest of Kentucky's eight state universities, NKU was founded in 1968 as Northern Kentucky State College, and gained university status in 1976, five years after its merger with the Salmon P. Chase College of Law. Since the early 1970s, NKU has engaged in an expansion campaign that continues unabated today.

NKU operates campuses in Highland Heights and Covington, offering 12 undergraduate associate degree programs and 54 baccalaureate degree programs. Graduate degree programs include accounting, business, computer science, education, nursing, public administration, technology, and law, as well as a joint law/master of business administration program. Nearly 12,000 students representing

AS A METROPOLITAN UNIVERSITY LOCATED JUST SEVEN MILES SOUTH OF DOWNTOWN CINCINNATI, NORTHERN KENTUCKY UNIVERSITY HAS THE OPPORTUNITY TO OFFER ITS STUDENTS AN ARRAY OF ADVANCED LEARNING OPPORTUNITIES UNIQUE AMONG KENTUCKY'S REGIONAL UNIVERSITIES.

43 states and 71 countries currently attend the university, attracted by its reputation for solid teaching, a strong and caring faculty, affordability, accessibility, and a diverse array of extracurricular activities. With an average undergraduate class size of just 23 and a student-faculty ratio of 17-to-1, NKU provides rigorous instruction with personalized attention.

NKU's rich extracurricular offerings are equally attractive. The university, which is considered a major force in the region's arts community, includes a theater department that is nationally recognized for its summer dinner theater and annual new play festival. Also, NKU's music department offers a wide variety of concerts and musical productions, many of which are presented in the 650-seat Greaves Concert Hall.

NKU is a member of the NCAA Division II and the Great Lakes Valley Conference. The university's 13 sports programs and cheerleading team excelled with several regional titles and one national championship in 2000. The men's basketball team has posted a 199-35 record over the 1995-2000 seasons, and played in national championship games—televised on CBS—in 1996 and 1997. The women's volleyball and soccer teams advanced to the final four in

1999-2000, while the women's basketball team won the school's first national championship in a game televised on ESPN2.

Adding to NKU's campus social scene are 11 chartered fraternities and sororities, as well as more than 100 student organizations, which provide unique opportunities to meet other students and develop personal and professional skills.

An Important Community Resource

NKU's response to the challenges of today's information age are framed by its relationship with the community. As a metropolitan university located just seven miles south of downtown Cincinnati, NKU has the opportunity to offer its students an array of advanced learning opportunities unique among Kentucky's regional universities, including working in partnership with the local community.

However, NKU regards its status as a metropolitan school not as a description of its geographic location, but as a characterization of its role in fostering the intellectual, social, economic, and civic vitality of the region. NKU serves as a vital educational resource for the community, while exposing its students to learning

opportunities beyond the confines of the campus.

NKU's involvement with the broader community includes a number of partnerships. The university currently serves more than 200 business and industry concerns, such as the Small Business Development Center and Office of Training and Development.

NKU has also developed unique partnerships with local employers to bring a taste of the real world to the university's campus. Through partnerships with Delta Air Lines and Fidelity Investments, students are able to earn valuable professional experience on campus while attending classes. The NKU Delta Reservations Center, which opened in 1997, employs about 200 students as customer service representatives, while the Fidelity Investments Customer Service Operations Center, which opened in 1999, employs more than 180 students who provide Fidelity customers with account information.

In partnership with Fidelity, the university has developed programs that include tax planning and investments designed to help students meet the educational requirements for professional exams. Through the Fifth Third Bank Entrepreneurship Institute, students learn about establishing, operating, and maintaining enterprises, as well as how to operate in an entrepreneurial manner within large, established organizations.

Excellence in the Sciences

NKU's latest expansion effort is the new, $38 million natural science building, which is currently under construction and scheduled to open in fall 2002. This state-of-the-art building will house the Center for Integrative Natural Science and Mathematics (CINSAM), a collaborative, interdisciplinary center that will strengthen preschool through 12th grade partnerships with the university, emphasize connections with industry, and feature an active learn-ing collaboration across education, the natural sciences, mathematics, and computer science. By creating CINSAM, the university addresses the region's needs for a cadre of well-prepared science and mathematics teachers in the elementary, middle, and secondary schools, and for a workforce capable of solving complex, technological problems that do not fit neatly into a single discipline. Equally important, the program addresses the need for a citizenry with a refined sense of inquiry and experience-based knowledge.

CINSAM represents one more way in which NKU is fulfilling its mission as an educational, cultural, and social center to stimulate economic development and foster the academic, artistic, and personal freedoms of its students. By living up to that educational mission, NKU prepares its students to be productive citizens, successful members of the business community, and advocates for lifelong learning.

Radisson Hotel Cincinnati

Hotels aren't often said to sparkle, but the term seems an apt description for the newly renovated Radisson Hotel Cincinnati. Having just emerged from a $7.5 million renovation, the Sharonville, Ohio, hotel is primed for business travelers who are destined for Cincinnati's northern suburbs. ● "We wanted the hotel to be as attractive as possible and to offer all the amenities that business travelers expect in a superior property,

while providing special benefits for those guests who would be traveling with children as well," says Adrian Perez, general manager. "We guarantee 100 percent satisfaction, and that's the standard we were holding ourselves to when we undertook the renovation."

Comfort, Convenience, and Service

Every element of the new Radisson was planned with business travelers' high standards in mind. Consequently, comfort, convenience, and service characterize the 14-story hotel. Comfort is evident the moment guests enter any one of the hotel's 350 guest rooms. Gutted as part of the renovation, the rooms include not only new decorative touches, such as new drapes, furniture, carpets, and wall coverings, but new tile in the bathrooms and new tubs. "We redid it all," Perez says. "We literally started from scratch so that we could be sure we were giving our guests all the comforts of home."

In fact, the new rooms take all types of guests' needs into consideration. Corporate travelers visiting any of the numerous businesses and Fortune 500 companies in the area will be pleased to discover that rooms include business-oriented amenities, such as telephones with voice mail,

THE RADISSON HOTEL CINCINNATI IS PRIMED FOR BUSINESS TRAVELERS WHO ARE DESTINED FOR CINCINNATI'S NORTHERN SUBURBS.

dataports, multiple phone lines, and workstations outfitted with power and communication jacks, ergonomic chairs, and glare-free lamps. Hospitality suites feature wet bars, conference and dining tables, and connecting bedrooms.

Families traveling with children will appreciate that rooms are outfitted with Playstation video games

and that the hotel's extensive selection of in-room, first-run movies includes a wide variety of films that are appropriate for children. Amenities like irons and ironing boards, coffeemakers, and a guest service laundry make everyone's life a little easier.

As comfortable as the Radisson's rooms may be, guests will want to get out and explore the rest of the hotel's facilities during their stays. Business travelers will most likely make use of the full-service business center that includes fax and copy services, as well as conveniences like free parking and automatic teller machines located in both the lobby and the parking lot. Those with recreation on their agenda will appreciate the indoor/outdoor swimming pool, the game room designed with kids in mind, and the extensive workout facilities, which include aerobic classes,

COMFORT IS EVIDENT THE MOMENT GUESTS ENTER ANY ONE OF THE RADISSON'S 350 GUEST ROOMS.

Nautilus equipment, and tennis courts, available at a conveniently located private fitness club.

Patrons seeking extra pampering will find it at the Hairy Cactus Day Spa and Wellness Center across the hotel's parking lot. Whether they need to have their tresses trimmed or a relaxing pedicure, guests will find the staff at the Hairy Cactus ready to accommodate their needs. Guests with a bit more wanderlust will want to explore nearby attractions, such as the TriCounty Mall or Paramount's King's Island, to which the hotel offers discounted passes.

Restaurant and Lounge Options

To find entertainment, the hotel's guests needn't look far. The Radisson offers a wide variety of creative, fun dining and recreation options. Next door to the Hairy Cactus is the hotel's rustic Red Dog Saloon. A dance club and a comedy club in its past incarnations, the bright red building, which looks as if it had been lifted from the set of the western movie favorite *Gunsmoke*, has undoubtedly caught the eye of anyone who has driven down Chester Road. As warm and inviting inside as it is out, the Red Dog features nightly entertainment, pool tables, darts, and a wooden floor generously sprinkled with peanut shells. "It's not a boring, nondescript hotel lounge," Perez says. "It's a place where you can kick back, be comfortable, and have a good time."

Within the hotel itself, McLeod's Lounge offers a more traditional lounge atmosphere. Patrons can enjoy a drink and catch a game before heading over to Vanessa Bistro and Lounge, the Radisson's acclaimed restaurant. There, guests can rub elbows with local residents who come to the hotel to savor Chef Mel Dacanay's tempting, European-style dishes.

Versatile Meeting Facilities

While offering services to individual guests, the Radisson also caters to groups. With 18,000 square feet of flexible meeting space and a location across the street from the bustling Sharonville Convention Center, the hotel simplifies the planning of any corporate function.

Divisible into nine sections that can accommodate smaller groups, the Grand Ballroom provides 8,320 square feet of unobstructed space and can hold as many as 48 exhibit booths. That makes the space perfect for hosting events for as few as 10 or as many as 1,150. The hotel's executive boardrooms are the answer for breakout sessions and smaller meetings. What's more, because the Radisson offers advanced audio-visual support, teleconferencing capabilities, and solid experience in facilitating meetings, groups of all sizes are assured successful, productive gatherings.

Couples planning weddings will be pleased to discover how easy the Radisson makes the process of getting ready for the big day. In addition to special discounted rates for wedding parties and guests, the

CLOCKWISE FROM TOP LEFT: RADISSON GUESTS WILL APPRECIATE THE HOTEL'S INDOOR/OUTDOOR SWIMMING POOL.

LOCATED ACROSS THE STREET FROM THE BUSTLING SHARONVILLE CONVENTION CENTER, THE RADISSON SIMPLIFIES THE PLANNING OF ANY FUNCTION.

THE RADISSON OFFERS A WIDE VARIETY OF CREATIVE, FUN DINING SUCH AS VANESSA'S BISTRO AND LOUNGE.

THE RADISSON'S GRAND BALLROOM IS DIVISIBLE INTO NINE SECTIONS THAT CAN ACCOMMODATE SMALLER GROUPS (TOP LEFT).

EVERY ELEMENT OF THE RADISSON WAS PLANNED WITH BUSINESS TRAVELERS' HIGH STANDARDS IN MIND (BOTTOM RIGHT).

hotel supplies couples with Radisson Reservations Envelopes. Couples need only slip an envelope in with their wedding invitations and out-of-town guests can return them directly to the hotel, allowing over-wrought brides and grooms to save valuable time.

When weddings, meetings, and other festivities are finished, the Radisson Hotel Cincinnati offers an important farewell gift: convenience. Given the hotel's easy access to Interstates 71 and 75, wedding guests and conference attendees will have no problem finding their way back

to either the Dayton International Airport, located 55 minutes north, or the Cincinnati/Northern Kentucky International Airport, located 40 minutes to the south.

Satisfaction Guaranteed

With so many services and amenities, satisfied guests return to the Radisson time and again. "There are no VIPs here," says Perez. "That's because every guest receives the VIP treatment. For example, every one of our guests receives turndown service in the evening. We want our guests to feel loyalty to us

and we understand that loyalty is earned. That's why each of our staff members is willing to go the extra mile for our guests."

All of the Radisson Hotel Cincinnati's 250 staffers are trained and empowered through the hotel's Yes, I Can program to meet guests' needs, solve any problems they might experience, and check back with them to make sure their concerns have been satisfactorily addressed.

"We have a very proactive staff," Perez explains. "Our staff members are constantly asking guests, 'Are you enjoying your stay?' or 'Do

you need anything?' We want to anticipate guests' needs whenever possible. If we can't anticipate those needs beforehand, we want to make sure we respond as quickly as possible when they arise."

While the Radisson's exemplary service makes the hotel the first choice among repeat travelers, its loyalty programs make selecting the hotel even more enticing. The Radisson Gold Rewards program enables travelers to earn points each time they stay at any Radisson hotel across the country. Points are redeemable for free hotel accommodations or for gifts and services provided by other Gold Reward partners, which include T.G.I. Friday's, Country Inns & Suites, FTD.com, Gold Connections, Skymall, MCI WorldCom, and National Car Rental. Alternatively, guests can earn miles toward free travel on Delta Airlines.

Travel agents can take advantage of the hotel's Look to Book program and earn awards for booking guests at Radisson hotels throughout the world. In doing so, they receive valuable prizes, while being assured their clients will be thrilled with their accommodations, thanks to Radisson's 100 Percent Satisfaction Guarantee.

"It's very simple," Perez says. "If, for any reason, guests are not completely delighted with our service and accommodations, they'll be fully reimbursed, no questions asked. That's the Radisson brand standard."

COMFORT, CONVENIENCE, AND SERVICE CHARACTERIZE THE 14-STORY RADISSON HOTEL (TOP LEFT).

HOSPITALITY SUITES FEATURE WET BARS, CONFERENCE AND DINING TABLES, AND CONNECTING BEDROOMS (BELOW).

The Regal
Cincinnati Hotel

WHEN JOHN VINKENBRINK, GENERAL MANAGER OF THE REGAL CINCINNATI HOTEL, SPEAKS OF THE NEW MILLENNIUM, HE'S REFERRING TO MORE THAN THE CALENDAR'S ROLLOVER. THAT'S BECAUSE THE REGAL, THE LARGEST HOTEL IN THE TRISTATE AREA, TOASTED THE DAWN OF THE 21ST CENTURY WITH MORE THAN A BOTTLE OF CHAMPAGNE; IT WELCOMED A NEW OWNERSHIP GROUP. ● MILLENNIUM HOTELS AND RESORTS, A LONDON-BASED OPERATOR OF FOUR-STAR HOTELS THROUGH-

out the world, including the Millennium Broadway in New York and the Millennium Commodore in Paris, purchased the Regal in late 1999. "Millennium is a first-class company," Vinkenbrink says, "and in acquiring the Regal, they recognized an opportunity to operate a premier property in a dynamic midwestern city."

Growing with the City

The view from the Regal's revolving rooftop restaurant, the acclaimed Seafood 32, bears testament to that dynamism. From 32 stories above the city's streets, diners can see the myriad changes taking place in Cincinnati. To the south, Paul Brown Stadium graces the riverfront, and the new Reds stadium is emerging. To the east, the Aronoff Center for the Arts and the vibrant Backstage District draw patrons from throughout the region. Just west of the hotel and connected by an enclosed skywalk, the soon-to-be-expanded Dr. Albert B. Sabin Cincinnati Convention Center draws exhibitors and conventioneers from all over the country.

Those types of projects have spawned a renaissance in Cincinnati, Vinkenbrink says, and the Regal is located in the heart of it

all. "The enthusiasm downtown is almost palpable," he says. "Cincinnati has become a major midwestern destination and the Regal is very much a part of it." With more than 800 guest rooms and 25,000 square feet of meeting space of its own, including two recently renovated ballrooms, the Regal itself is a major destination.

Not Just a Convention Hotel

Although its proximity to the convention center and to the numerous companies headquartered in downtown Cincinnati make the

hotel a popular choice with business travelers, the Regal serves a diverse array of guests. Meeting planners are thrilled to discover a hotel that can accommodate meetings and conventions of up to 1,500, while furnishing business travelers with such important amenities as two complimentary business centers with Internet access, printers, maps, fax machines, and photocopy services. They are equally grateful for the extensive collection of audiovisual equipment that can be rented through the hotel's on-site company.

CLOCKWISE FROM TOP:
AMONG MANY OF THE CITY'S MAJOR ATTRACTIONS, INCLUDING PAUL BROWN STADIUM, THE ARONOFF CENTER FOR THE ARTS, AND THE BACKSTAGE DISTRICT, THE REGAL CINCINNATI HOTEL IS AT THE FOREFRONT OF DOWNTOWN CINCINNATI'S RENAISSANCE.

WITH MORE THAN 800 GUEST ROOMS AND 25,000 SQUARE FEET OF MEETING SPACE OF ITS OWN, INCLUDING TWO RECENTLY RENOVATED BALLROOMS, THE REGAL IS ITSELF A MAJOR DESTINATION.

SEAFOOD 32'S CASUAL AMBIENCE, PANORAMIC VIEW, AND FANTASTIC MENU ARE AS MUCH A HIT WITH CINCINNATI RESIDENTS AS THEY ARE WITH VISITORS.

Weekend travelers appreciate the Regal's central location, which affords easy access to local attractions. Sports fans in town for Reds baseball and Bengals football games frequent the hotel, as do families eager to visit the nearby Children's Museum, the Cincinnati Art Museum, the Newport Aquarium, the Millennium Monument World Peace Bell, and the IMAX theater at the Museum Center at Union Terminal. Shoppers relish the chance to splurge at nearby Tiffany's, Saks Fifth Avenue, Lazarus, and the shops of Tower Place Mall.

What's more, the hotel offers an enormous selection of rooms. With accommodations ranging from 28 suites to the largest selection of double-occupancy rooms in the region, and a wide variety of nonsmoking and handicapped-accessible rooms, the Regal offers travelers a comfortable place to rest no matter what their needs.

Amenities Abound

We have a friendly staff that is dedicated to making sure our guests feel right at home, whether they're in town for business or pleasure," Vinkenbrink says. Hotel patrons appreciate the Regal's numerous amenities, convenience, and service—which are the hotel's watchwords—and its friendly staff goes out of its way to anticipate guests' needs and provide amenities they will appreciate.

Sun worshipers relish the hotel's outdoor swimming pool and sundeck, while fitness enthusiasts appreciate access to the nearby

Moore's Nautilus Athletic Club, one of the city's premier health clubs. The hotel meets guests' day-to-day needs by offering important amenities, such as an in-house gift and barber shop, an express checkout, underground valet parking, and laundry, valet, and shoeshine services.

A Treat for Every Palate

The hotel's diverse selection of restaurants and lounges is a draw as well. The splashy, contemporary Elm Street Grill always serves up fun and good food in a relaxed atmosphere. Martini's Lobby Bar, which serves snacks, light meals, and 33 varieties of martinis, is a great place to meet friends before a night on the town, while the High Spirits lounge on the 31st floor, which features live jazz, is the perfect setting for a romantic nightcap and last dance.

Although the hotel may house

mostly out-of-town guests, the Regal's charms aren't lost on locals, and its acclaimed Seafood 32 has a devoted following. The restaurant's casual ambience, panoramic view, and fantastic menu are as much a hit with Cincinnati residents as they are with visitors. Whether they opt for a light Dover sole sautéed in lemon and herb butter; a succulent, roasted rack of lamb; or any of the other savory dishes on the restaurant's tempting menu, diners can enjoy a casual, world-class meal at Seafood 32 without worrying about sticker shock.

"Cincinnatians know it's a fun place to go and that dinner with friends won't cost the month's mortgage," Vinkenbrink says. "Our acclaimed restaurants, along with amenities such as express checkout and valet parking, are designed to make staying at the Regal convenient and to make visiting Cincinnati a pleasure."

CLOCKWISE FROM TOP LEFT: FEATURING LIVE JAZZ, THE HIGH SPIRITS LOUNGE ON THE 31ST FLOOR IS THE PERFECT SETTING FOR A ROMANTIC NIGHTCAP AND LAST DANCE.

WITH ACCOMMODATIONS RANGING FROM 28 SUITES TO THE LARGEST SELECTION OF DOUBLE-OCCUPANCY ROOMS IN THE REGION, AND A WIDE VARIETY OF NON-SMOKING AND HANDICAPPED-ACCESSIBLE ROOMS, THE REGAL OFFERS TRAVELERS A COMFORTABLE PLACE TO REST NO MATTER WHAT THEIR NEEDS.

HOTEL PATRONS APPRECIATE THE REGAL'S NUMEROUS AMENITIES, CONVENIENCE, AND SERVICE—WHICH ARE THE HOTEL'S WATCHWORDS—AND ITS FRIENDLY STAFF GOES OUT OF ITS WAY TO ANTICIPATE GUESTS' NEEDS AND PROVIDE AMENITIES THEY WILL APPRECIATE.

THE SPLASHY, CONTEMPORARY ELM STREET GRILL SERVES UP FUN AND GOOD FOOD IN A RELAXED ATMOSPHERE.

It starts with a dream, then action, followed by grit and persistence—and even some disappointment. But that's how any venture becomes a success. The members of the Lindner family have turned their dreams into success in their own hometown, and Cincinnati has benefited from that success and from the family's influence and generosity throughout the years. ● The Lindners give of themselves and

have achieved much, but rarely call attention to their generosity or accomplishments. Carl H. Lindner Jr. built on the success of his family's dairy business, transforming American Financial Group (AFG) into the multibillion-dollar company it is today. He did this by working hard, adhering to religious beliefs and personal philosophies, surrounding himself with family and other top-notch people, and possessing an uncanny ability to recognize opportunities and take advantage of them.

Financial and insurance companies have long been at the heart of AFG's and Carl Lindner's operations. Founded in 1959, the company entered the property and casualty business in 1962 with the acquisition of Dempsey & Siders Agency. Today, its insurance operations are headed primarily by Great American Insurance, one of the country's largest property/casualty insurance groups, specializing in personal auto and a broad range of specialty insurance coverages. Another subsidiary, Great American Financial Resources, sells tax-sheltered annu-

ities and life and health insurance policies.

Beginnings as United Dairy Farmers

The seeds of the success that the Lindner family enjoys today were planted years ago in the suburb of Norwood. The Lindner patriarch, Carl H. Lindner Sr., dreamed of working for himself and nurturing a business. He began delivering milk by horse and carriage, and during the 1920s, opened a dairy in Cincinnati. Lindner later enlisted his children to help deliver milk and run the pasteurizing operations.

As the business flourished, Lindner envisioned a chain of stores to sell the dairy's products. On May 8, 1940, along with his wife, Clara, and their four children—Carl Jr., Richard, Robert, and Dorothy—Lindner opened the first United Dairy Farmers store in Norwood. Opening day sales were all of $8.28.

In the days when dairy products were delivered to the home, the Lindners' cash-and-carry milk store

became popular with customers because it offered lower prices. Milk was sold for 28 cents a gallon and ice cream for 17 cents a quart. Customers often furnished their own pails for the hand-dipped ice cream, so some quarts were a bit generous.

From the start, the Lindner siblings were involved in all facets of the business. Dorothy set up the bookkeeping operation; Carl directed marketing efforts and real estate acquisitions; Robert oversaw ice-cream and milk production; and Richard managed the physical facilities. Eventually, United Dairy Farmers added a second store in Norwood, a third in Silverton, and a fourth in St. Bernard. By 1950, there were nine stores. When his father died in 1952, Carl Jr. took charge and led the growth of United Dairy Farmers, which today operates approximately 250 convenience stores.

A Growing Family Operation

As the family continued to nurture the company's prosperity, the Lindners became involved in other pursuits. In 1959, American Financial Corporation was established as a public entity to invest in businesses away from the dairy operations. The company first bought three small savings and loans, which were combined and operated as Hunter Savings, and then also acquired a few small banks in the early 1960s. The first offices of American Financial were located at the original dairy plant on Montgomery Road in Norwood.

Like United Dairy Farmers, American Financial began as a family operation. As it grew, the two younger Lindner brothers acted as advisers, with Carl at the helm. Robert concentrated on running United Dairy Farmers, which today is still a family concern with three

The original United Dairy Farmers store—founded by Carl Lindner Sr., and a predecessor of the Lindner family's American Financial Group (AFG)—opened May 8, 1940, with opening day sales of $8.28.

of his sons—Bob, Brad, and David—holding key positions.

During the early 1960s, American Financial continued to make small acquisitions and started an equipment leasing company, partly to lease transportation and refrigeration equipment related to the growing dairy stores. The Lindner brothers also bought an interest in Thriftway grocery stores, which were ultimately owned and operated by Richard until he sold that company to Winn-Dixie in 1995.

The company has continued to grow through operations and acquisitions and remains a family business today. While Carl's three sons—Carl III, Craig, and Keith—all run major parts of the company, the extended family includes more than a dozen officers who, with Carl Lindner Jr. as leader, oversee day-to-day operations.

A Diverse Assemblage of Companies

The Lindners' financial roots are in Hunter Savings Association, a small savings and loan, which grew into Hamilton County's largest before merging with Provident Bank in 1991. American Financial's first major acquisition, however, took place in 1966. The purchase of a controlling interest in the Provident Bank more than doubled the size of American Financial, increasing its assets from $150 million to nearly $350 million. This move firmly established American Financial in the banking industry, increasing its capacity to perform financial functions.

In 1967, on the heels of the acquisition, American Financial moved into new headquarter offices in the Provident Tower at One East Fourth Street, where it remains today. With assets of about $12 billion, the Provident Financial Group is one of Greater Cincinnati's oldest banks, having served the community for almost 100 years. American Financial and members of the Lindner family own a 60 percent interest in Provident.

After establishing its banking operations, American Financial

turned toward insurance. In 1973, the company acquired National General Corporation, the parent of Great American Insurance, in a deal that brought even broader investment powers under the American Financial umbrella. The acquisition again doubled American Financial's size, increasing its assets of just over $1 billion to $2.3 billion.

Through subsidiaries, American Financial is engaged in a variety of other business activities, including the Sports Center at Kings Island, home of the Master Tennis Series, and a number of real estate holdings. Spread around the country, the

company's real estate operations include office space in various cities, including Le Pavillon Hotel in New Orleans, the Cincinnatian Hotel, the Driskill in Austin, the Chatham Bars Inn on Cape Cod, and apartment complexes in Florida, Kentucky, Louisiana, Minnesota, and Pennsylvania.

AFG owns a prestigious block in downtown Cincinnati—bounded by Third and Fourth streets and by Vine and Walnut streets—which includes the Provident Tower and the historic Dixie Terminal Building.

American Financial has been a longtime limited partner in the

THE UNIVERSITY OF CINCINNATI'S BUSINESS SCHOOL—LINDNER HALL—HAS BENEFITED FROM FUNDING PROVIDED BY AFG AND THE LINDNER FAMILY.

AFG REMAINS A FAMILY BUSINESS WITH (FROM LEFT) CRAIG, CARL JR., CARL III, AND KEITH LINDNER.

CARL LINDNER SR.'S CHILDREN RE-CREATED THE GOOD OLD DAYS WHEN THE FAMILY'S UNITED DAIRY FARMERS MT. ADAMS STORE OPENED (TOP).

XAVIER UNIVERSITY'S PHYSICS BUILDING WAS MADE POSSIBLE BY AFG AND LINDNER FAMILY CONTRIBUTIONS (BOTTOM).

company so it could remain intact and in Cincinnati. AFG's Hunter Savings also assumed the failed Home State Savings in the mid-1980s.

The Lindner family contributes to the Greater Cincinnati community in countless ways. The family provided funding for Lindner Hall at the University of Cincinnati's business school and for Xavier University's new physics building. The Lindners are also major contributors to Hebrew Union College, Cincinnati Hills Christian Academy, the Christ Hospital, and the Museum Center at Union Terminal.

Sawyer Point Park on the riverfront has benefited from the Lindners' generosity by way of a tennis complex and other facilities. The family gave a major gift to the Cincinnati Zoo for the Carl H. Lindner Family Center for Reproduction of Endangered Wildlife. And each year around Christmas, the Lindners express appreciation to employees by sponsoring private concerts at Music Hall; past shows have featured such well-known performers as Liza Minnelli, the Osmonds, Diana Ross, Bill Cosby, Paul Anka, Sammy Davis Jr., and Frank Sinatra.

Throughout Greater Cincinnati, Carl Lindner is known for his extraordinary loyalty. He forms personal and lasting relationships with people within the company, as well as with others in the city and around the country. American Financial has employed the same accounting and law firms for 40 years. Strong relationships with banks, printers, and other suppliers of products and services have been built over the years as well. Likewise, many people holding key positions in American Financial today began their careers with the Lindner family at the dairy or elsewhere.

Despite its vast holdings around the country, American Financial Group maintains strong ties to its hometown. Indeed, the Lindner family and American Financial have made indelible marks on the communities and the business history of Greater Cincinnati.

Cincinnati Reds baseball franchise. In 1999, Carl Lindner, along with other partners, acquired controlling interest and became managing general partner of the Reds. In February, Lindner and the club agreed to bring Ken Griffey Jr. home to Cincinnati. Then in July, the Reds announced that their new stadium, scheduled to open in 2003, will be known as Great American Ball Park under a 30-year agreement signed with the American Financial insurer.

An Important Force in Cincinnati

The Lindner family is fond of Cincinnati and has been tremendously loyal to its longtime home, with American Financial's acquisitions often being relocated to Cincinnati. The family has also acted a number of times to keep some area companies from leaving or failing. For example, when Taft Broadcasting Company was faced with a takeover from an out-of-town concern, American Financial bought the

1970-1980

1970
Great Oaks Institute of Technology and Career Development

1971
Metalex Manufacturing Inc.

1972
Cincilingua Inc.

1972
Paramount's Kings Island

1973
General Assembly, Inc.

1973
Portion Pac, Inc.

1974
Mazak Corporation

1977
Comair, the Delta Connection

1977
Haberer Registered Investment Advisor, Inc.

1978
kforce.com

1978
Van Melle USA, Inc.

1979
Williamsburg Homes

Great Oaks Institute of Technology and Career Development

REAT OAKS INSTITUTE OF TECHNOLOGY AND CAREER DEVELOPMENT SUMS UP ITS MISSION CONCISELY: TO "PROVIDE QUALITY WORKFORCE DEVELOPMENT PROGRAMS AND SERVICES TO MEET THE NEEDS OF OUR CUSTOMERS." THAT SIMPLE SUMMATION, HOWEVER, BELIES THE DEPTH AND BREADTH OF THE SCHOOL'S OFFERINGS. ● GREAT OAKS IS THE CAREER AND TECHNICAL EDUCATION DEPARTMENT FOR 36 AFFILIATED SCHOOL DISTRICTS. THE LARGEST INSTITUTE OF

its kind in the United States, Great Oaks covers 2,200 square miles and serves high school juniors and seniors from 38 high schools in 12 southwestern Ohio counties.

Although Great Oaks provides services through four career development centers—Diamond Oaks in western Hamilton County, Laurel Oaks in Wilmington, Live Oaks in Milford, and Scarlet Oaks in Sharonville—the institute's services extend beyond the borders of its campuses to encompass workforce, economic, and career development initiatives throughout the region.

Dedication to Workforce Development

Recognized by the National Center for Research in Vocational Education as one of 15 exemplary vocational institutions in the nation, Great Oaks uses workforce development programs to reach high school students and adults. Roughly 3,200 high school students were enrolled in the institute's technical programs and were pursuing 50 different career majors during the 1999-2000 academic year.

In addition, Great Oaks annually serves more than 70,000 adults with a range of full- and part-time skill training and self-enrichment programs. The institute also offers specialized training through both the Great Oaks School of Practical Nursing and the Great Oaks Police Academy. Its Virtual Institute for Professional Development helps workers meet various certification and training requirements through 600 fee-based courses provided via the Internet. For those seeking more rudimentary training, Great Oaks provides adult basic literacy education, GED preparation and testing, and English as a second language (ESL) classes.

Understanding that training is merely a means to an end and that employers require skill proficiency, Great Oaks stands behind its graduates, assuring employers who hire graduates through the Campus Placement Program that their new employees have the requisite skills to perform jobs efficiently and effectively. If a graduate falls short in any of the guaranteed competency areas, Great Oaks will retrain the employee at no cost.

Fostering a Healthy Economy

In addition to its career development centers, Great Oaks operates three economic development centers intended to promote the

THE CORPORATE OFFICE FOR GREAT OAKS INSTITUTE OF TECHNOLOGY AND CAREER DEVELOPMENT IS LOCATED ON THE SCARLET OAKS CAMPUS IN SHARONVILLE, OHIO.

region's economic health. Among the institute's innovative development programs is the Workforce Initiative Training Partnership, a recent partnership with Cincinnati State Technical and Community College. In collaboration with regional employers, the program seeks to develop a highly skilled, motivated workforce that will make Greater Cincinnati the economic hub of a super region, extending throughout the three-state area—Indiana, Kentucky, and Ohio.

Other development efforts include the Turning Point Center, a program designed to train welfare recipients for the workforce; the Center for Economic Opportunity in Washington Court House; and the Individual Development and Economic Advancement (IDEA) Center in Hillsboro. The latter two programs seek to meet the assessment and training needs of local businesses while providing training and counseling to residents of those communities.

Another Great Oaks initiative, Project Hire, targets individuals who may have been out of the workforce for a long period of time or who face barriers such as transportation or child care concerns that keep them from working. The program seeks to expand the available labor pool in a tight labor market by assessing the needs of potential employers and employees and bridging the gap between them.

Great Oaks helps place workers with disabilities through its Project Search program, a joint effort with Children's Hospital Medical Center. This effort trains workers with physical and mental disabilities to perform specific jobs in the health care field. The institute's Community Links program uses a similar model to train unemployed urban workers for health care jobs.

Careers, Not Just Jobs

Great Oaks' mission extends to career development. The institute acts as the career development services coordinator to all students, from kindergarten to 12th grade, in each of the 36 districts it serves. That means identifying field trip oppor-

tunities, providing guest speakers, or finding other ways to introduce students to the world of work. Such efforts help students realize that they can have fulfilling careers, rather than just jobs with paychecks.

To foster career awareness, the institute sponsors a weeklong High Tech Career Camp for students about to enter the ninth grade. In addition to teaching kids about technology, the camp exposes math and science instructors to various fields so they can incorporate real-world challenges and examples into their lesson plans. That dual purpose typifies Great Oaks' commitment to lifelong learning.

Students who don't have the opportunity to attend the camp are likewise immersed in technology. State-of-the-art tools are at the heart of the Great Oaks operation. Whether they're learning about automobile repair or the latest advancements in printing, students are exposed to the relevant technology in their fields. For example, with tools such as the Virtual Learning Academy, an Internet-based instruction program that expands learning opportunities for high school students while enabling them to advance at their

own pace, Great Oaks continually finds ways to use technology to enrich the learning process.

Whether Great Oaks is immersing its students in cutting-edge technologies or helping them acquire fundamental English or literacy skills, the institute is helping to meet the needs of all of its constituents—individuals, employers, or residents.

ART AND PRINTING TECHNOLOGY STUDENTS DEMONSTRATE THEIR SKILLS TO CLIFF MIGAL, GREAT OAKS PRESIDENT AND CEO (TOP).

THE RIGOROUS CURRICULUM AT GREAT OAKS INCLUDES ACADEMIC AND TECHNICAL COURSES (BOTTOM).

Metalex Manufacturing Inc.

WITH SERVICES ON THE CUTTING EDGE OF TECHNOLOGY, METALEX MANUFACTURING INC.'S CULTURE IS DEEPLY ROOTED IN TRADITIONS OF SERVICE AND VALUE. THE BLUE ASH, OHIO-BASED, HIGH-TECH CONTRACT MACHINE SHOP MANUFACTURES MISSION-CRITICAL COMPONENTS FOR CLIENTS SUCH AS NASA, PRATT & WHITNEY, AND BOEING ROCKETDYNE. METALEX PRIDES ITSELF ON SUCH FUNDAMENTALS AS COMMITMENT TO QUALITY, COST EFFICIENCY, ON-TIME

delivery, and respect for individuals as much as its reputation for machining excellence.

Werner and Sue Kummerle launched the family-owned Metalex business in 1971, which now operates three separate, state-of-the-art facilities. In addition to the main manufacturing building on Cornell Road, the Grooms Road facility performs precision grinding, certified welding, and assembly of large and small prototype and rollout projects. Large broaching systems for the automotive industry are built in the Deerfield Road plant.

The company excels at leveraging expertise and knowledge gained from diversified industrial arenas, and maximizes capabilities and resources to cost effectively service a broad spectrum of customers. Metalex produces first-of-its-kind prototypes for global aerospace clients, and is fully capable of meeting production requirements as well. The company's manufacturing technology and skills developed from the aerospace market and the design, build, and runoff of custom equipment—such as broaching systems and high-speed converters that produce consumer products—are reflected throughout the services it provides worldwide. In addition

ASTRONAUT MICHAEL LOPEZ-ALEGRIA VISITS METALEX MANUFACTURING INC., WHERE HE CONGRATULATES ONE OF THE COMPANY'S CRAFTSMEN FOR A JOB WELL DONE.

to parts for the space shuttle's main engines, Metalex clients supply such diverse products as automobiles, disposable diapers, aircraft engines, beverages, and silicon wafers for computer chips.

Working Together to Satisfy the Customer

Metalex defines itself as "a no-nonsense, performance-driven organization providing a win-win-win situation to our customers, our employees, and our company." That may sound like just another catchy tag line, but everyone within the organization takes it to heart.

The company operates under the ISO 9001 umbrella supported by the Metalex Pro-C scheduling system, and creates a business plan for all prototype, high-tech, and large assembly projects. This plan takes every aspect of the job into consideration.

The Metalex business plan outlines manufacturing processes from beginning to end in scrupulous detail, ensuring no costly misunderstandings or unpleasant surprises for the customer. Particulars such as cost, labor hours, and equipment needs are listed, allowing both the customer and Metalex to assess the project's personnel and resource needs, as

well as providing the basis for monitoring performance.

Before launching manufacturing cycles, Metalex's engineering staff and programming department finalize the work process guided by the business plan. This includes provisions for final routers and step-by-step descriptions of each operation, as well as determination of the fixtures and special tools needed during the manufacturing process. As part of the plan, Metalex presents customers with custom designs for the special requirements. The company's ability to quickly design and manufacture such tools sets it apart from other high-tech machine shops.

By carefully following this process, Metalex eliminates risking unwanted surprises, ensuring customer satisfaction. Customers are assured that projects are backed by skilled engineers and seasoned staff, as well as by detailed and carefully thought-out plans.

When Precision Matters

Exacting attention to detail is critical, given the nature of Metalex's work. Each and every client—whether in consumer goods, automobile manufacturing, or human spaceflight propulsion—demands precise, reliable equipment and chooses Metalex because of its

A SPECIAL CERTIFIED PROCESS IS USED TO WELD THIS HOUSING. METALEX IS QUALIFIED FOR ASME IX, AMS-STD-1595, AND IS NADCAP CERTIFIED.

proven track record. The company's uncompromising standards were certainly important to astronauts aboard the space shuttle Discovery, the first of NASA's fleet to be launched with Metalex-manufactured liquid oxygen inducers in the orbiter's main engines.

While up to 40 percent of Metalex's current business is with the aerospace industry, the company's expertise is far ranging. From airframes and space propulsion to high-speed converters and key modules for automobile transfer lines, Metalex is raising the bar in the precision machining business.

People Make the Difference

As important as Metalex's planning process may be, the firm's exceptional team of skilled employees is the key to its success. The company's some 130 professionals are highly trained and dedicated to customer satisfaction. That dedication reverberates throughout the entire organization, from the janitorial staff to the finance department.

Metalex's long-term commitment to customers means having the latest in technology, equipment, and systems, and also emphasizes cultivating the best working conditions possible for employees. With the understanding that properly trained, dedicated craftsmen are crucial to effective customer service, Metalex relies on a small-company mentality where individual employees make the difference.

Consequently, Metalex employees have professional development opportunities that emphasize continuous learning and cross training. Equally important, they are involved in planning and decision-making processes without being bogged down in no-value bureaucracy.

Organizationally, the company is divided into six business units: Sales, Service, Job Startup, Total Quality, Purchasing, and Employee Education & Training; Quotation, Processing, Design & Build Technical Unit; CNC Programming, CMM Programming & Processing Technical Unit; Machine Shop; Customer/Metalex Operations Support & Communications; and Financial Department. Each of these units is a specialized, high-performance area overseen by a business unit leader and consists of several technology centers. The technology centers— headed by individuals who work, and are experts in, a particular discipline—encourage and facilitate knowledge sharing, uncompromising quality, faster throughput time, and greater value to customers.

Because all employees are asked to think in terms of problem solving, the company has an innovative, can-do spirit. Metalex embraces challenging, first-time projects as readily as it welcomes routine work. With all assignments being unique, the company learns from each one, and, as a result, Metalex staffers are constantly learning and perfecting problem-solving skills.

Just as no one tool meets every need, no one person has all the answers. At Metalex, success is a mix of technology, craftsmanship, knowledge, open communications, teamwork, and pride of ownership— old-fashioned values for attaining space-age goals.

A METALEX TECHNOLOGY LEADER TEACHES A YOUNG APPRENTICE THE ART OF TOOLMAKING.

AN ISO-GRID CASING, ONE OF SEVERAL PROTOTYPE COMPONENTS METALEX PRODUCES FOR ENGINES BEING DEVELOPED TO POWER THE JOINT STRIKE FIGHTER, AMERICA'S NEXT GENERATION OF COMBAT AIRCRAFT.

Cincilingua Inc.

N 1972, HUBERT M. COLLET AND HIS WIFE MARINETTE, FOUNDED THE CINCILINGUA INC. INTENSIVE LANGUAGE TRAINING CENTER WITH THE GOAL OF TURNING THE CENTER INTO AN "ISOLATION BOOTH," WHERE EXECUTIVES COULD LEAVE THE PRESSURES OF PERSONAL AND BUSINESS COMMITMENTS BEHIND AND BE IMMERSED FULL-TIME IN A LANGUAGE WITHOUT THE DISTRACTIONS OF NORMAL WORK ACTIVITIES. ● THE COLLETS, WHO ALREADY HAD IO

CINCILINGUA INC. CURRENTLY OPERATES FROM ITS OWN BUILDING ON EAST FOURTH STREET IN DOWNTOWN CINCINNATI (LEFT).

PIERRE COLLET, DIRECTOR, AND HUBERT M. COLLET, PRESIDENT, CONTINUALLY DISCUSS WAYS TO ENSURE TOTAL QUALITY (RIGHT).

years of experience in language training in both France and the United States, felt that conversation-based immersion courses were the best means of helping busy executives reach a functional ability in a language in a very short period of time. To further facilitate language acquisition, they began offering all-inclusive, comprehensive language training packages, thus providing top-quality training at the lowest possible price.

Unlike other schools that attempt to satisfy every student by designing their programs on a very broad and generic basis, Cincilingua personalizes and individualizes each course based upon the needs of the student. In addition to grammar, listening, and pronunciation exercises, the terminology and situational vocabulary incorporated into each program are based on individual students' particular jobs or positions, thus allowing them to use the language where their needs actually begin—in important business situations. Each course is administered by highly qualified and experienced instructors, and is monitored by program coordinators to assure continuous progress. A high success rate has brought client satisfaction and return business.

Learning Language

The Cincilingua method, through its intensive training program, employs three basic principles: first, language is learned through an inductive process of associating certain sounds with certain concepts. Second, it is necessary to associate the concept directly with the sound in order to begin to think in the language. And third, direct association without translation is the shortest path to fluency.

Therefore, students learn to speak a second language much the way they learned to speak their mother tongues: through direct association, constant practice, and consistent correction. Instructors teach by speaking to the student in the target language and by requiring him or her to respond in the same language. This rapid, question-and-answer drilling technique sets the course's pace from the very beginning and characterizes the teaching throughout the course. Performed orally and exclusively in the target language, this drilling technique teaches the basics of the language. The student's progression will be steady and systematic, from general structures to technical and business matters.

When a student begins a course, he or she receives textbooks, which are used mainly in the evenings to reinforce material taught in class. The core of the course is what occurs in class—the presentation and practice of functional concepts. The instructor also keeps a notebook during

SANDRA CASTILLO

SANDRA CASTILLO

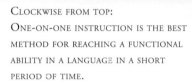

class, providing the students with a summary of every lesson. Thus, the student's attention is not divided between note taking and the lesson itself. The notebook also avoids repetition of material and mistakes in spelling and grammar that the student might make. Students take these notes home at the end of each class for review.

In addition, a synopsis of the day's class is recorded onto cassette tape, so that the student can study both the written and the spoken work simultaneously. The cassettes contain new words, expressions, and structures that were presented during the day.

An Ideal Location

Cincinnati has proved to be the ideal location for the Collets' center. Voted by *Places Rated Almanac*

as the most livable city in the United States, Cincinnati is safe, clean, easily accessible, and geographically located within a short distance of many of the top Fortune 500 companies. It offers the leisure opportunities of a large city, including sports events, excellent museums, and amusement parks, all in a friendly, small-town atmosphere and at very reasonable costs. Its many hotels ensure comfortable surroundings for short- and long-term stays.

From small beginnings, with only 10 classrooms and a small staff, Cincilingua showed steady growth, quickly necessitating expansion from its original location. The company currently operates from its own building on East Fourth Street in downtown Cincinnati. With 50 classrooms, ample administration offices, and a staff of more than 100

instructors, Cincilingua is exceeding the original dreams of the Collets.

The firm is most proud of the fact that it has become a top center for intensive training in the Midwest, counting as clients many major companies, such as General Motors, Ford, Chrysler, Dow Chemical, Eli Lilly, Caterpillar, Deere & Company, AT&T, Procter & Gamble, Toyota, and Honda. Cincilingua also has an excellent reputation as a center for intensive training in American English for executives from Mexico and Central and South America. Its future goals include expanding its market area to the entire United States, Asia, and Europe.

"Throughout the world," says Hubert M. Collet, "Cincilingua is becoming synonymous with cost-effective, efficient, intensive language training."

CLOCKWISE FROM TOP:
ONE-ON-ONE INSTRUCTION IS THE BEST METHOD FOR REACHING A FUNCTIONAL ABILITY IN A LANGUAGE IN A SHORT PERIOD OF TIME.

LUNCH WITH AN INSTRUCTOR IS AN INTEGRAL PART OF CLASS.

ALL OF CINCINNATI BECOMES A CLASSROOM FOR ENGLISH STUDENTS.

THE FIRM INDIVIDUALIZES EVERY COURSE BASED UPON THE NEEDS OF THE PARTICULAR STUDENT.

Paramount's Kings Island

PARAMOUNT'S KINGS ISLAND™ ISN'T AN ISLAND. IT'S A CITY WITH ITS OWN ZIP CODE, ITS OWN FIRE DEPARTMENT, ITS OWN GENERAL MANAGER WHO SERVES AS MAYOR, AND SOME 5,000 EMPLOYEES. NOT THAT THE MORE THAN 85 MILLION VISITORS WHO HAVE FLOCKED TO THE PARK SINCE 1972 NOTICE. TO THEM, KINGS ISLAND IS AN OASIS OF THRILLS AND FUN. ● ALTHOUGH MOST PEOPLE THINK OF PARAMOUNT'S KINGS ISLAND AS THE AMUSEMENT PARK LOCATED

off Interstate 71 in Mason, Ohio, the park actually traces its roots back much further. Kings Island's original owners got into the amusement park business in 1886 when they established Cincinnati's Coney Island.

Although the owners sold the Coney operation—which was often underwater during flood season—in the 1960s, several of its original attractions can be found at the new park, which opened in 1972. Among the historic rides still in operation today are a hand-carved, 1926 carousel featuring 18-karat-gold trim; flying scooters; Scrambler; and a classic log flume.

THE 700-ACRE PARAMOUNT'S KINGS ISLAND™, WHICH PARAMOUNT COMMUNICATIONS INC. PURCHASED IN 1992, IS THE LARGEST THEME PARK IN THE MIDWEST AND ONE OF THE LEADING INNOVATORS IN THE AMUSEMENT INDUSTRY.

King of Coasters

Historic though some of its holdings may be, Kings Island is anything but a museum relic. In fact, the 700-acre park, which Paramount Communications Inc. purchased in 1992, is the largest theme park in the Midwest and one of the leading innovators in the amusement industry.

With more than 85 live shows, rides, and attractions, Paramount's Kings Island is a critical mass of fun.

THE BEAST® OPENED IN 1979 AND REMAINS THE LONGEST WOODEN ROLLER COASTER IN THE WORLD.

Among the island's many attractions are the DROP ZONE™, the world's tallest gyro drop that enables riders to experience the thrill of a 315-foot, 67-mile-per-hour free fall; race car challenge DAYS OF THUNDER™; and WaterWorks, a 30-acre water park filled with water slides and a wave pool.

But it is the park's 13 roller coasters that are its hallmark. In 1972, the park christened The Racer, a roller coaster that faces both forward and backward. In 1979, it opened The Beast®, which, even after all these years, remains the longest wooden roller coaster in the world. Those landmark rides were followed by the King Cobra, the first stand-up looping roller coaster on the continent; the Vortex, the world's first six-loop coaster; and Flight of Fear™, an indoor, looping coaster that propels riders from zero to 54 miles per hour in just four seconds.

One might think it would be impossible to top such a choice list of rides, but in 2000, Paramount's Kings Island surpassed its own success when it unveiled Son of Beast™, the worlds' only looping wooden roller coaster, as well as the world's tallest and fastest such ride. The introduction of this ride marked the completion of a two-year, $40 million expansion that firmly cemented Kings Island's leadership position in the amusement industry.

Family Entertainment

Paramount's Kings Island isn't just for thrill seekers. The theme park includes two areas specifically designed for families with younger children. Hanna-Barbera Land™ includes rides and attractions based on familiar cartoons such as the Jetson's™, the Flintstones™, Yogi Bear™, and Scooby Doo™. New in 2001 was Nickelodeon Central™, an extravaganza of new rides, shows, and colorful characters. Guests are able to join the Wild Thornberry's™ as they journey down a river filled with whimsical adventure or fly with the Rugrats™ as they challenge Reptar. With the addition of the new Rugrat's inverted roller coaster, Paramount's Kings Island is the Kids' Coaster Capital of the World. In addition, the park features live shows suitable for the whole family.

With so many attractions, it's no wonder that Paramount's Kings Island is a leader in family entertainment. Thanks to Paramount Park's continued investment in rides, shows, and attractions, it's a position the park is likely to hold for generations to come.

Edward M. Haberer founded Haberer Registered Investment Advisor, Inc., a fee-only advisor, in 1977. His dream was to assist clients in the lifelong wealth creation experience within an environment of trust, making them feel as comfortable as possible. "At that time, banks, brokers, and a handful of investment advisors were courting high-net-worth individuals," Haberer recalls. "However, nobody was

providing unbiased, professional portfolio management to younger entrepreneurs and others who were just starting out. People needed someone they could totally trust in the management of their investment assets."

Some 23 years later, Haberer and the 16 members of his firm remain true to that mission. "A significant, ethical value system focused on the highest level of customer service permeates our organization," says Haberer. "We're focused on our clients' long-term success."

Cincinnati Roots

Because Haberer is a hometown firm, it does not owe allegiance to a large corporation in some faraway city. The firm has in-house analysts who conduct independent research, making decisions based on local clients' priorities and risk tolerance. That local focus remains a key part of what Haberer does to this day.

At the heart of Haberer's trust relationship with clients is the fee-only advisor structure. Unencumbered by commissions, the firm's investment decisions are inherently separate from conflict of interest. Clients simply pay a fee based on assets under management. The only incentive for Haberer to recommend any investment to a client is that it has the best reward-versus-risk profile based on that client's individual needs. There are no loads or sales fees. "Individual investors were very frustrated in years past by the lack of attention they received from banks and brokers," says Haberer. "There was, and still is, a need for unbiased advice."

Knowledge, Strength, Vigilance

Haberer uses three key words— knowledge, strength, and vigilance—as the summation of the firm's

background and commitment. "Knowledge isn't just about scholastic work," he says. "It's also about intuition. It means doing the right thing at the right time for the right reason. Strength relates to experience. Many of our staff members have been with the firm 10 years or more, and some are CFAs [Chartered Financial Analysts] or CPAs [Certified Public Accountants]. Vigilance, that's simple. After we make an investment for a client, we monitor it constantly. This is not just about performance; it's also about making sure that, over time, the investment remains a proper choice as the client moves through life's changes."

Part of this long-term vigilance approach applies to services such as estate planning, assisting clients in assuring a smooth transition of wealth from one generation to the next. Haberer works closely with outside attorneys, accountants, and other professionals in pursuit of clients' best interests. The local roots are evident, as Haberer employees develop working relationships with other Cincinnati professionals in related fields. Returning once again to the theme of avoiding conflicts of interest, clients know that these related professional services are unbundled—creating a natural system of checks and balances.

Clients learn that they can rely on Haberer to be both quarterback and watchdog on their behalf. "Many of our clients are Cincinnatians who don't want to focus on the challenges and vagaries of the market," Haberer says. "We take that responsibility off their shoulders. We believe that's what true professionals are supposed to do for their clients." Keeping knowledge, strength, and vigilance at the core of the firm's commitment, Haberer Registered Investment Advisor, Inc. continues to grow throughout the Cincinnati area.

EDWARD M. HABERER, PRESIDENT AND CEO OF HABERER REGISTERED INVESTMENT ADVISOR, INC., CONTINUES TO EMPHASIZE THE FIRM'S UNPARALLELED COMMITMENT TO THE SERVICE AND CONSISTENT PERFORMANCE THAT HAVE EARNED HABERER SO MANY SUCCESSFUL LONG-TERM CLIENT RELATIONSHIPS.

HABERER IS PROUD OF ITS TEAM APPROACH, PERSONAL SERVICE, AND DEPTH OF EXPERIENCE.

General Assembly, Inc.

GENERAL ASSEMBLY, INC. IS A SPECIALIZED EMPLOYMENT AND PRODUCTION SERVICE AFFILIATED WITH THE HAMILTON COUNTY BOARD OF MENTAL RETARDATION AND DEVELOPMENTAL DISABILITIES. GENERAL ASSEMBLY IS ABLE TO PROVIDE LOCAL BUSINESSES FULL-TIME EMPLOYEES, TEMPORARY EMPLOYEES, OR FULLY STAFFED PRODUCTION FACILITIES IN WHICH THE BUSINESSES' WORK CAN BE COMPLETED. THE COMPANY'S PRODUCTION FACILITIES ARE STRATEGICALLY

located throughout Hamilton County—with plants in Evendale, Fairfax, Green Township (Bridgetown), and north of Mount Healthy—making them convenient to businesses all over the tristate area. The plants are easily accessible from all interstate highways in the Cincinnati area, and have ample production, shipping, receiving, and warehouse space.

Simply Good Business

While the important social mission it serves may attract the companies that contract with General Assembly, these companies enter into a partnership with the firm because it makes irrefutable business sense. It is simply good business to have General Assembly address constantly fluctuating labor demands. With access to a labor pool of more than 1,800 dedicated workers, knowledgeable and skilled supervisors, and excellent quality control, a profitable relationship can exist for a company and General

Assembly. By forming this relationship, a company can add to its bottom line of profit maximization, and General Assembly can meet its bottom line of meaningful employment for Hamilton County citizens who have significant physical or mental disabilities.

Each General Assembly plant has a flexible production area, allowing for configuration based on the requirements of the business partner. The flexibility of the production area allows General Assembly to accommodate jobs of all sizes. The General Assembly supervisor has a dual role: to assure that business partners' projects are completed according to the specifications and deadlines, and to be an on-the-job trainer for the individuals with disabilities.

The company's business partners include large and small, local and multinational companies. Typical projects performed for General Assembly's business partners include bagging, collating, light assembly, preparing mailings, and custom packaging. Blister packing, L sealing, shrink-wrapping, weigh counting, stapling, and hot and cold gluing are some of the services available. Since most work is performed on a subcontract basis, the business partner is relieved of the burden of hiring and related payroll issues. Shipping can be arranged using General Assembly trucks or the business partners' trucks. The use of outside trucking firms, UPS, and FedEx further increases the options available to the business partner.

WITH ACCESS TO A LABOR POOL OF MORE THAN 1,800 DEDICATED WORKERS, KNOWLEDGEABLE AND SKILLED SUPERVISORS, AND EXCELLENT QUALITY CONTROL, A PROFITABLE RELATIONSHIP CAN EXIST FOR A COMPANY AND GENERAL ASSEMBLY, INC.

NOT ONLY CAN GENERAL ASSEMBLY BRING THE WORK TO ITS PLANTS, BUT IT CAN ALSO BRING ITS WORKERS TO A BUSINESS.

Component parts for assembly or packing projects can be sent from multiple suppliers directly to General Assembly plants, thus decreasing shipping, handling, and warehouse costs for the business partner.

An Eager Workforce

Not only can General Assembly bring work to its plants, but it can also bring its workers to a business. Since August 1999, more than 500 General Assembly employees have worked in business partners' plants. General Assembly assures that the right number of workers arrive at the business. Transportation arrangements are made by General Assembly through vendors such as van services or taxi companies to get the crew to work. This service is typically not included in the cost of doing business with General Assembly.

Many of General Assembly's business partners have hired the firm's workers. Unlike other temporary agencies, General Assembly does not charge either the business or the individual a placement fee. In fact, General Assembly will provide the business partner with support in training the new employee to learn the job, and is available for any retraining that may be needed if job responsibilities, duties, or work assignments change. General As-

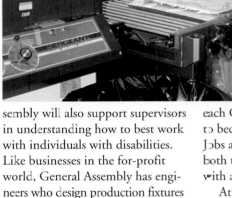

sembly will also support supervisors in understanding how to best work with individuals with disabilities. Like businesses in the for-profit world, General Assembly has engineers who design production fixtures and understand how to mold the production operations to the capability of the workers.

Attentive to Employees' Needs

General Assembly has been in the business of employing individuals with significant disabilities for more than 25 years. The company's supervisory staff is employed by the Hamilton County Board of Mental Retardation and Developmental Disabilities, and is trained in identifying the strengths, limitations, and adaptations needed for

each General Assembly employee to become a productive worker. Jobs are carefully assigned, assuring both the worker and the company with a win-win situation.

At a time when companies are struggling to fill positions, General Assembly's ranks continue to grow by approximately 70 workers each year. By entering into a business relationship with General Assembly, the business partner not only adds to its bottom line profit, but also actively supports General Assembly in its social mission: assuring that society's citizens with the most significant disabilities have the opportunity of enjoying a meaningful, productive life engaged in respected activities; making a just wage; and paying taxes.

CLOCKWISE FROM TOP LEFT:
THE FLEXIBILITY OF THE PRODUCTION AREA OF EACH GENERAL ASSEMBLY PLANT ALLOWS THE ORGANIZATION TO ACCOMMODATE JOBS OF ALL SIZES.

TYPICAL PROJECTS PERFORMED FOR GENERAL ASSEMBLY'S BUSINESS PARTNERS INCLUDE BAGGING, COLLATING, LIGHT ASSEMBLY, PREPARING MAILINGS, AND CUSTOM PACKAGING.

JOBS ARE CAREFULLY ASSIGNED TO EACH GENERAL ASSEMBLY WORKER, ASSURING BOTH THE WORKER AND THE COMPANY WITH A WIN-WIN SITUATION.

GENERAL ASSEMBLY WILL PROVIDE ITS BUSINESS PARTNERS WITH SUPPORT IN TRAINING NEW EMPLOYEES IN LEARNING THEIR JOBS.

Portion Pac, Inc.

Line up all the individual ketchup packets that Mason, Ohio-based Portion Pac, Inc. (PPI) produced in 2000 and they would circle the globe more than 19 times. While such tasty tidbits may fall into the category of fun facts, they also translate into big business for PPI, the nation's largest manufacturer of portion-control condiments. ● While the individual-sized portions may be small, the business

is huge and growing. Founded in 1973 by four former Serv-A-Portion employees, Portion Pac, Inc. in 1989 became a wholly owned subsidiary of H.J. Heinz Co. Today, PPI and Heinz produce more than 27 billion portion-control packets annually. That's an average of 108 million packets of condiments, dressings, and sauces per day.

Quality a Top Priority

Propelled by the growth of the quick-service restaurant industry, PPI's rapid rise from upstart company to industry leader is attributable to the quality of its product. "Customers benefit greatly from PPI's cost-saving and quality products," according to Managing Director Pete Jack. "Restaurant owners have confidence in us because we have a track record for cost-effective solutions to food-service challenges. Customer satisfaction has made PPI a portion-control leader since 1973.

We pride ourselves on working with well-known restaurants to formulate condiments and sauces to complement their food items."

To ensure quality, PPI pays careful attention to every detail. Customer satisfaction isn't simply based on how a product tastes. How the product looks and smells and how easy the package is to open are also important considerations. Consequently, PPI pays scrupulous attention to quality control.

Flexibility is important as well. PPI knows that customers' needs differ. That's why PPI designs and builds virtually every major piece of equipment the company uses. By manufacturing its own machines, PPI is able to provide faster turnaround, more reliable production, and the flexibility needed to respond to special requests from customers.

Flexibility is an important asset when a company produces as many different types of products as PPI

does. PPI manufactures more than 350 varieties and sizes of condiments, dressings, and sauces, including mustard, ketchup, mayonnaise, jam and jelly, salad dressing, table syrup, ice-cream toppings, taco sauce, salt and pepper, creamer, and more. To add to the variety, condiments are packaged in a wide variety of containers—including squeeze packs, dry packs, cups, and pourable packs—that seal in each product's flavor.

Good Things Come in Small Packages™

Quick-service restaurants are a mainstay of PPI's business. Long John Silver's was the first chain restaurant to sign on as a PPI customer. It has since been joined by the likes of Burger King, Carl's Jr., Jack in the Box, KFC, Hardee's, and Wendy's. Branded joint ventures represent an increasing share of PPI's business, and the firm has forged alliances to license, pack, and sell

PORTION PAC, INC. (PPI) MANUFACTURES MORE THAN 350 TYPES AND SIZES OF CONDIMENTS, DRESSINGS, AND SAUCES IN A WIDE VARIETY OF CONTAINERS.

▼ MILES WOLF

portion-control products from several of America's best-known brands including Log Cabin®, Mrs. Butterworth's®, Welch's®, French's®, SueBee®, Wish-Bone®, Musselman's®, ReaLemon®, and Jif® Peanut Butter.

PPI also manufactures a wide variety of high-quality house brands. Among the company's popular private label brands are Taste Pleasers Gourmet® dipping sauces and salad dressings, Chatsworth® dipping sauces, Madeira Farms® jams and table syrups, Salsa Del Sol® salsa and cheese dips, Sweet Pleasers Gourmet™ dessert toppings, and Squeezers® peanut butter and cheese products. In addition to its Mason, Ohio location, PPI also operates plants in Dallas, Texas; Jacksonville, Florida; and Los Angeles.

In May 1999, Heinz U.S.A. acquired Atlanta-based Thermo Pac, Inc. to complement PPI's operations. Thermo Pac's hot-fill capability allows PPI to offer its customers a wider array of products and services than ever before. Portion-control packets for packaged foods, like the cheese in macaroni and cheese and the fudge pouches in cake mixes, are an important part of Thermo Pac's business. With this additional capability, PPI can now offer a complete array of portion-control foods—from condiments, dressings, and cold-fill sauces to hot-fill sauces—for both the restaurant and the packaged food industries.

Because Thermo Pac, a major supplier to military food service, does a huge volume of business, the acquisition brings great economy to production, and allows PPI to offer existing and new customers even better cost benefits, along with the familiar benefits of portion control. What's more, because of the nature of Thermo Pac's products, the acquisition positions PPI to move beyond the food service industry and into the retail market.

In July 2000, Heinz U.S.A. acquired International DiverseFoods, Inc. in Nashville. The acquisition of International DiverseFoods provides PPI the opportunity to extend the company's capabilities into an extensive line of bulk food products, including sauces, condiments, salad dressings, syrups, batters, breading, and pancake, waffle, and biscuit mixes. The product mix makes International DiverseFoods a natural complement to PPI and Thermo Pac's product line, and assures PPI's ability to keep pace with the future growth of the food industry into the 21st century.

Dedicated Employees and the Community

While focusing on growing its business, PPI has never lost sight of its role as a corporate citizen. As part of its 25th anniversary celebration in 1998, the company donated funds to the Mason Police Department to purchase software that would update its neighborhood crime-watch systems. PPI's community support has similarly benefited the Special Olympics, March of Dimes, American Cancer Society, and Warren County United Way.

PPI is equally supportive of its 1,000-plus employees. "They are the reason why we have a national reputation for customer service, innovation, and great taste," Jack says. "Employees have always been an integral part of the success of PPI. The company's outstanding industry reputation for quality, flexibility, and speed of service is not possible without the continuing support of our loyal employees."

PPI MANUFACTURES A WIDE VARIETY OF HIGH-QUALITY HOUSE BRANDS, INCLUDING TASTE PLEASERS GOURMET® DIPPING SAUCES AND SALAD DRESSINGS.

SQUEEZERS® PEANUT BUTTER IS ANOTHER HOUSE BRAND MANUFACTURED BY PPI.

Mazak Corporation

To call Mazak Corporation a metal-cutting machine tool manufacturer would be like calling Secretariat a horse. Although technically accurate, the definition falls woefully short of the truth. Florence-based Mazak, which dubs itself "the other thoroughbred from Kentucky," is interested in providing clients more than just machines that fit their needs. Using the combined resources of its agile manufacturing plant,

national technology center, and national customer service and support center—each of which is headquartered in a dedicated facility on the Florence campus—Mazak produces solutions to clients' manufacturing challenges.

Award-Winning Manufacturing

Mazak's manufacturing plant, which opened its doors in 1974, may be the best advertising the company has because the facility incorporates the flexible manufacturing system (FMS) technology that Mazak touts to its clients, as well as computer-integrated manufacturing technology. The result is simple: the company has won accolades across the globe. Among the awards heaped upon the company have been the Society of Manufacturing Engineers' Award of Excellence, the Agility Forum Citation for Best Agile Practices, and the Philip B. Crosby Global Competition Award from the American Society for Competitiveness.

The key to Mazak's successful process starts with the company's manufacturing philosophy. Indeed, the Florence facility embodies the company's driving principles: to utilize manufacturing flexibility,

to vary its product mix, to rapidly adjust volumes in response to global and local demand, to shorten production lead time, to produce innovative products via new technology concepts, to be globally competitive, and to continuously improve.

The company achieves these lofty goals through a process that incorporates new, advanced materials; inventory principles; materials handling; machining processes; and assembly. The flexible manufacturing systems—which include a Mazak laser-cutting FMS for fabricated parts, a large casting FMS for structural parts, a prismatic-part FMS for precision housings, and an FMS for cylindrical parts—are scheduled and updated every day.

Only Mazak's outstanding quality rivals the company's impressive flexibility. The firm employs total quality management (TQM) processes throughout the facility. More than 40 quality circles meet weekly to discuss ideas on cost reduction, efficiency improvement, and error elimination.

Tomorrow's Technology Today

Mazak's goal is not merely to deliver a superior quality product that meets a client's needs.

As a supplier of capital equipment, the manufacturer is constantly working to create innovative hardware and software that improve customer operations.

The Mazak National Technology Center works to deliver just such a value-added product. By bringing together diverse technologies, ideas, and experience, the group works to develop and demonstrate solutions to clients' ever changing manufacturing needs.

The experts at the center work with clients to understand not only their technological needs and the shortcomings of existing technologies, but also their capital investment strategies and return on investment needs. That collaboration enables Mazak's engineers to understand all the issues at hand, and to devise solutions that meet both the manufacturing and the financial needs of the client.

Support for the Life of the Machine

The process of listening to and meeting the needs of the customer continues long after a Mazak machine is produced. The company's comprehensive customer support program, called OPTIMUM, begins even before a customer invests in

With headquarters located in Florence, Mazak Corporation dubs itself "the other thoroughbred from Kentucky."

Brian J. Papke, president of Mazak, has led the company to the point where it receives accolades from across the globe.

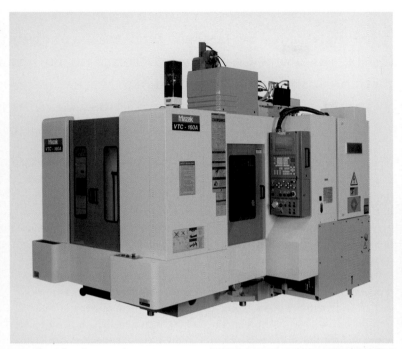

Mazak technology and continues throughout the life of the machine. The OPTIMUM program, which emphasizes quality, promptness, and readily available assistance, is administered through Mazak's National Customer Service and Support Center.

Located on the Florence campus, Mazak's 62,500-square-foot National Customer Service and Support Center houses field service, parts support, and 24-hour telephone technical assistance. The center evaluates every aspect of Mazak service from efficiency of installations to critical machine breakdowns and the determination of appropriate staffing levels. The center provides myriad services as well, including remanufacturing, spindle repair, Mazatrol single-source software and hardware support, centralized parts supply, customer training, and networking with the company's regional support centers and distributor locations.

Mazak understands that the measure of quality is not just how a machine performs when it leaves the factory floor. Rather, quality is tested daily across the nation during the life of the machine. Under those conditions, the true measure of quality is not only the machine's ability to perform, but also the Mazak staff's ability to service it promptly and efficiently. With that in mind, the company assures its clients that no matter where or

when a problem might arise, Mazak's solution-minded staff is only a phone call away. Should replacement parts be necessary, they will be shipped within 24 hours.

Because a machine's efficiency depends on the operator's ability to use it, Mazak offers an extensive training program. By assuring clients that their employees have the know-how to create new applications and programs, the proficiency in running the machine, and the skill in maintaining it, Mazak offers a comprehensive and professional training program. Classes in the designated 10,000-square-foot training facility cover all types of CNC programming, maintenance of Mazak machines, and maintenance of CNC systems. The company provides comprehensive training on automation systems and accessories as well, and can even

bring programming training to the client site if necessary.

No Detail Too Small

The company's attention to detail, which encompasses every aspect of design, manufacturing, innovation, and service, explains why Mazak has had so many laurels heaped upon it and why the company has credibility when talking to clients about optimal manufacturing processes in their own organizations. Through its own demonstrated ability to respond rapidly to customers' orders; work with customers to improve their production technology and optimize their operations; and provide fast, reliable customer support, Mazak has proved itself to be a thoroughbred in every sense of the word.

Comair, the Delta Connection

NEW COMPANIES MAKE HISTORY. ALMOST NONE MAKE IT TWICE. BUT WITH ITS MERGER IN JANUARY 2000 WITH LONGTIME PARTNER DELTA AIR LINES, COMAIR, THE DELTA CONNECTION IS POISED TO DO JUST THAT. ● AS AN INDEPENDENT REGIONAL AIRLINE, COMAIR CHANGED THE NATURE OF THE REGIONAL AIRLINE INDUSTRY IN 1993, WHEN IT INTRODUCED THE 50-SEAT CANADAIR REGIONAL JETS TO THE NORTH AMERICAN MARKET. THE REGIONAL JETS (RJS), POWERED

by engines made by Cincinnati-based GE Aircraft Engines, are replacing turboprop technology, establishing Cincinnati as the cradle of the RJ revolution. Moreover, regional jets have set a new industry standard for service and cemented Comair's position as a leader in innovation.

That quality, as well as Comair's consistent profitability and continual growth, inspired *Aviation Week and Space Technology* to name it the Best Managed Regional Airline in 1999. And in 2000, for the second time in less than a decade, *Air Transportation World* dubbed Comair Regional Airline of the Year, noting that "Comair is what other regional airlines aspire to be."

Excited by the speed and conve-

nience of Comair's RJs, passengers have flocked to the airline, making it one of the fastest-growing airlines in the industry. While competitors have tried to replicate the airline's success by introducing RJs of their own, Comair remains staunchly entrenched as the leader in the field; it operates more RJs than any other carrier. In December 2000, Comair introduced all-jet service to Cincinnati, a benefit the airline plans to extend to the rest of its markets by December 2001. The move is part of Delta Connection's plan to offer jet service throughout its entire route system.

Joining forces with Delta has enhanced Comair's commitment to innovation and improvement,

and has accelerated the regional jet movement that began nearly a decade ago. In spring 2000, Comair and its sister Delta Connection carrier Atlantic Southeast Airlines announced the largest regional jet order in history. The order, for up to 500 aircraft, brings tremendous opportunities to the travelers and communities served by these carriers.

"Customers benefit because RJs allow Delta Connection carriers to provide service in smaller markets—markets that may develop into big-jet markets," says David Siebenburgen, president and chief executive officer of Delta Connection, Inc., the Cincinnati-based entity that coordinates the operations of Delta Connection carriers.

The Delta Advantage

Important as Delta's financial backing is to Comair, it is just one of the many advantages associated with the marriage. While enabling Comair to continue to expand its services to new routes, the combination also intertwines Comair service with that of its parent company and other regional airlines in the Delta network. As part of Delta Connection, Comair is now able to connect its passengers to air service "from anywhere to everywhere," Siebenburgen says.

In addition, the partnership provides customers with an exemplary level of customer service, coordination of schedules, and numerous other conveniences. For example, passengers enjoy through fares, through ticketing, passenger check-in services, and credit in Delta Air Lines' SkyMiles program.

History in Cincinnati

Although a subsidiary of Atlanta-based Delta, Comair remains deeply rooted in Cincinnati, where Raymond and David Mueller

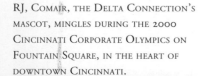

RJ, COMAIR, THE DELTA CONNECTION'S MASCOT, MINGLES DURING THE 2000 CINCINNATI CORPORATE OLYMPICS ON FOUNTAIN SQUARE, IN THE HEART OF DOWNTOWN CINCINNATI.

JIM CALLAWAY

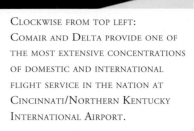

founded the company with a few small propeller-driven commuter airplanes in 1977. As demand for air service expanded, so did Comair as it converted to larger and more sophisticated turboprops before becoming a pioneer of the regional jet revolution.

Comair's long partnership with Delta, along with the growth brought by its use of regional jets, helped make the combination of Delta and Comair a powerfully positive force in Cincinnati and Northern Kentucky. Some 8,000 Comair and Delta employees call Cincinnati and Northern Kentucky home, and the airline contributes more than $1.4 million annually to community causes in the region.

Delta has been providing air service to Cincinnati for more than 50 years, and the airline brought jet service to the region in 1960.

Cincinnati is at the heart of the airline's operations. Delta designated Cincinnati/Northern Kentucky International Airport a major hub in 1986 and launched an ambitious initiative to expand its facilities at the airport. The airport is also the center of Comair's operations; Concourse C is Comair's largest hub. Completed in 1994, it is considered one of the most innovative regional jet facilities in the world and includes 53 gates and a number of stores, restaurants, and offices. Comair expanded the 60,000-square-foot Concourse C in 1999, adding 35,000 square feet. Including Comair's second hub at Orlando International Airport, the airline today serves more than 7 million customers a year in more than 90 cities in four countries, including 32 states in the United States.

Comair continues to expand its Northern Kentucky facilities. In

spring 2000, the airline christened a new, fixed-base operation that includes an aircraft hangar, customer service, and aircraft management facilities, and in fall 2000, unveiled its spacious, new headquarters building located across the street from the previous headquarters. That expansion paved the way for Comair to expand its Jet Express charter service business. In addition, Comair University, the regional carrier's corporate training and skills development program conducted in partnership with Thomas More College, is also located in Northern Kentucky.

While enhancing Comair's ties to the region, these state-of-the-art facilities and programs likewise ensure the airline will continue to enjoy its reputation for innovation well into the future. For Comair, the sky truly is the limit.

CLOCKWISE FROM TOP LEFT: COMAIR AND DELTA PROVIDE ONE OF THE MOST EXTENSIVE CONCENTRATIONS OF DOMESTIC AND INTERNATIONAL FLIGHT SERVICE IN THE NATION AT CINCINNATI/NORTHERN KENTUCKY INTERNATIONAL AIRPORT.

COMAIR'S CONCOURSE C IS ONE OF THE MOST INNOVATIVE REGIONAL JET PASSENGER FACILITIES IN THE WORLD.

COMAIR'S DEDICATED CUSTOMER SERVICE PROFESSIONALS ARE AMONG THE BEST TRAINED IN THE AIRLINE INDUSTRY.

TWO OF COMAIR JET EXPRESS' CHARTER AIRCRAFT STAND READY FOR ACTION IN THE COMPANY'S NEW GENERAL AVIATION FACILITY AT THE AIRPORT.

Van Melle USA, Inc.

ERLANGER, KENTUCKY, IS HOME TO AIRHEADS, ONE OF THE HOTTEST CANDIES ON THE MARKET TODAY. THE FIRST AIRHEADS WERE SHIPPED IN 1986, AND THE NAME WAS CREATED BY KENTUCKY SCHOOLCHILDREN. TODAY, MORE THAN 600 MILLION BARS ARE ENJOYED ANNUALLY. THE CHERRY, BLUE RASPBERRY, WATERMELON, GREEN APPLE, STRAWBERRY, ORANGE, AND THE EVER POPULAR WHITE MYSTERY HAVE BECOME A HALLMARK OF CONCESSION STANDS,

convenience stores, and retail establishments of every size and shape all over the country.

While Van Melle USA takes delight in its business, its mission is a serious one. The firm is a subsidiary of Holland-based Van Melle, N.V. Best known for its Mentos brand of candy, the Dutch firm employs some 4,100 workers through 25 operating companies.

In January 2001, Perfetti S.p.A.—the Italian privately owned chewing gum company—and Van Melle N.V., the Dutch confectionery group, jointly announced the intended merger of both companies to create a world-class confectionery group.

Van Melle has consistently valued its independence, even celebrating its centennial in 2000. However, the international confectionery market is experiencing consolidation and increasing competition, both at the retail and manufacturing levels, and therefore Perfetti and Van Melle have decided to join forces to strengthen their combined position in the global market.

Following the completion of the merger, it is intended that the combined group will be named Perfetti Van Melle. The new group will preserve the principles and values of both companies with respect to business strategy, employees, customers, consumers, and the environment.

WITH ITS CHEWY, CANDY TAFFY CALLED AIRHEADS, VAN MELLE USA, INC. IS A SUBSIDIARY OF HOLLAND-BASED VAN MELLE, N.V., BEST KNOWN FOR ITS MENTOS BRAND OF CANDY.

Fun Business, Serious Mission

The Erlanger-based subsidiary, which oversees all of the company's North American operations, seeks to meet the needs of Van Melle's approximately 170 local employees by ensuring that they are motivated and involved. Toward that end, senior management spon-

sors monthly meetings with staff members to share pertinent information about the company.

"We're a very people-oriented company," says Bob Howard, vice president of marketing. "It comes across in everything we do. People are our most precious resource."

Sweet Success

Consumers are the real beneficiaries of Van Melle's business.

Millions of candy lovers in 80 countries enjoy Van Melle candies. Although the company makes a variety of nonchocolate candies, it only markets Airheads and Mentos in the United States.

Van Melle USA manufactures some 4,800 pounds of chewy Airheads at its Erlanger plant every hour, five days a week. In November 1999, the company acquired an additional facility in Buffalo Grove to produce the new brand extension, Airheads Xtremes, which sell for a mere 15 cents each, or two for a quarter. "Airheads are very much a U.S.-focused brand, but they're very popular in the Caribbean and the Philippines as well," Howard notes.

Mentos are manufactured internationally and imported. Although the well-loved mint flavor is most familiar to the U.S. audience, Mentos are available in mixed fruit, cinnamon, and berry fresh flavors locally, and the product's black licorice flavor is a favorite in Europe.

THE ERLANGER, KENTUCKY-BASED VAN MELLE USA OVERSEES ALL OF THE COMPANY'S NORTH AMERICAN OPERATIONS.

Marketed as the Freshmaker, Mentos have become a cult favorite among candy connoisseurs.

Although the company is dedicated to growing its business, Howard says that Van Melle does not mind marketing just a few brands in the United States. "You can only be good at certain things, and we are very good at what we do," he says. "As a relatively small player in the world market, we have to focus on quality brands."

Benefits for the Children

Van Melle is equally careful about the way it approaches environmental resources. In fact, the company's environmental commitment and dedication to reducing any negative impact on the planet are part of its mission statement, making its commitment more than just corporatespeak. Van Melle requires its subsidiaries to invest 1 percent of their profits in improving the environment.

At Van Melle USA, the company's environmental initiatives include a massive internal recycling campaign, as well as a six-mile stretch of geo-

IN 1986, CHERRY BECAME THE FIRST FLAVOR SHIPPED. TODAY, THERE ARE SEVEN GREAT FLAVORS, WHICH ALSO INCLUDE STRAWBERRY, BLUE RASPBERRY, WATERMELON, GREEN APPLE, ORANGE, AND WHITE MYSTERY.

thermal piping that heats and cools the facility and dramatically reduces the amount of nonrenewable energy used by the site. Van Melle USA's headquarters, dedicated in 1997 and constructed around the shell of the company's older facility, includes an abundance of natural light and recycled building materials. "We didn't inherit the earth," Howard notes. "We just have it on loan for our children."

The payoff from Van Melle

USA, Inc.'s focus is plain to see in the fervid followings Airheads and Mentos have inspired. This proof of consumer devotion reminds Howard that his business, while based on the bottom line, is grounded in something sweeter. "We have a lot of school groups come through our factory here," he says. "All you have to do is watch the kids tour the factory and enjoy the candy to know that this business is really about the consumer."

Williamsburg Homes

WITH MORE THAN TWO DOZEN ACTIVE COMMUNITIES IN GREATER CINCINNATI AND DAYTON, WILLIAMSBURG HOMES HAS EARNED AN ENVIABLE REPUTATION AS ONE OF CINCINNATI'S LEADING HOME BUILDERS. THE FIRM IS WELL KNOWN FOR PROVIDING THOUSANDS OF ATTRACTIVE, SUPERIOR-DESIGNED, AWARD-WINNING, LUXURY HOMES TO BUYERS WHO DEMAND QUALITY PRODUCTS. ● "WE PREFER TO CREATE DESIRABLE NEIGHBORHOODS WHERE FAMILIES

can flourish and enjoy a sense of community," says Kevin Davis, president of Williamsburg Homes. "Walking paths, lakes, sidewalks, and pools are very common in our communities. We're also very selective of where we build, choosing some of the area's most desirable locations that offer convenience and accessibility to interstates, recreational facilities, and, most important, good schools."

Quality

Williamsburg Homes was founded in 1979, but its roots can be traced back more than 50 years before that date. The Ryan

brothers began building homes in 1947. They were following in the footsteps of their father, Edward Ryan, who had built his first house in 1925. For decades, the Ryans constructed thousands of homes in cities across the United States, all the while remaining dedicated to their family's commitment to quality and value.

In 1996, Williamsburg became a division of William Ryan Homes Inc., a company that created new neighborhoods in Illinois and Wisconsin. Today, backed by the Ryan family's experience, Williamsburg continues its mission: "to satisfy our customers' housing desires by building

high-quality, single-family homes and communities as economically as possible, exceeding our customers' expectations."

Value

Williamsburg's customers can select their dream homes from more than 50 innovative designs ranging in size from 1,400 to 4,000 square feet and in base price from $180,000 to more than $500,000. Floor plans are articulately designed to make efficient use of space so home owners can enjoy maximum value from every square foot. And Williamsburg homes not only are packed with standard features and amenities that are usually seen in more expensive homes, but also boast traditional architecture with all the modern conveniences today's families could want.

Plans generally include great rooms or oversized family rooms; spacious bedrooms featuring luxurious master suites with private baths and walk-in closets; up-to-date kitchens designed for both cooking and memory-making family interaction; an abundance of closet space; and basements. Williamsburg homes also come complete with landscaping packages, sodded front yards, concrete driveways, and sidewalks.

Williamsburg tailors each floor plan to meet the individual needs and style of the family that helps design it. "We want our customers to feel their homes are built just for them," says Davis. Buyers can choose from hundreds of options—some of which are upgrades—that can change any model's innovative floor plan into an exceptional custom plan. Moreover, full-time, professional interior design specialists at the in-house home store advise owners and offer them a personalized approach

FULL-TIME, PROFESSIONAL INTERIOR DESIGN SPECIALISTS AT WILLIAMSBURG HOMES' IN-HOUSE DECOR CENTER ADVISE OWNERS AND OFFER THEM A PERSONAL-IZED APPROACH IN THE SELECTION OF COUNTLESS NAME-BRAND ITEMS.

in the selection of countless name-brand items.

Service

The latest in technology is combined with pride in workmanship to give every Williamsburg home functionality, innovation, and classic style. "We use state-of-the-art, energy-efficient construction techniques, as well as the most durable building materials and appliances available," Davis explains. "Additionally, we employ professionals who work for our time-tested, dedicated team of industry leaders in specialized trades. Their collective talents, expertise, and old-world craftsmanship build homes with safety and permanence in mind—homes that reflect

Williamsburg Homes' commitment to excellence."

The firm's customer orientation and warranty programs ensure that each home will be built exactly as it was envisioned. As part of Williamsburg's unique Rest Assured home owner warranty program, owners have a quality assurance (QA) manager at their side from before the foundation is poured until a year after they are settled. This peerless program begins with the QA manager reviewing the individualized plan and selections with the owner.

In other phases of the construction process, the QA manager discusses the framing, electrical, plumbing, and ventilation work with the buyer, as well as demon-

strating and explaining equipment, warranties, and home owner maintenance responsibilities. Items requiring attention are noted and addressed within 30 days of the closing.

After the closing, 60-day, 11-month, and 23-month reviews are conducted to address any questions or concerns. To further increase a buyer's peace of mind, all Williamsburg homes are warranted by the company's Rest Assured warranty program.

"Isn't it nice to know that when you finally find the home you truly love, it also comes with one of the industry's best warranty programs?" says Davis. "It is just further proof that when you build a great home, you can offer a great warranty."

WILLIAMSBURG PLANS GENERALLY INCLUDE GREAT ROOMS OR OVERSIZED FAMILY ROOMS, SPACIOUS BEDROOMS FEATURING LUXURIOUS MASTER SUITES WITH PRIVATE BATHS AND WALK-IN CLOSETS, AND UP-TO-DATE KITCHENS DESIGNED FOR BOTH COOKING AND FAMILY INTERACTION.

kforce.com

IN A TIGHT LABOR MARKET, KFORCE.COM IS A PERSONNEL MANAGER'S BEST FRIEND. ONE OF THE NATION'S PREMIER SPECIALTY STAFFING FIRMS, KFORCE.COM PROVIDES EMPLOYERS WITH REGULAR CONSULTANTS AND TEMPORARY EMPLOYEES WHO SPECIALIZE IN AREAS SUCH AS INFORMATION TECHNOLOGY, FINANCE AND ACCOUNTING, HUMAN RESOURCES, HEALTH CARE, PHARMACEUTICAL, LEGAL, ENGINEERING, E-SOLUTIONS CONSULTING, SCIENTIFIC, INSURANCE, AND INVESTMENTS.

Although the kforce.com name is new, the company has more than 20 years of experience serving Cincinnati-area employers. Previously known as Romac International and Source Services Corporation, kforce.com has been recognized as an invaluable resource for identifying and delivering professional talent since 1978.

While many other staffing and consulting organizations take a buckshot approach to delivering talent, kforce.com specializes in two specific arenas, which it knows thoroughly. Because company recruiters have professional experience in their specialty areas, they understand the demands of specific positions and industries. As a result, kforce.com's corporate clients don't have to worry about educating a recruiter about their business because the firm understands the qualities and credentials candidates need in order to succeed in those organizations.

kforce.com doesn't just identify candidates for its corporate clients; it gets to know them. Through in-depth interviews, the recruiter learns about candidates' strengths and weaknesses, geographic preferences, and long-term goals. The recruiter then matches like-minded candidates with the right corporations.

With more than 100 offices nationwide, including two in Cincinnati, kforce.com knows where to find the talent. While firms struggle to find qualified professionals, kforce.com can simply turn to its database of hundreds of thousands of individuals to find potential matches.

Combining Expertise and Innovation

After recognizing the changing needs of the marketplace, kforce.com reinvented itself in January 2000 when the company merged its dedication to personalized service with the advanced technology of the Internet. The result was a firm that provided stability and support to more traditional companies, while offering the lower costs, shortened cycle times, and extended operating hours of the Web.

Today, corporate clients can cull through candidate résumés at kforce.com in the wee hours of the morning if they want to, knowing that they have the expertise of more than 2,000 career advocates, résumé editors, job-skills assessors, and other specialists backing them up. Whatever a client's style and desire, kforce.com offers the services to match.

The Short-Term Staffing Resource

Understanding that companies' staffing needs fluctuate, kforce.com stands ready to fill in temporary employment gaps and project staffing needs with exceptional workers. Because kforce.com has an extensive pool of highly trained contract and core employees upon which to draw, the firm can provide anything from an interim CFO to a lab technician at a moment's notice.

As a result, companies don't have to worry about getting the work accomplished when a key employee takes a vacation or parental leave. Similarly, companies can ratchet up staffing for a year-end audit or the launch of a Web site without worrying about being overstaffed during quiet periods. Best of all, companies can count on someone else to handle payroll and personnel issues. By providing employees who are more than qualified to tackle the job, kforce.com takes the worry out of professional staffing and lets companies get down to business.

ONE OF THE NATION'S PREMIER SPECIALTY STAFFING FIRMS, KFORCE.COM PROVIDES EMPLOYERS WITH REGULAR CONSULTANTS AND TEMPORARY EMPLOYEES WHO SPECIALIZE IN A WIDE VARIETY OF FIELDS.

1981-1990

1982
Custom Editorial Productions Inc.

1982
United Industrial Piping

1983
Balluff Inc.

1983
Belvedere Corporatipm

1984
Business Courier

1985
Adecco

1986
Ciber, Inc./DigiTerra, Inc.

1987
Comfort Suites

1987
The Payne Firm Inc.

1988
Lockwood Greene

1989
Aon Risk Services, Inc. of Ohio

Custom Editorial Productions Inc.

THE PEOPLE AT CUSTOM EDITORIAL PRODUCTIONS INC. (CEP) HAVE QUITE A JOB AHEAD. THEY MUST TRANSFER THE NUCLEAR WASTE FROM TWO SMALL STORAGE CONTAINERS INTO ONE LARGE CONTAINER. SPILLING ANY WASTE MEANS THOUSANDS OF DOLLARS IN FINES, NOT TO MENTION SERIOUS ENVIRONMENTAL CONSEQUENCES. TO COMPLICATE MATTERS, THERE IS NO INSTRUCTION MANUAL AND THE CLIENT IS INCOMMUNICADO. THEY HAVE A TANGLED WEB OF ROPES

attached to a bungee cord ring and 15 minutes to go.

The CEP team is intent on the task, but confident. After all, the nuclear waste is really only dried beans in coffee cans and the fictitious scenario is simply part of a team-building exercise at a company retreat. Although this particular challenge is new to the staff members, problem solving is familiar—it might as well be just another day on the job for the folks at CEP.

An Established and Growing Company

As a leader in the publishing services field, CEP is accustomed to complex projects and demanding schedules. The small staff—fewer than 20 associates—provides project management, writing, developmental editing, art preparation, page makeup, and editorial and design services to clients in a range of fields. Although the company performs many of the tasks usually associated with publishing, CEP is not a publisher. Rather, the firm performs all the behind-the-scenes work involved with developing and preparing products for manufacturing and market-

ing. These days, those products include traditional print materials, such as high school and college textbooks, professional books, scientific journals, and training manuals, as well as high-tech media, such as on-line instruction aids, CD-ROM testing tools, and Web-based content.

Mary Lou Motl, CEP founder and president, launched the business in 1982 during a week when more businesses failed than in any week since the Great Depression. Despite what some might have perceived as a bad omen, Motl confidently moved forward. Nearly 20 years later, Motl is a respected player not only in her field, but throughout the Cincinnati business community.

Through the years, CEP has developed a list of loyal clients, including publishers, professional societies, government entities, and corporations. Clients include Course Technology/Thomson Learning, Prentice Hall/Pearson, Centre Pointe Learning, Glencoe/McGraw-Hill, American Association of Petroleum Geologists, American Bar Association, Cincinnati Art Museum, Environmental Protection Agency, Rand Corporation, and Microsoft.

CEP's success springs from the premise that outsourcing writing, editing, design, and production services saves clients time and money. Publishers, in particular, benefit from CEP's services. Because textbook publishing is a seasonal industry, publishers can avoid hiring additional staffers by contracting with CEP during peak periods. For its part,

CLOCKWISE FROM TOP: "BECAUSE EVERYONE IS WORKING TOGETHER, CLIENTS CAN BE SURE THEY'RE GETTING THE MOST FROM EVERY ONE OF US," SAYS MARY LOU MOTL, CUSTOM EDITORIAL PRODUCTIONS INC. (CEP) FOUNDER AND PRESIDENT. "THE STAFF HERE IS UP TO ANY CHALLENGE."

THE SALTWATER AQUARIUM ADDS SPARKLE TO DAILY DISCUSSIONS AT CEP.

BASED IN CINCINNATI SINCE 1982, CEP PROVIDES PROJECT MANAGEMENT, WRITING, DEVELOPMENTAL EDITING, ART PREPARATION, PAGE MAKEUP, AND EDITORIAL AND DESIGN SERVICES TO CLIENTS IN A RANGE OF FIELDS.

CEP addresses its need for additional talent by turning to a reliable stable of freelancers. Because the organization can expand and contract with demand, CEP is always ready to meet clients' needs, but remains lean enough to ensure a low overhead, saving customers money. What's more, because CEP is continually upgrading its technology, clients benefit from the newest software without having to invest in it themselves.

But perhaps the primary reason clients turn to CEP again and again is because the company produces top-quality work and has, as Motl says, "a reputation for meeting the tightest, most outrageous deadlines." She adds, "We're known for our ability to get things done."

According to Motl, the company stays on top by anticipating what its clients will want next. As clients reposition and repurpose their materials, CEP offers tailored solutions. For instance, over the past several years, educational publishers have been looking for textbook support materials for today's high-tech class-

room. CEP has responded with CD-ROM-based testing software, customized PowerPoint presentations, on-line instructional aids, and distance learning programs. As new technologies and client needs emerge, CEP will be ready. "When a client approaches a problem, we want to have a solution to meet it," Motl says.

Interesting People
Doing Interesting Things

Visitors cannot walk through the CEP office without noticing the 300-gallon, saltwater fish tank. Like the fish in the aquarium, CEP people are bright and distinctive. For each project, a team of six or seven employees and freelancers is assembled. Each staff member brings a different set of strengths and skills to a project team, and each has a specific area of responsibility, such as manuscript development, copy editing, art production, page layout, proof reading, or project management. Because each team member takes ownership of a particular segment of the job with a project leader overseeing the opera-

tion in its entirety, attention to detail is balanced with project coordination and deadline management.

Although job tasks may be compartmentalized, the CEP environment is characterized by esprit de corps. Motl fosters a collegial workplace through company outings, including a staff retreat and an annual celebration of CEP's founding. The camaraderie has an important impact on CEP's clients and their projects: it fosters better communication among team members and makes CEP a fun place to work, both of which contribute to higher quality output.

"Because everyone is working together, clients can be sure they're getting the most from every one of us," Motl says. "The staff here is up to any challenge. We emphasize creative problem solving and teamwork. As a result, everyone has a real sense of ownership in the process. When you have such a talented group of people all working toward the same goal, you get the best results. That's what brings the clients back time after time."

CLOCKWISE FROM TOP: CEP STAFFERS ACCOMPLISH GREAT THINGS OUTSIDE OF WORK, TOO. BETSY NEWBERRY, MANAGER OF EDITORIAL SERVICES, IS A GOLFER, WHILE PROJECT EDITORS JANET BIXLER AND MEGAN SMITH-CREED ARE A GARDENER AND PASTRY CHEF, RESPECTIVELY. GENERAL MANAGER MARVIN GOOD IS AN AVID CHICAGO CUBS FAN, AND DEVELOPMENTAL EDITOR ROSE MARIE KUEBBING IS A BICYCLIST. AMY FRANCIS, PRODUCTION ASSISTANT, IS AN ART CRITIC AND VINCE IACOBUCCI, GRAPHICS SPECIALIST, IS A CARTOONIST.

United Industrial Piping

WHEN MARK W. MOSLEY FOUNDED UNITED INDUSTRIAL PIPING (UIP) IN 1982, THE COUNTRY WAS IN THE MIDST OF A RECESSION, AND THE CUSTOMER SERVICE REVOLUTION THAT WOULD TRANSFORM U.S. BUSINESS WAS JUST STARTING TO STIR. IT MIGHT NOT HAVE SEEMED LIKE A GOOD TIME TO START A MECHANICAL CONTRACTING BUSINESS WITH A RADICALLY DIFFERENT APPROACH TO CUSTOMER SERVICE, BUT, AS IT TURNED OUT, THE TIMING WAS PERFECT.

The result was a Cincinnati success story that continues to exceed even Mosley's expectations. UIP now employs approximately 200 people, with a blue-chip client list of primarily Fortune 100 manufacturers, along with a mix of regional and national clientele. In a construction trade once dominated by a project-to-project, low-bidder mentality, UIP has forged strong, lasting relationships with customers.

A New Approach

Prior to founding UIP, Mosley had accumulated an extensive background in mechanical contracting, where he learned his trade and observed some of the shortcomings that often prevented customers from getting what they expected or needed. "My goal in starting UIP was to offer the customer value and service," Mosley says. "At the time, the pricing structure in construction was outlandish. Productivity was down and prices were up. We set out to turn that around through increasing productivity and reducing cost by being an open shop contractor."

Implementing that philosophy meant changing some longtime beliefs and expectations. "I had to change the marketplace," Mosley says. "At the time we started, the marketplace had a large group of competitors offering roughly the same prices and the same performance. There were a lot of old, inflexible companies that turned out work to suit themselves, not the customer."

Mosley operated differently, focusing on customer satisfaction

CLOCKWISE FROM TOP RIGHT: "MY GOAL IN STARTING UNITED INDUSTRIAL PIPING (UIP) WAS TO OFFER THE CUSTOMER VALUE AND SERVICE," SAYS MARK W. MOSLEY, PRESIDENT.

UIP HAS BEEN HELPING CINCINNATI GROW SINCE 1982.

UIP HAS WON AWARDS FROM A NUMBER OF NATIONAL ORGANIZATIONS.

and impeccable quality. He trained his personnel in-house, where he had control over the thoroughness of instruction and could immerse employees in his philosophy of customer service. And Mosley concentrated on developing long-term relationships with customers rather than the traditional deal-to-deal approach. As a result, 90 percent of UIP's business is repeat business from its established customer base.

"A contractor would traditionally come in on a design and build just to the minimum specifications that the customer needed at that time," Mosley says. "I don't believe in that shortsighted approach. You have to look forward in your projections to what needs might be in the future. No business wants to get caught in the cost of shortsightedness. Every business wants to grow. You don't want to have to rip out a system down the road and put in something entirely new when your needs grow, because doing that winds up costing you much more in the end."

Keeping an eye on future needs has been an essential element of UIP's relationship-building approach. "When I sell to customers," Mosley says, "I tell them, 'I don't just want to come in and do one project for you. I want to be your contractor of choice. I want to be here for the long term.' That was a very different message from what they had been hearing. When a contractor's entire focus is based on the low bid, that low-bid mentality makes it virtually impossible to look out for the best interests of the customer."

A Key Link in Manufacturing Excellence

UIP is a mechanical contractor that specializes in fabricating piping systems to customer specifications for a wide variety of manufacturing applications, including fire protection and structural platforms. The company produces the piping used to move fluids, gases, and semisolids throughout facilities in the manufacturing process. Simply put, a manufacturing facility

cannot function without such piping, or without the mechanical expertise to make the piping work properly. UIP plays a crucial role in ensuring that those products are made properly and at the price and quality that meet consumer expectations. In that way, the company touches the lives of people in Cincinnati and throughout the entire world every day.

For instance, piping systems fabricated and installed by UIP carry pulp used to make paper, along with the ink used in printing presses, in order to produce newspapers and countless other printed materials. UIP systems are also used in processing a myriad of food and personal hygiene products purchased by millions of Americans daily. And labyrinths of piping created by UIP form intricate webs that move and process products of both the chemical and petroleum industries. The wide-ranging applications of UIP piping also include the automotive, steel, power generation, and pharmaceutical industries.

In addition to installation, piping maintenance service has become a fast-growing area of business for UIP. "When manufacturers look to cut costs, one of the first areas they examine is the maintenance department," Mosley says.

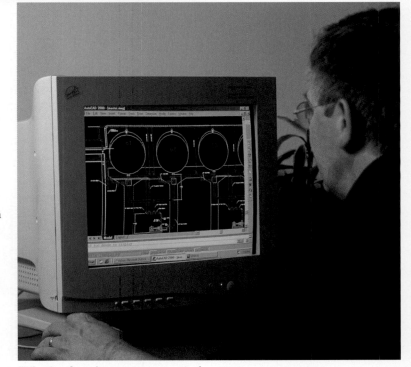

"They've found it more economical to outsource maintenance tasks than to complete them in-house. We can do it much more cost effectively than they can, because we can work for them on an as-needed basis."

A Continuum of Success

Today, UIP is one of the nation's leading mechanical contractors due to its performance in meeting or exceeding customer expectations. The company has been named among *Plumbing & Mechanical* magazine's top 100 mechanical contractors. UIP has enjoyed growth of 15 to 20 percent annually during its first two decades of operation in an industry that historically has been subject to major swings in sales.

"I had some large goals when I started the company," Mosley says. "From the very first, I knew that we had exceptional personnel, and those people have made exceptional success a standard for UIP."

Customer Satisfaction

U IP has worked to ensure that its customers' mechanical goals are met and their projects completed on time, with as little disruption as possible," Mosley says. "The ultimate goal for all manufacturers is to increase their production and productivity, and thus increase sales and the bottom line. When we go into a project, time is of the essence. The goal is to complete the project as quickly as possible, within quality specifications, allowing the customer to return to full-capacity production."

Beyond speed and convenience, doing the job right remains paramount for UIP, where quality is part of the culture. Says Mosley, "We double- and sometimes triple-check the product before it leaves our facility. And we have strict

customer satisfaction standards throughout the installation process, including final cleanup."

In-House Fabrication

U IP is one of only a handful of mechanical contractors in the Cincinnati region with in-house fabrication. The advantages are two-fold: in-house fabrication permits greatly improved quality and it mini-

mizes disruption at customer sites.

"In-house fabrication helps us meet or beat project schedules," Mosley says. "Fabricating pipe at the customer's site, on the other hand, can mean frequent delays and considerable disruption of the customer's business."

Team Project Building

U IP uses a sophisticated team-based approach on all of its projects. As many as 10 teams, each with three to six members, are involved in every project. "We treat every job, no matter what its size, as if it's the only job we have," Mosley says. "Every job receives the utmost attention. We're able to do that because of the team concept. Every project is reviewed on a daily basis, not only for production schedules, but also for material tracking, fabrication tracking, deliveries to the job site, installation, customer satisfaction, and, most important, safety."

Technology and Training

B ringing the most advanced technology and training to each job is another essential ingredient in UIP's success. For instance, the company was among the first mechanical contractors in Greater

A MAJOR PART OF UIP'S COMMITMENT TO SUPERIOR SERVICE IS ITS FOCUS ON SAFETY AND RELATED EMPLOYEE TRAINING.

INTRICATE MIXED GAS PIPING, PROCESS TUBING, AND INSTRUMENTATION FOR RESEARCH AND DEVELOPMENT FACILITIES AND FOOD-PROCESSING PLANTS ARE AMONG UIP'S SPECIALTIES.

Cincinnati to utilize AutoCAD. "Our piping detailers use this computerized system to double-check the designs and to ensure proper fit of the piping system for its intended location," Mosley says. "Also, AutoCAD makes in-house fabrication more efficient and accurate. Designs are field verified, and AutoCAD is used to create precise fabrication drawings. The result is the elimination of surprises and delays during the installation process."

With two staff inspectors certified by the American Welding Society (AWS), UIP is one of the nation's few mechanical contractors with this capability. In fact, the company is often called upon to provide inspections for power plants and other critical installations handled by other contractors. In addition, UIP has the experience to provide X-ray-quality welding in cases where strict specifications demand welds that meet the most thorough inspection requirements.

Attaining high-level welding capability comes only through a commitment to employee training. That commitment is embodied in UIP's full-time, on-staff trainers of welding technique, who focus on continuously upgrading technology and methods for safety, pipe-related installations, and the different processes UIP personnel encounter in the field. The company maintains a highly regarded in-house welding and piping training program in which graduates must demonstrate mastery of all skills before receiving certification.

"Technology is constantly changing, and we are always at work to stay on the leading edge through superior training that keeps our people current and our capabilities state of the art," says Mosley.

Committed to Safety

A major part of UIP's commitment to superior service is its focus on safety. The company has a full-time safety director, as well as a safety team of field employees that meets monthly to discuss every aspect of the job, including UIP personnel and customer safety. An in-house training center provides instruction to employee groups on a regular basis.

"Customers have recognized our safety program as one of the best in the industry," Mosley says. "It goes back again to education. If you're constantly exposed to a safety message, you're much more aware of safety and committed to making a safe effort every time out."

UIP meets or exceeds all Occupational Safety and Health Administration standards, and maintains a good workers' compensation claim record as the company strives to reach a goal of zero accidents.

Environmental Care

UIP has made it a policy over the years to develop relationships with clientele that have solid environmental records. Partnering with such companies places UIP in a much stronger market position, since resources can be dedicated to project work and not to dealing with the consequences of environmental irresponsibility.

"We do not want to be a part of a project that could result in hazardous spills or toxic discharges that would be damaging to the environment," Mosley says. "We take that posture not only because it could hurt our business, but also because we care about the quality of life in the community. We all have to live here, and doing work that is safe and environmentally responsible is the right thing to do."

Anticipating a Prosperous Future

Going forward into the next century, Mosley expects UIP to continue its steady, healthy growth by providing value, high quality, and total customer satisfaction. Piping installation and outsourcing of piping maintenance continue to be areas of particularly broad opportunity. "We are always looking for greater penetration in all areas of the market, both locally and beyond the tristate region," Mosley says. "A changing economy generally brings with it industrial changes, and that is an opportunity for UIP."

"Cincinnati is a progressive, value-oriented area," Mosley continues, mentioning the city's new stadiums, riverfront developments, area manufacturing, and industrial plant expansions as examples. "We have thrived in that type of business climate simply because we deeply believe in providing value and personal service to the customer. We feel our philosophy of business is in perfect step with the business community here and throughout the Midwest."

UIP HAS THE EXPERIENCE TO PROVIDE X-RAY-QUALITY WELDING IN CASES WHERE STRICT SPECIFICATIONS DEMAND WELDS THAT MEET THE MOST THOROUGH INSPECTION REQUIREMENTS.

Balluff Inc.

TUCKED AWAY IN THE WOODS OF FLORENCE, KENTUCKY, BALLUFF INC.'S PASTORAL SETTING BELIES ITS HIGH-TECH MISSION AND ITS PHENOMENAL GROWTH. THE GERMANY-BASED MANUFACTURER OF SENSORS AND TRANS-DUCERS HAS SEEN ITS SALES GROW AT AN ANNUAL RATE OF 25 PERCENT SINCE MOVING TO FLORENCE IN 1983, AND, ACCORDING TO PRESIDENT AND CEO KENT HOWARD, THAT GROWTH PROMISES CONTINUED SUCCESS IN THE YEARS TO COME. ● BALLUFF INC. IS A

subsidiary of the German Balluff GmbH & Co., an independently held manufacturer of sensors and trans-ducers, with more than 1,000 employ-ees and sales of more than $100 million. The Florence plant, home of Balluff's North American opera-tions, has a 43,000-square-foot facil-ity with more than 100 employees.

Emphasizing Solutions, Service, and Success

Among Balluff's products are transducers, precision switches, and industrial sensors. The firm's primary customers are metalworking, plastics, and automotive companies, which have provided a stable base for the company. Balluff's products are also found in a broad array of appli-cations. For example, Cincinnati Milcron, a world leader in plastic injection molding equipment, has standardized on Balluff transducers. Balluff's sensors are used to control, regulate, automate, position, and monitor manufacturing sequences. The firm's sensors can be found in Universal Studios' King Kong and Jaws exhibits in Orlando, as well as at the Beach, a Cincinnati-area water park, where they determine the size

and number of waves in the wave machine. Also, Balluff identifica-tion systems track the molds from which contact lenses are made.

By producing quality products and offering quick, reliable turn-around, Balluff has met customer demand and generated steady growth. The company adheres to a three-part mission statement emphasizing sensor solutions, superior service, and a commitment to its customers' success. Because the company manu-factures some 22,000 products, customers often turn to Balluff's technical support team for assistance in selecting the appropriate product. Balluff provides free samples for customers to test products on pro-duction equipment to ensure success-ful operation.

Balluff's products are of the high-est quality. The Florence manufac-turing facility meets the ISO 9001 international quality standard. The broadest of three ISO 9000 standards, ISO 9001 covers everything from design engineering and quality con-trol to manufacturing, training, and service. Still, Howard believes it is the company's service that sets it apart from its competitors. "Any-

body can sell sensors," he says. "It's the technical expertise and service that make the difference."

Howard, who succeeded John Goyer, the Balluff president and CEO who cemented the company's lead-ership position in the North American market, says the firm's mission reflects its values and its commitment to service. To meet customers' needs quickly, Balluff fills most orders the same day and, should a customer have a question, assistance is always available. "You won't get voice mail if you call here," Howard says. "A live person will answer your call and your questions."

An Employee-Friendly Environment

Balluff's concept of service applies not only to its customers, but to its employees as well. In addition to great benefits, such as a base four-week time-off package, full health benefits, and flexible schedules, Balluff's some 110 local employees enjoy a sense of ownership in the company that comes from empower-erment, and they are rewarded with a companywide profit sharing plan. Employees are challenged to solve

THE NORTH AMERICAN HEADQUARTERS OF BALLUFF, INC., LOCATED IN FLORENCE, KENTUCKY, HAS UNDERGONE THREE MAJOR EXPANSIONS IN THE LAST 15 YEARS.

problems for themselves and are given the tools to execute their decisions. In addition, the company pays 100 percent of employees' tuition for continuing education, even if the courses they select aren't job related. That's a fringe benefit Howard says exemplifies Balluff's overall commitment to positive thinking.

Balluff provides a number of small extras as well. Whether it's free coffee and popcorn in the lunchroom, or plants and skylights in the carpeted factory, Balluff is committed to making its Florence facility a pleasant and comfortable work environment. To ensure that the company is meeting the high standards

it sets for itself, Balluff conducts regular employee satisfaction surveys. Those types of initiatives have enabled Balluff to enjoy low employee turnover at a time when many of its competitors are losing their best workers.

Just as Balluff shares its success with its employees, the company works to benefit the community as a whole. The firm contributes to the Fine Arts Fund, United Way, Northern Kentucky University, and Thomas More College. In addition, Balluff employs students in co-op programs with Northern Kentucky University, GMI, Thomas More College, and University of Kentucky.

Forward Focus

Balluff, which has doubled the size of its current facility since moving to the site in 1986, expects to maintain its growth by pursuing its winning initiatives and expanding its e-commerce strategies. But the company's goals, like its values, aren't exclusively related to growing the business, Howard says. Although growth is vital, maintaining an impeccable record of customer and employee satisfaction is equally important.

"Customer service is our main point of differentiation," Howard says. "We want to be an easy company to do business with. But in order to maintain customer satisfaction, employees have to be happy with their jobs. We want to make sure that we continue to serve all of our constituents, now and in the future. Innovation is vital to keeping our competitive advantage and to exceeding our customers' expectations. At Balluff, we believe in the power and integrity of a professional workforce."

MANUFACTURING FACILITIES AT BALLUFF ARE FILLED WITH UNEXPECTED SURPRISES SUCH AS SKYLIGHTS, CARPETING, AND PLANTS (LEFT).

PRODUCING BALLUFF'S LEADING-EDGE SENSOR PRODUCTS REQUIRES EXCEPTIONAL ACCURACY AND RELIABILITY. TESTING AND CALIBRATION TAKE PLACE THROUGHOUT THE COMPANY'S MANUFACTURING PROCESS TO ENSURE TOP PERFORMANCE (RIGHT).

BALLUFF'S INDUCTIVE AND OPTICAL SENSORS REPRESENT A MAJORITY OF THE PRODUCTS USED FOR A WIDE VARIETY OF AUTOMATED MACHINES (LEFT).

BALLUFF'S MICROPULSE LINE OF LINEAR TRANSDUCERS PROVIDES THE CRITICAL MEASUREMENT FEEDBACK ESSENTIAL TO MANY AUTOMATED MACHINES (RIGHT).

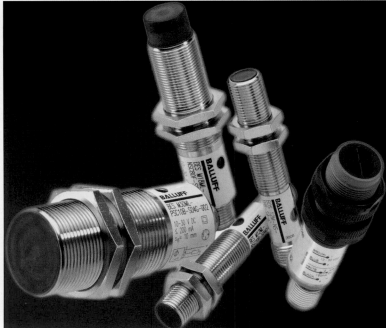

Belvedere Corporation

WHEN COMPANIES TALK ABOUT BUILDING ON TRADITION, THEY ARE OFTEN SPEAKING IN A RHETORICAL SENSE. BUT WHEN THE BELVEDERE CORPORATION USES THE PHRASE, THE COMPANY MEANS IT LITERALLY. KNOWN AS ONE OF THE CITY'S PREEMINENT REAL ESTATE MANAGEMENT AND DEVELOPMENT COMPANIES, BELVEDERE HAS MADE A NAME FOR ITSELF NOT ONLY BY BUILDING SHOWPLACES FOR THE FUTURE, BUT ALSO BY RESTORING CINCINNATI'S ARCHITECTURAL

jewels from bygone eras and using award-winning commercial development projects to revitalize entire communities.

A true understanding of the city has fueled Belvedere's success in Cincinnati. Steven Stein and brothers Stuart and Alex Warm, who founded the company in 1984, all grew up in the area and their families' histories have evolved with the city. Understanding the needs of the area's residents and business community, as well as the history and character of the local real estate market, has

enabled Belvedere to identify market opportunities outsiders might have missed and to create architectural gems that stand out as local landmarks.

Since undertaking its first project, the development of the 125 East Court Street building, Belvedere has undertaken numerous endeavors throughout the city. In the process, the firm has emerged as a full-service property management, development, and real estate services company responsible for more than $300 million in assets and more than

4 million square feet of office, hotel, retail, and parking facilities. Belvedere's areas of expertise include property management, leasing, renovation and construction oversight, financial analysis and projections, debt financing, and equity and joint ventures.

Specializing in Excellence

Among Belvedere's operating divisions are commercial office, retail, and industrial parks; hotels; and parking garages. The company's commercial office division has built

BELVEDERE CORPORATION TAKES CREDIT FOR THE RENOVATION OF THE CAREW TOWER COMPLEX, WHICH THE COMPANY PURCHASED IN EARLY 1990 (LEFT).

ONE OF BELVEDERE'S HALLMARK PROJECTS IS THE DEVELOPMENT OF THE CENTRAL PARKE BUSINESS PARK (RIGHT).

or renovated more than 2 million square feet of space in numerous properties. By owning and managing multiple properties, Belvedere allows tenants who outgrow one space the flexibility to relocate to another, and to choose from properties in different price ranges and locations.

Belvedere's retail group has developed and manages about 500,000 square feet of space, including the Carew Tower shopping center downtown and in various suburban strip centers. At the same time, the firm's office and industrial park division has built more than 2 million square feet of office space and corporate office parks in areas extending from Queensgate to Tri-County.

Belvedere's hotel division has renovated, owns, and oversees the management of approximately 30 percent of the downtown Cincinnati hotel market, while its garage division has developed and/or manages more than 1,000 spaces of garage parking in the area. In all, Belvedere manages and has an ownership interest in five downtown properties, including the URS Center, formerly the CBLD Center, and in another 33 properties sprinkled throughout the Cincinnati area.

Some of the company's hallmark projects include the renovation of the historic Vernon Manor Hotel and Central Parke. Belvedere likewise takes credit for the renovation of the Carew Tower complex,

which the company purchased in early 1990. An art deco masterpiece listed as a National Historic Landmark by the U.S. Department of the Interior, the complex includes the 600-room-plus Omni Netherland Plaza Hotel, which was awarded a 1998 Gold Award by *Meetings & Conventions* magazine.

Promoting Economic Development

Understanding that the importance of a building goes well beyond brick-and-mortar aesthetics, Belvedere is equally in tune with the economic impact its projects have on the neighborhoods where they are located. After General Motors closed its Norwood plant in 1986, Belvedere was able to pump new life into the neighborhood. The

company purchased the 60-acre site and developed Central Parke, a mixed-use development that includes more than 900,000 square feet of office, retail, and flexible business space. The complex, which brought more than 3,500 jobs to the city of Norwood, won the prestigious National Economic Development Partnership Award from the National Council for Urban Economic Development in 1997 and was highlighted in a *New York Times* article.

Belvedere's success lies in its commitment to quality. Because the company is closely integrated with Warm Bros. Construction, it is able to achieve the highest quality while realizing substantial savings. The impressive results can be seen in buildings such as the CBLD Center, a 26-story office, retail, and parking facility completed in 1989. The center, located at Seventh and Walnut streets downtown, includes 496,000 square feet of prime space just two blocks north of Fountain Square and is one of downtown's most sought-after addresses.

Whether a project is new construction or careful renovation of a historic property, Belvedere Corporation brings attention to detail, pride in workmanship, and a long-term view to each and every development. That attitude, coupled with attentive management and the expertise of its team of professionals, allows the firm to achieve stability and consistency in all of its projects.

THE VERNON MANOR HOTEL IS ANOTHER OF BELVEDERE'S RENOVATION PROJECTS.

THE CAREW TOWER COMPLEX INCLUDES THE 600-ROOM-PLUS OMNI NETHERLAND PLAZA HOTEL.

Business Courier

AT THE *Business Courier*, IT'S ALL BUSINESS ALL THE TIME. "ANYTIME MONEY CHANGES HANDS, WE'RE INTERESTED AND WANT TO BE TELLING OUR READERS WHAT'S GOING ON," SAYS DOUGLAS BOLTON, PUBLISHER, WHO RETURNED TO THE PAPER IN THE ORGANIZATION'S TOP SPOT IN LATE SUMMER 2000. ● THE *Business Courier* BEGAN ITS OPERATION IN 1984, AND HAS SEEN ITS BIGGEST GROWTH BETWEEN 1996 AND 2001. THE *Courier* PUBLISHES A WEEKLY BUSINESS NEWSPAPER,

delivered by mail each Friday, and is read by more than 75,000 businesspeople throughout Greater Cincinnati. The *Courier* also reports business news on its Web site, www.cincinnati.bcentral.com, providing readers with real-time local business news and headlines each business day.

"Our mission is to be the dominant provider of local business news and information to our readers," says Bolton, who was the paper's editor from late 1996 until November 1997, when he was named publisher of the *Courier*'s sister operation in Dayton.

"Through our weekly paper and the daily Web site, there's no reason why a businessperson in Greater Cincinnati should need any other source to keep up to date, well informed, and fully aware of the information they need to own or run a business or make critical career decisions," Bolton says.

The *Courier* employs a staff of some 15 editors and reporters, who help publish about 4,000 pages of business news annually—more than both Cincinnati daily newspapers combined. The paper also provides business news to listeners and viewers through news partnerships with WCPO-TV Channel 9 and WLW-AM 700.

The *Courier*'s editorial staff, led by Rob Daumeyer, editor, and Richard Curtis, managing editor, is supported by an advertising sales team of 12 professionals, two circulation sales and customer service account executives, and nine people in administrative, marketing, and production jobs. The *Courier*'s sales team, led by *Courier* veteran Jerry Mader, serve as consultants to local businesses, helping those businesses grow through marketing and advertising strategies aimed at reaching the highly educated and affluent readers of the *Courier* and its sister publications across the country.

Award-Winning Newspaper

Recent awards won by the *Courier* demonstrate its employees' commitment to producing a quality newspaper. The Society of American Business Editors &

DOUGLAS BOLTON SERVES AS PUBLISHER FOR THE *BUSINESS COURIER*.

THE *COURIER* IS READ BY MORE THAN 75,000 BUSINESSPEOPLE THROUGHOUT GREATER CINCINNATI.

MARK BOWEN

MARK BOWEN

Writers, a national journalism trade organization, recently named the *Courier* one of the five best weekly business newspapers in the country in its annual awards contest. The *Courier* had won the designation once before, in 1997. Other business journals winning the award recently are located in Detroit, San Francisco, Atlanta, and Boston.

The *Courier* was also recently rated by its own workers as the best workplace within American City Business Journals Inc., the Charlotte-based company that owns the *Courier* and 40 other business journals across the country. The workplace rating came in a poll of all American City workers. The *Courier*'s overall score of 4.35—on a one-to-five scale, with five being the best—was the best among all of American City's individual newspapers. The *Courier*'s operations department, coled by Kristin Davenport, art director, and Kim Spangler, business manager, was the highest ranking of American City's 160 individual departments.

American City

American City Business Journals Inc. is the United States' largest publisher of metropolitan weekly business newspapers. American City also is a major publisher of auto racing newspapers and magazines, as well as a sports annual, through

its Street & Smith's Sports Group. In addition, the company owns a national advertising sales firm and a commercial printing company. American City employs nearly 2,000 people, and its papers have a combined circulation approaching 450,000.

Ray Shaw is chairman and chief executive officer of American City, which he acquired in 1985 after retiring from the Dow Jones & Co. and the *Wall Street Journal*. At that time, American City owned 21 business weekly newspapers. Shaw had spent 29 years at Dow Jones, the last 10 as president and chief operating officer. During his tenure at Dow Jones, the company's annual revenues tripled to $1.7 billion.

In 1995, American City was purchased by Advance Publications, a long-established, privately held media company. Advance is the parent company of Condé Nast Publications, *The New Yorker* magazine, and *Parade* magazine, and is the owner of more than 20 daily newspapers throughout the country.

Through American City's and Advance's investments, the *Courier* has grown considerably since its conception by a group that would later become the nucleus of American City. The *Courier* took its biggest growth step when it acquired its rival, the *Greater Cincinnati Business Record*, in 1996 and merged the two

newspapers. Paid circulation nearly doubled to more than 12,000. Advertising revenue has also grown considerably since the merger, most years by double digits.

Business Veteran

A veteran for nearly 20 years of the journalism business—most of it spent in Cincinnati at the *Courier*, the *Business Record*, and the *Cincinnati Post*—Bolton hopes to build the *Business Courier*'s circulation even further with better marketing and continued improvement in the newspaper's news delivery.

"While my role as publisher includes the business operation of the newspaper, my roots are on the editorial side as a reporter and editor, and I strongly believe that the driving force of our newspaper must be the fair and accurate reporting and commenting on business news and issues that are important to our readers," says Bolton. "Local business news is our business, and we want to do a better job of delivering local business news, information, and commentary to our readers. We are mindful of our ability to influence what happens in the community, and we take that responsibility very seriously."

"THROUGH OUR WEEKLY PAPER AND THE DAILY WEB SITE, THERE'S NO REASON WHY A BUSINESSPERSON IN GREATER CINCINNATI SHOULD NEED ANY OTHER SOURCE TO KEEP UP TO DATE, WELL INFORMED, AND FULLY AWARE OF THE INFORMATION THEY NEED TO OWN OR RUN A BUSINESS OR MAKE CRITICAL CAREER DECISIONS," BOLTON SAYS.

As one of the world's largest employers, Adecco has something special to offer its clients: employees with the necessary skills for the job. Whether companies are looking for temporary associates or full-time employees, Adecco can meet their needs and provide a wide range of skills—from general clerical and industrial to more specialized computer, accounting, and technical capabilities. Adecco is ready to satisfy its clients' requirements with a global database of millions.

Adecco's Global Reach

The Adecco administration, serving more than 250,000 companies in 60 nations and catering to some 65,000 U.S. firms, knows about staffing. The company knows that running an efficient operation and maintaining a high level of customer service can be an overwhelming task for managers caught short-handed. To help alleviate that stress, Adecco professionals in more than 5,000 staffing offices worldwide are trained to identify employers' needs and fill the bill with professional staff members. On any given day, Adecco puts some 600,000 of its associates to work for employers around the globe.

Professionalism is only part of what Adecco brings to its clients. Through Job Shop kiosks located on college campuses and in malls, as well as the company's affiliation with on-line recruitment sites like monster.com, USAdecco.com, worknow.com, and jobs.com, Adecco puts the latest technology at its customers' disposal.

In addition, Adecco provides employers with highly tested asso-

ciates skilled in a broad variety of jobs. Adecco doesn't just test for skills; with the company's three-tiered testing program, Adecco evaluates a candidate's reliability, stress tolerance, and work conduct, and then goes one step further to consider his or her work style. As a result, an employer can be assured of getting workers who not only can do the job at hand, but are motivated to do it and have the styles that fit an employer's workplace. What's more, Adecco complements its core service of temporary staffing with several divisions and specialty com-

panies such as Adecco Career Group, Adecco Technical, Accountants on Call, Ajilon, BCI, and Lee Hecht Harrison.

People choose to work for Adecco for many reasons. The company's impressive benefit package and its ability to provide access to top employers worldwide are two main reasons. While Adecco serves companies of every shape and size, 90 percent of Fortune 500 employers rely on the company for staffing solutions. "Because employers of choice opt for Adecco, our temporary associates and full-time candidates have access to the premier jobs," says Stacey Jacobs, regional vice president.

In Cincinnati, some employers may be more familiar with the Olsten name than with the Adecco tag. That's likely to change, however, thanks to Adecco's August 2000 merger with Olsten of Cincinnati. Having served the Cincinnati market for more than three decades, Olsten understands the needs of local employers. That understanding, combined with Adecco's impressive resources, represents an enormous advantage for local employers. Today, area firms and employment candidates have access to 17 Adecco offices in the Greater Cincinnati area.

Serving more than 250,000 companies in 60 nations and catering to some 65,000 U.S. firms, Adecco provides employers with highly tested associates skilled in a broad variety of jobs.

SINCE OPENING ITS DOORS IN CINCINNATI IN 1989, AON RISK SERVICES, INC. OF OHIO HAS BEEN DEDICATED TO EARNING ITS CLIENTS' TRUST BY CONSISTENTLY DELIVERING ON ITS PROMISES. "TRUST IS THE MOST IMPORTANT FACTOR IN WHAT WE DO," MANAGING DIRECTOR CHARLES MILLER SAYS. "OUR REPUTATION DEPENDS ON IT. OVER THE LAST 1C YEARS, WE HAVE DEVELOPED A REPUTATION AND DEMONSTRATED COMPETENCY, AND THAT'S HOW WE'VE WON

our clients' trust."

That single-minded commitment, coupled with professional expertise and a deep-rooted understanding of clients' unique and complex needs, helps explain how Aon has built one of the largest property and casualty insurance brokerage and consulting practices in the tri-state area in a relatively short period of time.

Aon Interdependence

The driving force of the Aon business culture is interdependence, an internal initiative for bringing the vast resources of Aon's international network to bear for every client. Although the Cincinnati office is an independent and entrepreneurial operating subsidiary of Aon Corporation—a family of insurance brokerage, consulting, and consumer insurance companies serving clients and policyholders through global distribution networks—interdependence enables it to tap the parent company's international expertise. As a result, the Cincinnati office is able to draw on the resources and capabilities of Aon's global network of 44,000 employees. Given the ever shifting nature of risk, those resources are a tremendous asset to Aon clients.

"The world of risk is changing at an incredible pace," Miller explains. "Before, people worried about fire, injuries, products failing. Today, they have to consider a lot of other potential problems, including financial, human, technical, organizational, and physical risks." Whether they need to think about preventive claims services, ergonomics, or managing their legal risks, clients know they can turn to Aon. "The brokerage industry has changed," says Miller, noting that consulting is becoming an increasingly important part of the business. "Clients don't just turn to

Mayhew & Peper Photography

us for products, they turn to us for answers."

Aon professionals are committed to helping client companies grow. Clients are shown how to blend today's sophisticated risk management and financial tools into workable business solutions. Whether the client is an entrepreneur at the helm of a business, a CEO of a mid-size firm, or an executive making decisions for a multinational corporation, each individual has specific goals and objectives for his or her company. Aon wants its clients to be as successful as possible, and believes an unforeseen risk or liability should not sidetrack an organization's future.

Working as the client's partner, Aon analyzes the challenges and threats that could keep a company from achieving its business vision. Aon develops cutting-edge, financially integrated risk strategies and solutions, and conducts a comprehensive analysis of the client's business, responding with the full range of resources necessary to protect the company's financial future.

Aon is one of the largest insurance brokers and consultants in the tri-state area. Aon works to create a better environment for all by offering necessary insurance, risk management, and employee benefit services for the progress of all businesses, both public and private.

PROFESSIONAL EXPERTISE AND A DEEP-ROOTED UNDERSTANDING OF CLIENT NEEDS HELP EXPLAIN HOW AON RISK SERVICES, INC. OF OHIO HAS BUILT ONE OF THE LARGEST PROPERTY AND CASUALTY INSURANCE BROKERAGE AND CONSULTING PRACTICES IN THE TRI-STATE AREA. AON'S OFFICE DIRECTORS INCLUDE (FROM LEFT) JOHN PIHIR, CHARLES MILLER, VICTORIA McDONOUGH, JEFF BRANCA, TOM PURTELL, AND (NOT SHOWN) ANNE MULHOLLAND.

AON PROFESSIONALS BRUCE BRUMBAUGH AND KAREN BUTCHER (SEATED) WORK TO ASSIST CLIENTS WITH THEIR NEEDS.

Mayhew & Peper Photography

CIBER, Inc.

FOUNDED IN DETROIT IN 1974 TO SERVE THE INFORMATION TECHNOLOGY (IT) NEEDS OF THE GIANT AUTO INDUSTRY, CIBER, INC. (NYSE: CBR) HAS SINCE BECOME A LEADER IN PROVIDING E-BUSINESS SOLUTIONS FOR GLOBAL 2000, MIDDLE-MARKET, AND NEW-SCALING COMPANIES, AS WELL AS FOR ALL LEVELS OF GOVERNMENT. CIBER HAS GROWN EXPONENTIALLY SINCE ITS FOUNDING BY THREE PARTNERS, INCLUDING BOB STEVENSON, WHO BECAME ITS FULL OWNER IN 1978

and today acts as chairman of the publicly traded company's board of directors. In just five years, its consolidated revenues skyrocketed from $48 million in 1994 to some $720 million in 1999.

"Our growth is a testament to being in a great industry, our top-notch employees, and our commitment to excellence, as well as CIBER's evolving business model," says Mac Slingerlend, CIBER's president and CEO, who joined the company in 1989.

Backed by a 27-year history, CIBER has earned a reputation as the trusted technology leader transforming businesses to be agile, scalable, and connected. CIBER collaborates with customers to consistently and cost-effectively plan, execute, and deliver high-quality services and results. The company's seasoned professional consultants build long-term, trusted relationships, and bring a high level of energy, integrity, experience, and value to client work. Whether the target is businesses, consumers, employees or a combination, CIBER partners with companies to help them lead their competition. By partnering with best-in-class technology vendors, CIBER is able to remain objective while working with clients to determine the most appropriate hardware, software, and services to meet their business requirements.

CIBER's superior customer care and the depth and breadth of services have resulted in a significant 90 percent repeat business with customers, collaborating with them to make optimal use of technology today while planning for the future. More than 2,000 customers, including mid-market leaders, dot-coms, and many of the Fortune 500, rely on CIBER's expertise to leverage their investment in technology and guide them into the global digital economy.

Helping Businesses Conduct e-Business

Headquartered in Englewood, Colorado, since 1988, CIBER and its subsidiaries employ some 4,500 people in 35 offices across the United States, Canada, and Europe. CIBER's IT consulting services span all components of today's technology solutions including strategy and enterprise integration, Internet services, business intelligence, network integration and security, and outsourcing.

"Both the Internet and enabling technologies have changed the way the world does business—whether it's buying or selling products, or the way customers and companies relate," says Slingerlend. "It is changing the way society interacts and transforming the business world daily."

Located in Blue Ash since 1986, the Cincinnati CIBER office is available to help companies develop the Internet-technology foundation they need to conduct e-business capable of serving customers 24 hours a day. Recently, CIBER introduced the innovative .com in-a-box™ with which the company's IT staff quickly designs and conveniently maintains solutions that meet a client's Internet needs.

Growth and Recognition

CIBER's subsidiaries include DigiTerra, Inc., which provides end-to-end Internet solutions to middle-market companies, and Neovation, Inc., a global digital strategy agency. Both companies are headquartered in Englewood. In addition, CIBER entered into a joint venture with Denver-based Verio Inc., the world's largest Web-hosting company, to create Agilera.com, a leading application service provider (ASP).

CIBER insiders aren't the only ones to recognize the company's outstanding performance and innovation. *Forbes* magazine ranked CIBER among the nation's best small companies from 1994 to 1997. *Fortune* named CIBER one of the top 100 fastest-growing companies in 1998 and 1999. *Colorado Biz* magazine awarded CIBER its 1999 Company of the Year Award in the IT category, and *Smart Reseller* named CIBER to its list of smart companies in 1999 and 2000.

With such laudatory remarks from industry experts, CIBER will continue to blaze the way in the e-business arena for years to come—in the Cincinnati area and beyond.

FROM NETWORK INTEGRATION AND SECURITY SERVICE OFFERINGS TO WIRELESS INITIATIVES AND INTERNET SERVICES, CIBER, INC. PROVIDES CLIENTS WITH THE BEST POSSIBLE E-BUSINESS SOLUTIONS TO HELP THEM STAY CONNECTED AND COMPETITIVE.

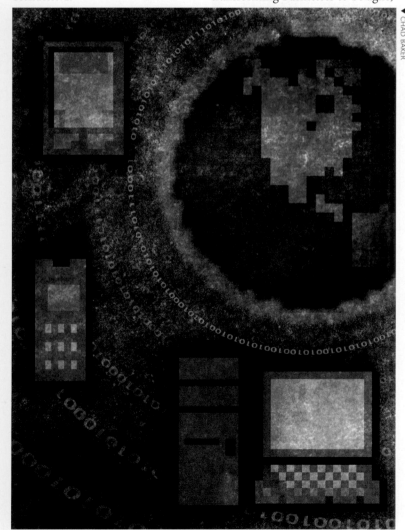

◄ CHAD BAKER

WITH MORE THAN 20 YEARS OF EXPERIENCE IN SYSTEMS INTEGRATION, DigiTerra, Inc. IS ANYTHING BUT A START-UP. FORMED IN APRIL 2000 AS A SUBSIDIARY OF CIBER, INC., THE SOFTWARE-ENABLED E-BUSINESS SOLUTION COMPANY'S PREDECESSORS—BUSINESS INFORMATION TECHNOLOGY AND THE SUMMIT GROUP—HAVE BEEN HELPING MID-SIZE FIRMS TACKLE BUSINESS AND INFORMATION TECHNOLOGY CHALLENGES FOR DECADES. ● DigiTerra TAKES A unique approach to problem solving by forming alliances with software suppliers and partnerships with customers. By collaborating with leading software companies, DigiTerra is able to offer customers a collection of leading software solutions in their respective industries, including e-business applications, customer relationship management, supply chain management, and enterprise resource planning. DigiTerra's history of having the right software package partnerships and timing as e-business evolves is its value proposition.

Keys to Success

Thanks to the company's strategic alliances, DigiTerra's consultants have a comprehensive understanding of available software. They also have access to the best training, better equipping them to handle clients' diverse needs and maintain a competitive edge. Because the company partners with a variety of firms, it isn't obligated to one supplier, so clients can rest assured that software selection is always in their best interest. Software vendors can count on DigiTerra, whose more than 1,000 employees serve clients through some 15 offices in the United States, Canada, and Europe, for access to companies that will benefit from their products.

DigiTerra partners with firms in the retail, higher education, health care, manufacturing and distribution, pharmaceutical, and public sector industries so that it can provide solutions on an ongoing basis. Dedicated account representatives, focused on client satisfaction, aim first to understand each client's circumstances and operations. By staying abreast of developments in their particular industry sectors, DigiTerra consultants can anticipate and respond to the changing needs of clients.

"Our staff includes experts who represent vertical industry segments and emerging technology," says Vice President Davison Schopmeyer, who oversees the Indiana, Kentucky, Michigan, and Ohio region. "That means we have the vision and the expertise to execute the technology effectively."

Building on Expertise

That expertise enables DigiTerra consultants to link customers and suppliers through strategy, e-business applications, industry-specific applications, business intelligence, business foundation applications, and technology infrastructure. By implementing solutions in each of those areas, DigiTerra strengthens the foundation upon which clients build their e-businesses, and better equips them to weather the competitive challenges posed by an increasingly digital world.

"Our methodology for linking customers with suppliers is key to both our clients' success and our own," Schopmeyer says. "We have the expertise and the partnerships, and we can guide a client through each step of the solution process."

DigiTerra has already formed partnerships with key software vendors, including e-business packages Commerce One, Ariba, Rightworks, and WebSphere; Siebel and Onyx in the customer relationship management world; Manhattan, Provia, Inrepa, Adexa, and SynQuest in supply chain; and enterprise resource planning packages such as Oracle, JD Edwards, PeopleSoft, Lawson, and SAP. As a reseller of IBM, Hewlett-Packard, Sun MicroSystems, Intermec, and Compaq, DigiTerra can also offer top-grade hardware, including printers and radio frequency technology equipment. "If you are looking at a software product, chances are we have some type of relationship with them," says Schopmeyer.

Strategically positioning itself to evolve and grow in challenging situations in which other high-technology solution providers may falter, DigiTerra's focus on quality practices and continuing development of expertise enable it to succeed in a competitive and dynamic industry.

DigiTerra Inc.'s full range of services and solutions helps companies realize e-business benefits through a powerful mix of experienced IT professionals, processes, and enabling technologies.

RYAN McVAY

TRAVELERS LOOKING FOR AFFORDABLE ACCOMMODATIONS NEED LOOK NO FURTHER THAN COMFORT SUITES. WHETHER THEY'RE IN CINCINNATI TO DO BUSINESS IN ONE OF THE CORPORATE OFFICE PARKS THAT PROLIFERATE THE AREA OR TO ENJOY A FAMILY WEEKEND AT NEARBY PARAMOUNT'S KINGS ISLAND, THE BLUE ASH HOTEL IS STRATEGICALLY LOCATED FOR TRAVELERS VISITING THE CITY'S NORTHERN SUBURBS. ● SINCE PURCHASING THE HOTEL IN APRIL 1999,

General Manager Rocky Patel has made numerous improvements. With more than 14 years of experience in the hotel business, Patel has owned and managed hotels in Arkansas, California, Kentucky, and Ohio. From his extensive experience, he has learned what guests want and expect from a quality hotel.

Visitors to the 50-suite hotel will notice something a little different as soon as they enter the immaculate lobby. The wrought-iron railings surrounding the tree-filled central atrium bring to mind the charm and architecture of New Orleans. Travelers can almost hear a Dixieland band as they check in with the friendly staff at the front desk.

Guests taking advantage of the hotel's convenient and abundant parking will appreciate the recently installed lights that surround the building and lot, as well as the electronic entrance doors that make life a bit easier for travelers laden with suitcases, laptops, and other travel accoutrements. Pristine guest suites, all of which have been updated, have a living room, bedroom, separate dressing area, and work area, affording travelers room to spread out and make themselves at home.

Suite amenities are designed with convenience in mind. Each suite includes two telephones with speakerphone and dataport features, and local telephone calls are complimentary. Suites are stocked with small appliances as well, so guests can press a shirt or enjoy a quick cup of coffee while they dress. Each suite includes a hair dryer, iron and ironing board, coffeemaker with complimentary coffee, mini-fridge, and microwave.

Guests who prefer a more leisurely start to the morning will want to take advantage of the hotel's free breakfast buffet, which includes an extensive, ever-changing variety of hot and cold items. Perusing a complimentary copy of *USA Today* while enjoying bacon and eggs or pancakes in the hotel's spacious dining area is a great way to ease into a busy day.

Location, Location, Location

Comfort Suites is ideally located for travelers planning to work or play in Cincinnati's northern suburbs during their visits. Situated

TRAVELERS LOOKING FOR AFFORDABLE ACCOMMODATIONS IN CINCINNATI NEED LOOK NO FURTHER THAN COMFORT SUITES.

on Reed Hartman Highway, it offers convenient access to both the Interstate 275 loop and the Ronald Reagan/Cross County Highway, but many corporate visitors needn't travel even that short distance. Located across the street from Procter & Gamble's Sharon Woods Technical Center, a short distance from Ethicon Endo-Surgery, and about seven miles from General Electric Aircraft Engines, the hotel is supremely well situated for travelers doing business in the area.

Comfort Suites' location is equally appealing to vacation travelers. During the busy summer months, the hotel is filled with families eager to enjoy a weekend at King's Island or The Beach water park. Tri-County and Kenwood malls are likewise only a short distance away, providing avid shoppers ample opportunity

to shop till they drop. For those with leisure on their minds, Sharon Woods—one of Hamilton County's premier parks—is also close by.

Both corporate and family travelers will appreciate a chance to sample some of Cincinnati's signature restaurants. Montgomery Inn, famed for its ribs and barbecue, is only a few miles away, as is Parkers Bar & Grill, which features American cuisine. Because no traveler can claim to have truly visited Cincinnati until he or she has sampled a "three-way," guests will be pleased to know Skyline Chili is just a block away.

Back at the Ranch

After an exhausting day of work or play, guests will find plenty of ways to unwind at the Comfort Suites. Exercise buffs can take ad-

vantage of the hotel's fitness room, rounding out their workouts with a relaxing steam sauna or a dip in the hotel's outdoor pool.

Guests wanting access to more extensive workout facilities can enjoy complimentary access to Bally Total Fitness, one of the area's best-known fitness facilities, by simply showing their room keys. Guests will want to reward themselves with a warm cookie and a cup of coffee, which the hotel provides each evening, before returning to their suites to enjoy a movie on HBO or catch a game on ESPN.

Comfort Suites' friendly, veteran staff stands ready to serve whatever its guests require. That attitude explains why the hotel, which offers a frequent traveler program, greets so many repeat visitors each year.

"We understand that, to a traveler, a room is pretty much a room," Patel says. "It's the service that truly differentiates a hotel, and Comfort Suites' staff is dedicated to delivering exceptional service."

CLOCKWISE FROM TOP LEFT: GUEST SUITES ARE DESIGNED WITH CONVENIENCE AND COMFORT IN MIND.

IN THE COMFORT SUITES LOBBY, THE WROUGHT-IRON RAILINGS SURROUNDING THE TREE-FILLED CENTRAL ATRIUM BRING TO MIND THE CHARM AND ARCHITECTURE OF NEW ORLEANS.

COMFORT SUITES PROVIDES A MEETING ROOM THAT CAN ACCOMMODATE 40 PEOPLE THEATRE STYLE. A BUSINESS CENTER FOR MAKING COPIES AND SENDING AND RECEIVING FAXES IS ALSO AVAILABLE.

The Payne Firm Inc.

an environmental consulting company, in 1987. "We solve complex problems in the environmental arena. But they aren't just environmental problems; they're business-related opportunities," Payne says.

Payne, a professional engineer, has been a faculty member of the American Law Institute-American Bar Association since 1988, and is a frequent lecturer on environmental issues. He says he challenges clients to consider environmental issues in a different light. "Our job is to bring value to the client," Payne says. "Environmental compliance has long been regarded as a cost liability. Often, we need to help our clients understand the potential ramifications that environmental issues may have on the company's financial performance and control."

Understanding the Forces at Work

Too often, environmental consultants work in a vacuum, Payne says. They fail to understand the problem at hand in the context of all the other forces affecting a client's business. "We're dealing with CFOs who want to be in compliance with regulations, but who also need to meet the demands of their own customers," Payne says. "They may have financial constraints or time constraints that impact the way they need to approach their environmental issues, and we ask them to share those challenges with us. We try to create a solution that takes all those challenges into consideration."

Payne believes that willingness to understand a client's business in its entirety is what sets the Payne Firm apart from its competitors. At his company, engineers and scientists aren't just consultants; they're partners working with a client to resolve acute situations and take proactive measures to ensure future compliance. "We use strategic environmental planning to help clients run their businesses better by understanding what they do," Payne says. At that point, the Payne Firm brings all its entrepreneurial spirit and technical expertise to bear on a problem in an attempt to forge an innovative solution. The firm's organizational structure is based on market sectors that focus on understanding the needs of various customer groups.

Finding solutions to complex problems encompasses extensive activity. The Payne Firm is available to help companies considering mergers or acquisitions assess real estate for possible environmental problems. Similarly, the firm can help companies integrate acquired businesses into their portfolio to maximize efficiency and profitability. The Payne Firm performs Brownfields property redevelopment assessments, soil and groundwater quality investigations, environmental risk assessments, compliance and safety audits, asbestos and lead paint identification and abatement management, and a variety of other environmental services. While the firm's clients vary

When John Payne founded the Payne Firm Inc. in 1987, he set out to avoid consultants describing problems in their own language.

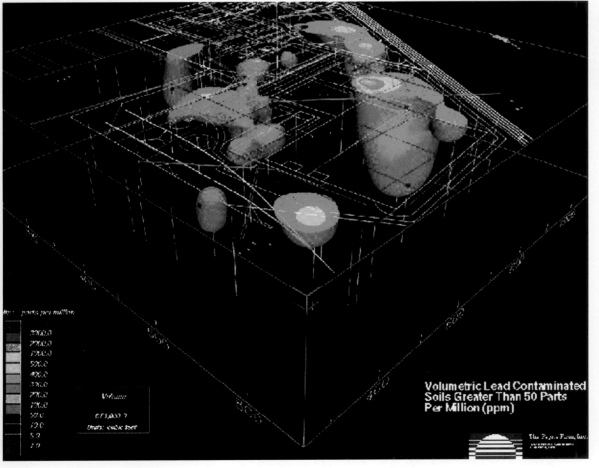

Volumetric Lead Contaminated Soils Greater Than 50 Parts Per Million (ppm)

tremendously—from small businesses and Fortune 100 concerns to some public sector clients—they all want to alleviate real and potential environmental liabilities.

Technical Focus, Clear Presentation

Understanding that clients don't want an environmental dictate from on high, the Payne Firm works hard to present its clients with options, and to communicate the pros and cons of those options in clear, nontechnical terms. The firm uses common business tools, such as decision-tree analyses and cash flow models, to help companies determine the solution that works best for their unique circumstances.

Those options and the common-sense manner in which they are presented are backed by solid, reliable technical expertise. The Payne Firm's staff represents a variety of technical disciplines, including environmental, civil, and chemical engineering; geology and hydrology; chemistry; risk assessment; wetlands management; and industrial hygiene and safety. The firm's scientists and engineers are among the top in the field. "We have high standards for performance and challenge our people every day," said Payne. "That has allowed us to attract and retain the best staff in the area."

Since the Payne Firm's founding, that combination has earned it an enviable reputation and a broad array of business. Although its only office is located in Blue Ash, the Payne Firm has worked in every state except Hawaii, as well as in many countries. Three-fourths of the firm's clients represent repeat customers.

Although market demand and the Payne Firm's client base would support a larger operation, Payne says he's happy to keep his firm, which includes some 35 staff members, a niche organization. Each member of his professional staff is required to be involved in business development activities, and is allotted a generous continuing education budget. In addition, the company holds informal continuing education sessions every Monday morning.

Weekly brown-bag sessions enable staff members and client representatives to present case studies and discuss industry trends.

To ensure that its staff is up to speed on the latest marketing and business developments, the Payne Firm sponsors an informal book club. Every few months, the entire staff—from the receptionist to the CEO—reads the same business book and discusses it to see if they can uncover any new insights to help improve their operations, as well as to get all staff members to "think like an owner." Those extra measures speak to the heart of the Payne Firm's mission. "We've formed a culture of like-minded, entrepreneurial individuals who think like business-people, not like technocrats," Payne says.

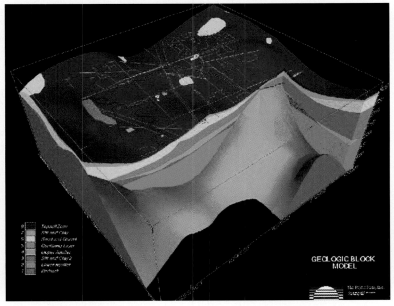

GEOLOGIC BLOCK MODEL

THE PAYNE FIRM BRINGS ALL OF ITS ENTREPRENEURIAL SPIRIT AND TECHNICAL EXPERTISE TO BEAR ON A PROBLEM IN AN ATTEMPT TO FORGE AN INNOVATIVE SOLUTION.

Lockwood Greene

Lockwood Greene has been a fixture in Cincinnati since 1988, but it began helping local businesses like the Baldwin Piano Company and the *Cincinnati Enquirer* with their manufacturing and facility needs as far back as the early 1900s. Located in the Blue Ash area, Lockwood Greene's Cincinnati office is focused on providing consulting, design, and construction for

process and industrial clients in the health and personal care, food and beverage, pharmaceutical, and general manufacturing industries.

Founded in 1832, Lockwood Greene is the oldest engineering company in the United States. Client trust and reliability have been well earned by Lockwood Greene during its nearly 170 years serving clients throughout Cincinnati and the world. The company has grown alongside and helped lead the development of America's industry. This experience has given the firm the unique perspective and understanding of business issues, manufacturing technologies, operational requirements, and regulatory mandates to help turn a client's

Although Lockwood Greene has been a part of the community since 1988, it began helping local businesses like the Baldwin Piano Company and the *Cincinnati Enquirer* with their manufacturing and facility needs as far back as the early 1900s (top right).

Lockwood Greene's consulting, engineering, architectural, and construction services provide results consistent with clients' expectations to optimize financial return, operational performance, competitive advantage, and global project delivery (bottom right and opposite).

capital investments into profitable and sustainable company growth.

Recently, the Cincinnati office played a major role in the design and construction of *Food Engineering*'s 1999 Plant of the Year for a food processing facility in Waterloo, Iowa.

In 1999, Lockwood Greene joined the J.A. Jones, Inc. family of companies, giving clients greater resources to offer life cycle advantage solutions to their business needs. This includes the ability to offer assistance from the project development stage all the way through maintenance, operations, and decommissioning from a complete design-build resource. Lockwood Greene also utilizes its Outcomes by Design® business process on every project to help ensure alignment with the client's project objectives.

For trust and reliability, Cincinnati industry can count on Lockwood Greene as its complete solutions provider for consulting, design,

1991-2001

1991
PHC Group

1992
Ethicon Endo-Surgery, Inc.

1993
ENTEX IT Service, Inc.

1993
LÛCRUM Inc.

1994
Keane, Inc.

1994
Premier Network Solutions, Inc.

1995
Application Objects, Inc.

1995
Attachmate Corporation

1995
The Health Alliance of Greater
   Cincinnati

1996
Process Plus

1996
Toyota Motor Manufacturing
   North America, Inc.

1998
Convergys Corporation

1999
Ashland Inc.

1999
Marriott Kingsgate Conference
   Center Hotel

Technically, PHC Group is a design and advertising agency. Practically, it's the ultimate customer service firm. President Pat Herb and her staff treat each client as if they were the firm's only account. "When I founded the company in 1991, I had two goals in mind: deliver personalized attention and a great product," says Herb. "That means meet any deadline, respond to any special request, and never settle for second best."

Technical Prowess and an Innovative Team

PHC's ability to deliver the most creative work on a consistent basis comes from its ongoing investment in state-of-the-art equipment and staff development. Herb sends her designers nationwide to learn the finer points of popular software programs and to stay current in the most up-to-date design tools. PHC also understands the importance of the right image for each customer, and that the advertising efforts need to be income-producing for that client. "We're constantly raising the bar," says Herb. Staff members are intent on producing the highest-quality, most eye-catching product, whether they're designing a national ad, a trade show display, direct mail, an annual report, a corporate logo, or product packaging.

In 1997, the agency introduced a separate department, PHCweb, which creates appealing, user-friendly Web sites that not only drive traffic, but also integrate corporate advertising goals into the final e-product. Several of PHC's client companies also require interactive CDs consisting of much of the same material. Having created Web sites for these clients, PHC is in a better position to provide this service efficiently.

Herb credits the fact that PHC trains its designers to use innovative technology—rather than teaching technicians how to design—for her company's success in often complex Web site work. "Half of our Web sites involve redoing existing sites that were originally designed by technicians who were unable to meet a client's communication goals," Herb explains. "Fortunately, we don't have those problems. As designers, we are already trained in grabbing people's attention and in customer-friendly navigation."

By weaving a set image throughout all media involved in a client's campaign, PHC can ensure that collateral materials work together to reinforce the desired message. This enables clients to get the most mileage out of their advertising efforts, whether they're speaking to consumers or to members of their industry group.

Making Business Easier for Clients

As the client's business partner, I believe we have an obligation to find innovative communication solutions that make sense financially," says Herb. "For example, if a particular layout looks as if it would result in wasted paper, we'll find a creative way to use the excess for that client."

In addition to its core staff members, PHC relies on an extensive support network, which enables the agency to serve even the largest clients' needs. Since personnel overhead isn't built into the PHC structure, companies with extensive in-house marketing departments aren't paying to duplicate their own resources. Likewise, this flexible structure enables PHC to maintain the prized assets of a small firm: agility and responsiveness.

Another advantage for PHC is its location. The agency provides regional, national, and international clients with easy access to Cincinnati's renowned printing industry. Moreover, Cincinnati is also an ideal location for a company that designs and distributes mass mailings and other bulk-distributed products, as 54 percent of the nation's population lives within 600 miles of the Queen City.

Perhaps the most high-profile testament to PHC Group's commitment to customers is its Web site, www.phcgroupinc.com. While the site does show a few samples of the agency's new-media work, that's not the main reason it exists. Rather, the Web site's real purpose is to visually communicate with PHC's clients. Each client's company uses a unique, protected password that enables it to privately view the progress PHC's professionals are making on its projects. "It would be too limiting to say that what is displayed on-line is our best effort," says Herb. "Every client gets our best work. We give 100 percent every day—and then we try to top ourselves."

PHC Group, Inc. office interiors, the creative team, and samples of their work.

Ethicon
Endo-Surgery, Inc.

ETHICON ENDO-SURGERY, INC., WITH HEADQUARTERS IN BLUE ASH, OHIO, IS AN OPERATING COMPANY OF JOHNSON & JOHNSON, THE WORLD'S MOST COMPREHENSIVE AND BROADLY BASED MANUFACTURER OF HEALTH CARE PRODUCTS. WITH $27.5 BILLION IN ANNUAL SALES, THE PARENT COMPANY SERVES THE CONSUMER, PHARMACEUTICAL AND MEDICAL DEVICE, AND DIAGNOSTIC MARKETS. ● GROUPED WITHIN JOHNSON & JOHNSON'S MEDICAL DEVICE BUSINESS SEGMENT, ETHICON

Endo-Surgery works with clinicians to develop less invasive products and procedures designed to improve life for people around the world. The company is the world leader in single-patient-use surgical instruments for less invasive procedures, as well as traditional surgical instruments. Its innovative products make it possible to perform surgery and diagnostic procedures through small punctures, rather than the long incisions required for traditional open surgery.

ETHICON ENDO-SURGERY, INC., WITH HEADQUARTERS IN BLUE ASH, OHIO, IS AN OPERATING COMPANY OF JOHNSON & JOHNSON, THE WORLD'S MOST COMPREHENSIVE AND BROADLY BASED MANUFACTURER OF HEALTH CARE PRODUCTS.

A History of Innovation

In April 1990, product directors from Ethicon, Inc., a Johnson & Johnson company in Somerville, New Jersey, began looking at the market for new, less invasive access devices called trocars. These devices, used to accommodate cameras called laparoscopes and other surgical instruments, were part of the emerging field of less invasive surgery.

By 1992, the Ethicon Endo-Surgery Institute in Cincinnati had

opened its doors to facilitate the training of physicians for this revolution in the world of medicine. That same year, Ethicon Endo-Surgery became a separate operating company of Johnson & Johnson, based in the Queen City.

"The company began by clearly focusing on four key strategies, which would later help us become market leaders," says Nick Valeriani, president. "Those remain our guiding principles: to help physicians develop new, less invasive procedures; to develop innovative products rapidly; to facilitate world-class education; and to create the most technically competent sales organization in the world."

More than 200 engineers from Johnson & Johnson and other industry leaders were hired. With the latest in computer-aided design systems and help from the Harvard Business School, the company put together multifunctional product development teams and reduced the cycle time for new product development to 12 months. The sales force originally numbered 200 representatives. Today, Ethicon Endo-Surgery's sales force comprises more than 600 associates in more than 50 countries around the world.

"The end result was that, by 1995, the company went from being a market follower to market leader in both the laparoscopic and traditional surgery market," says Valeriani. "Today, the company is the market leader and a high-growth global franchise for Johnson & Johnson because we stayed aligned around a single, unifying vision of transforming patient care through innovation."

Platforms for Growth

With the development of innovative new products for laparoscopic and traditional surgery

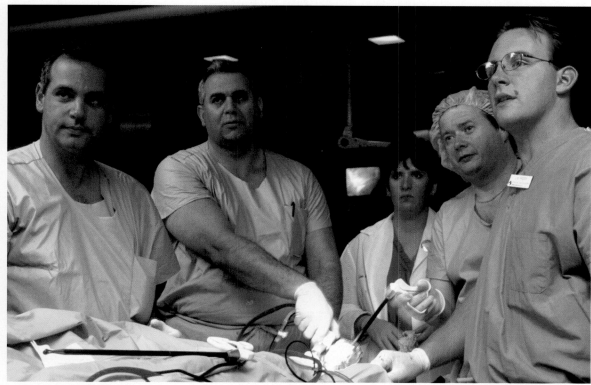

well in hand, the company began building its technology-based product portfolio. In 1995, the company acquired UltraCision, manufacturer of the Harmonic Scalpel®. The Harmonic Scalpel is an advanced surgical instrument that uses the power of ultrasonic energy to make surgical incisions with minimal tissue damage to the patient.

Following its acquisition of UltraCision, Ethicon Endo-Surgery began focusing on the development of innovative procedure-enabling devices for the Harmonic Scalpel. The firm's line of products has grown today to include blade designs that help facilitate procedures as varied as coronary artery bypasses and tonsillectomies. The company also

manufactures devices for the treatment of various male and female urologic disorders.

In 1997, Ethicon Endo-Surgery acquired Biopsys Medical, manufacturers of the Mammotome® Breast Biopsy System, which is highly accurate in helping doctors diagnose early-stage breast cancer. Then, in 1999, the company launched the ultrasound-guided Mammotome Hand-Held®. Like the original Mammotome, this system is designed to help physicians obtain the appropriate amount of breast tissue for definitive diagnosis without surgery. Both systems require only a single insertion and minimize the removal of surrounding healthy tissue. The procedure re-

quires only a local anesthetic and can be performed on an outpatient basis.

The company's Endo-Surgery Institute in Blue Ash is a world-class, state-of-the-art, professional educational and training facility. Here, renowned surgeons from around the world train visiting surgeons in the latest surgical procedures and techniques. The company also has similar training facilities in Norderstedt (Hamburg), Germany, and Sukegawa (Tokyo), Japan.

Ethicon Endo-Surgery's world-class manufacturing centers are located in Cincinnati, Albuquerque, Southington, Juárez, and Monterrey. The company sells and distributes its products in more than 50 countries around the world.

THE COMPANY'S ENDO-SURGERY INSTI-TUTE IN BLUE ASH IS A WORLD-CLASS, STATE-OF-THE-ART, PROFESSIONAL EDU-CATIONAL AND TRAINING FACILITY.

ENTEX IT Service, Inc.

Based in Rye Brook, New York, ENTEX IT Service, Inc. has been creating value for Fortune 1000 companies and other large, information-intensive businesses since its formation in August 1993. The company, a leading vendor-independent provider of distributed computing infrastructure services that manages more than 770,000 PC desktops and 30,000 servers, quickly staked a reputation for itself as a leader

in the information technology (IT) field. Today, ENTEX plans, builds, runs, and maintains the distributed computing information technology infrastructure for its customers. In addition, its some 5,000 employees provide consulting and resources to audit clients' networks, benchmark performance, and recommend comprehensive migration paths for e-business readiness. The company has performed more than 1 million desktop migrations and 30,000 server migrations to date.

Part of the Siemens Fold

With such an impressive track record, it's no surprise that the company attracted the attention of Siemens IT Service, which acquired ENTEX Information Services Inc. and relaunched it as ENTEX IT Service in April 2000. Siemens IT Service is part of the information and communications business segment of Siemens AG, a Berlin- and

Munich-based global powerhouse in electrical engineering and electronics with more than $75 billion in sales and approximately 443,000 employees worldwide.

In IT terms, the Siemens/ ENTEX union was a match made in heaven. Incorporation into the Siemens IT Service organization helped cement ENTEX's position as one of the strongest IT service providers in North America. At the same time, ENTEX forms a key element in the worldwide Siemens IT Service organization, which has revenues of nearly $2.2 billion and approximately 13,000 employees in more than 100 countries. The combination of Siemens' Unix expertise, in both the United States and Europe, and ENTEX's leadership in e-business infrastructure support services created a powerful new IT services organization, capable of supporting customers in the increasingly demanding e-business market.

ENTEX offers a comprehensive, vendor-independent portfolio of services available to customers both in North America and across the globe. Services include desktop and network outsourcing, field dispatch services, support services for Unix data center infrastructure, and a range of consulting services in the Unix/Windows NT arena.

Winning National Recognition

Siemens has not been the only organization to notice ENTEX. *PC Week* ranked ENTEX ninth in its Fast@Track 500 Annual Report, the industry's only report that ranks and profiles the fastest-moving e-business enterprises based solely on their levels of innovation in leveraging Internet-based technology for business advantage.

"ENTEX is a company that is pushing the limits of IT innovation to meet the challenges of e-business, and was selected as a Fast@Track

Since its formation in August 1993, ENTEX IT Service, Inc. has been creating value for Fortune 1000 companies and other large, information-intensive businesses.

THE ENTEX SOLUTION COMBINES HIGHLY SKILLED AND EXPERIENCED PEOPLE WITH PROVEN BEST-PRACTICE METHODOLOGIES DEVELOPED THROUGH REAL-WORLD USE WITH ENTEX'S MANY CUSTOMERS.

ENTEX HAS PERFORMED MORE THAN 1 MILLION DESKTOP MIGRATIONS AND 30,000 SERVER MIGRATIONS TO DATE.

500 because of its unique skills and methodologies in infrastructure consulting," says Eric Lundquist, editor in chief of *PC Week*. "They have clearly demonstrated their commitment to deploying cutting-edge technologies."

Creating Value through People

ENTEX understands that evaluating and deploying new technology requires capability, experience, and available resources. Because many organizations lack one or more of these critical elements, ENTEX creates value by filling the gaps in their expertise or managing the entire project from inception to completion.

The ENTEX solution combines highly skilled and experienced people with proven best-practice methodologies developed through real-world use with ENTEX's many customers. The results are projects delivered on time, within specification, and, most important, focused on the customer's business requirements.

Recognized for Excellence in Ohio

ENTEX recognizes that top-notch service can only be delivered by a knowledgeable workforce, and goes to great lengths to ensure its employees have access to the best, most innovative training programs. To fully support the growing range of computer technology that its customers use, ENTEX initiated its Technical Training Certification

program in hardware and software in January 1997. Technical marketing representatives participate in the program, and earn certification in notebook and desktop computers, local and wide-area networking, servers and printers, and forecasting customer technology needs. In addition, representatives are trained extensively in five of the most widely used Microsoft business software applications.

Continuous improvement in relationship and management skills was an important goal when ENTEX initiated its Employee/Management Development Training in August 1996. Today, 17 courses are offered through the program, including negotiation, team building, finance,

diversity appreciation, strategic planning, employee retention skills, and project management.

In 1998, ENTEX was recognized for its leadership in the training arena when former Ohio Governor George V. Voinovich honored the Mason office with the Governor's Workforce Excellence Award for the company's two training programs. "By investing in employee skills, ENTEX has become a leader in developing the world-class workforce that keeps Ohio globally competitive," Voinovich said when giving the award. "The training programs ENTEX developed will be used as a model to help other Ohio employers design strategies for lifelong employee learning."

LÛCRUM Incorporated

Digital strategies that improve the bottom line"—LÛCRUM Incorporated's tag line says it all. Although the company offers a tapestry of services, each one is, ultimately, an investment. "Our entire focus is on improving the bottom-line performance of our clients," says Ric Martin, vice president and chief operating officer. ● Founded in 1993 as Client Server Associates, LÛCRUM initially focused on

programming and reselling software. By 1999, the company had grown to be listed as number 272 on *Inc.* magazine's list of the nation's fastest-growing private companies. Over time, as the company increasingly focused on helping companies improve the way they accessed, managed, and used data, the name became less representative of the firm's business. The company was rechristened in January 2000.

"The name LÛCRUM is Latin for profit," explains John Bostick, founder and chief executive officer. "Our entire sales motion and system methodologies are based on improving the bottom-line performance of our clients. As such, the name perfectly defines our client mission."

Today, LÛCRUM focuses on three vertical markets—manufacturing, health care, and financial services—and four interrelated practice areas in strategic planning, e-business, customer relations management (CRM), and business intelligence. The company, which employs about 90 people locally, operates a downtown headquarters in Cincinnati, and a Sharonville office that focuses on sales and administration.

"The name LÛCRUM is Latin for profit," explains John Bostick, founder and chief executive officer of LÛCRUM Incorporated.

LÛCRUM Radio: Spreading the Word

LÛCRUM operates on a very simple premise: to survive the current digital revolution and prosper in the future, businesses must modify their old operating procedures. In the new environment, businesses must leverage their technological investments because communication, business knowledge, and computation hold the key to their continued survival and prosperity. To maximize those capabilities, LÛCRUM helps companies integrate, compile, assess, and man-

age data so they can make informed, strategic decisions.

LÛCRUM does not hold its cards close to its vest; rather, the company disseminates information and, in so doing, helps clients and would-be clients understand the complexities of today's technological world. The company's award-winning Web site includes excerpts from top business publications, as well as insights to help executives stay ahead of the curve. The key to LÛCRUM's marketing efforts, its Web site is visited by more than 3,500 people each month, an impressive tally for a site that is neither a retailer nor a search engine.

If the Web site is the foundation

of LÛCRUM's marketing campaign, LÛCRUM Radio is the heart of the Web site. Through features, such as a series of audio interviews with top CEOs, LÛCRUM Radio helps listeners understand the current spate of business challenges that companies face. More important, LÛCRUM Radio demonstrates how forward-thinking companies are using innovative strategies to get a leg up in the brave new world of business.

Through all of its business adventures, LÛCRUM Incorporated is on track to continue growing. Continuing to have its client base grow—and growing as a company as a whole—is leading LÛCRUM to the top of its field.

KEANE, INC.'S TAG LINE, "WE GET IT DONE," IS MORE THAN A CLEVER PLAY ON WORDS. IT IS A CONCISE STATEMENT OF FACT. ● HEADQUARTERED IN BOSTON, THIS INFORMATION TECHNOLOGY (IT) GIANT IS A $1 BILLION FIRM WITH A ROLL-UP-YOUR-SLEEVES APPROACH TO HELPING COMPANIES PLAN, BUILD, AND MANAGE APPLICATION SOFTWARE TO ACHIEVE A COMPETITIVE ADVANTAGE. THROUGH MORE THAN 40 BRANCH OFFICES IN NORTH AMERICA AND EUROPE, THE

company offers an array of technological services, including operations improvement consulting, e-solutions, customer relationship management, data warehousing, custom application development, and application outsourcing.

Founded in 1965, Keane employs more than 8,500 business and technical professionals. Consequently, when the 200-plus consultants from the Greater Cincinnati/Dayton branch walk into clients' offices, they bring a wealth of institutional knowledge and resources with them.

Individual Contributions Matter

Keane traces its success to its employees. Respect for the individual and for each person's unique perspective and input is one of Keane's core values. That respect is manifest in the company's commitment to local assignments for its consultants, its emphasis on ongoing paid training, and its recognition that employees need to balance their work commitments with their home lives. Such measures have earned Keane recognition by *Computerworld* magazine as one of the best places to work in information technology.

The benefits of creating a balanced and supportive work environment do not stop with employees, but flow to Keane's clients in a myriad of ways. A productive work environment fosters teamwork, a second core value at Keane. That enables the company to maximize the brainpower and problem-solving skills of its seasoned staff.

What's more, because Keane delivers its services through a network of branch offices and responds to the full software life cycle, it is able to establish long-term, value-added partnerships with its clients. This decentralized approach enables Keane to hire locally, and thus to control costs for clients while posi-

tively impacting the local economy.

Keane's emphasis on finding local solutions describes its community involvement as well. The Cincinnati branch office is a major contributor to the Juvenile Diabetes Foundation, National Conference for Community and Justice, Cystic Fibrosis Foundation, and Junior Achievement. In addition, the company is the official information technology partner for the new Contemporary Arts Center, having pledged to donate some $1 million in in-kind services. Keane also supports such diverse service and environmental organizations as United Way, Playhouse in the Park, March of Dimes, Earth Share, Emanuel Center, Family Services of Cincinnati, and One Way Farm.

Bringing Clients More

Ensuring client success is at the heart of Keane's value system. In fact, the company builds its client base by consistently delivering services above the client's expectations, on time and within budget.

Keane accomplishes this lofty aim by taking a holistic approach to problem solving, basing decisions

not on technology alone, but on its effects on business processes. Keane's solutions start with a customer's business strategy, and the firm uses that as a springboard for developing a technological strategy. Consequently, Keane aligns information technology goals more closely with its clients' business objectives, and enables clients themselves to deliver flexible, responsive service so they can enjoy a competitive advantage.

KEANE, INC. AND ITS EMPLOYEES SUPPORT A WIDE VARIETY OF LOCAL AND REGIONAL COMMUNITY PROGRAMS, INCLUDING THE 1999 JUVENILE DIABETES FOUNDATION WALK FOR THE CURE (TOP).

THE SENIOR MANAGEMENT TEAM AT KEANE'S GREATER CINCINNATI/DAYTON BRANCH INCLUDES (FROM LEFT) CRAIG SCHWEIGER, DIRECTOR OF SERVICE DELIVERY; YVONNE NABORS, OFFICE MANAGER; ROBERT E. KNAUER, AREA MANAGER; AND JAMES R. HALL JR., DIRECTOR OF STAFFING AND EMPLOYEE DEVELOPMENT (BOTTOM).

Success in business depends on connections, and no one knows that better than Premier Network Solutions, Inc. (PRENET). Founded in Cincinnati in 1994, PRENET has established a name for itself as a leading connectivity resource for businesses throughout the area. Understanding that commerce depends on each company's ability to communicate and share data with suppliers,

clients, and in-house users, PRENET offers companies an array of computer and telephone systems to meet their communications needs and solve their networking challenges.

Computer Network Solutions

Whether businesses need to network computers in the same building or systems in different countries, they have a pressing need to share information quickly. PRENET founders Steve Immerman, Mark Frees, and Stephen Berger—all of whom are Certified Network Engineers—understand that need and can design, implement, and maintain a system that suits every customer's requirements.

Premier specializes in both local area networks (LAN) and wide area networks (WAN). LANs connect users in an office and make it possible for them to combine resources. By enabling users to share files, printers, modems, and other resources, as well as by using servers to centralize management and back-office functions, LANs maximize existing resources, creating a synergy of data.

WANs perform the same function over larger geographic areas, enabling companies to enjoy the same connectivity with locations around the globe that they enjoy within the confines of their main building. Using WANs, PRENET helps clients share applications and data with other users across town or on another continent, keeping everyone well connected and up to date.

Facilitated Business Communication

Because computer and telephone systems have become intertwined, PRENET offers a comprehensive array of business communication solutions as well. "When we got started in 1994, there were still a lot of PCs that could not communicate with other systems in the organization," explains Immerman. "As we networked those systems, we realized that telephone systems would also need to be integrated. We really saw the two worlds drawing closer and closer.

"Increasingly, clients want computer features that require phone connectivity," Immerman says. "For example, they may want agents at their call centers to have account information pop up on their com-

Founded in Cincinnati in 1994, Premier Network Solutions, Inc. (PRENET) has established a name for itself as a leading connectivity resource for businesses throughout the area.

puter screens. These agents may also wish to work at home or remote locations. IP based solutions provide these capabilities." No matter what a client's communications preferences are, PRENET has a solution that facilitates round-the-clock communication.

Because systems are only as reliable as the cables upon which they function, PRENET can also provide a structured cabling foundation. By installing, maintaining, and documenting the infrastructure, PRENET ensures a stable base on which to build one or more networks. From start to finish, PRENET offers the complete solution.

PRENET's expertise in communications presented an ideal opportunity to segue into audiovisual system design and implementation. Because communication often depends on transmitting data to a sales conference or a training center, PRENET understands that top-notch audiovisual equipment is really just an extension of clients' communications systems. Companies interested in presentation systems can count on PRENET not just for the necessary screens and projectors, but also for design of the layout of the room to maximize communication as well.

Exemplary Customer Service

Although PRENET's client roster has grown with the firm's expanding menu of services, few names have disappeared. This loyalty shows that repeat work is the foundation of PRENET's business. As companies realize the value of their initial investment in PRENET-provided solutions, they are anxious to explore additional ways to improve efficiencies through

networking. When they do, they return to the company that helped them in the first place. "We're really committed to a long-term relationship with our clients," says Frees. "We want to maintain that high quality of service. We're very honest with them. We only recommend what they need, and we attempt to provide them with multiple solutions to their problems."

That is the kind of service that clients such as the Maisonette Group appreciate. "Generally I don't have any problems," says Michael Whelan, director of management information systems for the restaurant group and a longtime PRENET customer. "But if I do, I only have to make one phone call, and the problem ceases to exist." Because the group operates multiple restaurants around town, Whelan says he counts on PRENET for LAN and WAN support.

"PRENET is good at giving me alternatives to accomplish what I want to do," Whelan says. "They give me two or three ways to solve an issue, and present me with the costs, pros, and cons of each. That puts me in the position to make the decision that works best. They take my budgetary constraints into consideration and don't try to push the solution of the month. They've really got my best interests in mind."

PRENET's CLIENT ROSTER HAS GROWN WITH THE FIRM'S EXPANDING MENU OF SERVICES.

PRENET SPECIALIZES IN BOTH LOCAL AREA NETWORKS (LAN) AND WIDE AREA NETWORKS (WAN).

Application Objects, Inc.

WORKING FROM ITS CINCINNATI OFFICES ON THE 22ND FLOOR OF THE STAR BANK CENTER, APPLICATION OBJECTS, INC. (AOI) IS FOCUSED ON HELPING COMPANIES SOLVE BUSINESS PROBLEMS THROUGH THE CREATIVE USE OF LEADING-EDGE TECHNOLOGIES. FOUNDED BY ROB SULLIVAN, CHRISTOPHER TAULBEE, AND PATRICK LUCAS IN 1995, THE SOFTWARE CONSULTING FIRM SERVES ITS CLIENTS THROUGH THREE PRIMARY AREAS: SOFTWARE DEVELOPMENT, CONSULTING, AND

software training. While the company caters to myriad clients, AOI has developed particular expertise in working with travel, pharmaceutical, telecommunications, and financial services firms.

Although a young company by traditional measures, AOI is a venerable one by Internet standards. "As the Internet grew, our business expanded as well," says Sullivan, president and CEO. "We were working in the dot-com world before the term was even coined." The firm currently has some 30 employees working at offices in both Cincinnati and King of Prussia, Pennsylvania.

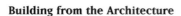

IN ADDITION TO ITS PRODUCTS, APPLICATION OBJECTS, INC. (AOI) OFFERS COMPREHENSIVE TECHNICAL TRAINING TO CUSTOMERS THAT IS THE SAME TYPE OF TRAINING THE COMPANY OFFERS ITS OWN CONSULTANTS.

Building from the Architecture

AOI provides products and services that enable it to design, build, and deploy systems using adaptable architecture devices. Because the company has an established track record, AOI brings institutional knowledge and experience to every engagement. Understanding that despite their varied individual technical problems, clients often require certain core capabilities, AOI offers a framework system that enables clients to tap the firm's considerable experience.

AOI has been actively involved in defining, confirming, implementing, deploying, and subsequently managing large-scale distributed system architectures for several years. From initial definition and deployment to consulting and support follow-through, the firm stands by its clients to ensure that their needs are met.

In addition to its products, AOI offers comprehensive technical training. Customers can take advantage of the same type of training the company offers its own consultants on subjects such as object orientation; distributed systems architecture; relational database theory; operations, administration, and maintenance; and development techniques. In addition, AOI offers database-specific classes in subjects such as Oracle, DB2, SQL*Server, and Sybase, as well as client-side development in VB, PowerBuilder, and Java, and server-side development in C, C++, Java, and COBOL.

"With the rapid change of tools, technologies, and methods, it is difficult for many companies to effectively implement internal programs to keep their technological edge," Sullivan says. "AOI provides comprehensive technical education in a range of subjects, each focused on providing customers with a balance between the leading edge and pragmatism."

AOI CREDITS ITS SUCCESS TO ITS PEOPLE. THE COMPANY'S TECHNICAL SPECIALISTS ARE AMONG THE TOP IN THE FIELD AND ARE WELL EQUIPPED TO MEET CUSTOMERS' NEEDS, WHATEVER THEY MIGHT BE.

A Framework for Success

At the heart of its software development services lies the AOI System Architecture Framework. The importance of architecture has been a prime topic in recent years, according to Sullivan. At its most basic level, architecture provides the framework for applications, the blueprint upon which they are built. Upon this technical infrastructure foundation, frameworks, components, and other approaches are layered to provide a robust approach to supporting the enterprise.

The software components that AOI designs function like interlocking building blocks that can be linked together and built upon to develop complex, integrated software systems. "Our architecture means that our team of professionals doesn't have to reinvent the wheel," says Sullivan. "They can take advantage of a product that pulls together and addresses many of the needs companies have in common." At the same time, he says, the highly trained AOI staff can address client-specific issues.

An emphasis on integrated solutions is evident in the company's approach to e-business. In developing an e-business solution, AOI seeks to establish clear and logical connections between a client's core business systems, data warehouse operations, and e-commerce activities. By linking those three functions through operational data storage, customer relationship management, and business intelligence,

AOI ensures that the client's e-business flows efficiently and that its Internet operations reflect the strengths of its business.

Specialists—Not Just Professionals

AOI credits its success to its people. The company's technical specialists are among the top in the field and are well equipped to meet customers' needs, whatever they might be.

The company's consultants are actively involved in defining, confirming, implementing, deploying, and managing high-performance, large-scale distributed systems. Their expertise includes technologies, frameworks, and architectures surrounding object-oriented, component-based development. Among the company's specific areas of skill are high-performance distribution systems architecture, large-scale

database and data warehousing systems, object-oriented methods, and applications development and deployment.

"Our consultants have a comprehensive knowledge in their areas of expertise," Sullivan says. "Access to intellectual property within the company, as well as access to other knowledgeable consultants, provides each person with a support network to better meet customer needs."

With core competencies in a range of specific technologies, such as development languages, relational database management systems, and operational environments, the AOI team has its bases covered. "This may be an emerging and growing field, but our people have been developing their expertise for years," Sullivan says. "They understand the issues clients face and have the knowledge, tools, and training to solve them."

CLOCKWISE FROM TOP LEFT: WORKING FROM ITS CINCINNATI OFFICES ON THE 22ND FLOOR OF THE STAR BANK CENTER, AOI IS FOCUSED ON HELPING COMPANIES SOLVE BUSINESS PROBLEMS THROUGH THE CREATIVE USE OF LEADING-EDGE TECHNOLOGIES.

AOI CURRENTLY HAS SOME 30 EMPLOYEES WORKING AT OFFICES IN BOTH CINCINNATI AND KING OF PRUSSIA, PENNSYLVANIA.

WITH CORE COMPETENCIES IN A RANGE OF SPECIFIC TECHNOLOGIES, SUCH AS DEVELOPMENT LANGUAGES, RELATIONAL DATABASE MANAGEMENT SYSTEMS, AND OPERATIONAL ENVIRONMENTS, THE AOI TEAM HAS ITS BASES COVERED.

Attachmate Corporation

SINCE ITS INCEPTION, ATTACHMATE CORPORATION HAS HELPED COMPANIES LINK CRUCIAL INFORMATION IN THEIR APPLICATIONS AND DATABASES ON MAINFRAME, MIDRANGE, OPEN-SYSTEM, AND INTERNET PLATFORMS. AS ONE OF THE PIONEERS IN HELPING CLIENTS LINK THEIR MAINFRAME AND PC NETWORKS, THE GROWING COMPANY HAS SINCE CARVED A NICHE FOR ITSELF AS THE PREMIER PROVIDER OF CONNECTIVITY SERVICES TO MAINFRAMES. ROUGHLY 80

percent of Fortune 500 and Global 2000 companies rely on Attachmate for the host access solutions they need to run their businesses.

One of the largest privately held PC-software companies in the world, Attachmate provides products that support a variety of e-business activities. Founded in 1982, the company maintains its headquarters in Bellevue, Washington. Offices in Cincinnati were established in 1995 as the company's client base grew. Attachmate employs some 1,900 workers—widely recognized for their expertise— through offices in more than 25 countries. Those workers are dedicated to helping companies improve their efficiency through greater connectivity, and their disciplines encompass development, support, marketing, sales, and management.

ONE OF THE LARGEST PRIVATELY HELD PC-SOFTWARE COMPANIES IN THE WORLD, ATTACHMATE PROVIDES PRODUCTS THAT SUPPORT A VARIETY OF E-BUSINESS ACTIVITIES.

For nearly 20 years, Attachmate has solved business problems for more than 12 million users worldwide with products, consulting

services, support, and strategic partnerships.

Service, Solutions, and Support

Attachmate helps clients solve connectivity problems across a number of different platforms. The company offers server- and client-based Web-to-host solutions—object-oriented development tools that can be used to secure Web-enabled companies to share information with internal users, business partners, customers, and the general public.

Attachmate Consulting Services supports the company's products by reducing the time to market with full-service, rapid design and deployment of host applications over the Web. If an organization has special needs or is constrained by time or lack of expertise, it can rely on Attachmate's team of experts to provide the right services for host access needs.

FOUNDED IN 1982, ATTACHMATE CORPORATION MAINTAINS ITS HEADQUARTERS IN BELLEVUE, WASHINGTON. OFFICES IN CINCINNATI WERE ESTABLISHED IN 1995 AS THE COMPANY'S CLIENT BASE GREW.

Serving Clients of Every Stripe

The advantages associated with Attachmate software and services aren't confined to a single industry or application. Users are as diverse as the problems they seek to solve.

For example, Attachmate helped Harbor Federal Savings Bank develop Harborline, a user-friendly, interactive site that provides quick Internet banking solutions for Harbor Federal's retail and commercial customers. Using Attachmate e-Vantage software, which is designed for organizations seeking to incorporate their current mainframe systems into e-business solutions, Attachmate created a system that can be accessed through a standard Web browser. The result: Harborline acts as a teller and loan officer for on-line users and provides the bank with a customized, secure, Web-to-host solution.

The U.S. Marine Corps uses Attachmate's e-Vantage Host Access Server solution to access payroll and personnel information located on mainframe computers in remote locations. The Attachmate e-Vantage solution, deployed to some 1,000 users in about 60 different locations overnight, enables the marines to move from a desktop-based "thick" to a server-based "thin" architecture, which is the basis for e-business applications. The solution, which works with any browser, provides the marines with the flexibility they need while providing greater speed and eliminating 80 percent of the failure points experienced with their previous system.

Attachmate's products and services have proven equally beneficial to international uses. In Italy, the Comune di Napoli, Naples' regional government, used e-Vantage Web-Publish to create an intranet presentation of election results to replace temporary terminals, green-screen presentations, and faxes.

High Tech in the Heartland

Although the company is an international powerhouse in the high-tech industry, Attachmate's Cincinnati offices are casual and relaxed. Understanding that high-tech talent can be found throughout the country and not just on the coasts, the Cincinnati office recruits employees who appreciate the company for its technical prowess and the community for its livability. That appreciation explains why Attachmate's nearly 200 local employees take such an active role in supporting the community. Cincinnati Junior Achievement, the Cincinnati Nature Center, Juvenile Diabetes, and the Cincinnati Free Store represent just a few of the organizations Attachmate and its employees support on an ongoing basis.

With the exceptional ability to provide innovative solutions for a diverse client base and a true dedication to the employees and community that maintain its force, Attachmate Corporation proves its enduring record of success in the Cincinnati area and beyond. Though growth and expansion are sure to come, the company will maintain its commitment to those core values and evolve with the industry in the future.

THE ADVANTAGES ASSOCIATED WITH ATTACHMATE SOFTWARE AND SERVICES AREN'T CONFINED TO A SINGLE INDUSTRY OR APPLICATION.

UNDERSTANDING THAT HIGH-TECH TALENT CAN BE FOUND THROUGHOUT THE COUNTRY AND NOT JUST ON THE COASTS, ATTACHMATE'S CINCINNATI OFFICE RECRUITS EMPLOYEES WHO APPRECIATE THE COMPANY FOR ITS TECHNICAL PROWESS AND THE COMMUNITY FOR ITS LIVABILITY.

The Health Alliance
of Greater Cincinnati

FORMED IN 1995 TO CREATE A REGIONAL, INTEGRATED SYSTEM TO RESPOND TO CHANGES IN THE HEALTH CARE ENVIRONMENT, THE HEALTH ALLIANCE OF GREATER CINCINNATI NETWORK OF HOSPITALS, PHYSICIANS' OFFICES, AND OUTPATIENT SERVICES ENCOMPASSES A COMPLETE SPECTRUM OF HEALTH CARE. TODAY, NO MATTER WHAT AN INDIVIDUAL'S HEALTH NEEDS, HE OR SHE CAN FIND THE NECESSARY CARE SIMPLY BY TAPPING INTO THE TRISTATE AREA'S

IN ADDITION TO SITES THROUGHOUT GREATER CINCINNATI, THE HEALTH ALLIANCE OFFERS MOBILE SCREENING SERVICES, SUCH AS MAMMOGRAPHY, THROUGHOUT THE COMMUNITY (TOP).

PHYSICIANS ARE AN INTEGRAL PART OF THE HEALTH ALLIANCE, WHICH INCLUDES THE LARGEST PRIMARY CARE PRACTICE IN THE TRISTATE AREA, AND MORE THAN 3,500 AFFILIATED PRIMARY AND SPECIALTY CARE PHYSICIANS THROUGHOUT THE COMMUNITY (LEFT).

THOUSANDS OF BABIES ENTER THE WORLD EACH YEAR AT HEALTH ALLIANCE FACILITIES (RIGHT).

largest health system.

Six member hospitals that comprise the Alliance trace their roots as far back as 1819, and collectively represent more than 600 years of Cincinnati history and employ some 13,000 workers.

Strengthened by Partnership

As strong as each of the Alliance hospitals is individually, they are strengthened by their partnership as they strive for a common standard of excellence. As a group, the Alliance sets the bar high, aiming to improve patient satisfaction, quality of care, financial performance, and market share.

"By combining our resources, we're constantly striving to be more effective and efficient," says Health Alliance President and Chief Executive Officer Jack Cook. "Through Alliance-wide services such as human resources, public relations and marketing, information services and technology, and laboratory, we can offer better support for our physicians, caregivers, hospitals, and facilities."

But the benefits of affiliation aren't simply a matter of shared expenses and expertise. Like any great team, the Alliance holds its members to the highest quality standards. Part of meeting those systemwide standards means delivering the best possible care in six areas of expertise: heart, cancer, orthopedic, behavioral, neuroscience, and emergency treatment.

Established Facilities

The six facilities that form Health Alliance have a storied history in the development of health care in the area.

The Christ Hospital, located in Mount Auburn, is a nationally recognized, not-for-profit, acute care institution specializing in cardiology, orthopedics, oncology, and women's services. The Christ Hospital was the first hospital in the region to perform coronary angioplasty, and has the region's only positron emission tomography unit, a remarkable imaging tool used for the detection of disease states.

Founded in 1819, the University Hospital, part of the University of Cincinnati's Medical Center, was the first hospital in the nation with a charter granting clinical teaching rights to a medical college. The hospital, which pioneered the first emergency medicine residency program in the United States, has the only heart and liver transplant programs in the region, and is the only hospital to offer Air Care, a medical helicopter service. In addition, the University Hospital, which offers 48 accredited residency programs for physicians in training as well as 19 specialty fellowships, has the world's first LEXAR high-precision radiotherapy/radiosurgery system.

The St. Luke Hospitals serve Northern Kentucky with hospital facilities in Fort Thomas and Florence, and a drug and alcohol treatment center in Falmouth. The hospital was the first in the tristate area to open a labor, delivery, recovery, and postpartum birthing center. The hospital was also the first to perform laser laparoscopic surgery.

The Jewish Hospital, the first Jewish-sponsored hospital in the

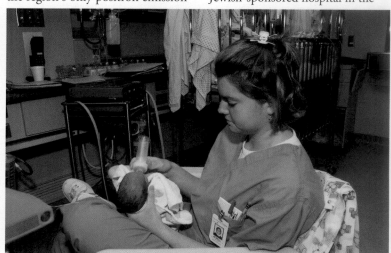

United States, opened in 1850 in response to a cholera epidemic that swept through Cincinnati. One of the earliest facilities to offer inpatient care, the hospital relocated to Kenwood in 1997 to serve the growing needs of Cincinnati's suburban east side. The hospital offers the only dedicated inpatient cancer care unit in Greater Cincinnati specializing in stem cell transplantation.

The Fort Hamilton Hospital, established in 1929, is a community hospital specializing in oncology, women's services, radiology, behavioral health, and chemical dependency treatment. Located in Hamilton, Ohio, Fort Hamilton was the first hospital in Butler County to be designated a cancer care treatment facility, as well as the first with a Level II childbirth center.

Forging Relationships

The Alliance's hospital network is complemented by Alliance Primary Care, the city's largest primary care physician group with more than 150 practitioners in more than 35 locations. The group, which includes internal medicine, family medicine, internal medicine/pediatric practitioners, and geriatric specialists, operates on the philosophy that the best medical care is

achieved when patients are allowed to establish strong relationships with their primary care physicians. To facilitate this, Alliance Primary Care has centralized many of the group's administrative functions so doctors can focus on patient care.

With its large network, the Health Alliance is able to draw on a wealth of resources to support patients' needs, no matter what they might be. For example, Alliance Laboratory Services is the largest nonprofit consolidated laboratory in the country.

The Alliance Institute for Integrative Medicine combines current medical technology with hands-on techniques, compassion, emotional self-help, spirituality, and alternative therapies such as acupuncture, chiropractics, energy medicine, and massage.

OccNet, the Alliance's occupational health services, provides employee physicals, drug screening services, physical therapy, and rehabilitation services.

The Health Alliance's support services benefit patients with highly specialized needs as well. For example, its comprehensive solid organ adult transplant program allows for liver, kidney, pancreas, simultaneous kidney and pancreas, and heart transplantation, while its Senior Care

Preferred program provides older consumers with a resource for medical treatment and general health information. Geriatric assessment centers offer specialized evaluation and care focused on the medical and mental concerns of senior adults.

In caring for members of the community, the Health Alliance is mindful of the needs of those who cannot afford to pay. Each year, the Alliance provides millions of dollars in uncompensated care—more than any other health care organization in the area—to patients who cannot afford health care. No matter what a patient's needs might be, the Alliance stands ready to help. That means not only delivering the highest quality care, but also delivering it in a compassionate and efficient way.

THE SIX HOSPITALS OF THE HEALTH ALLIANCE ARE THERE TO MEET PATIENT NEEDS FROM ROUTINE CARE TO THE MOST SOPHISTICATED CARE AVAILABLE IN THE COMMUNITY (ABOVE).

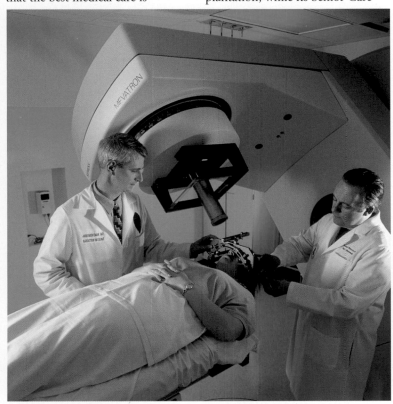

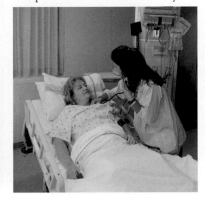

THE HEALTH ALLIANCE HOSPITALS OFFER STATE OF THE ART EQUIPMENT TO MEET THE HIGHLY SPECIALIZED NEEDS OF PATIENTS (LEFT).

THE HEALTH ALLIANCE GOAL IS TO PROVIDE THE HIGHEST QUALITY OF CARE IN A COMPASSIONATE AND EFFICIENT WAY (RIGHT).

Though the two descriptions "young and dynamic" and "seasoned and respected" may seem contradictory, they both characterize the way Process Plus does business. While the firm was founded only a few years ago, its principals have long-established reputations in the process and facilities engineering industry. Similarly, while Process Plus is carving a niche for itself as a bold and energetic young firm in the often

staid field of engineering, the company is doing so by building upon—and improving—the best that tradition has to offer.

Looking for a Better Way

Founded in 1996, Process Plus was based on a shared vision. Founders Bryan Speicher and Dan Prickel, with their seven partners, believed they could find a better way to conduct an engineering business. Since the fundamentals of engineering remain fairly constant from one firm to the other, the partners' "better way" had as much to do with running a business as it did with solving engineering challenges.

The better way meant assembling a staff whose technical proficiency was unassailable and whose skills would define the quality of the company's services. It meant providing service and customer orientation that were unparalleled in the marketplace, as well as creating a work environment where employees were motivated and able to influence the company's growth. The firm that Speicher and Prickel envisioned would do more than merely try to please its customers: the firm would stake its own success on their success by partnering with both customers and suppliers. And, above all, the firm would strive for excellence and continuous improvement through documented work processes that could be adapted to each customer's needs.

More than fanciful musing, those values have become the cornerstone upon which Process Plus was established. Weekly meetings ensure that all employees are kept abreast of corporate developments. Quarterly all-employee luncheons provide further means to distribute information and celebrate individuals with Above and Beyond awards. "Information isn't digested and distilled and passed through channels," Speicher says. "Everyone has a chance to hear the same news and to speak." As a result, three-dimensional computer-aided designs, project Web sites, interactive instrument databases, and process safety services have all come about from employee-led initiatives.

Further proof of the company's core values was shown in the first profit-sharing checks. They were issued to employees only; owners' checks were deferred.

Thanks to such bold and unambiguous actions, Process Plus quickly won recognition from potential clients and would-be employees. During its first four years in business, the company grew from two employees to 90, and its client list swelled from zero to 75. Revenues climbed to more than $6 million and the company, which had been leasing a building in Forest Park, Ohio, decided in late 1999 to purchase its own 32,000-square-foot facility.

Speicher believes Process Plus' success can be traced back to its values and its experience, which he says both potential customers and employees respect. However, he also says the company can't rest on its laurels. "Our values are a work in progress," Speicher says. They're always something we're trying to reach, never something we ever feel that we have fully achieved. They're our goals. The same is true of our mission statement. Our mission is to be the firm of choice. That's pretty brief, but the fact is you never get there either. You just work for continuous, constant improvement."

As part of that continuous improvement, Process Plus has partnered with other firms that complement the company's services. Process Plus also has an active mentoring program where employees can step out of their current roles to reach their full potential. These initiatives offer opportunities and abilities to meet customer needs beyond basic engineering services.

Minding the Details

Process Plus has forged its reputation in the chemical, food, pharmaceutical, and general industrial markets. While most of the company's clients are headquartered in Cincinnati, Process Plus has performed work for clients throughout the world. The fact that 95 percent of Process Plus clients return for follow-up projects is a testament to their satisfaction with the company's work.

Process Plus' services fall largely into three categories: process and

WHILE PROCESS PLUS WAS FOUNDED ONLY A FEW YEARS AGO, ITS PRINCIPALS HAVE LONG-ESTABLISHED REPUTATIONS IN THE PROCESS AND FACILITIES PLANNING INDUSTRY.

◀ JORDAN TATE

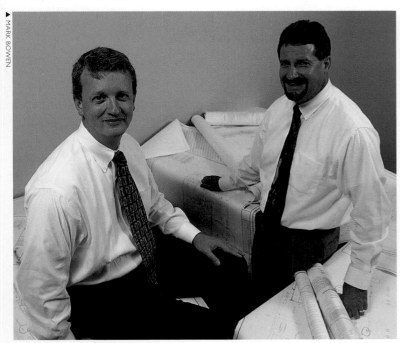

MARK BOWEN

JORDAN TATE

facilities engineering and design, plant automation and information systems, and construction and project services. Within those categories, Process Plus offers a broad array of

specialized services, enabling the company to meet a wide variety of needs.

"What people say to us that's most telling is that they come back for second projects because our folks

are very knowledgeable and competent, but at the same time, they don't put themselves on a pedestal," Speicher says. "Our consultants are very open and receptive to new ideas. We can tailor our services to meet client needs and demands because we're willing to be flexible. There's no rigid procedure book here. We're more solution oriented."

Winning Distinctions

Process Plus clients aren't the only ones who have taken notice. In 1999, the Greater Cincinnati Chamber of Commerce recognized the firm with a Pinnacle Award. That same year, the *Cincinnati Business Courier* selected Process Plus as a Small Business of the Year finalist, and the company is on track to make *Inc.* magazine's list of the 500 fastest-growing companies in the nation. The firm has earned the gratitude of the community for its sponsorship of local Cincinnati Pops concerts, for its participation in Habitat for Humanity projects, and for its informal involvement in area church projects.

According to Speicher, Process Plus' community involvement is not merely a gesture of goodwill, but is further evidence of the company's deeply held values. "All engineering firms offer basically the same services," Speicher says. "Our clients want a point of differentiation. The way we run our business, our commitment to our employees and their development, and our dedication to our customers' success is how we differentiate ourselves."

Toyota Motor Manufacturing North America, Inc. (TMMNA)

Toyota Motor Manufacturing North America, Inc. (TMMNA) wants to build more than cars. An important corporate member of the Northern Kentucky community since 1996, the U.S.-based parent company of Toyota's rapidly expanding North American manufacturing operations wants to build a community. ● "I want to establish a sense of community here," says Teruyuki Minoura, president and CEO of the Erlanger, Kentucky-based operation. "I sincerely look forward to building something special."

Streamlining Operations

As the parent company for Toyota's North American manufacturing operations, TMMNA oversees eight manufacturing facilities, including a plant in Georgetown, Kentucky, which produces nearly 500,000 Camrys, Avalons, and Siennas each year. The headquarters operation centralizes key manufacturing functions previously handled by the individual plants, such as purchasing, production engineering, quality control, and production planning. A second headquarters facility, Toyota Motor Sales (TMS), in Torrance, manages the company's national network of some 1,400 dealers, and is responsible for sales and marketing of Toyota vehicles in North America.

While no manufacturing is performed at the Erlanger facility itself, the headquarters provides important services to the plants. For example, Toyota's purchasing departments at each manufacturing plant used to buy their own parts, materials, services, and supplies directly, but now TMMNA has streamlined the process by consolidating North American purchasing at its headquarters office. Because the company annually buys nearly $13 billion worth of goods and services from more than 500 North American suppliers, this consolidation brought with it significant economies of scale, helping to reduce costs.

Improved efficiency is another benefit resulting from the establishment of TMMNA. With billions of dollars in construction and expansion projects under way across North America, TMMNA's engineering staff keeps everything under control.

The same is true for the company's production and quality control functions. Centralizing TMMNA's production control process speeds decision making in production planning, and facilitates better coordination among the manufacturing plants and between the plants and suppliers. Similarly, quality control is enhanced because TMMNA assures common standards and consistent policies for its plants and suppliers.

Economic Impact

Because Toyota's manufacturing investment in the United States now totals nearly $12 billion, the ripple effect of this long-term economic commitment to North America has a profound influence on local communities. Perhaps the most profound and obvious impact is on employment. While roughly 750 workers—or team members, as Toyota calls them—are employed at the Erlanger headquarters, many others in the area owe their jobs to TMMNA's presence.

TMMNA's drive to expand its production capacity in North America to more than 1 million vehicles per year has generated thousands of jobs. The company directly employs approximately 31,500 workers nationwide, and a recent economic impact study from the University of Michigan concluded that every new job created by Toyota generates an additional 5.5 jobs down-

Toyota Motor Manufacturing North America, Inc. (TMMNA) has been an important corporate member of the Northern Kentucky community since 1996.

stream for other Americans. So, roughly speaking, Toyota's some 20,000 manufacturing jobs in North America are actually responsible for some 110,000 jobs overall.

Many of these downstream jobs are at Toyota's 500 U.S. parts and materials suppliers, such as Sachs Automotive in Florence, Kentucky, which supplies shocks and struts to Toyota's North American plants. But the impact is even more profound than that. Milacron, for example, has hired additional workers over the years to help fill orders from Toyota for dozens of huge, multi-million-dollar plastic injection molding machines. And Toyota contracts with several firms that provide various services, especially construction, a practice that results in jobs for thousands of Americans at Toyota's various North American construction projects.

Part of the Community

The benefits of Toyota's impact are likely to grow as the company works toward its goal of building more vehicles in North America. Currently, about 60 percent of Toyotas sold in North America are built on this continent, and that percentage is growing. As the fourth-largest U.S. automaker,

Toyota believes its growth and continued success in the marketplace depend on its ability to understand and respect the unique qualities and needs of people and their local communities. Giving this important task the time and attention it deserves is another important reason TMMNA was established.

"Toyota is determined to become an active member of our new Northern Kentucky community," says Dennis Cuneo, senior vice president. "We have tried to demonstrate our good corporate citizenship through the volunteer activities of our team members, as well as through company contributions to several worthwhile local projects."

Team members at TMMNA

say they have found much to like about their new home. The location is convenient to Toyota's U.S. supply base and manufacturing plants, which are concentrated in the Midwest and the upper South. The Erlanger facility affords easy access to an international airport that provides direct connections to most places team members need to reach. What's more, the headquarters location offers a high quality of life for Toyota workers in the area.

And that's not to mention the warm and friendly reception neighbors extend to newcomers. That kind of welcome, Toyota Motor Manufacturing North America, Inc. has learned, is standard equipment in Northern Kentucky.

TOYOTA BELIEVES ITS GROWTH AND CONTINUED SUCCESS IN THE MARKETPLACE DEPEND ON ITS ABILITY TO UNDERSTAND AND RESPECT THE UNIQUE QUALITIES AND NEEDS OF PEOPLE AND THEIR LOCAL COMMUNITIES.

IN PREVIOUS GENERATIONS, THE MANTRA OF BUSINESS WAS "KNOW THINE ENEMY." TODAY, THE MAXIM MIGHT WELL BE "KNOW THY CUSTOMER." IN THE SERVICE-DRIVEN NEW ECONOMY, THE MAKE-OR-BREAK POINTS OF SURVIVAL ARE HOW FAST AND HOW WELL COMPANIES ANSWER THEIR TELEPHONES AND E-MAILS, HOW QUICKLY THEY RESPOND TO COMPLAINTS AND INQUIRIES, HOW ACTIVELY THEY PURSUE ADD-ON SALES, AND HOW THEY ADDRESS OTHER BUSINESS DYNAMICS.

That's where Convergys Corporation comes in.

Spun off from Cincinnati Bell in 1998, Cincinnati-based Convergys Corporation is the largest provider of outsourced billing and customer management services in the world. Using a combination of traditional and Internet-based customer relationship management (CRM) techniques, as well as highly sophisticated billing capabilities, Convergys helps its clients transform simple points of customer contact into important value, growth, and revenue drivers. The firm accomplishes these goals by enabling some of the world's most recognized companies to enter new consumer-driven markets quickly, differentiate their products and services, and maximize the value of each customer interaction.

Convergys adds value to the interaction between clients and their customers at every stage of the customer relationship. The firm brings new efficiencies to information management with sophisticated systems that track, manage, and bill for highly complex customer transactions and service usage. In addition, Convergys enhances the performance, efficiency, and cost-effectiveness of customer management and associated technical support functions.

"The key to Convergys' success is our focus on helping our clients enhance relationships at every stage of transactions and interactions with their customers," explains James Orr, Convergys' chairman, president, and CEO. "We enter the new millennium uniquely positioned to benefit directly from the changes brought about by technological developments and new business models that are shaping the future of commerce."

Despite its youth as an independent company, Convergys has tremendous scope. The firm employs more than 42,500 people in more than 50 cities worldwide. That scale has enabled Convergys to build strategic, long-term relationships with global leaders across business sectors, from communications and high-tech companies to health service and consumer goods providers.

Convergys serves those clients in a variety of ways. The firm's billing services group develops and manages software systems that collect, rate, and consolidate diverse, complex streams of data. That data is then transformed into more than 1.3 million bills per day, including about 41 percent of all those sent to U.S. wireless subscribers. Convergys' customer service representatives, acting on behalf of client firms, field more than 1 million customer interactions a day through sophisticated Web-enabled workstations and more than 40,000 toll-free telephone numbers that terminate in more than 40 state-of-the-art customer contact centers.

Serving Many Markets

Convergys, a member of the New York Stock Exchange (NYSE: CVG), serves clients in a wide variety of fields. The company specializes in telecommunications, cable and broadband, financial services, technology, utilities, health care, Internet, consumer products and packaged goods, and direct response firms. The firm's client list is a

THE CONVERGYS CENTER, LOCATED DOWNTOWN AT 600 VINE STREET, IS HOME TO MORE THAN 1,100 OF CONVERGYS' 2,100 EMPLOYEES IN CINCINNATI. CONVERGYS EMPLOYS APPROXIMATELY 1,000 SOFTWARE PROFESSIONALS IN THE GREATER CINCINNATI AREA. THESE SOFTWARE PROFESSIONALS DEVELOP AND MAINTAIN STATE-OF-THE-ART MANAGEMENT SYSTEMS TO SUPPORT THE WORLD'S LARGEST PROVIDERS OF TELEPHONY, WIRELESS, CABLE, AND BROADBAND INDUSTRIES.

virtual who's who of international firms, including AT&T, Microsoft Web TV, General Electric, Procter & Gamble, Lucent, Bell Atlantic, Cox Communications, Time Warner, Gateway, TeleWest, Compaq, Pfizer, DirecTV, Deutch Telecom, Hallmark, Palm Computing, Sprint PCS, France Telecom, Verizon Wireless, Toys "R" Us, Cisco Systems, and many more Fortune 500 companies.

Each of the markets Convergys serves faces a common challenge and a common solution. Increased competition and the need for brand differentiation are forcing companies operating in those sectors to strengthen customer loyalty if they are to remain competitive.

While mindful of their similarities, Convergys understands that each market also faces unique conditions. Each has specific customer management issues and the individual companies operating in the sectors require customer relationship management and information management solutions tailored to their own specific operations. With that in mind, Convergys' teams of industry-centric experts draw on their unparalleled experience in the sectors in which clients operate to craft customized solutions.

Because clients' needs differ, Convergys offers a suite of products and services to meet their needs. With services ranging from billing to customer management to employee care, Convergys' solutions fit its client's needs. The marketplace has already recognized the value Convergys brings to its clients. In only its second year of existence, Convergys was added to the Standard & Poor's 500 index.

Anticipating the Future

Although Convergys could well rest on its impressive laurels, Orr says the company's real opportunities are still on the horizon. While Convergys may well have originated the modern concept of customer relationship management, the field is still largely undeveloped. The company expects to enjoy dramatic revenue growth over the next several years and to expand its presence in overseas markets. Orr believes that, by 2005, Convergys could realize 30 percent of its revenues from international markets, which currently include the United States, Canada, Europe, and South America.

"In many ways, the true nature and promise of customer relationship management lies ahead, as it

expands and evolves with us," Orr explains. "We know the trend toward innovation in meeting new customer needs through rapidly evolving technology will grow unabated, and we intend to grow with it. With our resources, expertise, and experience, we will remain at the forefront of this evolution, and will remain uniquely positioned to take advantage of it on behalf of our clients and to the benefit of our shareholders."

JAMES F. ORR IS THE CHAIRMAN, PRESIDENT AND CHIEF EXECUTIVE OFFICER OF CONVERGYS CORPORATION, A MEMBER OF THE S&P 500 AND THE GLOBAL LEADER IN PROVIDING OUTSOURCED, INTEGRATED, BILLING AND CUSTOMER CARE SERVICES. WITH HEADQUARTERS IN CINCINNATI, CONVERGYS EMPLOYS MORE THAN 45,000 PEOPLE IN ITS 46 CUSTOMER CONTACT CENTERS AND IN ITS DATA CENTERS AND OTHER OFFICES IN THE UNITED STATES, CANADA, LATIN AMERICA, ISRAEL, AND EUROPE.

CONVERGYS CORPORATION'S INTEGRATED CONTACT CENTERS AROUND THE WORLD HELP TODAY'S LEADING COMPANIES ENHANCE CUSTOMER RELATIONSHIPS THROUGH A MIX OF TELEPHONE SUPPORT AND INTERNET-BASED CUSTOMER COMMUNICATIONS SERVICES. CONVERGYS' CUSTOMER SERVICE REPRESENTATIVES FIELD MORE THAN 1 MILLION PHONE CALLS A DAY ON BEHALF OF CLIENTS.

Ashland Inc.

SINCE RELOCATING ITS HEADQUARTERS TO COVINGTON IN JANUARY 1999, ASHLAND INC. MAY BE THE NEW KID ON THE BLOCK IN NORTHERN KENTUCKY CORPORATE CIRCLES, BUT ITS ROOTS IN THE STATE RUN DEEP. MOREOVER, MANY OF ITS DIVERSIFIED BUSINESSES HAVE BEEN WELL ESTABLISHED IN THE NORTHERN KENTUCKY/GREATER CINCINNATI MARKET FOR DECADES. ● FOUNDED BY PAUL G. BLAZER IN 1924 AS AN OIL REFINING SUBSIDIARY OF LEXINGTON-BASED SWISS

Oil Corporation, Ashland Inc. today is a multi-industry company with related businesses operating worldwide. Among them are four wholly owned divisions involved in chemicals and plastics distribution, specialty chemicals, branded motor oil and car care products, and highway construction. Ashland Inc. also owns a major stake in a petroleum refining and marketing joint venture.

Strategically Located in Covington

Considering the operations of Ashland—including a large corporate office that remains in Ashland, Kentucky—one of the major reasons the company chose to relocate its headquarters to Northern Kentucky is readily apparent. Geographically, Northern Kentucky is the hub of Ashland's operational wheel; the new office is encircled by its constituent parts.

Ashland Inc., which flourished in Ashland for 75 years, cherishes a long and valued history with Kentucky. Today, it celebrates that tradition from offices overlooking the booming Northern Kentucky riverfront, a vantage point less than a two-hour drive or a nonstop flight from any of Ashland's businesses.

Northeast from Ashland's Covington headquarters is Ashland Distribution Company in Dublin, Ohio, near Columbus. This offshoot is the largest distributor of industrial chemicals and plastics in North America, and operates more than 100 distribution centers in North America and Europe. Its annual sales exceed $3 billion.

Ashland Specialty Chemical Company is also based in Dublin. Reporting annual sales approaching $1.3 billion, it is a leading producer of six global lines of specialty chemicals, including foundry chemicals, adhesives, electronic chemicals, marine and water treatment chemicals, and polyester resins.

To the south of Ashland's Covington headquarters is The Valvoline Company, located in Lexington. Valvoline is a leading innovator and supplier of automotive products. Best known for Valvoline® motor oil, it also produces Zerex® antifreeze/coolant, SynPower® and Pyroil® automotive chemicals, and Eagle One® appearance products. The division operates or franchises 580 Valvoline Instant Oil Change service centers in 35 states, including 22 locations locally, as well as a motor oil packaging plant in Cincinnati. Valvoline's annual sales exceed $1 billion.

Ashland's APAC construction group is the nation's largest highway paver and contractor. It builds interstate highways, bridges, residential streets, and commercial driveways in 14 states in the Southeast and Midwest. APAC is based in Atlanta and generates $2.5 billion in annual sales.

In 1998, Ashland and Marathon Oil Company formed Marathon Ashland Petroleum LLC, a joint venture that combines the companies' major refining, marketing, and transportation operations. The joint venture, which is 38 percent owned by Ashland, is one of the nation's largest oil refiners and an

ASHLAND INC.'S CORPORATE HEAD-QUARTERS HAS BEEN LOCATED AT THE RIVERCENTER TOWERS IN COVINGTON, KENTUCKY, SINCE JANUARY 1999.

operator of more than 5,400 retail gasoline outlets.

Based in Findlay, Ohio, Marathon Ashland Petroleum operates a number of vital operations in the region. Speedway/SuperAmerica, the nation's second-largest convenience store chain, is headquartered in Springfield, Ohio, just 70 miles from Covington, and operates more than 300 outlets in the immediate area. In addition, Marathon Ashland Petroleum operates a terminal on the Ohio River in Cincinnati, which was acquired as part of Ashland's purchase of Tresler Oil.

Positioned for Performance

Given Covington's location at the heart of Ashland's diverse operations, the company made the strategic decision to move its headquarters 150 miles downriver. But Ashland isn't just geographically positioned for performance. The company's notable strengths include leading market share positions

in most of its businesses; efficient, low-cost production capabilities; marketing and distribution networks with critical mass and economies of scale; superior product quality and customer focus; and a long tradition of product innovation.

In recent years, Ashland has recast itself as a leader in providing goods and services to basic industrial markets. The company has inaugurated the 21st century geared for a new era of performance and driven by a desire to deliver value for shareholders; quality products and services for its customers; a challenging work environment for its employees; and positive, responsible, and ethical actions for the communities in which it operates.

Although Ashland's staff in Covington and the Greater Cincinnati area numbers only about 350, the new kid plans to make an important impact on the firm's adopted communities. "Even now, employees continue to tell me about the

many ways they've been warmly welcomed into the communities where they've settled and how pleased they are to be residents here," Chairman and CEO Paul Chellgren says.

Geography aside, Chellgren says Ashland was attracted to the Greater Cincinnati area because of its vibrant arts, sports, and entertainment communities; high-quality schools; natural beauty; and numerous other assets. Today, that attraction has developed into a deep and abiding affection that is spurring Ashland employees to get involved in their local communities and contribute to their continued prosperity.

"We have always been a community-minded company, so we looked for a place that offered the opportunity to become involved and work for the greater good of the entire region," Chellgren says. "We are convinced we've found that place here."

CLOCKWISE FROM TOP LEFT: ASHLAND IS A LEADER IN PROVIDING GOODS AND SERVICES TO BASIC INDUSTRIES, AND IS THE LARGEST U.S. DISTRIBUTOR OF THERMOPLASTICS. ONE OF ASHLAND'S NEARLY 100 DISTRIBUTION POINTS IS LOCATED IN CINCINNATI.

ASHLAND OFFERS CONSUMERS HIGH-QUALITY MOTOR OIL AND AUTOMOTIVE CHEMICALS THAT ARE PART OF THE VALVOLINE® FAMILY OF BRANDS.

WHEREVER ITS OPERATIONS MAY BE, ASHLAND GETS INVOLVED IN THE COMMUNITY BY DONATING TIME OR RESOURCES. IN 1999, THE COMPANY WAS THE OFFICIAL SPONSOR OF THE FIRST CINCINNATI BENGALS KIDS' DAY.

THE NATION'S LARGEST HIGHWAY CONTRACTOR THROUGH ITS APAC DIVISION, ASHLAND BUILDS HIGHWAYS, BRIDGES, AND AIRPORT SURFACES IN 14 STATES IN THE SOUTHEAST AND MIDWEST.

Marriott Kingsgate Conference Center Hotel

TUCKED BEHIND LUSH, GREEN HILLOCKS AND ADJACENT TO THE ARCHITECTURAL MASTERPIECE OF THE VONTZ CENTER FOR MOLECULAR RESEARCH ON THE UNIVERSITY OF CINCINNATI CAMPUS, THE MARRIOTT KINGSGATE CONFERENCE CENTER HOTEL IS EVIDENCE THAT FORM AND FUNCTION CAN NOT ONLY COEXIST, BUT CAN ALSO COMPLEMENT EACH OTHER. HOWEVER, WHILE THE CENTER'S FACILITY IS UNDENIABLY IMPRESSIVE—INCLUDING SWEEPING EXPANSES OF

windows and gently arching walls, a fountain, a sculpture garden, and landscaped earthworks—what attracts clients from around the Cincinnati area is the often invisible, state-of-the-art communications technology, wealth of amenities, and dedicated staff housed within the building.

Silicon Valley in Cincinnati

The Kingsgate, one of an elite handful of conference centers nationwide managed by Marriott Conference Centers, is a technical delight. The center offers 20,000 square feet of conference space in a total of 23 meeting rooms equipped with the latest in communication tools.

Facilities also include a 5,355-square-foot ballroom that can accommodate up to 540 visitors for theater-style seating or 360 for banquet dining. In addition, there are two boardrooms, two amphitheaters, seven large meeting rooms (named for each of Cincinnati's famed seven hills), and nine smaller breakout rooms.

Meeting rooms are equipped with computerized lighting options and individual climate control, sound-proof walls, tackable wall surfaces, and built-in white boards and screens. What's more, the meeting rooms are furnished with hard-surface writing tables—not banquet tables draped in white tablecloths—and ergonomically correct chairs designed for comfort during all-day meetings.

Designed to facilitate meetings ranging from small executive retreats to large symposiums, the center is equipped with enough high-tech equipment to impress even a dot-com CEO. Cutting-edge technology—including a T-3 Ethernet, audiovisual access connecting every meeting room and each of the 206 luxurious

THE MARRIOTT KINGSGATE CONFERENCE CENTER HOTEL IS ONE OF AN ELITE HANDFUL OF CONFERENCE CENTERS NATIONWIDE.

TWO BOARDROOMS, TWO AMPHITHEATERS, SEVEN LARGE MEETING ROOMS (NAMED FOR EACH OF CINCINNATI'S FAMED SEVEN HILLS), AND NINE SMALLER BREAKOUT ROOMS ARE PART OF THE KINGSGATE'S FACILITIES.

guest rooms, videoconferencing, and an enviable collection of audiovisual equipment—helps make meetings at the Kingsgate efficient and productive.

More Than Just Meeting Space

While technology may be at the heart of Kingsgate, Marriott hospitality and client comfort are essential parts of the conference center. Anyone who has ever endured a presentation in a darkened, windowless hotel ballroom will relish the center's open, airy atmosphere. Visitors gathered around the fireplace in the lobby will feel as if they are in a private club rather than a conference center. The contemporary furnishings invite guests to take a respite from the day's agenda, pluck a volume from the bookcase, and nestle into a sunny spot.

The center's dining services are equally enticing. After a thought-provoking meeting, guests will be grateful for the attention the Kingsgate's staff pays to break-time buffets. Guests can choose from hot appetizers, a variety of fresh fruits and yogurts, or chips and homemade cookies. And unlike some conference facilities, where the morning doughnuts harden on the counter all day, Kingsgate offers fresh and different fare throughout the day. Guests can also help themselves to hot coffee and tea, or to the juice, water, and soft drinks in the break-area refrigerators.

Mealtime is also an important part of the Kingsgate experience.

At Bistro 151, the center's bright and welcoming restaurant, conference attendees enjoy a full breakfast before starting their days. They return at lunchtime to peruse a buffet that includes an exhibition cooking station, a salad and fruit bar, and a dessert buffet. At dinnertime, the restaurant's menu includes such varied fare as lemon-thyme seared halibut with white bean stew and tomato, grilled pork loin with dried fruit chutney, and a variety of smoked specialties, such as prime rib with rosemary saffron. Finishing touches include tempting crème brûlée with berry garnish and key lime pie with gingered crème anglaise.

Guests not yet ready to turn in may want to work off the meal at the center's in-house fitness center or take advantage of the university's nearby tennis and racquetball courts and indoor pool. Those who would

rather watch than play can enjoy a drink and catch a game on television in the center's Tap Room.

Making Business Run Smoothly

Although the comfortable setting and delicious food may help visitors forget how hard they're working during their stay at the Kingsgate, the center's attentive staff never overlooks its mission. Staff members know how important it is for business travelers to maximize their time on the road. Toward that end, the center assigns a dedicated conference planner to each group to ensure travelers' needs are met. With free parking in its adjacent, 550-space garage and available transportation to the airport and business and entertainment outings, Kingsgate strives to eliminate the minor hassles that plague the business traveler.

Understanding how vital it is for businesspeople to stay on top of operations at home, the center provides a 24-hour business center and in-room facilities that make it easy to keep in touch. The one- and two-bedroom guest rooms are equipped with oversized desks, two telephone lines with dataports, and high-speed Internet access. Personal printers, fax machines, and copiers are available on request.

The Marriott Kingsgate Conference Center's business facilities are, in fact, so enviable that many guests will miss the high-speed modems and business services—not to mention the afternoon cookies—when they return home.

THE KINGSGATE'S MEETING ROOMS ARE EQUIPPED WITH COMPUTERIZED LIGHTING OPTIONS AND INDIVIDUAL CLIMATE CONTROL, SOUNDPROOF WALLS, TACKABLE WALL SURFACES, AND BUILT-IN WHITE BOARDS AND SCREENS.

WHILE TECHNOLOGY MAY BE AT THE HEART OF THE KINGSGATE, MARRIOTT HOSPITALITY AND CLIENT COMFORT ARE ESSENTIAL PARTS OF THE CONFERENCE CENTER.

Towery Publishing, Inc.

BEGINNING AS A SMALL PUBLISHER OF LOCAL NEWSPAPERS IN THE 1930S, TOWERY PUBLISHING, INC. TODAY PRODUCES A WIDE RANGE OF COMMUNITY-ORIENTED MATERIALS, INCLUDING BOOKS (URBAN TAPESTRY SERIES), BUSINESS DIRECTORIES, MAGAZINES, AND INTERNET PUBLICATIONS. BUILDING ON ITS LONG HERITAGE OF EXCELLENCE, THE COMPANY HAS BECOME GLOBAL IN SCOPE, WITH CITIES FROM SAN DIEGO TO SYDNEY REPRESENTED BY TOWERY PRODUCTS. IN ALL ITS ENDEAVORS,

this Memphis-based company strives to be synonymous with service, utility, and quality.

A Diversity of Community-Based Products

Over the years, Towery has become the largest producer of published materials for North American chambers of commerce. From membership directories that enhance business-to-business communication to visitor and relocation guides tailored to reflect the unique qualities of the communities they cover, the company's chamber-oriented materials offer comprehensive information on dozens of topics, including housing, education, leisure activities, health care, and local government.

In 1990, Towery launched the Urban Tapestry Series, an award-winning collection of oversized, hardbound photojournals detailing the people, history, culture, environment, and commerce of various metropolitan areas. These coffee-table books highlight a community through three basic elements: an introductory essay by a noted local individual, an exquisite collection of four-color photographs, and profiles of the companies and organizations that animate the area's business life.

To date, nearly 90 Urban Tapestry Series editions have been published in cities around the world, from New York to Vancouver to Sydney. Authors of the books' introductory essays include two former U.S. Presi-

dents—Gerald Ford (Grand Rapids) and Jimmy Carter (Atlanta); boxing great Muhammad Ali (Louisville); Canadian journalist Peter C. Newman (Vancouver); two network newscasters—CBS anchor Dan Rather (Austin) and ABC anchor Hugh Downs (Phoenix); NBC sportscaster Bob Costas (St. Louis); record-breaking quarterback Steve Young (San Francisco); best-selling mystery author Robert B. Parker (Boston), American Movie Classics host Nick Clooney (Cincinnati); former Texas first lady Nellie Connally (Houston); and former New York City Mayor Ed Koch (New York).

To maintain hands-on quality in all of its periodicals and books, Towery has long used the latest production methods available. The company was the first production environment in the United States to combine desktop publishing with color separations and image scanning to produce finished film suitable for burning plates for four-color printing. Today, Towery relies on state-of-the-art digital prepress services to produce more than 8,000 pages each year, containing well over 30,000 high-quality color images.

An Internet Pioneer

By combining its long-standing expertise in community-oriented published materials with advanced production capabilities, a global sales force, and extensive data management capabilities, Towery has emerged as a significant provider of Internet-based city information. In keeping with its overall focus on community resources, the company's Internet efforts represent a natural step in the evolution of the business.

The primary product lines within the Internet division are the introCity™ sites. Towery's introCity sites introduce newcomers, visitors, and longtime residents to every

STEVE DAVIS

TOWERY PUBLISHING, INC. PRESIDENT AND CEO J. ROBERT TOWERY HAS EXPANDED THE BUSINESS HIS PARENTS STARTED IN THE 1930S TO INCLUDE A GROWING ARRAY OF TRADITIONAL AND ELECTRONIC PUBLISHED MATERIALS, AS WELL AS INTERNET AND MULTIMEDIA SERVICES, THAT ARE MARKETED LOCALLY, NATIONALLY, AND INTERNATIONALLY.

facet of a particular community, while simultaneously placing the local chamber of commerce at the forefront of the city's Internet activity. The sites include newcomer information, calendars, photos, citywide business listings with everything from nightlife to shopping to family fun, and on-line maps pinpointing the exact location of businesses, schools, attractions, and much more.

Decades of Publishing Expertise

In 1972, current President and CEO J. Robert Towery succeeded his parents in managing the printing and publishing business they had founded nearly four decades earlier. Soon thereafter, he expanded the scope of the company's published materials to include *Memphis* magazine and other successful regional and national publications. In 1985, after selling its locally focused assets,

Towery began the trajectory on which it continues today, creating community-oriented materials that are often produced in conjunction with chambers of commerce and other business organizations.

Despite the decades of change, Towery himself follows a longstanding family philosophy of unmatched service and unflinching quality. That approach extends throughout the entire organization to include more than 120 employees at the Memphis headquarters, and more than 40 sales, marketing, and editorial staff traveling to and working in a growing list of client cities. All of its products, and more information about the company, are featured on the Internet at www.towery.com.

In summing up his company's steady growth, Towery restates the essential formula that has driven the business since its first pages were published: "The creative energies of our staff drive us toward innovation and invention. Our people make the highest possible demands on themselves, so I know that our future is secure if the ingredients for success remain a focus on service and quality."

TOWERY PUBLISHING WAS THE FIRST PRODUCTION ENVIRONMENT IN THE UNITED STATES TO COMBINE DESKTOP PUBLISHING WITH COLOR SEPARATIONS AND IMAGE SCANNING TO PRODUCE FINISHED FILM SUITABLE FOR BURNING PLATES FOR FOUR-COLOR PRINTING. TODAY, THE COMPANY'S STATE-OF-THE-ART NETWORK OF MACINTOSH AND WINDOWS WORKSTATIONS ALLOWS IT TO PRODUCE MORE THAN 8,000 PAGES EACH YEAR, CONTAINING MORE THAN 30,000 HIGH-QUALITY COLOR IMAGES.

THE TOWERY FAMILY'S PUBLISHING ROOTS CAN BE TRACED TO 1935, WHEN R.W. TOWERY (FAR LEFT) BEGAN PRODUCING A SERIES OF COMMUNITY HISTORIES IN TENNESSEE, MISSISSIPPI, AND TEXAS. THROUGHOUT THE COMPANY'S HISTORY, THE FOUNDING FAMILY HAS CONSISTENTLY EXHIBITED A COMMITMENT TO CLARITY, PRECISION, INNOVATION, AND VISION.

Library of Congress Cataloging-in-Publication Data

Cincinnati : majestic vision / introduction by Nick Clooney ; art direction by Bob Kimball.
  p. cm. – (Urban Tapestry series)
  "Sponsored by the Greater Cincinnati Chamber of Commerce."
  Includes index.
  ISBN 1-881096-90-4 (alk. paper)
  1. Cincinnati (Ohio)–Civilization. 2. Cincinnati (Ohio)–Pictorial works. 3. Cincinnati (Ohio)–Economic conditions. 4. Business enterprises–Ohio–Cincinnati. I. Greater Cincinnati Chamber of Commerce. II. Series.

F499.C55 C56 2001

977.1'78–dc21

Printed in China   2001027469

Towery Publishing, Inc.
The Towery Building
1835 Union Avenue
Memphis, TN 38104
www.towery.com

Publisher: J. Robert Towery **Executive Publisher:** Jenny McDowell **Marketing Director:** Carol Culpepper **Project Directors:** Candice Gilbert, Jeanne Schedel, Jim Tomlinson **Executive Editor:** David B. Dawson **Managing Editor:** Lynn Conlee **Senior Editors:** Carlisle Hacker, Brian L. Johnston **Profile Manager/Editor:** Sabrina Schroeder **Project Editor/Caption Writer:** Stephen M. Deusner **Editors:** Jay Adkins, Rebecca E. Farabough, Danna M. Greenfield, Ginny Reeves **Profile Writer:** Shelly Reese **Creative Director:** Brian Groppe **Photography Editor:** Jonathan Postal **Photographic Consultant:** Mark Bowen **Profile Designers:** Rebekah Barnhardt, Laurie Beck, Glen Marshall **Production Manager:** Brenda Pattat **Photography Coordinator:** Robin Lankford **Production Assistants:** Robert Barnett, Loretta Lane, Robert Parrish **Digital Color Supervisor:** Darin Ipema **Digital Color Technicians:** Eric Friedl, Mark Svetz **Digital Scanning Technician:** Brad Long **Print Coordinator:** Beverly Timmons

Photographers

Originally headquartered in London, **Allsport** has expanded to include offices in New York and Los Angeles. Its pictures have appeared in every major publication in the world, and the best of its portfolio has been displayed at elite photographic exhibitions at the Royal Photographic Society and the Olympic Museum in Lausanne.

Steve Baker is an international photographer who has contributed to more than 100 publications. With a degree in journalism from Indiana University, he is the proprietor of Highlight Photography, specializing in assignments for clients such as Eastman Kodak, Nike, Budweiser, the U.S. Olympic Committee, and Mobil Oil, which has commissioned seven exhibitions of his work since 1994. Baker is author and photographer of *Racing Is Everything*, and he has contributed to a number of Towery Urban Tapestry Series publications.

A Columbus native, **Rod Berry** owns and operates Rod Berry Photography, a stock agency covering a range of subjects from landscape to recreational activities. He works on freelance assignments and fine art photography, and his images have appeared in several galleries throughout the Midwest.

Originally from Chicago, **Scott Boehm** owns Boehm Photographic and specializes in photography and graphic design.

As owner and operator of Chris Cone Photography, **Chris Cone** specializes in corporate, editorial, annual report, and executive portrait photography. His images have been published by corporations, design firms, and ad agencies, as well as in consumer and trade publications.

Specializing in travel, historic, and inspirational photography, **Charlene Faris** is the owner and operator of Charlene Faris Photography. She has won numerous awards, including several from the National League of American Pen Women art shows, and was also nominated for a Pulitzer Prize in 1994 for wedding photos of

Lyle Lovett and Julia Roberts. Faris has contributed to numerous Towery Urban Tapestry Series publications.

A member of the Cincinnati Color Slide Club, **H. Jane Gahl** has had images published in Gibson greeting cards, calendars, booklets, and photography magazines. She specializes in sports, scenic, and manipulated still-life photography.

An award-winning photojournalist and documentary photographer, **Jon Hughes** has frequently contributed to local and national publications, ranging from the *Los Angeles Times* to the *Baltimore Sun*. He is the staff photographer for *Cincinnati City Beat*, an alternative newsweekly.

Marshall Johnson, an active member of the Louisville Photographic Society, specializes in landscape and nature photography. He has had images published in the *Louisville Voice-Tribune* and won first place in the Marie Shelby Botanical Gardens Photographic Exhibition in Sarasota, Florida.

Employed by the University of Cincinnati, **Colleen Kelley** specializes in photojournalism. Her images have appeared in *Architectural Digest*, *German Life*, the *Cincinnati Post*, *Cincinnati Enquirer*, *Cincinnati Business Courier*, *Catholic Telegraph*, and other publications.

Jean M. Landis is a member of the Cincinnati Color Slide Club and served as its president in 1998. She is a three-time winner in Pete's Photoworld Zoo Contest, was named Photographer of the Year in 1998 by Columbus State Community College, and received the Best of Show award at the Hamilton County Fair in 1999.

Specializing in travel and nature photography, **William Manning** conducts photography tours throughout North America, Europe, and Africa. His images have been published by American Airlines, Rand McNally, and most major calendar companies, and have appeared in such publications as *Readers Digest*, *ESPN* maga-

zine, *Time* magazine, and *Business Week*, among many others.

A member of the Cincinnati Color Slide Club, **Tim McGraw** specializes in nature photography and has had images published in the *Hamilton County Parks Visitors Guide*.

A freelance photographer, **Michael L. Mitchell** specializes in sports, photojournalism, fashion, and special event photography. His images have appeared in the *Cincinnati Post* and *Jet* magazine, and his clients include Coors Brewing Company, Cincinnati Convention and Visitors Bureau, CBS/Solar Records, and Motown Records.

Originally from Dayton, **Mary S. Moran** is a member of the Cincinnati Color Slide Club. From 1995 until 1999, she placed in the top three in the Cincinnati Zoo Photo Contest, and she won first place in the 1999 Cathedral Square Art Show photo category.

Owner of both Nemeth Photography and Image Quest Photography, **Mary Nemeth** has participated with other leading nature photographers in workshops throughout North America. Her images have appeared in calendars, magazines, and books, and she presents programs and judges photography for various groups in the tristate area.

A professional photographer for more than 30 years and a part-time teacher at the Art Academy of Cincinnati, **Paula Norton** owns Norton Photography 2 and specializes in commercial, stock, and event photography, as well as Polaroid image and emulsion transfers. Her pictures have appeared in *USA Today*, and her clients include the Cincinnati Chamber of Commerce, the Cincinnati Horticultural Society, and Clear Channel Radio.

Originally from Cincinnati, **Rick Norton** owns Rick Norton Photography and specializes in editorial and commercial photography. His clients

include theme parks, hospitals, and associations.

Judi Parks is an award-winning photojournalist living and working in the San Francisco Bay Area. Her work has been collected by museums and public collections in the United States and Europe, and her documentary series, *Home Sweet Home: Caring for America's Elderly*, was recently honored with the *Communication Arts-Design Annual* 1999 Award of Excellence for an unpublished series. Her images have appeared in numerous Towery publications.

For 17 consecutive years, **Vince Re** has won the Riverfest photo contest and has worked in such locations as Africa and China. He specializes in fireworks images from Riverfest and skyline views of Cincinnati.

Originally from Kentucky, **Gregory Rust** specializes in documentary photography. His clients include Xavier University, the Cincinnati Reds, and the Cincinnati Bengals.

A Columbus-based photographer, **Randall L. Schieber** studied photography and art at Kent State University. His images have appeared in publications such as *Ohio Magazine*, airplane travel magazines, posters and postcards, and Ohio calendars.

Originally from Detroit, Michigan, **Carl Schmitt** moved to Northern Kentucky more than 10 years ago. He has won numerous awards in competitions held by local clubs. His work has been exhibited in *Kentucky Moment VII, Cathedral Visions,* and Towery Publishing's *Northern Kentucky: Looking to the New Millennium.*

With a degree in graphic design and photography, **Chris Shenton A.R.P.S.** works for Norton Photography 2 and specializes in studio, advertising, and corporate photography. His clients include the Cincinnati Chamber of Commerce, Fidelity Investments, and many local companies.

A Cincinnati native, **Dan Tye** is a self-taught freelance photographer and has established his own company, the Art of Nature. Specializing in nature, wildlife, landscape, city skyline, and people photography, his images have appeared in several Cincinnati Chamber of Commerce and Towery publications, and he has won numerous awards for his photos.

A freelance photographer, **Tom Uhlman** works in the Cincinnati

area. His images have appeared through the Associated Press.

Lisa Ventre has had images published in the *New York Times, Chicago Tribune, Dallas Morning News,* and *Columbus Dispatch,* as well as on several news Web sites. Originally from Cincinnati, she specializes in photojournalism.

Specializing in nature photography, **William V. West** contributes his time and talent to the Hamilton County Park District and the Southwestern Ohio Historical Society.

Learning photography through workshops and lots of practice, **Leslie Wood** sells fine art photography through art shows and galleries. She specializes in images with strong graphic elements, and has won sec-

ond place for nature patterns at the Sierra Club photo contest and best in category at local art shows.

Other contributing photographers and organizations include the Cincinnati Historical Society Library, Mark Bowen Photography, L.J. Franklin, and Michael J. Pettypool. For further information about the photographers appearing in *Cincinnati: Majestic Vision,* please contact Towery Publishing.

Index
of Profiles